The Stage Year Book 1919

Lionel Carson

Alpha Editions

This edition published in 2020

ISBN : 9789354036408

Design and Setting By
Alpha Editions
www.alphaedis.com
email - alphaedis@gmail.com

As per information held with us this book is in Public Domain. This book is a reproduction of an important historical work. Alpha Editions uses the best technology to reproduce historical work in the same manner it was first published to preserve its original nature. Any marks or number seen are left intentionally to preserve its true form.

A BOON TO BOTH TEACHER AND BEGINNER.

FRANCIS, DAY & HUNTER,

Publishers of the New and Important Work,

THE FIVE C'S

By HENRY E. PETHER.

A REVOLUTION IN THE ART OF PIANOFORTE TUITION.

Enabling the Pupil to learn to read and play the whole of the notes on the Piano practically at sight.

PRICE TWO SHILLINGS.

Of all Music Dealers, and

FRANCIS, DAY & HUNTER,
138-140, Charing Cross Road, London, W.C.1.

New York: T. B. Harms and Francis, Day & Hunter, 62-64, West 45th Street.
Australia: Albert & Son, King Street, Sydney.

CHEMICAL CLEANING and DYEING COMPANY,
6, ARGYLL STREET, OXFORD CIRCUS, LONDON, W.

G. R. SANDERSON - - General Manager.

PIONEER
CLEANERS AND DYERS
TO THE THEATRICAL PROFESSION

Tableau Curtains, Box Draperies, and all Theatre Furnishings Cleaned at Special Contract Rates.

SHOW DRESSES AND COSTUMES CLEANED BETWEEN SHOWS

Artists' private Orders returned in 24 hours.

OUR VANS COLLECT AT ALL WEST END THEATRES NIGHTLY

PARCELS MAY BE LEFT WITH STAGE DOORKEEPERS.

Touring Managers can have their Wardrobes Cleaned between performances, when in or near London, by special arrangement.

Chemical Cleaning & Dyeing Company
(Next door to Palladium),

6, ARGYLL ST., OXFORD CIRCUS, LONDON, W.

TELEGRAMS "Cleaning," London.
TELEPHONE 1911-2 & 3300 Gerrard.

G. R. SANDERSON,
General Manager.

THE GUILDHALL SCHOOL OF MUSIC,
VICTORIA EMBANKMENT, E.C. 4.
(Near Blackfriars Bridge.)

*Established by the Corporation of London in 1880,
And under the Management and Control of the Music Committee.*

Principal - LANDON RONALD.

The Guildhall School of Music was established by the Corporation of the City of London in September, 1880, for the purpose of providing high-class instruction in the art and science of Music at moderate cost to the Student. The School is for Professional and Amateur Students.

The subjects taught in the School include :—Elocution, Gesture and Deportment, Stage Dancing, Fencing. and all Musical subjects.

Instruction in the above subjects is given daily from 8.30 a.m. till 8.30 p.m.

The year is divided into Three Terms, arranged to commence as follows :—Third Monday in September, Second Monday in January, Fourth Monday in April.

Students of any age are admitted at any time. Fees from £2 2s. 6d. to £10 10s. per term.

The only School in London or the Provinces possessing a fully equipped Theatre.

Students of the Guildhall School have played leading parts in the following Theatres and Companies :—The Moody-Manners Company, The Carl Rosa Company, Greet's Companies. The D'Oyly Carte Companies, The George Edwardes Companies, Mr. Seymour Hicks' Company, Drury Lane, The Gaiety. The Savoy, The Vaudeville, The Garrick, The Palace, &c., &c., &c.

The Stage Training given is of a thorough description, and opportunity is afforded pupils each term of taking part in performances in the School Theatre. Special attention given to Students of Grand Opera.

For Prospectus and all further particulars apply to
H. SAXE WYNDHAM, *Secretary.*
Telegraphic Address :—"EUPHONIUM, FLEET, LONDON." Telephone No.—Central 4459.

ANNUITIES.

Actors, Actresses, Dancers, Singers, Acting Managers, Stage Managers, Treasurers, Chorus Singers, Scenic Artists and Prompters should make provision for Old Age or Incapacitation by investing in the

ROYAL GENERAL THEATRICAL FUND,

WHICH OFFERS

GREATER ADVANTAGES

than can be obtained in any Insurance Office.

Write for full particulars as to Rules, Subscriptions, etc., to

CHARLES CRUIKSHANKS, Sec.,

55 & 56, GOSCHEN BUILDINGS, 12 & 13, HENRIETTA STREET, COVENT GARDEN, LONDON, W.C.

Mr. BENNETT SCOTT
Extends Hearty Greetings to all

and invites Artistes and Managers to call and hear the new SONG HITS demonstrated.

STAR MUSIC Co., 51, High St., New Oxford St.,
Ltd., LONDON, W.C.
Managing Director - - - BENNETT SCOTT.

Wires: SONGONIA, WESTCENT, LONDON.
'Phone: GERRARD 8146.

THE WORLD'S GREATEST BALLAD COMPOSER

HORATIO NICHOLLS

COMPOSER OF

"Blue Eyes."   "When God Gave You To Me."

"The Heart of a Rose."

"A Night of Romance."

"For You a Rose—For Me a Memory."

"Back From the Land of Yesterday."

"A Dream of Delight," etc.

Publishes all his Greatest Successes with

THE BALLAD HOUSE,

The LAWRENCE WRIGHT MUSIC CO.,

8, DENMARK STREET, CHARING CROSS ROAD,
LONDON, W.C.2.

Phone: REGENT 155.   Telegrams: "VOCABLE, W.C."

ACCURATE CHECK TAKER, Ltd.

TICKET ISSUING AND REGISTERING MACHINES
(March's Patents),

INDISPENSABLE.

Complete and Accurate Returns
for
ENTERTAINMENTS DUTY.

Over Four Thousand Machines Installed.

RECOGNISED AND ACCEPTED BY H.M. CUSTOMS.

For quotations, with full particulars, apply—
ACCURATE CHECK TAKER, Ltd.,
17 to 21, Tavistock Street, Covent Garden, London, W.C.
Telephone: REGENT 4685.   Telegrams: "UNRESERVED, RAND, LONDON."

ARTHUR PHILLIP'S
PRODUCTIONS.

Watch for them during the coming year.

P.A.:
Milton Farm, Westcott, near Dorking, Surrey.

'HALES STABLES'
Proprietor, S. GARDINER
The Universal Animal Provider.

Horses, and every kind of Animals provided for Stage and Film Spectacle, Horse and Pony Racing Tracks, also Miniature Ponies and Carriages for Cinderellas.

DRAKES FARM, NEASDEN LANE,
Phone—Willesden 842.   **NEASDEN, N.W. 10.**
London Stables:
King's Head Yard, Russell Street, Covent Garden, W.C.1.

WE LEAD, OTHERS TRY TO FOLLOW.

LIEUTENANT-COMMANDER ..
J. SEAGAR - ANDERSON, R.N.,
On Active Service, 8th August, 1914, to 26th November, 1918; now
Naval Secretary, Navy & Army Canteen Board,
Imperial Court, Knightsbridge, London, S.W.3.
Author of "NAVAL GAS," secured by A. P. De COURVILLE, Esq.
All Communications regarding future arrangements and Sketches ("The Death Drum," "The King's Ring," "Cuckoo" and "Cupid and the Cigarette") to be addressed to Sole Agents, Messrs. REEVES & LAMPORT, 18, Charing Cross Road. W.C. 2.
AND - **MISS SYBIL MELVILLE,**
Voluntary War Worker, for duration of hostilities, at Plymouth and Edinburgh;
AT LIBERTY SHORTLY FOR LONDON ONLY.

WEATHERLEY'S
Theatrical and Variety Agency,

IMPERIAL BUILDINGS,
WESTGATE ROAD,
NEWCASTLE-ON-TYNE.

ANIMALS
For The Stage——Cinema & Exhibition

Lions, Camels, Dogs, Horses, pigmy and cream Ponies (for Cinderella), Persian and midget Donkeys, Foreign Cattle and Sheep, Goats, etc.

Complete collections supplied to Pleasure Grounds, etc.

Wild and Tame.

State wants and apply for full particulars from

G. TYRWHITT-DRAKE, F.Z.S.,
Cobtree Manor, MAIDSTONE.

Telephone: 4 AYLESFORD.

Established in the Provinces, 10th October, 1906.
:: Established in London, 10th October, 1910. ::

ADAMS' AGENCY,
Theatrical and Musical,

122, SHAFTESBURY AVENUE, LONDON, W.
(Next to the Shaftesbury Theatre).

Telegraphic Address: "Shrieking, Ficcy, London." 'Phone: Gerrard 2092.

EVERY CLASS OF THEATRICAL AND VARIETY BUSINESS NEGOTIATED.

Sole Booking Agents—KEMBLE THEATRE, HEREFORD.

Permanent Address:
94, KENNINGTON PARK ROAD, LONDON. S.E.11.

Sixteenth Consecutive Year.

MR. W. V. GARROD.
PLAYS AND TOURS.

"ONE LAW FOR BOTH"
By W. V. Garrod.

"THE HEART OF A THIEF"
By W. V. Garrod. Booked by Mr. Charles Gulliver for The London Theatres of Varieties, Ltd.

"A WIFE FOR A DAY"
By W. V. Garrod. Booked by Mr. Charles Gulliver for The London Theatres of Varieties, Ltd.

"LOVE LEVELS ALL RANKS"
By W. V. Garrod.

"THE PRODIGAL PARSON"
22 years' success all over the English speaking world.

"A LOVE MARRIAGE"
By W. V. Garrod. Booked by Mr. Charles Gulliver for The London Theatres of Varieties, Ltd.

"THE MILLIONAIRE AND THE WOMAN"
By Charles Darrell.

"A PITMAN'S DAUGHTERS"
By Frank Price.

"THE ADMIRAL'S DAUGHTER"
By W. V. Garrod.

Telegrams: OSWASTOLL, WESTRAND, LONDON.   Telephone: GERRARD 7545. (2 lines).

STOLL OFFICES

COLISEUM BUILDINGS, CHARING CROSS, LONDON, W.C.

COLISEUM SYNDICATE, Ltd., THE OPERA HOUSE SYNDICATE, Ltd.; MIDDLESEX THEATRE OF VARIETIES, Ltd., HACKNEY AND SHEPHERD'S BUSH EMPIRE PALACES, Ltd., WOOD GREEN EMPIRE THEATRE OF VARIETIES, Ltd., MANCHESTER HIPPODROME AND ARDWICK EMPIRE, Ltd., LEICESTER PALACE THEATRE, Ltd., CHISWICK EMPIRE THEATRE OF VARIETIES, Ltd., CHATHAM EMPIRE THEATRE OF VARIETIES, Ltd., ST. AUGUSTINE'S PARADE HIPPODROME, BRISTOL, Ltd.

Chairman and Managing Director, OSWALD STOLL.
Secretary and Chief Accountant, W. S. GORDON MICHIE.
ARTISTES' DEPARTMENT: Negotiations—A. D. DAVIS; Dates—LLEWELLYN JOHNS.
Address all communications to the Managing Director.

London Coliseum
CHARING CROSS, Facing TRAFALGAR SQUARE.

Two Performances Daily at 2.30 and 7.45.   Rehearsals every Monday at 10 a.m.
PROPRIETORS .. .. COLISEUM SYNDICATE, LTD.

THE STOLL PICTURE THEATRE
(LONDON OPERA HOUSE), KINGSWAY

DAILY 2 to 10.30 (continuous).   PICTURES and VARIETIES.
PROPRIETORS .. .. THE OPERA HOUSE SYNDICATE, Ltd.

MANCHESTER HIPPODROME.
OXFORD STREET.
Two Performances Nightly at 6.30 and 8.35. Matinees Monday and Tuesday. Rehearsals every Monday at 12 noon.
Proprietors: THE MANCHESTER HIPPODROME AND ARDWICK EMPIRE, LTD.

SHEPHERD'S BUSH EMPIRE
SHEPHERD'S BUSH GREEN, LONDON, W.
Two Performances Nightly at 6.20 and 8.25. Rehearsals every Monday at 12.30 p.m.
Proprietors: HACKNEY AND SHEPHERD'S BUSH EMPIRE PALACES, LTD.

HACKNEY EMPIRE.
MARE STREET, LONDON, N.E.
Two Performances Nightly at 6.20 and 8.30. Rehearsals every Monday at 12 noon.
Proprietors: HACKNEY AND SHEPHERD'S BUSH EMPIRE PALACES, LTD.

LEICESTER PALACE.
BELGRAVE GATE.
Two Performances Nightly at 6.40 and 8.40. Rehearsals every Monday at 12 noon.

CHATHAM EMPIRE.
HIGH STREET.
Two Performances Nightly at 6.15 and 8.30. Rehearsals every Monday at 2 p.m.
Proprietors: CHATHAM EMPIRE THEATRE OF VARIETIES, LTD. Joint Managing Director—H. E. Davis, ex-Mayor of Gravesend.

BRISTOL HIPPODROME.
TRAMWAYS CENTRE.
Two Performances Nightly at 6.20 and 8.30. Rehearsals every Monday at 12 noon.
Proprietors: ST. AUGUSTINE'S PARADE HIPPODROME, BRISTOL, LTD.

CHISWICK EMPIRE.
CHISWICK HIGH ROAD, W.
Two Performances Nightly at 6.15 and 8.30. Rehearsals every Monday at 12 noon.
Proprietors: CHISWICK EMPIRE THEATRE OF VARIETIES, LTD.

WOOD GREEN EMPIRE.
HIGH ROAD, WOOD GREEN, LONDON, N.
Two Performances Nightly at 6.20 and 8.30. Rehearsals every Monday at 12.30 p.m.
Proprietors: WOOD GREEN EMPIRE THEATRE OF VARIETIES, LTD.

NEW MIDDLESEX THEATRE.
DRURY LANE, LONDON, W.C.
Two Performances Nightly at 6.15 and 8.20.
Proprietors: THE MIDDLESEX THEATRE OF VARIETIES, LTD.

ARDWICK EMPIRE.
ARDWICK GREEN.
Two Performances Nightly at 6.30 and 8.35. Rehearsals every Monday at 12.30 p.m.
Proprietors: MANCHESTER HIPPODROME AND ARDWICK EMPIRE, LTD.

BEDMINSTER HIPPODROME,
BRISTOL.
PICTURES & VARIETIES.
Proprietors: ST. AUGUSTINE'S PARADE HIPPODROME, BRISTOL, LTD.

FLORAL HALL, LEICESTER
(Adjoining Leicester Palace).
PICTURES.
Pro.: THE LEICESTER PALACE THEATRE, LTD.

THE PICTURE HOUSE, CHATHAM.
PICTURES.
Pro.: CHATHAM EMPIRE THEATRE OF VARIETIES, LTD.

IN ASSOCIATION WITH ## The Alhambra LEICESTER SQUARE.

Nightly, 7.40.   Matinees Wednesday, Thursday and Saturday at 2.15.
PROPRIETORS .. .. THE ALHAMBRA CO., LTD.

NOTE: All sketches played at the above theatres must be licensed by the Lord Chamberlain, and a copy of the license, together with script as licensed, must be sent to the Stoll offices at least 21 days before date of performance.

BAND PARTS REQUIRED.—14 different parts for English Orchestrations and 17 for Foreign Orchestrations. Bristol Hippodrome requires 20 parts, including three first violins and piano part for harp.

STAGE DEPARTMENT.—Songs proposed to be sung should be submitted and special stage requirements stated, in letters marked "Stage Department," by artistes three weeks before opening.

ADVERTISING MATTER.—Bills, Blocks, photographs, and specimens of pictorials really representing the act should be forwarded three weeks before opening.

COARSENESS, VULGARITY, &c., is not allowed.

ARTISTES' SCENERY AND PROPERTIES must be fireproofed or they cannot be brought into the theatre. This is by order of the Licensing Authorities.

WILLIAM HENRY
BROADHEAD & SON
OF
Manchester and Blackpool.

Operating the following Establishments:—

	Rehearsal.	'Phone.
Morecambe Winter Gardens	10.30 a.m.	8 Morecambe
Hulme Hippodrome, Manchester	2 p.m.	2388 Central
Pavilion, Liverpool	2 p.m.	1799 Royal
Empire, Ashton-under-Lyne	2 p.m.	95 Ashton
King's, Manchester	2 p.m.	655 Rusholme
Metropole, Manchester	2 p.m.	2392 Central
Hippodrome, Salford	2 p.m.	2394 Central
Osborne, Manchester	2 p.m.	2391 Central
Junction, Manchester	2 p.m.	2397 Central
Palace, Preston	2 p.m.	317 Preston
Hippodrome, Preston	11 a.m.	360 Preston
Crown, Eccles	2 p.m.	824 Eccles
Hippodrome, Queen's Park, Manchester	2 p.m.	2396 Central
Hippodrome, Bury	2 p.m.	146 Bury
Pavilion, Ashton-under-Lyne	2 p.m.	95 Ashton
Empress, Manchester	11 a.m.	2391 Central

Instructions to Artistes and Managers.

SONGS.
The words of all songs must be sent to the Resident Acting Manager fourteen days before opening.

SKETCHES.
The Lord Chamberlain's license must be obtained and must be produced to the Resident Acting Manager.

REHEARSALS.
Artistes should note the times of rehearsal as specified above. This clause in contracts will be strictly enforced.

BILL MATTER.
Full particulars of matter for Bills, Blocks, Specimens of Pictorials and Advertisements must be sent to the head office, Hulme Hippodrome, twenty-one days before opening. Failing this, artistes are liable to cancellation of engagements.

SCENERY, PROPERTIES AND ELECTRICAL INSTALLATIONS.
The Management cannot permit Scenery, Properties, etc., which have not been fireproofed, and Electrical Installations must be in accordance with the regulations of the Licensing Authorities.

All Communications re any of these Establishments to—

PERCY B. BROADHEAD,
The Hippodrome, Hulme, Manchester.

General District Manager - H. WINSTANLEY.
Secretary - - - - - W. H. ISHERWOOD.

Telegrams: "Broadheads, Manchester."   'Phones: City 5928 & 5929.

ERNEST C. ROLLS & Co.

IMPRESARIOS, THEATRICAL PRODUCERS.

Under the Personal Supervision of **ERNEST C. ROLLS**.
Musical Adviser, **HERMAN DAREWSKI**.
Secretary, **Miss A. MILLS**.

ERNEST C. ROLLS,
The Producer.

"The famous English Producer has set London agog by his out-of-the-way productions. A man of ideas, he never follows on old lines, hates conventional ruts, and snaps his fingers at tradition. Hence his success."—
Evening Standard.

"The Man with his finger on the pulse of the Entertainment World."

ERNEST C. ROLLS.

NOTE!!!
NEW ADDRESS!!

☛ "JENBIRD HOUSE,"

RUPERT STREET, LONDON, W. 1.

Tele. No. REGENT 4931.　　Telegrams, "JENBIRD," PICCY, LONDON.

AUDITIONS HELD WEEKLY.

Artists of all descriptions are invited to write in for appointment.

AUTHORS are invited to submit MSS. with a view to early production.

A few Artists who have been or are
UNDER THE ROLLS' BANNER.

Jennie Benson.	Robert Hale.	Phyllis Dare.	Nelson Keys.
Ivy Shilling.	John Humphries.	Phyllis Monkman.	Ralph Lynn.
Unity More.	George Clarke.	Renee Gratz.	Geo. Barrett.
Dithy Tarling.	Farr & Farland.	Marjorie Maxwell.	Stanley Brett.
Florence Wray.	Fred. A. Leslie.	Janette Denarber.	Tom Drew.
Amy Augarde.	Sims Wooley.	Mabel Finston.	Bert Gilbert.
Anne Croft.	Johnnie Schofield.	Mona Vivian.	Serge Morosoff.
Kathleen O'Hanlan.	Harry Ray.	Dorma Leigh.	George Wilbey.
Hope Charteris.	Max Darewski.	Dorothy Lena.	Jimmy Godden.

Etc., Etc.

ALWAYS AN OPENING FOR NEW TALENT.

The Right Brand.

LAKE

¶ THERE IS NO REASON WHY AN AGENCY SHOULD NOT HAVE THE COURAGE TO BRAND ITS GOODS.

¶ IF ANY ACT OR PERFORMANCE IS WORTHY OF RECOMMENDATION TO A MANAGEMENT IT SHOULD BEAR THE BRAND BY WHICH THE AGENT SHALL BE KNOWN.

¶ THE BRAND IS THE ONLY SAFEGUARD AGAINST IMPOSITION. IT IS THE ONLY GUARANTEE OF VALUE.

¶ BUT IT MUST BE THE RIGHT BRAND.

¶ IF YOU SEE THE BRAND **LAKE** ON ANY ACT YOU WILL KNOW "IT'S GOOD."

LAKE

LAKE'S AGENCY, 1a, Southampton Row, W.C. 1
Phone: MUSEUM 2176, 2177.   Wires: MOCCADORA, LONDON.

OPEN for PANTO 1919–1920

MORNY CASH,

THE LANCASHIRE :: :: LAD :: ::

MOSS TOUR.

Agents - - EDELSTEN & BURNS, Ltd.

LEON VINT

**142, LONG ACRE,
LONDON, W.C. 2.**

Telephone: Gerrard 6549.
Telegrams: 'Vinticon, Rand, London.'

"Oh, you Raymond! Merry Christmas."
—George Cooke.

VAUDEVILLE DEPARTMENT.

Conducting business with all the leading Tours in the World.

CAN ALWAYS PLACE REPUTED ACTS,

WHO ARE INVITED TO COMMUNICATE.

Manager, English Booking Dept. - TOM RICE.

3, LEICESTER STREET, LEICESTER SQUARE, W.C. 2

Telegrams: "AFFILTRUS, LONDON."

Telephones: REGENT 2620 (3 lines.)

SOUTH AFRICA

AFRICAN THEATRES, who control 99 % of the No. 1 Theatres in South Africa, require at once **ACTS OF EVERY DESCRIPTION**.

NOTHING TOO BIG.   NOTHING TOO SMALL.

Also DRAMATIC, COMEDY, MUSICAL COMEDY, and REVUE COMPANIES.

Sole Agents for
AFRICAN THEATRES.

AFRICAN FILM TRUST, LTD.

AFRICAN FILM PRODUCTIONS, LTD.

Sole Agents for
INDIA FILMS, LTD.
MIDDLE EAST FILMS, LTD.

Buyers for
THE WHOLE WORLD.

PLAYS BOUGHT AND SOLD.

Telegrams and Cables: "Affiltrus," London.

Telephone: Regent 2620 (3 lines).

American Branch: I.V.T.A., Ltd., Putnam Building, 1493 Broadway, New York City.

—— All Communications: General Manager or Secretary. ——

3, LEICESTER STREET, LONDON, W.C. 2

WEE GEORGIE WOOD

Photo] [Dobson

FULLY BOOKED.

Agent - - - E. EDELSTEN, Esq.

"I wonder why nobody ever kidnapped me?"

MAX DAREWSKI

Photo by E. O. Hoppé.

THE EMINENT
PIANIST, COMPOSER, AND CONDUCTOR.

Manager, JULIUS DAWSON.   Secretary, BERNARD FEILER.

All Business Communications to—

HARRY DAY, EFFINGHAM HOUSE, 1, ARUNDEL STREET, STRAND, W.C.2.

Telegraphic Address: "Terpsichore, Phone, London."
Phone: 5051-2-3 City.

TERENCE BYRON

Author-Producer,

395, CLAPHAM ROAD

LONDON, S.W.9.

ARCHIE GLEN ::

FRED KARNO'S
New Star Comedian.

No Slap Stick,
Real Artistic Comedy.

The Comedian who can bring a tear as well as a laugh.

Löis Barker & Percy Tarling

"THE GRUMBLERS"

In Humour and Music. Absolutely original. Written and composed by ourselves.

Booked 14 weeks this year, West End. Have played: Stoll, Moss, L.T.V., Variety Controlling Syndicate, Tours, and Victoria Palace. Booked into 1924.

For Vacancies apply: GEORGE BARCLAY,
Or permanent address:
"TANKERVILLE," 25, ELMFIELD RD., BROMLEY, KENT.
Phone: 1222 BROMLEY.

FRED FUTVOYE
JUVENILE OR LIGHT COMEDY.

WHO'LL GIVE THIS YOUNGSTER A CHANCE?

4½ Years H.M.'s Forces.

ALL PARTICULARS:
F. FUTVOYE,
109, Albany Road, S.E.

ELLA SHIELDS

"BURLINGTON BERTIE."

Eternally grateful to the Great British Public for their constant expressions of love and esteem—which are reciprocated to the full, and compensate for any of the sorrows of life.

My heart goes out to those splendid fellows, the blinded soldiers, and I hope that it may be my privilege on many more occasions to help them with song ("Burlington Bertie," I know, is their great favourite) or story.

MERIT

IS THE RULING FACTOR IN

"COLEMAN"

BRANDED PRODUCTIONS

WHICH

MERIT
ATTENTION
SUPPORT
PRAISE
INTEREST
SUCCESS

THE COLEMAN SERVICE IS DIFFERENT

It is a highly systemised organisation which combines all the forces that make for success, and guarantees complete satisfaction to the Proprietor, the Artist, and the Public.

THE COLEMAN SERVICE IS EFFICIENT

It gives the Public Branded productions, and the Proprietor shows that play to capacity. If you want to share in our success, write for particulars of our forthcoming productions.

There is nothing second-hand and ancient in Coleman Branded Productions; they are well ahead of the times.

Fothcoming "Coleman" No. 1 Productions that are different:—

"THE RAJAH'S RUBY." A Musical Play with thrills and laughs.

"DARK HOURS." A West End Problem Play of paramount interest.

"THE EXPERIMENT." A cynical Fable, with a Moral.

Coleman Branded Productions will commence Touring with the Declaration of Peace and the release of our "Pivotal" Principals.

Write in now to:—

THE GEOFFREY COLEMAN SYNDICATES,
18, CHARING CROSS ROAD, LONDON, W.C. 2.

Incorporating THE GEOFFREY COLEMAN THEATRICAL SYND. LTD.; THE GEOFFREY COLEMAN (NORTHERN) SYND. LTD.; THE GEOFFREY COLEMAN (SOUTHERN) SYND. LTD.

Interviews can only be given by Appointment.

STANLEY KIRKBY AND HARRY HUDSON
IN HUMOUR AND HARMONY.

Business Communications to TOM RICE, The I.V.T.A., Ltd., 3, Leicester St. LONDON, W.C. 2.

Booked by all the Leading Variety Tours.

JAMES S. CHARTERS, STAGE MANAGER.

Present Engagement - BLACK'S THEATRE, SUNDERLAND.

LATEST REFERENCES.

"IT'S A BARGAIN" REVUE. 19-1-18.

This is to certify that Mr. JAMES S. CHARTERS has acted for me as Stage Manager for a period of six months, during which time he has given every satisfaction. He is honest, sober, and trustworthy. For some weeks he has acted as "Front of the House" Manager, in which capacity he showed his honesty and interest.

(Signed) ARCHIE PITT.

EMPIRE THEATRE, LIVERPOOL (Deputy) Stage Manager.

KING'S THEATRE, SOUTHSEA, Stage Manager.

JAMES S. CHARTERS was employed at this Theatre as Stage Manager for a period of six months, during which time he has given every satisfaction, leaving here of his own accord.

Yours faithfully, R. H. HOLLANDS, Acting Manager.

THEATRE ROYAL, WORTHING.

To whom it may concern. June 2nd, 1916.

JAMES S. CHARTERS has been in my employ as Stage Manager and Scenic Artist for about 3 years, and during the whole of that period I have found him punctual, a most conscientious, willing and obliging worker, and most capable as Stage Manager, and I am highly pleased with all the different scenes he has painted for me.

(Signed) C. A. SEEBOLD.

MARTIN HARVEY'S COMPANY (two engagements) over 7 years.

During which time Mr. CHARTERS had the distinguished honour of assisting at four Royal Command Performances and one "State Command Performance" for their Majesties the late King Edward VII and Queen Alexandra, and the King and Queen of Sweden at Windsor Castle, 28th Nov. 1908.

Mr. JAMES S. CHARTERS, Stage Manager, Black's Theatre (late King's), Sunderland, has had another offer to return to Mr. Martin Harvey's Company at double increase of previous salary (having been in the Company over 7 years). He also received the same day an offer from Miss Violet Vanbrugh's Manager to be his Stage Manager for his London Theatre and to tour. However, Mr. Black, his employer, recognises his abilities also and does not wish to lose him. He has again risen his salary, for the third time inside of 10 months, but then, JAMES S. CHARTERS is "some" Stage Manager.—(Era, Advert).

"I thank you, you are always my good friend."—Henry VIII.

Yours sincerely, VIOLET VANBRUGH.

Have been 32 years in the business, and only this week have I got to like it, thanks to Mr. CHARTERS. ERNEST SHAND.

In each of the foregoing engagements Mr. Charters left of his own accord, and on each occasion was asked to reconsider his decision, usually at an increased salary.

THE
THEATRES MUTUAL INSURANCE
COMPANY, LTD.

79, PALL MALL, LONDON, S.W.1.

Telephone: REGENT 5567 (2 lines).   Reg. Tel. Address: EAGLE INSURANCE, CHARLES, LONDON.

DIRECTORS:
J. F. ELLISTON *(Chairman)*.
W. E. ALLEN.   J. GARDINER, A.C.A.
S. A. BENNETT, F.C.L.I.   JOHN HART.
MILTON BODE.   FRED. W. WARDEN.

SECRETARY:
W. G. HALL, F.S.A.A.
MANAGER:
A. F. HENDERSON,
Late Lessee Grand Theatre, Fulham.
Late General Manager for Sir Chas. Wyndham.

The Directors of THE THEATRES MUTUAL INSURANCE COMPANY, LTD., have much pleasure in announcing that arrangements have now been completed under which all the Policies issued by this Company will be GUARANTEED by

THE EAGLE STAR AND BRITISH DOMINIONS
INSURANCE COMPANY, LTD.,

Assets exceed **£16,000,000 (Sixteen Millions).** Under this arrangement "THE THEATRES MUTUAL" is in a position to deal with all Insurances incidental to the Theatrical Business, irrespective of the amount, and is able to offer impregnable Security.

The Manager or a Representative of the Company will be very pleased to answer any enquiry or keep any appointment that may be made.

Particulars of Comprehensive "All Risks" Policies will be sent on application to

THE MANAGER,

79, PALL MALL, LONDON, S.W.1.

Telephone: GERRARD 7630.

MADAME MAY WALTER

Dramatic, Variety and Musical Agent.

Orchestras—Ladies' and Gentlemen's.

Over 8,000 Musical Selections.

3, MACCLESFIELD ST., SHAFTESBURY AVENUE, W.

DROITWICH.—SALTERS' HALL.

Well-furnished excellent Hall for Concerts, Theatricals, etc., with large Seating Accommodation on Floor and in Gallery. Licensed for Plays. The Hall contains Permanent Stage, with Proscenium, Tableau Curtains, Dressing Rooms, and other appointments. No picture shows.—For terms of booking, apply

J. H. HOLLYER, Secretary, Corbett Estate, **DROITWICH.**

Before fixing up your Curtain, Slides or Programme Advertising rights **CONSULT DARBY'S.** Get our Quotation. We pay the Top Price, and rents always in advance. *EXCLUSIVE AND ARTISTICALLY-DESIGNED ADVERTISING CURTAINS, SLIDES, AND PROGRAMMES.*

DARBY'S ADVERTISING AGENCY, LTD., THEATRE ADVERTISING EXPERTS.

Tel.: Croydon 1087.   109, ST. JAMES' ROAD, CROYDON.

FLORA CROMER

In her latest and greatest successes,

"Ta-ra-ra Boom-de-aye"

AND

"Inky-Pinky Parlez Vous."

The rage of London and the Provinces.

3, BRIXTON HILL   -   -   -   S.W.

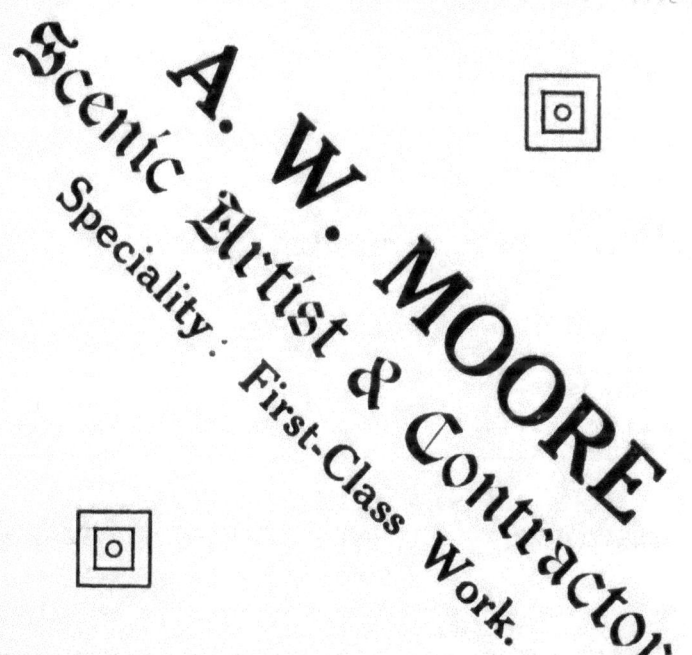

A. W. MOORE
Scenic Artist & Contractor
Speciality: First-Class Work.

Contracts successfully completed in 1918 include the Scenery for several of Moss Empires Principal Halls.

For Address see Card in "The Stage."

MUSIC HALL ARTISTS' RAILWAY ASSOCIATION.
Founded February, 1897.

President, BRANSBY WILLIAMS.   *Chairman of Committee*, BRUCE GREEN.
Vice-Chairman, JIM OBO.   *Hon. Treasurer*, CHARLES COBORN.

Terms of Membership, 5s. entrance fee and 7s. 6d. annual subscription.

Advantages of Membership: 25% Reduction on all Railways in the United Kingdom when travelling in parties of five or more. Free Insurance against accidents and loss of luggage. Free Medical and Free Legal Advice. All Variety Artists not Members should send for Prospectus from—

C. DOUGLAS STUART, Secretary, 18, **CHARING CROSS ROAD, W.C.**

VARIETY ARTISTS' BENEVOLENT FUND & INSTITUTION.
Founded December, 1907.

President .. .. .. GEORGE ROBEY.
Chairman of Committee, BRUCE GREEN.   *Vice-Chairman*, W. H. ATLAS.
Hon. Treasurer, HARRY BLAKE.

Committee Meetings are held Every Wednesday at 12 o'clock.
Established for the Relief, by Grants or Loans, of *bond-fide* Variety Artists only.
FUNDS URGENTLY NEEDED. All cases are carefully investigated.
Donations should be sent to—

C. DOUGLAS STUART, Secretary, 18, **CHARING CROSS ROAD, W.C.**

THE BENEVOLENT INSTITUTION.
"BRINSWORTH," STAINES ROAD, TWICKENHAM, NOW OPEN.

Candidates for admission, who must be genuine old performers, should apply to the Committee. Annual Subscriptions earnestly required for the maintenance of the Institution.

C. DOUGLAS STUART, Secretary, 18, Charing Cross Road, **W.C.**

The Beneficent Order of Terriers.
93, WESTMINSTER BRIDGE ROAD, LONDON, S.E.1.
(Over the London County and Westminster Bank.)

PRESIDENT .. .. BRUCE GREEN.

A Society for Variety Performers.

Any bona-fide Variety Performer over the age of 18 and under 50 is eligible for membership.
ENTRANCE FEE.. .. .. SEVEN GUINEAS
WEEKLY SUBSCRIPTION, CLASS A.. .. .. ONE SHILLING
CLASS B.. ONE SHILLING AND SIXPENCE

Grants in case of Sickness, Death, etc. Free Medical Attendance. Free Legal Advice.
Insurance of Properties against Loss by Fire. Emergency Loans.
GRAND CEREMONIAL MEETING EVERY SUNDAY EVENING at the HEADQUARTERS at 6.30 p.m.

For full particulars of the unrivalled advantages of membership, apply to **ARTHUR WERE**, Secretary.

FOOT COMFORT.
GARDNER'S Corn, Bunion, Chilblain and Rheumatic Ointment.

Absolutely cures Gouty, Tender, Weak or Swollen Feet, Hard or Soft Corns, Stiff or Enlarged Joints, Bunions, Chilblains, Chaps, Piles and Rheumatism, etc., on any part of the body. Sold for over 30 years. POST FREE, 1s. 3d.

GARDNER & RENDALL, Chiropodists and Foot Specialists,
85, REGENT STREET, LONDON, W.

Corns and Ingrowing toe nails painlessly extracted. Mr. Gardner will be pleased to advise anyone who calls.

J. RAYMOND KIRBY

Patent Apparatus for Aerial Stage Effects.

THE "PETER PAN" FLYING FIRM.

A few Artists we have flown:

Miss Eva Embury	Miss Nina Boucicault	Mr. Cyril Maude
Miss Pauline Chase	Miss Unity More	Mr. Henry Ainley
Miss Madge Titheradge	Mr. Seymour Hicks	Mr. Courtice Pounds

Flying Ballets arranged for Pantomime, Revues, &c.

GREAT ATTRACTION—"AEROPLANE" which "Loops the Loop" with Occupant.

FLYING EFFECTS ARRANGED FOR FAIRY PLAYS, etc.

Address all communications to:

110, TULSE HILL, BRIXTON, S.W.2.

Telephone: BRIXTON 2407.

LITTLE MAISIE DAWN

JUVENILE PARTS
SPECIALITY DANCER

Martell's Studio
20, FITZROY ST., W. 1.

Gladys Archbutt & A. E. Story's
PRODUCTIONS, LIMITED,
18, CHARING CROSS ROAD, W.C.

TELLING THE TALE

First-class Company now Touring, including
MISS GLADYS ARCHBUTT & MR. A. E. STORY.

Authors are invited to submit MSS. for early production.

Demobilised Actors are invited to place their names on our Books.

GERALD DE BEAUREPAIRE, AUTHOR, PLAYWRIGHT, and VERSATILE ACTOR,

Writer of original plays, sketches, scenarios, and adaptor of novels and plays, etc., for the bioscope screen.

Writing Commissions Invited. : ; Ideas written up.

Own Original Plays and Sketches for Sale or to Let.   Very Latest Scripts include:—
"An Actor's Romance" (6-reel Screen-play, accepted by Barker's Pictures, Ltd.), "Japhet in Search of a Father" (adapted from the Novel of the late Capt. Marryat, for the National Cinema Productions, Ltd.), "The Rule of God," "The Silent Witness," and many others.

OWN DRAMATIC TOUR SHORTLY.

Address:— 62, FOXBOURNE ROAD, BALHAM, S.W. 17.

THE
STAGE YEAR BOOK
For Twelve Years 1908-1919.

A Few Complete Sets are in Stock.

PRICE, Bound in Cloth, **26s.** Carr'age paid.
,,   Paper Covers, **14s.**   ,,   ,,

Apply, The Manager, "THE STAGE" Offices,
16, York Street, Covent Garden, London, W.C

JACK LAURIE
PRESENTS

THE WINFIELDS & JACK

(Two Ladies and a Gent)

IN A NOVEL AND REFINED

HARMONY, COMEDY, RAGTIME, and PIANO ACT.

Thanks to the following for Contracts during the past twelve months: Messrs. Geo. Campbell, Frank Hardie, E. & C. Dixon, H. Zahl, Moss Empires, Ltd.

P.A., 304, STRONE ROAD, MANOR PARK, LONDON, E. 12.

RICHARD HUNTLEY,

MANAGER.

FIRST-CLASS COMPANIES can be booked and entire tours arranged for No. 1 or No. 2 Towns at Home or Abroad.   25 years' booking experience.

TERMS, 5% ON NETT.

Permanent Address, 2, North Lodge Terrace, Darlington.

HENRY CLAY and NELLY NYE.

BARITONE and PRODUCER.   VIOLINIST and PIANIST.

Expert Concert Party Providers and Producers.

P.a., 106, Tressillian Road, Brockley, London, S.E.

LESLIE MAYNE.

LEADING BUSINESS.

Perm. add.: 24, Richford Street, Hammersmith, London, W. 6

Wires: Cymric, Glasgow.   Phone: 2298 Central.

LLEWELLYN DAVID'S AGENCY,

HOWARD CHAMBERS, HOWARD STREET, GLASGOW.

Wanted: REVUES, PANTOS, and ACTS OF REPUTE

Send Day Bill and Date Sheet.

THEATRICAL LADIES' GUILD.

Founder   -   -   MRS. CARSON.
President   MISS IRENE VANBRUGH.

3, Bayley Street, Bedford Square, LONDON, W.C.

Mr. ARTHUR YOUNG

Present Address: 2nd.-Lt. A. H. Young, 1st Batt. Gloucestershire Regt., B.E.F., Germany.
Permanent Address: 157. Sefton Park Road, Ashley Down, Bristol.

Young men character parts in Shakespearean and Modern Plays.

Last Engagement, "Harry Leyton" in "The Thief," with Miss Madge McIntosh.
(*Vide Press*, Dundee.—" Particularly excellent being Mr. Young in a difficult and trying part.")

OFFERS OR PROPOSALS INVITED FOR SUMMER.

REGINALD NORTH,

"Alfred" in SOLDIER BOY.

APOLLO THEATRE, W.

MONTAGUE & HART

Theatrical and Variety Agents.

Business Management and Sole Agency undertaken for a limited number of Star Artistes.

ALBION HOUSE, 59, NEW OXFORD ST., W.C.1.

Phone, 2780 Museum.   Grams, Eugatnom, Westcent.

GORDON STEWART

Light Character Comedian, Revue, etc.
Brilliant Pianist and Accompanist.

Just Finished Three Years' Active Service in France.

All Coms. to 105, ELGIN AVENUE, W. 9.

PROFESSIONAL CARDS.

M. VANE-TEMPEST.
ACTORS' ASSOCIATION.

TED E. ROSE.
Comedian and Dancer.
All coms., P.A., 67, Claremont Road, Portsmouth, Hants.

STANLEY MAUDE.
Character Actor, Stage and Business Manager.   Now in fourth year of service as Corporal in the M.T.A.S.C. First-class offers invited for Autumn. Address, C/o "The Stage."

Comedy. Melody. Versatility.
HARRY MASKELL.
Versatile Entertainer.   Perm. add., 50, Leconfield Road, Canonbury, N.5

Pte. D. LINDSAY FYNN.
Stage Manager or Master Carpenter. Best Refs.
All coms., 48, Lower Beechwood Avenue, Ranelagh, Dublin.

Mr. RONALD DOUGLAS.
Basso. Concerts. London only.
"Cintra," Tudor Road, New Barnet.   'Phone, Barnet 24.

Mr. ARTHUR FREDERICKS.
The Versatile Entertainer.
93, Churchill Road, Willesden Green, London, N.W, 2.

BERT NORMAN.
Comedian.
Permanent Address, 17, Marlboro' Hill, Bristol.

HY. L. PARKER.
The Laugh-raiser and Mirth-producer.
Oxford and Bucks Light Infantry.

GEORGE E. ROE.
Pianist-Composer. Bands Provided. Concerts Arranged.
13, Acton Street, London, W.C.1.

MATTHEW BOULTON.
4, Cranworth Gardens, S.W. 9.

VIOLETTE CAMPBELLE & CO.
The Original.
"All Ladies Camouflage Show."   Per. add., "The Stage" Office, London.

PROFESSIONAL CARDS.

Two Certainties. THE PANTHER and
SAMMY FOSTER.
The Comedian with a Gallop. c/o "Stage."

JACK PATTERSON.
The Boy in the White Suit. Eccentric Change Juggler. Playing the Principal Tours.
Coms., E. H. Granville or Jack Goodson, Ltd. P.A. 286, Coldharbour Lane, Brixton, S.W.

TERESA EVANS
Mezzo Soprano. Concerts, Banquets, and At Homes.
25, Giesbach Road, Highgate, N.19.

A. E. STORY
Comedian. Lead, Oh I Say, Telling the Tale.
P.A.: Eccentric Club, Ryder Street, W.

Mr. CHARLES R. STONE
Play-Actor and Film-Actor.
Address: A.A., 51, Millbrook Road, Brixton, S.W.1.

GLADYS ARCHBUTT
Lead, Telling the Tale.
P.A.: 18, Charing Cross Road, W.C.

CHESNEY ALLEN
A Pre-War Artiste. Leads and Light Comedy.
All coms., 78, Rectory Lane, Tooting Bec, S.W.17.

Capt. G. STEER FLINDERS
Fifth year of Service, B.E.F. France.
Shortly Demobilised. Offers, c/o "The Stage."

MISS ETHEL MONTON.
Star Lead.
Perm. Add.:
6, Burleigh Mansions, Charing Cross Road, London, W.C. 'Phone: Gerrard 6088

CHRISTIAN MORROW
Character Comedy.
Dower House, Gestingthorpe, Essex.

LOUIS VICTOR JAUME
"He of the Phenomenal Voice." The Great Anglo-French Versatile Robust Tenor and Pianist.
Touring with The Ryewodes Trio. All coms. to P.A., 65, Cairo Road, Walthamstow, E.

MISS R. SMITH (Mrs. R. HARRIS)
Theatrical Wardrobe Mistress. Second to none.
P.A.: 8, St. Anne Street, Chester.

PROFESSIONAL CARDS.

E. R. MORRIS
Address, c/o "The Stage."

Established 1912.
SYD. MOORINGS
Theatrical and Variety Agency.   Address see "Stage" weekly.

FRED E. FOSTER
L/Corpl., R.A.S.C.   Character Comedian and Stage Manager.
2, Calabria Road, Highbury.

SYDNEY EWART.
PRODUCER.
All Communications, 21, Cumberland Mansions, West End Lane, London, N.W.

MARK HENRY.
The Refined Character Comedian.
Coms., Irish Club, Charing Cross Road, or 7, Keith Grove, Shepherds Bush, W.

MISS ANNIE SAKER.
LYCEUM THEATRE.

HARRY NICHOLLS.
RUPERT COTTAGE, BEDFORD PARK, W.

MR. ERIC H. ALBURY.
4th Year of Service with the R.A.M.C. (T.F.), Somewhere in France.
Address, c/o "The Stage" Offices.

J. COURT HARVARD.
Character, Comedy, Old Men.
For Address, see Weekly Card in "Stage" and "Era."

H. J. SNELSON.
General Theatrical Manager, 17, Leicester Street, W.C. 2.
Wires: Snelson, "Advancement," London.   'Phone: Gerrard 451; House 'Phone, Hampstead 5104.

B. SHEREK.
Theatrical and Variety Agent.   17, Lisle Street, London, W.C. 2.
Telegrams: "Sherekium, London."   Telephone: Gerrard 550 (2 lines).

CHARLES CRAYFORD,
"The Kentish Mystic,"
46, WATLING STREET, BEXLEY HEATH, KENT.

THE ST. CLEMENTS PRESS OFFICE EQUIPMENT DEPARTMENT holds large stocks of Envelopes, Files, Dating Stamps, and all the miscellaneous articles required in a completely equipped office, and will gladly quote you current prices at any time. Ring Holborn 5800.

OFFICE EQUIPMENT SPECIALISTS
PORTUGAL STREET
W.C.2

Wires :
Printshop, Estrand
London

DAY AND NIGHT PRINTERS

VAUDEVILLE PRODUCTIONS, LIMITED.

Telegrams: "Wylicarro, Ox, London."

Wylie-Tate Productions

Telephone: 4669 } Museum. 4670

Staged by GUS SOHLKE.

Produced under the personal supervision of
JULIAN WYLIE & JAS. W. TATE.

The Passing Show of 1919.
With ELLA RETFORD, HARRY ANGERS, IVEY LATIMER, FRED TOOZE, BERT ESCOTT and ALFIE KEEN, Etc.

The Follies of 1919.
With JIMMY LEARMOUTH, ANNIE CROFT, JIMMY GLOVER, WALLACE LUPINO, REGINALD SHARLAND, ELSIE PRINCE, GREEN & ELLIS, and WILLIE GARVEY, Etc.

Any Lady? (Second Edition)
With LUPINO LANE, HORACE MILLS, CLAIRE ROMAINE, RENEE REEL, LENNOX LOCHNER, Etc.

IN PREPARATION.
A New Musical Piece.
With NEIL KENYON, Etc

IN PREPARATION. (By arrangement with Messrs. Grossmith & Laurillard)
"Mr. Manhattan"
With FRED DUPREZ.

All Communications to—
STANLEY RHEIM, General Manager, 25-27, Oxford St., W.1

BUY

ALL
BRITISH
Grease
Paints

Obtainable from all their
London and Provincial Branches.

555 BRANCHES
THROUGHOUT
THE COUNTRY.

BOOTS PURE DRUG CO., LTD.

"The Stage" Year Book

1919

EDITED BY LIONEL CARSON

London:
—— "THE STAGE" OFFICES ——
16, York Street, Covent Garden

[Foulsham & Banfield.

Mr. HERMAN DAREWSKI.
The leading Revue Composer and Music Publisher.

CONTENTS.

	PAGE
Academy of Dramatic Art	72
Actors' Association	55
Actors' Benevolent Fund	57
Actors' Church Union	60
Actors' Day	60
Actors' Orphanage Fund	58
Adelaide Neilson Fund	62
America, Authors of the Year	145
America, Fires in Theatres	144
America, New Theatres Opened	144
America, Obituary	149
America, Plays of the Year	123
Annual Meetings	6
Authors of the Year	113
Beneficent Order of Terriers	72
Birmingham Repertory Theatre	69
Books of the Year. By L. H. Jacobsen	8
Catholic Stage Guild	61
Circuits	112
Concert Artists' Benevolent Association	74
Concert Party Proprietors' Association	74
Concert and Plays at the Front	19
Critics' Circle	74
Drama of the Year, The. By E. A. Baughan	1
Drama in America, The. By St. Clair Bayfield	41
Dublin Repertory Theatre	69
Fires in British Theatres	22
Grand Order of Water Rats	72
Incorporated Stage Society, The	62
Kinematograph Associations	75
King George's Pension Fund	61
Legal Cases	154
Legal Cases (Index to same)	168
Liverpool Repertory Theatre	68
London Seasons	48
London Theatres—Plays Produced	109

CONTENTS—continued.

	PAGE
Manchester, Gaiety	68
Masonic Lodges	49
Music Hall Artists' Railway Association	70
Music Hall Ladies' Guild	71
Obituary	121
Paris Stage, The. By Tor. du Arozarena	37
Performing Right Society	73
Play Actors	62
Playgoers' Clubs	67
Play-Producing Societies	62
Plays of the Year (alphabetically arranged, with full Casts)	79
Plays produced during 1917 which concluded their runs during 1918	108
Provincial Entertainment Proprietors' and Managers' Association	56
Repertory Theatres	68
Roll of Honour	118
Royalty at the Theatre	111
Society of Authors	57
Society of West End Theatre Managers	55
Staff Organisations	77
Stage Needlework Guild	59
Theatres Alliance, The	56
Theatrical Clubs	64
Theatrical Ladies' Guild	59
Theatrical Managers' Association	55
Theatrical Organisations	55
Touring Managers' Association	56
Trade Unionism for Actors. By Sydney Valentine	7
Travelling Theatre Managers' Association	56
United Billposters' Association	73
Variety Artists' Benevolent Fund and Institution	70
Variety Artists' Federation	69
Variety Organisations	69
Variety Year, The. By Arthur Coles Armstrong	31
War Time Stage, The. By Bernard Weller	23

Edmond T. Guinn, *Sculptor*   **EDWIN BOOTH**   Edwin S. Dodge, *Architect*

Memorial to the founder of "The Players," erected by the Club
in Gramercy Park, New York, unveiled on November 13, 1918.

THE DRAMA OF THE YEAR.

By E. A. BAUGHAN.

THAT the London stage should have carried on through more than four years of the most terrible war the world has known is one of those things which the historian of the future will not easily understand. How difficult it has been only managers know. True, 1918 was not quite as bad as previous years. Except after the two air-raids in February, when almost half the theatres in London abandoned evening performances for a week or so, we were not much troubled by bombs, and May saw the end of the Huns' stupid misunderstanding of the psychology of British peoples. But there were some black weeks when the last offensive of the Boches seemed very dangerous even to the most optimistic among us. Then came Foch's shrewd attacks for an opening, and the final knock-out blow when the enemy was bewildered and breathless. The theatre has been a most accurate barometer of the state of the war. When the news was bad the theatres were empty; when the news was good they filled again; and at the end of 1918 a stall was more difficult to buy than a box of matches. We were lifted on a wave of theatrical prosperity. Managers deserve their good fortune if only for the dogged way in which they carried on in the early years of the war.

That is the financial side of the past year. The artistic reverse does not call for jubilation. It was a barren year, and no one can say that the renewed prosperity of the theatres promises anything of moment. Perhaps that is hardly to be expected. We must wait patiently until the tide of reaction has flowed and the ebb has begun. This is not the place for a consideration of the effect the war will ultimately exercise on our dramatic art. Some prophets say one thing; some, another. We may be very sure, however, that the four years of war and the consequent change in the conditions of society—changes that have as yet hardly begun—will be reflected in our drama. For some little while we shall mark time, closing up our ranks for (it is to be hoped) a great advance. There should be a glorious future for the theatre, and in the vast reconstruction schemes surely some little corner may be found for the encouragement and development of the dramatic art as a factor in the real civilisation for which the war has made us yearn. Surely the re-birth of nations will not be materialistic only.

TRUE WAR PLAYS.

We must not be discouraged by the poor effect the war has had on our art as yet. We are too near the stupendous catastrophe; most of us have been too intimately involved in its terrors or in the sufferings entailed by them. Consequently we find that the war plays of the past year have dealt mostly with the circumstances of war as convenient machinery for comedy or melodrama. From many of these plays you could strip the outer shell of war and find the old kernel of crook-melodrama. Already the war has been turned to advantage by dramatists anxious to find the least line of resistance for the crisis of their plots. Almost alone among the true war plays of the war stand Sir James Barrie's "The Well-Remembered Voice" and Paul Gsell's play on Poulbot's pictures, "Les Gosses dans les Ruines." There was infinite and natural pathos in the duologue between the father and his dead son's voice in Barrie's play. Much depended, of course, on the actor who undertook the part of the father. For nearly half the play he has to act a thinking part, while the boy's mother conducts a spiritualistic séance in another part of the room. With that subtle dramatic art which is characteristic of Barrie at his best, the audience was gradually prepared for the dénouement. Sir Johnston Forbes-Robertson was the very actor for the part of the father. His grand reticence and tender humour struck just the right note. In spite of its painfulness in dealing with a sorrow which must have been actually experienced by many of the audience "The Well-Remembered Voice" had the effect of a solace by reason of its sustained

1

optimism. After all, Sir James Barrie has written the best war plays. "The Unspoken Word" might be considered a prologue to "The Well-Remembered Voice," and, in its own way, was quite as true a picture of the war spirit of our nation. "The Old Lady Shows Her Medals" and even "Der Tag" were far above the level of ordinary war dramas. The last-named play suffered from a mixture of dream and reality, a mixture which is never effective on the stage. The other true war play, "The Kiddies in the Ruins," adapted from the French by Brigadier-General Cannot, showed us a devastated French village inhabited by old men, women, and children who hide in cellars and behind the ruins of their houses until the hated Boches have gone. But over this misery the spirit of the children easily is conqueror. They play their own Kaiser-game and inspire the French soldiers, who re-occupy the village, to rebuild their homes instead of flying from its ruins. So shall be healed the wounds of the stricken land, whose blasted soil shows the naked chalk beneath, like the bones of a long-dead man. As in Barrie's play, a note of fine optimism was struck. The future is with our children, and for their sake we must endure and reconstruct and, if we can, imitate the high-spirited optimism of their youth. Both these plays were remarkable achievements, considering that they were written in the midst of a state of war which did not encourage optimism. No other war plays reached the same level.

Herbert Thomas's "Out of Hell," produced at the Ambassadors on January 4, had the merit of treating an ordinary spy-drama with reticence and a certain simplicity which is not usual in plays by actors. There was interest, too, in the different points of view of two sisters, one of whom had married a German officer. Some such tragedy must have been common during the war. The play was otherwise remarkable for the fact that it was acted by only two players, who doubled parts. This was not really an advantage to the play. Without being a fine expression of the war-spirit, "Out of Hell" did present something of the heroism of mothers who gave their all to their country. Sir Arthur Pinero's wordless play, "Monica's Blue Boy," was another of the pieces in which the war was part of the web and woof, and not merely an applied decoration. Laurence Cowen's "The Hidden Hand," produced on July 4 at the Strand Theatre, was another. Mr. Bottomley described this as something more than a play: with equal truth the description might be put differently. In essence it was an ordinary spy play disfigured by an attempt to present one of the characters as Saint-George, with appropriate rhetorical declamation. "The Hidden Hand" was just a play of the moment, and in every sense was dramatic journalism of a crude and popular type. It belongs to the category of "true war plays" only in the sense that the action was centred on the kind of spy who was the special product of the war. You could not alter the character without knocking the bottom out of the play. Most of the other war plays could easily be reconstructed into ordinary melodramas or crook dramas if necessary.

Plays of War's Circumstance.

Sir Hall Caine's "The Prime Minister" is an instance of what I mean. Externally it was supposed to give us a dramatic picture of the sitting of the Cabinet on the eve of declaration of war, and of the peril of the naturalised German spy in London. In essence it was the old melodrama of a woman's self-sacrifice for love, brought about by the sudden change in characterisation dear to the dramatist of situation. Except for the scene of the Cabinet, which was so rhetorical and unnatural in treatment as to lose all impressiveness, the melodrama in essence might have been presented as anything but a war play. "The Prime Minister" must be judged by a high standard, for it had high pretensions. The other war plays of the year have simply and naturally drawn on the circumstances of war for exciting situations. Austin Page's "By Pigeon Post" was one of the most successful of these. It was an ingenious melodrama, fresh as to its subject and characterisation, but rather overloaded with detailed explanations. Mr. Page may claim the honour, I think, of being the first dramatist since the war to give us a lady doctor and a lady chauffeur, just as Sir Hall Caine, by the way, was the first dramatist to present an air-raid in London.

The Navy has inspired four plays, three by English authors and one by a Frenchman. Walter Hackett's "The Freedom of the Seas" is amusing and exciting when once it puts out to sea. The first act, which presents the hero as all kinds of a nincompoop, is incredibly foolish. The rest of the play is saved by an exciting spy episode and by the amusing characterisation of an old master of a tramp steamer, after W. W. Jacobs. Mrs. Clifford Mills's "The Luck of the Navy" does not pretend to be anything more than a straightforward spy drama with a background of naval officers. Seymour Hicks and Arthur Shirley's "Jolly Jack Tar" is more successful than either of these plays in giving some idea of the spirit of the Navy. It is a curious, ramshackle piece, being a mixture of melodrama, musical comedy (quite out of place), and kinematograph. The moving pictures, in some cases having no connection with the drama other than the office of creating a naval atmosphere, are interesting in themselves. The melodrama of the piece is well worked up, and there is a most exciting fight. On the first night it was generally thought that the scene of the prisoners' camp in Germany was unnecessarily painful. As a picture of what our men have suffered it was not realistic enough, and the authors had relied too much on sentiment. This scene was afterwards differently played, at any rate as far as its dénouement is concerned. Without being very elaborately staged "Jolly Jack Tar" is splendidly stage-managed, and the attack on the Zeebrugge Mole is very thrilling. Of the three English naval plays the melodrama at the Prince's did breathe something of the spirit of our Navy. None of these three plays is on the same plane, however, as Claude Farrère and Lucien Nepoty's "La Veille d'Armes," adapted into English by Michael Morton with the title of "In the Night Watch," and produced at the redecorated Oxford. In essence the play is yet another version of the eternal triangle, but with a difference. In the English adaptation, at any rate, the young wife of the elderly husband (the captain of a French cruiser) is more flighty than caring. Dramatically it seems rather hard lines that she should be carried out to sea when indulging in an assignation through sheer pique at what looks like her husband's indifference. The triangle is broken by the death of the lover in action—a thrilling stage picture. The court-martial in the last act is a safe stage convention, but it is a very impressive court-martial. There is originality in the husband's simple belief in his wife's tale of how she came to be on board and was able to clear him of the charge of want of care. Whether that is due to the adapter or the original authors I do not know. The play is interesting as showing the differences of discipline in the French Navy and our own, and is remarkably well acted by a fine cast. In spite of its obvious theatricality and artificiality, "In the Night Watch" is a well-knit and effective melodrama. Not much need be said of "The Female Hun" at the Lyceum. It contains at least one original scene, in which a British officer shoots his German wife on discovering her treachery. Sydney Blow and Douglas Hoare's "The Live Wire" was simply a crook play camouflaged with war.

And that ends the list of plays dealing directly with the war. None of them can be said to be worthy of the subject, with the exception of Barrie's "A Well-Remembered Voice," but then the titanic struggle through which we have just emerged can hardly be treated adequately until our dramatists can see it as a whole. Possibly the dramatist of the future will find his greatest inspiration in dealing with the war from the point of view of the social upheaval it has caused and is causing. That playwrights should attempt to ignore it will be a grave mistake. In the meantime one must expect the circumstances of the war to be employed merely as a background. After all, human beings and the clash of their minds, will and temperament must, as always, be the proper subject for drama. Our playwrights might try to deal a little more fairly with our side. In most of the war plays I have mentioned the German spies have the best of it dramatically. One and all go to their death undismayed, and are upheld by an unquestioning devotion to their country; whereas our naval and military officers spout slang, leave important documents about, and generally suggest profound inefficiency. Although our playwrights do not seem aware of the fact, we have a very wide-awake secret service. Someone should write a play showing how easily German spies have been duped and how the Germans have paid through the nose for secrets that were not secrets at all. The Dover Barrage would be a good title for a comedy spy-play.

Plays With References to the War.

So far I have dealt with all-war plays. There have been several comedies, however, which have used the circumstances of war in a very slight manner. Alfred Sutro's "Uncle Anyhow" was one of these. Probably it was written before the war, and the inventor of aeroplanes was made to concentrate his talents on a new bombing machine as an afterthought. The comedy itself, originally produced by Miss Horniman's company under the title of "The Two Miss Farndons," had considerable charm, especially in the character of a young girl who gradually realises that she is in love. It did not represent Mr. Sutro at his best, but was a pleasant enough little comedy. Arnold Bennett's brilliant "The Title" deals with a different aspect of war, the bestowing of honours for war-work—a very fruitful subject for satirical comedy. In the conduct of situations and in the writing of dialogue Mr. Bennett has acquired the sense of the theatre—occasionally one wishes he had not been quite so thorough in the attainment of that accomplishment; but he has yet to learn that plot, however slight, is an important factor in drama, and that although a novelist may, but should not, end his story mechanically, a dramatist *must* bring his play to a brilliant full-stop. R. C. Carton and Justin Huntly McCarthy's "Nurse Benson" is slightly connected with the war, but very slightly—a trifle of a V.C. hero and the pseudo profession of the heroine. The piece is a curious mixture of styles, and I wonder which author introduced a pair of melodramatic schemers quite out of tone with the piece. The heroine herself is not consistently drawn, but the play is amusing, and has an admirable last act, in which it reaches the level of real comedy. H. V. Esmond's "The Law Divine" is to some extent connected with the war, although it originally may not have been. It is a pleasant play, and ambles along gaily. The action of the piece is continuous, except for an interval before a supper party. The curtains do not disturb the scenes. The stage is darkened, and the last comer is illumined with limelight at the end of each act.

Among the plays connected with the war must be mentioned Gerolamo Rovetta's "Romanticismo." It deals with the attempt of Italy to throw off the Austrian yoke, and so was to some extent topical. Originally acted in Italian by a company of amateurs, it was afterwards produced in an English version. The war is dealt with more or less in several musical comedies and revues, notably "The Officers' Mess," "Soldier Boy," and "Buzz-Buzz."

SERIOUS PRE-WAR DRAMA.

Apart from war melodramas, light comedy has been the staple commodity at the theatres. There are a few faint signs that playgoers of the future may demand something more solid than light comedy and revue. Some critics pin their faith to a new-born interest in Shakespeare, apparently on the strength of the Shakespearean performances at the "Old Vic." and of the successful revival of "Twelfth Night" at the Court. J. Bernard Fagan's production is among the best we have had in my memory, but, after all, "Twelfth Night" is a very amusing comedy, quite as amusing as any modern revue. I should not like to argue from its success any marked inclination to Shakespearean drama as a whole. Nor can much be made of the performances at the "Old Vic.," where "Love's Labours Lost" and "Measure for Measure" were added to the repertory. The position of the "Old Vic." is peculiar. "Maritana" and the old operas are successful there, but you could not truthfully argue from that a possible success for old-fashioned opera elsewhere. Serious drama of any sort seems as dead as a doornail. So far as the problem play is concerned, we need not bewail its death, but drama will deteriorate if the future gives us nothing but comedies, or such "serious" plays as the popular "Eyes of Youth," by Max Marcin and C. Guenon, and Cosmo Hamilton's "Scandal." Eugene Waler's "The Knife" was sensational enough, but the plea put forward that it is justifiable to experiment on the body of a living criminal for the good of mankind in general was marred by the usual theatrical begging of the question, for in this case the criminal had actually outraged the girl to whom the vivisector is engaged. The play was labelled as a "warning," but who should be warned by it we did not learn. However, it was exciting if very unpleasant. Matheson Lang's translation of "Le Chevalier au Masque" under the title of "The Purple Mask" is an effective costume drama of the type of "The Scarlet Pimpernel." In quite another category was "The Lover's Heart," by Hamilton Leslie and John Dymock, a play founded on a tale of Boccaccio. The first act was quite in the right vein, and generally the situations and incidents had the proper atmosphere, but neither of the authors had the power of writing fantastic dialogue. In this respect the play was very matter-of-fact. "The Chinese Puzzle," by Marian Bower and Leon M. Lion, is a thoroughly effective comedy-melodrama, with an unusual and picturesque setting, and gives great opportunities of acting to Miss Ethel Irving and Mr. Lion himself. Its successful run was suspended at Christmas to make way for the usual revival of "Peter Pan." Perhaps the most noticeable serious play of the year was Benedict James and Milton Goldsmith's "The Little Brother," an adaptation of "The Rabbi and the Priest," a very popular American novel. Had the play a subtler psychology and less ornate dialogue it would have been powerful drama, for the situations are good and the characters intrinsically true. Without having read the book it is impossible to say how far Mr. James was responsible for the theatrical style of treatment, but that treatment certainly marred what might have been a fine play.

The tale of serious drama is not long. The principal productions of the Stage Societies were "Manfred," with Schumann's music, Congreve's "The Way of the World," Arthur Symons's translation of D'Annunzio's "La Città Morte," Pierre Louys and Pierre Frondaie's "The Girl and the Puppet," and Verhaeren's "Philip II.," and a special matinée of "L'Aiglon," with Miss Marie Löhr in Mme. Bernhardt's part, completes the list.

Pre-War Comedies.

If the year has been disappointing in regard to serious comedies and plays—barren, in fact—it has given us several light comedies which compare well with anything produced in pre-war days. Avery Hopwood's "Fair and Warmer," amusing if a trifle risqué, and "Roxana," a replica of "Romance," in giving Miss Doris Keane another "capricious" part; "The Naughty Wife," Douglas Murray's "The Man from Toronto," and James Montgomery's "Nothing But the Truth," are, with "Nurse Benson," "The Law Divine," and "The Title," the most successful comedies of the year. The last three had references to the war; the others were distinctly pre-war light comedies. In the success of these plays the taste of the past year may be gauged. One and all are light trifles which gave, and are giving, entertainment and relief from the worries of war, and so were justified of their being. Somerset Maugham's "Love in a Cottage" was neither quite light nor quite serious comedy, but tried to steer a course between the two. There seemed some lack of psychological consistency in the heroine. The treatment of the play continually swung from farce to tragedy and back. Sir Arthur Pinero's "The Freaks" was a mistake, and so was R. S. Hichens's "Press the Button." In "Too Much Money" Mr. Zangwill made very self-conscious fun, which, somehow or other, was not so humorous as he seems to have imagined it was. A. A. Milne's "Belinda" was an advance on his other stage work. His characteristic dialogue tells on the stage, but he has yet to learn that you must have a distinct objective, either of situation or idea, in a stage play. There was really no idea in "Belinda," and there was not a strong enough plot to take its place. In a sense Arnold Bennett's "The Title" suffers from the same faults. Our literary men seldom take the theatre seriously. Ernest Denny's "Marmaduke" enabled Mr. Dennis Eadie to double the parts of a man of the world who has lost his memory and a drunken wastrel, the real Marmaduke. The play was brightly written, and the "doubling" was well managed. Finally, Max Marcin's "Cheating Cheaters" was a good example of the hustling crook-drama with its inevitable "surprise." Of the farces, W. W. Ellis's "A Week End," Martin Henry and Hannaford Bennett's "You Never Know, Y'Know," and Salisbury Field and Margaret Mayo's "Be Careful, Baby" fulfilled the purposes for which they were written.

Revues and Musical Comedies.

The prophets who predicted the gradual death of the revue must consult the omens again. Revue and musical comedy were never more alive. "The Lilac Domino," "Going Up," "Soldier Boy," and, possibly, "The Officers' Mess" bid fair to follow the example of "The Boy," "The Maid of the Mountains," "Yes, Uncle," and "Chu Chin Chow." For these last four pieces it has been impossible to buy seats since the armistice was signed. At the same time revues are very successful, although they do not have quite such a long run. "Hullo, America," "Box o' Tricks," "The Bing Boys on Broadway," "Tails Up," "Buzz-Buzz," and "As You Were" prove that the revue as a form of entertainment is anything but dead. If only revue writers could manage to connect their numbers by a central idea the revue would be more entertaining than it is. The inconsequence of most of these pieces is a little trying. In "As You Were" the central idea helps to make it the most brilliant of the revues. This review of the year must not be closed without reference to the productions of the historical Christmas of 1918. "Peter Pan" and "When the Rainbow Ends" were duly revived, and there were pantomimes at the Lyceum and Drury Lane. In addition, a new management, of which Mr. Arnold Bennett is the leading spirit, produced a children's revue and pantomime, "Make Believe," at the Hammersmith Lyric. A. A. Milne and C. E. Barton wrote the book and lyrics.

It is difficult, in finishing this review of the dramatic year in London, to refrain from prophecy. What will the future hold for the theatre? Shall we still be content with trifling light comedies and musical plays and revues? Will the war, and all it has meant to the world, have no effect on drama? Is a National Theatre to remain always an impracticable dream? Will a civilisation, shaken to its very foundations and eager to reform itself, continue to ignore one of the most human acts by which great ideas may be expressed and noble actions set forth? I will not dare answer these questions, but will content myself with pointing to the history of English drama after the great Elizabethan days.

ANNUAL MEETINGS, etc.

January 6.—The annual installation meeting of the Grand Order of Water Rats was held in the Lodge Room at the Vaudeville Club.

January 20.—The annual general meeting of the Touchstone Club took place at Oddenino's Imperial Restaurant, with Mr. Harry Nicholls in the chair.

January 27.—The annual general meeting of the Variety Artists' Federation was held at the Rehearsal Theatre, Maiden Lane, Mr. Fred Russell presiding.

January 27.—The annual meeting of the Beneficent Order of Terriers was held in the Terriers' Lodge, with Mr. Harry Gribben in the chair.

February 24.—The annual general meeting of the members of the Stage Staff Branch (London) of the National Association of Theatrical Employees took place at the Holborn Empire.

February 27.—The annual general meeting of the Variety Artists' Benevolent Fund and Institution took place at the Rehearsal Theatre, Maiden Lane, with Mr. Bruce Green in the chair.

March 10.—The annual general meeting of the Actors' Association took place at the Ambassadors', Sir Johnston Forbes-Robertson presiding.

March 19.—The annual general meeting of the Actors' Benevolent Fund was held at the St. James's, Sir Squire Bancroft presiding.

March 21.—The annual meeting of the Theatrical Managers' Association was held at the offices, 52, Shaftesbury Avenue, with Mr. Tom B. Davis in the chair.

March 22.—The annual general meeting of the Critics' Circle was held in the hall of the Institute of Journalists, Tudor Street, with Mr. E. F. Spence in the chair.

March 22.—The annual general meeting of the Royal General Theatrical Fund was held at the offices of the fund, Goschen Buildings, Henrietta Street, with Mr. Charles Rock in the chair.

April 30.—The annual general meeting of the Yorick Club took place at St. George's House, St. Martin's Lane.

May 3.—The annual meeting of the Provincial Entertainments Proprietors' and Managers' Association was held at the Victoria Hotel, Manchester, Mr. Matthew Montgomery presiding.

May 7.—The annual general meeting of the Rehearsal Club took place at the St. James's, with Mr. Gerald du Maurier in the chair.

May 12.—The Magicians' Club held their annual séance at the Bijou, Bedford Street, with Mr. David Devant in the chair.

June 18.—The annual meeting of the Actors' Church Union took place at St. Anne's Rectory, Soho, with the President, the Bishop of Winchester, in the chair.

June 28.—The annual general meeting of the Touring Managers' Association took place at Water House, Strand.

July 12.—The annual meeting of the Catholic Stage Guild was held at the Vaudeville, with the Right Hon. Lord Morris in the chair.

November 12.—The annual general meeting of the Music Hall Ladies' Guild was held at the Board Room, 18, Charing Cross Road, with Mrs. Charles Coborn in the chair.

December 6.—The annual general meeting of the Theatrical Ladies' Guild was held at the St. James's, with Miss Irene Vanbrugh in the chair.

December 22.—The sixth annual meeting of the "Charley's Aunt" Club was held at the Royal Albert Hall Theatre, with the President, Mrs. Brandon Thomas, in the chair.

PLAYS OF THE YEAR.

"GOING UP" AT THE GAIETY.

PLAYS OF THE YEAR.

"NURSE BENSON" AT THE GLOBE.

Mr. Nelson Ramsay, Miss Marie Louise, Mr. Geo. Elton, Miss Lottie Venne, Miss Violet Farebrother.

"*Daily Mirror.*"

PLAYS OF THE YEAR.

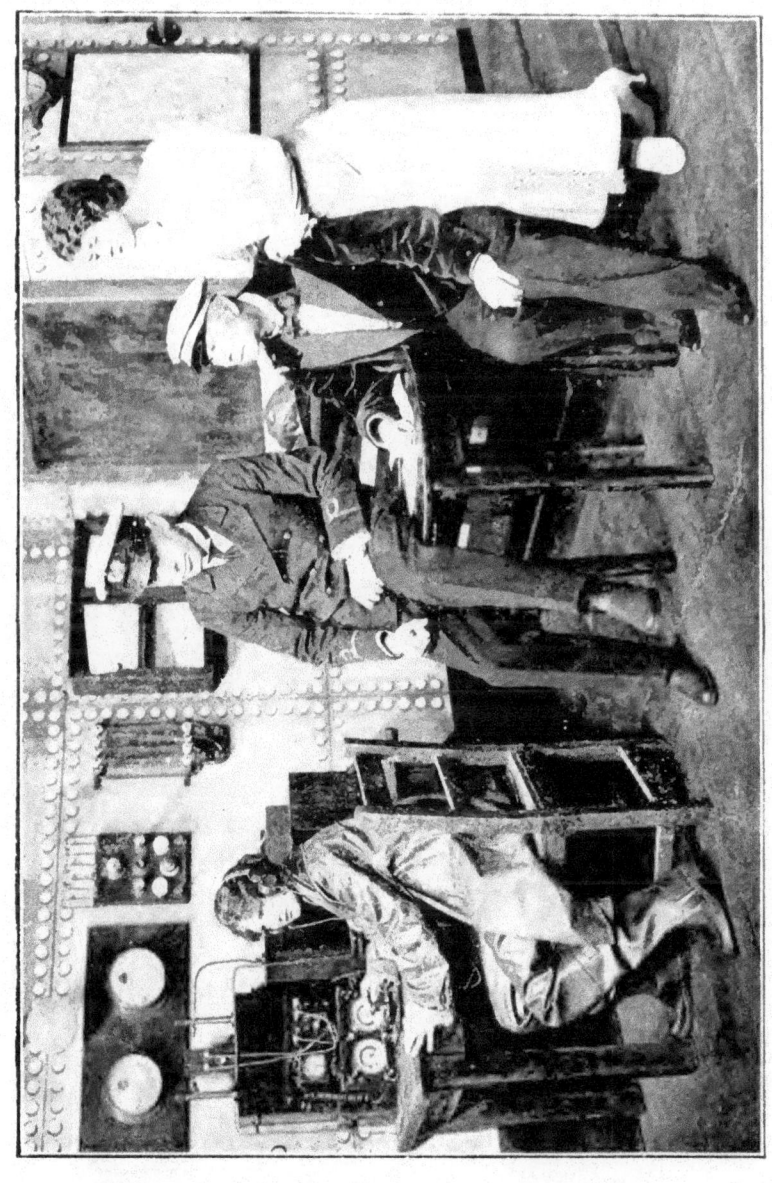

"THE FREEDOM OF THE SEAS" AT THE HAYMARKET.

PLAYS OF THE YEAR.

"ROXANA" AT THE LYRIC.

Miss Athene Seyler, Mr. Eric Harrison, Miss Doris Keane, and Mr. Basil Sydney.

PLAYS OF THE YEAR.

"BOX O' TRICKS" AT THE LONDON HIPPODROME.
Miss Cissie Bramshaw and Chorus.

PLAYS OF THE YEAR.

"THE KNIFE" AT THE COMEDY.

Helen Haye, Kyrle Bellew, Aubrey Smith, Stephen Ewart, Farren Soutar, Marguerite Collier, Sam Livesey, Norman Page.

Stage Photo Co.

PLAYS OF THE YEAR

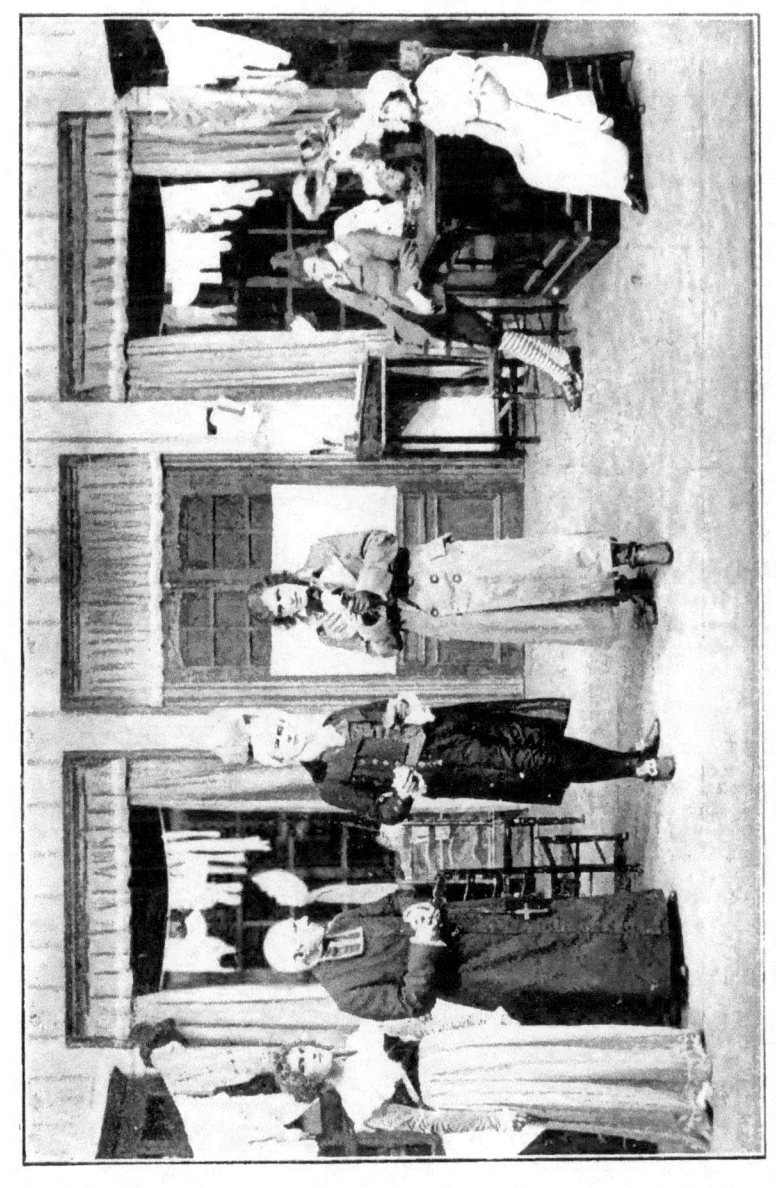

"THE PURPLE MASK" AT THE PRINCES, AND AFTERWARDS AT THE SCALA.
Group includes Miss Amy Brandon Thomas, Mr. Hodges Cooper, Mr. Matheson Lang, and Miss Aline Mortyn.

PLAYS OF THE YEAR.

"SOLDIER BOY" AT THE APOLLO.
Mr. Laurence Leonard, Miss Sinna St. Clair, Miss Winifred Barnes.

Stage Photo Co.

PLAYS OF THE YEAR.

"THE NAUGHTY WIFE" AT THE PLAYHOUSE.

PLAYS OF THE YEAR.

"NOTHING BUT THE TRUTH" AT THE SAVOY.

Foulsham & Banfield

Group includes Mr. Paul Arthur, Miss Zoe Gordon, Mr. Percival Clark, Mr. Chas. Glenney, Mr. A. E. Matthews, Miss Dorothy Minto, and Miss Henrietta Watson.

PLAYS OF THE YEAR.

"FAIR AND WARMER" AT THE PRINCE OF WALES'S.
Margaret Bannerman, Geo. Belpher, David Miller, Ronald Squire, Fay Compton.

PLAYS OF THE YEAR.

Foulsham & Banfield.

"THE MAN FROM TORONTO."
Miss Iris Hoey and Mr. George Tully.

TRADE UNIONISM FOR ACTORS.

By SYDNEY VALENTINE.

THE year 1919 should be a notable one in the annals of the theatrical profession, for it heralds the birth of a trade union for actors and actresses. The new union begins its existence as a lusty and promising infant, and it rests with actors and actresses to see that it grows to maturity and proves to be of valuable and permanent usefulness in the world of the theatre.

The old Actors' Association, after over a quarter of a century of existence, had failed to do anything to remedy the evils which have been growing up steadily during the past decade, and the only thing to be done was to wind it up and start afresh. The overwhelming majority by which it was decided to do so proves that the actor had fully realised this necessity.

We are living in a democratic age in which the worker intends to obtain a fairer share of the profits resulting from his labours.

The conditions under which the actor earns his living have radically changed during the past five-and-twenty years.

The terms on which an actor was engaged, which were fair and equitable in the past, are no longer so under the altered conditions.

Whereas an actor used to be engaged for a season, or a year or more, in this age of "specialising" he is usually engaged only for one play at a time, which may be, and often is, a failure, and he has to start all over again. In other words, he has to "gamble" for his living. And it is a gamble in which he always takes his share of the losses, but not of the profits. Now this is obviously a foolish way of earning one's living. But it is of no use to blame the manager for taking advantage of the actor's foolishness. Until the millennium arrives and alters human nature we cannot expect anything else.

It is the actor's business to see that the manager does not take advantage of him. And in order that the actor may be strong enough to look after his interests it is necessary for him to combine.

The only way in which this can be done lawfully is by forming a trade union, which gives him the right of "collective bargaining." But the trade union must embrace the bulk of the members of the trade in question before it can exercise this right of collective bargaining. It is therefore the duty of every member of the union to do his or her utmost to prevent any actor or actress from remaining outside. And that is not all. Every member of the union must regard the good of the community as a whole as the object to be worked for, and not the selfish interest of the individual. This means conforming to discipline, without which no enterprise can hope to be successful.

When once a trade union is firmly established its power is great, and should never be abused.

Every actor and actress who joins the new trade union should do so with the honest intention of doing something to better the conditions under which we actors have to earn a living.

There need be no strife with the manager who deals fairly with his employees.

It is a question of business, and it is perfectly legitimate for each side to try to make the best bargain, so long as everything is honest and straightforward. If, on the other hand, there is anything "crooked" or unfair in the transaction, the union has a perfect right to use its power to the utmost.

The origin of trade unionism was the necessity of workmen combining to *protect* themselves against injustice and wrong. That should be the object of the Actors' Union. Defence, not Defiance.

BOOKS OF THE YEAR.

BY L. H. JACOBSEN.

FOR the fifth, and, as we all hope, the last time, we have to be content with what may be termed a "war edition" of "Books of the Year"; but, all the same, as with 1917 at any rate, one's record of books on topics connected with various departments of stage work is, for 1918, once more an interesting, if not a very extensive, one. Important volumes have been issued in the sections of biographical recollections, Shakespearean studies, and general criticism, to name the chief only, and a good deal of the matter therein contained has been such as to call for detailed comment and for judiciously-exercised transcription as well. The main points are set forth below under various headings, and hence one has been able again to display with some success skill in the noble art of window-dressing. As there is every likelihood that an Armistice Christmas will be followed by an Early Peace, one may look forward with confidence to renewed publishing activity and to good book seasons throughout the year of 1919. So sanguine a tone has not been justified since the now far-off spring of 1914.

Books About the Bard.

Ever one of the most faithful among the band of faithful, Mrs. Charlotte Carmichael Stopes issued through George Bell and Sons, Limited (8s. 6d. net). a second edition of her volume of collected essays and papers, styled "Shakespeare's Environment," just in time for the Birthday Celebrations. She included therein two of her 1916 Commemoration papers—the prose piece, "In Memory of Shakespeare, Time's Laureate," and the verses, "The Making of Shakespeare," the latter from "The Book of Homage." This second issue of "Shakespeare's Environment" was rendered notable by the insertion of a beautifully-coloured frontispiece apropos of the reprint of "The True Story of the Stratford Bust," this being a reproduction of Miss Estella Canziani's able study of one of the Shakespeare portraits in presenting "the face enlarged and coloured from Dugdale's engraving of Shakespeare's Tomb in his 'Warwickshire,' 1656." In this work the daughter of a much-lamented lady artist, the late Louisa Starr-Canziani, had been induced by the indefatigably zealous Mrs. Stopes to treat the face "as a sitter, and yet to paint it with the colours of the tomb."

"Shakespeare's Workmanship."

Under this title T. Fisher Unwin, Limited, sent forth, at 15s. net, a second impression of Sir Arthur Quiller-Couch's scholarly attempt at Shakespearean criticism and analysis. The volume, which has won golden opinions from all sorts of persons, is formed of detailed and searching discussions of the characters, management of plot, method of workmanship, and measure of success attained, in some of the most famous plays, for instance, "Hamlet," "The Merchant of Venice," "The Tempest," "Cymbeline," "Macbeth," and so on, and "Q's" thoughtful studies ought to be read carefully by earnest Shakespeare-lovers.

"Shakespeare and the Stage."

In this handsomely-bound, well-printed, and most excellently illustrated treatise (published at 15s. by Davis and Orioli) Maurice Jonas, author, also, of "Notes of an Art Collector," set forth his refreshingly independent, commonsense, and unbiassed views on many vexed questions of Shakespearean scholarship and controversy, besides cramming the book with interesting and sometimes new matter. It contained, among other things, a most useful "Complete List of Theatrical Terms Used by Shakespeare in His Plays and Poems, Arranged in Alphabetical

Order," and more valuable still were the numerous reproductions of rare title-pages of old plays. These had been made in facsimile for Mr. Jonas by Mr. H. Franklin Waghorn, who paid many visits to the British Museum for that purpose, and the blocks for all the facsimile photographs were executed by Mr. Fleming. Merely to study these alone the Shakespearean enthusiast should take account of Mr. Jonas's book. Among its longest and most interesting sections were those on "The Theatres," "London Theatrical Companies," "Shakespeare as an Actor," and "Court Performances," all full of facts, many of them no doubt familiar to students of the stage, and the illustrations included views of the Swan, Rose, Second Fortune, Red Bull, and other Elizabethan or Jacobean playhouses.

GENEVIÈVE WARD'S RECOLLECTIONS.

There was full justification for that veteran tragédienne Geneviève Ward having the literary assistance of Richard Whiteing in the putting together of her book of recollections of a long life, styled "Both Sides of the Curtain," and published by Cassells at 10s. 6d. net. Mr. Whiteing it was who wrote the *Manchester Guardian* notice of her appearance as Lady Macbeth at the Royal, Manchester, as far back as 1873; she was seen in the same famous rôle at Drury Lane in 1876, when she "organised the performance for the benefit of the American Centennial Fund in honour of the 100th anniversary of the Declaration of Independence"; and only quite lately has one witnessed Miss Ward's deeply impressive acting of an Old Style Lady Macbeth, which was among the most interesting features of the recent Drury Lane Pageant. Her book, marked (as the reminiscences of other famous players have been) by a certain acerbity of tone and frank criticism of others here and there, is full of well-told anecdotes and of sayings imbued with the wisdom or assurance that experience gives; and it is finely illustrated, the frontispiece being a reproduction in colours from the painting by Hugh G. Rivière, and other portraits showing the distinguished actress in such rôles as those of the ambitious Thane's blood-guilty wife, Queen Katharine, Stephanie de Mohrivart in her celebrated assumption given in "Forget-Me-Not," Volumnia, Elinor in "Becket," Margaret of Anjou, the Blind Queen, in "The Virgin Goddess," and the Duchess in "The Aristocrat," which part she was playing when she received her "eightieth birthday address" from Sir George Alexander, Mr. Louis N. Parker, and the members of the St. James's Company.

Miss Ward has recorded that she has travelled "about 85,000 miles, all on business," including a trip round the world and sixteen crossings of the Atlantic, and that in drama (not counting opera) she played "in seventy-seven pieces, great and small, and by a large proportion mainly the former. Shakespeare was a large contributor, and the rest were important ventures in ancient or modern work." A paragraph calling for transcription begins: "No wonder the actors are sometimes tempted to lose sight of the distinction between themselves and the characters they play. They are kings and queens in a way, and the incense they breathe exceeds in pungency anything offered to the most popular rulers of the world." She goes on: "It was a great epoch for us, perhaps as great as any in theatrical annals. We were admired, honoured, respected—aye, there's the rub. The palmy days of the stage did not end with the dynasties of the Kembles. The Victorian was a great age in that, as in all else."

A PEN-PICTURE OF SALA.

Miss Ward has taken from her album a few characteristic drawings by George Augustus Sala wherewith to adorn this volume, and of "G. A. S." himself she speaks in terms of warm affection, thus: "Kind and constant friend! I had the greatest respect and admiration for him to the last. He took his art of journalism seriously, for no one laboured more assiduously for the instruction by amusement of the million then coming into its own. On the surface he seemed but the gossamer creature of an hour, touching literature, art, society, and manners. But the touch was light only because the hand was sure—every anecdote was in its place, as carefully edited to the very pauses and inflections and for the terminal words, as if he had conned it in triple proof."

TEACHING FOR THE FRENCH STAGE.

Another extract from "Both Sides of the Curtain" deals with the training that Geneviève Ward received in Paris. She says: "The teaching for the French stage is the most thorough thing of the kind in the world. I studied privately under Regnier; beginners go first to the school of the Conservatoire, where many of the greatest actors of the Français take the classes in turn for a fee that does little more than cover the cost of their cab fares. No single thing is omitted—gesture, declamation, the search for the author's innermost meaning; above all, the sense of the absolute unity of the performance in the due subordination of the part to the whole. No nicety of the grammar of the art is beneath the notice of the master."

IRVING AS CRIMINOLOGIST.

Now that he is free from the trammels of war work, Mr. H. B. Irving may be able to take up again his literary as well as professional labours and thus provide us with a successor to those admirable books of his, "The Life of Judge Jeffreys" and "Studies of French Criminals of the Nineteenth Century," followed quite recently by his volume entitled "A Book of Remarkable Criminals" (Cassells, 7s. 6d. net). In this work, dedicated to E. V. Lucas, "H. B." treated in full the careers of such notorious murderers as Charles Peace, Robert Butler, Prof. Webster, H. H. Holmes, and various French criminals, whose stories, taken singly or together, bear out a statement made by Mr. Irving in his Introduction: "A judge once told the present writer that he did not often go to the theatre because none of the dramas which he saw on the stage seemed to him equal in intensity to those of real life which came before him in the course of his duties." This Introduction, as has previously been pointed out, is full of apt comparisons and parallels drawn from the plays of Shakespeare, with whose gallery of infamous evil-doers the men already mentioned and many others may fairly be classed, and, indeed, the studies in the book may thus be said to satisfy the legal mind, as well as helping to appease the pretty general and natural craving for strong drama. The subjects chosen have given the writer scope both for his well-known bent towards the analysis of criminal motives and for the display of the at once closely reasoned and sufficiently coloured literary method required to make a treatise of this sort something better than a mere Newgate Calendar. Perhaps Mr. Irving might have some of these strange and appalling life stories dramatised for his own stage purposes: they might afford him the chance of enriching the modern theatre with some more brilliant character impersonations.

"OLD SAWS AND MODERN INSTANCES."

That ripe scholar and distinguished man of letters W. L. Courtney adapted one of the melancholy Jaques's famous aphorisms from his "All the world's a stage" speech to serve as the label of a deeply interesting series of essays, most of them dealing with theatrical matters and dramatic themes. Published by Chapman and Hall at 10s. 6d. net, "Old Saws and Modern Instances" contained ably-thought-out comparisons of Thomas Hardy as a dramatist with Æschylus, and of Eugène Brieux with Euripides, besides other notable papers on "The Idea of Comedy" and on "Realistic Drama." To these but cursory reference can now be made, as much more detailed note is required of Mr. Courtney's both generous and eminently judicious appreciation of Sir Herbert Tree, of whom he says he had been a friend "for more than a quarter of a century—a rather intimate friend, with whom he would discuss matters concerning which he would remain silent with others. He talked freely with me because he thought (and I hope he thought rightly) that I would understand him and sympathise with him." This renders all the more valuable Mr. Courtney's frank summing up of the merits and the main characteristics, both as actor and as manager, of the man whose loss so many of us are still deploring. Hence I feel called upon to make a few extracts from a volume that ought to be in the hands of every thoughtful student of the stage. Better examples of true criticism could with difficulty be found, and Mr. Courtney should regard the choosing of these quotations as "a sincere form of flattery."

TREE'S VERSATILITY.

"Versatility was Tree's chief characteristic, or, as some might say, his besetting sin. Versatile he undoubtedly was; he tried to show his skill in very different fields of dramatic work. He essayed tragic rôles—at one time he was very anxious to act King Lear as a pendant or culmination to his Macbeth, his Othello, his Hamlet. He was a comedian either with or without a touch of melodrama; he made his name originally in farce, as those know who saw his Private Secretary. Versatility is undoubtedly a perilous gift. You know how a versatile man is supposed to waste himself and his talents in many channels of activity and to succeed in none. I have said a 'so-called versatile man,' because no man is really versatile; he only thinks he is, or is idly so reported by others. There is always one thing he does which is better than others, despite his many-sidedness, and, if he is wise, he will discover what it is and cultivate it to the best of his ability. Tree liked to be considered many-sided; indeed, he resented any suggestion to the contrary, and for this reason, I suppose, wrote two books, though he ostentatiously declared that he was not a book-reader. His restless and unbounded activity was compelled to show itself in various fields. I do not think I ever came across any man who was more pertinaciously and assiduously alive. He was 'a dragon for work,' as they say, and had a greater range of vivid interests—literary, political, social, and dramatic—than most of us can lay claim to. His quick alertness of spirit, his ready apprehension, his humour—which at times verged on the *macabre*—made him a most stimulating companion. He always saw objects from the less obvious standpoints, and delighted in all that was unconventional and paradoxical. His wit was never mordant, nor was it always very pointed. And his epigrams were for the most part ebullitions of high spirits."

His Contributions to the Stage.

"What were the positive contributions of Herbert Tree to the English stage? Here there is some room for dissent and disagreement. I will only put down certain facts in the form in which they appear to me. Remember, in the first place, that he inherited a great tradition from Henry Irving, who had set a magnificent example of stage production at the Lyceum. Tree was at first content to carry on the tradition on similar lines. He produced plays with extreme care for detail and many appeals to the eye. There was never anything slipshod either in the method of stage representation or in the attention paid to what diplomats call 'imponderabilia.' Indeed, it was the care taken over the minutiæ which guaranteed the effectiveness of the whole. Thanks in especial to Irving and Tree, London stage production reached a higher level of completeness and finish than was to be seen in foreign capitals. Sarah Bernhardt and other foreign visitors acknowledged that in this respect they did not do things better in France. Gradually Tree bettered the examples of his predecessors. His critics said he over-elaborated his effects; his friends were never tired of welcoming new grades of beauty. I take only two instances out of many which offer themselves in recollection.

"Probably there was never a more beautiful stage picture than Olivia's pleasaunce in 'Twelfth Night.' We talk of the hanging gardens of Babylon as of something legendary and rare. Here before our eyes were to be seen Olivia's hanging gardens, a dream of exquisite and appealing beauty which seemed to bring out the more clearly by contrast the vulgarity and coarseness of Sir Toby Belch and Sir Andrew Ague-Cheek, while it enhanced the delicacy of Viola and Olivia herself. The other example I will take from 'A Midsummer Night's Dream.' You will recall that though the scene is supposed to be laid in the neighbourhood of Athens, the feeling, the atmosphere of the play belong essentially to Stratford and England. Accordingly, Tree gave us. alternately with some marble seats and olive-trees, splendid glimpses of British forests, in which the fairies ran wild and Bottom and his companions rehearsed their uncouth theatricals. Anything more restful to the eye than these glades of sylvan beauty I have never seen on any stage. I used to drop into the theatre while the play was going on just to realise once more the solemn delightful effect of the old beeches sheltering the wayward fancies of Oberon, Titania, and Puck, and providing a rehearsal ground for Pyramus and Thisbe. I must also add something about the elaborate scene at the end of the play, when the pillars of the Duke's palace glow with internal light to enable the fairies to carry on their domestic tasks of making everything clean and sweet for the mortals. It was beautiful, but perhaps too elaborate. One missed in this case the note of simplicity, the wise sobriety of an accomplished artist who would not strive 'to do better than well' lest he should 'confound his skill in covetousness.' There were charming pictures, too, in 'The Tempest,' little sea-fairies peeping round the edges of the rocks, while Ariel sported in the pools, which one remembers with gratitude. But, indeed, the time would fail me if I were to recount half the wonders which the magician Tree displayed before our eyes in play after play. You may call him a consummate decorator if you like."

NOT MERELY DECORATION.

"Tree soon realised that decoration in itself could only please the groundlings or the dilettantes, and that the main matter of consequence was the spirit in which the whole adventure was attempted. What was the character of the adventure? It was to give the British stage dignity as well as charm, high seriousness as well as æsthetic adornment. It was for this reason that from time to time he put before his public—a *clientèle*, by the way, which was always steadily growing—stately performances of Shakespearean plays, incidentally proving that our great English dramatist did not necessarily spell bankruptcy, but. judiciously treated, might be made to yield a fair percentage of profit. He varied his programme with lighter fare as a matter of course. A man who had undertaken the responsibility of so large a theatre as His Majesty's was bound to keep a steady eye on the booking-office and replenish his coffers now and again by popular appeals. Unfortunately, our public is not always spurred and exalted to finer issues; and though Shakespeare, under special conditions, can become almost popular, a certain melodramatic blatancy—or at least insistence—has a more distinct pecuniary appeal. Where theatres are not supported by municipalities or the State, the lessee and manager is forced to 'go here and there and make himself a motley to the view' for base considerations of solvency. But Tree did not forget the higher obligations of the position he had attained. As head of the profession, he realised his responsibilities. He was full of the idea of the importance of the theatrical art as a main instrument of culture, and as a most necessary element in civic and social life. He did not work merely for his own hand, but upheld the claims of his calling. He instituted a Shakespearean week—a most costly undertaking—in order to keep alive our indebtedness to the Elizabethan stage. He presided at meetings, made speeches, inaugurated movements, pushed and encouraged various policies, in order to prove that actors were important elements in the community who had their proper functions in the body politic."

THE REALISM OF BRIEUX.

Mr. Courtney's analysis of the method of Brieux also calls for notice. He says: "I come now to the consideration of that so-called realistic method which is especially illustrated in Brieux's 'Les Avariés,' and in Ibsen's 'Ghosts.' Realism is. of course, an ambiguous word, because it involves one or two assumptions which are not always verifiable. There is no greater realism in describing details which most people would pass over as either unsavoury or unnecessary than there is in other forms of dramatic or literary art which do not think it necessary to emphasise the sordid or the unclean. In the one case, as in the other, the artist is making use of that principle which is his by nature—the principle of selection. He uses the materials which are necessary for his purpose, and he disregards the others. An artist painting a picture groups together various elements, not so much copying Nature as adapting Nature to his uses. A dramatist who would be called romantic proceeds in precisely the same fashion, throwing into high relief the figures of his hero and his heroine. and emphasising the sentiments and emotions appropriate in such cases. But what we sometimes forget is that the so-called realist has a precisely similar method of working. He, too, is occupied with arranging a picture, and, in order to bring out his scheme, he emphasises certain points and allows others to recede into the background. He uses his characters, not like independent personages, but rather as vehicles for illustrating the purpose or lesson which he has in mind. From this point of view the realist is just as unreal as the romantic dramatist. Or, to put the matter otherwise. he has the same justification which the artist claims for himself, selection being of the very essence of the artist's problem.

"We must not, therefore, take it for granted that because Brieux wrote the play which, in the English translation, is called 'Damaged Goods,' or because Ibsen wrote a play which is called 'Ghosts,' they are necessarily nearer the ultimate truth of things than, let us say, Victor Hugo, with his romantic drama. We call it realism when the materials are sordid, and we call it romantic when the materials are sentimental or emotional. But the artist is a free worker; he can manipulate as he desires. Even the man whom we might call the most thorough-going of realists probably has some dream or ideal, which, tarnished as it may be, yet has in his eyes all the value of the Beautiful, however he may construe it. The question of truth hardly enters into these considerations. The dream of the artist is always true of him, and true for all those who see eye to eye with him in his work.

"To me, I confess, the whole question of what we vaguely call realism ought to be envisaged from another standpoint. If we look at the matter historically, knowing as we do that in the history of art progress is made by a series of spiral actions and reactions, we discover that romance, pursued up to a certain point, produces a feeling of satiety or unreality, and therefore naturally gives place to an opposite theory which calls itself logical and scientific. After Victor Hugo came Zola, Ibsen, and Brieux, just as in an earlier stage of the process of development the remoteness and frigidity of the classical drama gave place to Victor Hugo's romantic enthusiasm. The important thing, however, to notice is that the different artistic attitudes correspond to different periods in the evolution of a nation or of humanity at large. Nothing is clearer than the fact that what we sometimes call the Victorian outlook—that is to say, the attitude towards men and things congenial to the nineteenth century, is in large measure superseded, and it is interesting and important for us to recognise how the generation which we may call Georgian re-acts against its predecessor. It would have been impossible in the Victorian era to produce for the public plays like 'Les Avariés' and 'Ghosts.' Why? Because the theory of art was different; the temper of the public was different; the atmosphere was different. The appeal of the nineteenth century was to the heart; that of the twentieth century is to logical processes of the intellect. The office of drama is to popularise, as it were, scientific conceptions, to make use of scientific principles, to illustrate them in some imagined scheme, and thus to convey and metamorphose drama into a tract for the times."

Pinero on Merrick.

Hodder and Stoughton have been publishing a collected edition of the works of Leonard Merrick, and all these ably-written stories, including such novels of theatrical life as "When Love Flies Out of the Window," "The Actor-Manager," and "The Position of Peggy Harper," have had their value and interest enhanced by introductions from various distinguished pens. for instance, those of Sir James M. Barrie, Maurice Hewlett, H. G. Wells, G. K. Chesterton, and Granville Barker. To the book last-named this introductory matter has been contributed in some pungent and trenchantly-phrased pages by Sir Arthur Pinero, who begins: "It is, I believe, an open secret that Mr. Merrick was once upon a time 'on the stage,' and the reason I have been asked to write a short introduction is, I suppose, that I also was an actor in my early days." Mr. Merrick's lifelike portraits of Press-boomed stars, old players the victims of their own vices, bogus managers, agents, and so forth, have led Pinero to deliver some further broadsides against sundry "ornaments" (?) of the lower strata of the profession.

Bogus the Enemy.

In this story Mr. Merrick thus described a bogus manager named Armytage:— "The advertiser was evidently attired for the occasion. He wore a frock-coat in combination with a summer waistcoat, much crumpled, and the trousers of a tweed suit. A garnet pin ornamented the wrong portion of a made-up tie." This, Sir Arthur observes, ' is neither Impressionism nor Realism, in the sense that these words are bandied about. It is a plain, straightforward, apparently effortless account of a man's apparel. Every stroke, as in a skilful etching, being 'in the right place,' the imagination is stimulated to evolve from it the whole history of the miserable Armytage. Struggle, defeat, the fight for life, the pitiful roguery—all is suggested, as it were, upon the bitten plate." Ending his introduction to this brilliant story of stage life with the repetition of an àpropos "wig" yarn, Pinero winds up: "Alas! in the theatre of books, as well as in the theatre of plays, a vast number of people are still looking for wigs. And Mr. Merrick's characters wear none, being the creatures not only of keen observation, but of a strict literary integrity."

"Training for the Stage."

This was the title of a volume in Lippincott's Training Series issued in this country at 5s. net by the J. B. Lippincott Company, Philadelphia and London. This book—a well-intentioned one, if not combining anything very fresh or useful—was put together by Arthur Hornblow, editor of an American publication, *The Theatre Magazine*, and it had a Foreword by David Belasco. In this that well-known dramatist and producer said, among other things: "There is one thing the stage beginner need never fear: the profession is not so overcrowded that there is not always room for real talent. As a matter of fact, good actors to-day are hard to find. Managers need actors more than actors need managers. In preparing a play for the stage the first requisite is to see that it is properly cast; and so important do I consider this part of the work that I have often spent a year in selecting a suitable company. It is then that the manager must call into service all his knowledge of human nature." He ended: "Intelligence is desirable, but it is secondary. The merely 'brainy' actor is never a great actor on the stage." (A very debatable proposition, many of us may think.) "The heart is greater than the brain." Carefully compiled, Mr. Hornblow's treatise will probably have served its purpose with many ambitious stage aspirants. Noteworthy Appendices were those giving the Standard Theatrical Contract and General Rules for the Guidance of Actors during Performance proposed and drawn up by the Actors' Equity Association.

"Colour Studies in Paris."

Known for years as a critic of independent outlook, as a dramatist, and as a writer of picturesque and florid style, Arthur Symons collected some of his essays and articles best worth preserving under the above heading in a book issued at 7s. 6d. net by Chapman and Hall. He has much to say about Paul Verlaine, Stephane Mallarmé, Aristide Bruant, Petrus Borel, "et hoc genus omne," and one class of readers will be attracted thereby; but for one's own special purposes more interest attaches to the passages, pen-pictures, crayon-drawings, what you will, in which Mr. Symons set down his impressions of Yvette Guilbert as far back as 1900, and of such landmarks of Bohemian Paris as Montmartre and the Gingerbread Fair at Vincennes, his vivid descriptions of which may be paralleled with Charpentier's scenes of revelry, as shown in "Louise." Excellent writing in abundance is to be found in other sections of "Colour Studies in Paris," four excerpts from which may be taken, with due apologies to both author and publishers. The nature of these transcribed passages is indicated clearly enough by the headings now chosen for them.

The Gingerbread Fair at Vincennes.

"It is at night, towards nine o'clock, that the fair is at its best. The painted faces, the crude colours, assume their right aspect, become harmonious under the artificial light. The dancing pinks and reds whirl on the platforms, flash into the gaslight, disappear for an instant into a solid shadow against the light, emerge vividly. The moving black masses surge to and fro before the booths; from the side one sees lines of rigid figures, faces that the light shows in eager profile. Outside the Théâtre Cocherie there is a shifting light, which turns a dazzling glitter, moment by moment, across the road; it plunges like a sword into one of the trees opposite, casts a glow as of white fire over the transfigured green of leaves and branches, and then falls off, baffled by the impenetrable leafage. As the light drops suddenly on the crowd, an instant before only dimly visible, it throws into fierce relief the intent eyes, the gaping mouths, the unshaven cheeks, darting into the hollows of broken teeth, pointing cruelly at every scar and wrinkle."

At Montmartre.

"Still, if some of the glories of Montmartre are gone, Montmartre remains, and it remains unique. In no other city can I recall anything in itself so sordidly picturesque as those crawling heights which lead up to the Butte, so wonderful as the vision of the city which the Butte gives one. Night after night I have been up to this odd, fascinating little corner, merely to look at all I had left behind, and I have been struck by the attraction which this view obviously has for the somewhat unpleasant and unimpressionable people who inhabit the neighbourhood. Aristide Bruant's heroes and heroines, the lady on her way to Saint Lazare, the gentleman—who knows?—perhaps to La Roquette; they rest from their labour at times, and, leaning over the wooden paling, I am sure, enjoy Paris impressionistically. Perhaps this is one of the gifts of the *esprit Montmartre*, that philosophy of the pavement which has always been more or less localised in this district. Here at Montmartre, of course, and of it essentially, are almost all the public balls, the really Parisian café-concerts, which exist in Paris. The establishments in the Champs-Elysées are after an order of their own; the Folies-Bergère is an unsuccessful attempt to imitate an English music hall and a successful attempt to attract the English public; but amusing Paris, and Paris which amuses itself, goes to Montmartre. The cabaret of Aristide Bruant has lost something of its special character since Bruant took to singing at the Ambassadeurs: the Concert Lisbonne, which was once so pleasantly eccentric, has become ordinary. But there is still the true ring of Montmartre in the Carillon, that homely little place in the Rue de la Tour d'Auvergne, and the baser kind of Montmartre wit in the Concert des Concierges, not far off. And then, to end the evening, is there not the Rat Mort, of which a conscientious English lady novelist once gave so fanciful a picture? The Rat Mort, which ends the evening, sums up Montmartre; not prudently, but with 'some emotions and a moral.' "

YVETTE GUILBERT IN 1900.

" Her gamut in the purely comic is wide. With an inflection of the voice, a bend of that curious, long, thin body which seems to be embodied gesture, she can suggest, she can portray the humour that is dry, ironical, coarse (I will admit), unctuous even. Her voice can be sweet or harsh; it can chirp, lilt, chuckle, stutter; it can moan or laugh, be tipsy or distinguished. Nowhere is she conventional; nowhere does she even resemble any other French singer. Voice, face, gestures, pantomime, all are different, all are purely her own. She is a creature of contrasts, and suggests at once all that is innocent and all that is perverse. She has the pure blue eyes of a child—eyes that are cloudless, that gleam with a wicked ingenuousness, that close in the utter abasement of weariness, that open wide in all the expressionlessness of surprise. Her naïveté is perfect, and perfect, too, is that strange, subtle smile of comprehension that closes the period. A great impersonal artist, depending, as she does, entirely on her expressive power, her dramatic capabilities, her gift for being moved, for rendering the emotions of those in whom we do not look for just that kind of emotion, she affects one all the time as being, after all, removed from what she sings of—an artist whose sympathy is an instinct, a divination. There is something automatic in all fine histrionic genius, and I find some of the charm of the automaton in Yvette Guilbert."

WOMAN À LA WATTEAU.

" For Watteau a woman is the most beautiful thing in the world—something of a toy, perhaps, or an ornament, flowers. or jewels; and her clothes must be as beautiful as herself. He paints what no one else has painted : a *frisson* made woman. But he paints without desire. with a kind of tender, melancholy respect for the soul of the flesh, embodied in fine silks, fragile, loving to be loved. For him she is a bibelot, not a mistress, and he has made her after his own heart. He paints her cheek and her face with the same tenderness, the same passionate ecstasy. And he has put into her eyes not only that dainty malice with which she fights and conquers, but also that dainty mystery with which she attracts and retains."

SOME PUBLISHED PLAYS.

A fair number of notable plays were issued in book form during the year. The list of these included Maurice Maeterlinck's war drama, "The Burgomaster of Stilemonde" (recently produced by Mr. Martin Harvey), translated, as with other works by the once-styled " Belgian Shakespeare," by A. Teixeira de Mattos, and published by Methuen at 5s. net; C. Haddon Chambers's delightful comedy, " The Saving Grace " (successful on both sides of the Atlantic), Heinemann, 5s. net; John Drinkwater's ambitious Birmingham Repertory play, "Abraham Lincoln" (lately criticised in full), Sidgwick and Jackson, 2s. net; and Gwen Lally's "Jezebel," A. L. Humphreys, 2s. 6d. net. This last, from the pen of a versatile lady, writer, entertainer, and brilliant male impersonator, was styled in its "Author's Note" the first Biblical play "passed" by the Censor in this country. Effectively couched in blank verse, perhaps "Jezebel" may, by-and-bye, receive regular stage representation, in addition to the so-called copyright performance it had six years ago. Mention might be made also of a few popular plays turned into novels. Thus, from Hurst and Blackett (6s. 9d. net) there came Justin Huntly McCarthy's version in book form of "Nurse Benson," and in like manner "novelisations" of "Mr. Wu" and "The Purple Mask" were made by Louise Jordan Miln.

MUSICAL MONOGRAPHS.

Two more of Richard Northcott's admirably compiled booklets, invaluable to all intelligent students of matters operatic, were sent forth from the Press Printers, Limited, the subjects being "Beethoven's 'Fidelio' in London" and "Gounod's Operas in London," preceded by Notes, full of new and first-hand matter, on the life of the French composer, whose centenary had been celebrated in the summer. Both these monographs, like all the others from Mr. Northcott's pen, were crammed full with interesting dates, statistics, and carefully-verified references to the achievements of famous operatic artists. The Beethoven book opens with this somewhat melancholy paragraph : "Though the symphonies and overtures of Beethoven are familiar to English musicians, his opera has never become popular in this country. Placed on a lofty pinnacle in solitary grandeur, 'Fidelio' is gazed at reverentially, but its beauties are seldom appreciated. Undoubtedly the chilly gloominess of the story detracts from its potential fascination, but this defect is more than compensated for by gorgeous, elevating music. During the eighteen years' reign of Thérèse Tietjens it was heard occasionally in London, but since her death in 1877 it has aroused enthusiasm only from a select circle of art-lovers, and rarely have box-office receipts equalled stage expenses." In support of the often-made statement that the self-called "musician of love" will be remembered chiefly as the composer of "Faust," Mr. Northcott clinches the argument with these seemingly conclusive figures :—" There were 155 performances of 'Faust' at Her Majesty's; up to October 1, 1918, there have been 93 at Drury Lane and 344 at Covent Garden. In addition, I have records of 128 performances at other places of entertainment in London. As a contrast to these figures it may be mentioned that 124 performances of 'Roméo et Juliette' have been given at Covent Garden and 6 at Drury Lane; while 'Philémon et Baucis' can only boast of 30 representations at the Bow Street house and 4 at Drury Lane. In the British Museum Index 187 pages are devoted to Gounod's compositions and arrangements thereof, of which 73 relate solely to 'Faust.'"

MUSINGS OF A MUSICIAN.

Late on in the year, at the beginning of December, Macmillan and Co., Limited, issued, at 12s. 6d. net, "Musings and Memories of a Musician," by Sir George Henschel, Mus. Doc., the frequent references to foreign celebrities in which render advisable the transcription of this sentence from the author's prefatory note : "This book was written and in type before the war." More interesting than Sir George Henschel's gossip about his upbringing, early efforts, and wanderings are his accounts of meetings with many eminent personages, and more interesting and important still are the particulars which he gives concerning his laudable and zealous labours in connection with the Boston Symphony Orchestra, the London Symphony Concerts, and the Scottish Orchestra. Passages with regard to these excellent organisations are quoted below. The book, which is adorned with a fine portrait of the author in comparatively early or middle life, contains references to such distinguished musicians (alive or dead) as Sir Charles Santley, Sir Hubert Parry, Sarasate, the Rubinsteins. Adelina Patti, Sir Alexander Mackenzie, Hans Richter, Moscheles. Joachim, Brahms. Sir Charles Halle, Michael Costa, Boïto, César Cui, Tschaikowsky, Jenny Lind. Verdi, Edward Lloyd, Marie Brema, and so on and so on ; and there are allusions also to a good many theatrical notabilities, including Sir George Alexander, Sir Henry Irving, Ellen Terry, Mary Anderson, and Kate Terry-Lewis.

HENSCHEL'S EXORDIUM.

With the following apt illustration drawn from stage doings Sir George Henschel begins his musings :—"Shakespeare's 'All the World's a Stage' must appear of particular aptness and truth to the man who, approaching three score and ten of the Patriarch, reviews his past with the object of writing down his reminiscences. Looking back on the events of his life, he sees them as he would so many scenes in an old stage-play, upon which the curtain has fallen long ago, and the men and women who appeared in them pass before his spiritual vision like actors and actresses; some, having stirred his imagination, kindled the fire of his enthusiasm; some touched him to tears, provoked his mirth; some, perhaps, exceeded his expectations, some fallen short of them; but all having left some mark, some impression on his mind, lasting for a longer or a shorter period, according to their part and to the manner in which it was acted. I shall never forget a little incident at the Court Theatre of Weimar long years ago. The play had been Shakespeare's 'King Lear.' It was exceedingly well done as a whole, and the impersonation, in particular of the chief actor—a member of the regular company—of the tragic and majestically pathetic figure of the aged king was a wonderfully fine and powerful performance. At the end of the play, amid the enthusiasm of the crowded house, the chief actor was vociferously called before the curtain over and over again. At last, when recalled for the tenth time or so, he seemed quite overcome with emotion on receiving so great an ovation in the historical playhouse which could boast the traditions of Goethe and Schiller, and, bowing deeply, he was heard to mutter—audible, however, to part of the audience —'I think I've merited it.' This, many people, and some of the Press, considered a great piece of arrogance and self-conceit on the part of the actor, whilst I emphatically held with the few who, in that no doubt unusual utterance, could see nothing but the innocent, in the excitement of the moment thoughtlessly escaped, expression of the artist's consciousness of having given, having done his best; and I have often thought since then how it would by no means be a deplorable state of things if more of the actors on the stage of life could make their exits with that consciousness, whether unnoticed or amid the plaudits of the multitude."

RULES FOR THE BOSTON SYMPHONY ORCHESTRA.

Very fitting and to the point will be found the rules appended :—

"To the Members of the Boston Symphony Orchestra.

"Gentlemen,—I beg leave to say a few words to you now in order to avoid waste of time after our work has once begun. Wherever a body of men are working together for one and the same end, as you and I, the utmost of unity and mutual understanding is required in order to achieve anything that is great and good. Every one of us, engaged for the concerts we are on the point of beginning, has been engaged because his powers, his talents have been considered valuable for the purpose. Every one of us, therefore, should have a like interest as well as a like share in the success of our work, and it is in this regard that I address you now, calling your attention to the following points, with which I urgently beg of you to acquaint yourselves thoroughly :—

"Let us be punctual. Better ten minutes before than one minute behind the time appointed.

"Tuning will cease the moment the conductor gives the sign for doing so.

"No member of the orchestra, even if his presence be not needed for the moment, will leave the hall during the time of the rehearsals and concerts without the consent of the conductor. The folios containing the parts will be closed after each rehearsal and concert.

"Inasmuch as we are engaged for musical purposes, we will not talk of private matters during rehearsals and concerts.

"Hoping that, thus working together with perfect understanding, our labours will be crowned with success, I am, gentlemen, your obedient servant, G. H."

HIS WORK WITH THE SCOTTISH ORCHESTRA.

"Those concerts with the Scottish Orchestra, recalling, by the absence of a committee and consequent perfect freedom and independence as regards programmes and rehearsals, those happy years of my first experiences in Boston, were a great joy to me, though to conduct over seventy concerts in Glasgow, Edinburgh, and a number of smaller towns north of the Tweed, and at the same time keep up the London Symphony Concerts as I did from '93 to '95 was, with all the rehearsals I insisted upon having, rather too much of a good thing, necessitating living mostly in hotels and doing a good amount of night travelling, and threatening to make a sort of 'quick-charge artist' of me, for usually there was, between the end of the concert and my jumping into the waiting cab to catch the train for London, barely time to change from evening clothes to travelling suit. But, with all that, my heart and mind were in my work, and their power over matter is truly wonderful. Try, for instance, to move your wrist and arm in strict rhythm as a mechanical physical exercise, and after less than five minutes you will be utterly tired out and forced to give it up. The Ninth Symphony takes more than sixty minutes' conducting, and at the end of it you feel like doing it all over again. At least, I did."

A VALEDICTORY.

The Memories are summarised thus:—

"In laying down my pen I cast a last surveying glance over the past, and, with feelings of sadness and keen disappointment, realise how grievously short of my aspirations and endeavours has fallen what I have been able to accomplish in my life. Is it perhaps that my natural talents have been too diffuse—I even dabbled in painting, and often regretted not having chosen it as a profession—and that, instead of concentrating all my energies upon one object from the beginning, I allowed them to be scattered over too many, thus achieving nothing notable in any? Two things only I can think of which conscience permits me to contemplate with something resembling satisfaction. One is: I have never betrayed my art by consciously stooping to the unworthy, to the commonplace; the other: music at present in England is on a very high level. Nowhere in the world, for instance, can there now be found orchestras superior to the best we have here. If it really could be, as generous and forbearing friends would have me believe, that by founding thirty years ago, at a time when there was no opportunity of hearing orchestral music during the winter season in London proper, the London Symphony Concerts, and, in the face of great difficulties, conducting them for eleven years, I have given the impetus, or even in some measure contributed to the marvellous development of music, creative and recreative, in this beloved land, I should die content in the thought of not, after all, having lived in vain."

MISCELLANEOUS.

March 5.—A complimentary luncheon was given at the Criterion Restaurant in honour of Mr. George Robey, to mark the excellent work he had done in connection with war charities. Sir William Henry Dunn was in the chair.

March 17.—A recognition dinner was given by the O.P. Club at the Criterion Restaurant to mark the appreciation of playgoers of the work done by the theatrical and variety professions in entertaining soldiers at home and abroad, and in raising large sums of money for various war funds and charities. The Right Hon. Lord Lambourne, C.V.O., was in the chair.

May 14.—The Music Hall Ladies' Guild held an Eastern Bazaar at the Savoy Hotel in aid of the funds for the widows and orphans of the variety profession. the Princess Royal and Princess Maud being present.

August 15.—Mr. Fred Terry was the guest at luncheon, at the Savoy Restaurant, of various managers throughout the kingdom whose theatres he visits, when he was presented with his portrait, painted by Mr. Frank Daniell.

October 6.—A dinner was given by the O.P. Club at the Criterion to Mr. Arthur Collins in celebration of his twenty-one years' management of Drury Lane Theatre.

November 17.—The Beneficent Order of Terriers gave a banquet at the Boulogne Restaurant in honour of Terrier Jack Harris, who had been a prisoner of war in Germany.

December 17.—A matinée was given at His Majesty's on behalf of King George's Pension Fund for Actors and Actresses. The Royal box was occupied by the King and Queen, Queen Alexandra, Princess Mary, Prince Albert, and Princess Victoria. The programme in the main consisted of a triple bill—an act of "Masks and Faces," scenes from "Macbeth," and "A Pantomime Rehearsal." Interesting features of the occasion were the appearance of Sir Squire and Lady Bancroft, as actor and speaker respectively; Miss Mary Anderson in the part of Lady Macbeth for the first time in the West End; and Mr. Weedon Grossmith's resumption of his old rôle of Lord Arthur Pomeroy in "A Pantomime Rehearsal." Lady Bancroft announced during the afternoon that the receipts had reached the sum of £2,000 odd.

CONCERTS AND PLAYS AT THE FRONT.

DURING the war the dramatic and musical professions have done a great national service. Their help in raising money for war charities will be difficult to value; but it would be quite impossible to appraise the value of the work that has been done for the armies through the Concerts at the Front organisation, because such a work is incalculable. Our armies, recruited suddenly from civilian life and hurried across to a foreign country, were called upon to endure not only danger and physical hardships, but the more subtle and more difficult privations of the cessation of all intellectual and recreative interests, loneliness of spirit in strange lands under strict discipline, and boredom.

The Napoleonic dictum that an army marches on its stomach can be matched by the aphorism that an army fights with its morale and wins with its nerves, and no one can tell what the music and cheerfulness and happiness taken across to France by the "Lena Ashwell Concert Parties" have meant to our men during the four years of war, when the armies went through grimmer, darker days than were generally realised.

The work started in the early days of 1915, when, at the request of the Ladies' Auxiliary Committee of the Y.M.C.A., Miss Lena Ashwell undertook to send a concert party to France. The men in the great base camps were dull, they were just realising that the war was going to be a long weary business, and that they were exiles in a strange country. They badly needed some form of recreation. Miss Ashwell raised the necessary funds for the experiment among her own friends, chose the musicians, and they crossed to Havre under the auspices of the Y.M.C.A. The first concerts were such an enormous success, the enthusiasm aroused among all ranks of the army they visited was so spontaneous and sincere, that Miss Ashwell decided that the appeals for more concerts that reached her from every part of France where the British armies were established could not be refused. The result has been the growth and development of the "Concerts at the Front" organisation, which has sent out over 800 artists during its four years of work, and given concerts and plays at the rate of 14,000 performances a year to many millions of men from all parts of the Empire.

It is not possible in so limited a space to give the full list of 800 names, but among the many popular artists who have been out to France with the concert parties during the war are: Miss Carrie Tubb, Miss Phyllis Lett, Miss Beatrice Eveline, Miss Margery Bentwich, Miss Auriol Jones, Mr. Gervase Elwes, Mr. Herbert Fryer, Mr. Charles Tree, Mr. Frederick Ranalow, Mr. Walter Hyde, etc., and Miss Ashwell herself has been out on many occasions.

At the end of 1918 there were twenty concert and dramatic parties continually in France, each party giving two or three performances a day to different audiences.

Two principles were established at the very beginning, and have been rigidly adhered to: (a) that only professional musicians and artists should be sent out to undertake what was extremely arduous work; (b) and that a high standard of performance should be maintained. Only good music is included in the programme, only good plays chosen, and the wisdom of this decision has been proved by its success. Every musician, every actor and actress who has been to France with the concert parties has the same experience and the same tale to tell of the almost bewildering enthusiasm of their audiences and the extraordinarily high level of the armies' taste in music and drama. The question: "What music do the men like best?" is difficult to answer, because they like anything that is simple and good, whether it is new or old—old familiar ballads, "Loch Lomond" and "Annie Laurie," "Drink to me only with thine eyes"; old Folk-songs which were new to them, but learned at once, such as "The Keys of Heaven" or "'Twas on a Monday morning"; songs or duets from operas, from "Carmen," "Samson and Delilah," or Gounod's "Romeo and Juliet"; instrumental solos or concerted music by Chopin,

Bach, Handel, Beethoven, Tschaikowsky, Dvorak, etc.; modern music—Elgar, Roger Quilter—all were extremely popular. Each concert party consisted of seven artists: a soprano, contralto, bass, tenor, violinist or 'cellist, pianist and accompanist, a conjurer, a ventriloquist, or entertainer, or someone to recite, so that the programmes might be as varied as possible.

One-third of the work was hospital work. Every afternoon the concerts were given in hospitals. The sick and wounded who were well enough to be moved would be gathered into the largest hall, ward, or tent, and those who were too ill to be moved would be visited in the "serious cases" wards and sung or played to, for however weak or ill the patients were they always wanted music, and it seemed to help them, not only by diverting their thoughts and giving them something pleasant to look forward to and think about, but in so many cases the music actually seemed to lessen their pain. And in cases of shell-shock or when the wounded were brought in straight from the trenches the music and the atmosphere of a concert were an enormous help in rallying the men's vitality and in helping to dispel from their minds the horrors they had passed through on the battlefield. The hospital audiences were necessarily smaller and quieter than the exuberant audiences that thronged the huts at the evening performances, but their pleasure and satisfaction were intense. One boy who was at a hospital concert the day before he returned to the front, wrote: "We all agreed that we would go back to the trenches and fight all the better for the happy remembrance. I was feeling rather lonely, not having anybody to write to me while I was out there. I began to feel I was fighting for no one until that cheery party came along. I can even now fancy I can hear the sweet notes of the violin." That was before the second battle of Ypres, when the boy was wounded four times and gassed.

The other daily performances were and are given in huts, in hangars, or marquees, or out of doors—wherever, in fact, the largest audiences can be collected; and the anxiety of the men to get in is such that they will wait hours beforehand—perhaps 800 men will squeeze into a hut that could hold 500 with comfort, and another 800 will be crowded round the hut outside, 8 or 9 deep all round, to hear what they can through the doors and windows. The largest huts hold 2,000 men. And it is difficult to say which is the most moving, the breathless silence with which these audiences listen to every item on the programme or the deafening applause with which they encore everything that appeals to them.

Some of the camps visited are far away from the great bases, lonely aircraft camps, or forage camps, or lumber camps in the heart of French forests, and the advent of a concert party is the only entertainment or pleasure that reaches them.

After the work had been growing for a year permission was received for concert parties to be sent up to the firing line. The firing line parties had to be composed of men only, as no women were allowed beyond a certain danger zone. These firing line concert parties, who travelled with gas masks, and sang and played to armed audiences straight from the trenches, had the unique experiences of giving concerts under shell fire to the accompaniment of the roar of cannon—our own cannon, for they went right among our artillery, and the enemy's, and they learned to "carry on" under the most trying conditions. In the winter the cold was intense, for the concert hall was very often a barn perforated with shell holes, and often the darkness was only relieved by a few bits of candle. It was "unhealthy" to show lights so near the Hun trenches, and frequently the enemy would start shelling the immediate neighbourhood in the middle of the concert, but nothing disturbed the concerts. Often another concert had to be given immediately after the first was over, because as the audience filed out at one door a second audience, which had been waiting outside for an hour and a-half, possibly in a blizzard or a snowstorm, filed in at another, and the concert would begin all over again. Then the concert party would visit a clearing station hospital, where the men lay on stretchers as they were carried in from the trenches. The doctors would be working at one end of the room, which was probably some school in peace time, and the concert party would be installed at the other end, and however difficult it was to begin to sing or play in such a scene of pain and suffering the performers were encouraged by the evident pleasure and enjoyment the music gave. Often apparently grievously wounded men would stop groaning to try to join in the chorus of a song they knew, or to try to applaud.

The hospital work was so valuable that a special concert party was sent out to Malta when that island was one vast hospital camp with the sick and wounded from Gallipoli and Salonika. That concert party had the satisfaction of visiting part of the fleet that was in Mediterranean waters. It gave concerts on the decks of cruisers to audiences of naval heroes from Suvla Bay and the Dardanelles, and other concerts in harbours to crews of minesweepers and submarines, and in the autumn of 1916 a concert party went still further afield. It went out to Egypt for six months, but that concert party remained over two years, visiting not only our troops encamped all over Egypt and spending Christmas in the Libyan desert, but followed the armies into Sinai, and finally was with General Allenby's victorious armies in Palestine when he defeated the Turks. Concerts were given to our troops in Jaffa, in the Holy Land, in Jerusalem itself; and after one concert given at Jerusalem to an audience of many nationalities and various creeds, including Indians, Moslems, priests of different denominations and religious communities as well as officers, nurses, and men of the British armies, the Military Governor wrote a letter of gratitude and appreciation to say that the work of the concert party by "uniting in friendly merriment the various and often conflicting nationalities and religions has been of definite political value to the military administration."

The dramatic side of the work developed gradually. At first a few one-act plays were taken out—some of Miss Gertrude Jennings's—and were played wherever a platform and curtain could be improvised. In hospitals a stage could be made of tables with Red Cross screens for scenery; in the camps the companies managed with sugar boxes and brown Army blankets, if nothing else was available. And anything that could be borrowed on the spot did duty for properties. In one tea-party scene in a Mayfair drawing-room, ginger-beer bottles had to be used as tea-things. In spite of all scenic shortcomings the little plays were so popular that Miss Ashwell made a bolder experiment, and took out a small company to give scenes from "Macbeth." She played Lady Macbeth. And this war-time celebration of Shakespeare's Tercentenary in France, given without scenery—unless Army blankets be counted as scenery—was appreciated enormously. On one occasion, when a programme of one-act comedies had been arranged as the most suitable both for the audience and for the building—a great bare hangar—the men sent three deputations during the day to beg for "Macbeth" instead. The bill was changed, and they had the tragedy.

Sheridan's "School for Scandal" was a great success, too. It was first performed out of doors in a wood, with a backcloth of flags, with the audience sitting on the grass and dangerously overcrowding the branches of trees. Then men's admiration for the play was intensified by their delight over the pretty dresses—the whole army grew so sick of the all-prevailing khaki uniform that the sight of civilian clothes was a joy to them, and the gaily coloured clothes partly accounted for the especial popularity of costume plays.

One after another seven repertory dramatic companies were formed and sent out to different bases, and a small theatre was taken in Paris in 1918 for the entertainment of men on leave there. Altogether 80 plays have been successfully produced. These dramatic companies have had strange difficulties to overcome, not only difficulties of scenery and properties, which in many cases they have had to set to work to make themselves out of any odds and ends of wood, canvas and paint they could beg, borrow, or otherwise acquire from the armies to whom they were ministering, but difficulties of personnel. For part of their work was to help the men themselves to take a practical part in the production—to find and rehearse promising amateurs to supplement the cast—and then to find, possibly at the last moment, that such useful recruits had marching orders, and would be unable to appear. But no difficulties really daunted the enterprising stage managers, among whom have been Miss Cicely Hamilton, Miss Mary Barton, Mrs. Penelope Wheeler, Miss Marie Ault, Mr. H. Lomas, and Mr. Oswald Marshall.

The work in the war zone has entailed not only extraordinary difficulties upon all concerned, but very definite dangers—danger from submarines by sea and bombs on land. The firing line parties were in the danger zone in the line, but the concert parties at the bases were in continual air raids. One dramatic party was actually bombed out of its billets night after night, and finally took refuge by night in the neighbouring forest, camping out to sleep and going into the town every day to give two performances more or less peacefully.

But in spite of dangers and difficulties, the work was carried on for four arduous years, Miss Ashwell, as honorary organiser, being responsible not only for every detail of the organisation, but for the work of raising the necessary funds to pay for it. And the work is not yet over; until the armies are demobilised hundreds of thousands of men from all over the world—England, Scotland, Ireland, Wales,

Canada, Australia, New Zealand, South Africa, India, and the smaller Overseas Dominions—will be exiles in a strange land needing the recreation and relaxation and inspiration that music and drama are in the world to give to those who pass through.

LIST OF PLAYS PRODUCED IN FRANCE BY THE "CONCERTS AT THE FRONT" REPERTORY DRAMATIC COMPANIES.

SIR JAMES BARRIE.—"The Old Lady Shows Her Medals," "Rosalind," "Seven Women," "The Twelve Pound Look."

HAROLD BRIGHOUSE.—"The Price of Coal."

HADDON CHAMBERS.—"The Tyranny of Tears," "Sir Antony."

CECIL CLAY.—"The Pantomime Rehearsal."

W. J. COLEBY.—"Her Point of View."

HUBERT HENRY DAVIES.—"The Mollusc," "Cousin Kate."

OLIPHANT DOWN.—"The Maker of Dreams."

GERALD DUNN.—"Dear Little Wife."

JAMES B. FAGAN.—"The Fourth of August."

FREDERICK FENN.—"The Convict on the Hearth," "'Op o' Me Thumb" (with Richard Pryce).

OLIVER GOLDSMITH.—"She Stoops to Conquer."

LADY GREGORY.—"The Workhouse Ward."

CICELY HAMILTON.—"Just to Get Married," "A Mystery Play."

COSMO HAMILTON.—"Box B," "Jerry and a Sunbeam," "Soldiers' Daughters."

CYRIL HARCOURT.—"Wanted a Husband."

ROBERT HIGGINBOTTOM. — "Kitty," "Clearly and Concisely."

CAPT. HARWOOD AND TENNYSON JESSE.—"Billeted."

STANLEY HOUGHTON.—"The Dear Departed," "The Younger Generation."

KEBLE HOWARD.—"Compromising Martha."

W. W. JACOBS.—"The Monkey's Paw," "The Ghost of Jerry Bundler."

GERTRUDE JENNINGS.—"Acid Drops," "The Bathroom Door," "Between the Soup and the Savoury," "Five Birds in a Cage," "Mother o' Pearl," "Poached Eggs and Pearls," "The Rest Cure."

G. AND J. LANDA.—"Red 'Ria."

LEON M. LION.—"Mobswoman."

COSMO GORDON LENNOX.—"The Marriage of Kitty."

CAPT. MARSHALL.—"His Excellency the Governor."

J. E. SACKVILLE MARTIN.—"Cupid and the Styx."

NORMAN McKINNEL.—"The Bishop's Candlesticks."

ARTHUR MORRISON.—"That Brute Simmons."

LEOPOLD MONTAGUE.—"The Crystal Gazer."

SOMERSET MAUGHAM. — "Caroline," "Smith."

DAISY McGEOGH.—"The Collaborators."

HARTLEY MANNERS.—"The Queen's Messenger."

HAROLD OWEN.—"A Little Fowl Play."

MRS. GEORGE PASTON.—"Feed the Brute," "'Tilda's New Hat."

SIR ARTHUR PINERO.—"The Playgoers."

ROSEMARY REES.—"Her Dearest Friend."

GERTRUDE ROBINS.—"Loving as We Do," "Makeshifts."

HENRY SETON AND NIEL LYONS.—"A Penny a Bunch."

HENRY SETON.—"The Link."

SHAKESPEARE.—"Macbeth," "The Taming of the Shrew," "The Merchant of Venice," "Twelfth Night."

SHERIDAN.—"The School for Scandal."

BERNARD SHAW.—"Candida," "You Never Can Tell."

GITHA SOWERBY.—"Before Breakfast."

ALFRED SUTRO.—"The Open Door," "The Marriage Will Not Take Place."

HAROLD TERRY.—"General Post."

GIDEON WARREN.—"Punctured."

OSCAR WILDE.—"The Importance of Being Earnest."

GEOFFREY WILKINSON.—"Releasing a Man."

FIRES IN BRITISH THEATRES.

September 5.—Royal, Colchester. Practically destroyed.

September 5.—Grand, Glasgow. Seriously damaged.

MISS LENA ASHWELL.

CONCERT PARTY.—STAGE AND AUDIENCE.

CAIRO SKATING THEATRE.
An open-air audience in Egypt.

MISS LENA ASHWELL'S CONCERT PARTY.

THE WAR-TIME STAGE.

By BERNARD WELLER.

BY the armistice of Monday, November 11, 1918, in the fifth year of the great war, fighting ceased on all fronts. After the long agony of strife, terrible and pauseless, after the going down of the principal enemy, deserted by her allies, in a swift cataclysm of defeat and revolution, peace and rejoicing for the forces of right and civilisation. Little wonder that the people of this country, victors upon every field and masters of the great seas, in the words of the old Psalmist lifted up their hearts in gladness. By a wise decision, the theatres and other places of amusement were not closed on this night, and in them, as in the streets throughout the day and far into the night, there were scenes of natural enthusiasm. The stage, as it always has been and always will be, is the mirror of popular life. There was little or no excess. Too much lay nearly within the memory of men and women, too much confronted them in the problems of peace, not to temper joy with a sense of the price that had been paid and was yet to be paid for the war that had engulfed Europe in its vasty jaws. There seemed on this historic night a peculiar rapport between auditorium and stage. No doubt the public in places of amusement had at the back of its mind—subconsciously, for the triumph of a just cause was the ruling emotion of all—an appreciation of the sturdy and strenuous ways in which the stage took up from the first and continued untiringly its share in the war. All actors fit for service joined up—by far the greater number of them before conscription came in. The elder actors and the actresses remained, and between them they kept in being a grievously depleted stage. They, and with them the managers, did more than that. They stimulated patriotism. They raised—with no thought of profit to themselves, and indeed at a heavy loss to themselves—some millions of money for war funds by their art. By the same means they cheered soldiers at the front and the base, in camp at home, in hospital. Withal they helped to keep the public in good spirits—a public worn with work and racked with the toll of the war upon health and life. It would be idle to say that the resources of the stage, working within limitations, restricted, specially taxed, unhelped officially, did not show some amount of weakening. But they were never exhausted; and the spirit to go on and to do a necessary public task was as strong in the fifth year of the war as in the first. The Government came, however tardily, and without offering any material assistance, to a recognition of the fact that it was a political and indeed national interest for amusements to be maintained. As the war lengthened and the conditions of life became harder, as the strain upon the endurance of the people grew, the value of the recreative work of the stage increased; and even a Government that had shown itself slow in imagination became alive to this position. The public had always been so. There was a note in the demonstrations of armistice night in theatres and other houses that gave assurance that the public had not forgotten.

OFFICIAL OBLIQUITY.

And there was matter enough for lively and grateful remembrance. The stage had done much—incredibly much—in the circumstances. It might have done still more provided the authorities had adopted towards it a policy of open encouragement and practical support, instead of one that was in effect negative and restrictive. It would appear to have been the official view that, whatever happened, and however it was treated, the stage might confidently be left to maintain its traffic. That view was not taken in the case of other industries, some of which were made certified occupations, and others of which were assisted by way of grant or subsidy. Consider for the moment the situation of the stage at the beginning of 1918, in the fourth year of the war. It had been stripped of its man-power available for military service, industrially conscripted by means of the Restricted Occupations Order, singled out for special taxation, which has meant a surcharge of 5s. on every £1 coming to the pay-boxes; restricted in lighting, in poster advertising, in the sale of refreshments and tobacco, and in other things; crippled in transit arrangements, by limited passenger and goods services and by fares 50 per cent. up and luggage rates heavily increased—just as the movement of the public has been hampered by inadequate rail and road facilities—compelled to pay more for labour and material; and, with it all, peculiarly subject to the effects of war depressions and in particular of air raid disturbances. Thus the stage had been obliged to struggle against continual odds. Yet, while requisitions for war services continued to be made upon managers and artists, and continued cheerfully to be met by them, on the other hand the calling of which they were members remained without any concessions of a kind that would enable them to a better to carry out such services and at the same time to keep the stage in a soundly productive state, for their own benefit and also the benefit of the public. Here and there was a little lip service. On a public occasion at which he was unable to be present, the Earl of Derby, then War Secretary, in a letter said:—

"I should like to have borne testimony to those in the theatrical profession who have done such extraordinarily good service in cheering our men, whether they be in health or in sickness. While many people out of their wealth have given large sums of money, the theatrical profession have given something which is even more valuable, and that is devoted service, which has brought, besides large sums of money for charity, a cheerfulness to our men which has made them, at all events for the moment, forget the dangers which they have to face."

Such tributes were agreeable reading, but little more, for throughout 1918 the steady constriction of theatrical affairs went on, directly and indirectly Though the Restricted Occupations Order was withdrawn—not simply against the stage, but generally—this fact was of slight advantage in view of the question of the new Military Service Act. A Government that acted logically upon the professions of Ministers that the supply of amusements was essential national service would have provided for the exemption of a certain proportion of managers and artists. But no provision of this sort was made, and the stage was faced with the prospect of all its man-power up to the age of fifty-one being called up. How places of amusement were to be managed, plays played, and stages set in these circumstances did not concern the Government. Every possible endeavour was made to keep places of amusement open, but the supply was inevitably reduced, and anything might have happened. At the best, the further yield of men from the stage could be only a thousand or two. Seeing the special position of the stage, to whose arts a proportion of men under fifty-one was essential, and seeing the national work that the stage was doing, was it worth while to carry the depletion farther than it had gone? These considerations, however, did not influence the Government. There was no measure of exemption, and the provisions of the Act were applied by the Tribunals with a minimum of relief in the cases of managers, artists, and other stage workers.

The 10.30 Bar.

Things began to look exceptionally dark for places of amusement in the early months of the year. That was literally so in regard to an Order in Council affecting lighting. Before the appearance of this Order business in town had suffered—if only temporarily in its worst aspects—by the air raids of January 28, February 17, and March 7. The proposal under which places of amusement in certain parts of the kingdom, including London, would be closed at 9.30 p.m., was not, however, put forward as a precautionary measure against raids. It was said officially that the sole reason for the projected Order was to conserve coal used in lighting, heating, and transport. It is noteworthy that the restriction was suggested for only a comparatively small part of the country—to the south of a line drawn from Bristol to Walton-on-the-Naze, which included the areas most open to aircraft attack. There appeared to be no purpose in trying to save fuel in, say, a tithe of the United Kingdom and allowing the old consumption elsewhere. If the real reason was a fear of aircraft attacks on a large scale, why raise a false issue? But any such reason was disavowed. The sole reason was stated to be the necessity for saving fuel. That being the case, so drastic a step, with so little to justify it, and with such serious consequences for the stage and also for both the public and the Army, who derived so much refreshment from the stage, looked like one more blunder from the departmental chiefs, who, in a spasmodic and drastic use of their wide powers, were doing the country more harm than good, and at the same time paralysing industries of which they had no technical knowledge. On March 15 the Coal Controller, Mr. Guy Calthrop, acting with the authority of the Board of Trade, notified managers of the impending Order, prescribing 9.30 p.m. as the latest time to which places of entertainment, in common with clubs and restaurants, should be allowed to remain open. The Coal Controller perhaps recognised the seriousness of any such restriction in relation to places of amusement, and he suggested that a deputation of managers from the different branches of amusements should see him and let him hear their views. Managers naturally appreciated this preliminary step by Mr. Calthrop. The Joint Committee of the Entertainment Industry formed in connection with the abortive National Service campaign—which harassed public amusements without producing any practical results—was called together for a meeting on March 18, and managers were thus in a position to state their case in a representative way. But managers found that Mr. Calthrop was ready to meet them but not their very reasonable views. He asked for a patriotic compliance. He overlooked the fact that managers were none the less patriotic because they objected to requisitions that were ill-considered and unworkable. Managers then referred the matter to Sir Albert Stanley, the President of the Board of Trade, who met them on March 20. This timely action fortunately saved the situation—or at all events averted its worst consequences, for the public as well as the managers. The project of throwing upon the streets the immense public in need of recreation as early as 9.30 p.m. (technically 9.30 p.m., but really 8.30 p.m.), or, in other words, before nightfall in summer, with nothing to do and nowhere to go—this foolish project was abandoned as hastily as it had been conceived. The authorities perhaps began to realise the social condition of London, especially the younger elements of London, in such circumstances. Managers clearly expressed their willingness to sacrifice their own interests to any national necessity. But they h... ...ve much difficulty in bringing home to so competent a man in industrial affairs as Sir Albert Stanley that the 9.30 proposal, while not securing its objects, would cripple the necessary evening supply of amusements. The saving of fuel in connection with the lighting of places of amusement was very problematical. The public, wherever it was, would need light after 9.30 p.m., and it could be more economically served with light in places of amusement than elsewhere. Moreover, if places of amusement started their performances an hour or an hour and a half earlier, the consumption of light would be increased. As to transport, the coal carried for the purpose of making electricity or gas was, in regard to places of amusement, relatively inconsiderable, and the passenger traffic of the public attending places of amusement could be discharged with less pressure when not conflicting—as it would have done under the proposed conditions—with the ordinary traffic. The wonder is that so uncalled-for and so unworkable a proposal should ever have been seriously contemplated by anyone in authority. The amendment that Sir Albert Stanley made in the draft Order was the substitution of 10.30 p.m. for 9.30 p.m. as the closing time. He also extended the operation of the Order to the whole of Great Britain. The restriction came into force on April 2. The new times of commencement at the theatres varied from 6.45 p.m. to 8.30 p.m., with 7.30 p.m. and 8 p.m. as the prevailing times. The twice-nightly music halls were rather harder hit than the theatres, which could leave out the first pieces. In general, these halls started half an hour or more earlier, and the new starting times that established themselves and continued until the withdrawal of the Order on December 23 averaged 6.15 p.m. for the first houses, with 8.30 p.m. for the second. The immediate consequences of the new curfew were a blow to the majority of managers, and the libraries also lost heavily. But the 10.30 bar was not entirely responsible for the fall in business at this period. The war news from the Western front was grave; leave was stopped, and khaki for the time all but disappeared from places of amusement. The public gradually adapted itself to the early closing conditions. But with train services reduced, the motor omnibuses ceasing to run late, and taxicabs limited in number, it became necessary for the central London houses to end their performances as soon after 10 p.m. as possible—no easy task, for it was difficult to speed up performances with working staffs cut down to the smallest dimensions through scarcity of labour. Managers had a further lighting trouble in the requirement that the consumption of light should be one-sixth less than in the previous year. This uniform reduction overlooked the fact that a manager who might have been running a piece or pieces with interior scenes requiring comparatively little light would be hard put to comply with the regulation when staging a musical comedy or a revue, say, with exterior scenes, or scenes calling for brilliant illumination.

The Paper Trouble.

In addition to these and other restrictions—the total prohibition of children under fourteen performing on the stage, contained in the Education Bill, was at the last moment, though passed into law, postponed in operation for three years—managers had to comply with the paper restrictions and the restrictions on the sale of goods in their houses. The existing paper restrictions were modified by a new Order taking effect on February 1. In the first place the restrictions from February 1 upon posters that were printed or partly printed on or before March 2, 1917, and were actually in stock on October 22, 1917, were removed. In the second place, the prohibition of advertising circulars after January 31—a prohibition that would have cut away a cheap and effective form of publicity—was withdrawn. Advertising circulars were permitted for a further period covering the year. The limitation upon the amount of printing of advertising circulars, however, was continued. This limitation was the same as the former one—i.e., one-third of weight of printing used within a certain period, specified as from February 1, 1917, to January 31, 1918. An advertising circular is one distributed by hand or through the post. If it is exhibited it becomes a poster. This distinction is material. Daybills, lithos, and the like are, if exhibited, posters, and in those circumstances the weight restriction does not apply to them. The concessions as to posters was at all events welcomed by managers who had large stocks of printing and by lessees with plenty of wall space at their disposal. Managers became free to exhibit such posters as they liked, provided the posters were begun on or before March 2, 1917, and were in stock on October 22, 1917, irrespective of size or number. Hitherto they had been allowed to exhibit on any one station (a) only one stock poster exceeding in size 2,400 square inches and (b) only a combination of posters of lesser size not exceeding in the aggregate a superficial area of 2,400 square inches. New posters, however, were restricted under the Order to 2,400 square inches, whether singly or in combination, on any one station. By new posters were meant posters of which the printing was begun after March 2, 1917. Thus touring managers who did not happen to have placed their orders in time for part-printing by March 2 were under a severe handicap in comparison with those who did. The latter had been enabled to have their stocks of printing—usually, on the instalment plan, large stocks, covering several tours—completed without regard, as it turned out, to the size of their posters. The former could not compete in the matter of the larger posters; and in point of quantity, if they were expected to supply the thousands of pictorial sheets, bills, lithos, etc., that managers with plants laid down were able to supply out of their completed stocks, could only do so at double or treble the old prices. Subsequently the Controller of Paper sanctioned a practice that had grown up in relation to old posters. He laid it down that posters printed on the back of old posters might be exhibited without restrictions, provided they bore the imprint :—"Printed on the reverse side of posters which were in stock before March 2, 1917." Also that new posters not exceeding in all the area of a 4-sheet d.c. might be exhibited on the same hoarding as any number of old posters, or of old posters printed on the reverse side, whether they did or did not refer to the same subject or business; and, further, that old posters and date-expired day-bills and double-crowns might be reversed and used for blanking. On the other hand, no new paper must be used for blanking. The paper trouble, however, was not yet at an end, for managers were summoned on May 15 to a meeting to discuss the reduction of programmes in size. The Controller wanted a programme not exceeding in size a 4 pp. crown quarto, or the equivalent in superficial measurement. Ultimately a 8 pp. crown quarto or equivalent was the maximum size fixed. This reduction meant a considerable loss in advertisement revenue to managers.

Sales in Theatres.

In regard to sales in theatres, an Order made by the Food Controller confined the sale of sweets by retail to certain shopkeepers. Only those shopkeepers whose rateable value was not more than £40 per annum, or whose receipts from the sale of sweets were at least 20 per cent. of the gross receipts, were allowed to continue this part of their businesses. The former class were not affected by the Order. The latter class might not carry on the sale of sweets after May 31, except under licenses. Of course, places of amusement did not sell chocolates and other sweets to the extent named, and therefore they lost this source of revenue, which, while not a fifth of their receipts, yet formed a useful addition in times when every little helped. The position was that sweets might be sold in places of amusement up to May 31, and provided application was made for license until June 30. These arrangements gave two months in which to clear out stocks, but this concession, which applied generally, was not a large one. With bars subject to 9.30 closing, and with other sales under the shop closing and similar regulations, managers, who usually let these departments to catering firms at substantial weekly rentals, had a useful source of income very greatly diminished.

TAXATION.

It will be seen from this rapid and incomplete summary how much—how cumulatively much—managers had to contend with in the fifth year of the war. And superimposed upon it all was the Entertainments Tax. Except for some trivial adjustments, which were chiefly of benefit to the picture houses that, with their small working expenses and minimum demand upon labour, were the best able to bear the tax, the high rates set in the 1917 Finance Act were maintained by the Chancellor of the Exchequer. In his Budget speech in April, Mr. Bonar Law said that the tax had yielded £5,000,000, or nearly £500,000 more than the estimate, in spite of the fact that the duty was put in force three months later than had been intended. He described the tax as one productive and easily collected. True, it is easily collected, because the trouble and also the cost thereof have been imposed on managers, who have been made to pay for the privilege of being their own tax collectors. Mr. Bonar Law even declined a request from managers to recoup themselves for the actual expenses of collection. How long the tax will remain productive, or at all events as productive as it has been, in view of a policy of continuously increasing repression, remains to be seen. The costs of stage production have mounted in all directions, in material, in labour, in transit. Yet managers of places have not, following the course of all other trades, raised their prices. Their expenses have gone up enormously, but managers are dealing with the public on the old terms—a policy for which they received no credit. On the contrary, they were mulcted in special taxation. The Government raised their prices for them and took the difference—this huge sum, under the new scale of the tax, of five millions for the last nine months of the financial year: on a full year it would on this basis have amounted to more than £6,000,000. Yet, immense as their difficulties have been, managers have succeeded in keeping places of amusement in full activity—that is to say, so far as keeping them open goes. That has only been possible because of the ever-increasing need of the public for entertainment and the consequent large attendance. As has been said, there were periods when this attendance had its sudden checks, but these periods were few and brief; and, simply in relation to receipts —by no means the same thing as profits, as the returns of many of the limited companies have shown—it may be that the last year of the war holds a record. No peace year probably ever saw such abounding gross receipts.

THE PROVINCIAL TRAFFIC.—LODGINGS.

Except for the fulness of attendance at places of amusement, the provincial traffic has been conducted at even greater disadvantage than the town Last year in an aggravated degree the manning of companies was extremely arduous; every sort of labour was short, the cost of materials was heavy, railway travelling was expensive, and the paper order and other restrictions pressed both hardly and unequally on managers. Further, managers on tour, and artists with them, had to bear with bad train services, bad luggage arrangements, bad food supplies—which affected them with special severity before the ration coupons came in—and after they arrived at their towns, worn out with journeys made in these circumstances, bad accommodation.

Many of the ills of the touring system might have been minimised if not entirely remedied by the adoption of a few co-ordinated measures. In spite of the cost of travelling, with the 50 per cent. extra on passenger fares, and the extra goods and luggage charges in addition, of scanty and slow trains, of labour for loading and unloading difficult to obtain, and of the unpunctual delivery of goods in transit, the itinerary for a tour was still not mapped out so that the different towns could be taken by easy and economical stages. Little or nothing was done, by joint effort, to grapple with these difficulties, as they might have been grappled with. Absurdly long railway journeys continued to be made; weekly and even semi-weekly changes of venue went on almost as freely as ever; and tired companies arrived at their destinations with in the majority of cases no resting places arranged for them in advance. If only comparatively short journeys were taken companies would reach their towns early in the day, and if fortnightly visits were made instead of weekly, as they could be by a large proportion of companies, fewer lodgings would be required by the artists concerned, and there would be less unreadiness on the part of landladies to let their rooms, as the occupancy would not be so temporary in character. The lodging problem last year became acute. The professional demand for accommodation was much larger than it had been. The aggregate of theatrical companies, revue companies, concert parties, and variety artists travelling in the provinces was greatly increased. In addition, owing to the growth of the fortnight's notice the duration of engagements has become more uncertain than ever, and without a tour list in front of him and a knowledge that his contract holds good for the towns on the list an artist is not justified in incurring liabilities the onus of which will fall upon him. Hence the recent tendency to leave the finding of rooms until the day of arrival in a town. Then the supply, which was something like a special supply, was heavily encroached upon by non-professional demands—from munition and other war-workers, from soldiers in training and wounded soldiers, freely billeted out by the military authorities; from holiday-makers, who last summer were immensely above the average in numbers; and from refugees, air-raid and otherwise. Hence artists found that the usual lodgings, never very large in number and seldom satisfactory in quality, were practically unobtainable in many parts of the country, and had everywhere risen greatly in cost. Very great hardships were suffered. To give a case by no means exceptional: Four actresses, after a twelve hours' journey, reached a town at 11 p.m. The town was pitch dark, and the four tramped its streets in a flood of rain. Finally, they had to spend the night in a cell at the police station. Leaving the cell at 7 a.m. they again set out in the search for rooms, and only after seven hours, once more in the rain, did they find any accommodation, and ther at an exorbitant price. There were bitter complaints of similar experiences in every sort of town, large as well as small. The small reserve of apartments for professionals seems either to have been swept away or rendered impracticable by force of competition.

ACTORS' CONTRACTS.

In the midst of apparent plenty—judging from the size of audiences—there were therefore hard times for actors on tour. In certain salaries—particularly for the younger men—the scales increased, but not proportionately to the rise in the cost of living; and the salaries of actresses especially remained inadequate. Working conditions were not improved by the way in which managers, at a loss for skilled artists, recruited their companies with incompetent and irresponsible performers, some of whom failed to keep their contractual obligations. The tendency of some of these latter to terminate their engagements without notice served in part to raise the whole question of actors' contracts, of which much was heard during the year, although managers held aloof from the practical remedy of a standard equitable contract. The reproduction of a number of current contracts in THE STAGE brought this question to a head; and the Actors' Association failing to obtain for actors a redress long overdue decided to reconstruct itself on a trade union basis. Mr. Sydney Valentine, as Chairman of the Council, was specially energetic in this course, and he and the other members of the Council had the satisfaction of seeing their proposals adopted by overwhelming majorities at the two statutory meetings by which, on November 1 and November 23, the Association as a limited liability company was wound up and the decision to form a trade union come to. Just prior to the first meeting the leading London actors issued a hotly-worded letter, addressed to "the non-union members of the Green Room Club." This letter, based on a clause in one of the contracts referred to, declared that "If we actors were one and indivisible we could stop this traffic in human bodies and souls in six months." The clause, however, was no worse than many others in the contracts, if as bad. The contracts, indeed, let in a flood of light

THE VARIETY YEAR.

By ARTHUR COLES ARMSTRONG.

WORKERS in the variety profession, from the highest to the most humble, have every legitimate reason to congratulate themselves upon the gallant and self-sacrificing part they have played in the glorious national triumphs of 1918. The year that has closed in over the sorrows and anxieties of war has seen a crescendo effort in their battle against the powers of darkness and despondency; and our Lady Variety is more radiant and resplendent than ever—smiling through her tears, and with a steady and confident regard for the future. It is difficult to appraise her work for humanity during the crawling years of hideous war. Nor would the task be an altogether desirable one. To have given gold and brought happiness to countless thousands; to have distributed with lavish and equal care the smile in the hospital ward and the robust chorus in the camp; to have uprooted despair and planted in its place the bright seed of hope—who is to estimate the precise value of these things to the achievement of final victory? To those who gave them they must ever be their own exceeding great reward; to those who received them, is not their heartening influence side by side with the manœuvrings of Foch and the hammer blows of Haig? The thought must have been uppermost in the mind of the King when he paid a considered tribute to variety by selecting a variety theatre—the Alhambra—as the first house of amusement, with the exception of war charity performances, to be visited by him since the outbreak of hostilities. Three days after the signing of the Armistice the King, the Queen, and Princess Mary witnessed " The Bing Boys on Broadway," and wonderful enthusiasm prevailed during the evening. At the close of the performance His Majesty said to Mr. Oswald Stoll : " I felt anxious to show my personal appreciation of the handsome way in which a popular entertainment industry has helped in the war with great sums of money, untiring service, and many sad sacrifices "—a just tribute, justly and gracefully paid. As for the sacrifices, if the variety profession can claim no special distinction over any other section of the community in having responded cheerfully and readily to the call, it can at least rest in the comforting knowledge of having made the general burden of sacrifice easier to bear. Those who sing the songs of a nation—songs of laughter and tears, or songs of sadness and hope—have the soul of a nation largely in their keeping. There have been songs in the variety theatres through all the sadness of these sad years, and the singers, many of them with bruised and aching hearts, are singing still, and will go on singing. A nation that can sing, both in sorrow and in triumph, is mightier than an army with banners.

TRIALS AND TRIBULATIONS.

In an artistic and productive sense, the variety world, like the theatrical world, may be said to have been marking time during 1918. From a material point of view, however, the variety theatre has enjoyed a consistent level of prosperity, in spite of wartime trials and tribulations and the shadow of " Dora," with her threat of pains and penalties. Houses in London have been wonderfully patronised—over 3,000,000 persons had paid for admission to the Palladium up to the beginning of December, for instance—and the same happy condition of affairs has prevailed in the provinces. The reason, of course, is not far to seek. Times of national stress invariably bring with them an increased need for amusement; but, apart from that, this right and tight little island has been a sort of clearing house for armies on their way to and from the Continent. London—in fact, England—has never been so full, and houses of amusement have flourished accordingly. On the debit side there have been the aforementioned trials and tribulations. In the spring of the year, for instance, there was the hair-raising proposal to close houses of entertainment at 9.30, and people were but half appeased when that unearthly hour was altered to 10.30. In a very short time, however, artists and audiences adapted themselves to the novel conditions, and earlier hours of opening and quickened and slightly curtailed performances solved the problem. On the other hand, the laws regulating the sales of sweetmeats, cigars, and cigarettes in the auditorium may be said to have caused some inconvenience and a certain loss of revenue. As for the paper shortage, such fears as were entertained have not been fully realised. If there has been a scarcity of paper on the walls, there has been a welcome scarcity of "paper" in the auditorium. In the autumn the possibility of a serious epidemic gave theatres the novel experience of being under the purview of the sanitary inspector.

WAR FUNDS.

One of the greatest triumphs of the variety world during the past year has been its increased success and activity in the raising of war funds. The variety profession has thousands, nay, millions, of pounds to its credit for the alleviation of suffering and distress caused by the war, and there is scarcely any war fund or charity—detestable word!—that has not benefited through the music hall and its large-hearted workers. At great personal trouble and expense, artists, big and little, have thrown themselves into the splendid cause, and where all have been so painstaking and self-sacrificing in the effort to bring a little sunshine into grey lives any picking out of particular individuals would seem to be almost invidious. No variety survey of the past year, however, would be complete without mention of that prince of "beggars," Mr. George Robey, whose wonderful record had its fitting recognition at a luncheon at the Criterion Restaurant in March, when, in the presence of a representative gathering, he was presented with an address and a solid silver tea and coffee service for his enterprise in organising special concerts and his weird and wonderful skill as an auctioneer. Up to the date of that happy gathering—happy on an exclusively vegetarian menu protected by a barrage of champagne—Mr. Robey had collected £50,000; he was careful to explain, in a feeling speech, that such a result would have been impossible without the whole-hearted co-operation of his brother and sister artists. He has gone on collecting ever since, and the best pens in England have been hard put to it to do justice to his prowess as an auctioneer. At Mr. George Robey's concerts thousands of pounds invariably changed hands—one of them, at the London Coliseum, realised the splendid total of £14,050, and even stray coppers strained at their moorings.

Among other successful raisers of war funds—it is impossible to name them all—have been Mr. Harry Tate and Mr. Harry Lauder, the first-named mainly by means of concerts—one of which realised £7,000—and Mr. Lauder with his Million Pound Fund for Scottish Sailors and Soldiers. Mr. Frank Allen, on the managerial side, had raised, by August, something like £75,000 by special matinées, and Mr. Walter de Frece, and of course, Mr. Oswald Stoll, have also been well to the fore in the halls under their control. Nor must the special appeals made from the variety stage on behalf of the Red Cross, the War Bonds Campaign (with Mr. Herman Darewski as honorary organiser of the scheme), and so on, be forgotten. Mr. Julien Henry, to name no other, was particularly successful in his appeals at the London Coliseum in the first-named connection; and the combined music hall collections ran into many thousands of pounds. One of these days, perhaps, it will be possible to get at the exact amount raised by the variety profession for war funds. The figures will astonish some people. In the meanwhile, one can but re-echo the opinion of Mr. Harry Lauder that the Government, after the tribute of the King, should pay the profession an official compliment for the splendid work it has accomplished during the great struggle.

THE WAR SEAL FOUNDATION.

Mr. Oswald Stoll's War Seal Foundation scheme may be mentioned in this survey by reason of its close connection, through Mr. Stoll, with the variety profession. It is one of the noblest and most practical of all schemes designed for the care and future comfort of men broken in the war, and 1918 saw immense progress with the range of flats at Fulham. Readers will require no further information about one of the best housing schemes of modern times, a scheme that will reflect lasting credit upon its founder. If all good things came into being by the simple process of licking a stamp, there would be no need for a League of Nations. Visiting the block of flats in October, Sir Arthur Stanley said, in a letter to Mr.

Stoll: "I feel confident that they will meet a real need and will bring comfort and happiness to many men who otherwise would have been separated from their families. I look upon this as not only one of the best, but also one of the kindest bits of war work that I have seen, and I feel sure that it will always be a source of legitimate satisfaction and pride to yourself and to all your coadjutors to know that you have brought home-life and consequent happiness to many who have suffered in the Great Cause, and to whom these blessings would otherwise have been denied."

REVUES.

In a former Year Book article the present writer put the question, Will peace kill the revue? and answered it by saying that it lies in the fact that peace will abolish nothing but the false, the unnecessary, and the improperly-labelled, that the future of real, legitimate revue is assured. Peace—real official peace—is already tinting the horizon, and there is no cause to go back upon the opinion. Revue, together with what has passed for revue, has rendered inestimable service to the variety theatre. In many instances it has kept it open and enabled it to carry on during wartime; and wartime audiences have been very easy to please. But there is no reason to suppose that the future public, with the burden of war troubles off their shoulders, will leave their critical faculties entirely at home whenever they go to a variety theatre. They will demand infinitely better material than that supplied, for instance, by a certain type of touring revue, some recent specimens of which have been shockingly bad and grossly inartistic. The enemies of the late James McNeil Whistler used to declare that he shied pots of paint at various pieces of canvas and called them pictures. In the variety theatres we have had various get-rich-quick gentlemen shying scenery and costumes, songs, and verbal gibberish at an audience, and calling themselves revue authors and producers. All that sort of thing must disappear. The war is over; we have had our fireworks in Hyde Park—with a prospect of more to follow, and it is time to set the variety theatre in order in the matter of revue. That it will be done is past all question. There are many good revues to point the way, although your heaven-sent revue author is a comparatively rare bird. In parenthesis, it may be said here that the death from wounds, early in the year, of Lieutenant Charles H. Bovill was a sad loss to English revue. He had pulsed the requirements of a revue audience to a nicety, and possessed much of the necessary Gallic touch. Many excellent producers are still with us, particularly Mr. Charles B. Cochran, who has fathered some of the best revues upon this side of the channel. Incidentally, Mr. Cochran has restored revue to the London Pavilion, which had previously gone over to drama; while a similar process in favour of revue has taken place at the Palace under the reign of Sir Alfred Butt. It would appear that the Oxford, which is another Cochran house, is to be lost for some time to both revue and variety

A list of the principal revues of the year will be found in another place. Those that may be mentioned here as having caught the particular fancy of audiences during 1918 include, among others, the Albert de Courville production, by Wal Pink and Frederick C. Chappelle, entitled "Hotch-Potch," first seen at Penge, and afterwards revived at the Duke of York's Theatre; "The Bing Boys on Broadway," by George Grossmith, Fred Thompson, Harry M. Vernon, Nat D. Ayer, and others, at the Alhambra; "Box o' Tricks," by Albert de Courville, Wal Pink, Dave Stamper, and Frederick C. Chappelle, at the London Hippodrome; "Jack in the Box," by Joseph Hayman and Max Darewski, at Birmingham; "The Passing Show of 1918," a Wylie-Tate production, at Birmingham; "Happy Go Lucky," an Albert de Courville production, at the Finsbury Park Empire; "Hullo, America!" by J. Hastings Turner and Herman Finck, at the Palace; "Ciro's Frolics," by R. P. Weston, Bert Lee, and Melville Gideon, which had its first London production at the Kilburn Empire, after a lengthy run in the provinces; and "As You Were," by Arthur Wimperis and Herman Darewski, and Edouard Mathé, at the London Pavilion. The list, it will be observed, is considerably shorter than that of the previous year, a circumstance due to a large extent to the marking-time policy already alluded to. The revue, however, is still the staple fare in variety. In addition to the gentlemen mentioned above, Messrs. George Shurley, Ernest C. Rolls, Karl F. Hooper, Harry Day, P. L. Flers, Fred Karno, William J. Wilson, Clifford Grey, Lew Lake, Robert Reilly, Fred Allandale, and others have been represented in the revue activities of 1918.

More Sketches?

With popular taste turning from the more nondescript type of touring revue, something of a revival may be expected in the direction of the sketch, or one-act play, of a serious, comical, or musical character. Such a revival would follow very naturally upon the weeding-out process among revues, and there is every indication that the time is ripe for it. The sketch of a former decade, of rough and ready construction and characterisation, can never return, but there is already a growing demand for the neatly-dovetailed and carefully-written one-act piece— a demand voiced by such an experienced entertainment-caterer as Mr. Charles Gulliver, who also quite recently offered a prize of £50 for a suitable manuscript. As Mr. Gulliver put it, "there is a distinct demand for half-hour sketches in the music halls. The coming of peace makes a change from the war sketch essential. Many artists go on giving the old stuff because no one studies their needs and supplies them with the right material." Most of the one-act plays seen in the variety theatres during the past year have been well worth their production, and the list of their authors has included J. M. Barrie, George Bernard Shaw, Alfred Sutro, W. W. Jacobs, Conan Doyle, Arthur W. Pinero, Cosmo Gordon Lennox, James Bernard Fagan, Harry M. Vernon, A. A. Milne, and other practised writers.

Prominent Players in Variety.

The one-act play, or play excerpt, has naturally brought many well-known players from the theatres to the field of variety. During the past year Miss Ellen Terry again graced the vaudeville stage in Shakespearean scenes, and Misses Violet and Irene Vanbrugh have been welcome visitors. Others have included Mr. Dion Boucicault, Miss Madge Titheradge, Mr. Nigel Playfair, Mr. Arthur Bourchier, Miss Lillah McCarthy (in a Shaw piece), Mr. Arthur Sinclair, and his company of Irish players, Mr. H. B. Irving, Mr. Rutland Barrington, Miss Clare Greet, Mrs. Langtry, Miss Viola Tree, Mr. George Barrett, Mr. Stanley Logan, and Mr. Herbert Waring. Sir George Alexander, who died in March, was, of course, a frequent player in the variety theatres.

A Revival of Ballet.

The lengthy season of the Serge Diaghileff Russian Ballet at the London Coliseum has been one of the artistic events of the variety year, and has served to revive an interest in ballet which has had its effect in other quarters. The Russian artists again displayed all their love for vivid colour effects; and there have been Bakst scenery and costumes in plenty for those who revel in such vagaries of freakish beauty. The Russian company included some notably artistic dancers, and Londoners will not readily forget the splendid artistry of such performers as Léonide Massine, Lydia Lopokova, Lubov Tchernicheva (whose performance of Cleopatra, first seen in London at Drury Lane in 1914, was repeated several times), Lydia Sokolova, and Stanislas Idzikovsky, one of the nimblest and most impish of harlequins of the present generation. Not a little of the fine effects produced by the Russians came from the orchestra scores of such masters of tone and melody as Schumann, Tschaikowsky, Rimsky-Korsakoff, Glazounov, Arensky, Tcherpnin, and others, all of which were artistically interpreted by the London Coliseum orchestra under the bâton of M. Henry Defosse. Certain events in the great world war may have inspired different thoughts and feelings about Russians in the more practical affairs of life, but there can be no possible doubt as to their supremacy in the art of ballet. They are easily first in the world of choregraphy, and art has no frontier line.

The Russian season at the London Coliseum commenced in September, and is to continue well into the spring of 1919. The full repertory of ballets includes "Cleopatra," "Good Humoured Ladies," "Papillons," "Prince Igor," "Scheherazade," "Les Sylphides," "Children's Tales," "Midnight Sun," "Carnaval," "Sadko," "The Enchanted Princess," "Spectre de la Rose," "Pekronshka," "L'Oiseau de Feu," "The Nightingale," "Thamar," and "L'Apres-Midi d'un Faune."

The Sir Thomas Beecham opera ballet and chorus, under the conductorship of Messrs. Percy Pitt, Eugene Goossens, Julius Harrison, and Wynn Reeves, began a three weeks' engagement at the Palladium in September, with excerpts from "Faust," "Phœbus and Pan," and "Carmen," the principal dancers including Mlle. Ninette de Valois and Misses Louise Maisie, Eily Gerald, and Anna Ouka;

and in December, at the same house, Mr. Napoleon Lambelet presented and conducted performances of the Butterfly ballet from "Valentine," with Misses Marjorie Stevens and Anna Bromova in leading parts. Both seasons, if not so ambitious as that of the Russians, enjoyed much success. The year's ballets should also include a delightful little piece by Sir Frederic Cowen entitled "Cupid's Conspiracy," with Mlle. Lydia Kyasht in the leading rôle. It was produced at the London Coliseum on the last day of 1917, but ran well into 1918. Sir Frederic Cowen conducted the orchestra at all performances.

NAVAL AND MILITARY CONCERT PARTIES.

The advent during 1918 of several concert parties composed of men from the naval and military services demands at least a passing notice, if only for the fact that such combinations, excellent though they may be, must of necessity belong exclusively to wartime. Perhaps the best was that known as The Dumbells, of the Third Canadian Division, who achieved marked success at the Victoria Palace, and afterwards at the London Coliseum. On the day following the signing of the Armistice, by the way, The Dumbells produced "The Pirates of Penzance" in its entirety at Mons, a town they had entered the previous day. A party of New Zealanders also did well at the Victoria Palace, where, later on, the "That" Quartet, composed of American sailors from Admiral Sims's flagship, "Nevada," were particularly popular. At the London Coliseum there was another Service party, the "See Toos," of the Second Canadian Division, who also came in for a cordial welcome. The First Army Headquarters Concert Party, "Les Rouges et Noirs," made a first appearance in London at the Beaver Hut Theatre (the Little) in December; and among other parties were the Diamond Troupe at the Court, and the Anzac Coves, who visited several houses. It was to the credit of these Service parties that their applause was invariably gained by legitimate artistic means, and not on account of the increased wartime popularity of khaki or blue. Quite a feature of their performances was the excellence of their "female impersonators."

THE PROFESSIONAL CHARITIES.

Members of the profession, in spite of their incurable regard for wartime and other charities, have, of course, not been entirely unmindful of their own. At the annual general meeting of the Variety Artists' Benevolent Fund held at the end of February, at which Mr. George Robey was unanimously elected President, it was made evident that, owing to the stress of war, the financial affairs of the Fund were not nearly so satisfactory as could be wished. It is still an unwelcome fact that the variety profession, ever open to the call of outside charities, pays insufficient attention to its own. The following extract from the annual report speaks for itself :—"It has been computed that the variety profession has raised for various charities connected with the war upwards of £5,000,000 (up to February). All the Benevolent Fund requires is £3,000!"

BRINSWORTH.

Nor can it be said that the funds for the upkeep and maintenance of Brinsworth have as yet been placed upon a satisfactory basis. At a special meeting held at the London Hippodrome in April for the purpose of drawing professional and public attention to the pressing needs of the V.A.B.F. and I., which, by the way, was very poorly attended, Mr. George Robey and other speakers referred to the deplorable hand-to-mouth condition of affairs, and the urgent need for a proper sinking fund. It was at this meeting that Mr. Joe Elvin inaugurated the Bing Boys Society, since called the Bings, in aid of Brinsworth, the title being chosen in honour of Mr. Robey. The Bings are in a line with the Hambones.

It may be mentioned that Mr. Frank Allen has arranged to hold an annual matinée at each of his halls on behalf of the funds of Brinsworth. Such a scheme should place matters upon a regular and permanent basis, and it is to be hoped that it will be imitated by other managers throughout the country.

The Music Hall Ladies' Guild, who continue their noble work among the poorer members of the profession, have had a fairly satisfactory wartime year. The ladies are "out" for £20,000 as a sinking fund for their proposed Orphanage. The street collection on Forget-Me-Not Day was twice as successful as that of last year.

THE V.A.F. AND OTHER SOCIETIES.

At the twelfth annual general meeting of the Variety Artists' Federation held in January, with the Chairman, Mr. Fred Russell, presiding, it was reported that the affairs of the Federation remained in an eminently satisfactory condition, notwithstanding some inevitable falling off in membership owing to the war.

A special meeting of the V.A.F. was called at a later date to discuss the desirability of Parliamentary representation of the profession through the Federation, and it was a generally accepted idea that Mr. Fred Russell should have contested one of the Brixton divisions in the Labour interest. Mr. Russell withdrew his candidature later on, however, owing to ill-health, and the matter remains in abeyance.

The Music Hall Artists' Railway Association, at their annual general meeting in October, reported satisfactory financial progress under war conditions.

The Grand Order of Water Rats and the Beneficent Order of Terriers carry along their good work, although they have been restricted on the social side owing to the war.

SONG NOTES.

As in the previous year, there has been great activity among the song publishing firms, particularly prominent being the houses of Francis and Day, the Herman Darewski Company, the Lawrence Wright Company, the Star Company, Osborne and Company, West and Company, Silberman and Grock, the Newman Publishing Company, Ascherberg, Hopwood, and Crew, and others. The ballad of domestic or sympathetic sentiment has again been uppermost in public favour, while great attention has been paid during the year to the song of purely ephemeral interest. Quite a number of the last-named have been published upon the quick sale principle. At the time of writing there is a revival of what is known as Jazz music.

OBITUARY.

Variety, alas! has paid its full toll of dead in the great war, and there were many vacant chairs around the Christmas table. In the thought of those who lie asleep across the seas in a little plot of earth that is for ever England, as Rupert Brooke so beautifully puts it, those of us who are left behind stand in affectionate memory and deep gratitude. *Dulce et decorum est pro patria mori.* There has also been a thinning out of the ranks of the civilians. Two of the largest-hearted men of the profession have passed away in the lovable persons of Eugene Stratton—"Uncle Gene"—and Paul Cinquevalli. Others whose loss we mourn include W. J. Ashcroft, Edward Towers, Lieutenant C. H. Bovill, Mark Sheridan (who died in such tragic circumstances at Glasgow), Fred Higham (the well-known agent), Cooper Mitchell, "Buster" Brown, Dick Burge, Little Tony, C. J. Scarisbrick, Harry Anderson, George Fairburn, Mrs. Lena Guilbert Ford (who wrote the lyric of "Keep the Home Fires Burning," and was killed in a London air raid), Charles William Poole, Richard Wake, Chung Ling Soo (William Elsworth Robinson, who was accidentally shot on the stage at the Wood Green Empire), Jack Woolf, Ronald F. Wakley, Walter Dickson (of the Empire directorate), Sir Henry Tozer, Sadrenne Storri, Anna Held, Arthur Playfair, L. M. Stewart, Rev. Thomas Horne (the showman's parson), Bonny Browning, Bu Val, Captain Tom Maltby, Billy Cragg, Harry Thornton, Walter Subtel, Mamie Graham, Bob Barry, Olive Sinclair, Lou Romah, Jack Delaine, Will Mayne, and Phil Ray.

L'ENVOI.

The war is over and the Boche is beaten—that must be the one dominating circumstance in any record of the year 1918. The variety profession has had a big hand in the securing of victory, and everything points to a great and glorious future. But at present, as has been said earlier in this article, variety is marking time. After the shouting and the tumult—a period of calm. We have breasted the torrents—for the moment we lie "pleased and panting in a pool." The future can hold nothing but good.

> Gone is the dawn with its lurking fears
> On a night of tearless weeping;
> Gone is the ache of the tremulous years
> With sorrow and death in their keeping;
> O ever the quiet of coming years,
> And the loved ones around us sleeping.

THE PARIS STAGE.

By TOR. DU AROZARENA.

CONSIDERING the difficulties with which the theatre has been obliged to cope in nearly every quarter of the world, the Paris stage has undoubtedly suffered more than any other among the Allied nations during the past year. Its proximity to the front made it sensitive to every fluctuation in the tide of war, and while there was an atmosphere of uncertainty in the theatrical world of London and New York, in Paris one had to contend, not only with the possible effect of reverses on the public moral, but with the imminent danger to the daily life and fortunes of all. It was an exciting game of chance that managers and actors played with Fate, and looking backward a Frenchman can feel with satisfaction that they have upheld the honour of their calling and recovered their glove. True, the Allied troops continually passing through the capital added largely to the playgoing public, but one must remember that they invariably preferred a music hall to the effort of following the story of a play in a foreign tongue. The result has not been wholly fortunate, for while Variety was never so flourishing as now, the Drama has suffered grievously, and the stage has been inundated by spectacular entertainments that are—or aim to be—enjoyable to the eye rather than to the intellect. In fact, with but a few exceptions, the serious dramatists showed no inclination to give their works, and thus aid in upholding the glory of the French Drama even at a personal loss, and the young playwrights were away in the trenches and unable to take advantage of the openings thus offered them. Now that the war is over, we are like to have an avalanche of plays from the four years' accumulated stock of celebrated authors, and the young playwrights will go begging as before.

Conditions During the Year.

The early part of last winter was marked by a more optimistic spirit among managers. They still showed an unaccountable tendency to produce war plays, for which there was no demand; but towards mid-winter things brightened perceptibly. An unusual number of English and American plays had been introduced, though the choice was unfortunately poor. However, H. A. Yachell's "Quinneys" did very well at the Gymnase, and Mme. Réjane scored a notable success with that curious melodrama of Bayard Veiller, "The 13th Chair." The critics, of course, treated all these importations with characteristic disdain, but the public thronged to see Mme. Réjane.

Just as the best bridge players traverse periods of ill luck, so in the theatre there are always one or two players who fail, often for several consecutive seasons, to draw the public. Thus, Lucien Guitry, unable to find a suitable part, was driven to the expedient of writing "Grand-Père" for himself, with partial success; but when this autumn he appeared in his second effort, "L'archevêque et ses fils," it proved to be so loosely constructed that it was hastily withdrawn from the Porte-St.-Martin and replaced by a revival of "Samson." In like manner did Max Déarly flounder through a mass of English farce until the recent success of "Nothing but the Truth" seems to have brought his troubles to an end. On the whole, however, conditions were steadily improving during the first months of 1918. One of the foremost French dramatists, G. de Porto-Riche, had given a new play, "Le Marchand d'Estampes." The Comédie-Française had produced "La Triomphatrice" of Mme. Lenéru, practically the only woman dramatist in Paris; Henri Bataille announced a new play for Réjane; Gémier had made his momentous production of "Antony and Cleopatra," and Sacha Guitry had given his picturesque "Duburau"; the Porte-St.-Martin had given Henry Kistermaeckers's "Un Soir au Front," while the Renaissance, Gymnase, Nouvel-Ambigu, Bouffes-Parisiens, and Palais-Royal, etc., were playing successful farces. It was then that the sudden and almost nightly air raids began to spread havoc in the city, followed by a daily bombardment with long-range guns. While the material damage was comparatively slight, it must be owned that something like panic reigned in Paris for several weeks, and the stations were besieged by the rich population fleeing to the country. A severe commercial crisis followed, and as it is the wealthy who make up the prosperity of the theatres, these were faced with utter ruin. Many were obliged to close immediately, others attempted to remain open at a loss in order to save their artists from becoming wholly destitute. M. Gémier changed the hour of his performances to 5 o'clock, M. Sacha Guitry adopted a daily matinée policy, and several others followed their example. The Prefect of Police issued an order that all theatres were to close not only in case of air raids, but upon days of bombardment as well. This rendered the position of managers impossible, and a delegation, supported by M. Huguenet on behalf of the Actors' Association, succeeded in having the order revoked. An announcement was to be made as soon as the bombardment began, allowing the timid among the audience to retire without preventing the performance from going on.

Nevertheless, the season was killed. Receipts had dwindled as low as £6, and the Comédie-Française and Palais-Royal alone remained open through the summer, with several music halls. During the worst days of the German offensive, M. Rip showed great courage in bringing out a new revue at the Théâtre Michel, and indeed his revues were to be seen in several theatres at that time, an example of French humour rising above adversity. The autumn season began unusually late; most of the theatres opened with revivals, and managers have shown such caution this time in making plans that it is doubtful if they will have adequate means of meeting the requirements of peace for some time.

Principal Productions of 1918.

Of the leading dramatists whose works have appeared during the year none has fulfilled our expectations or given us of his best. "Le Marchand d'Estamps," by G. de Porto-Riche, was not unworthy of thought, but the obscure pessimism of the play rendered it unsympathetic. Henry Kistermaeckers gave us a tawdry war melodrama, well written in parts, but highly improbable. The war would seem to be a fatal subject among dramatists. Even M. Bernstein was disappointing in "L'Elévation" last year, for M. Bernstein is a realist, and, although the idea was nobly conceived, he lacked the spirituality required of the last act. Henry Bataille, whose new play, "Notre Image," was postponed last spring, and has just been produced by Mme. Réjane, has also put forth an interesting idea which bears the intellectual symbolism that characterises his work; but it possesses neither the depth of psychological research of "Les Flambeaux," nor the humanity of "Poliche" and at times it wanders like the talk of an old man. M. Sacha Guitry made a worthy effort in "Duburau," the most serious thing he has yet attempted; but as far as productions are concerned, the principal feature of the year was unquestionably Gémier's staging of "Antony and Cleopatra" under the auspices of the Société Shakespeare. The modernism of his treatment was displayed with a lavish harmony of scene and costume, beautifully sustained by the music of Henri Rabeau, and culminating in a stupendously effective tableau of Cleopatra's banquet before the battle. At the top of an immense stairway lay the lovers fanned by slaves, while below them, in a mad medley of Oriental colours, thronged the courtiers, dancers, wrestlers, singers, and courtesans in riotous confusion, until the lamps burnt low, the throng subsided exhausted upon the steps, and in the still grey dawn the voice of a woman arose, singing plaintively afar. Gémier has been severely criticised for inserting this mute tableau between two scenes of Shakespeare's tragedy. I can only say that I deeply admire it, for apart from its striking effectiveness it admirably portrayed the downfall of the General, seeking to drown his humiliation and remorse in the depths of revelry, and rolling to the ultimate abyss with the enchantress whose slave he had become.

Of recent productions, that of "Esope" at the Comédie-Française is the most interesting.

Repertory Theatres.

With the exception of "La Triomphatrice," no new play of importance was produced at the Comédie-Française; "Turcaret," "Les Fausses Confidences," and "La Princesse Georges" were among the most conspicuous revivals. At the outbreak of the war, Albert Carré, who had just been appointed manager after the death of

Jules Clartie, was called away upon military duty and replaced by Emile Fabre, a playwright of considerable standing. M. Fabre's administration has been such a happy one that when, in October, a quarrel arose between the Isola brothers and M. Gheusi, managers of the Opéra-Comique, culminating in the latter's dismissal, the Minister of Fine Arts decided to appoint Albert Carré co-manager of the Opéra-Comique (which he directed for many years) with the Isolas, and definitely maintain M. Fabre at the Comédie-Française. Let us hope that in future he will be induced to give us more of the classical repertory rather than revivals of contemporary successes. He is now striving to solve the financial problem of the Pensionnaires (minor actors, who, unlike the Sociétaires, have no shares in the theatre). During certain months when receipts were poor the salary of many of these young people dwindled as low as £7. It was impossible to ask the State for a larger allowance at such a time. My distinguished confrère, Emile Mas, has taken up the question in *La Verite* with his passionate love for the Comédie-Française, but as yet no solution has been reached.

Paul Gavault has done some splendid work at the Odéon, and so far averted the ruin that has attended all his predecessors. At the Opéra a dreary lethargy exists as of old, but the Théâtre des Champs-Elysées has re-opened once more, and is now the home of an excellent Italian opera company.

There have been quite a number of English performances in Paris this year. Foremost among these are those of Miss Lena Ashwell's company at the Théâtre Albert I. After opening during the worst days of last spring it has become a great success, thanks largely to the skilful management of Mr. Oswald Marshall, and I hope that it will remain here permanently. Miss Dorothy Rundell, who replaced Miss Doris Keane in "Romance" during its London production, has won all hearts by her personal charm and delicate sensibility, while Miss Brenda Harvey's spontaneous naturalness and girlish freshness of manner are altogether delightful after the sophisticated paint and powder of some French acting. Besides Mr. Marshall the company includes such dependable actors as Mr. Allan Wade, Mr. Robert Minster, etc., and in addition to repertory plays they are presenting the latest London successes. An attempt to launch an American revue at the Théâtre Marigny failed miserably owing to the poorness of the mounting, but Mr. de Courville's "Zig-Zag" is doing splendidly at the Folies-Bergère.

ACTING OF THE YEAR.

The past year has shown some notable performances on the part of several actors and actresses, but there have been few discoveries of new talent. Mme. Réjane gave a wonderfully simple and moving characterisation of the fortune teller in "The 13th Chair." Mme. Piérat, now in complete possession of her brilliant talent, has appeared in many parts at the Comédie-Française, from "La Princesse Georges" of Dumas fils to "Amoureuse" of de Porto-Riche, and Mlle. Lecomte, of whom we see far too little, was delightful as the coquettish and winsome little Baroness in "Turcaret," of which Bernard gave so rich and finished a performance. But the most artistic triumphs of the year were undoubtedly won by de Max, and this is all the more significant, because notwithstanding his huge reputation on the Boulevards, he met with considerable opposition when elected sociétaire last year. It was said that he was out of place at the Comédie-Française because, as a Roumanian, he could not grasp the spirit of French classics, but his magnificent portrayal of Nero in "Britannicus," and his Esope, have been the saving of French classics since the death of Mounet-Sully, which threatened their decline. In his versatile art, de Max—who has played everything from Greek tragedy to revues—possesses those rare qualities in a tragedian—fancy and humour. Perhaps his finest achievement lately was the Monk in "Le Cloître," admirable for its spiritual beauty and human feeling. Not that de Max is always perfect; he is too great an artist for that, but he has the "feu sacré" which, when he is in the mood, can bear us away with him, far from the busy hubbub of the world to a realm of dreams.

In opposition to this was the modernism of Gémier's Antony in "Antony and Cleopatra." Curiously enough in so masterful an actor, the power and authority of the commander were barely felt; above all, he was the lover, and the utter enslavement of the man, who in the agony of his despair and dishonour forgets all at a word from the woman he loves, was expressed with puissant realism.

The year revealed one remarkable actress, Mlle. Yvonne Printemps, who had appeared unostentatiously in revues and played a small part in Sacha Guitry's "Jean de la Fontaine," became his leading lady, and essayed her first serious rôle as Marie Duplessis in "Duburau." She combines a strange fascination and deep clear voice to a humorous elfin spirit, and I should not be surprised to see her become one of the leading emotional actresses of the next few years as well. Her portrayal of Nono in a revival of that play was a living and pitiful study. Mlle. Jane Renouardt, who has enjoyed quite a vogue of late, was seen in "Quinneys" and other comedies. At present she is supporting Réjane in a difficult and ungrateful part of Nôtre Image that does not suit her.

Musical comedy has been the stepping-stone of several talented young people: Mlle. Regina Camier came into prominence at L'Abri, the underground War theatre, in the witty revue "1918"; although her part was small, she showed such grace and charm that M. Quinson has given her a leading part in "Le Filon," the new farce at the Palais-Royal. Mlle. Pierrette Madd also won recognition at the Abri, and is now starring in a musical comedy at the Bouffes-Parisiens; Mlle. Denise Gray made a decided hit in a minor part of "La Petite Femme de Loth," which, by the way, was a failure, and Mlle. Peggy Vere stepped successfully from the ranks of the chorus girls at Mayol's.

VARIETY.

The Variety theatres have taken a huge predominance in Paris during the season, and the Alhambra and Olympia, the Folies Bergère and Casino are packed to the doors at every performance. English songs and English dancers are the order of the day, and since the American Jazz band took the audience of the Casino by storm there have been would-be Jazz bands in every music hall and little theatre in Paris.

While the revue at "L'Abri," the cellar theatre, was the wittiest, the last revue at the Casino has been the best from a spectacular point of view. There is one truly remarkable scene in an opium den, and a dream dance by Mlle. Mistinguett and Mr. Oy-Ra that was very effective. A host of little playhouses and cabaret chantants have opened up, and the moving pictures are doing a huge business with American films.

EDMOND ROSTAND.

And now at the very end of the year when the Drama seemed about to revive and take up its mission once more, comes the unexpected blow of Rostand's death. The loss is immeasurably great, not only because Edmond Rostand was the greatest French dramatist of his day, but because his genius possessed that delicacy and spiritual nobility that are most needed to-day.

It seems almost futile to recall the career of one so famous throughout the world. Born at Marseilles in 1868, he published his first—and only—book of poems, "Les Musardises," while yet a student. He wrote a one-act play, "Les Deux Pierrots," for the Comédie-Française, but as that theatre had revived de Banville's play on a similar subject he was asked to submit something different, and thus in 1894 "Les Romanesques," that charming fantasy, came to be written. Shortly afterwards he married Mlle. Rosemonde Gérard, a descendant of one of Napoleon's Marshals, and herself a poetess of high attainment. His next play was "La Princesse Lointaine," produced by Sarah Bernhardt at the Renaissance, with Guitry and de Max, and this was followed by "La Samaritaine." Coquelin, always in search of new parts and young authors, asked him for a play, and in 1897 he produced "Cyrano de Bergerac," that pure masterpiece of beauty and dramatic art, and one of the most successful plays ever written. It was played thousands of times, and carried the fame of the author to every country in the world. In 1900 "L'Aiglon" gave Sarah Bernhardt one of her greatest triumphs, but shortly afterwards Rostand was obliged to seek the tranquillity of his beautiful home at Cambo on account of his precarious health. Here he continued to work on "Chantecler," in which he had centred all his hopes and dreams, but continual illness and vexations retarded its production, he was never satisfied with his work, and when it was finally put into rehearsal the sudden death of Coquelin prevented the play from being produced until a year or two later. Edmond Rostand's prodigious success made him the butt of the envious, and realists and modernists did all in their power to lessen his reputation. But the people and the world will come to realise the true greatness of the man who was so pre-eminently a poet, and who in the magic of his art has caught all that is noblest in spirit and ideals of the French race.

THE PARIS STAGE.

MLLE. MARIE LECONTI,
Sociétaire of the Comédie Française.

[Reutlinger.

THE PARIS STAGE.

[*Bert.*

MLLE. REGINA CAURIE,
in the Revue "L'Abri."

THE PARIS STAGE.

[Talma.

MISTINGUETT
in the Revue at the Casino.

THE PARIS STAGE.

(Henri Manuel.

MLLE. DENISE GREY,
who appeared in "La Petite Femme de Lotto."

THE PARIS STAGE.

Henri Manuel.

MLLE. PIERRETTE MADD,
appearing in musical comedy at the Bouffes Parisiens.

THE PARIS STAGE.

[Walery.

MLLE. JANE MARNAC,
who appeared in "La Reine Joyeuse."

THE PARIS STAGE.

NAPIRKOWSKA,
in the Revue at the Casino, Paris.

THE PARIS STAGE.

[Henri Manuel.

MME. PIÉRAT,
"La Marche Nuptial" at the Comédie Française.

THE PARIS STAGE.

Henri Manuel.

JEAN RENOUARDT,
who has played leading parts in "Quinneys" and "Notre Image."

THE PARIS STAGE.

[H. M. Talma.

MLLE. YVONNE PRINTEMPS,
who has won success in the leading parts in "Duburean" and "Nono" with Sacha Guitry.

THE PARIS STAGE.

[Talma.

"ESTHER" AT THE COMÉDIE FRANÇAISE.

THE PARIS STAGE.

"DUBUREAU."
Sacha Guitry and Mlle. Yvonne Printemps.
[*Talma.*

THE DRAMA IN AMERICA.

By ST. CLAIR BAYFIELD.

A GREAT deal of pluck and enterprise has been shown by American managers of the business end of the theatrical life in the face of adverse circumstances due to war conditions. These produced heavy taxes, limitation of electrical lighting, of advertising, difficulties about fuel, difficulties of travel and of transportation, vastly added expense in these directions, scarcity of young actors, Liberty Loan considerations, and the disadvantage of having to heckle patrons in the interests of this necessary work, the conservation by the professional classes of money spent on amusement during the war. Actors' salaries were not lowered. No new and successful dramatists have appeared. New York City theatres have done a booming business chiefly by the patronage of transients; but the touring companies have suffered much bad business, and from enormous difficulties and expenses. Touring companies have been entirely shut off from portions of the States owing to first consideration of transportation necessary for the war, and lack of trucks and passenger accommodation. The managers have "carried on" despite these conditions, but those with small capital have been pushed to the wall.

PLAYS RUNNING FROM PRECEDING YEAR.

"Business Before Pleasure" (Cohan and Harris), a sequel to "Perlmutter," opened on August 15, 1917, and continued to big business into the month of June, 1918. "Lombardi, Limited," by Frederick and Fanny Hatton, was an unsavoury but swiftly moving play, with comedy that overpowered and hid its bad taste. "Parlour, Bedroom, and Bath" (A. H. Woods), farce comedy, ran from December 24 to the middle of July, and four companies went on tour with it.
"Polly With a Past" (Belasco), a light comedy, starring Ina Claire, produced September 6, 1917, ran to the second week of June.
"Seven Days' Leave" ran from January 17 to the end of May. Reginald Carrington as Stephen Darrell gave an excellent performance.
An adaptation from boy stories of Booth Tarkington was a charming comedy, "Seventeen" (Stuart Walker, manager). In this a remarkably skilfully drawn sketch was given by Paul Kelly of a boy of seventeen in calf-love. This play ran from January 21 into July.
"A Tailor-Made Man," a comedy with a hero who was determined to rise in the world and did so, finished an immensely successful run in July, having opened August 27, 1917. (Cohan and Harris, managers.)
"The Copperhead," a stirring drama of the Civil War, ran from February 18 until the end of May. The part of Milt Shanks, a secret service agent, who allowed himself to be thought a slacker for the good of his country, gave a really great opportunity for Lionel Barrymore's acting ability.
"Eyes of Youth," since produced in London, which had opened here August 22, 1917, with Marjorie Rambeau in the leading part, despite an accident to the star, which resulted in the part being filled by two substitutes, continued a prosperous run, only closing in July of 1918.
"The Man Who Stayed at Home" ("The White Feather") was popular for a run of sixteen weeks.
"Tiger Rose" (Belasco) completed its run in New York the end of October, 1918, having opened October 3, 1917—a pictorial melodrama.
A musical extravaganza, "Jack o' Lantern," a good vehicle for the delicious humour of Fred Stone, closed about the same time, after a triumphant season starting October 16, 1917. An entertainment of a similar kind (Shubert) at the Winter Garden, called "Sinbad," started February 14, and is still running in December to immense business with Al Jolson as star.
"Flo, Flo" (Cort), lyrics by E. Paulton, music by Silvio Hein, opened December

2*

20, 1917, and for a long time was run at a loss. Eventually it became a "winner," running over six months. Girl comedy, light music, and dances.

The Raymond Hitchcock musical play of the season, "Hitchy Koo," was but half a "go."

"Going Up" (Cohan and Harris) was a musical farce founded on a comedy, "The Aviator." Frank Craven's acting of a courageous man who imagined he was a coward was excellent. The piece had the usual musical comedy dressings. Opened December 25, 1917, running prosperously right through summer and into October, 1918. Three companies went on tour.

"Maytime" (Shubert), four-act play with music. Closed in September, 1918, having run to enormous business since production at the Shubert, September 9, 1917. Afterwards shifted to 44th Street Theatre, February 18, to Broadhurst Theatre, April 1, Lyric Theatre, August 5, and back to the Broadhurst, September 9.

"The Rainbow Girl," an adaptation for musical comedy of Jerome K. Jerome's "Fanny and the Servant Problem," had a prosperous run from April 1, 1917, to end of June, 1918. Lyrics, Wolff; music, Hirsch. Sydney Greenstreet made comedy out of a butler. (Klaw and Erlanger, managers.)

PLAYS PRODUCED DURING THE 1918 SEASON.

The best things artistically are "Redemption" and "The Betrothal." Other good pieces included "The Better 'Ole" and that capital American humorous play, "Lightnin'," "Daddies," despite its children; "Three Wise Fools," a theatrical contraption of good old men, and a *so* good boy and girl lover; "Be Calm, Camilla," a delicate bit of clever dialogue ever so charmingly set; "Remnant," another theatrical play with sentimental appeal. In drama : "Tiger! Tiger!" a high-notch record for Belasco; "Three Faces East," more interesting because of mystery than of war, produced August 13. "Under Orders," produced August 20. "The Unknown Purple," produced September 14. "Forever After," "The Big Chance," and "The Riddle Woman."

In musical comedy : "Little Simplicity," "The Girl Behind the Gun" (September 16), "Sometime" (October 4), "Ladies First" (October 24), "The Canary" (November 4), "Gloriana" (October 28). In extravaganza, "Sinbad" scored an enormous success. "The Midnight Revue" is atop of the Century, and Ziegfeld's Follies in the roof theatre of New Amsterdam. "Everything" is another huge show at the Hippodrome. The fifth New York Princess Theatre musical production opened February 1, and ran on into June (Messrs. F. Ray Comstock and William Gest, managers.) "Oh, Lady! Lady!" a typical chorusless tinkling melody Princess production.

LACK OF PLAYS.

A great number of legitimate houses in the smaller towns were converted into "movie" houses because the theatres were unable to obtain plays. Theatrical travel out of New York was curtailed by a bulletin issued by Director-General McAdoo, the Pennsylvania and New York Central being particularly affected at the time of scarcity of fuel. Baggage cars were very difficult to obtain. In January of 1918 there were only fifty-one attractions playing outside of the four biggest cities.

REDUCED PRICES.

As an offset against increased theatre taxes and economy amongst the public a bait to draw theatre-goers was thrown out by reducing the prices at New York theatres. At the Park, where "Seven Days' Leave" was played, seats were offered at from 25c. to $1.50, with three hundred seats at $1, and on one matinée a week no seat cost more than $1. One of the most popular stars, Miss Margaret Anglin, in "Billeted," made a reduction of 50c. a seat, and the firm of Comstock and Gest also reduced prices to their great success "Chu Chin Chow." Arthur Hopkins reduced prices for his successful play, "The Gypsy Trail." Profit-sharing schemes between managers and actors were proposed, but were only carried out in one or two cases where a failing play encouraged the idea.

THE SEASON SINCE AUGUST.

The 1918 Fall season opened prosperously despite the drain upon the public purse by the Liberty Loans, but in October the disastrous check caused last season by war conditions was reflected this season as a consequence of the "flu" epidemic, and afterwards by the evolution from war to peace conditions. But, as I write this, prospects are bright for the future, with expectation of better railway conditions and soldiers expected home from the front.

The influenza epidemic closed the theatres throughout the entire country, with the exception of New York City, for about four weeks or more. In this giant country, companies of players were suddenly left upon their own resources, in many cases thousands of miles away from their homes in New York. Companies "run" by corporations with small capital were stranded, and were helped out in some cases by the public. Of the bigger managers, David Belasco was out of pocket to the tune of $1,500 for one company alone, and his actual money loss on the "Boomerang" company was no less than $2,500, as well as the cost of the printing for twenty dates. Messrs. Klaw and Erlanger were compelled to pay out no less than $25,000 without value received, including advances of salary to actors, railway fares, rebooking of dates, switching of routes, etc. This amount is not all a bad debt, but it exemplifies the necessity of large capital for theatrical management in this huge country. Companies suddenly ceased playing in St. Louis—about twenty-six hours by rail from New York, Kansas City, about 1,600 miles from New York, Detroit about 1,000 miles away, Chicago 1,200 miles away, and this in the face of a 65 per cent. war increase in cost of railway transportation. Consequent upon these conditions the small manager has gone under for the present, and the "big" fellow alone remains with capital for the busy times that are expected with peace conditions.

Many actors died from the results of influenza—Messrs. Cohan and Harris alone reported the deaths of five actors in their employment. The theatres were closed by Municipal orders. Masks were worn in many cities to prevent communicating of the disease by coughing and spitting. In San Francisco the masking order was not rescinded until after the theatres had re-opened, and there appeared the unique sight of an audience wearing masks. The actors on the stage were excused from wearing masks by a special order. Special directions were given to the audiences of New York theatres before the performances by an official spokesman; people were instructed not to crowd, spit, cough, etc. The New York theatres were nearly emptied owing to the fear of contagion, but, actually the theatres were safer to be in owing to the stringent regulations as to sanitation and airing than were the overcrowded, dusty streets. Elliot, Comstock, and Gest had to bring in no fewer than six companies. New York theatres remained open, but receipts fell. The Ziegfeld Follies, the biggest attraction in the United States to-day, fell from $20,000 to $7,000 a week in takings. Plays that were struggling went to the storehouse, and plays that had promised well for a season's run, by the time the epidemic was over were second favourites to newer productions. With the signing of the armistice war plays fell from favour. One of the biggest draws, "Where Poppies Bloom," took its departure for the road, others closed down, and the London play, "By Pigeon Post," produced on the day of the armistice, closed after a showing of five weeks.

Following the armistice, theatrical business immediately showed very great improvement in the whole eastern section of the country—pre-holiday weeks showed unprecedented business.

War Conditions in 1918.

The U.S. Fuel Administration prohibited unnecessary lighting of the streets, and not only were the theatres affected by dark streets, but theatrical advertising by electric signs was prohibited except upon certain nights a week, and then within prescribed limits. From January until summertime the theatres were short of coal for heating purposes, and the unexampled cold weather of last winter compelled theatres to close up, and others could not be heated to a comfortable degree.

A direct effect of the reduction in the number of companies on tour, owing to transportation difficulties and advanced rates, has given the lesser cities a better average of attractions, for only the companies of big organisations have been able to travel, but they have encountered little competition.

In cities employing many women moving pictures and very low-priced entertainments did well, whilst higher-class attractions "froze." Where there were camps, munition factories, and shipyards business was good, but there, too, high prices could not draw. In the Eastern States things were best because of the many lines of rail radiating from the theatrical capital—New York. Musical plays were popular if not too high priced. Some cities, formerly theatrical slumps, showed much improvement. A place called Bethlehem, in Pennsylvania, formerly 4,000, has an increased population of 15,000, and many other cities have increased in proportion.

The regulations as to theatre lighting were made when the fuel famine was on.

Directional signs could only be lighted from one half hour after sunset until one half hour after commencement of performance. Advertising signs only operated from 7.45 to 11 p.m.

THE WAR TAX ON THEATRES.

The collection of a 10 per cent. war tax upon theatre tickets affected business only when it was first laid on. New York has been the chief port of embarkation for troops, and relatives of the soldiers came to New York in large numbers and the theatres made a great deal of money. There are fifty-three legitimate theatres in Manhattan and the Bronx, and none of them has been dark for any great length of time. Stock companies increased in number owing to transportation difficulties and did good business, but the country seems willing and anxious to be visited again by travelling companies of Metropolitan organisation. Prosperity has been brought to the South by the planting of sixteen training camps in the Southern States, and the deploying of railway traffic to southern ports, and last, but not least, the high price of and a heavy crop of cotton, and war industries. The South has unaccustomed pocket money, and a Southern theatrical tour offers better opportunity for profits than ever before.

INCOME-TAX.

Under the new law every unmarried person whose income exceeds $1,000, and every married person whose income exceeds $2,000 had to pay income-tax. Figures regarding members of the theatrical profession showed that 914 actors, singers, and musicians have a total income of $11,128,000—an average of $12,000—about £2,040. Five of these incomes were in excess of $150,000.

In New York City alone, appeals to the theatres gained subscriptions to the Liberty Loan amounting to $35,000,000. The well-known managers, Messrs. Klaw and Erlanger, subscribed $50,000 each.

Messrs. Edward H. Sothern and Winthrop Ames went to France as members of the Y.M.C.A. Committee, and made arrangements so that U.S. soldiers received good theatrical entertainment, and at regular intervals, by arrangement with actors at home who volunteered for this service.

The Allied Theatrical interests raised $42,124,780 in subscriptions for the Fourth Liberty Loan.

German plays, copyrighted under the International Treaty, have forfeited the protection of that Act during war time. Those who adapted German works for the American stage have paid a fee to the U.S. Government.

RISE IN THE COST OF TRANSPORTATION.

Before the armistice cost of railway transportation had risen 65 per cent. There was a war tax on cost of transportation; another on Pullmans, and another on transportation whilst occupying a Pullman. Hauling scenery cost about $15 a load, instead of $5 to $8, and trunk delivery rose from 35c. a piece to 80c. Baggage cars were extremely hard to obtain, and consequently most companies missed some of their dates. Sleeping accommodation was very often unobtainable, and travelling-companies frequently spent nights sitting up in day coaches. Stage hands have been ruder and more expensive than ever before.

WAR EFFORTS.

The Stage Women's War Relief has been in existence twenty months, and has developed so successfully that it is amongst the foremost of the War Relief Societies. The executive committee is of sixteen women connected with the stage. There are branches of the Society in several important cities. Those, however, of the stage alone are permitted to volunteer to work in the workroom which opens at 366, Fifth Avenue at 10 a.m. each day. In the year, over 100 cases of clothing have been sent to the Allied armies. An ingenious use of waste leather is in collecting old scraps of leather and making them into wind-proof jackets. The organisation looks after the interests of the families of men at the front. Autographs of well-known actresses in the wind-proof jackets are eagerly sought for by wounded men.

In one year the Stage Women's War Relief raised 6,265,858 dollars for the Liberty Loans, and through their efforts thousands of dollars have been raised for the Red Cross, Thrift Stamp and other Government "drives." The Association has donated 9,000 dollars to the Free Milk for France Fund, and 1,000 dollars for Serbian Relief. A fund for assisting the needy families of professional men in service is constantly being enlarged. Surgical dressings, hospital supplies, baby garments, clothes, and knitted articles have totalled 32,648, and 192,000 have been distributed.

A Service House is established in New York offering sleeping accommodation to ninety men, and entertaining an average of 600 men in the Sunday Canteen. Free entertainments are sent to camps and base hospitals every day, and two free Sunday performances of current Broadway attractions are given under the auspices of the Stage Women's War Relief. Through the co-operation of the vaudeville managers, a free Thursday morning performance is given in the largest vaudeville theatre in New York City (the Palace), for wounded and convalescent soldiers and sailors. Motor transportation is furnished by the Motor Corps of America, and the Red Cross serves a luncheon at the canteen.

A division of films producing two-reel feature pictures, is conducted by the organisation, with celebrated artists, well known scenario writers, and managers contributing their services. The income derived from these films is used for War Relief and Reconstruction work.

A play entitled "When a Fellow Needs a Friend," by Harvey O. Higgins and Harry Ford, was written and devoted to raising funds. A special performance at the New Amsterdam Theatre raised 3,460 dollars. It is being played throughout the country, and the receipts are given to the fund.

A STAR CAST ACTING FOR THE RED CROSS.

"Out There," the popular war play, written by J. Hartley Manners, went on a three weeks' tour of the bigger cities of the country under the management of George C. Tyler, with a cast consisting entirely of distinguished actors called in this country "an all-star cast," in aid of the funds of the Red Cross. This company acted the play in seventeen cities and raised the sum of 683,248 dollars for the Red Cross. Mr. John P. Toohey, one of the most able press agents in the country, looked after advertising, or what in the United States is called "publicity." The artists gave their services entirely free of charge and paid their own expenses. Mme. Eleonora de Cisneros, the well-known opera prima donna, sang at the close of each performance. Mrs. Fiske delivered a Red Cross appeal, and Mr. Burr McIntosh, though temporarily crippled and on crutches, by his oratory succeeded in selling autographed programmes for a total of 165,000 dollars. The cast consisted of Miss Laurette Taylor, Miss Helen Ware, Miss Beryl Mercer, Mr. H. B. Warner, Mr. James T. Powers, and Mr. George Arliss. The following well-known actors played small parts: Mr. Chauncey Olcott, an Irish character; the Cockney, Mr. O. P. Heggie; the Canadian, Mr. James K. Hackett; the Scotchman, Mr. George MacFarlane; the American, Mr. George M. Cohan; Gabrielle, Miss Julia Arthur.

THE ACTORS' EQUITY ASSOCIATION.

The A.E.A. set a certain date—November 4, 1918—on and after which every member of the Association must insist upon a Standard Contract upon every engagement. The Standard Contract is that which was agreed upon by the Managers' Association and the Actors' Equity Association as being equitable in November, 1917. Twelve hundred members, including forty-seven stars, signed a pledge that they would insist upon receiving these contracts. Since this declaration of policy, Messrs. Shubert have agreed to use the Standard Contract and have begun to do so. During the year the Association has affiliated with the British and the Australian Associations.

A classified list of disengaged actors who are members of the Association has been established, and each manager receives, each week, this disengaged list. To avail themselves of this, the members of the Association have merely to send a postcard to their Association announcing that they are at liberty. The managers have warmly endorsed this plan. An Executive Committee of five members has been formed to systematise the working of the Association, and a salaried position of Executive Secretary has been created, and is filled by Mr. Frank Gilmore.

A NOTABLE PUBLICATION.

The Life of David Belasco, by the late William Winter, was published in November. It is written in a spirit of fearless truth, and is full of encyclopædic information.

German Operas and Plays.

The royalties from several operas and plays owned by enemies to the United States were taken over by Mr. A. Mitchell Palmer, Alien Property Custodian, and the proceeds invested in Liberty Bonds. Among the plays are "Madame X." and "The Concert," and in light opera, "Her Soldier Boy," "Alone at Last," "The Star Gazers," "The Dollar Princess," "Gipsy Love," "Pom-Pom," and "The Riviera Girl."

Ticket Speculating.

Ticket speculators still act as middlemen in the sale of tickets and make theatre-going expensive, driving people of moderate means away from the theatre by exorbitant charges. That man of ideals Arthur Hopkins attempted to fight them "on his own," and was defeated. Good seats are seldom to be had at the box office. Tickets for a popular success are usually bought at a 25 per cent. premium above the printed price. Visitors to New York have been acquiescent to this. When the cast has been a distinguished one and the out-of-town-try-out a success, managers frequently have relieved themselves of much speculation by selling out to ticket speculators for eight weeks. The large influx of soldiers and sailors and their friends into New York has encouraged these conditions. Consequently, the majority of New York's permanent population looks upon theatre-going as an expensive luxury, but moving picture attractions as within its means.

Shuberts, and Klaw and Erlanger.

The agreement which existed for six years between Messrs. Klaw and Erlanger, and Messrs. Shuberts, for pooling interests and relative to booking arrangements, has terminated, and the two firms are now in clean-out competition. The split came following a disagreement as to payments. Its effects have been strongly felt in smaller cities where only a few first-class theatres are available. In Philadelphia, the Shuberts have built a new theatre almost opposite the Broad Street, which belongs to their opponents.

Among the producers who have been booking through the Shuberts are William A. Brady, Arthur Hammerstein, Oliver Morosco, Elizabeth Marbury, Comstock, Elliott and Gest, Richard Walton Tully, and Arthur Hopkins. Those who have booked with Klaw and Erlanger have been George C. Tyler, Cohan and Harris, David Belasco, the Charles Frohman Company, Henry W. Savage, and Charles B. Dillingham. The Selwyns and A. H. Woods have recently had attractions playing in New York in both Klaw and Erlanger and Shubert houses.

The Players' Club.

On November 13 a *statue of the founder of this charming old club was unveiled in Gramercy Park opposite the club house. The statue is the creation of Messrs. Quinn and Edwin S. Dodge, who competed with many others by models and sketches, and were given the award by a jury of sculptors in 1914. In this statue, the great American actor, Edwin Booth, is shown at about thirty-five years of age in the character of Hamlet. The cost of the Memorial was met by voluntary contributions from the membership of the Players. It is the property of the Club. The Memorial is the first of its kind to an actor in this country. The presentation of the Memorial was a most impressive ceremony attended by many hundreds of people of importance. The Rev. George Clark Houghton, D.D., Rector of the Church of the Transfiguration—affectionately known by actors and their friends as "The Little Church Around the Corner"—invoked a blessing and offered up a very beautiful prayer, composed for the occasion by the reverend gentleman; Mr. Howard Kyle, Treasurer of the Booth Memorial Fund, was met by Mr. John Drew, the President of the Club, in front of the statue, and in a graceful speech announced the statue was ready to be unveiled. The great muffling cloth was parted by young Mr. Edwin Booth Grosman, a grandson of Edwin Booth, whilst Mr. Guy Nicholls, Librarian of the Club, swept the veil clear of Hamlet's chair. This sudden disclosure of the statue elicited tremendous applause. Both Mr. Edwin Booth Grosman, his children, and his parents were present—three generations of Booths. The plot of earth surrounding the monument is planted with pachysandras, which

[*A picture of the statue serves as the frontispiece to THE STAGE YEAR BOOK.—EDITOR.]

THE AMERICAN STAGE.

MISS LILLIAN LORRAINE PLAYING IN "ZIEGFELD'S FOLLIES."

THE AMERICAN STAGE.

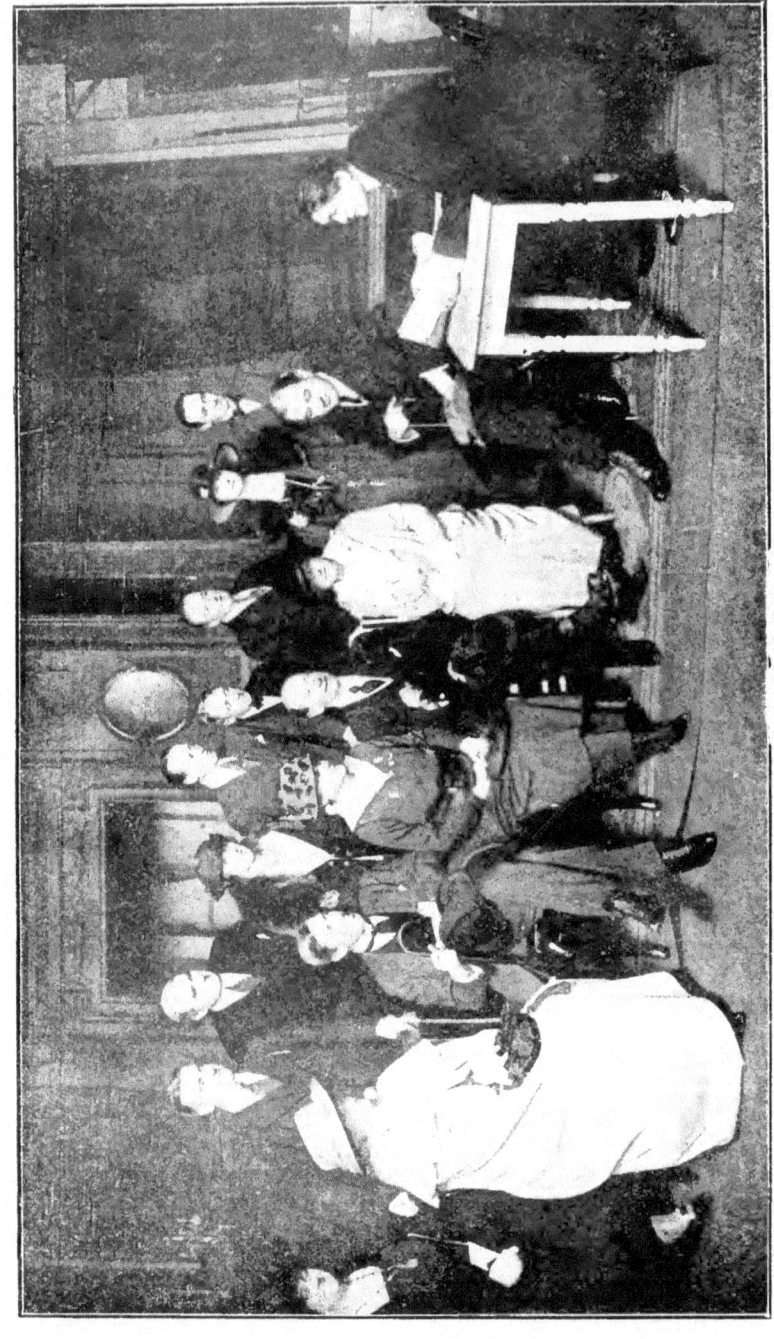

"OUT THERE."

The All-Star Cast of "Out There," by J. Hartley Manners. This company toured in aid of Red Cross Funds, and in three weeks in seventeen cities raised $585,248, nearly £150,000. Seated, left to right, Miss Eleanor de Cisneros, Mrs. Fiske, Mr. George Arliss, Miss Julia Arthur, Mr. James T. Powers, Miss Beryl Mercer. Standing, left to right, Mr. George McFarlane, Mr. James K. Hackett, Mr. J. Hartley Manners, Mr. H. B. Warner, Mr. George M. Cohan, Mr. Chauncey Olcott, Miss Helen Ware, and Mr. O. P. Heggie. At table, Mr. Hartley Manners.

THE AMERICAN STAGE.

ELSIE FERGUSON, [Paul Thompson.
is autographing one of the famous wind-proof jackets made at the Stage Women's War Relief Factory.

THE AMERICAN STAGE

MISS DOROTHY CUMMING.

THE AMERICAN STAGE.

"SINBAD," AT THE WINTER GARDEN, NEW YORK.
"Beauties" appearing with AL JOLSON.

THE AMERICAN STAGE.

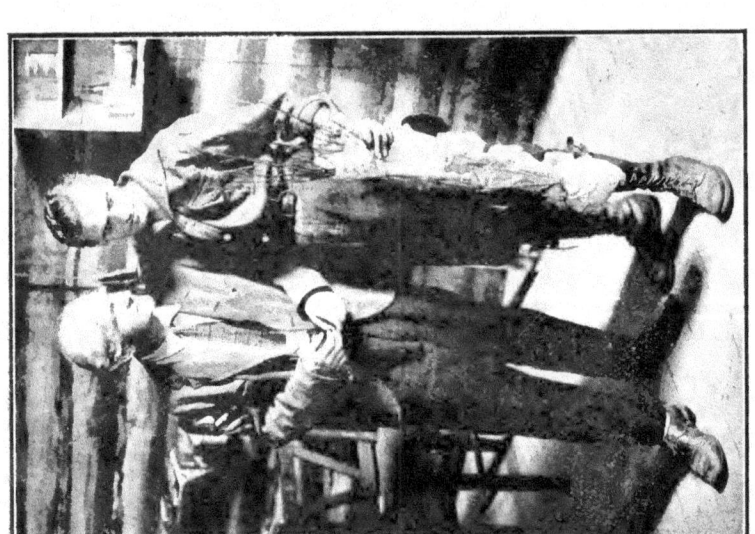

"LIGHTNIN'."
Mr. Frank Bacon as Lightnin' Bill Jones and Mr. Ralph Morgan as John Marvin.

"THREE FACES EAST" AT THE COHAN AND HARRIS, N.Y.C.
Mr. Emmett Corrigan and Miss Violet Heming.

THE AMERICAN STAGE.

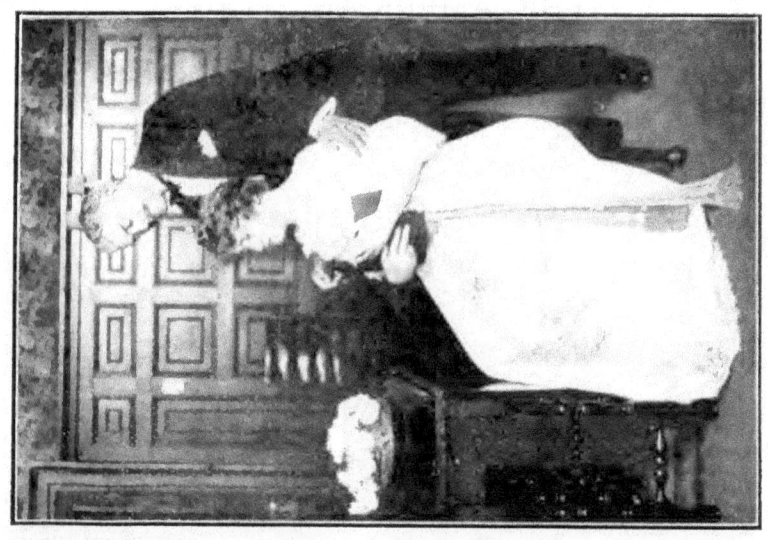

"TIGER! TIGER!!" AT THE BELASCO.
Miss Frances Starr.

"THE SAVING GRACE" AT THE EMPIRE.

THE AMERICAN STAGE.

"REDEMPTION" AT THE PLYMOUTH.

Miss Maude Hannaford and Mr. Manart Kippen with Lisa's mother and sister.

[White.

THE AMERICAN STAGE.

"LIGHTNIN'" AT THE GAIETY, NEW YORK.
The Court Room Scene.

THE AMERICAN STAGE.

"THE GIRL BEHIND THE GUN."

Principals.—Mr. John E. Hazzard, Miss Ada Meade, Mr. Frank Doane, Miss Wilda Bennett, Mr. Donald Brian.

THE AMERICAN STAGE.

"THE BETTER 'OLE."
Mr. Colin Campbell, Mr. Coburn, Mrs. Coburn, and Mr. Chas. McNaughton.

THE AMERICAN STAGE.

MR. DAVID WARFIELD.

THE AMERICAN STAGE.

MISS EUGENIE YOUNG,
in "The Better 'Ole."

THE AMERICAN STAGE.

MISS LILLIAN LORRAINE PLAYING IN "ZIEGFELD'S FOLLIES."

THE AMERICAN STAGE.

"DADDIES" AT THE BELASCO.
One of Daddie's kids.

MISS LAURETTE TAYLOR.

THE AMERICAN STAGE.

"REDEMPTION" AT THE PLYMOUTH. [*White.*
Miss Maude Hannaford, Miss Zeffie Tillbury, and Mr. Russ Whytal.

"HUMPTY DUMPTY" AT THE LYCEUM. [*White.*
Miss Clara T. Bracy, Mr. Otis Skinner, and Miss Beryl Mercer.

spreads as it grows and is likely to be a large patch of green by spring. Professor Brander Matthews (Dramatic Literature, Columbia University) made a notable address.

THE LIBERTY THEATRES.

These theatres were found to be difficult to manage profitably owing to the big jumps by rail between camp and camp, and in the sixteen camps situated in the South the Summer heat kept the men out of doors. Few actors with big names visited the camps until this Fall, when a new system of booking companies pursuing a regular tour was followed.

The Washington Square Players, at the Comedy Theatre, broke up in May after twelve of their number had gone to the war. The organisation started on its career years ago at the little Bandbox Theatre on East Fifty-Seventh Street. The Players have brought forward many excellent one-act plays and several amateur actors, after training in their ranks, have been successful on Broadway. This band of enthusiasts set out to make the stage artistic; at least they succeeded in encouraging art upon the stage and exposing much foolish theatricalism.

SCENIC ART.

The art of Robert Edmond Jones has created a striking example in stage settings—it does away with long waits between acts for laboursome scene-shifting, and reduces limitations to the art of the dramatist, whilst it encourages strong suggestion. Flatness is a main principle, elimination of unnecessary detail, and strong effect by creation of atmosphere inherent to the scene. In " Redemption," Mr. Jones has eleven scenes, each one a thing of beauty. By the old, cumbersome methods, the setting of the scenes would have taken at least three-quarters of an hour. The artist takes complete charge of everything in the picture including the furniture, props and lights, thereby gaining unity of effect. Mr. Jones attracted much attention by his treatment of the Ibsen plays done by Mme. Nazimova last spring and recently of the modern comedy "Be Calm, Camilla." He has also completely illustrated the book of the community play written for the American Red Cross, by Percy Mackeye, "The Roll Call."

Joseph Urban's art is still extremely popular. It is one of a system of roundness, of reliefs, carried from the footlights into and through the whole picture. It is realism, massive material built according to the dramatist's description of the scene, vividism coloured and beautiful, but trusting nothing to suggestion or imagination. His setting for "By Pigeon Post" was exceedingly successful. He has also done many extremely beautiful sets for the Ziegfeld Follies.

LONDON SEASONS.

MR. ARTHUR SINCLAIR and his company, the Irish Players, including several members of the Abbey, Dublin, organisation, opened a season at the Court on Easter Monday, April 1, with a double bill, consisting of "Tactics" and "Fox and Geese." During the second week a triple bill—"The Building Fund," "The Coiner," and "Duty"—was presented. J. M. Synge's "The Playboy of the Western World" formed the third week's offering, and was played until the conclusion of the season on May 4.

Mr. Arthur Sinclair and his company, the Irish Players, including several members of the Abbey, Dublin, organisation, opened a season at the Court on Easter Monday, April 1, with a double bill, consisting of "Tactics" and "Fox and Geese." During the second week a triple bill—"The Building Fund," "The Coiner," and "Duty"—was presented. J. M. Synge's "The Playboy of the Western World" formed the third week's offering, and was played until the conclusion of the season on May 4.

The Players of the Gate opened a four weeks' season at the Kennington on Monday, June 6, with W. S. Gilbert's "The Palace of Truth," and a one-act play by Jack Edwards, entitled "A Colour Scheme." These two pieces were played until the Thursday night, when "Romeo and Juliet" was given and retained in the bill for the remainder of the week. "As You Like It" and "Candida" constituted the programme for the following week. "The Mollusc" followed, and "Outcast" was played for the fourth and last week of the season, which terminated on Saturday, June 29.

The Diaghileff Russian Ballet from the Theatre St. Martin, Petrograd, gave a season of ballet at the London Coliseum, beginning on Thursday, September 5, when "Cleopatra" and "The Good-Humoured Ladies" were presented, the latter being new to London. On the following Monday Tschaikowsky's "The Enchanted Princess" and Borodine's "Prince Igor" were given. "The Midnight Sun" was produced for the first time in England on November 21. On December 23 three divertissements entitled "The Children's Tales" were presented. Other ballets presented during the season included "Carnaval," "Papillons," and "Scheherazade."

The Carl Rosa Opera Company opened a six weeks' season at the Shaftesbury on Monday, May 6, with a performance of "Carmen." The bill for the rest of the week consisted of "Tannhäuser," "Tales of Hoffmann," "La Bohême," "The Merry Wives of Windsor," "Jeanie Deans," "Madame Butterfly," and "Il Trovatore." The operas given during this season were "Cavalleria Rusticana," "Pagliacci," "Faust," "Maritana," "Don Giovanni," "The Marriage of Figaro," "Mignon," "Rigoletto," "The Bohemian Girl," etc. On Friday, June 7, "Dante and Beatrice," a new opera by Eden Phillpotts and W. J. Miller, was produced. The jubilee of the Carl Rosa Opera Company was celebrated on Monday, June 10, a matinée in aid of the Prisoners of War Fund of the Royal Regiment of Artillery being given in honour of the occasion. The programme consisted of excerpts from "The Merry Wives of Windsor," "Pagliacci," "Tales of Hoffmann," etc. The season ended on June 15.

On Saturday afternoon, March 2, Sir Thomas Beecham opened a five weeks' spring season at Drury Lane, "The Marriage of Figaro" being given at the first performance. During this visit, which ended on Saturday, April 16, the operas presented were those which had been given during previous seasons.

The company returned to Drury Lane on June 3 for a two months' summer season, opening with "Othello." On Friday, June 14, "The Valkyrie" was produced, Sir Thomas conducting. "La Tosca," "The Magic Flute," "Il Trovatore," "Romeo and Juliet," "La Bohême," "Madame Butterfly," "Aïda," "Tristan and Isolda," "The Seraglio," "The Marriage of Figaro," "Tannhäuser," "Faust," "Carmen," "Louise," "Samson and Delilah," "The Boatswain's Mate," "Pagliacci" and "Cavalleria Rusticana," "Boris Godounov," "Coq d'Or," etc., were given during the rest of the season, which ended on July 27.

MASONIC LODGES.

A RECORD OF MASONIC LODGES AND CHAPTERS, MEMBERS OF WHICH ARE CONNECTED WITH THE DRAMATIC, MUSICAL, AND VARIETY PROFESSIONS.

LODGE OF ASAPH, No. 1319.

Consecrated 1870.

Held at Freemasons' Hall, Great Queen Street, London, W.C., on the fourth Tuesday in February, March, May, June, October, and November. Installation in November.

OFFICERS, 1918-19.

Algernon Rose	W.M.
R. D. Cox	I.P.M.
E. A. Pickering	S.W.
Harry Locket	J.W.
Rev. Canon Besley, P.G.C.	Chaplain.
Chas. Cruikshanks, P.A.G.Std.B.	Treasurer.
Herbert Chenery, P.M., L.R.	Secretary.
Roland D. Cox	Assistant Sec.
Marcus Saunders	S.D.
C. McLaren	J.D.
E. W. Whitmore	D.C.
George H. Dyball	A.D.C.
W. Barrett	Almoner.
Tom Clare	Organist.
Joseph Batten	Ass. Organist.
Bertram Iles	I.G.
W. Foster Harfield	} Stewards.
Geo. Shurley	
E. J. Nesbitt	Tyler.

PAST MASTERS.		G.L. RANK.
E. Stanton Jones	1870— 1	—
Charles Coote	1871— 2	—
John M. Chamberlin	1872— 3	—
James Weaver	1873— 4	P.G.Std.B.
Edward Frewin	1874— 5	—
Charles S. Jekyll	1875— 6	P.G.O.
William A. Tinney	1876— 7	—
Edward Terry	1877— 8	P.G., Treasr.
George Buckland	1878— 9	—
Edward Swanborough	1879—80	—
Charles Wellard	1880— 1	—
W. Meyer Lutz	1881— 2	—
John Maclean	1882— 3	—
Frederick Delevanti	1883— 4	—
Charles E. Tinney	1884— 5	—
William J. Kent	1885— 6	—
Henry J. Tinney	1886— 7	—
William Lestocq	1887— 8	P.A.G.D.C.
James D. Beveridge, L.R.	1889—90	—
T. de B. Holmes	1890— 1	—
Alfred E. Bishop	1891— 2	—
W. Sydney Penley	1892— 3	P.G., Treasr.
J. Ed. Hambleton, L.R.	1893— 4	—
Francis H. Macklin	1894— 5	—
Charles C. Cruikshanks	1895— 6	P.A.G.Std.B.
Samuel Johnson	1896— 7	—
W. John Holloway	1897— 8	—
Luigi Lablache	1898— 9	—
Charles Blount Powell	1899—1900	—
James W. Mathews	1900— 1	P.A.G.D.C.
Algernon Syms, L.R.	1901— 2	—
Louis Honig	1902— 3	—
Akerman May, L.R.	1903— 4	—
Herbert Leonard	1904— 5	—
Edward W. Whitmore, L.R.	1905— 6	—
E. H. Bull, L.R.	1906— 7	—
Herbert Chenery, L.R.	1907— 8	—
Ernest H. Paterson	1908— 9	—
Chris. Hilton	1909—10	—
A. B. Tapping	1910—11	—
Albert Le Fre, L.R.	1911—12	—
Frank Lister	1912—13	—

Lodge of Asaph—*Continued.*

PAST MASTERS.		G.L. RANK.
Tom Clare, L.R.	1913—14	—
W. E. Holloway	1914—15	—
Geo. H. Dyball	1915—16	—
Rev. W. P. Besley	1916—17	P.G.C.
R. Douglas Cox	1917—18	—

Address of Secretary—
78, Addison Gardens,
Kensington, W. 14.

Address of Assistant Secretary—
12, Blakemore Road,
Streatham, S.W. 16.

CHAPTER OF ASAPH, No. 1319.

Consecrated 1875.

Held at Freemasons' Hall, Great Queen Street, London, W.C., on the fourth Monday in February, April, June, and November. Installation in June.

OFFICERS, 1918-19.

E. H. Paterson	M.E.Z.
J. H. Ryley	I.P.Z.
Tom Clare	H.
Douglas Gordon	J.
Harry Nicholls	Treasurer.
Herbert Chenery	Scribe E.
A. E. George	Scribe N.
A. B. Tapping	P.S.
E. Vivian Reynolds	1st A.S.
A. E. Stenning	2nd A.S.
E. W. Whitmore	D.C.
Charles Macdona	Organist.
John Gilbert	Janitor.

PAST PRINCIPALS.	WHEN IN CHAIR.	G.C. RANK.
James Weaver	1877	P.A.G.D.C.
James E. Hambleton	1896	—
Harry Nicholls	1898	P.D.G.D.C.
James D. Beveridge, L.R.	1903	—
Edward W. Whitmore	1908	—
Clarence T. Coggin	1909	—
F. Stewart	1911	—
George A. Keen	1913	—
C. W. A. Trollope	1914	—
Herbert Chenery	1915	—
A. P. Oxley	1916	—
J. H. Ryley	1917	—
Robert D. Cummings		P.A.G.D.C.

Address of Scribe E.—
78, Addison Gardens,
Kensington, W. 14.

LIVERPOOL DRAMATIC LODGE. No. 1609.

Consecrated 1876.

Held at Masonic Temple, 22, Hope Street, Liverpool, on the fourth Tuesday in every month except June, July, and December. Installation in October.

OFFICERS, 1918-19.

John Breeze	W.M.
William Crompton	I.P.M.

Liverpool Dramatic Lodge—Continued.
OFFICERS, 1918-19—Continued.

Albert Moore	S.W.
Frank Stokes	J.W.
Wm. Savage, P.Pr.G.Tr.	Treasurer.
W. D. Jones, P.M.	Secretary.
E. Baxter, P.Pr.G. S. of W.	D.C.
John Waters	S.D.
Leslie Green	J.D.
W. Wright	Organist.
R. H. Benson	Asst. Sec.
J. A. Moore	I.G.
H. Hildyard	S. Std.
J. Mulligan	J. Std.
T. McLean, T. Pearse, A. Angers, J. Kiernan, T. Wood, T. Roberts, F. H. Crossley, and J. F. Reddington	Assistant Stewards.
W. Read	Tyler.
F. Coles, P.M.	Group Rpve.
T. R. Robertson	Charity Rpve.

PAST MASTERS.	WHEN W.M.	G.L. RANK.
W. W. Sandbrook	1880 and 1889	P.P.G.D.
W. Savage	1882	P.P.G., Treas.
J. Fineberg	1890	P.P.G.D.
H. Fineberg	1896	—
E. Baxter	1898	P.P.G.S. of W.
H. C. Arnold	1901—2	P.P.G.D.
W. G. T. Hargrave	1903	P.G.S.(I.O.M.).
J. J. Hewson	1904	P.G.D.C.
T. R. Robertson	1905	—
R. T. Palmer, P.M.	1906—14	—
W. D. Jones	1907	—
H. C. Arnold, Jun.	1912	—
Frank M. Coker ("Fred Coles")	1913	—
George Smith	1915—16	—
Edwin Haigh	1916—17	—
William Crompton	1917—18	—
O. E. B. Limbrick, 1620		—
T. Bush, 249		P.P.G.D.C.
S. Haden Jones, 1299		P.P.G.P.
G. B. Wright, 307		—
R. Goffin, 3292		—

Address of Secretary—
100, Seel Street, Liverpool.

DRURY LANE LODGE, No. 2127.
Consecrated 1885.

Held at the Theatre Royal, Drury Lane, London, W.C., on the second Tuesday in February, March, April, and November. Installation in February.

OFFICERS, 1918-19.

E. T. Pryor	W.M.
Joseph C. Harker, L.R.	I.P.M.
A. Steffens Hardy	S.W.
Joseph A. Myer	J.W.
Rev. G. Russell Gipps, M.A.	Chaplain.
Prov. G. C. (Warwickshire)	
Thomas Catling, P.M., P.A.G.D.C.	Treasurer.
James Powell, P.M., P.A.G. Reg.	Secretary.
Albert G. Neville, P.M., P.G.D.	D.C.
Richard Northcott	S.D.
A. E. Stenning	J.D.
Frank Braine	Almoner
Harold Kendal Grimston	Organist
A. Blomfield Jackson, P.M., L.R.	Assistant Sec.
Albert Ward	I.G.
Lieut. Comdr. J. Powell, R.N., Shad Frost, Dr. G. G. Howitt, and J. M. Brown	Stewards
E. J. Nesbitt	Tyler.

PAST MASTERS.	WHEN W.M.	G. L. RANK.
The Earl of Londesborough	1886	P.G.W.
Sir Augustus Harris	1887	P.G., Treas.
Sir John E. Gorst, Q.C., M.P.	1888	P.G.W.
Adm. Sir E. A. Inglefield	1889	P.G.W.
Sir Henry A. Isaacs (Lord Mayor)	1890	P.G.W.

Drury Lane Lodge—Continued.

PAST MASTERS.	WHEN W.M.	G. L. RANK.
James Fernandez	1891	P.A.G.D.C.
Sir S. B. Bancroft	1892	P.G.D.
Harry Nicholls	1893	P.G.Std.B.
Thomas Catling	1894	P.A.G.D.C.
Oscar Barrett	1895	—
Henry Neville	{1896 1897}	P.A.G.D.C.
Gerald Maxwell	1898	P.A.G.D.C.
Guy Repton	1899	P.G.D.
Lionel Rignold	1900	L.R.
J. H. Barnes	1901	—
Luigi Lablache	1902	L.R.
Albert G. Neville	1903	P.G.D.
A. Rashleigh Phipps	1904	—
H. Nye Chart	1905	—
Clarence T. Coggin	1906	A. G. Supt. W.
S. H. Tatham Armitage	1907	P.G.D.
James Powell	1908	P.A.G.Reg.
Rt. Hon. Lord Athlumney	1909	P.G.W.
Bedford McNeill	1919	L.R. P.P.G.D.Stffs.
A. Blomfield Jackson	1911	L.R.
Col. H. Walker	1912	P.G.S.B.
Blake Adams	1913	—
W. Bruce Smith	1914	—
J. H. Ryley	1915	L.R.
Dr. W. Wilson, L.R.	1916	—
J. C. Harker, L.R.	1917	—

Address of Secretary—
34, Essex Street, Strand, W.C. 2.

MANCHESTER DRAMATIC LODGE, No. 2387.
Consecrated 1891.

Held at Freemasons' Hall, Cooper Street, Manchester, on the fourth Thursday in January, February, March, April, May, June, September, October, and November.

Installation in April.

OFFICERS, 1918-19.

Fred Thorpe	W.M.
M. J. Tench	I.P.M.
E. Catling	S.W.
Ellis H. Bennett	J.W.
Chas. Swinn, P.P.G.D.	Treasurer.
J. Butterworth, P.P.G. Swd. B.	Secretary.
A. E. Wait, P.M.	Acting Sec.
Frank Ogden, P.M., P.M.	S.D.
E. Smethurst	J.D.
J. J. Bennett, P.M.	D.C.
E. H. C. Roberts, P.M.	A.D.C.
Harry Greenwood, P.P.G.D.	Organist.
Nelson Firth	Asst. ,,
James Chapman	I.G.
F. Blackhurst, M. Solomons, Nelson Firth, B. A. Rhodes, G. Dale, F. Bliss, H. George, A. Lees	Stewards.
E. Roberts, Prov. G.T.	Tyler.

PAST MASTERS.*	WHEN W.M.	PROV. G.L. RANK.
Chas. Swinn	1895	P.P.G.J.D.
John Butterworth	1900	P.P.G.Swd.B.
J. Pitt Hardacre	1901	—
T. Ll. Marsden	1902	P.P.G.J.D.
Harry S. Greenwood, P.P. G. Organist	1903	
Nelson Stokes	1904	—
Phillip Joseph	1906	—
James J. Bennett	1907	—
Arthur E. Wait	1909	—
S. Fielder	1910	—
Tom Cook	1911	—
John Bentley	1912	—

* At present Members of the Lodge.

MASONIC LODGES. 51

Manchester Dramatic Lodge—*Continued*.

Past Masters.	When W.M.	Prov. G.L. Rank.
Peter Lawton..	1880	P.P.J.G.D.
Manby Willson	1913	—
H. O. Roberts..	1914	—
E. Lorimer Wilson..	1915	—
F. Green	1916	—
M. J. Tench	1917	—

Address of Acting Secretary—
47, Clifton Road,
Prestwich, Manchester.

GUILDHALL SCHOOL OF MUSIC LODGE, No. 2454.
Consecrated 1892.

Held at the Holborn Restaurant, High Holborn, London, W.C., on the second Monday in February, March, May, November, and December.
Installation in February.

OFFICERS, 1918-19.

Landon Ronald, G.O.	W.M.
Frederick J. Griffiths	I.P.M.
Bernard Turner	S.W.
Henry Burgess, P.P.G.D., Herts.	J.W.
Walter Morrow, P.M., L.R. (21st Year)..	Treasurer.
George F. Smith (died Sept., 1918), P.P.G.O. Essex, P.G.O. (25th Year)..	Secretary.
Arthur H. Lines, P.M., P.P.G.S.D,Herts., P.G.Purst...	D.C.
Walter Hubbard	S.D.
James Saker..	J.D.
E. Lewis Arney	Asst. D.C.
F. Harold Hankins, P.Dep.G.O...	Organist
David Beardwell, P.M., L.R., P.P.G.O. Herts., P.Dep.G.O. ..	Asst. Sec.
Robert Carr	I.G.
Charles Whittaker and Albert Garcia	Stewards.
George Coop, P.M.	Tyler.

Past Masters.	When In Chair.	G.L. Rank.
T. Hastings Miller	1893	P.G.Swd.Br.
Geo. F. Smith..	1893— 4	P.G.O.
W. Henry Thomas	1894— 5	P.G.O.
Henry Gadsby	1895— 6	—
Henry Guy, L.R.	1896— 7	—
William H. Cummings, Mus. Doc., Dublin	1897— 8	P.G.O.
William Hy. Wheeler	1898— 9	—
Walter Syckelmoore	1899—1900	—
David Beardwell	1900— 1	P.Dep.G.O.
W. Rogers	1901— 2	P.P.G.Dep. D.C.
Thomas R. Busby	1902— 3	P.Dep.G.O.
Albert E. Rowarth	1903— 4	P.Dep.G.O.
George H. Dawson	1904— 5	—
Arthur L. Simmons..	1905— 6	—
Montague Borwell	1906— 7	—
G. A. Hustler Hinchliff	1907— 8	—
Sir T. Brooke-Hitching	1908— 9	P.G.D.
Arthur H. Lines	1909—10	P.P.G.S.D., Herts. P.G.P.
H. Turnpenny	1910—11	—
George K. Lang	1911—12	P.P.G.D, Herts.
F. Harold Hankins..	1912—13	P.P.G.O., Herts. Dep.G.O.
Mortlake Mann	1913—14	—
J. Ben Johnson	1914—15	—
E. Lewis Arney	1915—16	—
Frederick J. Griffiths	1916—17	—
and to Feb. 1918.		

Address of Acting Secretary—
David Beardwell,
1, Norbury Cresent,
Norbury, S.W.16

GUILDHALL SCHOOL OF MUSIC CHAPTER, No. 2454.
Consecrated 1900.

Held at the Holborn Restaurant, High Holborn London, W.C., on the fourth Friday in March June, and October.
Installation in March.

OFFICERS, 1918-19.

John W. Pare, M.D.	M.E.Z.
Robert J. Hatfield, P.A.G.D.C.	I.P.Z.
Francis Findlay	H.
W. Hunter Johnston	J.
W. Henry Thomas, P.G.O.	Treasurer.
David Beardwell, P.G.O.	Scribe E.
Carlos Sobrino	Scribe N.
Frederick G. Stubbings	P.S.
Stanley Udale	1st A.S.
Henry T. R. Morden	2nd A.S.
George Coop	Janitor

Past Principals.	When In Chair.	G.C. Rank.
T. Hastings Miller	1900— 1	P.G.Std.B.
Dr. W. H. Cummings	1901— 2	P.G.O.
W. H. Thomas	1902— 3	P.G.O.
Thomas R. Busby	1903— 4	P.G.O.
Fountain Meen	1904— 5	P.G.O.
Charles E. Tinney	1905— 6	—
David Beardwell	1906— 7	P.G.O.
Walter Morrow	1907— 8	—
Albert E. Rowarth	1908— 9	—
F. Harold Hankins	1909—10	P.G.O.
George F. Smith	1910—11	P.G.O.
Arthur L. Simmons..	1911—12	—
Hugo T. Chadfield	1912—13	—
G. K. Lang	1913—14	—
Arthur H. Lines	1914—15	P.A.G.D.C.
C. H. Allan Gill	1915—16	P.G.O.
Robert J. Hatfield	1916—17	P.A.G.D.C.
John W. Pare, M.D.	1917—18	—

Address of Scribe E.—
1, Norbury Crescent,
Norbury, S.W.

GREEN ROOM LODGE, No. 2957.
Consecrated 1903.

Held at the Imperial Restaurant, 60, Regent Street, London, W., on the first Friday in April, May, June, November, and December.
Installation in May.

OFFICERS, 1918-19.

J. R. Crauford	W.M.
A. E. George	I.P.M.
A. A. Harris	S.W.
Charles Doran	J.W.
Rev. W. P. Besley, P.G.C.	Chaplain.
W. Lestocq, P.A.G.D.C.	Treasurer.
Harry Nicholls, P.M., P.A.G.Std.B.	Secretary
Frederick Ross	S.D.
Leslie Stiles	J.D.
Vivian Reynolds, P.M.	D.C.
Robert Minster	Almoner
Lewis Sydney..	Organist
J. H. Ryley, P.M., L.R.	Assistant Sec.
Henry Ainley..	I.G.
Hubert Harben	1st Steward
Frank Arlton	2nd Steward
Spencer Geach	3rd Steward
S. Major Jones	4th Steward
E. J. Nesbitt	Tyler

Past Masters.	When W.M.	G.L. Rank.
Harry Nicholls	1903— 4	P.G. Std. B.
J. D. Beveridge, L.R...	1904— 5	—
Gerald Maxwell..	1905— 6	P.A.G.D.C.
Herbert Leonard	1906— 7	—
Akerman May, L.R.	1907— 8	—
E. H. Bull, L.R.	1908— 9	—
Charles Macdona, L.R.	1909—10	—
Hubert Willis	1910—11	—
J. H. Ryley, L.R.	1911—12	—
Blake Adams (deceased)	1912—13	—

Green Room Lodge—*Continued.*

Past Masters	When W.M.	G.L. Rank
E. Vivian Reynolds	1913—14—15	—
Douglas Gordon	1915—16	—
A. E. Rayner	1916—17	—
A. E. George	1917—18	—

Address of Secretary—
Rupert Cottage,
Bedford Park, W. 4.

LYRIC LODGE, No. 3016.
Consecrated 1904.

Held at the Imperial Restaurant, Regent Street, London, W., on the fourth Saturday in February, March, October, and November.
Installation in February.

OFFICERS, 1918-19.

Harry J. Barclay	W.M.
Charles E. White	I.P.M.
Walter Walters	S.W.
F. de Lara	J.W.
Rev. Chas. E. L. Wright, M.A., P.G.D.	Chaplain.
J. A. Stovell, P.M., P.P.G.D., Surrey	Treasurer.
G. H. E. Goodman, L.R., P.M.	Secretary.
P. T. Goodbau	S.D.
Emil F. Clare	J.D.
Tom Clare, L.R., P.M.	D.C.
T. G. Greenin	A.D.C.
Alfred Hill, P.M. 1556	Almoner.
W. E. Manaton	Organist.
Ernest Shields	I.G.
C. G. Raymond, G. E. Newman, R. J. Scott, and W. L. Adams	Stewards.
J. Bailey, L.R.	Tyler.

Past Masters.	When W.M.	G.L. Rank.
W. S. Penley	1904— 5	P.G. Treasr.
Joseph Harrison	1905— 6	P.A.G.D.C.
Charles Bertram	1906—7	—
J. A. Stovell	1907— 8	—
Sir George Pragnell	1908— 9	—
P. A Ransom	1909—10	—
Tom Clare	1910—11	—
Harry T. Dummett	1911—12	—
G. H. E. Goodman	1912—13	—
Wilson James Lakeman	1913—14	—
D. Lorne Wallet	1914—15	—
Thos. F. Noakes	1915—16	—
J. H. Willey	1916—17	—
Charles E. White	1917—18	—

Address of Secretary—
44, Bedford Row, W.C. 1.

LYRIC CHAPTER, No. 3016.
Consecrated 1910.

Held at Freemasons' Hall, Great Queen Street, London, W.C., on the third Saturday in January, March and November.
Installation in January.

OFFICERS "ELECT," 1918-19.

Wilson James Lakeman	M.E.Z.
Alfred Hill	I.P.Z.
Walter Walters	H.
Algernon Fox	J.
J. A. Stovell	Treasurer.
G. H. E. Goodman	Scribe E.
F. de Lara	Scribe N.
Emil F. Clare	P.S.
James Lake	1st A.S.
W. L. Adams	2nd A.S.
A. E. MaNickolds	Organist.
J. Strong	Steward.
J. Bailey	Janitor.

Lyric Chapter—*Continued.*

Past Principals.	When in Chair.
Tom Clare	1910—11—12
John A. Stovell	1912—13
P. A. Ransom	1913—14
Thos. F. Noakes	1914—15
J. H. Willey	1915—16
G. H. E. Goodman	1916—17
Alfred Hill	1917—18

Address of Scribe E.—
44, Bedford Row, W.C. 1.

ORCHESTRAL LODGE, No. 3028.
Consecrated 1904.

Held at the Holborn Restaurant, High Holborn, London, W.C., on the fourth Thursday in March, May, September, and December.
Installation in March.

OFFICERS, 1918-19.

Victor Watson	W.M.
Edwin F. James, P.M., P.P.G.O., Surrey	I.P.M.
Cecil Dorling	S.W.
Jesse Stamp	J. W.
John Solomon	Treasurer.
Thomas R. Busby, P.Dep.G.O.	Secretary.
Frank Stewart, L.R.	D.C.
Charles E. Fairweather	S.D.
John Eyre	J.D.
Frank M. Reade	Organist.
John Ansell	I.G.
Harry Jackson and James Brown	Stewards.
J. Whiteman	Tyler.

Past Masters.	When W.M.	G.L. Rank.
Thomas R. Busby	1904— 5	P.Dep.G. Organist.
Albert E. Rowarth, L.	1905— 6	D.G. Organist
W. A Sutch	1906— 7	—
Frank Stewart, L.R.	1907— 8	—
John H. Calcott	1908— 9	—
James Breeden	1909—10	—
Edward W. Whitmore, L.R.	1910—11	—
Frank James, L.R.	1911—12	—
Robert Gray	1912—13	—
W. Silvester	1913—14	—
H. Vander Meerschen	1914—15	—
Herbert Goom	1915—16	—
Charles Appleford	1916—17	—
Edwin F. James, P.P.G.O.	1917—18	—

Address of Secretary—
175, Brigstock Road,
Thornton Heath,
Surrey.

ORCHESTRAL CHAPTER, No. 3028.
Consecrated 1906.

Held at the Holborn Restaurant, High Holborn, London, W.C., on the third Friday in April, June and December.
Installation in April.

OFFICERS, 1918-19.

David Beardwell	M.E.Z.
Walter Morrow	I.P.Z.
Charles Appleford	H.
Albert Victor Watson	J.
Thomas R. Busby	Treasurer.
Thomas R. Busby *(pro tem.)*	Scribe E.
Frank R Moore	Scribe N.
R. Jesse Stamp	P.S.
J. Whiteman	Janitor.

MASONIC LODGES. 53

Orchestral Chapter—*Continued*.

Past Principals.	When In Chair.	G.C. Rank.
Thomas R. Busby	1906— 7	P.G.O.
J. Edward Hambleton	1907— 8	—
Albert E. Rowarth	1908— 9	—
Frank Stewart	1909—10	—
Edward Whitmore	1910—11	—
H. G. Hambleton	1911—12	—
Robert Gray	1912—13	—
Edwin F. James	1913 14	—
Frank G. James	1914—15	—
William Silvester	1915—16	—
Do. do.	1916—17	—
Walter Morrow	1917—18	—

Address of Scribe E.—
175, Brigstock Road,
Thornton Heath,
Surrey.

CHELSEA LODGE, No. 3098.

Consecrated 1905.

Held at the Town Hall, Chelsea, London, S.W., on the third Friday in March, April, May, June, July, August, September, and October.
Installation in May.

OFFICERS, 1918-19.

Ernest Smith (Erne Chester)	W.M.
Douglas White	I.P.M.
William J. Wells (Frank Hardie)	S.W.
Harold G. Hickmott (Harold Finden)	J.W.
Frederick B. Box	Chaplain.
Wolfe S. Lyon, P.A.G.P.	Treasurer.
C. J. Doughty, L.R.	Secretary.
James E. Young (Jimmie Athlone)	S.D.
Ernest A. Warsaw	J.D.
Albert le Fre, P.M.L.R.	D.C.
W. H. Hitch, P.M.L.R.	Almoner.
Henry W. May	Organist.
J. B. H. Green (Bruce Green)	I.G.
Amandus C. Linden and Alfred D. Toledano (Alfred Daniels)	} Stewards.
J. H. McNaughton	Tyler.

Past Masters.	When W.M.	G.L. Rank.
James W. Mathews	1905— 6	P.A.G.
Albert le Fre	1906— 7	—
Theodore Schreiber	1907— 8	—
Henry Coutts	1908— 9	—
Walter H. Hitch	1909—10	—
Harry Bawn	1910—11	—
Walter F. K. Walton	1911—12	—
George H. Dyball	1912—13	—
Ernest T. R. Lester	1913—14	—
W. H. Roberts (Atlas)	1914—15	—
Albert Brady	1915—16	—
H. W. J. Church	1916—17	—
Douglas White	1917—18	—

Address of Secretary—
3, Whittingstall Mansions,
Fulham, S.W.

CHELSEA CHAPTER, No. 3098.

Consecrated 1907.

Held at Freemasons' Hall, Great Queen Street, London, W.C., on the fourth Friday in March, June, September, and November.
Installation in June.

OFFICERS, 1918-19.

Albert Ashton	M.E.Z.
John H. McNaughton	I.P.Z.
Phillip Sheridan	H.
Phineas Headworth (Fred Lyster)	J.

Chelsea Chapter—*Continued*.

OFFICERS—*Continued*.

W. S. Lyon, P.A.G.D.C.	Treasurer.
C. J. Doughty, P.Z.	Scribe E.
Francis E. M. Stephens (C. Douglas Stuart)	} Scribe N.
John E. Pinder	P.S.
E. T. R. Lester	1st A.S.
Albert Brady (Felino)	2nd A.S.
William J. Wells (Frank Hardie)	D.C.
Fred W. Allwood	Organist.
J. Athlone and J. Sterzelly	Stewards.
John Gilbert	Janitor.

Past Principals.	When In Chair.	G.C. Rank.
James W. Mathews	1907— 8	P.A.G.D.C.
Albert le Fre	1908— 9	—
Herbert Chenery	1909—10	—
Henry Coutts	1910—11	—
Walter H. Hitch	1911—12	—
Harry Bawn	1912—13	—
W. H. Roberts (Atlas)	1913—14	—
Chas. J. Doughty	1914—15	—
George H. Dyball	1915—16	—
Arthur T. Chamberlain	1916—17	—
John H. McNaughton	1917—18	—

Address of Scribe E.—
3, Whittingstall Mansions,
Fulham, S.W.

BOHEMIAN LODGE, No. 3294.

Consecrated 1908.

Held at Masonic Hall, Oliver Street, Birkenhead, on the fourth Friday in January, February, March, April, May, September, October, and November.
Installation in May.

OFFICERS, 1918-19.

J. Livingston	W.M.
Fred. A. Parker	I.P.M.
A. N. McLeod	S.W.
T. Pearse	J.W.
W. H. Huish	Chaplain.
W J. Kerr, P.P.G.W.	Treasurer.
Robt. E. Goffin P.P.G.P.	Secretary.
Louis Best	S.D.
Ronald Edge	J.D.
H. Keays-Bentley, P.P.G.W.	D.C.
F. Weston	A.D.C.
J. G. Agamozong Lawson	Almoner.
J. F. Swift, P.P.G.W.	Organist.
Arthur Richards	I.G.
Robt. Linaker	Asst. Sec.
Robt. Rilley	S.S.
R. La'ham	J.S.
Arthur Rudd, F. V. Swift, W. Ballinger, J. M. King, W. A. Pratt, A. Sydney, S. A. Jones, A. T. Willis, J. H. Rigby, L. J. Simpson, F. V. Ross, Timothy Coop	} Stewards.
George Swallow	Charity Rpstv.
John Scott, P.P.G.S. of W., W.L.	Tyler.

Past Masters.	When W.M.	G.L. Rank.
A. J. Shelley-Thompson	1908— 9	{ P.P.G.W., Cheshire.
H. R. Romer	1909—10	{ P.P.G.D., Cheshire.
W. S. Tafner	1910—11	P.P.A.G.D.C.
Henry Mathison	1911—12	—
Wm. Jones	1913—14	—
R. E. Goffin	1914—15	{ P.P.G.Pursvt. Cheshire.
Geo. Mathison	1915—16	—
Frank Weston	1916—17	—
Fred A. Parker	1917—18	—

Address of Secretary—
8, Pickering Road,
New Brighton, Cheshire.

PROSCENIUM LODGE, No. 3435.

Consecrated 1910.

Held at the Town Hall, King's Road, Chelsea, S.W., on the first Tuesday in March, April, May, June, July, August, September, and October. Installation in March.

OFFICERS, 1918-19.

Phineas Headworth (Fred Lyster)	W.M.
Benjamin J. Whiteley	I.P.M.
William Dufton	S.W.
Reginald H. S. Roberts	J.W.
W. S. Lyon, P.A.G.P.	Treasurer.
C. J, Doughty, P.M., L.R.	Secretary.
Francis E. M. Stephens (C.) Douglas Stuart)	S.D.
Fred W. Allwood	J.D.
G. H. Dyball	D.C.
Albert le Fre, P.M., L.R.	Almoner.
Ernest J. Headworth	Organist.
Arthur E. Were	I.G.
Jack Enzer, E. J. S. Stephens (Stanley J. Damerell), Tom Morton, and Jack Sterzeliy	Stewards.
J. H. McNaughton	Tyler.

Past Masters.	When W.M.
Albert le Fre	1910—11
W. H. Roberts (Atlas)	1911—12
Chas. J. Doughty	1912—13
William Jas. Wells (Frank Hardie)	1913—14
George A. Keen	1914—15
Harry Bawn	1915—16
Stanley Palmer	1916—17
Benjamin J. Whiteley	1917—18

Address of Secretary—
3, Whittingstall Mansions,
Fulham, S.W.

DRAMATIC MARK LODGE, No. 487

Consecrated 1895.

Held at Mark Masons' Hall, Great Queen Street, London, W.C., on the second Thursday in February, fourth Thursday in March, and the second Thursday in October, November and December. Installation in December.

OFFICERS, 1918-19.

W. H. Roberts	W.M.
Douglas Gordon	I.P.M.
A. H. Hunt	S.W.
E. Vivian Reynolds	J.W.
Cecil Burton	M.O.
Albert Collings	S.O.
A. M. Latham	J.O.
Rev. C. E. L. Wright, P.G.C.	Chaplain.
Charles Cruikshanks, P.M., P.A.G.D.C.	Treasurer.
Clarence Sounes	Reg. of Marks
Will Sparks, G.S.	Secretary.
James Sharpe	S.D.
A. E. George	J.D.
George Harvey	D.C.
Joseph Batten	Organist.
W. Bishop	I.G.
H. Rees	1st Steward.
A. E. Mallinson	2nd Steward.
F. Banchini	Tyler.

Dramatic Mark Lodge—*Continued*.

Past Masters.		G.L. Rank.
Harry Nicholls	1895— 6	P.G.Std.B.
Rev. C. E. L. Wright	1896— 7	P.G.C.
Charles Cruikshanks	1897— 8	A.G.D.C.
W. A. Tinney	1898— 9	—
Harry Nicholls	1899—1900	P.G.Std.B.
H. G. Danby	1900— 1	—
W. J. Holloway	1901— 2	—
Herbert Leonard	1902— 3	—
Thomas Fraser	1903— 4	P.G., Treasr
E. H. Paterson	1904— 5	—
The Rt. Hon. the Lord Athlumney	1905— 6	P.G.W.
A. G. Duck (D.M.)		
Clarence T. Coggin	1906— 7	—
J. E. Hambleton	1907— 8	—
G. A. Keen	1908— 9	—
W. J. Keen	1909—10	—
W. Hotten George	1910—11	—
Chris Hilton	1911—12	—
James Powell	1912—13	—
J. H. Ryley	1913—14	—
Alfred Ellis	1914—15	—
Tom Clare	1915—16	—
Will Sparks	1916—17	—
Douglas Gordon	1917—18	—

Address of Secretary—
32, Walbrook, E.C.

DRAMATIC LODGE OF ROYAL ARK MARINERS, No. 487.

Consecrated 1901.

Held at Mark Masons' Hall, Great Queen Street, London, on the first Thursday in the months of January, April and October in every year, and at such other periods as the W.C.N. for the time being shall appoint.

Installation in April.

OFFICERS, 1918-19.

James Powell	W.C.N.
A. M. Latham	I.P.C.N.
James Sharpe	S.W.J.
F. H. Buckmaster	J.W.S.
Will Sparks	Treasurer.
A. M. Latham	Scribe.
Cecil Burton	D.C.
W. E. Lincoln	S.D.
Tom Clare	J.D.
A. E. George	Guardian.
G. A. Keen	Steward.
F. Banchini	Warder.

Past Commanders.	When in Chair.
Charles Cruikshanks	1901— 2
Harry Nicholls	1902— 3
Rev. C. E. L. Wright	1903— 4
Herbert Leonard	1904— 5
Thomas Fraser	1905— 6
,,	1906— 7
A. M. Scarff	1907— 8
Chris Hilton	1913—14
W. H. Roberts	1914—15
W. J. C. Nourse	1915—16
Dr. J. J. Pitcairn	1916—17
A. M. Latham	1917—18

Address of Scribe—
4, Paper Buildings,
Temple, E.C. 4.

THEATRICAL ORGANISATIONS.

THE ACTORS' ASSOCIATION.

After many meetings and discussions the Actors' Association was, by an overwhelming majority, dissolved and reformed as a Trade Union. The following were elected as the Council. Miss Eva Moore and Miss Lena Ashwell were subsequently disqualified on the ground that they were manageresses.

Sydney Valentine, C. V. France, Sydney Paxton, Alfred Lugg, Eva Moore, Henry Vibart, Ben Webster, Norman McKinnel, Henry Ainley, James Carew, Lilian Braithwaite, Allan Aynesworth, J. Fisher White, Geo. Tully, Julian Royce, W. G. Fay, Ernest Hendrie, Lennox Pawle, O. B. Clarence, Lena Ashwell, Dawson Milward, Henry Oscar, Dennis Neilson Terry, Gerald Ames, Frank Arlton, Phyllis Broughton, Madge McIntosh, A. Harding Steerman, Lucy Sibley, Lisa Coleman.

Secretary, Alfred Lugg. Offices, 32, Regent Street, Piccadilly Circus. W. Telephone, Gerrard 1753.

THE THEATRICAL MANAGERS' ASSOCIATION.

President, Mr. Tom B. Davis. Hon. Treasurer, Mr. Fred W. Warden, Royal Opera House, Belfast. Vice-Presidents, Mr. J. F. Elliston, Mr. W. W. Kelly, and Mr. Milton Bode. Secretary, Mr. H. W. Rowland.

The monthly meetings are held on the third Thursday in each month, and are open to all members, Council meetings having been discontinued.

THE THEATRICAL MANAGERS' ASSOCIATION, LIMITED.

Registered Offices, 52, Shaftesbury Avenue, London, W. 1.

Formed for acquiring the assets and conducting the financial business of the above Association.

DIRECTORS.

Mr. Tom B. Davis (President),
Mr. Milton Bode,
Mr. J. F. Elliston,
Mr. Robert Evett,
Mr. Fred Fredericks,

Mr. W. W. Kelly,
Mr. Walter Melville,
Mr. Fred W. Warden.
Secretary, Mr. H. W. Rowland.
('Phone : Regent 1651.)

THEATRICAL MANAGERS' ASSOCIATION.

The Association has 70 members, and represents about 100 of the leading theatres in the country, also many touring companies.

The Association is now established in its own conveniently situated offices, 52, Shaftesbury Avenue, where meetings are held, and members can also use them for their personal business. Telephone, Regent 1651.

THE SOCIETY OF WEST END THEATRE MANAGERS.

The Society of West End Theatre Managers consists of 28 members, including the hon. members, Sir Squire Bancroft, Sir J. Forbes-Robertson, and Sir John Hare.

President, Mr. J. M. Gatti; Vice-President, Mr. J. E. Vedrenne. Members: Mr. Oscar Asche, Sir Squire Bancroft, Mr. Dion Boucicault, Sir Alfred Butt, Mr. Arthur Chudleigh, Mr. C. B. Cochran, Mr. André Charlot, Miss Gladys Cooper, Mr. Frank Curzon, Mr. Tom B. Davis, Mr. Gerald du Maurier, Mr. Dennis Eadie, Mr. Robert Evett, Mr. P. M. Faraday, Sir J. Forbes-Robertson, Mr. J. M. Gatti, Mr. Rocco Gatti, Mr. George Grossmith, Sir John Hare, Mr. Frederick Harrison, Mr. Percy Hutchison, Mr. H. B. Irving, Mr. J. Herbert Jay, Miss Marie Löhr, Mr. Edward Laurillard, Mr. G. H. Miller, Mr. F. W. Tibbetts and Mr. J. E. Vedrenne.

Theatres controlled are the Adelphi, Ambassadors, Apollo, Comedy, Criterion, Daly's, Empire, Gaiety, Garrick, Globe, Haymarket, His Majesty's, Kingsway, Lyric, New, Oxford, Pavilion, Princes, Playhouse, Prince of Wales', Queen's, Royalty, St. James's, St. Martin's, Savoy, Shaftesbury, Strand, Vaudeville, and Wyndham's.

Meetings are held each month. The Committee meet when required.

Secretary, Mr. H. E. B. Butler, 18, Austin Friars, E.C. 2. Tel.: 7869 London Wall.

THE THEATRES' ALLIANCE.

This Association was formed in the year 1904, under the name of the Suburban Theatre Managers' Association, but in the year 1908, in consequence of the widening influence of the Association, the name was changed to the Theatres' Alliance, and provincial managers became eligible for membership and joined in considerable numbers. The objects of the Association are, *inter alia*, the discussion and settlement by arbitration or otherwise of matters of common interest to theatrical managers or proprietors; the affording to members of a central means for inter-communication and encouragement, by meetings or otherwise, of the direct exchange of opinions and ideas regarding theatres; the taking when necessary of concerted action, and the institution or defence of proceedings, legal or otherwise.

The members have special terms and privileges in connection with insurance and other matters, by which considerable saving can be effected.

The subscription is £2 2s. per annum for each theatre for which a member is registered. The Officers of the Alliance are:—President, Mr. J. B. Mulholland; Vice-President and Hon. Treasurer, Mr. F. Fredericks; Hon. Auditor, Mr. William Bailey; Secretary, Mr. J. Moberley Sharp, 75/77, Shaftesbury Avenue, W.1.

The members meet monthly on the first Thursday in the month to discuss and deal with any matters of general or particular interest that may arise.

Application for membership should be made to the Secretary, 75/77, Shaftesbury Avenue, W.1. Telephone, Gerrard 6450.

THE TOURING MANAGERS' ASSOCIATION.

The objects of this Association are to advance and to protect the interests of Touring Theatrical Managers, and by the promotion of a system of arbitration to endeavour to avoid litigation between managers and artists.

Meetings are held on the last Friday of each month.

Chairman, Bernard Hishin; Vice-Chairman, Cecil Barth; Hon. Treasurer, Hubert Woodward; Hon. Solicitor, Alfred De Freece; Hon. Secretary, Arthur Gibbons, 1 and 2, King Street, Covent Garden, W.C.2.

PROVINCIAL ENTERTAINMENT PROPRIETORS' AND MANAGERS' ASSOCIATION, LIMITED.

This Association was started in 1913. Has a membership of 87, covering 203 places of amusement in the provinces. President: Mr. Percy B. Broadhead (Manchester); Vice-Presidents:—Messrs. Ernest Dottridge (Oldham), Will Sley (Manchester), Matthew Montgomery (Liverpool), E. P. Lawton (Sheffield). Executive Committee:—Messrs. D. J. Clarke (Birkenhead), J. F. Elliston (Bolton), John Harrison (Manchester), J. C. Imeson (Middlesbrough), Harry McKelvie (Glasgow), H. D. Moorhouse (Manchester), Wm. Robinson (Halifax), G. E. Smith (Dewsbury), Wilberforce Turner (Salford), and Fred Waller (Blackpool). Secretary: P. Percival, 73, Bridge Street, Manchester. Telephone: 537 City.

The Association was very active in opposing the increase in the Entertainments Tax.

The annual meeting of the Association was held on March 30 at the Victoria Hotel, Manchester.

TRAVELLING THEATRE MANAGERS' ASSOCIATION.

An Association formed in 1907 among managers and proprietors of portable theatres. One of the principal matters to which the Association turned its early attention was (working hand-in-hand with the Copyright Play Protection Association) that of preventing the pirating of plays in portable theatres. By leasing the portable rights of plays and letting them out to their members the Association has been able to put a certain amount of check on piracy and to bring the price of copyright plays well within the limited reach of its members. It is not a large body, and, possibly handicapped by a lack of funds, it has not sought much in the way of reform amongst portable theatres beyond that already mentioned in the way of piracy prevention, and even in this direction the Association can do but little, as many portable managers are not members, and its authority, of course, does not extend beyond its membership. The officers for the current year are:—Mr. A. E. Drinkwater, chairman; Mr. E. Ebley, vice-chairman; Messrs. John Johnson, Wm. Haggar, and E. Ebley. Secretary, F. L. Loveridge.

On March 1, 1918, the Association moved back to their old office (which they had to vacate owing to the war) at 219, Folkestone Road, Dover.

At the meeting in September at the Carlton Hotel, Cardiff, all business was suspended for another year, but this resolution will now be cancelled on account of the Armistice.

THE INCORPORATED SOCIETY OF AUTHORS, PLAYWRIGHTS, AND COMPOSERS.

Under a Dramatic Sub-Committee of the Society of Authors, Playwrights, and Composers the dramatists of Great Britain are able to act as an independent section of that body, save on the question of finance. The dramatists now members of the Society number over 250, comprising nearly all the best-known authors. The Dramatic Sub-Committee is composed of the following:—Mr. Dion Clayton Calthrop, Mr. G. Haddon Chambers, Mr. C. B. Fernald, Mr. Anstey Guthrie, Miss Cicely Hamilton, Mr. Monckton Hoffe, Mr. Justin Huntly McCarthy (Chairman), Mr. Edward Knoblock, Mr. Richard Pryce, Mr. Arthur Shirley, Miss E. M. Symonds, and Mr. J. E. Harold Terry.

The questions dealt with by the Dramatic Sub-Committee have been many and varied, comprising such important issues to dramatic authors as Copyright, Domestic, Colonial, and International; the Managerial Treaty, Kinematograph Film Contracts. Amateur Fees, Foreign Agents. The meetings, and the subjects discussed, are chronicled fully month by month in *The Author*, the organ of the Society, and in the yearly Report. Owing to the growing importance of kinematograph contracts, on the recommendation of the Dramatic Sub-Committee the Committee of Management appointed a Special Sub-Committee to deal with all matters relating to the marketing of film rights of members' works, and the representatives of the dramatic authors have places on that Sub-Committee which meets monthly.

On the recommendation of the Sub-Committee to the Committee of Management, cases are carried through the Courts on behalf of dramatic authors. These cases comprise claims for infringement of copyright at home and abroad, actions for breach of agreements, claims for unpaid authors' fees, questions of plagarism by one dramatist against another. These last-mentioned cases are very carefully investigated by the Sub-Committee, and members of that body very often help the member, if the claim seems a sound one, by giving evidence on his or her behalf. The Sub-Committee have decided, owing to the large percentage of dramatic cases taken up by the Society without any liability for costs to the member, that in those cases where fees are recovered through the intervention of the Society's solicitors 10 per cent. of the fees must be handed over to the Society's funds. During 1918 the Society has recovered over £2,000 for members of the dramatic profession in Great Britain and the United States.

There is, in addition, a Collection Bureau attached to the Society. This Bureau collects authors' fees on contracts at home and abroad. Amateur fees, equally with professional fees, are collected by the Bureau.

The Society has, as well, a Register of Scenarios and Plays. For a fee of 2/6 per act, a member is able to deposit with the Society a copy of his play immediately he has completed it. The evidence of the date of completion of his work, which he thus obtains, may prove of importance should his work be pirated subsequently, or should its originality be challenged by another party.

Secretary, Mr. G. Herbert Thring. 1, Central Buildings, Tothill Street, Westminster, S.W. Telephone, Victoria 374.

ACTORS' BENEVOLENT FUND.

The object of the Actors' Benevolent Fund, which was established in 1882, is to help by allowances, gifts, and loans, old or distressed actors and actresses, managers, stage managers, and acting-managers, and their wives and orphans, and choristers whose efforts are entirely devoted to theatrical work.

At the time the Year Book went to press the Fund was without a President owing to the death of Sir Charles Wyndham. The Vice-Presidents are Lady Wyndham, Mr. Martin Harvey and Mr. Gerald du Maurier. Mr. Harry Nicholls is Hon. Treasurer, and Mr. Martin Harvey and Mr. Gerald du Maurier are the Hon. Trustees.

The members of the Executive Committee are as follow:—

Mr. Allan Aynesworth,
Mr. Clifton Alderson,
Mr. Stanley Bell,
Mr. J. D. Beveridge,
Mr. Dion Boucicault,
Mr. E. H. Bull,
Mr. Robert Courtneidge,
Mr. Charles Cruikshanks,
Mr. A. E. George,
Mr. J. Bannister Howard,
Mr. H. B. Irving,
Mr. S. Major Jones,
Mr. Alfred Lester,
Mr. Cyril Maude,
Mr. M. R. Morand,
Mr. Sydney Paxton,
Mr. Lionel Rignold,
Mr. Frederick Ross,
Mr. A. B. Tapping,
Mr. Arthur Wontner,

The Secretary of the Fund is Mr. C. I. Coltson, and the offices are at 8, Adam Street, Strand.

The Annual General Meeting was held on March 19, at the St. James's, with Sir Squire Bancroft in the chair. The accounts showed an income of £5,796 16s. 9d., including £1,133 15s. 11d. by way of subscriptions, and £1,327 13s. 10d., THE STAGE'S special appeal. The total expenditure amounted to £6,533 1s. 11d.

The following is a list of the Local Centres of the Fund:—Blackburn, Prince's, Mr. E. H. Page; Bradford, Royal and Opera House, Mr. J. Hart; Bristol, Prince's, Mr. J. Ellis Miller; Cardiff, New, Mr. R. Redford; Carlisle, His Majesty's, Mr. Thomas Courtice; Dublin, Gaiety, Mr. Charles Hyland; Edinburgh, Lyceum, Mr. G. T. Minshull; Leeds, Grand and Opera House, Mr. J. Wynn Miller; Newcastle-on-Tyne, Tyne, Mr. F. C. Sutcliffe; Paisley, Paisley, Mr. J. H. Savile; Scarborough, Londesborough, Mr. W. A. Waddington; Sheffield, Lyceum, Mr. J. E. B. Beaumont; Southampton, Grand, Mr. Arthur Weston.

THE ACTORS' ORPHANAGE FUND.

Founded in 1896 by Mrs. C. L. Carson. Mr. Gerald du Maurier is the President. Vice-Presidents are Lady Bancroft, Mrs. C. L. Carson, Miss Winifred Emery, Mr. Cyril Maude, Miss Ellen Terry and Lady Tree. Trustees are Mr. Arthur Bourchier, Mr. Charles Cruikshanks, Mr. Harry Nicholls, Mr. Cyril Maude, and Mr. Anslow J. Austin. Hon. Treasurer, Mr. C. Aubrey Smith; and Hon. Secretary, Mr. A. J. Austin, Goldsmith Building, Inner Temple, E.C.4.

The aim of the Fund is to board, clothe, and educate destitute children of actors and actresses, and to fit them for useful positions in after life.

DEFINITION OF DESTITUTE CHILDREN.—By destitute children is meant—
  (a) A fatherless and motherless child.
  (b) A child of whom one parent is dead, or incapacitated; the other living, but unable to support it.
  (c) A child whose father is permanently and entirely unable, by reason of mental or physical affliction, to contribute to the support of the child, the mother living but unable to support it.

The Orphanage was moved from Croydon in May, 1915, to Langley Place, Langley, Bucks. The present Home is a charming old mansion situate in its own grounds, part of which is cultivated, thereby lessening the cost of maintenance.

The staff consists of a Matron, Assistant Matron, Resident Master, a Mistress living out, and domestic staff.

ROYAL GENERAL THEATRICAL FUND.

The Royal General Theatrical Fund, which has the King, the Queen, and Queen Alexandra as its patrons, was instituted January 22, 1839, and Incorporated by Royal Charter January 29, 1853. It is for the purpose of granting annuities regulated by the rate of quarterly subscriptions paid by members in accordance with the published scale to actors and actresses, dancers, singers, acting managers, stage managers, treasurers, chorus singers, scenic artists, and prompters on attaining the age of sixty. Quarterly payments cease at sixty, when the annuity becomes due. A member may surrender his membership and be refunded half the amount paid in subscriptions. If a member dies before he qualifies for an annuity, then the whole of the amount paid in subscriptions is returned to his legal representatives. If he dies after the age of sixty his legal representatives are entitled to claim one year's annuity as from the date of his death. A Samaritan Fund has also been established designed for the relief, by way of annuity, according to the discretion of the directors, of any member who having paid his subscriptions for a period of seven years, may subsequently become permanently incapacitated from earning his living.

President, Mr. Fred Terry. Trustees, Sir Squire Bancroft, Sir W. H. Goschen, K.B.E., and Mr. H. B. Irving; Chairman of the Association, Mr. M. R. Morand; Honorary Treasurer, Mr. Charles Rock. Directors: Messrs. Lionel Carson, Lewis Casson, H. Cooper Cliffe, Charles Doran, Henry Doughty, Alfred Goddard, Douglas Gordon, the Hon. Sir W. H. Goschen, K.B.E., Edmund Gwenn, Herbert B. Hays, H. B. Irving, L. Cairns James, Herbert Lyndon, Frank Ridley, Walter L. Rignold, Bassett Roe, Frank Weathersby, Wallace Widdicombe, Hubert Willis, and H. Saxe Wyndham. Secretary, Charles Cruikshanks, 55 and 56, Goschen Buildings, 12 and 13, Henrietta Street, Covent Garden, London, W.C.2.

Office hours, Tuesdays and Fridays, 11 to 4. No dinner was held in 1918, but a list of donations was opened, and over £460 was received.

THEATRICAL LADIES' GUILD.

Founder, Mrs. C. L. Carson; President, Miss Irene Vanbrugh; Chairwoman of Committee, Dame May Whitty, D.B.E. Vice-Presidents, Lady Burnand, Mrs. Alfred Bishop, Miss Lilian Braithwaite, Miss Phyllis Broughton, Mrs. Edward Compton, Miss Eva Moore, Dame May Whitty, D.B.E.; Trustees, Miss Vane Featherston and Miss Helen Ferrers; Members of the Executive Committee, Miss Victoria Addison, Miss Lena Ashwell, O.B.E., Miss Ada Blanche, Mrs. John Douglass, Miss Vane Featherston, Lady Forbes-Robertson, Miss Helen Ferrers, Mrs. G. P. Huntley, Mrs. Synge-Hutchinson, Mrs. H. B. Irving, Miss Lindsay Jardine, Miss Clara Jecks, Miss Marie Löhr, Mrs. Gerald du Maurier, Mrs. Raleigh, Miss Louise Stopford, Miss Hilda Trevelyan, Miss May Warley, Miss Frances Wetherall.

Every member has to pay not less than 1s. per year, and to contribute 1s. or more towards buying material. The Guild helps mothers (members of the theatrical profession) during the period of their maternity by a complete outfit for mother and child, in special cases doctors' fees being paid. The Guild also provides second-hand clothing for stage purposes and for private wear to the poorer members of the profession. Ladies not connected with the theatrical profession can be elected as honorary members on payment of a donation of not less than 2s. 6d. They can then attend the weekly Bee meetings, the annual general meeting, and all social functions in connection with the Guild, but they have no voting powers.

The Guild is allied to the Needle and Thimble Guild, Edinburgh, and the Stage Needlework Guild, which annually contribute clothing and sums of money.

The Annual General Meeting was held at the St. James's on December 6, with Miss Irene Vanbrugh in the chair. The accounts showed that the Guild, for the financial year ended June 30, 1918, had received £1,299 16s. 3d., while the expenses of administration amounted to £371 18s. 4d. A sum of £155 16s. 11d. was spent in assisting necessitous cases. Bee meetings every Friday, 3 p.m. to 5 p.m.

Secretary, Miss Lorna Ridler. Offices: 3, Bayley Street, Bedford Square, London, W.C.1.

THE STAGE NEEDLEWORK GUILD.

The Stage Needlework Guild was founded in 1895 by Miss Louise Stopford as a branch of the Theatrical Ladies' Guild. Its object is to provide new clothing for the poorer members (men, women and children) of the theatrical profession and the working staffs of the London and Provincial theatres. The Stage Needlework Guild undertakes only supplying clothing for purposes of distribution. It hands the garments, after an exhibition usually held in December, to the Theatrical Ladies' Guild. There is one president, Miss Louise Stopford. There are unlimited vice-presidents, the qualification for such a position being an undertaking to find at least five associates.

Rules.—All members to contribute two new useful garments (at least) every year, and pay a subscription of 6d. (at least) to cover printing and postage expenses, or contribute 2s. 6d. (at least) in lieu of clothing. Men can become associates by contributing 2s. 6d. (at least) per annum, which will be used in buying articles which women cannot make (such as blankets, etc.).

Address, Miss Louise Stopford, 19, Belgrave Road, London, S.W.

ACTORS' DAY.

The initiation of Actors' Day took place on Thursday, October 18, 1906.

The annual Collection falls on the third Thursday in October in each year. Owing, however, to the conditions prevailing on account of the war the Committee decided that no money should be collected during the period of the war. All those who were on the register in 1913, therefore, remain on the register as though they had contributed.

Conditions.—All who contribute one night's salary, or fees, once a year are on the register. Actors, actresses, authors, managers, whether actor-manager, theatre manager, touring manager, business or acting manager, or stage manager, are eligible. The Fund helps no one who is not on the register. All not playing on Actors' Day, but who have, in previous years, when playing, contributed their night's salary, will remain on the register, provided they notify the Committee of the fact. Those on the register may apply for benefit. The Committee may authorise grants or loans to contributors, in case of sickness or urgent need.

The Advisory Board decided that in consequence of the war no collection should be held in 1914. This decision was of course to relieve members from the obligation to subscribe to the Fund at a time when many of them might find it difficult to do so; and the Board have seen no reason to alter their views within the last four years. Although no collection has been made since 1913, the Fund has been able to make grants and loans to members, and in no single case has refused to consider and deal as generously as possible with all the applications received.

Trustees : Mr. Robert Courtneidge, Miss A. E. Horniman, and Mr. Edmund Gwenn.

The Advisory Board stands as follows :—

Chairman, Mr. Henry Ainley. Mr. Sydney Valentine, Mr. A. E. Drinkwater, Mr. Story Gofton, Mr. C. Seymour, Mr. Norman V. Norman, Mr. Cecil Barth, Mr. Walter Maxwell, Mr. H. A. Saintsbury, Mr. Cyril Cattley, and Mr. Claude King.

Secretary, Mr. W. G. Fay, Dudley House, 37, Southampton Street, Strand, London, W.C.

ACTORS' CHURCH UNION.

The object of the Actors' Church Union is to endeavour to make special provision to meet the spiritual needs of those members of the Church who are engaged in the dramatic profession.

The chaplains (nominated by the President with the approval of the Bishop of the Diocese) endeavour to render any service in their power to the theatrical members of the Union, and are glad to be notified of any case of illness or other emergency which may need their help.

The Actors' Church Union is in no sense a mission to the Stage. It does not regard actors and actresses as in any way different from other people, nor as needing any "special treatment." It looks upon them simply as members of the Church who, on account of the constant travelling which their profession involves, are deprived of many of those spiritual advantages which are enjoyed by other Churchmen whose mode of life permits them to have a fixed place of residence and to attend some particular church.

In London the Union in many instances, through its chaplains, has been able to co-operate with the Actors' Benevolent Fund, the Music Hall Ladies' Guild and other theatrical charities in looking after cases of distress.

One special feature of the work of the A.C.U. is the lodging-house register, containing addresses in the various towns recommended by the local chaplains. The register is published in the A.C.U. Directory, and is issued to all members.

The Union also attempts to organise something in the way of entertainment and friendly social intercourse to alleviate the monotony of life on tour.

Any member of the dramatic profession may become a member of the A.C.U. on payment of an annual subscription of 1s. 6d., which is required to defray the printing and postage expenses connected with the Union.

The A.C.U. is promoting the formation of Hostels for the care of Actors' children while their parents are on tour. The Hon. Treasurers are Sir Johnston Forbes-Robertson and Mr. H. B. Irving. Contributions should be sent to Rev. Donald Hole, 28, Soho Square, W.1.

President, the Right Rev. the Lord Bishop of Winchester; Patrons, His Grace the Archbishop of Canterbury, His Grace the Archbishop of York, The Most Rev. the Primate of All Ireland, The Most Rev. the Lord Archbishop of Dublin, The Most

Rev. the Lord Primus of Scotland; V.P. and Chairman, The Right Rev. the Lord Bishop of Willesden; Vice-Presidents, Right Rev. the Lord Bishop of London, Right Rev. the Lord Bishop of Southwark, Right Rev. the Lord Bishop of Oxford, Right Rev. the Lord Bishop of Birmingham, Right Rev. the Lord Bishop of Down, Right Rev. the Lord Bishop of Sheffield, Right Rev. the Lord Bishop of Bristol, Right Rev. Bishop Browne, Right Rev. the Lord Bishop of Lichfield, Right Rev. Bishop Welldon, Right Rev. the Lord Bishop of Glasgow, Right Rev. the Lord Bishop of Argyll and the Isles, Right Rev. the Lord Bishop of Southampton, Right Rev. the Lord Bishop of Burnley, Sir Charles Wyndham, Sir John Hare, Mr. Ben Greet, Mr. Martin Harvey, Mr. H. B. Irving, Mr. Charles Manners, Mr. Cyril Maude; Committee, Rev. Wm. Cree, Rev. Wynn Healey, Rev. A. D. V. Magee, Rev. A. M. Dale, Rev. W. E. Kingsbury, Rev. P. W. Bischoff, Rev. F. W. Chambers, Rev. G. C. Wilton, Mr. Fortescue Harrison, Rev. Thomas Varney, Mrs. Donald Hole, Miss C. Chambers, Miss E. G. Clarke, Mrs. Murray, Mr. G. Munro Miller, Miss Lilian Baylis, Madame Isabel Beresford, Miss Lilian Braithwaite, Miss Phyllis Broughton, Mr. Charles Coborn, Mrs. Carson, Mrs. Edward Compton, Miss Winifred Emery, Miss Harriet Greet, Miss Georgina Hamilton, Mrs. H. B. Irving, Mr. Charles Windermere, Mr. Fewlass Llewellyn, Mr. C. Douglas Stuart, Mr. Kenneth Barnes, Mr. Hubert Greenwood; Hon. Treasurer, Mr. G. Munro Miller, Barton St. Mary, East Grinstead, Sussex; Hon. Lady Correspondent and Visitor, Miss Clarke, 10, The Grove, Ealing, W.5; Organising Secretary, Rev. Donald Hole, A.C.U. Headquarters, 28, Soho Square, W.1; Hon. Assistant Secretary, Rev. W. E. Kingsbury, A.C.U. Headquarters, 28, Soho Square, W.1.

The A.C.U. Annual Directory (price 7½d. post free) can be obtained from the Secretary.

CATHOLIC STAGE GUILD.

The objects of the Catholic Stage Guild, founded in 1911, are to help Catholic artists on tour and to place them in touch with the local Catholic clergy. The means by which these are accomplished are by distributing in the theatres cards giving the hours of Mass and name of priest; forwarding names of members to the priests in the towns visited; and furthering social intercourse among the members. Membership is open to artists, or those engaged on the staff, or in other ways connected with the work of the theatre, and the minimum subscription is 1s. per annum for Members and 2s. 6d. per annum for Associates. Secretary, Miss Margaret Mackenzie, 21, Beauchamp Place, Brompton Road, S.W.3. Telephone, 1986 Western. Office hours, week-days, 11 a.m.—4 p.m.; Saturday excepted.

The Annual General Meeting was held at the Vaudeville on July 12, 1918. The Right Hon. Ford Morris, P.C., K.C.M.G,, of Newfoundland, in the chair.

KING GEORGE'S PENSION FUND.

This Fund was founded on the amount derived from the first Gala performance given in an English theatre (apart from those given at Covent Garden). The performance was given in 1911 at His Majesty's Theatre in connection with the functions which marked the Coronation. On December 17, 1918, a special performance was given at His Majesty's, in the presence of the King and Queen, of a triple bill consisting of an act of "Masks and Faces," scenes from "Macbeth," and "A Pantomime Rehearsal." The President is Colonel Sir Douglas Dawson, G.C.V.O., C.B., C.M.G. The Trustees are Sir Squire Bancroft, Sir John Hare, Mr. H. B. Irving, and Mr. Dion Boucicault. General Committee includes Mr. Oscar Asche, Sir Frank Benson, Mr. J. D. Beveride, Mr. Dion Boucicault, Mr. Arthur Collins, Mr. Gerald du Maurier, Mr. Weedon Grossmith, Mr. George Grossmith, Mr. Martin Harvey, Mr. Charles Hawtrey, Mr. H. B. Irving, Mr. Cyril Maude, Mr. Harry Nicholls, Sir Johnston Forbes-Robertson, and Mr. Fred Terry. Mr. H. B. Irving is the Hon. Secretary, Mr. Stanley J. Passmore, the Assistant Hon. Secretary, and Mr. H. S. Lambart, Hon. Treasurer. Address: His Majesty's Theatre, Haymarket, W.

No person is eligible to receive a pension under the age of 60 years, nor unless he or she shall have been an Actor or Actress for at least 15 years, unless he or she shall be certified by two medical men to be suffering from blindness, paralysis, or other affliction which in the opinion of the Committee incapacitates him or her from earning a livelihood, in which case he or she may be granted a pension "without the 60 or 15 years' qualification." The amount of the annuity is in each case determined by the Committee, but in no case may exceed the maximum amount fixed from time to time by the Court.

ADELAIDE NEILSON FUND.

Miss Lilian Adelaide Neilson, who was born in 1850, and died in 1880 in Paris in the zenith of her fame, endowed a fund for charity to be applied in emergency cases—for indigent actors and actresses only. The fund is administered by the present trustees, Sir Squire Bancroft, Mr. Arthur Bourchier, and Mr. H. B. Irving.

PLAY-PRODUCING SOCIETIES.

THE INCORPORATED STAGE SOCIETY.

This Society was founded in 1899 and incorporated in 1904. Council of Management : Major Ashley Dukes, Sir Almeric Fitzroy, K.C.B., K.C.V.O., Mr. W. L. George, Mrs. Gordon-Stables, Mr. H. A. Hertz, Mr. E. J. Horniman, Mr. W. S. Kennedy (Hon. Treasurer), Mr. Lee Mathews, Mr. F. H. Mitchell, Mr. T. Sturge Moore, Allan Wade, Miss Magdalen Ponsonby, Mr. G. Bernard Shaw, Mr. Charles E. Wheeler, Mr. Frederick Whelen, Mr. Norman Wilkinson.

Address, 36, Southampton Street, Strand, W.C. Telephone: Gerrard 6907.

The year's productions of this Society were as follow :—

December 16, revival of "The Philosopher of Butterbiggens," by the late Harold Chapin ; " Fêtes Galantes," ballet comique, by Mme. Donnet; and "Vote by Ballot," a new play in one act, by Granville Barker, Court.

February 24, "The Dead City," (La Citta Morta). A Tragedy in Five Acts, by Gabriele D'Annunzio. Translated by Arthur Symons, Court.

May 12, "The Way of the World," a Comedy in Five Acts, by William Congreve (1669 [1670]—1729), King's Hall, Covent Garden.

July 28, "Manfred," a Tragedy in five scenes, by Byron, Theatre Royal, Drury Lane.

THE PLAY ACTORS.

This Society was founded in May, 1907, by members of the Actors' Association for the production of original works by English authors, Shakespearean plays, and other classic works, and translations of well-known foreign works, and to benefit the position of the working actor and actress.

The membership consists of two degrees—acting membership and ordinary or associate. Only professional players who are members of the Actors' Association are admitted to the first, and from these the various plays presented and produced are cast. Associates' subscriptions are from 5s. (for gallery) to £1 1s. (stall), according to the position and the number of seats desired by the members.

No plays were produced during 1915, 1916, 1917, and 1918, owing to the war.

The Council are willing to produce original works, when such plays have been approved by the Reading Committee. All MSS. should be sent to the Secretary of the Reading Committee, Mr. A. M. Heathcote, Lower Faringdon, Alton, Hants. Secretary, Miss Ruth Parrott, Court Theatre, Sloane Square, S.W.

THE DRAMA SOCIETY.

This Society, of which Mr. Rathmell Wilson is the director, was founded October, 1911. Full particulars may be obtained from the Secretary, The Drama Society, c/o Actors' Association, 32, Regent Street, W.1.

The Society's performances will be resumed shortly. No performances have been given since May 26, 1914, when "Dido and Æneas," by A. von Herder, was produced at the Ambassadors'.

THE PIONEER PLAYERS.

This Society was formed in 1911 with the object of producing plays which may be outside the province of the commercial theatre, but are none the less sincere manifestations of the dramatic spirit.

PLAY PRODUCING SOCIETIES. 63

President, Miss Ellen Terry. Hon. Secretary, Miss Christopher St. John. Hon. Stage Director, Miss Edith Craig. Address, 31, Bedford Street, Strand. Tel., Gerrard 3873.

In 1918 the Society produced: Literature, "The Girl and the Puppet," by Pierre Louys; "Romanticismo," by Rovetta; and "The Earlier Works of Roderick Athelstane," by H. F. Rubinstein.

WOMEN WRITERS' SUFFRAGE LEAGUE.

The object of the Women Writers' Suffrage League, which was founded in 1908 by Miss Cicely Hamilton and Miss Bessie Hatton, was to obtain the Parliamentary Franchise for women on equal terms with men.

The qualification for membership is the publication or production of a book, article, story, poem, or play for which the author has received payment, with a subscription of 2s. 6d., to be paid annually.

President: Miss Elizabeth Robins. Chairman of Committee: Miss Peggy Webling. Vice-Presidents: Lady Blake, Mrs. Herbert Cohen, Miss Cicely Hamilton, Miss Beatrice Harraden, Miss Bessie Hatton, Mrs. Belloc-Lowndes, Mrs. Meynell, Mrs. Baillie Reynolds, Mrs. Flora Annie Steel, Miss Evelyn Sharp, Miss May Sinclair, Miss Symonds (George Paston), Mrs. Margaret Woods, Mrs. Zangwill. Committee: Mrs. Benson, Mrs. Herbert Cohen, Miss Susan Carpenter, Mrs. Greenwood, Miss Annie Himes, Mrs. Romanné-James, Lady Muir Mackenzie, Mrs. Nevinson. Hon. Solicitor: Mr. Reginald C. Watson. Hon. Treasurer: Mrs. Benson. Hon. Secretary: Mrs. Susan Carpenter. Hon. Assistant Secretary: Mrs. Greenwood.

All communications should be addressed to the Hon. Sec., 144, High Holborn, W.C.

STOCKPORT GARRICK SOCIETY.

This Society was founded eighteen years ago for the purposes of studying the drama and giving an opportunity to unknown authors to have their works put on without any cost to them. The performances are private. Last year it produced "T'Marsdens," a comedy in three acts by James R. Gregson; "Pinwiddie's Profession," a comedy by Ross Hills, both of which will probably appear on the professional stage at a later date. A public performance was also given of Bernard Shaw's "You Never Can Tell."

Officers:—President, Alderman Johnstone; Secretary, Chas. J. Nairne, 45, Garners Lane, Stockport; Treasurer, Arthur Gibbons. Headquarters, Garrick Chambers, Stockport. A monthly magazine is also published.

ALTRINCHAM GARRICK SOCIETY.

The Altrincham Garrick Society was founded in 1913 by Mr. W. S. Nixon, of the Stockport Garrick Society, on lines similar to those on which it is run. Its objects are to foster the higher forms of dramatic art and literature. The Society is anxious to encourage rising dramatists by the production of new plays, and invites them to submit MS. copies. President, Mr. Edward Acton, M.A. (President of the Manchester Playgoers' Society); Secretary, Mr. W. S. Nixon; Headquarters, "Garrick Rooms," Kingsway, Altrincham. Membership, 130. The activities of the Society have been temporarily suspended, but it is intended to resume productions immediately after demobilisation of the forces.

IRISH PLAYWRIGHTS' ASSOCIATION.

Founded 1917. Aims mainly at the prevention of unauthorised and unpaid-for performances of members' plays. Subscription: Members, £1 1s. per annum; Associates, 10s. 6d. per annum. Committee: Bernard Duffy, Edward McNulty, D. C. Maher, H. Bailey, William Boyle. Hon. Treasurer, T. C. Murray. Hon. Secretary, T. King Moylan, 8, Villiers Road, Rathgar, Dublin; American Correspondent, Seumas O'Brien, 275, Wyckoff Street, Brooklyn, New York.

During the year the Association has published in handy form a list of its members' plays available to amateurs, with particulars of number of acts, characters, publisher's name, acting fee and agent. The Association also acts as agent for its members.

The directors of the Abbey Theatre having expressed their willingness to consider a fresh form of agreement which would be acceptable to the majority of Irish authors, the Association submitted a draft contract which was practically agreed to *in toto*.

In addition the Association has done much useful work in recovering fees for amateur performances after the author or his agent had failed to collect.

THEATRICAL CLUBS.

THE GARRICK CLUB.

The Garrick Club, Garrick Street, Covent Garden, was founded in 1831. Its objects are defined as follow :—"The Garrick Club is instituted for the general patronage of the drama, for the purpose of combining a club, on economic principles, with the advantages of a Literary Society, for bringing together the supporters of the Drama, and for the foundation of a theatrical library with works on Costume." The club possesses a collection of more than 600 theatrical portraits and other pictures, and numerous theatrical relics. Secretary, Mr. Charles J. Fitch.

THE SAVAGE CLUB.

The Savage Club, 6 and 7, Adelphi Terrace, Strand, London, W.C., is for the association of gentlemen connected professionally with Literature, Art, Science, the Drama, or Music. Trustees, Conrad W. Cooke, Yeend King, V.P.R.I.; Sir W. P. Treloar. Committee :— John T. Day, J. W. Gilmer, E. Hope Goddard, Reginald Groome, Fred Grundy, E. C. Heath Hosken, Bart Kennedy, G. K. Menzies, H. G. Montgomery, Rafael Sabatini, Cornwallis H. Smith, Carl St. Amory; Hon. Treasurer, Reginald Geard; Hon. Secretary, David Urquhart; Hon. Solicitor, R. H. Humphreys; Hon. Auditors and Scrutineers, Thomas Catling and Achille Bazire; Hon. Librarian, J. W. Gilmer.

THE ECCENTRIC CLUB.

The Eccentric Club, 9-11, Ryder Street, St. James's Street, S.W. (founded 1890), is constituted for the purpose of promoting social intercourse amongst gentlemen connected, directly or indirectly, with Literature, Art, Music, the Drama, Science, Sport, and Commerce. The President is Sir Charles Wyndham, the Hon. Secretary J. A. Harrison. The Committee are as follow :—G. S. Allen, Major H. Bateman, H. Montague Bates, W. J. W. Beard, Frederick Bishop, Captain W. R. Bennett, Neal Christey, Barnet Cohen, Walter de Frece, G. F. Cripps, Alfred Ellis, W. E. Garstin, H. J. Homer, Thomas Honey, W. S. Hooper, Sydney Jousiffe, Percy Leftwich, John Le Hay, T. Richards, W. J. Dayer Smith, Ernest Stuart. The Club moved into its new premises in Ryder Street in December, 1914. Telephone : 1723 Regent, 3 lines.

THE GREEN ROOM CLUB.

The Green Room Club was founded in 1877 for the association of gentlemen of the dramatic and artistic professions. The Committee are vested with power to elect others than those engaged in dramatic, literary, and artistic professions as members of the club. The larger proportion of the members are actors. The club for a number of years was situated in Bedford Street, whence it moved to its present premises in Leicester Square in 1902. The late Duke of Beaufort was the first President of the club. Sir Squire Bancroft is the present President.

The Green Room Club includes amongst its treasured possessions valuable pieces of autographed plate, the gifts or legacies of various members and celebrities in the dramatic profession. Mr. Henry Neville, by whose death during 1910 the club lost one of its most popular members, left a small legacy to the club in order that it might purchase a memento of him in the shape of a silver tankard.

Secretary, Miss Beatrice K. Huggins.—Address, 46, Leicester Square.

THE TOUCHSTONE CLUB.

This club was formed at a meeting held on October 16, 1911, at the Rehearsal Theatre, when the late Mr. Harry Paulton was elected President; Mr. Harry Nicholls, Honorary Secretary; and Mr. Charles Cruikshanks, Honorary Treasurer. Membership is limited only to actors, that is to say, those who at the time of joining are not managers, business or acting managers, musical directors, authors, critics, journalists, etc., and only those who have been in the profession for 21 years or more are eligible for membership. Owing to the death of Mr. Harry Paulton, Mr. Harry Nicholls is now president, and Mr. Charles Cruikshanks hon. secretary and treasurer. The Committee include Messrs. Frank Arlton, J. H. Barnes, Leonard Pagden, Henry Arncliffe, and, ex officio, the President, the Treasurer, and the Secretary. For some time the Club House was situated at the Adelphi Hotel, Strand, but the club is now without a home. The Committee hold their meetings meanwhile at the offices of the Royal General Theatrical Fund.

THE REHEARSAL CLUB.

The Rehearsal Club (29, Leicester Square) was founded in 1892 with the view to furnishing a quiet retreat to which minor actresses might resort between the hours of rehearsals and matinées and the evening performance.

The members' subscription is 2s. per quarter. The club is open from 11 a.m. to 7.30 p.m., and contains comfortable reading, resting, and refreshment rooms, the first well supplied with books, papers, and magazines. Anyone wishing to see the club will be gladly shown over by one of the committee or the matron.

President, H.R.H. Princess Helena Victoria; Vice-President, the Lady Louisa Magenis. Committee: Chair, Lady Maud B. Wilbraham, Lady Alexander, Lady Bancroft, Lady Bedford, Mrs. Bayne Chapman, Mrs. Gilmour, Miss Alice Gladstone, Mrs. Max Hecht, Mrs. R. S. Henderson, Mrs. Kendal, Mrs. George Marjoribanks, Mrs. Cyril Maude, Mrs. Mayne, Mrs. Frank Pownall, Miss Constance Rivington, Lady Tree, Eleonora Lady Trevelyan. Hon. Treasurer, Mrs. Mayne, 101, Queen's Gate, S.W.; Hon. Secretary, Mrs. George Marjoribanks, 22, Hans Road, S.W.; Secretary, Miss Murray, Rehearsal Club, 29, Leicester Square.

THEATRE GIRLS' CLUB.

59, Greek Street, Soho Square. This residential club began its fifth year in January, 1919. It was started to receive girls earning small salaries, girls looking for work, girls who are rehearsing, and girls who have been "out" a long time through various causes—illness, ill-luck, etc., etc. Such are helped to start again. This is a Club for non-resident members also; they can obtain meals at low prices, use the club rooms and pianos, and spend the intervals of train journeys (the club is open all Sunday) for the very small annual subscription of 2s. 6d.

Mrs. Edward Compton, the Hon. Secretary, receives all applications for entrance, and also very gratefully any subscriptions or donations. Cheques to be crossed London and South-Western Bank, Earl's Court Branch, Theatre Girls' Club Account.

THE LYCEUM CLUB.

The Lyceum Club was founded in 1904, the aim being "to focus the work of women of all nations in art, literature, science," and other professional fields. The interests of dramatists were not, however, fully represented till the Dramatists' Section was formed in 1914.

The season of 1917-18 began on October 31 with a lecture by Miss Agnes Platt on "Plots for Plays from Private Life."

On November 9 Mrs. Leo Myers arranged an entertainment for the annual Soldiers' Tea.

On December 19 the annual dinner was given, at which Miss Dorothy Brandon, author of "Wild Heather," took the chair.

Several play readings were given in the course of the year, including Winifred St. Clair's "The Patch of Purple," Mrs. Leo Myers' "The New Order," Mrs. Vigo's

"Settled Out of Court," and Bertha N. G. Graham's "Land of the Free." Miss Elsie Fogerty arranged a reading of Miss Openshaw's poetic play "Roses," followed by Sybil Bristowe's "Spring Time Fantasy." Mrs. Herbert Cohen's play of Jewish life, "The Lonely Festival," was read on May 29.

Lectures were given by Mr. Leonard Courtney on the plays of Brieux, by Mrs. Gordon Ascher on "Memories of the Stage," when Mrs. Jessie Porter took the chair. Mr. Hugh Mytton spoke on "The Drama and Professionalism," with special reference to the study of Shakespeare. The lecture has since led to the formation of a Shakespeare Study Circle in the Club under the presidency of Miss Winifred St. Clair.

A matinee in aid of the Vanguard Farm for Disabled Soldiers and Sailors at Sutton Valence was given on November 8 at the New Middlesex. Four plays were given, "John the Stoic," by Gertrude M. Saunders, produced by Henry Millar; "The Level Crossing," the prize play of the Lyceum Club Competition of 1915, produced by H. A. Saintsbury; "Sara," by Bertha N. Graham, produced by Yorke Stephens; "'Im," by Olive Lethbridge, produced by Frank Cochrane. As the result of the matinee it is hoped to send between £250 and £300 to the charity.

The Dramatic Dinner of 1918 boasted a particularly good guest list, headed by Sir Edward Marshall Hall, K.C., M.P., Miss Edyth Olive, Mr. Captain Aplin, and many others.

The Advisory Board for 1918-19 consists of Miss Jessica Solomon, Chair; Mrs. Herbert Cohen, Vice-Chair; Mrs. Gordon Ascher, Hon. Sec.; Miss Gwen John, Miss B. N. Graham, Mrs. Leo Myers, Miss Agnes Platt, Mrs. Bowman, Miss Sybil Ruskin, Mrs. Bromley Taylor, Miss Laura Smithson, Miss Sybil Bristowe, Miss Muriel Dawbarn, Miss Crosby Heath, Mrs. Arthur Binstead, Mrs. Greenaway, and Mrs. Jessie Porter.

THE DRAMATISTS' CLUB.

President, Sir A. W. Pinero; Vice-President, W. J. Locke; Executive Committee, J. E. Harold Terry, W. J. Locke, G. R. Sims. Hon. Sec., C. B. Fernald, 4, Marlborough Road, N.W.8.

The club, founded in 1909, for "dramatists of established reputation," meets at intervals at luncheon; the "objects of the club being the promotion of the interests of dramatists and of their social good-fellowship." Members are elected by invitation only.

ACTORS' SWORD CLUB.

Suspended during the period of the war.

THE ACTRESSES' FOIL CLUB.

The Actresses' Foil Club is the ladies' branch of the Actors' Sword Club, and is formed on similar lines to that Club. The President is Miss Irene Vanbrugh. The Committee are: Miss Esmé Beringer, Miss Gracie Leigh, Miss Alexandra Carlisle, Miss Mary Mackenzie. Hon. Secretary, Miss Ruth Maitland, 32, Basil Street, Knightsbridge, W.C. A six-monthly subscription of 5s. entitles members to meet and fence together at three London Salles d'Armes.

THE MAGICIANS' CLUB.

The objects of the club (established 1911) are to encourage friendly and social intercourse among persons interested in conjuring and similar arts; to encourage the science of conjuring and to watch the interests of the profession generally; to assist members with legal advice, etc. The subscription is £1 1s. per year for London members, and 10s. 6d. for country. "Socials" and entertainments are held at regular intervals. The annual séance was held in October.

President: Mr. Harry Houdini; Honorary Treasurer, Mr. Will Goldston; Secretary, "Hermalin"; Bankers, London City and Midland, Bedford Row Branch. Address, 14, Green Street, London, W.C. Telephone No. Regent 3304.

PLAYGOERS' CLUBS.

THE PLAYGOERS' CLUB.

This club was founded in 1884 to encourage social intercourse amongst those interested in the Drama, and to afford facilities for the discussion of all matters connected with the theatre. Debates on new plays are a feature in the club, and in addition, lectures, concerts, dinners, dances, etc., are held to which members have the privilege of inviting guests. There are a golfing society and a Masonic Lodge and Chapter in connection with the club, and it exchanges courtesies with the Manchester Playgoers' Club, the Bristol and other provincial Playgoers' clubs.

The club occupies commodious premises above the Leicester Square Tube Station in Cranbourn Street and Charing Cross Road, where ample accommodation is provided for the membership. Annual subscription, £3 3s.; entrance fee, £2 2s., in addition to which every member must on election take up one 10s. (fully paid) share in the Playgoers' Club, Limited.

Officers and Committee:—President, Mr. Will Sparks; Vice-President, Mr. J. S. Cotman; Trustee, Mr. Louis E. Harfeld; Hon. Treasurer, Mr. James Sharpe; Committee, Messrs. Henry Rees, S. G. Hobbs, T. B. Blurton, F. E. Healey, Harry Hart, F. G. E. Jones, W. H. Watts; Hon. Sec., Mr. A. F. Spencer; Hon. Librarian, Mr. E. H. Shear; Hon. Architect, Mr. H. E. Pollard.

Excellent work has been done by the Playgoers' Club in connection with its Christmas Pantomime Fund. Thousands of children who possibly otherwise would have little chance of witnessing one of the hardy annuals have been annually taken to pantomimes. The war, however, has naturally restricted its activity in this as well as in other directions. It has, however, succeeded in maintaining its special character, and keeps its place as one of the leading Bohemian institutions. It is the home also of the Billiards Control Club, the governing authority of amateur billiards. Secretary, Mr. G. H. Nelson.

THE O.P. CLUB.

The O.P. Club was founded and opened in the year 1900 by a body of playgoers interested in the pursuit and progress of the drama, and desirous of establishing an institution which would foster and conserve the love of playgoing in a broad and catholic spirit. Its headquarters are at Craven Street, Strand, W.C.2. President, Lord Leverhulme; Vice-President, Mr. Murray Griffith; Trustee, Mr. Carl Hentschel; Hon. Treasurer, Mr. J. Bernard Dickson; Hon. Secretary, Mr. John Evans; Acting Hon. Secretary, Mr. J. T. C. Dickinson

In addition to lectures, various entertainments and visits of large bodies of members to theatres, the Club makes a feature of its dinners. One was given recently to Mr. Arthur Collins in commemoration of his completing 21 years of management of Drury Lane Theatre. In that connection the Club was able to raise the sum of £1,000 for the help of theatrical charities. Early last spring the Club also gave a successful dinner in recognition of the great services rendered in the cause of charity by members of the theatrical and music hall professions, Lord Lambourne occupying the chair. The Club is very prosperous, with funds in hand.

THE GALLERY FIRST NIGHTERS' CLUB.

The Gallery First Nighters' Club was founded in 1896, "to maintain the right of playgoers to give free and independent criticism in the theatre, and to afford facilities for social intercourse among gallery first nighters." Genuine gallery playgoers alone are eligible for membership. The club holds frequent debates on subjects connected with the Drama. Other functions include the annual dinner, held at Frascati's in February, suppers, concerts, etc. Ladies are invited to the annual dinner and the debates.

Since the outbreak of war the Club may be said to be in a state of suspended animation. A large proportion of the members are of military age, and the inevitable dislocation of affairs has taken place. In the meantime communications should be addressed to the President, Mr. H. S. Doswell, 24, Pandora Road, West Hampstead, N.W.

Among the better-known members of the Club who fought in the war are L. H. Kenny, killed in action; Percy Jackson, killed in action; J. C. Chalmers, killed in action; James Kenny, who was wounded in the Dardanelles; John Page, Royal Fusiliers; James Campbell, R.A.S.C., M.T.; W. G. Sear, Northumberland Fusiliers; L. Arnold, discharged owing to blindness; Fred Page, discharged; Percy House, H. F. Whitworth, Moss Mansell, J. L. O'Riordan (wounded), Arthur T. Ellis, and G. F. Wright.

REPERTORY THEATRES.

GAIETY THEATRE, MANCHESTER.

By THOS. F. HUNTER.

The principles and aims of the Repertory movement were maintained as far as possible by Miss Horniman during the year 1918.

The most ambitious repertory effort here during 1918 was the talented company organised and run personally by Mr. Dion Boucicault and Miss Irene Vanbrugh for a six weeks' season, from September 23 to November 2. The series of West End plays produced included "Caroline," "Trelawny of the Wells," "Belinda," and "His Excellency the Governor." The venture proved a huge success.

Another company, who included several members of Miss Horniman's late repertory company, i.e., Miss Irene Rooke, Mrs. A. B. Tapping, and Mr. Douglas Gordon, producer, etc., revived the comedy "Humpty Dumpty" under the title of "Wigs Win," which was followed with "Miss Hobbs" and "Lady Huntsworth's Experiment," each play running two weeks.

The Christmas attraction of 1917-18 was "Where the Rainbow Ends," which had a successful run of five weeks from December 20, 1917, to January 26, 1918. On January 28 Messrs. Murray King and Charles Clark's company opened with "Romance," which had a run of nine weeks.

During the spring and autumn seasons the following plays were staged by touring companies:—"Damaged Goods," "Billeted," "The Little Brother," and "Sinners."

On May 13 an organised company revived Cicely Hamilton's play "Phyl." A special matinée was given on November 20 by Miss Jean Sterling McKinley in her old English ballads, assisted by Mr. Harcourt Williams.

On December 21 "Alice in Wonderland" was revived.

New plays produced at the Gaiety, Manchester, during 1918 were:—"Sixes and Sevens," by Susanne R. Day; "The Bubble," by Edward Locke, and produced by Ben Nathan; and "The Farringdon Case," by C. A. Castell.

THE PLAYHOUSE, LIVERPOOL.

By J. JAMES HEWSON.

That the Chairman of the last annual meeting of the shareholders of this theatre was in a position to announce that the year's working showed a profit of £881, against a large loss on the previous year, was very pleasant reading, not only for the shareholders, but for those who have watched the progress of this theatre from its inception under its present régime. The directors have had a weary, uphill struggle to maintain a smiling front on their undertaking They have courageously stuck to it, and through all its past vicissitudes have looked for a day with trust and belief that that day would bring with it a little relief, encouragement, and reward; and it would appear that their faith is being justified.

From the fantastic vagaries of the opening years they have emerged into the broader and more sedate atmosphere of sound theatrical methods and principles, and if their earlier venture had been initiated and conducted on these lines we venture to say that the troubles which have been experienced and overcome would never have become imminent, and the theatre long ago would have strongly established itself in public favour, as it now seems likely to do.

We can definitely trace the commencement of the sound business principles of management, from the artists' and staff commonwealth, the consolidation of these by Mr. Max Jerome—to whom the directors recently paid a well-deserved compliment—and the continuance of them by Mr. A. S. Pigott, the present manager, who has succeeded Mr. Jerome, the latter having relinquished the management owing to a temporary breakdown in health.

The theatre is undoubtedly occupying a unique position, in that it is providing a home for that class of stage play, comedy, and drama which is in danger of becoming a *rara avis* in the provinces under the avalanche of lighter and more evanescent fare at present. The theatre, too, has achieved and maintains the wholesome and much to be desired family atmosphere, as well as a successful appeal to a broader general public.

The changes in the company have been more frequent of late, and if by this individuality has become less marked the changes in the personnel have been perhaps a little more interesting from time to time.

The new plays which have during the past season seen the light here have not been of a very distinguished character, none of them having risen above the level of sympathetic regard and respectful admiration. Among these new pieces were "After the War," by Gertrude Jennings; "Robin's Father," by Rudolf Besier and Hugh Walpole; "Fancy Dress," a one-act play, by Capt. Merivale; and "The Call of the Road," an adaptation of Tom Gallon's "Great Gay Road," by Mrs. Geo. Norman and David Ellis. Each of these plays ran between two and three weeks, except this last one, which had to be withdrawn owing to the arrangements for the revival of "Fragments," the Christmas bill. Otherwise the play would have enjoyed a much longer run, which it deserved.

Interesting and popular revivals have been made of " Peter's Mother," "Lady Frederick," and " The Adventure of Lady Ursula." The spring season is to see the production of Sir James Barrie's " The Little Minister," in which the stock company will be augmented by several Scotch artists; a new play by Capt. Bernard Merivale, and a revival of "His House in Order," followed by several new plays by well-known authors.

It will thus be gathered that the theatre is likely to continue in its present stimulating and satisfactory condition.

ABBEY THEATRE, DUBLIN.

Directors: Mr. W. B. Yeats and Lady Gregory; Manager, Mr. Fred O'Donovan; Secretary, Mr. C. S. Millington.

During 1918 the following plays were produced:—"Aliens," play, in one act, by Rose McKenna, March 12; "Atonement," play, in three acts, by Dorothy McArdle, December 17; "The Grabber," in three acts, by Edward Barrett. November 12; "Hanrahan's Oath," comedy, in one act, by Lady Gregory, January 29; "Her Ladyship," comedy, in three acts, by Chas. McEvoy, June 24; "Little Bit of Youth," comedy, in one act, by Christian Callister, May 28; "Spring," play, in one act, by T. C. Muray, January 7; "When Love Came Over the Hills," play, in one act, by W. R. Fearon and Roy Nesbit, January 22.

BIRMINGHAM REPERTORY THEATRE.

Lessee, Mr. Barry V. Jackson; General Manager, Mr. John Drinkwater; Business Manager, Mr. Bache Matthews. Situated in Station Street, Birmingham. Telephone, Mid. 2471 and 2472.

HAMPSTEAD GARDEN SUBURB LITERARY THEATRE.

All activity has ceased until after the War.

VARIETY ORGANISATIONS.

VARIETY ARTISTS' FEDERATION.

Founded February 18, 1906. Registered under the Trades Union Acts, 1871 and 1876. Offices, 18, Charing Cross Road London, W.C. 2. Telephone, Gerrard 6950. Telegraphic address, Artifedera, Westrand, London. Affiliated to L'Union Syndicale des Artistes Lyriques of France, the Australian Vaudeville Artists' Federation, and the Trades Union Congress. Officers:—Chairman, Mr. Fred Russell; Secretary, Mr.

Fred Herbert; Trustees, Messrs. Joe Elvin, Paul Martinetti, and J. W. Cragg; Treasurer, Mr. G. H. Chirgwin; Accountant, Mr. W. H. McCarthy. Executive Committee meetings are held every Thursday at the offices at 12.30.

The Federation aims at the abolition of all abuses detrimental to the interests and welfare of the music hall profession. It provides its members with financial assistance as regards railroad fares in the United Kingdom, free legal advice, and free legal protection and fire insurance. There is also a death levy of 6d. per head per member in full benefit. Entrance fee, 5s.; Weekly subscription, 6d.

The Executive are as follow:— Jos. Alexandre, Martin Adeson, W. H. Atlas, F. E. (Lieut.) Albini, Charles Austin, A. B. Astor, Wilkie Bard, Leo Bliss, Signor Borelli, Sid Bandon, Harry Barrett, Edwin Barwick, Monte Bayly, Harry Blake, Burnetti, G. H. Chirgwin, S. J. Chapman, Tom Clare, Fred Curran, Morny Cash, W. J. Churchill, Will Cody, Chas. Cohan, Whit Cunliffe, Dave Carter, Syd Crossley, Tom E. Conover, Harry Claff, Geo. D'Albert, Sam J. Downing, John Donald, Harry Delevine, Captain de Villiers, Percy Delevine, Robert Dunning, Johnny Dwyer, Marriott Edgar, Seth Egbert, George French, W. F. Frame, James Foreman, A. E. Godfrey, Horace Goldin, Arthur Gallimore, J. W. Gallagher, W. E. Gillin, Chas. Grantley, Bruce Green, Harry Gribben, Fred Griffiths, Gus Garrick, Arthur Hall, Rowland Hill, Geo. Hughes, Carl Hertz, Mr. Hymack, Martin Henderson, Harry Jee, Tom E. Hood, Cecil W. Huxter, Lew Lake, Ted Karno, Chas. Kasrac, Fred Kitchen, Stanley Kirkby, Neil Kenyon, J. W. Knowles, Albert Le Fre, Harry Lauder, Jay Laurier, Fred. Latimar, J. P. Ling, John Le Hay, James Learmouth, Fred Maple, James Mooney, J. C. McMahon, Steve McCarthy, Harry Marvello, Orpheus, Jim Obo, Ben Obo, Jack Pleasants, Courtice Pounds, Charles Rich, W. B. Raby, J. W. Rickaby, Geo. Ross, Harry Radford, F. V. St. Clair, Fred Sinclair, Ryder Slone, Max Sterling, Jean Schwiler, Bob Stevens, George Sanford, Albert Schafer, Alfred Sutcliffe, Harry Tate, Harry Taft, Joe Tennyson, Thora, Deane Tribune, Chas. Ulrick, Chris Van Bern, Bert Vasco, Albert Voyce, Horace Wheatley, Erne Warsaw, Jack Williams, Albert Whelan, John Warren, Ben Whiteley, Howard Ward, Charles R. Whittle, Major Charles. J. Miller Sutcliffe, E. Story Gofton, Lauderdale Maitland, Griff, Tom E. Cliffe, Fred Day, Wal Langtry, Tom E. Reno, Tom Gott, Stanley J. Damerell, Fred Dunstone, and Harry Marlow.

The Annual General Meeting was held on Sunday, January 27, at the Criterion Restaurant, with Mr. Fred Russell, presiding. The balance sheet showed that subscription stamps sold amounted to £3,064 19s. 6d. Funds in hand were represented by £14,019.

MUSIC HALL ARTISTS' RAILWAY ASSOCIATION.

Founded on February 2, 1897. Head offices, 18, Charing Cross Road, London, W.C. Secretary, Mr. C. Douglas Stuart. Branch offices in Cardiff: Agent, Mr. W. F. Moss; Glasgow: Agent, Mr. John Alexander; Liverpool: Agent, Mr. Tom McKay; and Manchester: Agent, Mr. Fred Slingsby. Officers for the current year:— Hon. President, Mr. Bransby Williams; Hon. Vice-Presidents, Lieut. Albini, Mr. Charles Austin, Mr. Harry Blake, Mr. Charles Coborn, Mr. Arthur Gallimore, Mr. Harry Gribben, Mr. Fied Herbert, Mr. Ben Obo, Mr. Fred Russell, and Mr. Albert Voyce; Hon. Trustees, Messrs. J. W. Cragg, G. H. Chirgwin and Syd Walker; Hon. Treasurer, Mr. Charles Coborn; Chairman of Committee, Mr. Bruce Green, Vice-Chairman, Mr. Jim Obo; Hon. Solicitor, Mr. Eugene Judge (Judge and Priestly).

The annual subscription is 7s. 6d., children, 5s., and entrance fee 5s. The financial position of the Association has improved considerably during the past 12 months, and at the end of the financial year there was a balance of £200 invested in War Loan Stock, and over £500 current account, and £70 in hand. In spite of the many members who have answered their country's call, there were only 121 less members than in the previous year, and the total number is 4,800.

VARIETY ARTISTS' BENEVOLENT FUND AND INSTITUTION.
(With which is Amalgamated the Music Hall Benevolent Institution and the Music Hall Home.)

Founded on December 4, 1907. Offices, 18, Charing Cross Road, W.C.; Secretary, Mr. C. Douglas Stuart. The work of the society consists in the granting of relief to the deserving poor of the variety profession, and the direction of the Institution of

"Brinsworth," Staines Road, Twickenham, where over thirty old performers of both sexes are housed, fed and clothed.

Committee Meetings to consider applications for relief are held every Wednesday at 12 o'clock.

The officers of the Variety Artists' Benevolent Fund and Institution are as follow:—President, George Robey; Vice-Presidents, Charles Austin, G. H. Chirgwin, George Graves, Wal Pink, Harry Tate; Hon. Trustees, J. W. Cragg, Joe Elvin, Harry Lauder; Hon. Treasurer, Harry Blake; Auditors, Messrs. Jackson, Pixley & Co.

Executive Committee, 1918:—Robert Abel, Lieut. Albini, Gus Atlas, W. H. Atlas, Sid Baker, Jack Barker, W. Barrett, Edwin Barwick, Monte Bayly, Henri Bekker, Dick Bell, A. Borelli, Burnetti, Tom E. Cliffe, Harry Claff, Chas. Coborn, Syd Crossley, Walter Dale, Stanley J. Dameroll, H. M. Darsie, Fred Day, A. de Brean, Captain de Villiers, Marriott Edgar, Seth Egbert, Harry Falls, Albert Felino, Fred Fields, Harold Finden, J. W. Gallagher, Arthur Gallimore, Ken Gallimore, Gus Garrick, W. E. Gillin, Chas. Grantley, Bruce Green, H. Gribben, H. Griff, James Guidery, Jack Harris, A. P. Hemsley, Martin Henderson, Alf Herald, George Herd, Fred Hughes, Jack Hurst, Hymack, C. Kasrac, James Kellino, W. Kellino, J. W. Knowles, Albert le Fre, Alf Leonard, Harry Marlow, Harry Marvello, H. Mason, Fred McNaughton, Gus McNaughton, Frank Melvin, Tom J. Morton, W. W. Mosford, Ben Obo, Jim Obo, Dave O'Toole, Tom Packer, Pharos, Reginald Prince, W. B. Raby, Phil Ray, Tom Reno, Arthur Rigby, Cecil Rutland, George Sanford, Albert Schafer, Norris Smith, Geo. H. Smythson, F. V. St. Clair, Jack Sterzelly, Will Titman, Chris van Bern, Albert Voyce, Syd Walker, Wm. Welsh, Horace Wheatley, Horace White, Ben Whiteley, Bert Williams, and Fred Woellhaf. Chairman, Bruce Green; Vice-Chairman, W. H. Atlas; Secretary, C. Douglas Stuart.

Under the distinguished presidentship for this year of Mr. George Robey the Benevolent Fund and Institution has received an increased amount of support. The President's Special List of Donations exceed £2,000, another £1,000 has been received from the Performer Appeal Fund, over £600 through the 5 per cent. Charity matinee fund. Through the proceeds of a Sunday night Concert at the Hippodrome, Brighton, and a matinee at the Empire, Shepherd's Bush, £100 was realised, which was invested in War Loan, as well as another £1,000. Nearly £2,500 was expended in relief and loans and the maintenance and upkeep of the Benevolent Institution at Brinsworth, Twickenham, during the first ten months of the year. Fourteen artists who died in poverty were buried at the expense of the Fund. The President is generously giving £10 a week, and has promised to give a Sunday concert early in the new year in aid of the Fund, the proceeds to be devoted to the foundation of a permanent reserve fund. There are 30 inmates in the Institution, and over 60 weekly pensioners who receive outdoor relief.

THE MUSIC HALL LADIES' GUILD.

The Guild was formed on September 23, 1906, with the object of assisting the wives of artists, who, through lack of employment, illness, or confinement, are in want of help, by supplying proper medical aid, food, coal, or other necessaries as may be required. Also, in cases of confinement, to lend a supply of suitable baby clothes for the first month, to be returned at the expiration of that time; to assist widows of artists to find suitable employment, to find employment for children of poor artists and orphans, to supply necessitous artists with free clothing; to give stage or other clothing to artists who may require it, to visit the sick, etc. The officers of the Guild are as follows:—President, Miss Vesta Tilley; Vice-Presidents, Mrs. Chas. Coborn and Mrs. Lewis Levey; Hon. Treasurer, Miss Lottie Albert; Executive Committee: Mrs. Harry Bawn, Miss Maggie Bowman, Miss Bessie Clifford, Mrs. Ethel Cosgrove, Miss Milita Dolores, Mrs. Gintaro, Mrs. Charles Kasrac, Mrs. Fred Millis, Miss Ettie Osborn, Miss Irene Rose, Miss Louie Vere.

Hon. Auditors: Messrs. Jackson, Pixley and Co., E.C. Hon. Solicitor: Mr. Harold Seyd, 312, Regent Street, W. Hon. Counsel: Mr. E. F. Lever.

Committee meetings are held every Wednesday, at the offices, 3, Newport House, 16, Great Newport Street, W.C. Secretary, Mrs. R. Davis.

The Guild during 1918 sent over sixty children for a fortnight's holiday at the seaside or in the country. One hundred children with their mothers were given a happy day's outing on July 8 at Karsino, Hampton Court. The annual matinée was held at the Victoria Palace on December 17, and was attended by the Queen and Princess Mary. A bazaar was held for two days at the Savoy Hotel on May 14 and 15, being opened the first day by the Princess Royal, and the second day by Lady Tree. The Eighth Annual Forget-Me-Not Day was held on June 25, and brought in £272 5s. 2d., which was divided between the Guild and the Variety Artists' Benevolent Fund and Institution.

THE GRAND ORDER OF WATER RATS.

This Society was founded in 1890. Its headquarters are the Vaudeville Club, 98, Charing Cross Road, W.C. For the present year the officers are as follow:— King Rat, Wm. Banquier (Apollo); Prince Rat, Morny Cash; Scribe Rat, W. H. McCarthy; Test Rat, John B. Barton; Musical Rat, Alf. Leonard; Bait Rat, R. Protti; Collecting Rat, Forest Tell; Trustees, J. W. Cragg and Charles Austin.

THE BENEFICENT ORDER OF TERRIERS.

The Order, founded in December, 1912, by the active members (variety performers) of the Terriers' Association (now dissolved), has held a meeting almost every Sunday evening during the past year.

The Order has "carried on" as usual throughout the war. All claims for benefits have been paid in full. Further, all members in the Army and Navy have been exempt from payment of subscriptions.

A fund has also been started to assist the service members upon their discharge. Two members have been killed, about fifteen wounded, and one is still missing.

The only function has been the welcome home banquet to Terrier Jack Harris, upon his return from Germany, where he was a prisoner of war for three years.

The Grand Rally of the Order was held in November.

The Order holds a meeting every Sunday evening in the Terriers Lodge, 93, Westminster Bridge Road, S.E.1 (over the London County and Westminster Bank). The Lodge is open each day for the convenience of members. Letters may be addressed there, and facilities for correspondence, telephone, etc., are provided.

The entrance fee is now £7 7s., and the weekly subscription from 1s.

MISCELLANEOUS.

ACADEMY OF DRAMATIC ART.

The Academy of Dramatic Art (62-64, Gower Street, London, W.C.1.) was founded by the late Sir Herbert Tree in 1904. It was reconstituted in 1906, and is now vested in the following Council:—

Sir Squire Bancroft (President),
Sir James Barrie, Bart.,
Sir John Hare,
Sir Arthur Pinero,
Sir Johnston Forbes-Robertson,
Mr. Cyril Maude,
Mr. G. Bernard Shaw,
Miss Irene Vanbrugh.
Mr. H. B. Irving,
Mr. Gerald du Maurier.

Administrator.—Mr. C. M. Lowne.

The aim of the Academy is to provide a thorough training for the dramatic stage in England, and to encourage those who show talent and discourage those who do not. There is a qualifying test, consisting of two recitations, three times annually, at the commencement of each term, January, May, and October. Two scholarships of one year's free tuition are awarded to the best lady and gentleman students each term; thus, there are six scholarships in the year.

The training consists of voice production, elocution, Delsarte gesture, dancing, fencing, rehearsal classes; also lectures on subjects connected with the drama and French diction (optional). The ordinary course takes four terms, but students can enter for a single term. The fee per term is £12 12s., and the entrance fee £1 1s. The French diction classes are £1 1s. extra for regular students. The average number of students each term during the past year has been 90.

There is a body of ninety-two Associates, consisting of distinguished members of the theatrical and literary professions. The Council and Associates take voluntarily an active part in the work of the Academy. During 1918 the following ladies and gentlemen assisted at qualifying tests, scholarship competitions, and prize-judging, etc. :—Sir Johnston Forbes-Robertson, Lady Forbes-Robertson, Miss Gertrude Burnett, Mr. Herbert Bunston, Mr. Donald Calthrop, Miss Fay Davis, Colonel Robert Loraine, Mr. Dawson Milward, Miss Eva Moore, Mr. Norman Page, Mr. G. Bernard Shaw, Miss Irene Vanbrugh, Mr. Herbert Waring and Miss Henrietta Watson.

The last students' public performance took place at Wyndham's Theatre, and the following programme was performed:—"Poached Eggs and Pearls"; Scenes from "Paolo and Francesca," and "A Midsummer Night's Dream"; "Maurice's Own Idea," by Miles Malleson; "Sur la Lisière d'un Bois," by Victor Hugo, a play in mime and dances. The Bancroft Gold Medal was awarded to Miss A. Turner Robertson; Miss Kay Deane and Miss Molly Burton gaining the Silver and Bronze Medals. The Vedrenne and Eadie Award (of a year's engagement) was given to Miss Winifred McCarthy.

There are four different divisions and usually eight different classes, including a children's class. Each class consists of twelve to fifteen students, and forms, as it were, a company. Plays rehearsed in the acting classes are performed at the end of each term, providing generally over thirty performances, each of about three hours' duration. A variety of plays from Shakespearean tragedy to modern farce are taken. The aim of the Academy is in the first place to afford a practical training, to be of use both to the student and to the manager.

The Academy is not a source of profit to any of its Governing Body. Any surplus in funds is applied to the enlargement of the premises and the improvement of the training.

The Council, assisted by a generous gift of £1,000 from Sir Squire Bancroft, have constructed a theatre for the students on a site adjoining the present premises. The stage is about the size of that at the Duke of York's, and the auditorium will seat 300 comfortably, having a dress circle and boxes. The theatre, though practically completed, has not yet been opened owing to the war. It will be a great addition to the practical value of the training at the Academy. The present stage and auditorium will also be kept in use.

THE PERFORMING RIGHTS SOCIETY, LIMITED.

Established to issue licenses for the performance of its copyright music by orchestras, pianists, etc., at theatres, music halls, cinemas, concerts, hotels, restaurants, and in all other places of public resort. The Copyright Act of 1911 prohibits such performance without the written permission of the copyright owners, and the Society's license gives the permission required by the Act for over a million modern works in its repertory and in those of the affiliated Societies of France, Italy, and six other countries. Offices: 61-63, Shaftesbury Avenue, London, W. Tel.: Gerrard 7403.

THE UNITED BILLPOSTERS' ASSOCIATION.

President: Sir James Owen, J.P., Exeter; Vice-President, Mr. J. M. Godfrey, Portsmouth; Committee, Councillor Joseph Crookes Grime, J.P., Manchester; Councillor Charles Pascall, London; Mr. L. Rockley, Nottingham; Mr. David Allen, M.A., LL.B., B.L., Dublin; Mr. John Hill, Reading; Mr. W. H. Breare, J.P., Harrogate; Alderman J. Duckworth, J.P., Accrington; Mr. Cyril Sheldon, Leeds; Mr. Walter Hill, London; County Councillor David Weston, J.P., Enfield, Middlesex; Consultant Secretary, Mr. G. F. Smith, 12, John Street, Bedford Row, W.C.; Secretary, Mr. C. G. Wright. Offices, 4 and 5, Warwick Court, Holborn, London. Telephone, 6447 Holborn.

This Association, which had been in existence for many years, was registered in June, 1890, for the protection and advancement of common trade interests.

It has a committee of management, governed by a president, vice-president and ten other members, which meets monthly. The Association has a membership of between 600 and 700, comprising practically the whole of the Billposting contractors in the kingdom.

It has also (jointly with other associations) a Committee of Censors, whose duty is the examination of posters of questionable taste which may be sent them, and whose views upon them are communicated to the members. It has also a Parliamentary Committee to watch all proposed legislation and bye-laws.

THE CRITICS' CIRCLE.

The Critics' Circle was founded in May, 1913, in affiliation to the Institute of Journalists, to promote the professional interests of dramatic and musical critics, and to facilitate social intercourse and the exchange of views upon artistic and other matters. In its relations with the Institute of Journalists the Circle acts as an auxiliary committee, advising the Council of the London District on such questions as concern dramatic and musical criticism. At the same time it has power to act independently, and its members are not all of them necessarily members of the Institute. The Circle now includes 90 members. Officers and committee for 1917-18:—President, G. E. Morrison; Vice-President, E. F. Spence; Committee, William Archer, E. A. Baughan, J. M. Bulloch, Harold Child, J. T. Grein, Alfred Kalisch, Charles Palmer, A. F. Robbins, John Parker, H. M. Walbrook; Hon. Treasurer, Bernard Weller; Hon. Librarian, G. E. Morrison; Assist. Hon. Librarian, Willson Disher; Chairman, Music Committee, Herman Klein; Hon. Secretary, Music Committee, H. A. Scott; Hon. Sec., S. R. Littlewood, Hall of the Institute, Tudor Street, E.C. 4. Club Room, No. 16 at the Institute.

CONCERT SOCIETIES.

THE CONCERT ARTISTS' BENEVOLENT ASSOCIATION.

President, Mr. George Ashton; Vice-Presidents, Messrs. Tom Clare and Bruce Smith; Chairman, Mr. Harold Montague; Hon. Treasurer, Mr. Harry Crozleigh: Hon. Solicitor, Mr. William Sparks; Hon. Auditors, Messrs. Cole, Dickin, and Hills; Hon. Secretary, Mr. Osborne Pearston; and Committee, Messrs. Charles Morton, Harry Briden, Alfred Thomas, Charles Connell, Alan Adair, A. E. Nicholds, Alan Stainer, George Bolton, Herbert Townsend, David Beveridge, Dion Lane, Sydney Locklynne, Fred Wildon, Percy E. Barkshire, and Eric Williams.

The Association consists of ladies and gentlemen who are professional vocalists, instrumentalists, and entertainers. It has been established since 1897, and is managed by an annually elected Committee of fifteen members.

The Association is for the purpose of relieving the sick and needy, promoting sociability, providing legal and medical advice, furnishing a central address, redressing grievances, giving opportunity for discussion upon all matters connected with the concert artists' profession, and publishing a list of members for the use and guidance of entertainment promoters. The Association is willing to act as arbitrator when any dispute concerning its members' interests is brought to its notice.

The Annual General Meeting was held on Sunday, May 12, at the Criterion Restaurant, with Mr. William Sparks in the chair. The balance sheet showed £308 7s. 6d. as received by way of income, and an expenditure of £301.

The Association has its Benevolent Fund and Special Sickness Fund. During the year a number of "At Homes" are held on certain Sunday evenings, when members have the opportunity of appearing. These "At Homes" are attended by organisers of concerts and others, and the advantage to the artist appearing is obvious.

The entrance fee is 5s. Annual subscription £1 1s. For country members resident over forty miles beyond London the annual subscription is 10s. 6d. The funds in hand exceed £2,000.

Applications for new membership should be made to the Secretary, 9 and 10, Pancras Lane, London, E.C. 4.

CONCERT PARTY PROPRIETORS' ASSOCIATION.

Formed in November, 1913. Objects, to safeguard the interests of concert party proprietors generally, to receive and deal with suggestions for the benefit of members' interests, to establish, by means of meetings and written correspondence, a closer friendship amongst members, and generally to deal with all matters of complaint brought before the executive of the Association.

Only bonâ fide proprietors of concert parties, either resident or touring, are eligible for membership. The Association is governed by a Council, elected annually. Offices: 28, Wellington Street, Covent Garden, London, W.C.

KINEMATOGRAPH ASSOCIATIONS.

INCORPORATED ASSOCIATION OF KINEMATOGRAPH MANUFACTURERS, LTD.

Office, 62, Strand, W.C. Secretary, J. Brooke Wilkinson. Formed to protect the interests of manufacturers and publishers of films.

THE CINEMATOGRAPH EXHIBITORS' ASSOCIATION OF GREAT BRITAIN AND IRELAND (Reg. No. 1622 T.)

Secretary, W. Gavazzi King, Broadmead House, Panton Street, Haymarket. Tel: Regent 6452.

President, A. E. Newbould; Vice-President, A. Cunningham; General Secretary, W. Gavazzi King; Treasurer, Matt. Raymond; Solicitor, Norman Hart; Auditors, A. F. Stoy and Co.; Hon. Consulting Accountants, Sydney Jeffreys and Co.

General Council:—Birmingham and Midlands Branch, G. F. McDonald, Wm. Astley; Bradford and District, R. Richardson; Bristol and West of England, Tom Channing; Scottish Branch. J. J. Bennell, J. Welsh, Matt Waddell. R. C. Buchanan; Hull and District, Robert Freeman; Leicestershire County, A. Mynard; Leeds and District, Bert Rutter, J. Briggs; Liverpool and Cheshire, S. H. Carter, W. H. Huish; London and Home Counties, A. J. Gale, E. M. Barker, F. R. Goodwin, W. H. Percy; Manchester and District, Fred Carlton, C. A. Wood; Northern Branch, S. Bacon, F. W. Morrison, Thos. Thomson; North Staffordshire, Bert Miller; Notts and Derby, H. B. Stone, J. N. Nutt; Sheffield and District, W. H. Ravenscroft; South Wales and Monmouthshire, H. V. Davies, W. Stone, Rowland Williams; Hants and Isle of Wight, H. J. Hood, S. J. Flatau; Eastern Counties, F. H. Cooper.

CONSTITUTION.

The Society consists of A, B, C, and D members. Every branch has powers as provided by these rules, and is subject, in accordance with them, to the control and direction of the Council, but every branch can appoint its own officers and conduct its own business in the manner set forth in Rule X. hereof.

The objects of the Association are:—

(a) To promote goodwill and a good understanding between all proprietors of kinemas and other places of entertainment, and between them and such persons as work for them, and between them and the manufacturers and the renters of films.

(b) To provide a fund for the protection of the interests of the members of the Association, to relieve them when in distress, and to protect them from oppression.

(c) To secure unity of action among proprietors of kinemas and other places of entertainment.

(d) To promote by all lawful means the adoption of fair working rules and customs of the trade.

(e) To organise means to secure, and, if at any time considered necessary, themselves supply, means whereby a free and unrestricted circulation of films and other trade requisites may be secured for members of the Association.

(f) To resist, by all lawful means, the imposition by public authorities, or other persons, of terms and conditions upon the trade which are unreasonable or unnecessary.

(g) To secure legislation for the protection of the interests of members, and to promote or oppose and join in promoting or opposing Bills in Parliament.

(h) To adopt such means of making known the operations of the Association as may seem to the Council expedient.

(i) To adopt any means which in the opinion of the Council may be incidental o conducive to the above objects.

MEMBERSHIP OF THE ASSOCIATION.

1. The Association shall consist of :—
   (a) Proprietors of kinemas and other places of amusement approved by the Council of the Association.
   (b) Directors, shareholders, or secretaries of any company, owning or controlling such halls or places of amusement, who shall be nominated by the company and approved by the Council of the Association.

A member may nominate a representative to act for him and on his behalf, provided that such representative has been duly approved by the Council.

2. Any qualified person may be nominated by a member of the Association, and shall sign a form of application for membership. The Council shall elect or reject the candidate at the next Council meeting held, after the nomination paper and signed form of application have been received by the General Council for seven days. The Council shall vote by ballot, and one vote in three shall reject the candidate. A rejected candidate shall have the right to appeal to General Meeting.

FINANCE.

The Association shall collect funds for the furtherance of its objects, and for the benefit of distressed, persecuted, or unfortunate members. Money shall be received from the following sources:—

1. All members, other than members of the Cinematograph Exhibitors' Association, Limited, shall pay on election an entrance fee of 5s.

2. The members shall consist of four classes, namely, A, B, C, and D. The first three classes shall pay an annual subscription at the following rates, namely:—Members who are proprietors of any hall or halls, place or places of entertainment, or are the authorised nominee of any company, or proprietor of any hall or place of entertainment, duly appointed by resolution of the Board of any such company, and signed by the Chairman and Secretary, or by the proprietor, as the case may be, which comes within class A, an annual subscription of £3 3s. in respect of each hall specified and declared as provided for in clause 4 of this rule. Members who are similarly proprietors of or nominees in respect of a hall or place which comes within class B, an annual subscription of £2 2s. in respect of each hall specified and declared as provided for in clause 4 of this rule. Members who are similarly proprietors of, or nominees in respect of a hall or place which comes within class C, an annual subscription of £1 1s. in respect of each hall specified and declared as provided for in clause 4 of this rule. Class D consists of hon. members who are eligible for branch or district offices, subject to the approval of the Council.

BRANCHES.

Birmingham and Midlands.—Secretary, L. Wheatcroft, C.A., Newton Chambers, 43, Cannon Street, Birmingham. Chairman, G. F. McDonald, Rookery Picture House, Handsworth, Birmingham.

Blackpool.—Secretary, H. A. Deakin, Talbot Chambers, Blackpool.

Bradford and District.—Secretary, A. E. Shields, Lion Chambers, 29, Kirkgate. Bradford. Chairman, W. Goodall, Goodall's Pictures Ltd., Albion Street, Cleckheaton.

Bristol and West of England.—Secretary, Tom Channing, Baldwin Chambers, Baldwin Street, Bristol. Chairman, Alex. Grant, Cinema Theatre, Castle Street, Bristol.

Scottish Branch.—Secretary, J. Welsh, 79, West Regent Street, Glasgow. Chairman, J. J. Bennell, 81, Dunlop Street, Glasgow.

Hampshire and Isle of Wight.—Secretary, S. A. Gough, Shirley Electric Theatre, Southampton. Chairman, H. J. Hood, The Palladium, Southampton.

Hull and District.—Secretary, G. J. Morgan, Hessle Road Picture Palace, Hull. Chairman, R. Freeman, Tower Picture House (Hull), Ltd., Jameson Chambers, Jameson Street, Hull.

Leicestershire.—Secretary, A. Mynard, House Imperial, Narborough Road, Leicester. Chairman, F. D. Gray, Olympia Picture Hall, Narborough Road, Leicester.

Leeds and District.—Secretary, Wm. Clayton, 72, Albion Street, Leeds. Chairman, H. B. Hylton, 2, Ayresome Terrace, Street Lane, Roundhay, Leeds.

Liverpool and Cheshire.—Secretary, W. H. Huish, 39, Blackfriars Street, Manchester. Chairman, Councillor E. Haigh, 10, Commutation Row, Liverpool.

London and Home Counties.—Secretary, Percy Young, 213, Shaftesbury Avenue, W.C.2. Chairman, F. R. Goodwin, 213, Shaftesbury Avenue, W.C. 2.

Manchester and District.—Secretary, W. H. Huish, 39, Blackfriars Street, Manchester. Chairman, J. B. Midgeley, Jun., 83, Bridge Street, Manchester.

Eastern Counties.—Secretary, W. Waters, 98, Prince of Wales Road, Norwich. Chairman, F. H. Cooper, 98, Prince of Wales Road, Norwich.

North Staffordshire.—Secretary, Bert Miller, King's Theatre, Newcastle-under-Lyme, Staffs. Chairman, Councillor G. H. Barber, Palace, Tunstall, Staffs.

Nottinghamshire and Derbyshire.—Secretary, P. H. Henshaw, 15, Long Row, Nottingham. Chairman, H. B. Stone, 2, Forman Street, Nottingham.

Northern Branch.—Secretary, Alfred Smith, 71, Westgate Road, Newcastle-on-Tyne. Chairman, J. Coverdale Bell, 6, Dilston Road, Newcastle-on-Tyne.

Sheffield and District.—Secretary, G. E. Wright, 55, Norfolk Street, Sheffield. Chairman, W. H. Ravenscroft, Cinema House, Fargate, Sheffield.

South Wales and Monmouthshire.—Secretary, G. R. Dewar, 4, Park Place, Cardiff. Chairman, Will Stone, New Hippodrome, Tonypandy.

NATIONAL ASSOCIATION OF KINEMATOGRAPH OPERATORS.
(Branch No. 10, N.A.T.E.)

This Association was established in April, 1907. Its members are qualified operators of animated picture apparatus.

Objects:—(a) To protect and promote the interests of qualified operators, and to raise the status of their profession. (b) To encourage among its members a knowledge of the science of new inventions affecting their business. (c) To establish a standard of proficiency by a qualifying examination. (d) To secure the recognition of a minimum rate of pay for each class of work. (e) To establish an employment register, and to assist members with legal advice and assistance at the discretion of the Committee.

Entrance fee, 3s. Contributions, section a, 3d. per week; section b, 4d. per week.

Certificates are issued to members passing an examination, particulars of which are supplied on application.

Full particulars of membership and benefits supplied post free on application to the Secretary, at King's Chambers, Portugal Street. Telephone, 1305 Holborn. Telegraphic Address, Stageland, Estrand, London, W.C.

STAFF ORGANISATIONS.

NATIONAL ASSOCIATION OF THEATRICAL EMPLOYEES.

This Association was established on August 20, 1890. It represents those employed in the various stage departments in the use of stage scenery, properties, electrical fittings, animated picture machines, comprising stage managers, heads of departments, carpenters, electricians, kinematograph operators, property men, stagemen, and in fact all men and women employed on the mechanical or administrative staff of a dramatic, variety, or picture theatre, theatrical, or cinematographic business or industry.

It is affiliated with the General Federation of Trade Unions, the Trade Union Congress, London and Provincial Trades and Labour Councils. The chief office is King's Chambers, Portugal Street, London, W.C. Telephone, 1305 Holborn. Telegraphic Address, Stageland, Estrand, London.

Summary of Objects.—To raise the status of each class and grade of employees by maintaining a minimum rate of pay, definite working rules, and the provision of sick, funeral, and benevolent benefits for members. The Association has Branches in various parts of the United Kingdom. The entrance fee is 3s., including copy of rules and membership card. The contributions and benefits are as follows:—(a) TRADE SECTION MEMBERS.—Open to employees over 18 years of age. Contributions, 3d. per week. Benefits: Trade protection; Dispute pay, a sum equal to one-half of the normal earnings at the time, from theatre work, not exceeding the sum of 20s. per week; Legal advice free; Legal assistance in approved circumstances; Grants from the Benevolent Fund subject to the discretion of the Committee. (b) TRADE AND FUNERAL FUND SECTION MEMBERS —Open to those under 40 years of age at time of joining. Contribution 4d. per week. Benefits, in addition to all the benefits provided for class (a) members, the following sums at death :— £10 on the death of a member, £5 on the death of a member's wife or husband, after 12 months' membership.

The constitution of the Association permits any grade or section of employees eligible to join to form a branch. or all sections to combine in one branch in any locality. The aim of the organisation is to enrol all eligible men with touring companies, and those resident in every theatrical centre in the United Kingdom.

The National Executive Committee is selected from the members residing within twenty miles of the Chief office, but it is open to any branch to nominate any member to one of the general offices.

During 1918 the membership was about 10,000.

The Association is affiliated with the Australian Federation of Stage Employees.

Any man or woman between the ages of 16 and 65 engaged in any capacity in the entertainment world may apply to join the Association for the purposes of the Act, irrespective of whether he or she is eligible or ineligible to join the Association for its other purposes.

THE DRAMATIC AND VARIETY THEATRE (Employees') PROVIDENT ASSOCIATION.

This fund is a separate and independent fund for special purposes. It is not a part of any Approved Society, although it is managed by the Executive Committee of the National Association of Theatrical Employees.

It is for those who wish to make provision for more assistance during sickness than the National Health Insurance Act provides. It combines the savings bank principle with the co-operative method of providing sickness benefit and sums at death. That is to say, the members' contributions not needed to assist members in any one year are divided at the end of the year between the members.

This Association is open to any man employed in the entertainment world over eighteen and under forty-five years of age whose application is accepted by the Committee.

Entrance Fee.—1s. 3d., including membership card and book of rules. Revised contributions :—Class A.—7d. per week. Class B.—3½d. per week. Annual division of the surplus General Funds. In December of each year, each member receives an equal share for equal period of membership (Class A full share, Class B half share), less 1s. deducted to carry on the membership, and if required 1s. for the Benevolent Fund.

King's Chambers, Portugal Street, London, W.C. Telegraphic address : "Stageland, Estrand, London." Telephone : 1305 Holborn.

HEADS OF DEPARTMENTS ASSOCIATION.

This Association is a branch of the N.A.T.E. and was established in November, 1902. It consists exclusively of stage managers, scenic artists, master carpenters, chief electricians, master propertymen, and master gasmen of dramatic, variety, and picture theatres. Membership is open to those connected with any theatre, music hall, or touring company in the United Kingdom who have held such positions for at least six months, and are otherwise qualified. The entrance fee is 3s. The contribution varies from 3d., 4d., to 6d. per week, according to benefit desired and age of applicant. Sick pay is assured to those subscribing for same.

The Association has a benevolent fund, and affords free legal advice to members. Office, King's Chambers, Portugal Street, London, W.C. Telephone, 1305 Holborn. Telegraphic Address, "Stageland, Estrand, London."

AMALGAMATED MUSICIANS' UNION.

Has a membership of over 12,000. General offices, Avenue Chambers, Southampton Row, London, W.C.1. Tel.: Museum, 4427. Registered Office : 135, Moss Lane East, Manchester. Has branches in most of the important cities. General Secretary, Mr. J. B. Williams.

PLAYS OF THE YEAR.

BEING A COMPLETE LIST WITH CASTS OF NEW PLAYS, SKETCHES, AND IMPORTANT REVIVALS AT THEATRES AND MUSIC HALLS IN THE UNITED KINGDOM DURING THE YEAR 1918.

ABSENT-MINDED HUSBAND, THE, play, in one act, by Henry Seton. May 13.
Daisy Dimrose ....Miss Nora Wadeley
James Souter ....Mr. James Lindsay
Lily Lancaster ....Miss Louie Pounds
—Palace, Chelsea.

ABRAHAM LINCOLN, play, in six scenes, by John Drinkwater. Presented by the Birmingham Repertory Company. October 12. —Repertory, Birmingham.

ACROSS THE SANDS OF TIME, drama, in four acts, by Dorothy Mullord. March 11. —Battersea Palace.

AFTER DINNER, musical cocktail, by Leedham Stanley and A. Patrick Wilson. November 4.
Bunny ....Mr. Bernard Knowles
George ....Mr. G. W. Sala
Stan ....Mr. Leedham Stanley
Zoe ....Miss Zoe Corner
Vera ....Miss Vera Moore
Rosalie ....Miss Rosalie Carter
Norah ....Miss Norah Doran
—Alexandra, Stoke Newington.

AFTER THE BALL, musical comedy burlesque, book and lyrics by Jerold Robinson, music by Donovan Maher. October 7.—Hippodrome, Margate.

AFTER THE TRIAL, "a timely one-act play," by Laura Leycester. January 14.
Capt. Stephen Andrews ....Mr. Percy Rhodes
Iris ....Miss Laura Leycester
Mrs. Barford ....Miss Mildred Cotell
Wallie Jackson ....Mr. Willox Cadogan
Raby ....Miss Dorothy Smith
—Euston Theatre of Varieties.

AFTER THE WAR, play, in three acts, by Gertrude E. Jennings. September 27.
Mrs. Eastwood ....Miss Dorothy Green
Cona Edison ....Miss Doris Lloyd
Lieut.-Colonel Eastwood, D.S.O.
Mr. Lancelot Jupton
Jemima ....Miss Dora Gregory
Austin Murray ....Mr. Otho Stuart
Lady Florence Hay ....Miss Joan Rogers
Pauline Ashcroft ....Miss Margery Bryce
Nancy Courthorpe ....Miss Edith Reynolds
Mr. Carnsby ....Mr. Arthur Fayne
Mrs. Carnsby (A) ....Miss Freda Fay
—Playhouse, Liverpool.

AIGLON, L' (THE EAGLET), play, in six acts, by Edmond Rostand, translated by Louis N. Parker. Presented at a matinée in aid of the King's Fund. November 19.
Maria Louisa ....Miss Lettice Fairfax
A Maid of Honour ....Miss Olivia Glynne
Another Maid of Honour
Miss Barbara Hannay
The Marquis of Bombelles
Mr. F. Kinsey Pelle
Theresa de Loget ....Miss Hazel Jones

Aiglon, L' (The Eaglet) (Cont.).
Tibertius de Loget ....Mr. Arthur Applin
A Country Doctor ....Mr. Douglas Munro
Prince Metternich ....Mr. Clifton Alderson
Baron Friedrich Von Genz ..Mr. Roy Byford
The Attaché of the French Embassy
Mr. Frederic Worlock
The Archduchess Sophia of Austria
Miss Vane Featherston
A Lady ....Miss Violet Farebrother
Another Lady ....Miss Mabel Love
Lord Cowley ....Mr. Henry Byatt
Scaramp ....Miss Malise Sheridan
An Austrian Sergeant ..Mr. G. Dickson-Kenwin
Count Moritz von Dietrichstein
Mr. H. Hamilton Stewart
Francis Charles ....Miss Marie Löhr
A Little Archduchess .....Miss Babs Farren
A Little Archduke ....Miss Sunday Wilshin
A Tailor ....Mr. Peter Gawthorne
Countess Napoleone Camerata
Miss Doris Lytton
Baron Von Obenaus ....Mr. George Elton
Fanny Elssler ....Miss Mavis Yorke
Count Sedlnizky ....Mr. Henry Vibart
First Lackey ....Mr. Fred Hill
Second Lackey ....Mr. A. Fitzmaurice
Third Lackey ....Mr. Eric Cowley
Fourth Lackey ....Mr. A. Stevenson
A Chamberlain ....Mr. Howard Sturge
Dr. Malfatti ....Mr. William Lugg
Capt. Foresti ....Mr. Ivo Dawson
Count Prokesch ....Mr. Cowley Wright
Marshal Marmont ....Mr. Fred Kerr
Flambeau ....Mr. Lyn Harding
A Woman ....Miss Blanche Stanley
Francis I. (Emperor of Austria)
Mr. Dawson Milward
A Peasant ....Mr. G. Barclay
An Old Woman ....Miss Haidée Wright
A Tyrolese ....Mr. Clifford Mollison
A Mountaineer ....Mr. A. White
An Austrian Veteran .....Mr. Ben Greet
General Hartmann ....Mr. Julian Roce

AIRMAN'S WIFE, THE, spy play, by Charles Darrell (October 28, Alexandra, Birmingham). December 2.
Flight Commander Hector Baird
Mr. Stanley S. Gordon
Herr Franz Von Hengrin.Mr. A. Edward Brooke
Andrew Moffit, "Andy"..Mr. C. Elton-Morgan
Air Mechanic Cowd ......Mr. Fred Webber
Air Mechanic Sharland ....Mr. John Turner
Frau Solga Stel'er ......Miss Flo Norman
Mrs. Gertrude Baird ....Miss Hariette Lovdall
Carrie Baird ....Miss Edna Vena
Loyale Armadale ....Miss Nina Vaughton
—Imperial, Canning Town.

ALIEN, THE, play, by W. A. Tremayne (Produced in America, June 3. at His Majesty's, Montreal). November 11.—Royal Court. Warrington.

ALIENS, play, in one act, by Rose McKenna. March 12.
Mary Lynch .... Miss Maureen Delany
Fergus Lynch .... Mr. Arthur Shields
Kathleen Lynch .... Miss Irene Kelly
Patrick Kane .... Mr. Louis O'Connor
Con Foley .... Mr. Fred Harford
—Abbey, Dublin.

ALICE IN SUNDER-LAND, musical farce, by Lance-Cpl. H. R. Hammond (Kenneth Barton), music by Lieut. E. P. May. January 31.—Hylton Castle Camp.

ALL A DREAM, revue, in five scenes, by Billy Clarkson. Principal artists: Miss Billie Rudge, Miss Grace Collins, Mr. Tom Webb, Mr. Bill Hallett, Mr. George Farnley, and Mr. Harry Rickards. March 25.—Palace, Northampton.

ALL ALONE, THE, play, in four acts, by Henry O'Hanlon. June 17.
Esmond, Everard ....Mr. Paul Farrel
Mrs. Everard ....Miss Katherine MacCormack
Michael Clery ....Mr. W. Reddin
Andrew Arnold ....Mr. P. Hayden
Sheila Clery ....Miss Molly O'Brien
Sean Hammond ....Mr. Harold Deane
Agnes ....Miss Aoife Taaffe
Syra ....Miss Columba O'Carroll
—Hardwick Street, Dublin.

ALL DRESSED UP, musical farcical revue, in three scenes, by Wallace Parnell, with music by Vere Barker. Principal artists: Mr. Ray Kay, Miss Vera Rochdale, Mr. Frank St. Clair, Mr. Billy Firman. March 19. Empire, Penge.

ALL OVER THE SHOP, musical comedy revue, by Joseph L. Barry, music by Herbert Barnes. Principal artists: Mr. Billy Bernhart, Miss Hilda Mascott, Mr. Ken Barton, Mr. Tommy Way, Mr. Dan Doyle, Miss Elsie French, Miss Nita Van Biene. September 23.—Alexandra, Birmingham.

ALL WRONG, farce, in one act, by Francis Nordstrom. Presented by Albert Whelan (June 17, Pavilion, Glasgow). October 7.
Gale Thorne ....Miss Mary Livingston
Tom Thorne ....Mr. W. T. Ellwanger
—Holborn Empire.

ALLOTMENTS, revue. Played by Mr. Dandy Page, Miss Nan Crane, Miss Violet Lester, Mr. Austin Webb, Mr. James Stephens, Miss Gladwyn Carmyle, Miss Lucie Victor, Miss E. Hodgkinson. April 29.—Granville, Walham Green.

AN EGYPTIAN FANTASIA, dumb-show piece, invented and produced by Erica Beale. Presented at a matinée in aid of the funds of the Charing Cross Hospital. April 19.
Princess Suri-Sama ......Mlle. Arlette Ravenna
Baba-el-Yan ....M. Layos Olza
Miru ....Lady Willoughby William Williams
Fan Bearer ....Lady Muir Mackenzie
Namuras ....Lady Hewitt
A Slave ....Miss Cherry Malotte
—Shaftesbury.

AN OLD CLOWN'S IDOL, sketch, by Bruce Smith, incidental music by Harry Pepper. Produced by Ernest D'Auban. Played by Whimsical Walker and company. March 11.—Collins's, Islington.

AND AFTERWARDS: A PEACE-TIME WARNING, play, in one act, by Gertrude R. Wiskin and Martin Lewis. October 6.—Victoria Palace.

ANNAJANSKA, THE WILD GRAND DUCHESS, play, in one act, "from the Russian of Gregory Biessipoff." January 21.

Annajanska, The Wild Grand Duchess (Cont.).
Annajanska, the wild Grand Duchess
.................................Miss Lillah McCarthy
General Strammfest ......Mr. Randal Ayrton
Schneidekind ....Mr. Henry Miller
First Soldier ....Mr. Drelincourt Odlum
—London Coliseum

ANY LADY, revue, book and lyrics by R. P. Weston and Bert Lee, music by Bert Lee. Staged by Gus Sohlke. Principal artists: Mr. Horace Mills, Mr. Lupino Lane, Miss Claire Romaine, Miss Joyce St. Clair. August 5.—Hippodrome, Liverpool.

ARCADIAN ATALANTA, Greek mime, music by Granville Bantock and others. Presented at the opening of the Fogerty-Ginner season. March 11.—Court (matinée).

AMOUR, MEDECIN, L', Molière's comedy (originally produced September 22, 1665). Presented at the second performance of the second season of the French Players. March 24.—Queen's (matinée).

ASTHARA, verse play, in three acts, by Dorothy M. C. McArdle. May 24.
Asthara ....Miss Elisabeth Young
Una ....Miss Mona MacArdle
Horgel ....Miss Penhallow
Cattine ....Miss Lorna MacDonald
Thorgyn ....Mr. Paul Farrel
Derg ....Mr. Leonard
Ruorc ....Mr. Dillon
—Little, Dublin.

AS YOU WERE, fantastic revue, by Arthur Wimperis, adapted from Rip's "Plus ca Change," music by Herman Darewski and Edouard Mathe. Staged by Frank Collins, dances arranged by A. H. Majilton. Principal artists: Mlle. Alice Delysia, Mr. John Humphries, M. Leon Morton, Mr. Clifford Morgan, Miss Mona Vivian, Miss Daisy Hancox, Mr. Strafford Moss, Mr. Hayden Coffin, Miss Polly Prim, Mr. Edward Stillward. August 3.—London Pavilion.

ATONEMENT, play, in three acts, by Dorothy McArdle. December 17.
Mrs. Farraher ....Miss Margaret Nicholls
Shawn Farraher ....Mr. Fred O'Donovan
Bridie Farraher ......Miss Columba O'Carroll
Daniel Huggard ....Mr. Fred Harford
Donagh Huggard ....Mr. Arthur Shields
Father MacCarthy ....Mr. Peter Nolan
—Abbey, Dublin.

AWAY FROM THE MOSS, comedy, in three acts, by George S. Morshiel. November 25.
Brice Walker ....Mr. Walter Kennedy
Matt Mulvenna ....Mr. Norman Gray
Aunt O'Hay ....Miss Irene Boyd
Peggy O'Hay ....Miss Moya Reynolds
P.J.M. Slattery ....Mr. J. G. Abbey
Pat O'Kennedy ....Mr. C. K. Ayre
Barney Bruan ....Mr. Gerald Macnamara
Jerry Mulrooney ....Mr. Wm. Johnston
A Bar-tender ....Mr. Wm. J. Black
—Grand Opera House, Belfast.

BABES IN THE WOOD, THE, revue-pantomime. Presented by the London Divisional (58th Div.) Concert Party, "The Goods," at six special matinées. March 11.—The Middlesex.

BACK FROM OVERSEAS, play, by Wilson Howard. May 24.—Royal, Dewsbury.

BACK TO BLIGHTY, naval spy play, in five acts, by Ivy Maurice. September 16.—Palace, Barnoldswick.

BEAUTY SPOTS, musical farce. Presented by Vincent Erne and company. August 25.—Collins's.

PLAYS OF THE YEAR.

BE CAREFUL, BABY, farce, in three acts, dramatised by Salisbury Field and Margaret Mayo from the book of Mr. Field (produced in America under the title of "Twin Beds," May 4, 1914, at the Nixon, Pittsburgh; Fulton, New York, August 14, 1914). March 30.—Royal, Plymouth, April 17.—Transferred to Prince's, June 24. Last performance (the 102nd), July 13.
Harry Hawkins .... Mr. Edward Combermere
Signor Monti .... Mr. Griffith Humphreys
Andrew Larkin .... Mr. Lawrence Hanray
Blanche Hawkins .. Miss Margaret Bannerman
Signora Monti.. .... Miss Helen Raymond
Amanda .... Miss Dorothy Hanson
Norah .... Miss Peggy Doran
—Apollo.

BELINDA, an "April folly," in three acts, by A. A. Milne. April 8. Last performance (the 72nd), June 8.
Belinda Tremayne ...... Miss Irene Vanbrugh
Delia .... Miss Isobel Elsom
Harold Baxter .... Mr. Dion Boucicault
Claude Devenish .... Mr. Dennis Neilson-Terry
John Tremayne .... Mr. Ben Webster
Betty .... Miss Anne Walden
—New.

BELOW STREET LEVEL, sketch, by Jessica Solomon. May 2,—Rehearsal, Maiden Lane.

BERT AND 'ERB, adaptation of an episode in "Half-past Eight," by Hugh E. Wright. —February 18.
Lysistrata .... Miss Madoline Rees
Theta .... Miss Betty Denard
Iota .... Miss Florence Nutkins
Althra .... Miss Ethel Thompson
Newotica .... Miss Mary Machie
Amprosa .... Miss Zoe Lang
Beta .... Miss Esme Willard
Bert .... Mr. Fred Edwards
'Erb .... Mr. Syd. Russell
—Palace, East Ham.

BETTY AT BAY, play, in four acts, by Jessie Porter (March 11, Court, Liverpool). April 9. Last performance (the 53rd). May 18.
Betty .... Miss Christine Silver
Adams .... Master Roy Lennol
Geoffrey .... Master Teddy Hayward
Jimmy .... Master Hugo Charpentier
Babs .... Miss Elaine Bisley
Lucy .... Miss Frances Davis
Lady Muriel Naylor .... Miss Evelyn Hope
Michael Hylton .... Mr. Arthur Whitby
Mrs. Devlin.................... Miss Fortescue
Dick Fellowes .... Mr. Eric Cowey
Styles .... Miss Kathleen Sinclair
Sir Charles Fellowes, Bart. .. Mr. J. H. Barnes
Brooks .... Miss Cecilia Loftus
—Strand.

BETTY WAKES UP, comedy, with music, in three acts, by Maisie Robson and John S. Millward, lyrics by Percy Ford, music by Kingsford, Shortland (September 2, Palace, Rugeley). September 9.
Philip Strangeways .... Mr. John S. Millward
Stanforth Dorien .... Mr. Walter Gilbert
Walters .... Mr. Arthur de Marr
Inspector Wilson .... Mr. George Wallace
Madame Delecia .... Miss Frances Mather
Martha .... Miss Kathleen Emmett
Asta Neilson .... Miss Edith Giddings
Cissie Delaney .... Miss Gertrude Harber
Betty .... Miss Maisie Robson
—Hippodrome, Maidenhead.

BEWARE GERMANS, war drama, by A. Myddleton-Myles, November 11.
Arthur Guyver, M.P. .... Mr. Fred de Vere
Leslie Chesham, R.A.F. .... Mr. Douglas Carlile
Adeline Cobourne .... Miss May Hullatt
Thomas Pelham, alias "Atkins"
.... Mr. Arthur Page

Beware Germans (Cont.).
Oswald Shoeman .... Mr. A. Myddleton-Myles
Sir Henry Colbourne .. Mr. Harry C. Robinson
Lucy Pelham .... Miss Daisy Cook
Carmen, Higglewig .... Miss May Emery
Binnie Belper .... Miss Muriel Haydn
Florence Cooley .... Miss Gwen Shilton
Inspector of Police ...... Mr. Walter Grahame
Several Policemen on Strike
Messrs. Hobbs, Kent, and Tees
—Palace, Battersea.

BIDDY, Irish comedy sketch. Produced by E. Holman Clark. November 4.
Capt. Lord Seymour .... Mr. Neil Curtis
Lady Aurora Bellairs .... Miss Mary Morrell
Mrs. Marjoribanks Smythe..Miss Norah Balfour
Biddy .... Miss Judith Wogan
—Palace, East Ham.

BILL IN A FIX, sketch. January 23.—Hippodrome, Richmond.

BING BOYS ON BROADWAY, THE, revue, in two acts and nine scenes, "told" by George Grossmith and Fred Thompson, written by Fred Thompson and Harry M. Vernon, music by Nat. D. Ayer, lyrics by Clifford Grey. Produced by Harry M. Vernon, staged by Gus Sohlke. Principal artists: Mr. George Robey, Miss Violet Loraine, Mr. Arthur Finn, Mr. Dan Agar, Miss Kitty Fielder, the Misses Lorna and Toots Pounds, Mr. Peter Wiser, Miss Bessie Clifford, Mr. Pip Powell, Miss Lou Edwards, Mr. E. Jack Caldwell, Miss Marjorie Carlisle, Mr. Joe Milton, Mr. George Robinson, Mr Albert Brouett, Mr. Fred Rigg, Mr. Frank Leslie, Miss Freda Large, Miss Maxime Craven, and Miss Mollie Molteno. February 16.—Alhambra.

BIRD IN HAND, fairy play, by Laurence Housman. Produced at a matinée in aid of the Sisters of Mercy homes for working women and girls. January 4.
Professor Braintree ...... Mr. J. Fisher White
Miss Tuckey .... Miss Daisy Weekes
Dr. Locum .... Mr. E. H. Paterson
Elfrida .... Miss Agnes Buddeley
Bird in Hand .... Miss Jean Vivian-Rees
—Vaudeville.

BIRDS OF PARADISE, musical comedy revue, book by Herbert Sargent, music by Patrick Thayer. Principal artists: Mr. Rupert Hazel, Mr. Frank G. Sort, Miss Florence Vie, Miss Kitty Emson, Miss Poppy Lake, Mr. Douglas Maclaren. November 18.—Empire, Wolverhampton.

BIRTHDAYS, musical comedy revue. October 23.—Pavilion, Ashington.

BLACK BOOK, THE, melodrama, in prelude and three acts, by Leonard Mortimer. July 15.
Hamilton Cleek .... Mr. Leonard Mortimer
Dr. David Howard .... Mr. Richard Custance
Dr. Eustace Baskerville ..Mr. Albert McLean
Prof. Brano Krultz .... Mr. Herbert Walmsley
Chickles .... Mr. Louis Gaye
Rev. Joseph Howard .... Mr. Lawrence Derrick
Nancy Howard .... Miss Marion Brereton
Briggs .... Mr. George Mason
Reema Sax .... Miss Ivy Sheppard
Hypathia Hilda Mason .... Miss Peggy Wyse
Mrs. Hammond .... Miss Mabel Wilton
Betty Lyle .... Miss Ida Clifford
—Grand, Croydon.

BLAME THE CINEMA, play, in one act, by Martin Lane. February 4.
The Lady .... Mrs. Langtry
The Lover .... Mr. Walter Pearce
The Butler .... Mr. Henry Deas
—London Coliseum.

BLIND MAN'S BUFF, play, in one act, by Ernest Bramah. April 22.
Hugh Darragh ....Mr. Watkin Wynne
Kato Kuromi ....Mr. George Belmore
John Beringer Huise ......Mr. Herbert Wills
Tims ....} Mr. D. S. Crewe
Inspector Beedel ....
Violet Darragh ....Miss Jessie Danvers
Max Carrados ....Mr. Gilbert Heron
—Palace, Chelsea.

BOBO, musical comedy, in four scenes. February 11.—Middlesex.

BOITE A JOJOUX, LA, ballet for children, by André Hellé, music by Claude Debussy. Presented at the opening of the Fogerty-Ginner season. March 11.—Court (matinée).

BOX O' TRICKS, revue, in seventeen scenes, by Albert de Courville and Wal Pink, with additional lyrics by Douglas Forbes, Leslie Haslam, and Harry Graham, music by Dave Stamper and Frederick Chappelle, staged by Ned Wayburn, and produced by Albert de Courville. Principal artists: Miss Shirley Kellogg, Mr. Harry Tate, Miss Cicely Debenham, Miss Daphne Pollard, Mr. Tom Macnaughton, Mr. Fred Allandale, Mr. Ralph Riggs, Miss Katherine Witchie, Miss Marion Peake, Mr. Harry Frankiss, Miss Dorothy Jay, Mr. Tom Tweedly, Mr. Ronald Stewart, Mr. H. A. Kennedy, Mr. H. Beesley, and the Ten Loonies. March 7.—London Hippodrome.

BOY COMES HOME, THE, comedy, in one act, by A. A. Milne. September 9.
Philip ....Mr. Owen Nares
Uncle James ....Mr. Tom Reynolds
Aunt Emily ....Miss Dorothy Radford
Mary ....Miss Ada Dick
Mrs. Higgins ....Miss Rachel de Solla
—Victoria Palace.

BOY WANTED, musical comedy, by James Salter and George Rowlands, music by George Shaw. November 18.—Hippodrome, Margate.

BROKEN DOLL, A, play, by Gladys Hastings-Walton (December 31, 1917, Royal, Barnsley). May 27.—Royal, Woolwich.

BUBBLE, THE, comedy, in four acts, by Edward Locke (produced in America, January 18, 1915, Schenectady; April 5, 1915, Booth, New York). September 9.—Gaiety, Manchester, October 28.
Jacob Cohen ....Mr. Ben Nathan
Joseph Marks ......Mr. Lauderdale Maitland
David Goldsmith ....Mr. Ronald Colman
Mrs. Cohen ....Miss Joan Pereira
Rosa ....Miss Annie Trilnick
—Wimbledon.

BUBBLES FROM BUBBLY, extract from the revue "Bubbly" (May 5. 1917, Comedy). Played by Miss Phyllis Monkman, Mr. Jack Buchanan, Mr. Gilbert Childs, Mr. Douglas Phillips, Miss Margaret Campbell, etc. April 22.—London Coliseum.

BUILDING FUND, THE, William Boyle's comedy (April 25, 1905, Abbey, Dublin). Presented by the Irish Players during the second week of their London season. April 8.—Court.

BULLDOG BREED, THE, dramatic naval episode, in one act, by Wing Commander Charles F. Noyes and Lieut. José Levy. February 18.
The Captain .... Mr. Athol Forde
Lieut.-Commander Leveson
        Mr. A. Lambert Emson
Lieut. Meyer ....Mr. William Luff
C.P.O. Bowline ....Mr. Hubert Willis
Ship's Doctor ....Mr. Wordley Hulse
Sentry ....Mr. T. R. Robertson
—Empire, Finsbury Park.

BURGOMASTER OF STILEMONDE, THE, an English version of a play, in three acts, by Maurice Maeterlinck. October 4.
Cyrille van Belle, Burgomaster of Stilemonde ....Mr. Martin Harvey
Isabelle ....Miss N. de Silva
Floris ....Mr. Vere Bennett
Major Baron von Rochow ......Mr. Fred Grove
Lieut. Otto Hilmer ......Mr. Walter Pearce
Lieut. Karl von Schaunberg..Mr. Leo Casselli
The Municipal Secretary ..Mr. Alfred Tibberson
Claus ....Mr. Rutland Barrington
Jean Gileon ....Mr. J. Cooke Beresford
Burgomaster's Footman ......Mr. Roger Alwyn
German Sergeant ....Mr. Alfred Fisher
German Soldier ....Mr. Leonard Cassell
—Lyceum, Edinburgh.

BUZZ BUZZ, revue, by Arthur Wimperis and Ronald Jeans, music by Herman Darewski, musical numbers staged by J. W. Jackson, costumes and scenery under the supervision of Arthur Weigall. Principal artists: Miss Margaret Bannerman, Mr. Caleb Porter, Mr. Nelson Keys, Mr. Walter Williams, Miss Gertrude Lawrence, Miss Vera Lennox, Mr. Albert Wallace, Mr. Dan O'Neill, Miss Poppy Dale, Miss Doris Llewelyn, Miss Gladys Miles, Miss Violet Leicester, Miss Eunice Broadwood, Mr. William Pringle. December 20.—Vaudeville.

BY PIGEON POST, play, in three acts, by Austin Page. March 30 (produced in America, at the Broad Street, Philadelphia, November 12, George M. Cohan; New York, November 25). Last performance (the 378th), December 14.
Blondel .... Mr. Hubert Willis
Laeken .... Mr. A. E. George
Captain Paul Chalfoat ....Mr. Arthur Wontner
Madame Chalfont ....Miss Kate Phillips
Major Pierre Vaudry ....Mr. Hugh Buckler
Dr. Marie Latour ......Miss Madge Titheridge
Colonel Laroque ....Mr. A. S. Homewood
Margot Latour ....Miss Dorothy Lane
General Delapierre ....Mr. C. V. France
—Garrick.

CALL OF THE ROAD, THE, adaptation of Tom Gallon's novel, "The Great Gay Road," in a prologue and three acts, arranged by Mrs. George Norman and David Ellis. December 4.
Bill ....Mr. Frank Fay
Perkins ....Mr. Paul Hansell
Joe ....Mr. Richard Bird
Mrs. Grogan ....Miss Freda Fay
Hilray Tolfrey Kite ....Mr. Lancelot Hilton
Policeman ....Mr. Howard Leslie
Nancy ....Miss Doris Lloyd
Azrien Vieary ....Miss Margery Bryce
Rodney Foster ....Mr. Richard Bird
Backus ....Mr. Arthur Fayne
Sir Crespin Vickery ....Mr. L. Hawkins
Colonel Trigg ....Mr. Frank Fay
—Playhouse, Liverpool.

CALLED UP, play, in eight scenes, by E. Vivian Edmonds. July 18.
Reggie Travers ......Mr. E. Vivian Edmonds
Bill Blower ....Mr. Frank Fountain
Eric Mullins ....Mr. Rupert W. H. Corri
Enoch Hargraves ....Mr. John F. Preston
Mr. Smith ....Mr. J. Andrian Byrne
Samuel Butterworth ......Mr. Fred G. Kay
Billy Blair ....Mr. Ernest Vasey
Fritz ....Mr. Ernest C. Winn
Mr. Sykes ....Mr. Tom Howard
Rhoda Hargraves .. Miss Minnie Watersford
Matilda Hargraves ....Miss Florence Davis
Lilian Alice Jinks ....Miss H. Graham Edwins
Mary Darling ....Miss Gladys Ford-Howitt
—Royal, Barnsley.

PLAYS OF THE YEAR.

CAMOUFLAGE, war musical comedy, in ten scenes, book and lyrics by Alfred Parker, music by Lawrence Wright, dances and ensembles by George Shurley, the whole originated and produced by Joe Peterman (March 4, King's, Portsmouth). March 11.

Kaiser .... Mr. Richard F. Symons
Herr Von Golo .... Mr. George P. Polson
The Crown Prince ..... Mr. William Wilfred
Admiral Von Tirpitz ...... Mr. G. Harris
General Hindenburg ...... Mr. Harry Turner
Hans .... Mr. S. C. Saltmarsh
Fritz .... Mr. George S. Young
Willie Woodbine .... Mr. Billy Anstell

CAST.

Herr Von Golo .... Mr. George P. Polson
Squib Woodbine .... Mr. Billy Anstell
Dash the Daring ...... Mr. George S. Young
Lieut. Jack Hainsworth, R.N.
        Mr. Hampson Lawton
Admiral J. T. Fancourt, R.N.
        Mr. V. Watkin Wynne
George Smith, alias Otto Schmidt
        Mr. William Wilfred
James Dawson .... Mr. S. C. Saltmarsh
Joe Smith .... Mr. M. Harris
Saltey Jack .... Mr. Harry Turner
P.O. Hackett, R.N. ... Mr. G. Harris
James Fenton .... Mr. Richard F. Symons
Marie Torpedo .... Miss M. Mack
The Duchess of Taytree ... Miss Mary Polson
Lady Freidrichs, known as Sonia
        Miss Mildred Cottell
Peg Magdalen .... Miss Prue Temple
        —The Middlesex.

CARRY ON, Scottish spy play, in four acts, by G. Gordon Jefferson and R. F. Morrison. August 5. (Title afterwards changed to "The Secret Aeroplane.")

Sir John Douglas ..... Mr. William S. Palmer
Capt. Stanley Douglas .. Mr. Jerrold Heather
Colonel Maxwell, V.C. .. Mr. Fred A. Marston
Capt. Rudolph von Essenbourg
        Mr. Robert Ferris
Sgt. Sandy M'Allister .. Mr. Robert Robertson
Hamel Clentz .... Mr. J. Halston Crimmins
Mary Wilson .... Miss Lalla Stanhope
Carline von Krechner .. Miss Leah Corentez
Maggie M'Allister .... Miss Lily Leoni
Wilfred Martin .... Mr. Robert James
Jimmy Morris .... Mr. John Higgins
Bobby Paterson .... Mr. David Anson
        —Paisley, Paisley.

CELESTIAL BRIDE, A. farce-comedy, by H. Chance Newton, music by John Crook. December 9.—Hippodrome, Balham.

CERTIFICATES, piece, by Charles Baldwin, music by Snell Robinson. Presented by the Six Brothers Luck. November 18.—Empire, New Cross.

CHANDELIER, LE, Alfred de Musset's comedy. Presented at the second performance of the second season of the French Players. March 24.—Queen's (matinée).

CHANGE OF TACTICS, A. comedy sketch, in one scene, by Cyril Fitch and Margaret Kaye. June 24.

Sergeant Bleary .... Mr. Tom Wall's
Miss Dulcie Ducle .... Miss Eva Kelly
Colonel Cobbly .... Mr. George de Lara
Private No. 6 .... Mr. Tom Tindall
Lieut. Donald Wobmondsey..Mr. G. P. Huntley
        —London Coliseum

CHARLEY'S AUNT, revival of Brandon Thomas's farce (February 29, 1892, Bury St. Edmunds; December 21, 1892, Royalty). December 16.—Garrick.

CHEATING CHEATERS, play, in four acts, by Max Marcin (produced in America, June 19, 1916, at the Savoy, Asbury Park, N.J.;

Cheating Cheaters (Cont.).

August 9, 1916, Eltinge, New York). February 4. Last performance (the 67th), March 30.

Steve Wilson .... Mr. Sam Livesey
Antonio Verdi .... Mr. Henry Adnes
George Brockton ...... Mr. Brandon Hurst
Neil Brockton .... Miss Barbara Gott
Nan Carey (alias Ruth Brockton)
        Miss Shirley Kellogg
Ira Lazarre .... Mr. George Elton
Mrs. Palmer .... Miss Helen Haye
Grace Palmer .... Miss Kyrle Bellew
Tom Palmer .... Mr. Alec Fraser
Edward Palmer .... Mr. J. H. Barnes
Phil Preston .... Mr. Michael Sherbrooke
Martin T. Hanley ..... Mr. George Stephenson
Holmes .... Mr. William Ralston
        —Strand.

CHILDREN'S TALES, THE, music by M. Lladoff. Presented by the Russian Ballet. December 25.—London Coliseum.

CHINESE PUZZLE, THE, play, in four acts, by Marion Bower and Leon M. Lion (July 1, Shakespeare, Liverpool). July 21. (Produced in America, June 24, Poli's, Washington.) Run suspended on December 14 with the 102nd performance.

Naomi Melsham .... Miss Ethel Irving
Mrs. Melsham .... Miss Ruth Mackay
Victoria Cresswell ... Miss Ellen O'Malley
Aimée de Villeseptier .. Miss Mercia Cameron
Lady de la Haye ...... Miss Lilian Braithwaite
Paul Marketel .... Mr. Ellie Norwood
Sir Roger de la Haye . Mr. John Howell
Armand de Rochecorbon..Mr. G. de Warfaz
Hon. William Hirst ... Mr. Reginald Malcolm
Aaron Quant .... Mr. R. Carey Fairfax
Sir Aylmer Brent ..... Mr. George Mallett
Littleport .... Mr. E. Ashley Marvin
Dr. Fu Yang .... Mr. R. Ossulston Riche
Fee Sing .... Mr. A. B. Imeson
The Marquis Chi Lung . Mr. Leon M. Lion
        —New.

CHINESE SILK, sketch, in dumb show. Presented by Mlle. Andree d'Henry. July 1.—Hippodrome, Portsmouth.

CINDERELLA, ballet. Produced by Miss Margret Morris, and performed by her pupils, December 21.—Margaret Morris, Chelsea (matinée).

CIRO'S FROLICS, revue, in eight episodes, book, music, and lyrics by R. P. Weston and Bert Lee, additional lyrics by Melville Gideon (October 29, 1917, Hippodrome, Portsmouth). Principal artists: Miss Beth Tate, the Two Bobs, Mr. Tubby Edlin, Miss Nora Moore, Sinclaris and Dalva, Mr. L Leon, Mr. Fred Foster, Miss Lynox. November 25.—Empire, Kilburn.

COME WHAT MAY, South African play, in three acts by Patrick O'Malley (February 18, Royal, Worthing). March 4.

John Bretor .... Mr. F. Rawson Buckley
Robert Robertson ..... Mr. Charles Vane
Hon. Charles Moffit .. Mr. Oliver McKenzie
Manchier .... Mr. Howard Coveney
Jacob .... Mr. Percy Lyle
A Black "Boy" .... Mr. Wm. Baker
Maud Robertson .... Miss Maud Cressall
Kate O'Brien .... Miss Bessie Bedford
Grace Treasure .. Miss Grace Denbeigh Russell
        —Grand, Croydon.

COINER, THE, Bernard Duffy's comedy (December 8, 1915, Grand Opera House, Belfast). Presented by the Irish Players during the second week of their London season. April 8.—Court.

COQ D'OR, LE, English version of N. Rimsky-Korsakow's opera, by Edward Agate. Presented by the Beecham Opera Company. (The opera was given by the Russian company at Drury Lane on June 15, 1914.) July 19.—Drury Lane.

CORNER SHOP, THE, play, in one act, by James Sexton and Michael O'Mahony. May 20.
Mrs. Fitzgerald ....Miss Doris Lloyd
Mary Joyce ....Miss Mary Goulden
Tom Fitzgerald ....Mr. Terence O'Brien
Mat Hannigan ....Mr. Clive Woods
Dermot Fitzgerald ....Mr. Frank Milray
—Playhouse, Liverpool.

CORTEGE, modern harlequinade, by H. R. Barbor, music by Granville Bantock. Presented at the opening of the Fogerty-Ginner season. March 11.—Court (matinée).

COURRIER DE LYON, LE, adaptation of "The Lyons Mail" (March 16, 1850, Gaîté, Paris; June 26, 1854, Princess's, London). Presented by the officers of the 5th Batt. of the Middlesex Regiment at four military charity matinées. February 8.—Court.

CRY OF THE CHILDREN, THE, Russian sketch, by Percival H. T. Sykes. January 3.—Euston Theatre of Varieties.

CRYSTALS, comic playlet, by Bert Lee, R. P. Weston, Geo. W. Pilkington, and Jane Smith (December 2, Empire, Liverpool). December 16.
William Huntley ....Mr. Adolph Luck
Major Claude Gatling ......Mr. Brian Daly
Mabel Chetwynd ....Miss Kathleen Barbor
Paulette ....Mlle. Rie Costa
Browning ....:......Mr. Fred Rea
Smith........................Mr. Fred Gretton
Jimmy Josser ....Mr. Ernie Lotinga
—Palace, Hammersmith.

CUDDDLESOME GHOST, A. sketch, by Frederick H. U. Bowman. June 24.
Cuthbert Stone..Mr. Frederick H. U. Bowman
Jimmy Jellyface ....Mr. Andy Wilson
Mabel Melrose ....Miss Theresa Foote
—Park Royal, Liverpool.

CUPID IN A CARAVAN, comedy, in three acts, by Ernest Goodwin (originally produced at a matinée on February 9, Empire, Swindon), June 24. Last performance (the eighth), June 29.
Bamfield ....Mr. Bromley Challenor
Monk ....Mr. Alexander Bradley
Ifflestein ....Mr. H. Tripp Edgar
Jarge Gubbins ....Mr. Charles F. Lloyd
P.C. 99 ....Mr. J. W. Wilkinson
Bertha Babbage ....Miss Minnie Leslie
Mrs. Grampette ....Miss Julia Bassett
Anne Grampette ....Miss Lucy Sibley
Miss Doubledaisy ......Miss Dorothy Duncan
Maid ....Miss Beatrice Scott
Rose Nufegente ....Miss Marjorie Bellairs
—Kingsway.

CUSHY JOB, A, comedy playlet, in one act, by Capt. E. C. Baker (January 7, Hippodrome, Sheffield). February 4.
Corporal .... Mr. Howard Law
Mrs. 'Iggins .... Miss Fanny Wallace
Capt. B. .... Mr. Fred Hill
Sebastian ....} Mr. Andrew Storm
Goldsilverstein ....}
Peggy Perkins ....Miss Mary Allen
Joyce ....Miss Molly Suffield
Frances ....} Miss Lillian Wallace
Mrs. B. ....}
—Surrey.

DABCHICK, M.P., play, by Haddon Scott. July 3.—Metropole, Glasgow.

DAMAGED GOODS, revival of Brieux's play (produced privately by the Authors' Producing Society, February 16, 1914, Little), by Mr. James Bernard Fagan. August 31. —Court. Last performance (the 56th), October 19.

DANTE AND BEATRICE, opera, in three scenes, music by Eden Philpotts, book by W. J. Miller. Presented by the Carl Rosa Opera Company. June 7.—Shaftesbury.

DAUGHTER OF FRANCE, A, war sketch, by Lucienne Deroyle. August 12.
H.H. Prince Oscar Von Frankhamen
    Mr. Albert Ward
Mlle. Marie D'Avricourt..Miss Lois Heatherley
Adolph ....Mr. James Manning
—Empress, Brixton.

DAWKINS, sketch, by Mrs. O. C. Greenaway. Produced at a matinée in aid of the funds of the Charing Cross Hospital. April 19.
Hon. Mary Carter ....Miss Isabel Ohmead
Gertie Gates ....Miss Mary O'Farrell
Louisa Robb ....Miss Milsom Rees
Jimmy Dawkins ....Mr. Arthur Cleave
—Shaftesbury.

DEAD CITY, THE, tragedy, in five acts, by Gabriele d'Annunzio, translated by Arthur Symons. Presented by the Stage Society, February 25.
Bianca Maria .... Miss Barbara Everest
Anna .... Miss Maire O'Neill
The Nurse .... Miss Evelyn Hall
Alessandro .... Mr. William Stack
Leonardo .... Mr. Robert Farquharson
—Court.

DEAR SIR,—UNLESS, sketch, by Michael Morris. February 4.
The Hon. Tony Marsh ....Mr. Stanley Logan
Snaith ....Mr. Ben Field
Samuel Snaith ......Mr. Townsend Whiting
The Lady Aileen ....Miss Doris Mansell
—London Coliseum.

DECISION, THE, playlet, presented by Mr. Alec Maclean at a performance given in aid of the Red Cross. November 30.—Town Hall, Amersham.

DEVONSHIRE CREAM, musical comedy, in five scenes, book by Jay Henn, music by Edwin Turner and Bert Sedgebeer.—August 11.
Simon Slop ....Mr. Jack McKenzie
Roy Royston ....Mr. Dan Robson
Tom Binnacle ....Mr. Wil Spicer
Peter Potts ....Mr. Tom Morrison
Peter Slyne ....Mr. George Curtis
Goliath ....Mr. J. Leonard
Lady Violet ....Miss Gladys Rossiter
Winkles ....Miss Jenny Hackett
Peggy ....Miss Daisy Rentone
Betty ....Miss Maud Holden
Rosie ....Miss Peggy Glynn
Elsie ....Miss Viola Rene
—Alhambra, Stourbridge.

DIVORCE OR DISHONOUR, drama, in six scenes, by Frederick H. U. Bowman. August 19.
Desmond Kay ....Mr. Walter H. Wilson
Stephen Gledsdale ....Mr. Eric Morden
Dr. Joseph Trench ....Mr. John Durant
Roger Beverly ....Mr. C. Alan Hineson
Lionel Kirk ....Mr. Joseph Poulton
Pat Sumner ....Mr. Fred Rignold
Dolly Adair ....Miss May Day
Annie Elvira ....Miss Maudie B. Douglas
Florence Beverley ....Miss Violet Ingram
—Grand, Plymouth.

DOG SHOW, THE, farcical sketch, in three acts, by Will Vasey. March 4.

PLAYS OF THE YEAR. 85

Dog Show, The (Cont.).
Billy Brisket .... Mr. Reg. Bolton
Cecil .... Mr. Geo. Green
Dorothy Tompkins .... Miss Susie Belmore
Hans Velldam .... Mr. J. P. Marsden
Horatio Tompkins .... Mr. Hy Egglinton
Captain Hardbake ...... Mr. Arthur Stratton
—Empire, Rotherham.

✓ **DOMES OF SILENCE**, sketch, by Dion Clayton Calthrop. Produced at the Theatrical Garden Party. June 25.—Royal Botanic Gardens.

DOMESTIC AGENCY, THE, playlet, by J. St. Aubyn. Presented by the pupils of the Florence Etlinger Dramatic School. November 15.—60, Paddington Street, W.

DUTY, Seumas O'Brien's farce of County Cork rural life (December 16, 1913, Abbey, Dublin). Presented by the Irish Players during the second week of their London season. April 3.—Court.

DUTY! AND THE GIRL play, by Clifford Rean. July 22.—Royal, Stratford.

EARLIER WORKS OF SIR RODERICK ATHELSTANE, THE, "a romantic biographical fragment," in three acts and an epilogue, by H. F. Rubenstein. Presented by the Pioneer Players. June 2.
Roderick Athelstane ...... Mr. Leon M. Lion
Stanley Hull .... Mr. E. J. Caldwell
Gwendolen Athelstane.. Miss Gwen Richardson
Mr. Athelstane .... Mr. George Goodwin
Percival Athelstane .... Master Barrie Livesey
Silvia Panton .... Miss Elsie Margetson
Hilda Dickins .... Miss Helena Millais
Mr. Panton .... Mr. Sydney Pease
—King's Hall, Covent Garden.

EDE'S TROUBLE, play, in one act, by Mrs. Harold Gorst. May 29.—Studio Club.

END OF THE TRAIL, THE, melodrama, in nine scenes, by Ruth A. Zillwood (January 14. Junction, Manchester). August 26.
Stanley Brent .... Mr. Harold Lyndon
Blackwolf .... Mr. Robert Montegle
Ratty Roper .... Mr. Bert Madil
Ah Wah .... Mr. Charles Foster
Peter Arden .... Mr. Peter Snel
Father Clark .... Mr. Edgar Mendonca
Reverend Mother .... Miss Evie Conway
Miriam Arden .... Miss Iza Lyndon
Kitty Marlow .... Mr. Edie Macklin
—Palace, Battersea.

EVERYBODY'S HUSBAND, play, by Gilbert Cannan (originally produced by the Birmingham Repertory Company, April 14, 1917). Presented at four performances in aid of the British Red Cross Society by the teachers and pupils of Miss Maud Gibson's academy. June 29.—Court.

EXCUSES; OR, WHY THEY WERE LATE, revue, in two acts, by Capt. E. Green Foley, R.A.M.C. Presented by the Summerdown Convalescent Camp. September 30.—Pier, Eastbourne.

EYES OF YOUTH, play, in three acts, by Max Marcin and Charles Guernon. Produced by Mr. Ian Robertson. (Produced in America, May 12, 1917, Stamford, Conn.; Maxine Elliott, New York, August 22, 1917.) September 2.
Asa Ashling .... Mr. Lyston Lyle
Kenneth Ashling ...... Mr. Robert Maclachlan
Rita Ashling .... Miss Maud Buchanan
Louis Anthony .... Mr. Percival Keitley
Peter Judson .... Mr. Evan Thomas
Robert Goring .... Mr. James Lindsay
Paolo Salvo .... Mr. E. Dagnall
Gina Ashling .... Miss Gertrude Elliott
A Yogi .... Mr. Ian Robertson
Joan .... Miss Dorothy Paget

Eyes of Youth (Cont.).
Picquard .... Mr. Herman de Lange
Groitz .... Mr. Arthur Viroux
Alfred Brooks .... Mr. H. A. Young
Percival Blake .... Mr. Bassett Roe
Judge Singleton .. Mr. John Hastings Batson
Court Stenographer ...... Mr. Harold Simpson
Clarence Morgan ...... Mr. C. Jervis Walter
Dick Brownell .... Mr. Alec Alves
Opera Singer .... Miss Elsie Cochrane
School Children: Sunday Wilshin, Nina Starace, Dinka Starace, Connie Webster, Ruby Hilary, Pippyn Manning, Elaine Bisley, Phyllis Calvert, Phil Seppings, Roger Cutbush, Sydney Moyle, William Jackson.
—St. James's.

FACE FROM THE PAST, A, play, in six scenes, by Alfred Beckett and Kathleen Mayne. May 20.
Capt. Hon. Leslie d'Alroy .. Mr. Alfred Beckett
Robert Gray .... Mr. Geo. D. Knight
Karl Schmidt .... Mr. Jack Gibson
Frederich von Kuehlmann
          Mr. Stephen Stormont
Pte. Joe Blake .... Mr. Len Dalmer
Baron von Gottch .... Mr. E. Mann
Marion Redfern .... Miss Marie Danvers
"Nemo," Le Petit Hero.. Miss Queenie Malcolm
Dollie Dimple .... Miss Emilie Davies
Vere Gray .... Miss Kathleen Mayne
—Empire, Oswestry.

✓ **FAIR AND WARMER**, farce, in three acts, by Avery Hopwood (produced in America, October 25, 1915, Empire, Syracuse; November 6, 1915, Eltinge, New York; May 6, Prince's, Manchester). May 14.
Billy Bartlett .... Mr. David Miller
Laura Bartlett .... Miss Margaret Halstan
Jack Wheeler .... Mr. Ronald Squire
Blanche ("Blanny") Wheeler
          Miss Fay Compton
Philip Evans .... Mr. George Relph
Tessie .... Miss Billie Carleton
Harrigan .... Mr. James Prior
Pete Mealy .... Mr. George Elliston
—Prince of Wales's.

FAIRY OF THE WELL, THE, dance scene, arranged by Miss Olive Richardson, music arranged by Miss Florence Wooderson. Presented by the pupils of the Gordon House School of Elocution, Dancing, Music, and Dramatic Art at a performance in aid of the Battersea and Clapham War Hospital Supply Depôt. June 1.—Court.

FANCY DRESS, play, in one act, by Bernard Merivale. September 7.
Butterfly .... Miss Doris Lloyd
Domino .... Mr. Paul Hansell
Shepherd .... Mr. Lancelot Hilton
Convict .... Mr. Otho Stuart
Warder .... Mr. Howard Leslie
—Playhouse, Liverpool.

FARRINGDON CASE, THE, comedy, in three acts, by C. A. Castell. November 18.
Diana Quest .... Miss Sybil Arundale
Mary .... Mrs. A. B. Tapping
Mrs. Chevrell .... Miss Eileen Munro
Mr. Chevrell .... Mr. Percy Jackson
Tom Quest .... Mr. Gordon Bailey
Admiral Dale .... Mr. Farren Soutar
Rosamund .... Miss Mary O'Farrell
Virginia Leeven ...... Miss Joy Chatwyn
Miss Cutler .... Miss Olivia West
Batton .... Mr. George P. Lester
Billy Bellamy .... Mr. Vernon Crabtree
Capt. Macgregor ...... Mr. C. Osbourne
Jim Chevrell .... Mr. George Relph
—Gaiety, Manchester.

FEMALE HUN, THE, play, in four acts, by Walter Melville. Produced by Walter and Frederick Melville, music composed by Ernest Vousden, scenery by H. K. Browne and Lyceum Studio. October 2. Run suspended on December 21 (the 105th performance).
Capt. Dennis Maxwell .. Mr. Herbert Mansfield
Lieut. Eddie Laurence ...... Mr. Bert Randall
Pte. Bill Baxter .... Mr. Leslie Carter
Susan Baker .... Miss Dorrie Eyre
Weiss .... Mr. Philip Hay
John Brown .... Mr. F. Joynson-Powell
Von Stein .... Mr. Arthur Nicholas
Baron Arnheim .... Mr. Chris Olgar
Grace Pearson .... Miss Gladys Mason
General Grant .... Mr. Sam Livesey
Julian D'Arcy .... Mr. J. C. Aubrey
Lord Pitcher .... Mr. Hugh Montgomery
George Wilson .... Mr. Ernest E. Norris
Lutz .... Mr. A. Percy
Topnitzer .... Mr. Horace Mears
Sir Archibald Blackford.. Mr. Jerrold Manville
Betty Blackford .... Miss Hilda Vaughan
Constance Vivian .... Miss Annie Saker
—Lyceum.

FIDDLE-DE-DEE, revue, in seven scenes. Produced by Albert de Courville. Principal artists: Mr. Stan Paskin, Miss Mona Vivian, Miss Kitty Emson, Mr. Dare Phillips, Mr. James Hooper, Miss McCarthy, Miss Malinson, Mr. Walton, Miss Margery Daw, Mr. Mannering. May 27.—Empire, Finsbury Park.

FIDDLESTICKS, revue. Presented by Bert Tupman. October 28.—Bedford, Camden Town.

FISHER GIRL, THE, revue, by Dick Ray. November 11.—Bedford, Camden Town.

FIVE NIGHTS, play, by Victoria Cross (April 1, Grand, Swansea). June 10. (A dramatised version of Victoria Cross's novel of the same name was produced in America at the Grand Opera House, Brooklyn, August 31, 1914.)
Trevor .... Mr. Philip Anthony
Morey .... Mr. Thomas Barry
Capt. Lawton .... Mr. Allen H. Leamy
Hop Lee .... Mr. Tim Ryley
Miss Fothergill .... Miss Muriel Langley
Veronica .... Miss Sylvia Bassano
Suzee .... Miss Betta Charna
Trevor's Manservant .... Mr. C. Hillier
Viola's Maid .... Miss Lena Anson
Maid at Hotel in 'Frisco.... Miss Ruth Manning
Trevor's Nurse at 'Frisco.. Miss Muriel Gaffney
Trevor's Doctor at 'Frisco.. Mr. Rhodes Watson
Ticket Agent .... Mr. George F. Watts
The Costumier .... Miss Ernestine Jack
Viola .... Miss Phyllis Joyce
—Borough, Stratford.

FLASH FRED, sketch, by Percy Bradshaw. Played by George Clarke and company. April 1.—Empire, New Cross.

FLASHLIGHTS, revue, by P. T. Selbit, music by George A. Stephens and Vincent Exley (September 30, Hippodrome, Dover). October 28.—The Middlesex.

FLORA, musical comedy, in three acts, by Harry Grattan, music by Herman Darewski and Melville Gideon, lyrics by James Heard and Davy Burnaby. March 12. Last performance (the 72nd), May 7.
Cokeby .... Mr Alfred Phillips
Horace Lobley .... Mr. Willie Hartill
Miss Maple .... Miss Cecily Guiver
Mrs. Brapwick .... Miss Veronica Brady
Philernina Brapwick .... Miss Florence Bayfield
Jack Foruner .... Mr. Walter Williams
Hamilton P. Brapwick .... Mr. Lennox Pawle
Lucas Whittle .... Mr Jo Nightingale

Flora (Cont.).
Gwendoline Brapwick .. Miss Blanche Tomlin
Flora Brapwick .... Miss Gertie Millar
The Vicar .... Mr. Wyndham Guise
Mr. Griffen, F.R.H.S. .... Mr Murri Moncrieff
The Earl of Knowse ...... Mr Ralph Lynn
Mrs. Merwyn .... Miss Holford Beringer
Daphne Dalrymple .... Miss Elsie Gregory
Nissie Noggie .... Miss Helen Beltramo
Nadjy b.nks .... Miss Kathleen Vincent
Cooie Koigh .... Miss Cooie Emney
Trixie Tripp .... Miss Flora Le Breton
Marquis of Ince .... Mr. George Grundy
The Hon. Charles Dudley.. Mr. Arthur Wellesley
—Prince of Wales's.

FLOWER GIRL'S DREAM, THE, children's ballet. Played by the pupils of Miss Flo Martell and Miss Amy Elstob. March 30. —Grand, Croydon.

FOLLOW THE GIRLS, musical comedy revue, written and produced by Harry Curwen. August 26.
Rosie Reval .... Miss Gertie Zack
Dorothy .... Miss Margot Steed
Vi .... Miss Vi Trevelyan
Fifi .... Miss Lauri Purvis
Teddie Verral .... Mr. Lawzon Frazier
Cuthbert .... Mr. George Rall
Billy Buster .... Mr. Harold Baker
—Grand, Accrington.

FOR HIS LADY'S HONOUR, drama, by Lodge Percy and Henrietta Schrier. March 18.
Lieut. Jack Seymour .... Mr. William Hayward
Capt. Ferdinand .... Mr. John William
Colonel Boocasin .... Mr. Dane Clark
Isaacs .... Mr. Fred Blake
Lieut. Nicholas .... Miss Louisa Bates
Geraldine de Marenso.. Miss Kathleen Harrowby
Lucy Layton .... Miss Annie Graham
Kathleen Isaacs .... Miss Marie Horn
Maria Thesilger .... Miss Ruby Lee
—Dalston.

FOR THE FLAG, drama, in nine scenes, by M.P. Run under the auspices of the Federation for Discharged and Demobilised Sailors and Soldiers. September 2.
Capt. Edward Montague .... Mr. Harold Heath
Van Der Blom .... Mr. William Grainger
Harry Wilcox .... Mr. Louis Gaye
Fritz .... Mr. Alfred W. Beale
Lord Sussex .... Mr. Edward Maples
Jules .... Mr. Fred Mace
German Officer .... Mr. Jack H. Beale
Sergt. Brown .... Mr. Albert Bramber
Signalman Williams .... Mr. George Carter
P.C. Hawkins .... Mr. Arthur Bogue
Delphine .... Miss May Hallet
Lady Marjorie .... Miss Renée Bevan
Irma Montague .... Miss Clarice Amber
—Empire, Edmonton.

FORTUNE'S IDOL, musical comedy revue, in five scenes, book by Billy Clarkson, music composed and arranged by Billy Clarkson. Principal artists: Mr. Billy Bell, Miss Flo Guest, Mr. Fred Ramsdale, the Hendreas, Mr. Tom Webb, the Four Emeralds. May 6.—Hippodrome, Stoke-on-Trent.

FOURTEEN DAYS' LEAVE, drama, in four acts, by J. Leicester Jackson. November 4. —Princess's, Glasgow.

FOX AND GEESE, comedy, in three acts, by Susanne R. Day and G. D. Cummins (February 2, 1917, Abbey, Dublin). Presented by the Irish Players at the opening of their London season. April 1.—Court.

FRAGMENTS, revue, in five scenes, by P. T. Selbit. Principal artists: Mr. Ben Taylor, Miss Bonny Browning, Mr. Syd le Fre, Miss Silvia Petina, Mr. Donald Brown, Miss Peggy Dare. May 27.—Palace, Bath.

FRAGMENTS FROM FRANCE, piece, in two acts, by ex-Sergt. Wilson Bennett and Capt. John Maclaren. Presented by the Silver Badge Players. (November 4, Horne Bay). December 9.

'Erb 'Iggins .... Mr. Will Bennett
Horace Hartley ...... Mr. Alec P. Henderson
Sid Grainger .... Mr. Jack Heaney
Bert Griggs .... Mr. Harry Creeve
Old Gent .... Mr. L. S. Stafford
Tommins .... Mr. Wilfred Fowler
Sergt.-Major .... Mr. Jackson Fowler
Capt. Trevor .... Mr. Robert S. Bevan
Colonel Whyte .... Mr. George Parsons
French Pu.u .... Miss Camille Gillard
Mrs. 'Oskins .... Miss Camille Norreys
Lady Owen Astor ...... Miss Fanny Loader
Connie .... Miss Anita Sennett
" Ria " .... Miss Winnie Braemar
—Dalston.

FREAKS, THE, "an Idyll of Suburbia," in three acts, by Sir Arthur Pinero. February 14. Last performance (the 51st), March 30.

ORDINARY MORTALS.

Mrs. Herrick (née Smith) .. Miss Irene Rooke
Ronald .... Mr. Leslie Howard
Sheila .... Miss Isobel Elsom
Lady Ball-Jennings .... Miss Helen Ferrers
Sir Norton Ball-Jennings .... Mr. Fred Kerr
Revd. Stephen Glyn ...... Mr. C. V. France
Mr. Edward Waterfield, M.R.C.S.
                                Mr. Nigel Playfair
Collingridge .... Miss Anne Walden
Luff .... Miss Dorothy Stephen

EXTRAORDINARY MORTALS.

Horatio Tilney .... Mr. Ben Webster
James Edddowes .... Mr. Walter Lake
Thomas Quincy Pratt ...... Miss Katie Snow
Julie Maud Pratt ...... Miss Babs Farren
Rosa Balmano .... Miss Laura Cowie
—New.

FREEDOM OF ALSACE, THE, sketch. Played by Mr. Frederick Ross and company. December 2.—Olympia, Shoreditch.

FREEDOM OF THE SEAS, THE, play, in three acts, by Walter Hackett. August 1.

George Smith .... Mr. Dennis Eadie
Horatio Gamp .... Mr. Vincent Sternroyd
Daniel Harcourt .... Mr. E. Holman Clark
Stanley Bolton .... Mr. Tom Reynolds
Phyllis Harcourt .... Miss Billie Carleton
Harry Jackson .... Mr. F. Randle Ayrton
Nils Bergstrom .... Mr. James Carew
Ginger Brown .... Mr. Charles Groves
O'Hara .... Mr. Henry Scatchard
Adoniram Wallace ... Mr. Sydney Valentine
Jenny Weathersbee ...... Miss Marion Lorne
Lieut.-Commander Claude Sullivan, R.N.
                            Mr. Dennis Wyndham
—Haymarket.

GAY RIVER, THE, musical comedy, in one act, by G. E. Cornille-Pescud. August 19.

Peter Peploe .... Robt. F. Douglas
Dolly Pennington .... Phyllis St. Cair
Doris Marriott .... Gladys Connor
Jack Conyingham .... Cyril Dane
Selina Flopp .... Hilda Barry
Polly Wannington .... Betty Gordon
Archibald Vere de Vere Chumpleigh
                                Harry Messey
—Alexandra, Stoke Newington.

GERMAN SHELL, A, sketch, by J. J. Mannix (February 25, Hippodrome, Altrincham). July 29.

Michael Flynn .... Mr. Charles Carte
Thomas Flynn .... Mr. Alfred Sanders
Margaret Flynn .... Miss Lizzie Gordon
Jim Flynn .... Mr. Ernest Montefiore
—Palace, Hammersmith.

GETTING RID OF HER, farcical Scottish sketch, in one act. April 15.

Mr. Thomas McBlain .. Mr. George Westland
Emmeline .... Miss Bunty Scott
Wardress .... Miss Jean Fraser
Mrs. McGusky .... Miss Lillan Urquhart
—Palace, Chelsea.

GINGER GIRL, THE, revue, in four scenes, by Paul Pelham and Thomas McGhee. Invented by Willie Bona. August 26.—Bedford, Camden Town.

GIRL, THE, musical comedy revue, in two acts, by Q. Cole and Henry Ca vert, music by Milton Webb. September 23.—Pavilion, Leicester.

GIRL AND THE PUPPET, THE, play, by Pierre Louys and Pierre Frondaie, translated by Dr. Chalmers Mitchell. Presented by the Pioneer Players. February 17.

Don Ramon .... Mr. Herbert Norris
Bianca .... Miss Enid Lorimer
A Masker .... Mr. Miles Malleson
Ferger .... Mr. Stephen T. Ewart
Don Mateo .... Mr. Allan Jeayes
A Gipsy .... Miss Honor Bright
Concha Perez .... Miss Joan Vivian-Rees
Miguel .... Mr. Basil Gordon
Le Morento .... Mr. Jean Varda
Senora Perez .... Miss Joan Pereira
Pipa .... Miss Stella Rho
Mercedes .... Miss Olive Richardson
Pablo .... Miss Iré Cameron
French Sailor .... Mr. Julian Andrews
English Sailor .... Mr. C. Wordley Hulse
American Sailor .... Mr. Henry Oscar
Gu!de .... Mr. Herbert Norris
English Tourist .. Mr. H. Armytage Sanders
Second Tourist .... Mr. Neil Curtis
—Prince's.

GIRL IN THE BATH, musical farce, in three scenes, by Roland R. Gibson, Granville Fulton, and Frank Dix, music by Hubert Bath, additional numbers by Donovan Parsons and Patrick Thayer (March 25, Hippodrome, Boscombe). April 22.

Sir Toby Rayne .... Mr. James Stevenson
Alphonse Vernet .... Mr. Gaston de Pamel
Baron Delgourki .... Mr. Albert Le Fre
Bottle .... Mr. Harry Wright
Hon. Jimmy Fairfax .... Mr. Syd Le Fre
Mr. Sobienski .... Mr. Mick Webber
Mr. Chung .... Mr. Jack Levey
Chow Chow .... Mr. E. F. Saxon
Liang .... Mr. W. Frewer
Ah Ping .... Mr. Oswald Vernon
Princess Mitzi .... Miss Doris Mervyn
Mme. Papi .... Miss Violet Parry
Fi Fi .... Miss Nelle O'Bery
Lady Payne .... Miss Florence Wilton
Flo .... Miss Winnie West
Gertie .... Miss Cynthia Mertagh
Maisie .... Miss Joan Clarkson
Dolly .... Miss Rose Birks
Trixie .... Miss Jeanne Deauville
Toots .... Miss Winnie Pollock
—King's, Hammersmith.

GIRL FROM CANADA, THE, drama, in five scenes, by Frank Price (June 24, Palace, Newcastle-on-Tyne). September 23.—Royal, Stratford.

GIRL WHO CHANGED HER MIND, THE, play, by Clifford Rean (April 12, Royal, Liverpool). October 21.—Royal, Stratford.

GLASS HOUSES, play, by Dorothy Massingham. March 9.

John Stephens ...... Mr. Joseph A. Dodd
Mrs. Stephens .... Miss Cathleen Orford
Grace .... Miss Margaret Chatwin
Maggie .... Miss Maud Gill
Mary .... Miss Dorothy Taylor

Glass Houses (Cont.).
Bert .... Mr. Christian Morrow
George .... Mr. Maurice Neville
Maid .... Miss Sidney Leon
—Repertory, Birmingham.

GOING UP, musical comedy, in three acts, book by James Montgomery and Otto Harbak, lyrics by Otto Harbak, music by Louis Hirsch (based upon James Montgomery's play "The Aviator." September 23, 1911, Lyceum, Sheffield; produced in America, November 15, 1917, Apollo, Atlantic City; Liberty, New York, December 25, 1917; May 13, Prince's, Manchester). May 22.
Miss Zonne .... Miss Ruby Miller
John Gordon .... Mr. Clifton Alderson
F. H. Douglas .... Mr. Arthur Chesney
Mrs. Douglas .... Miss Elaine Inescort
Jules Gaillard .... Mr. Henry de Bray
Grace Douglas .... Miss Marjorie Gordon
Madeline Manners ...... Miss Evelyn Laye
Hopkinson Brown .... Mr. Austin Melford
Robert Street .... Mr. Joseph Coyne
James Brookes .... Mr. Franklyn Bellamy
Sam Robinson .... Mr. Roy Byford
Louis .... Mr. Louis Mathyl
—Gaiety.

GOLD STRIPE, a comedy, by Matthew Boulton. Played by Miss Florence Steventon, Miss Amy Lorraine, Mr. Fred Fraser, and Mr. Stewart Dawson. February 18.—Palace, Tottenham.

GOOD-BYE, 1918, revue, by Capt. A. J. Elphinstone, music by Driver Lex Holmes. Produced by the No. 1 Reserve Horse Transport, A.S.C., in aid of the St. Dunstan's Hostel for Blinded Soldiers, December 16.—Regimental Institute, Park Royal.

GOOD-HUMOURED LADIES, THE, choreographic scenario, by Leonide Massine, founded upon the eighteenth-century Italian comedies of Carlo Goldini, music, orchestrated, and arranged by Vincenzo Tommasini, by Domenico Scarlatti. Presented by the Russian Ballet. September 5.—London Coliseum.

GOOD OLD TIMES, revue, by Frederick H. U. Bowman, December 9.—Pavilion, Northwich.

GRABBER, THE, play, in three act, by Edward Barret. November 12.
John Foley .... Mr. Fred O'Donovan
Mrs. Foley .... Miss Maureen Delany
Their Daughter .... Miss Muriel Munro
The Son .... Mr. F. I. MacCormack
Pats Wall .... Mr. Peter Nolan
His Son .... Mr. Arthur Shields
Policemen .... { Mr. Hubert Maguire
                        { Mr. Fred Harford
—Abbey, Dublin.

GREAT MOMENT, THE, playlet, by Gwen Lally. Presented at a matinée in aid of Lady Smith-Dorrien's Hospital Bag Fund. December 3.—St. James's.

GREAT SCOTT, revue, by Charles Baldwin (September 23, Ramsgate). October 7.—Bedford, Camden Town.

GREEN PLUMS, THE, by Boccioni. Presented by the Plough Players. December 8.—Lyric, Hammersmith.

H.M.S. "PINAFORE," W. S. Gilbert and Arthur Sullivan's opera (May 25, 1878, Opéra Comique). Presented at a matinée in aid of the funds of the Military Orthopædic Hospital, Shepherd's Bush, when all the male parts were filled by wounded officers and men. February 9.—King's, Hammersmith.

H.M.S. "VICTORIOUS," patriotic scena, produced by T. C. Fairbairn, music composed, arranged, and orchestrated by Vincent Thomas, Arthur Fagge, and Alfred Dove. December 16.—Victoria Palace.

HANRAHAN'S OATH, comedy, in one act, by Lady Gregory. January 29.
Mary Gillis .... Miss Maureen Delany
Margaret Rooney .... Miss May Craig
Owen Hanrahan .... Mr. Fred O'Donovan
Coey .... Mr. Arthur Shields
Mrs. Coey .... Miss Christine Hayden
Michael Feeney .... Mr. Peter Nolan
—Abbey, Dublin.

HARBURY PEARLS, THE, farcical sketch, by J. Wilkie Rusk. Presented at a concert for soldiers and sailors. December 1.
Flash Harvey .... Mr. Martin Lewis
Sylvia .... Miss Fay Compton
Dodger Dan .... Mr. George Thorne
—Victoria Palace.

HAPPY-GO-LUCKY, revue, book by A. P. de Courville and Wal Pink, music by Frederick Chapelle, staged by Frank Smithson, produced by Albert de Courville. Principal artists: Miss Dorothy Ward, Mr. Shaun Glenville, Miss Betty Green, Miss Gaby Condor, Mr. Cedric Percival, Mr. Harry Gibson. August 26.—Empire, Finsbury Park.

HAVE A NIBBLE, revue, in three scenes. Produced by Tom Seymour. Principal artists: Mr. Joe Robins, Mr. Percy Lyle, Miss Hilda Playfair, Miss Queenie Valerie. April 29.—Hippodrome, Cheltenham.

HELLO, THERE! revue. August 26.—Royal, Woolwich.

HER BRIDAL HOUR, for the first time in London, a comedy-drama, by Herbert Sidney. July 1.
Andrew Heritage .... Mr. Oswald Lingard
William Sturdy .... Mr. A. W. Norman
John Drummond .... Mr. Dane Clark
Joey Kint .... Mr. Arthur Eacott-Davies
Cornelia Heritage ..... Miss Madge Heyton
Barbara Heritage ...... Miss Annie Graham
Mary Foley .... Miss Amy Manfree
Mona Drummond .... Miss Ruby Lee
—Royal, Edmonton.

HER LADYSHIP, comedy, in three acts, by Charles McEvoy. Produced by Mr. Franklin Dyall and Miss Mary Merrall. June 24.
George Tamworth .... Mr. Harry Barford
Cameron .... Mr. Louis O'Connor
Henrietta Tamworth .... Miss Mary Raby
Gloria Tamworth .... Miss Edith Smith
Thelma Tamworth .... Miss Lilian Yates
Mr. Pyke .... Mr. J. R. La Fane
Mr. Hodson .... Mr. Antony Holles
Mrs. Cameron .... Miss Elizabeth Campbell
Annie .... Miss Marry Merrall
Tristram Tamworth ..... Mr. Franklin Dyall
Andrew Loom .... Mr. J. A. Keogh
Mr. Nestor .... Mr. W. Earle Grey
—Abbey, Dublin.

HER SECOND CHANCE, play, by Lodge-Percy and Henrietta Schrier. April 8.
Ned Marsden .... Mr. Geoffrey L. Carlile
Phil Murkett .... Mr. Josh H. Hybert
Steve Ingersol .... Mr. Sidney Jacques
Dennis Le Grand .... Mr. Walter Dale
Eva Steele .... Miss Madge Soutter
Norah Steele .... Miss Gipsy Alexander
Mattie Steele .... Miss Julie Burns
Lily Marsden .... Miss Henrietta Schrier
—Royal, Stratford.

HI-DIDDLE-DIDDLE, muscial comedy revue, book and lyrics by Syd Walker and Percival Langley, music by Dudley Powell and John Hatton (August 12, Royal, Edinburgh). Principal artists: Miss Maudie Vera, Mr. George Gee, Mr. Syd Walker, Miss Margaret Phillips, Mr. Reg. Bromlow, Miss Tina Bromlow, Mr. Fred Leon. November 11.—Hippodrome, Ilford.

PLAYS OF THE YEAR.

HIDDEN HAND, THE, play, in three acts, by Laurence Cowen (May 27, Court, Liverpool). July 4. Last performance (the 165th), November 23.

Lady Adela Fitzwarren ....Mrs. Saba Raleigh
Montmorency Fortescue Curzon
    Mr. Stanley Drewitt
Mary Marshall ....Miss Peggy Primrose
John Marshall, M.P. ..Mr. Leonard Shepherd
Mrs. Marshall ....Miss Maud Snelton
Elsa Rosenbaum ....Miss Molly Terraine
Lieut. Stephen English, R.N. Mr. Kenneth Kent
Sir Charles Rosenbaum, Bt., M.P.
    Mr. D. Lewis Mannering
Fritz von Schafhausen..Mr. Michael Sherbrooke
Capt. the Rev. Christian St. George D.S.O.
    Mr. William Stack
Andrew Ross ....Mr. James Howard
Robert Greig ....Mr. Lionel Wilson
Mr. Volkman ....Mr. Howard Ringe
Mr. Lessing ....Mr. Horace James
Lieut. Otto Steinbruick
    Mr. Alexander Lubimof
    —Strand.

HIGH PRESSURE, revue, in four acts, by Cecil Sankey, music by John Esmond. July 8.—Palace, Watford.

HIS AUSTRALIAN WIFE, play, in four acts, by Leila Zillwood (July 29, Metropole, Glasgow). August 19.

Jack Meredith ....Mr. Harry Wood
The Growler ....Mr. Arthur Barton
The Sheriff ....Mr. Harry Harrold
Smiling Bill ....Mr. Harwood Cooper
Billy Tiddleback ....Mr. Albert Williams
Sentry Joe ....Mr. Gerald Maude
Sergt. Bates ....Mr. Tom Owen
Tess ....Miss Lydia Audre
Olive Meredith ....Miss Marie Cotton
Sophy Smart ....Miss Edie Williams
Rose Watson ....Miss Annie Burnette
Comfort Lady ....Miss Dora Guy
A Flapper ....Miss Minnie Harris
Little Ned (Jack's son)..Miss Kathleen May
    —Royal, Stratford.

HIS DEAREST WISH, farce, in one act, by A. Patrick Wilson. May 30.

Rosabel Lee ....Miss Mabel Coleman
Nancy Lee ....Miss Lally Wynne
Archie Hudson ......Mr. A. Patrick Wilson
Priscilla ....Miss Doris Champion
    —Alexandra, N.

HIS GOOD ANGEL, domestic play, by Lodge-Percy and Henrietta Schrier (January 21, Royal, Yarmouth). March 25.

Ralph Monckton........Mr. Edward Warden
Jack Craven ....Mr. Roland Howard
Captain Boniface ....Mr. J. Edmund Wildash
Mrs. Monckton ....Miss Maud Elliott
Mamie Monckton ....Miss Gwen Percy
Hon. Mrs. Craven ....Miss Sidney Crowe
Miss Phipps ....Miss Georgie Longraine
Kathleen ....Miss Marie Ensor
Grace Wyndham ......Miss Beatrice Western
    —Dalston.

HIS KINDRED SPIRIT, comedy, in one act, by John Dore. June 17.—Empire, Dublin.

HIS ROYAL HAPPINESS, play, in four acts, by Sara Jeannette Duncan. (Produced in America, January 4, 1915, at the Princess's, Toronto.) November 4.

Mrs. Phipps ....Miss Grace Lane
Kate Carrol ....Miss Molly Stuart
Bettine D'Orsay ....Miss Iris de Villiers
Hilary Lanchester ......Miss Adah Rothwell
Major Calder ....Mr. Stephen Wentworth
Bookey ....Mr. Jack Bligh
Prince Alfred .. ..Mr. G. H. Mulcaster
Colonel Vandeleur ....Mr. Frank Royde

His Royal Happiness (Cont.).
Dr. Morrow ....Mr. F. G. Thurstans
Sir Randolph Perry ..Mr. Arthur Bawtree
Ex-President Lanchester ..Mr. Julius Knight
Abe ....Mr. Jeff Coates
Princess Henrietta ....Miss Helen Haye
Lady A'thea Dawe ....Miss Molly Stuart
Arthur Youghall ....Mr. Dennis Wyndham
Austin ....Mr. Geo. Anderson
Lord Caversham ....Mr. Sydney Paxton
Sir Bute Rivers ....Mr. F. C Thurstans
    —Devonshire Park, Eastbourne.

HIS WIFE'S SECRET, play, in one act, by the Vicar of Birdham. September 16.

Camilla Weldon ....Miss Ray Godcharle
Jack Weldon ....Mr. Hugh Higgins
    —Hippodrome, Cheltenham.

HOLD FAST, revue, by Robert Reilly (August 26 Hippodrome, Aldershot). September 2.
—Empire, Kingston.

HOME FROM THE TRENCHES, drama, in three acts and ten scenes, by Arthur Jefferson (May 29, Grand, Nottingham). July 8.

Silas Hardman ....Mr. Chas. E. Johnson
Neville Hardman ....Mr. Edgar T. Hayes
Peter Wilson ....Mr. J. Spencer
Corporal Dennison ....Mr. Wilfrid Launceston
Charlie Goodall . ...Mr. Richard Wilson
Horace Hopkins ....Mr. Harry Emmerson
Inspector Ward ....Mr. George Gormley
Detective Adams ....Mr. Felix Jackson
Detective Walker ......Mr. Dennis Walters
P.C. Harrison ....Mr. Percy Blair
P.C. Drake ....Mr. W. Jones
Bessie Dennison ....Miss Ada Oak'ey
Pattie Hopkins ....Miss L. Addison
Myra Gray ....Miss Betty Seymour
Muriel Miranda Peabody ..Miss Nellie Wilson
    —Grand, Croydon.

HOME SERVICE, drama, in four acts, by Capt. Cecil F. Armstrong. Produced by the Convalescent Comedy Company from Summerdown Camp. April 22.

George Smith ....Pte. H. Twinberrow
Curtis Smith
    2nd Lieut. R. S. Summerhays, A.S.C.
Mrs. Curtis Smith ....Miss Phyllis Smyth
Georgina Smith ....Miss Elsie Davidson
Albert Schmidt
    Captain Cecil F. Armstrong, A.S.C.
Gertrude Schmidt ......Mme. Constance Lyall
Britten Schmidt
    Capt. E. Green Foley, R.A.M.C.
Old Funnell ....L/Cpl. Laurie Howard
Young Funnell ....Pte. J. Bulbeck
Mrs. Funnell ....Mrs. Horace Green
Gladys ....Mrs. M. MacFadden
A Clerk ....Captain Stuart Rose
Mr. Burnstone ....Staff-Sergt. T. Hoyland
Two Policemen
    Bombr. Castello and Cpl. Davis
    —Devonshire Park, Eastbourne.

HOME WRECKERS, THE, farce, by Maud Williamson. July 1.

Bob Bagshaw ....Mr. Alfred Woods
Euphrosue ....Miss Maud Williamson
Gustaras ....Mr. Leslie Norman Clare
Clementine ....Miss Dorothy Woods
    —Empress, Brixton.

HON. GERTRUDE, THE, sketch, by Henry Seton. June 17.

The Hon. Gertrude ......Miss Esmé Beringer
Mrs. Briggs ....Miss Mary Brough
Lady Fatiborham ....Miss May Holford
Pte. Herbert Briggs, V.C. Mr. Gerald Valentine
    —Empress, Brixton.

HOTCH-POTCH, revue, by A'bert de Courville and Wal Pink, music by Frederick G. Chappelle, staged by Frank Smithson. Principal artists: Miss Flora Courtenay, Miss Nora Delany, Mr. Fred Kitchen, Miss Florence Smithers, Mr. Chris Olgar, Mr. Wally Walford, Mr. Charles Stern, Miss Ida Rose. January 14.—Empire, Penge. (Presented in the West End at the Duke of York's, May 2.)

HOW DO YOU LIKE IT? revue, by Mrs. F. G. Kimberley. Principal artists: Miss Ruby Kimberley, Miss Adeline Ruby, Miss Ruby Bradford, Mr. Tom H. Solly, Miss Lill Clifford, Miss Ruby Mildred, Mr. Eric Wingfield, Mr. George Millard, the Five Weetmans. June 24.—Grand, Brighton.

HULA MAID, THE, revue. September 30.—Playhouse, Faversham.

HULLO! AMERICA, revue, in two acts and eight scenes, by J. Hastings Turner, with music composed and arranged by Herman Finck, lyrics by Clifford Grey, colour schemes and costumes by Comelli, and staging by Gus Sohlke. Principal artists: Miss Elsie Janis, Mr. Owen Nares, Mr. Stanley Lupino, Mr. Robert Reilly, Miss Irene Magley, Miss Edris Coombs, Miss Marjorie Essex, Miss Madeleine Seymour, Mr. Will West, Mr. Wilbur Lenton. September 25.—Palace.

HUNDRED YEARS AGO, A. Presented by the pupils of the Gordon House School of Elocution, Dancing, Music, and Dramatic Art at a performance in aid of the Battersea and Clapham War Hospital Supply Depôt. June 1.—Court.

IGNORANCE, play, in three acts, by Clifford Rean (October 28, King's, Gainsborough). November 18.

The Doctor ....Mr. G. Raymond Wallace
The Parson ....Mr. John Worth
The Landlord ....Mr. Josh A. Hybert
The Boy ....Mr. Phil Holles
The Mother ....Miss Clara Santley
The School Teacher ....Miss Maude Steeple
The Child ....Miss Nancy Lawrence
The Girl ....Miss Gertrude Gilbert
—Royal, Stratford.

'IM, play, in one act, by Olive Lethbridge. Produced at a matinée arranged by the Dramatists' Advisory Board of the Lyceum Club in aid of the Vanguard Fund for Disabled Sailors and Soldiers. November 8.—The Middlesex.

IN THE LIGHT OF DAY, dramatic play, in one act, by H. C. Gilbard Stevens. September 4.

Benet Cunningham ......Mr. Lionel Williams
Edward O'Rourke ......⎫
Father O'Rafferty........⎬ Mr. Arthur Hare
Shelagh O'Rourke ....Miss Alice de Grey
Derek Mayne ....Mr. Herbert Norris
—The Little.

IN THE NIGHT WATCH, play, in three acts, freely adapted from Claude Farrère and Lucien Nepoty's "La Veille d'Armes," by Michael Morton. December 2.

Capt. de la Croix de Corlaix..Mr. C. V. France
Lieut. Brambourg ....Mr. C. M. Hallard
Lieut. D'Artelle ....Mr. Dennis Wyndham
Commander Fargasson ....Mr. H. K. Ayliff
Lieut.-Commander Dulec
Mr. Griffith Humphreys
Engineer-Lieut. Birodat ....Mr. Ernest Ruston
Dr. Ribot ....Mr. Henry Oscar
Seaman Le Duc ....Mr. A. E. George

In the Night Watch (Cont.).

Quartermaster Dagorne ......Mr. Edgar Bruce
Ship's Boy ....Mr. George Ayre
Vice-Admiral Fogat ....Mr. Herbert Leonard
Rear-Admiral de Lutzen ....Mr. A. Lubimoff
Rear-Admiral de Challemont
Mr. Griffith Humphreys
Commander Mobraye ....Mr. Henry Wenman
Capt. de l'Estissac ......Mr. Lionel Williams
Clerk of the Court ......Mr. Edgar Bruce
Eugénie de Corlaix ....Miss Madge Titheradge
Alice Perlet ....Miss Jessie Bateman
—The Oxford.

IRISHMAN'S HOME, AN, play, in two acts, by L. G. Redmond Howard and Capt. Harry Carson. November 18.

Sir John Redfern ....Mr. R. H. McCandless
Frank Redfern ....Mr. Jackson Graham
Doran ....Mr. Jack McGibbon
James ....Mr. Desmond Crean
First Lieut. Seagrave ..Mr. McClelland Marten
First Lieut. ....Mr. B. Nolan
Second Lieut. ....Mr. Cecil Young
First Nationalist ......Mr. Louis Vincent
Second Nationalist ....Mr. W. B. Lindsay
First Orangeman ....Mr. M. McDonald
Second Orangeman ....Mr. J. McGettrick
Lady Redfern ....Miss Eileen Adair
Dora ....Miss Irene Boyd
Cardinal ....Mr. Desmond Aird
Willie Doran ....Master R. Shaw
—Empire, Belfast.

IS IT SAFE? musical comedy revue, by Donovan Parsons and Reginald Relste, music by Mary Watson. April 1.—Empire, Southend.

IT'S TOPPING, revue, in three scenes, by Gilbert Payne (July 29, Hippodrome, Mexborough). November 4.—Bedford, Camden Town.

IT'S A WALK OVER, revue, in ten scenes, by Lindsay and Harte. Principal artists: Lindsay and Harte, Miss Doreen Lyndon, Miss Ruby McCormick, Mr. Jack Ross, Wee Jimmie Stewart, Flossy Hogg and Cowden, Mr. Dan Young, and the Eight Walk Over Girls. December 23.—Olympia, Glasgow.

JACK IN THE BOX, musical extravaganza, in five scenes, book by Joseph Hayman, music composed and arranged by Max Darewski (April 15, Grand, Birmingham). June 24.

Betty .... Miss Blanche Mayne.
Nellie Worth ....Miss Helena Carmen.
Jack Gillingham ....Mr. Alec Chentrens.
Cheerful Willie ....Mr. L. N. Kirk.
Cuthbert ....Mr. Harold Wellesley.
Algernon ....Mr. George Hestor.
Dancer ....Miss Eunice McGlenn.
Mary Chaplin Pickwood..Miss Dorothy Millar.
—Hippodrome, Ilford.

JACK ON LEAVE, drama, in four acts, by Kennedy Allen and Eva Lewes. May 27.

Jack Meadows ....Mr. John Malley
Bill Blinker ....Mr. Louis Weston
Silas Slammer ....Mr. A. Walford
Lord Langdale ....Mr. Jas. P. Millar
Daniel Danks ....Mr. Fred Mace
Sam Meadows ....Mr. Alfred Harris
Kara Elphinstone ....Miss Blanche Lee
Ellen Gomersall ....Miss Theresa Karney
Mary Clements ....Miss Madge Malley
—Grand, Croydon.

JEW AMONG THE THORNS, THE, arranged and produced by Mrs. Bright Morris. Presented by the pupils of Miss Margaret Morris. December 21.—Margaret Morris, Chelsea (matinée).

PLAYS OF THE YEAR.

JESS O' THE CARAVAN, drama, in four acts, by Ben Landeck (March 4, Eden, Bishop Auckland), May 13.

James Hartfield	Mr. Jas. P. Millar
Wilkins	Mr. Paul Barry-Lewers
Ronald Vernon	Mr. Reginald Hartey
Frank Crawford	Mr. Kenneth Gordon
Davie Dockerty	Mr. Louis Weston
Mr. Taylor	Mr. Paul Lorimer
Mr. Brittnall	Mr. Alf Johnson
Nina Hartfield	Miss Amy Hardcastle
Violet Vernon	Miss Muriel Carlton
Mrs. Smith	Miss Helen Hartley
Mrs. Crawford	Miss Dora Naylor
Jess o' the Caravan	Miss René Belle Douglas

—Royal, Stratford.

JIM MASON, MINESWEEPER, nautical play, by Horace Stanley. December 16.

Jim Mason	Mr. Denbigh J. Douglas
Sir James Ogden	Mr. J. O. Stewart
Harry Lestock	Mr. Ernest Fare
Jeremiah Nutts	Mr. Lonnen Meadows
Fred Flutter	Mr. Alec W. Wynne
Lavender Moore	Miss Maud Morton Powell
Marion Mason	Miss Jessie Paterson
Susan Griggle	Miss Ellie Macintosh

—Royal, Sunderland.

JOLLY JACK TAR, nautical musical drama, in a prologue and two acts, by Seymour Hicks and Arthur Shirley, music by Herman Darewski, lyrics by Davy Burnaby, James Heard, and John P. Harrington, staged by Frank Collins, scenery designed and executed by John Bull, naval details supervised by two Commanders of the Royal Navy. November 29.

Lord Howard of Effingham	Mr. Mark Stanley
Sir Walter Raleigh	Mr. H. Brough Robertson
Sir Francis Drake	Mr. Wilfred Lyndon
Admiral Frobisher	Mr. Ernest Warburton
Admiral Hawkins	Mr. Charles Rock
Ben Bartim's	Mr. Ambrose Manning
Bill Bright	Mr. Dick Webb
Bob Merry	Mr. Albert Bruno
Admiral Beatty	Mr. Fred Osborne
Mrs. Fleet	Miss May Beatty
Tida	Miss Elsie Donalds
Jennie	Miss Maudie Dunham
Mr. Bessing	Mr. Sam Livesey
Charlie Knox	Mr. Teddy Hayward
Lady Breton	Miss Mary Fenner
Betty	Miss Joan Clarkson
Von Kroppen	Mr. Charles Rock
Karl	Mr. Mark Stanley
First Yokel	Mr. J. David Marquand
Gamekeeper	Mr. Fred Osborne
Donkey Man	Mr. Jack Witten
British Naval Officer	Mr. Ernest Warburton
Von Zegers	Mr. H. Brough Robertson
The Captain	Mr. Mark Stanley
Sentry	Mr. Allan Black
Yeoman of Signals	Mr. Wilfred Lyndon
The Shade of Nelson	Mr. Murri Moncrieff
The Shade of Cornwell	Mr. George Cornwall
Commander Gardner	Mr. Jack Edwards
Lieut. Blake	Mr. Ernest Warburton
Major Hamilton	Mr. H. Brough Robertson
Ikey	Mr. Robert Howard
John Willy	Mr. Ernest Warburton
McIntosh	Mr. Murri Moncrieff
Blimy	Mr. A. Cramer Kingsley
Archibald	Mr. Jack Edwards
First Sentry	Mr. Charles Rock
German Officer	Mr. Mark Stanley
Second Sentry	Mr. Bertram D'Arcy
Smith, V.C.	Mr. H. Brough Robertson
O'Gorman	Mr. Wilfred Lyndon
A Female Hun	Miss Violet Lindsay
Jim	Mr. Stanley Donaldson

—Princes.

JOLLY TIMES, musical burlesque, in seven scenes, book by H. Goring and John H. Howitt, music composed and arranged by Max Darewski (November 18, Empire, Bristol). Principal artists: Mr. Jos. Alexandre, Mr. Billie Finan, Mr. Adrian Burgon, Miss Florence Williams, Miss Dolly Vernon, Miss Madge Merle, Mr. Charles L. Vivian. November 25.—The Middlesex.

JOHN THE STOIC, play, in one act, by Gertrude M. Saunders. Produced at a matinée arranged by the Dramatists' Advisory Board of the Lyceum Club in aid of the Vanguard Farm for Disabled Sailors and Soldiers. November 8.—The Middlesex.

JUST IMPEDIMENT, THE, comedy-drama, in four acts, by C. H. Abbott. May 27.

Marquis of Camford	Mr. A. Harding Steerman
George Tallentyre	Mr. Randolph McLeod
Diana Lady St. Aubyn	Miss Dorothy Palcock
Nurse Francoise	Miss Keith Lytton
Ruth	Miss Helena Pickard

—Kennington.

JUST MY LUCK, musical comedy, book and lyrics by George Lestocq and Wybert Stanford, music by Sullivan Brooke and Sheridan Gordon, additional numbers by Arthur Anderson. June 10.

Manager of the Hotel Peltapole	Mr. Herbert Lewis
Alec	Mr. Len Teel
George	Mr. James Herbert
Kitty	Miss Nance Haines
Maud	Miss Elsie Norris
Chi Chi	Miss Blanche Le Roy
Hotel Porter	Miss Maisie Pickard
An Old Man	Mr. James Thorpe
Principal Dancer	Miss Marcelle Wilson
Interpreter at the Hotel	Mr. Jack Hill
Mindi	Miss Alberta Flahey

—Dalston.

K.C., THE, comedy, in three acts, by Dion Titheradge. April 29.

David Hyslop	Mr. Clive Woods
Beagle	Mr. John Cecil
Dorothea Oddington	Miss Doris Lloyd
Arthur Dawson	Mr. Rex Gerrard
Sir Benjamin Oddington	Mr. Percy Foster
Inspector Hitchin	Mr. Reginald Galty
Lilian Alvin	Miss Eileen Thorndike

—Playhouse, Liverpool.

KHAKI AND KLOGS, play, in three acts, by Arthur Shirley. July 1.

Jack Curzon	Mr. Jack McCaig
Stephen Rainhill	Miss Hilda Beverley
Harriet Rainhill	Miss Maysie Wright
Orgustus John	Mr. Frank Caffrey
Cyril Lingwood	Mr. Sydney Clewlow
Capt. Ferrars	Mr. J. B. Stanley
Mr. Halton	Mr. Terry Davies
Mrs. Boaker	Miss Laurie O'Neill
Julie Amaund	Miss Marjorie Denville
Adelaide Curzon	Miss Edith Rutland

—Royal, Oldham.

KIDDIES IN THE RUINS, THE, episode, in one scene, adapted from the French of Paul Gsell and Francisque Poulbot by Brigadier-General J. E. Cannot, C.M.G., D.S.O., introduced into "The Better 'Ole." June 27.

Maurice Regnard	Mr. Frederick Ross
Père Honoré	Mr. Keith Shepherd
Père Martin	Mr. Herbert H. Young
Père Fortuné	Mr. Harry Danby
Père Mathieu	Mr. Frank Adair
Cpl. Jules Lelong	Mr. David Clarkson
Trooper Henri Laval	Mr. C. Lifford Delph
Trooper Emile Marchand	Mr. Frederick Baker
Trooper Francois Boucher	Mr. A. Way
Francoise Regnard	Miss Sybil Thorndike
Nini Regnard	Miss Monica Morgan

Kiddies in the Ruins, The (Cont.).
Jeannot Regnard ......Miss Fernand Mertens
Amee ....Miss Violette Kemplen
A Soldier Cyclist ....Mr. Victor Robson
  Women and children of the Village: Florence Wood, Gladys Ffolliott, Ruby Kertheen, Therese Nordblom, Hugo Charpentier, Katie Snow, Ella Lowes, Julia Belas, Albert Lock, Frank Worth, Ben Wendy, Sydney Pinner, and Jill Sanders.—Oxford.

KING OF DUBLIN, THE, musical play, by Edward McNulty and Tom Madden.— April 15.—Queen's, Dublin.

KITTY BREAKS LOOSE, play, in three acts, by Kingston Stack. Presented in aid of the Wounded Soldiers' Social Entertainment Fund. May 14.—Wyndham's.

KNIFE, THE, a "Warning," in a prelude and three acts, by Eugene Walter (produced in America, February 20, 1917, Harmanus Bleecker Hall, Albany; April 12, 1917, Bijou, New York). April 10. (Transferred to the Queen's, May 27.) Last performance (the 151st), August 3.
Dr. Robert Manning .... Mr. C. Aubrey Smith
William Meredith ...... Mr. J. Farren Soutar
Wm. Scott, jun. .... Mr. Stephen T. Ewart
Ellis .... Mr. Norman Page
James Bristol .... Mr. Sam Livesey
Edward .... Mr. J. Graham Pockett
Kate Tarleton ....Miss Kyrle Bellew
Dr. Louise Meredith .... Miss Helen Haye
Mammy .... Miss Barbara Gott
Stella Hill .... Miss Muriel Barnby
Nurse .... Miss Marguerite Cellier
—Comedy.

LADY EMMA'S ROMANCE, comedy, in three acts, by Herbert Thomas. February 4.
Lady Emma Jones .... Miss May Palfrey
Jennings .... Miss Gwynne Herbert
Florence Lauderdale .... Miss Dorothy Tetley
Reginald Pierpoint .... Mr. Pat Somerset
Montagu Leroy .... Mr. H. G. Bellamy
Police-Sergeant Blogg .... Mr. E. V. Rae
Mr. Lang .... Mr. Cyril Fairlie
Mrs. Pierpoint .... Mrs. Leslie James
Mrs. Lauderdale .... Mrs. Lena Dalphine
Mr. Faulkener ...... Mr. G. Beresford Innes
Mr. Denezie .... Mr. Ernest Griffin
Mr. Smithers .... Mr. Ivan Leslie
Clerk .... Mr. James Bendall
Usher .... Mr. Sydney Littlejohn
Juror .... Mr. Nevill Wyatt
Mrs. Niggs .... Miss Drusilla Wills
The Judge .... Mr. Weedon Grossmith
—Royal, Bournemouth.

LAST VIENNE, THE, romantic play, in one act, by C. C. Charsley. June 5.
Fernand Count de Vienne..Mr. A. J. Makepeace
Raoul, Seigneur de Posay ..Mr. P. A. O'Reilly
The King of France ....Mr. D. Shine
Jean ....Mr. C. C. Charsley
Le Comte de Touraine......Mr. J. H. Power
Marie de Posay ....Miss N. Swain
Charles, Jules, Jacques..Messrs. W. Hatton, E. B. Pilley, and W. H. Fulford
Noble ....Mr. W. J. Wall
—Empire, Coventry.

LAVENDER, musical comedy sketch, by Leslie Stiles, music by Howard Carr. Played by Miss Ada Davis, Mr. Dewey Gibson, Mr. Tom Tindall, and Miss Polly Emery. April 8.—Palace, South London.

LAW DIVINE, THE, comedy, in four acts, by H. V. Esmond. August 29.
Jack la Bas ....Mr. H. V. Esmond
Edie la Bas ....Miss Jessie Winter
Bill la Bas ....Mr. John Williams
Kate Hayne ....Miss Margaret Watson

Law Divine, The (Cont.).
Claudia Meriton ....Miss Doris Lytton
Daphne Gray ....Miss Barbara Hoffe
Mrs. Gaythorne ....Miss Marie Illington
Ted Campion ....Mr. Pat Somerset
Nellie ....Miss Lesley Winter
Elizabeth ....Miss Dorothy Charles
—Wyndham's.

LEGION OF HONOUR, THE, romantic play, in three acts, by the Baroness Orczy (founded on her novel "A Sheaf of Bluebells"). May 27.
Ronnay de Maurel ....Mr. Julius Knight
Comte de Puisave ......Mr. Charles J. Barber
Comte de Courson ....Mr. Will Smith
Laurant Marquis de Mortain..Mr. Owen Cassidy
Baron de Ritter ....Mr. A. B. Lyons
Mattieu ....Mr. Edmund Despard
Maturin .... Mr. Lawrence Kelly
Paul Leroux ....Mr. Herbert Leonard
Pierre Despres ....Mr. Fred Laurence
Gervais ....Mr. Bert Orkney
Marcel ....Mr. Edgar Pearson
Mme. La Marquise de Mortain
         Miss Frances Wetherall
Annette, wife of Mattieu..Miss Marie Hassell
Fernande de Courson..Miss Mary Fairbankes
—Royal, Bradford.

LIFT, SIR? comedy, in one act, by Rita Bromley Taylor. December 16.
Captain Gordon ....Mr. Gerald Norman
Peters ....Mr. Arthur Jackson
Ginette ....Mlle. Marguerite Schaltiel
—Palace, Chelsea.

LIGHTS OUT, revue, in three acts, book and lyrics by Jack Davidson, music by Sydney Twinn, additional musical numbers by Herbert E. Haines. Presented by the A. O. C. Dideot Concert Party. December 7.—White City.

LILAC DOMINO, THE, operette, in three acts, book by Harry B. Smith, music by Charles Cuvillier, additional dialogue and re-written lyrics by S. J. Adair Fitzgerald. (Produced in America, October 28, 1914, at the Forty-fourth Street, New York.) February 21. Still running.
Cornelius Cleveden .... Mr. A. Stewart Pigott
Léonie Forde ....Miss Josephine Earle
Elliston Deyn ....Mr. Vincent Sullivan
Prosper Woodhouse ....Mr. Frank Lalor
Norman J. Calmain ...... Mr. Edwin Wilson
Maximilian .... Mr. George Rayne
The Honourable André d'Aubigny
         Mr. Jamieson Dodds
Carabana .... Mr. Dallas Anderson
Georgine .... Miss Clara Butterworth
The Baroness de Villiers
         Miss Andrée Corday
Parker .... Mr. Frank Wyllie
—The Empire.

LITTLE BIT OF YOUTH, A, comedy, in one act, by Christian Callister. May 28.
Mrs. Harman ....Miss Margaret Nicholls
Mathew ....Mr. Louis O'Connor
Ethel Riley ....Miss Craig
Edith Martin ....Miss Kelly
Norah McGill ....Miss Christine Hayden
Hudson ....Mr. Fred Harford
—Abbey, Dublin.

LITTLE BROTHER, THE, play, in prologue and three acts, by Benedict James. February 6. (Produced in America at the Royal, Alexandra, Toronto, October 7; Belmont, New York, November 25.) Last performance (the 60th), April 6.
Isaac Elkantrovitch ...... Mr. Sydney Paxton
Blume .... Miss Helen Temple
Mordecai .... Miss Kathleen Cope
Marie .... Miss Mary Grey
Uncle Tulpin .... Mr. Roy Byford

Little Brother, The (Cont.).
Thaddeus .... Mr Corney Grain
Shlomke .... Mr. Ben Nathan
Shmul ....Mr. Corney Grain
Scene.—Russian Poland, 1876. Room in Elkantrovitch's House.

CHARACTERS IN PLAY.
Rabbi Elkan ....Mr. J. Fisher White
George Lub n .... Mr. Ronald Colman
Judith .... Miss Cecily Byrne
Bridget .... Miss Mignon O'Doherty
Vanderlinde .... Mr. Sydney Paxton
Mrs. Lomas .... Miss Hilda Davies
Rube Samuels .... Mr. Roy Byford
Shinovitch .... Mr. Ben Nathan
Father Petrovitch .... Mr. Lyn Harding
—Ambassadors.

LITTLE MISS MODESTY, musical comedy revue, by T. W. Ivory and Kenneth Morrison (September 23, Palace, Weston-super-Mare). December 2.
Sir John Modesty ....Mr. Reg. Varley
Dick Carr ....Mr. Claude Leslie
Annanias Jones ....Mr. Parky Knight
Mara Lestrange ....Miss Phyllis Hume
Kitty ....Miss Florence Phillips
Lady Notting Hill ....Miss F. Dorrie
Betty Berkeley ....Miss Hamilton
Gertie Grovenor ....Miss C. Newton
Victoria ....Miss Queenie Steadman
Zobedia ....Miss Lily Booth
Pomadie ....Miss Lennie Taylor
Nasma ....Miss Alice Emery
Daisy Cheyne ....Miss Vera Dudley
Lili Valli ....Miss Mary Drury
Lettice Leaf ....Miss Freda Clarke
Cressie Waters ....Miss Barbara Curzon
Little Miss Modesty .....Miss Gay Silvani
—Hippodrome, Rotherhithe.

LITTLE MISS VANITY, revue, lyrics by Herbert Rule, music by Burton Manning and W. Leigh, written by O. W. Bellamy-Brettoner. (March 4, Pavilion, Leicester.) December 30.—Imperial, Canning Town.

LITTLE LOST SISTER, American play, in four acts, by Edward E. Rose. October 7.
John Boland ....Mr. Percy E. Hubbard
Harry Boland ....Mr. Harry Norman
Michael Grogan ....Mr. Charles Nevi'l
Martin Druce ....Mr. Hary Lington
Harvey Spencer ....Mr. George Brunswick
Carter Anson ....Mr. Peter Fayre
Tom Welcome ....Mr. Gerald Banks
Jack ....Mr. Jack James
Red ....Mr. Percy Proy
Andy ....Mr. William Way
Mary Randall ....Miss Julie Kennard
Patience Welcome ....Miss Greta Wood
Elsie Welcome ....Miss Irene Barnett
Martha Welcome ...Miss Stella Carmichael
—Dalston.

LIVE WIRE, THE, play, in three acts, by Sydney Blow and Douglas Hoare. August 30 Last performance (the 84th), November 2.
Mulligan ....Mr. George Shelton
Betty Byrne ....Miss Hilda Trevelyan
Sir Hartley Merstbam ..Mr. C. M. Hallard
Christina Anderson ....Miss Helen Morris
Mervyn Chester ....Mr. Alex Scott-Gatty
Inspector Woods ....Mr. Henry Daas
P.C. Weldon ....Mr. Albert Sims
Wilfred Carpenter ("Chin.")
                        Mr. Donald Calthrop
Gibson ....Mr. W. Ford-Hamilton
Inspector Dew ....Mr. Douglas Phillips
—St. Martin's.

LIZA, playlet, by Mrs. Emily Taylor. Presented at the soldiers' and sailors' concert. August 13.—Victoria Palace.

LOLA, burlesque revue, book by W. T. Ivory, music by Kenneth Morrison (July 29, Hippodrome, Sheerness). Principal artists: Miss Lola de Liane, Mr. Jack Christie, Mr. Jack Marks, Mr. Maurice Heath, Mr. Doff Doc. Mr. Julius Pront, Miss Lydia Lee, Miss Winnie Oxford. August 19.—The Middlesex.

LOOK PLEASANT, musical comedy, by Herbert C. Sargent, music by Robert Reaby (March 11, Hippodrome, Devonport). March 25.—The Middlesex.

LOST LEADER, THE, play, in three acts, by Lennox Robinson. February 19.
Augustus Smith..............Mr. Eric Gorman
Lucius Lenihan..........Mr. Fred O'Donovan
Mary Lenihan................Miss May Craig
Dr. James Powell-Harper..Mr. W. Earle Grey
Frank Ormbsy...........Miss Louis O'Connor
Kate Buckley............Miss Maureen Delany
Peter Cooney, J.P............Mr. Peter Nolan
James Clancy............Mr. Hubert McGuire
Major John White, J.P. ....Mr. Fred Harford
Michael O'Connor..........Mr. Bryan Herbert
Tomas Houlihan............Mr. Arthur Shields
Long John Flavin........Mr. Maurice Esmonde
—Abbey, Dublin.

LOT 79, farcical adventure, in three acts, by Rida Johnson Young (produced in America under the title of "Buried Treasure," June 19, 1916, at the Apollo, Atlantic City; presented as "Captain Kidd, Jun.," November 13, 1916. Cohan and Harris, New York). April 30, 1917, Pier, Eastbourne, April 29. Last performance (the 17th), May 4.
Andrew MacTavish ....Mr. Alfred Bishop
An Expressman ..:..........Mr. Bryan Powley
Mary MacTavish ....Miss Hilda Trevelyan
Jim Anderson ....Mr. Percy Hutchison
George Brent ....Mr. Lyston Lyle
Marion Fenton ....Miss Amy Brandon-Thomas
William Carleton ....Mr. Frank Denton
Lemuel Bush ....Mr. Fred Lewis
Susan Bush ....Miss Dora Gregory
Samuel Dickins ....Mr. F. G. Thurstans
Greyson ....Mr. Arthur Cullin
—Queen's.

LOVE AND KISSES, musical phantasy, in three scenes, by Thomas Courtice. May 13.
Sugar Plum Fairy ....Miss Cecile Maule-Cole
Dinkie ....Miss Ivy Judd
Twee ....Miss Gwen Noel
The Chimney Sweep ..Miss Marjorie Fountain
The Imps' Fairy Messenger..Miss Edith Verdune
Swish, the Khaki Boy ....Miss Winnie Wilde
Dickie ....Miss Primrose Carpentier
Jacob, the Cat }
The "Tommy" }........Master B. Lockwood
Charlie Chaplin }
Pansy ....Miss Noreena Feist
Flower Girl ....Miss Doena Ward
Newsboy ....Miss Marjorie Fountain
Eton Boy ....Miss Maisie Wells
—King's, Hammersmith.

LOVE AND THE LAW, drama, by Charles Darrell. March 4—Elephant and Castle.

LOVE IN A COTTAGE, play, in four acts, by W. Somerset Maugham. January 26. Last performance (the 127th), May 18.
Sybil Bruce .... Miss Marie Löhr
Mrs. Butterfield .... Miss Haidee Wright
Jane Raymond .... Miss Ellen O'Malley
Eleanor Dawson .... Miss Margaret Watson
Constance Dawson .... Miss Marie Wright
Mrs. Palmer .... Miss Vane Featherston
Lady Barchester ...... Miss Malise Sheridan
Marquise de Saintorme.. Miss Barbara Hannay
Hortense .... Miss Ida McGill
Dr. Bell .... Mr. G. H. Mulcaster
Owen Butterfield ...... Mr. Sydney Valentine
Martin Arrol .... Mr. W. Gayer Mackay
Sir Peter Ellingham .. Mr. Whitworth Jones

Love in a Cottage (Cont.).
Rev. Archibald Palmer .. Mr. Heath Haviland
Lord Barchester ...... Mr. E. Vivian Reynolds
Rogers .... Mr. J. Dickson Kenwin
Chef d'Orchestre .... Mr. F. Marshall
An Italian Waiter .... Mr. F. G. Carson
—Globe.

LOVER D'OLIVETTE, LE, sketch, by Mlle. Juliette Mylo. Presented at an Anglo-French matinée. February 7.—Court.

LOVING HEART, THE, romantic play, in four acts, by Henrietta Leslie and John Dymock. June 12. Last performance (the 29th), July 6.
The King of France ......Mr. Alfred Brydon
Arnald, Count of Ventadour .. Mr. Basil Gill
Duke Jerome of Navarre ......Mr. Geo. Barran
The Magister Pasquinus Trismegistus
 Mr. George R. Foss
Miles ....Mr. Russell Thorndike
Messer Guido Baldo D'Anguilara
 Mr. Charles B. Bedells
Messer Jacopo ....Mr. Arthur Claremont
Beppo ....Mr. Charles R. Rose
Bernard ....Mr. Elliot O'Donnell
Bernard's Brother ......Mr. Leonard Calvert
Mario ....Mr. Hampton Gordon
Jaques ....Mr. Leonard Calvert
A Page ....Miss Babs Farren
Blanchefleur ....Miss Muriel Pratt
Flaminea ....Miss Rosina Filippi
Isabella ....Miss Barbara Everset
Peroneda ....Miss Elinor Foster
Laura ....Miss Rita John
Melisande ....Miss Hilda Davies
—New.

LUCK OF THE NAVY, THE, spy play of naval interest, in three acts, by Mrs. Clifford Mills (August 1, Royal, Bournemouth). August 5.
Lieut. Clive Stanton, V.C., R.N.
 Mr. Percy Hutchison
Sub-Lieut. Louis Peel, R.N. ..Mr. A. B. Imeson
Engineer-Comr. Perrin, R.N. ..Mr. C. F. Collings
Midshipman Wing Eden ....Mr. Patrick Ludlow
Admiral Maybridge, R.N. ..Mr. Alfred Bishop
Francois ....Mr. Trevor Spencer
Schaffer ....Mr Edward O'Neill
Briggs ....Mr. Tom Redmond
Police Inspector ....Mr. H. A. Mather
An Airman ....Mr. John Byron
Mrs. Gordon Peel ....Miss Ruth Mackay
Cynthia Eden ....Miss Mary Glynne
Dora Green ....Miss Elsie Stranack
Anna ....Miss Mary Byron
Maidservant ....Miss Violet Harley
Newspaper Boy ....Master Barry Livesey
—Queen's.

MAID OF THE SOUTH, revue, by John Warr. August 19.—Bedford, Camden Town.

MAKE BELIEVE, children's revue and pantomime, written by A. A. Milne, lyrics by C. E. Burton, music by George Dorlay. December 24.
Scissors ....Miss Baddeley
Paste ....Miss Hermione Baddeley
A Girl ....Miss Marjory Holman
A Boy ....Master Roy Lennard
 The Play (by A. A. Milne).
Act 1.—The Princess and the Woodcutter.
 The Woodcutter, Mr. Barclay; the Princess, Miss Holman; the King, Mr. Kinsey Peile; the Queen, Miss Rosa Lynd; the Blue Prince, Mr. Stanley Drewitt; the Red Prince, Mr. Herbert Marshall; the Yellow Prince, Mr. Stephen Thomas; the Page, Miss Lilian Simpson.
 Act 2.—Oliver's Island.
 Scene 1.—The Heal Nursery.
 Oliver, Master Lennard; Jill, Miss Holman; Miss Pinninger, Miss Jean Cadell; the Rev. Lemuel Smilax, Mr. Drewitt; the Doctor, Mr. Peile; Aunt Jane, Miss Lynd.

Make Believe (Cont.).
 Scene 2.—The Island.
 Oliver, Master Lennard; Jill, Miss Holman; the Pirate Chief, Mr. Barclay; First Pirate, Mr. Herbert Marshall; Second Pirate, Mr. Stephen Thomas; Steward, Master Frank Worth; Dusky Maiden, Miss Betty Chester; Miss Pinninger, Miss Cadell; Fluffkins, Mr. Peile; Jane, Miss Lynd; Missionary, Mr. Drewitt; the Cassowary, Miss Hannah Hart; Cannibal, Mr. Gordon; Pirates, Dusky Maidens, Fireflies, etc.

Act 3.—Father Christmas and the Hubbard Family.
 Scene 1.—The Home of the Hubbards.
 Mr. Hubbard, Mr. Peile; Mrs. Hubbard, Miss Lynd.

Scene 2.—Outside the Home of the Hubbards.
 Peter Ableways, Mr. Barclay; Jonas Humphrey, Mr. Ford Hamilton; Jennifer Ling, Miss Carmen Judah; Martha Powitt, Miss Maud Millar; Mr. Hubbard, Mr. Peile; Liz, Miss Purcell; Bill, Mr. H. Marshall; A Policeman, Mr. Thomas.

 Scene 3.—As for Scene 1.
 Scene 4.—The Hall of Father Christmas.
 Father Christmas, Mr. Barclay; Mr. Hubbard, Mr. Peile; Mrs. Hubbard, Miss Lynd; First Usher, Mr. Gordon; Baron Bluebeard, Mr. Marshall; Mr. Robinson Crusoe, Master Lennard; Goldilocks, Miss Wooller; Red Riding Hood, Miss Holman; Punchinello, Miss Hart; A Cracker, Miss O. B. Bangs; Toys, etc.
—Lyric, Hammersmith.

MALEFILATRES, LES, play, by Georges de Porto-Riche. Presented by the French Players. May 26.—Court.

MAN FROM TORONTO, THE, comedy, in three acts, by Douglas Murray. May 30.
Mr. Priestley ....Mr. Eric Lewis
Bobby Gilmour ....Mr. Henry Daniell
Fergus Wimbush ....Mr. George Tully
Ruth Wimbush ....Miss Marion Ashworth
Ada Wimbush ....Miss Gwen Gwynne
Mrs. Hubbard ....Miss Ada Palmer
Minnie ....Miss Phœbe Hodgson
Martha ....Miss Margaret Moffat
Mrs. Calthorpe ....Miss Iris Hoey
—Royalty.

MAN SHE BOUGHT, THE, drama, in three acts, by Walter Saltoun. February 11.
Jim Stanley ...... Mr. Henry Earlesmere
Bert Mayfield ...... Mr. Joe Raymond
Bob Elliot .... Mr. Edwin Clarke
Mrs. Elliot .... Miss Louise Millward
Mrs. Murphy ...... Miss Eileen O'Connor
Vic. Stanley .... Miss Nancy Newell
Sybil .... Miss Marguerite Estiville
Enid .... Miss Phyllis Claude
—Royal, Stratford.

MAN WHO MADE GOOD, THE, melodrama, in three acts, by C. Vernon Proctor (January 21, Metropole, Glasgow). April 15.
General John Sheldrake ..Mr. Conrad Clerke
Harry Sheldrake ....Mr. Frank V. Fenn
Vernon Sheldrake ....Mr. Cyril Grier
Betty Sheldrake ....Miss Florrie McInnes
Alice Sheldrake ....Miss Edna Lester
Esther Bastion ....Miss Laurie Adair
Bartlett ....Mr. Archie Grant
Rose Giller ....Miss Dora Weber
Mark Tapley Topper ....Mr. Alan Carruthers
Martha Topper ....Miss Amy Wood
—Elephant.

MANFRED, revival of Lord Byron's dramatic poem, with Robert Schumann's music, by the Incorporated Stage Society, in conjunction with Sir Thomas Beecham, in aid of various charities. July 28.—Drury Lane.

PLAYS OF THE YEAR. 95

MARIA MARTEN; OR, THE RED BARN, melodramatic romance, by Mary Austin and John Maclaren (March 4, King's, Colne). August 5.—Royal, Stratford.

MARRIAGE (K)NOT, THE, revuesical comedy, by E. C. Jazon. July 8.—The Middlesex.

MARRIAGE OF OBERON, THE, masque, in two scenes, by Lewis Cornwall, music by Jean Mars. May 13.

Fate .... Miss Noreena Feist
Past ....Miss Connie Wilde
Present ....Miss Queenie Anderson
Future ....Miss Edith Verdune
Dame Dara ....Miss Queenie Anderson
Spackleback Toad ..Master Bertie Lockwood
Mrs. Fieldmouse ....Miss Maisie Wells
Magnificent Mole ....Master Bertie Lockwood
Sir Flitterback Cockchaffer
                    Miss Primrose Carpentier
Lady Cockchaffer ....Miss Doris Tully
Beetretta Cockchaffer ..Miss Marjorie Fountain
Mrs. Homely ....Miss Maisie Wells
The Golden Fairy ......Miss Connie Wilde
The Star of Destiny ...Miss Cecile Maule-Cole
Queen of the Rainbow ..Miss Edith Verdune
Woodland Nymph ......Miss Marjorie Fountain
Titania ....Miss Dorma Ward
Oberon ....Miss Winnie Wilde
                  —King's, Hammersmith.

MARRIED MAN'S SWEETHEART, A, drama, by Walter Saltoun (produced under the title of "The Serpent in the Garden." June 28, Royal, Dewsbury). September 30.

Henry Ardleigh, afterwards Paul Leigh
                  Mr. Henry Earlesmere
Noel Cheshunt ......Mr. Geo. E. Merrifield
Richard Cameron ....Mr. John Cullen
Peitro Marini ....Mr. Edwin Clarke
Detective Ferrars ....Mr. William Ross
Wilson ....Mr. Ernest Archer
Jane ....Miss Winnie Braemar
Commissionaire ....Miss Elsie Cherry
Duchess of Studleigh......Miss Minnie Webb
Lady Allicia ....Miss Marguerite Estiville
Sonia Cameron ....Miss Holly Haslewood
                  —Royal, Woolwich.

MARRIED ON LEAVE, drama, by Dorothy Mulford. April 15.—Royal, Woolwich.

MARMADUKE, comedy, in three acts, by Ernest Denny. June 19. Last performance (the 47th), July 27.

Marmaduke ....Mr. Dennis Eadie
Mortimer Gregory ......Mr. Sydney Valentine
Dr. Keeling ....Mr. Vincent Sternroyd
Christopher Deacon ....Mr. F. Randle Ayrton
Walter ....Mr. E. H. Brooke
Lady Althea Gregory ....Miss Mary Jerrold
Lady Susan Keppel ....Miss Helen Rous
Patricia O'Brien ....Miss Mary O'Farrell
Beatrice Wyley ....Miss Muriel Pope
Mary Pollock ....Miss Helen Morris
Dawson ....Miss Margaret Murray
                  —Haymarket.

MARRYIN' OF MARGET BELLA, THE, Belfast sketch, by Cathal O'Byrne. Played by Mr. Joe Keenan, Miss Peggy McCurdy, Mr. A. Charters, Mr. Barney Sullivan, Mr. James Hodgens Miss Bride O'Gorman, Mr. Frank O'Leary, Miss Mary Crothers, Miss Jane McAteer, Miss Nellie O'Hagan, Miss Annie Cullen. July 29.—Empire, Belfast.

MASTER BUILDER, THE, revival of Ibsen's play (February 20, 1893, Trafalgar Square) by Mr. Leigh Lovel and company. May 13.—Court. Last performance (the 16th), May 25.

MASTER WAYFARER, operetta, by J. E. Harold Terry, songs by Arthur Scott Craven, music by Howard Carr (produced at the Belgian Red Cross (Ealing Depôt), matinée, December 4, 1917, Apolo). April 20.
The Wayfarer ....Mr. Hayden Coffin
The Man ....Mr. Bryan Powley
The Villain ....Mr. John Howell
The Maid ....Miss Elsie Stranack
                  —Queen's.

MAURICE'S OWN IDEA, play, by Miles Malleson. Produced at a matinée given by the students of the Academy of Dramatic Art. March 26.—Wyndham's.

MAYOR FOR A DAY, musical play, book by Jack F. O'Connor, music by "Primus." Played by Mr. Arthur Roberts and company. June 17.—Pavilion, Leicester.

McTAGGART, THE, Scotch comedy, in one act, by W. A. Tremayne. September 13.—Little.

MEN IN POSSESSION, THE, comedy, in three acts, by J. Bernard M'Carthy. March 11.—Empire, Dublin

MIDNIGHT SUN, THE, Russian ballet, scenes, dances, and choreography by Leonide Massine, music by Rimsky-Korsakoff. Presented by the Serge Diaghileff Russian Ballet. November 21.—London Coliseum.

MILL GIRL AND THE MINER, THE, drama, by Stuart Lomath. April 29.—Palace, Battersea.

MISS ROBINSON, play, in three scenes, by Elizabeth Baker. November 9.
Walter Vintage ....Mr. Arthur Claremont
Agnes Vintage ......Miss Margaret Chatwin
Lister, ...Mr. Christian Morrow
Horace ....Mr. Eric Ross
Angela Robinson....Miss Dorothy Massingham
Mrs. Robinson ....Miss Cathleen Orford
Ivy ....Miss Dorothy Taylor
Mabel ....Miss Sydney Leon
Billy Arden ....Mr. H. Victor Tandy
Pollock ....Mr. Reginald Gatty
Mattie Hine ....Miss Mary Raby
                  —Repertory, Birmingham.

MISTRESS NELL, play, by George C. Hazelton. May 23.—King's, Glasgow.

MIXED HONEYMOON, A, sketch. Played by Mr. Syd Cotterell and company. November 18.—Hippodrome, Rotherhithe.

MONEY FOR NOTHING, farce, in three acts, by George Rollit. May 6.
Capt. Archie Fitzgerald ..Mr. Julian Royce.
Charles Clifton ....Mr. Alan Nichols.
Matthew McDougal ....Mr. Clive Currie.
Fred ....Mr. Jack O'Shea.
A Butcher ....Mr. John McNally.
Inspector O'Hara ....Mr. Benedict Butler.
Yorkshire Backer ....Mr. Tom Burt.
Sergt.-Major Dolan ......Mr. Frank Warren.
Gunter's Man ....Mr. H. E. Browne.
Assistant from Streeters ......Mr. J. Greene.
Messenger Boy ....Mr. George Hamilton.
Fishmonger's Boy ....Mr. F. E. Saxby.
Mabel ....Miss Dorothé Brett.
Dot ....Miss Hilda Charteris.
Miss Banneran ....Miss Edie Casson
"Baby" Berkeley ......Miss Louie Beckman.
A Coster Donah ....Miss Wynne Bronte.
Girl from Lee's ....Miss A. Christopher.
Girl from Gainsborough's ..Miss Ivy Gardiner.
Girl from White's ....Miss Celia Clay.
Bella ....Miss Ethel Callanan.
                  —Prince's, Bristol.

MONEY FOR NOTHING, sketch, by Gladys Lloyd. May 2.—Rehearsal, Maiden Lane.

MONICA'S BLUE BOY, musical playlet without words, by Arthur Pinero and Frederic Cowen. April 8. Last performance (the 48th), May 18.
Mr. Miffle .... Mr. Eric Lewis
Doris .... Miss Dorothy Stephen
Ruby .... Miss Georgina Milne
Beryl .... Miss Esmé Biddle
Monica .... Miss Mary Glynne
Sarah .... Miss Anne Walden
Pte. Lance Lovejoy .... Mr. Martin Lewis
—New.

MOONBEAM, A, by F. T. Marinette. Presented by the Plough Players. December 8. —Lyric, Hammersmith.

MORALS OF VANDA, THE, comedy, in three acts, by A. G. Rhode. April 1.
Dr. Carlyon .... Mr. William Stack
Vanda Mortimer .... Miss Hazel May
Joseph Mortimer .... Mr. H. K. Ayliff
Leonard Mortimer .... Mr. Leslie Howard
Elsmere Grant ...... Mr. Rupert Stutfield
Rev. Robert Checksfield Mr. Walter Raymond
Elizabeth Checksfield .. Miss Lillian Tweed
Binks .... Mr. Benedick Butler
Ellen .... Miss Elsie Donalds
Charles .... Mr. Gerald Johns
Leeson .... Miss Helen Colville
First Detective .... Mr. Julian Gade
Second Detective .... Mr. James Ford
Lady Gruber .... Miss Frances Wetherall
—Grand, Croydon.

MOTHER GOOSE; OR, THE LAY OF AN EGG, pantomime. Produced by a company of fifty naval officers, petty officers, and men. November 9.—Gymnasium, Royal Naval Barracks, Chatham.

MOTHER OR MISTRESS? play, by Lodge-Percy and Henrietta Schrier. August 12.
Colonel Bidlington Biggs
          Mr. Geoffrey Broughton
Raphael Bidlington Biggs
          Miss Sidney Crowe
Reginald Bidlington Biggs
          Mr. Geoffrey L. Carlile
Sergeant Cox .... Mr. Thomas Marshall
Newton Richards ...... Mr. William Hayward
Mrs. Schwarin .... } Miss Marie de Yonson
Lucinda Wild .... }
Fräulein Anna Schwarin
          Miss Kathleen Harrowby
Nerissa Matthews .... Miss Mamie Stockton
Nancy Pellington .... Miss Claire Huntley
Miranda Cox .... Miss Henrietta Schrier
—Royal, Stratford.

MOVIES, farce, in one act, by Thomas King Moylan. March 4.
Darby Spillane .... Mr. Arthur Sinclair
Paddy Farrel ...... Mr. J. A. O'Rourke
Barney Doyle .... Mr. Fred Jeffs
Susie Cahill .... Miss Kathleen Drago
Bridgy O'Brien .... Miss Nan Fitzgerald
Bolton Hereward .... Mr. Sydney Morgan
Nash Milvale ... . Mr. Harry Hutchinson
" Signorina Pipperetto " .. Miss Nora Desmond
—Empire, Dublin.

MRS. MULLIGAN'S MILLIONS, comedy, in three acts, by Edward McNulty. June 24. —Empire, Dublin.

MY AUNT FROM NEW YORK, farcical comedy, in three acts, by Herbert Shelley. October 10.
Harry Brampton .... Mr. Herbert Shelley
Joseph Whitmore .... Mr. Arthur Temple
Robert Perkins, P.C. ...... Mr. Will West
Samuel Cheeseman ...... Mr. Thomas Brooks
Hiram Q. Jefferson .. Mr. C. Lindo Courtenay
Miss Adelaide Brampton ... Miss Rhoda Larkin
Poppy Perkins .... Miss May Dana
Mrs. Joseph Whitmore ...... Miss Mabel Marte
Jessie Cheeseman .... Miss Florence Huntley
Eva Brampton .... Miss Florence Rutter
—Royal, Edinburgh.

NAUGHTY OLIVETTE, comedy playlet, in one act (produced under its French title of "Le Loyer d'Olivette" at an Anglo-French matinée on February 7 at the Court). Played by Mlle. Juliette Mylo and company. April 8.—Chelsea, Palace.

NAUGHTY WIFE, THE, comedy, in three acts, by Fred Jackson, "elaborated and revised" by Edgar Selwyn. (Produced under the title of "Losing Eloise," November 17, 1917, at the Harris, New York.) April 11.
Eloise Farrington .... Miss Gladys Cooper
Carter .... Mr. H. R. Hignett
Hilary Farrington .... Mr. Charles Hawtrey
Darrell McKnight .... Mr. Stanley Logan
Annette .... Miss Mona Harrison
Nora Gail .... Miss Ellis Jeffreys
Thompson .... Mr. Ernest Graham
Bishop Kennelly .... Mr. Herbert Bunston
—Playhouse.

NELL'S LUCK, sketch. April 1.
Mr. Gardner .... Mr. Harry Lofting
Jim .... Mr. D. Tremayne
Mrs. Gardner .... Miss Ada Roscoe
Nell .... Miss Mary Neil
—Euston.

NIBS, play, by Thornley Dodge. September 30. —Grand, Peterborough.

NOTHING BUT THE TRUTH, farcical comedy, in three acts, by James Montgomery, from the novel by Frederick Isham (produced in America, March 13, 1916, at the Shubert, Newark; September 14, 1916, Longacre, New York. January 28, Devonshire Park, Eastbourne). February 5.
Robert Bennett .... Mr. A. E. Matthews
E. M. Ralston .... Mr. Charles Glenney
Richard Donnelly .... Mr. Perceval Clark
Clarence Van Dusen ...... Mr. Paul Arthur
Rev. Dr. Doran .... Mr. O. B. Clarence
Mabel Jackson .... Miss Dorothy Minto
Sabel Jackson .... Miss Zoë Gordon
Martha .... Miss Marie Leman
Ethel Clark .... Miss Norah Fleming
Mrs. E. M. Ralston ...... Miss Henrietta Watson
Gwendolyn Ralston ...... Miss Renée Kelly
—Savoy.

NUNS OF ARDBOE, THE, opera, by Addison Price. Presented by the H. B. Phillips Opera Company. May 3.
Antoinette .... Miss Florence Morden
The Abbess .... Miss Gladys Parr
O'Corra .... Mr. John Pegg
Moyra .... Miss Dorothy Yorke
Kathleen .... Miss Ann Hassal
Eileen .... Miss Florence Parry
—Shakespeare, Liverpool.

NURSE BENSON, play, in four acts, by R. C. Carton and Justin Huntly M'Carthy. June 21.
Lord Messiger .... Mr. Fred Kerr
Brooke Stanway .... Mr. Dawson Millward
Joseph Tibbenham .... Mr. George Elton
Capt. Tibbenham, V.C.
          Mr. F. Pennington-Gush
Ray Marrison .... Mr. Nelson Ramsay
Sergt. Hinks .... Mr. Chas. B. Vaughan
Moxon .... Mr. E. Vivian Reynolds
Smeeton .... Mr. Douglas Munro
Finchett .... Mr. E. A. Walker
Johns .... Mr. G. Dickson-Kenwin
Lady Gillian Dunsmore .... Miss Marie Löhr
Mrs. Tibbenham .... Miss Lottie Venne
Mrs. Marrison .... Miss Violet Farebrother
Nurse Benson .... Miss Blanche Stanley
Watts .... Miss Marjorie Battiss
—Globe.

PLAYS OF THE YEAR.

OH! ALEXANDER, farce, in three acts, by Bay Dumaresq. December 2.
Freece .... Mr. Harry Phydora
Mr. Pettifer .... Mr. Mark Paton
Kyrle .... Mr. Lionel Westlake
Glory Rose .... Miss Pauline Hugen
Mr. Boom .... Mr. Charles Windermere
Mrs. Junk .... Miss Lily Griffin
The Grand Duchess .... Miss Réné Vivian
Ermyntrude Baker .... Miss Mabel Rees
The Grand Duke .... Mr. Chas. F. Lloyd
Baker .... Mr. Harry Phydora
—Palace, Watford.

OH! JOY, American musical comedy, in two acts, book by Guy Bolton and P. G. Wodehouse, music by Jerome Kern, additional numbers and lyrics by Clifford Grey and Julian Frank. (Produced in America under the title of "Oh! Boy," January 20, 1917, Schenectady; February 20, 1917, Princess's, New York.) December 16.
Briggs .... Mr. Hal Gordon
Jane Packard .... Miss Isabel Jeans
Polly Andrus .... Miss Ida Benson
Jim Marvin .... Mr. Billy Leonard
George Budd .... Mr. Tom Powers
Lou Ellen Carter .... Miss Dot Temple
Jackie Sampson .... Miss Beatrice Lillie
Constable Simms .... Mr. Fred Russell
Sir John Carter, J.P. ..... Mr. Tom Payne
Lady Carter .... Miss Diana Durand
Miss Penelope Budd ...... Miss He'en Rous
A Club Waiter .... Mr. Lucien Mussière
—Prince's, Manchester.

OCEAN WAVES, revue, by Albert de Courville, Wal Pink, and H. C. Sargent, music by F. W. Chappelle (December 3, 1917, Empire Palace, Edinburgh). Principal artistes: Mr. Billy Leonard, Mr. Jesse Jacobson, Ridiculous Recco, Miss Jennie Hartley, Miss Isabel Scott, Miss Doris Leslie, Miss Kitty Kirwan, Mr. Billy Leon. May 13.—Empire, New Cross.

O'DEMPSEY, THE, comedy, in three acts, by William Boyle. Produced by the Irish Players. June 4.
Jeremiah Dempsey .... Mr. Arthur Sinclair
Mrs. Catherine Dempsey .. Miss Nora Desmond
Mary Kate O'Neill .... Mrs. Nan Fitzgerald
Brian O'Neill .... Mr. Harry Hutchinson
Mike O'Flanigan .... Mr. Fred A. Jeffs
Tim O'Murphy .... Mr. Sydney J. Morgan
Owney Goveran .... Mr. J. A. O'Rourke
Susie .... Miss Kathleen Drago
Mickey .... Mr. J. M. Bridgman
—Opera House, Cork.

OH! BOY, American revue, by Alrod Alled (July 22, Hippodrome, Margate). Principal artistes: Mr. George Belmore, Mr. Francis Hugo, Mr. Charles Maverne, Miss Moira O'Connor, Miss Maisie Danvers, Miss Agnes Marchand, Miss Gladys Paget. July 29.—Empire, Edmonton.

OFFICERS' MESS, THE, musical farce, in three acts, by Sydney Blow and Douglas Hoare, music by Philip Braham, dances and ensembles by George Shurley, additional lyrics by Davy Burnaby. Produced by Sydney Blow (September 16, Royal, Plymouth). November 7.
Phœbe .... Miss Dorice Gorman
Philip Bolton .... Mr. Murray Moore
Mary .... Miss Elsie Stevens
Joan .... Miss Thelma Morgan
Tommy .... Master Roger Livesey
Hoskins .... Mr. Harry Cole
Ivy Challis .... Miss Violet Gould
Major Bramsgrove .... Mr. Herbert Sparling
Capt. Hardbottle .... Mr. Evan Thomas
Lieut. Turnbull .... Mr. Ralph Lynn
Phyllis .... Miss Beryl Harrison
Esmé .... Miss Ruby Loraine
Sadie .... Miss Dorothy Cecil
Angela .... Miss Lilian Daimler
Peggy .... Miss Estelle Watt

Officers' Mess, The (Cont.).
Babs .... Miss Evie Graham
Mrs. Makepeace .... Miss Betty Ward
Mr. Tinkerton .... Mr. M. R. Morand
Sergeant .... Mr. H. B. Lane
Cora Merville .... Miss Odette Myrtil
A Jeweller .... Mr. George Howley
Mr. Hardbottle .... Mr. Ernest Hendrie
Mrs. Hardbottle .... Miss Sybil Carlisle
Martha .... Miss Flora le Breton
Kitty Cavanagh .... Miss Peggy Kurton
Gordon .... Miss Stella Marris
—St. Martin's.

OH! DOCTOR, farcical piece, by P. T. Selbit, songs and music by J. Weston-Hill and Vincent Exley (March 4, Palace, Bath). April 29.
Dr. Sticky Bax .... Mr. George Jackley
Winkle .... Miss Ray Holgate
The Dinky Nurse .... Miss Lilian Farrar
The Wife .... Miss Diana Morrow
A Friend .... Mr. Frank Herald
Chemist .... Mr. James Herbert
A Patient .... Miss Evelyn Griffiths
Maid .... Miss Lily Evans
—The Middlesex.

OLD BILL'S BABY, comedy sketch, by Ernest G. Batley. November 11.—Collins's, Islington.

OLD DOWN AND OUT, sketch, by A. Patrick Wilson. May 27.
Molly .... Miss Doris Champion
Jack Brent .... Mr. Raymond Langley
"Old Down and Out" .... Mr. Frank Denis
—Alexandra, N.

ON LEAVE FOR HIS WEDDING, play, by Clifford Rean (June 10, Royal, West Bromwich). August 19.—Elephant.

ONE OF THE BIRDS, sketch, by Arthur Wilson. November 4.—Hippodrome, Balham.

OUT OF HELL, drama, in four acts, by Herbert Thomas. (Produced in America under the title of "My Boy." May 6, Parson's, Hartford; as "Under Orders," August 20, Eltinge, New York.) January 5. Last performance (the 31st), February 2.
Mrs. Ford .... } Miss Frances Ivor
Frau Hartzmann ....
Arthur Ford .... } Mr. H. Brough Robertson
Carl Hartzmann ....
—Ambassadors.

OUTSIDE THE LINES, play, in one act, by Charles Kean. October 7.—Palace, Walthamstow.

PACIFIST, THE, play, by John G. Brandon. October 28.
Richard Brunner .... Mr. Geo. Pickett
Mrs. Garritt .... Miss Phyllis Manners
A Poor Woman .... Miss Edith Madelle
Sergt. Mardon .... Mr. Harry Gilbey
Dr. Madge Verrinder, M.D.
Miss Dorothy Wilmer
—Empress, Brixton.

PAGEANT OF DRURY LANE THEATRE, 1663-1918, THE, written and presented to Arthur Collins and the Theatrical Charities by Louis N. Parker in celebration of the twenty-one years of management of Drury Lane Theatre by Arthur Collins. September 27.—Theatre Royal, Drury Lane (matinée).

PAGEANT OF FREEDOM, THE. Louis N. Parker's Pageant presented by Mme. Clara Butt for a series of seven performances in aid of the British Red Cross Society and the Order of St. John. May 7.—Queen's Hall.

PAN LAUGHS, pantomime dansante. By A. Weigall, music by Manuel Gomez. Presented at the opening of a season of dances by Lady Constance Stewart-Richardson, M. Alex Goudin, and Mr. Michael Michell. June 3.—Court.

3

PARTED AT THE CHURCH, drama, by Horace Stanley. February 25.—Palace, Rugeley.

PASSATISMO, by Bruno Corra and Emilio Settimelli. Presented by the Plough Players. December 8.—Lyric, Hammersmith.

PASSING SHOW OF 1918, THE, revue, in eleven scenes, book by Lauri Wylie, lyrics by Clifford Harris and Valentine, mise-enscène by Julian Wylie, music composed, selected, and arranged by Jas. W. Tate, staged by Gus Sohlke. Principal artists: Miss Ella Retford, Mr. Harry Angers, Little Keene, Mr. Telam Rayne, Miss Paulette del Baye, Miss Zelinda Davis. July 8.—Royal, Birmingham.

PAULINA, prologue to a three-act play. Produced by Miss Marion McCarthy at an Anglo-French matinée. February 7.—Court.

PAUV'YETTE, sketch, by Mlle. Juliette Mylo. Presented at an Anglo-French matinée. February 7.—Court.

PEG O' MY HEART, revival of J. Hartley Manners' play (originally produced in America, December 20, 1912. Court, New York; in England, October 5, 1914. Devonshire Park, Eastbourne; October 10, 1914. Comedy) by Mr. Alfred Butt. April 24. Last performance (the 43rd), May 24.—St. James's.

PEG OF THE PAVEMENT, play, by Aimée Grattan-Clyndes. November 4.—Palace, Redditch.

PETER PAN, revival of Sir J. M. Barrie's play (December 27, 1904. Duke of York's) by Mr. Dion Boucicault. December 19.—New (matinée).

PETTICOAT FAIR, musical comedy, by Robert Courtneidge, music by Arthur Wood. December 23.

Admiral Hornby	Mr. Edwin Brett
Harry Hornby	Mr. Harry Ray
Tom	Mr. Walter Passmore
Tipper	Mr. W. A. Haines
Mr. Tovey	Mr. William Cromwell
The Chef	Mr. Leo Frank'yn
Frances Talbot	Miss Ethel Oliver
Lady Broughton	Miss Emmeline Orford
Susan	Miss Dorma Leigh

—Hippodrome, Newcastle.

PHEW! "extravagant farce," in six scenes, by Fred Karno and John Gerant (January 28, Empire, Nottingham). April 22.

Robin Rudd	Mr. George Goodfellow
Nurse Lettice Hope	Miss Jennie Gregson
Dr. Brownlow	Mr. Drelincourt Odlum
Mr. Hargreaves	Mr. Scott Alexander
Dick Rudd	Mr. Harry Paulo
Tony Rudd	Mr. James Leslie
William Ormroyd	Mr. Emlyn Davis
Thomas Smith	Mr. G. Newark
Garge	Mr. William Clayton
Phœbe Ormroyd	Miss Lucie Evelyn
Araminta Rudd	Miss Mercia Russell
Millicent Languid	Miss Ruby Wentworth
Millie	Miss Elsie Stirling

—Empire, Finsbury Park.

PHILIP II., tragedy, in three acts, by Emile Verhaeren, translated by F. S. Flint, costumes and scenery designed by Glyn Philpot, music by Eugene Goossens, jun., the play produced by George de Warfaz, presented by The Plough. September 29.

Philip II.	Mr. H. R. Hignett
Don Carlos	Mr. George de Warfaz
Countess de Clermont	Miss Muriel Pratt
Fray Bernardo	Mr. Tom Heslewood
Don Juan of Austria	Mr. Reginald Malcolm
Duke de Feria	Mr. Arthur de Robin

Philip II. (Cont.).

A Soldier	Mr. Vivian Forbes
Don Francisco de Hoyos	Mr. A. T. Jones

—Court.

PHYL, revival of Cicely Hamilton's three-act play (March 10, 1913, West Pier, Brighton). May 13.

Betty Ponsonby	Miss Peggi Andrews
Olive Ponsonby	Miss Genee Andrews
Mabel Ponsonby	Miss Coletto O'Neill
Maid	Miss Betty Warton
Cathy Chester	Miss Henrietta Leverett
Phyllis Chester	Miss Marie Blanche
Jack Folliott	Mr. Philip Knox
Mrs. Ponsonby	Miss Jess Dorynne
Waiter	Mr. Mick Webber
Mr. Westmacott	Mr. A. G. Paulton

—Gaiety, Manchester.

PLAYBOY OF THE WESTERN WORLD, THE, J. M. Synge's play (June 10, 1907, Great Queen Street). Presented by the Irish Players during the third week of their London season. April 15.—Court.

PLAYTHING OF AN HOUR, THE, play, in three acts, by C. Vernon Proctor. December 30.

Stephen Ollerton	Mr. H. A. Langlots
Lieut. Frank Ollerton, R.N.	
	Mr. Alfred D. Adams
George Ollerton	Mr. Frank V. Fenn
Joseph Jipp, A.B.	Mr. Allan Carruthers
Martha Ollerton	Miss Amy Wood
Connie Ol'erton	Miss Florence MacInnes
Joan Chelford	Miss Margnerite Cryer
Jeannette Palissy	Miss Louie Adams
Meg Lees	Miss Bett Emery

—Metropole, Gasgow.

PLUM AND APPLE, a "merry musical mixture in one pot," by Leedam Stanley and A Patrick Wilson, music by Rosalie Carter. November 11.

George	Mr. G. W. Sola
Bunny	Mr. Bernard Knowles
Stan	Mr. Leedham Stanley
Zoe	Miss Zoe Corner
Vera	Miss Vera Moore
Rosalie	Miss Rosalie Carter
Norah	Miss Norah Doran

—Alexandra, Stoke Newington.

POLITESSE, LA, play, by J. M. Barrie. Produced at a matinée in aid of Lady Lytton's Hospital. June 28.—Wyndham's.

PRESS THE BUTTON, an absurdity, in three acts, by Robert Hichens. May 23. Last performance (the 11th), May 31.

Lord Anthony Fitzurse	Mr. F. Kinsey Peile
The Count of Camerano	Mr. F. Pennington-Gush
Maynard	Mr. Alfam Aynesworth
Macclesfield	Mr. Stanley Cooke
Sir Chewson Polgate	Mr. Arthur Helmore
Talbot Bulstrode	Mr. E. M. Robson
First Policeman	Mr. Charles Bishop
Second Policeman	Mr. G. Langley-Bill
Boy	Master Arthur Samson
Lady Anthony Fitzurse	Miss Marie Löhr
The Ex-Queen of Paradise Islands	
	Miss Lottie Venne
Mme. de Regnier	Miss Vane Featherston
Emma Tapp	Miss Pollie Emery
Housekeeper	Miss Margaret Watson

—Globe.

PRIDE OF THE REGIMENT, THE, drama, by Mrs. F. G. Kimberley (December 10, 1917, Royal, Wolverhampton). March 4.
—Empire, Edmonton.

PRINCESS GIOIA, THE, ballet, by Colin MacLeod Campbell. Presented by Miss Doris Norman's pupils at a matinée in aid of the St. Dunstan's Hostel for Blinded Soldiers. February 5.—Court.

PLAYS OF THE YEAR.

PRIME MINISTER, THE, drama, in four acts, by Hall Caine (produced in America under the title of "Margaret Schiller," at Atlantic City, January 14, 1916; New Amsterdam, New York, January 31, 1916). March 30. Last performance (the 66th), May 25.

Rt. Hon. Sir Robert Temple Mr. C. M. Hallard
Lord Burnley .... Mr. Vincent Sternroyd
Mr. Dundas .... Mr. Howard Sturge
Sir Richard Carfax .. .. Mr. H. A. Young
Admiral Sir Charles Hallam Mr. Ernest Ruston
Sir Malcolm Clark .... Mr. Allan Jeayes
Galloway .... Mr. Gilbert Porteous
Dr. Gottfried Schiller .... Mr. Henry Vibart
Friedrich Schiller ...... Mr. A. B. Imeson
Otto Schiler .... Mr. Wilfred Fletcher
Dr. Hoffmann .... Mr. Arthur Ewart
Lady Dorothy Nugent .. Miss Joy Chatwyn
Peggy .... Miss Vesta Sylva
Mrs. Schiller .... Mrs. A. B. Tapping
Freda Michel .... Miss D. Holmes-Gore
Margaret Schiller ...... Miss Ethel Irving
—Royalty.

PRINCESS AND THE SWINEHERD, THE, version of Hans Christian Andersen's story, arranged by Mrs. Bright Morris. Presented by the pupils of Miss Margaret Morris. December 21.—Margaret Morris, Chelsea (matinée).

PRIVATE PINKER ON LEAVE, sketch, by Frederick H. U. Bowman. December 12.
George Rivington ...... Mr. F. H. U. Bowman
Pte. Charlie Pinker ...... Mr. Andy Wilson
Maisie Pinker .... Miss Cecelia Crawford
—Westminster Music Hall, Liverpool.

PRINCESS POSY, musical play, by Vincent Douglass, music and lyrics by Amos Parker. December 26 (matinée).
Sir John Guy .... Mr. Henry Herne
Lady Margaret Guy .. Miss Victoria Wright
Gerald Guy .... Mr. Roy Oakleigh
Gerald (in the Fantasy) ..Mr. Melville Phillips
Philosopher Joe .... Mr. Wilfrid Shine
Posy .... Miss Violette Kemp'in
Posy (in the Fantasy).. Miss Queenie Stanley
Nap .... Mr. Melville Phillips
Hanky }
Panky } .... Purcella Brothers
Mr. Moon .... Mr. Alfred Clinton
Cupid .... Miss Vivienne Bennett
Pierrot .... Miss Irene Dene
Pierette .... Hilda Dugdale
Fifinella .... Miss Daphne Delamere
Tick }
Tock } .... Brothers Webb
Ned .... Miss Primrose Carpentiere
Pann .... Mr. Walter Long
Tricolour .... Miss Vio'ette Kemplin
Columbine .... Miss Betty d'Alby
Tommy................ Miss Eileen Galvin
Mr. Stork .... Mr. Donald Thorpe
Mrs. Stork .... Miss Sybil Hicks
—Winter Gardens, New Brighton.

PROFITEER, THE, play, in six scenes, by C. Vernon Proctor (April 1, New Hall, Bargoed). May 6.
Gideon Blackiston .... Mr. Cyril Grier
Harry Blackiston .... Mr. Bert Bannister
Teddy Parker .... Mr. Victor Mason
Jane Higgs .... Miss Winnie Webster
Norah Ruston .... Miss Sybil Hammersley
Rosie Selfridge .... M'ss Betty Emery
Eva Loring .... Miss Dolly Wright
Wilhelmina Kay "Old Wheezy"
                        Miss Kathleen Magee
—Elephant and Cast'e.

PROFITEERS, THE, play, in one act, adapted from the French of Pierre Veber (Anglicised version of "Gonzague." March 16, 1917, Ambassadors), by Walter Hackett. June 3.

Profiteers, The (Cont.).
Horace Parkyns .... Mr. Fred Lewis
Matilda Parkyns .... Miss Florence Vie
Henrietta Parkyns ...... Miss Mona Fraser
Thomas Middleton .... Mr. John Keating
Mrs. Middleton .... Miss Gladys Ffolliott
Genevieve Middleton ... Miss Joan Lockton
Julia Middleton .... Miss Molly Lumley
Poderigo Lopez .... Mr. A. H. Majilton
Mrs. Lopez .... Miss Sybil Thorndike
Sir Ernest Blythe ...... Mr. Harold Bradly
Mr. Stanley, M.P. .. Mr. A. Cramer Kingsley
Mrs. Stanley .... Miss Ruth Rose
Mr. Jennings .... Mr. Dmitri Vetter
Karl Spitzenberger ...... Mr. Fernand Leane
Marie .... Miss Eva Embury
Zedekiah Dubois .... M. Leon Morton
—London Pavilion.

PROPER CASE, A, comedy sketch, by Bernard P. Macdonald. July 8.
Eustace Linkin ....Mr. Bernard MacDonald
Agnes Linkin .... Miss Beatrice Webb
P.C. Puncey .... Mr. Alfred Wellesley
—Granville, Walham Green.

PROPOSAL, THE, comedy, in one act, by Anton Tchekoff, translated by Julius West. Presented at a matinée in aid of Lady Smith-Dorrien's Hospital Bag Fund. December 3.—St. James's.

PURITAN GIRL, THE, revue, in three scenes, book, lyrics, and music by Frederic Hendries. Principal artists: Miss Florence Harrington, M'ss Rosa Thornbury, Mr. Ted Stan'ey, Miss Nancie Storey, Mr. Bert Davis, Miss Boy Marris, Miss Jessie Hewitt. October 21.—Exchange, Spalding.

PURPLE MASK, THE, romantic comedy, in four acts, from "Le Chevalier au Masque," by Paul Amont and Jean Manoussi, adapted by Charles Latour (April 22, Royal, Plymouth). Transferred to Princes, September 16; to Scala November 11. July 10.
A Customer .... Miss Gwen Compton
Constance .... Miss Nona Wynne
Another Customer........ Miss Margaret Varde
Majolin .... Mr. Henry Vibart
Irene .... Miss Dorothy Rinley
Laurette .... Miss Alice Moffat
Dominique .... Mr. Russell Thorndike
Capt. Lavernais .... Mr. Walter Menpes
Fouché .... Mr. Ernest H. Paterson
Brisquet............ Mr. C. H. Croker-King
Valentine Boudet .. Miss Amy Brandon-Thomas
The Abbé Brochard .... Mr. Horton Cooper
Armand Comte de Trevières Mr. Matheson Lang
Roche .... Mr. Fred Russell
Mme. Anais.......... Miss Margaret Varde
Sabine .... Miss Betty Belloc
Bernard .... Mr. Walter Plinge
The Vicomte de Morsanne.. Mr. Frederic Sargent
The Baron de Vivonne.. Mr. Leyton Cancellor
Mme. Breau .... Miss Alice Phillips
Bastien .... Mr. Herbert Rea
A Sergeant of Gendarmes .. Mr. Chas. R Stone
Keeper of the Toll House ..Mr. W. R. Stavely
The Duc de Châteaubriand.. Mr. Alfred Brandon
—Lyric.

QUEEN AND THE KNAVE, THE, romantic play, in eight scenes, by Emma Litchfield. July 29.
Hugo Dareford ....Mr. Conrad E. Stratford
Tallard .... Mr. J. Russell Bogue
Victor Stirling .... Mr. T. C. Jackson
Poderio .... Mr. M. Leonard Pierney
Grinaway .... Mr. Sydney Bryant
Princess Helen of Daimba
                Miss Winifred Rutland
Carnoetta .... M'ss Claire Elkington
Rosalind .... Miss Rose Carr

Queen and the Knave, The (Cont.).
Roland ....Miss Gertie Moody
Nedecia, Queen of Moravia
　　　　　　　　Miss Emma Litchfield
　　　　　　　　　—Royal, Whitehaven.
QUITS, comedietta, by George W. Botell. August 19.
Peter Wyatt ....Mr. George Morgan
Patty ....Miss Irene Wallace
　　　　　　　　　—Royal, Newcastle.

RATIONS, revue, by Bert Lee and R. P. Weston (April 1, Hippodrome, Colchester). Principal artists: Mr. Robb Wilton, Miss Winnie Collins, Mr. Frank H. St. Clair, Mr. Jack Mann, Mr. Harry Davis, Miss Florence Palmer, Miss Maisie Craig, Mr. Billy Adams, Mr. Arthur Bright. July 8.—Empire, Stratford.

REAL SPORTS, musical, sporting, naval, and military play, by Arthur Rosebery, music by Ernest Vousden, additional lyrics by Leslie Hawkins. August 5.

Ria Breeze ....Mr. Dave O'Toole
Sgt.-Major Bob Breeze ....Mr. Will Priestley
Padgy ....Mr. Clifton Dane
Colonel Sterling ....Mr. Fred A. Ellis
Count Romanoff ....Mr. Edgar C. Milton
Jim ....Mr. Tony Snape
Dick ....Mr. Clifton Dane
Bill ....Mr. Fred A. Ellis
Charlie ....Mr. Fred Richards
Willie Clarkson ....Mr. Tony Snape
Bob Cash ....Mr. Fred Richards
Spot ....Mr. Sammy Sands
Flora ....Princess Delhi
Jack ....Miss Beattie Browning
Tom ....Miss May Grayce
Cora ....Miss Grace Vasey
Kitty ....Miss Hetty Gale
　　　　　　　　　—Borough, Stratford

REALITIES, "the new Ibsen play." Presented by Mr. Austin Fryers. February 18.
Pastor Manders ....Mr. H. K. Ayliff
Oswald Alving ....M. George de Warfaaz
Johannes Kjerulf ....Mr. William Lawrence
Regina ....Miss Madeleine Clayton
Aimée de Tassère ....Miss Rita Thom
Mrs. Alving ....Miss Madge McIntosh
　　　　　　　　　—Court.

RED HUSSAR, THE, revival of H. P. Stephens's comic opera (November 3, 1889, Lyric). September 2.—Shakespeare, Liverpool. September 30.—The Middlesex.

REPORTED MISSING, play, by Alfred Denville. May 27.
Dr. Bates, R.A.M.C. ....Mr. Reginald Harley
Pte. Egbert Podgers ....Mr. Terry Davies
Lieut. Egbert Podgers ..Mr. Frank Caffrey
Capt. Jack Meredith ....Mr. Alfred Denville
Pte. Joe Meredith ......Mr. Jack McCaig
Sergt. Bill Jones ......Mr. S. Clewlow
Postal Telegraph Boy ...Mr. J. B. Stanley
Ptes. Brown, White, Bailey, Smith
　　　　　　　　The Shaw Glee Singers
Yvonne Douciet ....Miss Marjorie Denville
Mrs. Podgers ....Miss Maysie Wright
Mary Meredith ....Miss Godfrey Turner
　　　　　　　　　—Royal, Oldham.

ROBIN'S FATHER, play, in three acts, by Rudolf Besier and Hugh Walpole. November 1.
Eustace Leigh ....Mr. Lancelot Hilton
Sir Jeremy Leigh ....Mr. Arthur Payne
Dahlia Bristowe ....Miss Dorothy Green
Robin Leigh ....Mr. Paul Hansell
Claire Leigh ....Miss Margary Bryce
Harry Leigh ....Mr. Otho Stuart
　　　　　　　　　—Playhouse, Liverpool.

ROLL OF HONOUR, melodrama, in seven scenes, by Gladys Hastings-Walton (December 24, 1917, Grand Junction, Manchester). January 21.
Jim Smith ....Mr. Jerrold Heather
Major Hugh Ramsdale....Mr. J. O. Stevenson
Philip Ramsdale........Miss G. Hastings-Walton
Sergeant Jock MacTavish..Mr. Fred Gresham
Anton ....Mr. H. Hacker
Karl von Wurlberg.......Mr. Gilbert Elvin
Lady Rose Tregarthen....Miss Dallas Yorke
Poll Binks..............Miss Frances D'Albert
Liz Smith ....Miss Lean Corentez
　　　　　　　　　—Royal, Stratford.

ROMANTIC LOVER, THE, play, by J. Bernard McCarthy. August 26.—Empire, Dublin.

ROMANTICISMO. drama, by Gerolamo Rovetta. Presented by an Italian company, under the direction of Chevalier Ugo Catani, in aid of the Italian Hospital and the Queen's Hospital, Frognal. March 12.—Comedy. (A second performance of the play in English by an English company was given on March 19.) The play was put on at the Ambassadors for a short run on June 8. It ran for 33 performances, ending on July 6.

ROSE MARY, stage version of Dante Gabriel Rossetti's ballad, arranged, designed, and produced by Miss Fogerty, music by Walter Mudie. Presented at the opening of the Fogerty-Ginner season. March 11.—Court (matinée).

ROSE OF PICARDY, THE, musical comedietta, in one act, by G. E. Cornille-Pescud. September 2.
Cecile St. Ayr ....Margaret Fletcher
Eugenie ....Betty Gordon
Raoul de Chatillon .....Kennett Harding
Marcelle Belaire ....Hilda Barry
Schmidt ....Robt. F. W. Douglas
Margot ....Isobel Dorothy
Corporal Dods ....Harry Massey
　　　　　　—Alexandra, Stoke Newington.

ROSES OF PICARDY, musical military play, by Evelyn Thomas. August 5.
Duke of Southwick (afterwards General)
　　　　　　　　Mr. Sutton West
Duchess of Southwick ...Miss Violet Lewis
Capt. Lord Arthur Parkin..Mr. A. S. Mayne
Rector of Southwick ....Mr. Webster Lake
Jack Chester ....Mr. Harry Fraser
Jenefer Graham ....Miss Frances Murray
Billy Jones ....Mr. J. Collier
Sally Gee ....Miss Margot Grenville
Some of the B.E.F.
　　　　Privates Harris, Morley, Beilby
　　　　　　　　—Hippodrome, Cannock.

ROSETTE, comic opera, in two acts, written by W. Beresford Inglis, music by George Henry Martin. April 29.
Barry Williams ....Mr. W. Beresford Inglis
Sidney ....Mr. James Anderson
Capt. Williams ....Mr. Percy Wilding
M. Morand ....Mr. George Ross
No. 22 ....Mr. Neil C. Gemmell
No. 14 ....Mr. Campbell George
No. 7 ....Mr. Arthur M. Steven
No. 9 ....Mr. Theo. Lowe
The Statue ....Mr. Geo. Hope
Griggs ....Mr. J. Lavis Angus
Edith ....Miss Winifred M. Macdougall
Mrs. Williams .....Miss Dorothy A. Lawrence
Martha ....Miss Millie Wilson
Rosette ....Miss Marjorie E. Macdougall
　　　　　　　　　—Royal, Glasgow.

ROSY ISLAND. musical comedy, in four scenes. Produced by Tom Major. June 3.—Empire, Garston.

PLAYS OF THE YEAR. 101

ROXANA, comedy, in three acts, by Avery
  Hopwood (produced at a stage-right per-
  formance, under the title of "Nobody's
  Widow," October 20, 1910, Dalston; pre-
  sented in America under the same title
  October 25, 1910, Euclid Avenue Opera
  House, Cleveland; November 15, 1910, Hud-
  son, New York). September 9, Devonshire
  Park, Eastbourne. September 18.
Betty Jackson ....Miss Athene Seyler
Fanny Owens ....Miss Mona Mangan
Ned Stephens ....Mr. Eric Harrison
Countess Manuelo Valencia....Miss Stella Rho
Duke of Moreland ....Mr. Basil Sydney
Count de Favier ....Mr. Ivo Dawson
Sadie ....Miss Dorothy Tetley
Peter ....Mr. Ernest Trimingham
Roxana Clayton ....Miss Doris Keane
                                —Lyric.
RUINED LIVES, play, in ten scenes, by Mrs.
  F. G. Kimberley (September 2, Grand,
  Brighton). September 9.
Geoffrey Rousden ....Mr. Arthur E. Pringle
Alfred Wade ....Mr. Tom Beasley
Jack Canning ....Mr. Charles Buxton
Dr. Grant Regis ....Mr. Clarke Nicholson
P.C. Wilson ....Mr. Will Nicholson
Mrs. Edith Lyme ....Miss Mona Gray
Clara Canning ....Miss Jennie Clare
Hilda Sidone ....Miss Isla Garnet-Vayne
Enid Wade ....Miss Roma Pendrous
                     —Elephant and Castle.
SABLE AND GOLD, play, in three acts, by
  Maurice Dalton. September 16.
John Parke ....Mr. Peter Nolan
Ann Parke ....Miss Maureen Delany
Gregory Parke ....Mr. Fred O'Donovan
Eileen Parke ....Miss May Craig
Paul Keller ....Mr. Louis O'Connor
Agnes O'Neill ....Miss Una Bourke
                     —Abbey, Dublin.
SACRIFICE OF ISAAC, THE. Presented by
  the Plough Players. December 8.—Lyric,
  Hammersmith.

SACRIFICE, play, by Sir Rabindranath Tagore.
  Presented by the Indian Art and Dramatic
  Society. February 9.
Gunavati .... Miss Barbara Everest
Raghupati .... Mr. Norman V. Norman
Govinda .... Mr. H. K. Ayliff
Jalsing .... Miss Edyth Goodall
Aparna .... Miss Hazel Jones
Nakshatra .... Mr. Eric Ross
Chandpal ...., ... Mr. W. F. Pearce
Nayan Rai .... Mr. Loftus Hare
Queen's Attendant .... Miss Eleanor Street
Druva ....,..... Master Eric Deacon.
      —King George's Hall, Central Y.M.C.A.

SALOME, Oscar Wilde's play (May 10, 1905,
  Bijou, Bayswater). Presented at a private
  performance given by the Independent
  Theatre, with Miss Maud Allan as Salomé.
  April 12.—Court.

SALVAGE, sketch, by Captain E. J. Solano.
  Presented at a matinée in aid of the
  Prisoners of War Fund for the Worcesters.
  July 5.—Queen's.

SARA, play, in one act, by Bertha N. Graham.
  Produced at a matinée arranged by the
  Dramatists' Advisory Board of the Lyceum
  Club in aid of the Vanguard Farm for Dis-
  ab'ed Sailors and Soldiers. November 8.—
  The Middlesex.

SAVING MONEY, farce, by Nita Faydon. Produced by the students of the Florence
  Etlinger School. December 13.—Paddington Street, W.

SCANDAL, play, in four acts, by Cosmo
  Hamilton. December 7.
Pelham Franklin ......Mr. Arthur Bourchier
Malcolm Fraser ......Mr. Alex. Scott-Gatty
Lord Wickham ....Mr. Stan'ey Lathbury
Sutherland York ....Mr. William Stack

Scandal (Cont.).
Major Alex. Thatcher ......Mr. Fred Lewis
Courtney Borner ....Mr. Noel Coward
Pewsey ....Mr. Gilbert Laye
Lady Wickham ....Miss Millie Hylton
The Hon. Honoria Hinchliffe
                     Miss Gladys Ffolliott
Mrs. Lee-Reeves ....Miss Esmé Beringer
Mrs. Claude Larpent ....Miss Mary Robson
Mrs. Lester Keene ....Miss Clare Greet
Regina Waterhouse ....Miss Norah Swinburne
Hélène ....Miss Hazel Hamilton
The Hon. Beatrix Hinchcliffe
                     Miss Kyrle Bellew
                          —Strand.
SECOND SPRING, A, comedy, by Godwin
  Bulger. July 15.
Leslie Surridge ....Mr. Rex Gerard
Parrack ....Mr. Harold Jenkins
Mrs. Percy Darnell ..Miss Gertrude Gilbert
James Darnell ....Mr. H. Lane Bayliff
Ursula Darnell ....Miss Doris Lloyd
Harry Folland ....Mr. Frank Milray
Muriel Darnell ....Miss Madge McIntosh
Stephen Griggs ....Mr. Reginald Gatty
                     —Playhouse, Liverpool.
SECRET AEROPLANE, THE. (See "Carry
  On.")

SECRET SERVICE GIRL, THE, drama, in two
  acts, by Royce Carleton. December 16.
Capt. Jack Bennett ......Mr. Royce Carleton
Henry Miller ....Mr. Rich Minster
Alf Bairnsfather ....Mr. W. Carr
Sir Horace Brunton ....Mr. G. Robarts
Delilah Sabine ....Miss Ethel Edwards
Rosie Bawn ....Miss Josephine Middleton
Penelope Pipsqueak .. Miss Margaret Cotten
Susie Spratt ....Miss Janet Stark
Mrs. Winning ....Miss Katherine Clark
Pearl Winning ....Miss Valerie Crespin
                     —Imperial, Canning Town.
SERPENT IN THE GARDEN, THE, play, by
  Walter Saltoun. June 28. (Title after-
  wards changed to "A Married Man's
  Sweetheart.")
Henry Ardleigh, afterwards Paul Leigh
                     Mr. Henry Earlesmere
Noel Cheshunt ....Mr. Wm. Priestley
Richard Cameron...........Mr. Arthur Elliott
Peitro Marini ....Mr. Edwin Clarke
Wilson ....Mr. Ernest Archer
Jane ....Miss Winnie Braemar
Detective Ferrars ....Mr. William Ross
Commissionaire ....Miss Elsie Cherry
Duchess of Studleigh ...Miss Minnie Webb
Lady Alicia ....Miss Marguerite Estiville
Sonia Cameron ....Miss Cissie Bellamy
                     —Royal, Dewsbury.
SETTLING DAY, a playlet with a moral, by
  Denton Spencer. June 10.
Wallie Belmore, D.C.M. ..Mr. Albert Brasque
Nellie Belmore ....Miss Cora Duncan
                     —Empire, Edmonton.
SHANGHAI, spectacular operette, in two acts,
  by Wm. Carey Duncan and Lauri Wylie,
  music by Isidor Witmark, production by
  William J. Wilson. August 28. Last (131st)
  performance, December 7.
Fo Pah ....Mr. Dennis Hoey
Fee Fum ....Mr. Ewart Drake
Zu Zu ....Miss Louie Brooks
K. Pete Dark ....Mr. Ray Kay
Flast Pansy ....Mr. Betty Bush
Constance Keys ....Miss Joan Hay
Algernon Bay ....Mr. Bert Coote
Wong Ho ....Mr. Harry Claff
Kin Foo ....Mr. Harry Dearth
Fan Tan ....Miss Dorothy Brunton
Hu Du ....Mr. Alfred Lester
Ah Sing ....Mr. Fred Wright
Sen Sen ....Miss Blanche Tomlin
Première Danseuse ....Miss Ivy Shilling
Premier Danseur ....Mr. Paul Jakovleff
                     —Theatre Royal, Drury Lane.

SIGNS OF THE TIMES, extravaganza, by Mrs. D. C. F. Harding. Produced at an Anglo-French matinée. February 7.—Court.

SINCERITY, play, in one act, by Gerald Macnamara. May 31.
Hiram Gurdy ....Mr. J. G. Abbey
Mrs. Gurdy ....Miss Evelyn Fitzgerald
Master Gurdy ....Mr. Laurence M'Larnon
Dan Kelly ....Mr. Rutherford Mayne
Bridget ....Miss Marion Crimmins
Rebecca ....Miss Rose M'Quillan
—Gaiety, Dublin.

SINNERS, play, in three acts, by Brandon Fleming. June 3.
Sir Noel Barchester ....Mr. H. K. Ayliff
John Lynton ....Mr. Dennis Wyndham
Robert Ransom ....Mr. Leslie Howard
James Mountford ....Mr. Wilfred E. Payne
A Maid ....Miss Ruth Brook
Marion Barchester ..Miss Eva Leonard Boyne
Lady Barchester ....Miss Gertrude Sterroll
Ruth Carleon ....Miss Marga La Rubia
—Prince of Wales's, Birmingham.

SINNERS BOTH, drama, in four acts, by Herbert Thomas. September 19.
Rose Hutchins ....Miss Frances Ivor
Ebenezer Jones ....Mr. Herbert Thomas
—Grand, Croydon.

SISTERS, THE, James Shirley's comedy (originally produced in 1652). Presented by the Graystoke Place College Dramatic Club. July 6.—Birkbeck.

SIXES AND SEVENS, comedy, in three acts, by Susanne R. Day. May 27.
Jane Fairfax ....Miss Anne Beaufort
Carter ....Miss Alice Calvert
Lady Anne ....Miss Clara Nicholls
John Morse ....Mr. Arthur Hare
Glodagh Dymley ....Miss Grace Lane
Howard Bellingham ....Mr. Guy Vivian
Willy Gillman ....Mr. Cecil G. Calvert
—Gaiety, Manchester.

SIXES AND SEVENS, revue, by Capt. W. F. Helmore. Produced by the 67th Division Theatrical Company. January 1.—St. Margaret's Hall, Canterbury.

SKIPPER'S SUBMARINE, THE, comedy, in two acts, by Charles K. Ayre. July 29.
Peter Rooney ....Mr. Fred O'Donovan
Mary Anne ....Miss Esmé Ward
Minnie ....Miss Nora Clancy
William Burns ....Mr. F. J. MacCormac
Constable McLoughlin ..Mr. Maurice Esmond
Sam Dawson ....Mr. Eric Gorman
Dick Green ....Mr. Hubert Maguire
Johann Faber ....Mr. Fred Harford
—Empire, Dublin.

SMITH OF THE LOAMSHIRES, play, in one act, by Charles Bushell. May 1.
M. Dulac ....Cadet Chas. Bushell
Capt. Lawrence ....Cadet J. Olivere Jones
Lieut. Edgar ....Cadet Sydney Herbert
Lieut. Smith ....Cadet Arthur Young
Servant to M. Dulac .....Cadet C. H. Walker
—No. 7 Officer Cadet Battalion's Theatre, Moore Park, Kilworth.

SNEEZING CHARM, THE, an Arabian Night's phantasy, in a prologue and four acts, by Clifford Bax. Presented by "The Plough" Society. June 9.—Court.

SOLDIER BOY, American musical comedy, in two acts, book by Rida Johnson Young and Edgar Wallace, music by S. Rombeau and Frederick Chappello (produced in America, April 3, 1916, Shubert, Newark; December 6, 1916, Astor, New York). (June 10, Prince's, Manchester.) June 26.

Soldier Boy (Cont.).
Alfred Appledore ....Mr. Reginald North
Frank de Launay ....Mr. Dewey Gibson
Alan Teniers ....Mr. Lawrence Leonard
Marlene de Launay ......Miss Winifred Barnes
Nora ....Miss Fanny Olive
Boy ....Miss Winnie Shotter
Teddy McLane ....Mr. Fred Duprez
Monty Mainwaring ....Mr. Billy Leonard
Désirée ....Miss Vera Wilkinson
Vitus Appledore ....Mr. E. W. Thomas
Comte de Belleville ....Mr. Arthur Pitt
Amy Lee ....Miss Maisie Gay
Mme. de Launay ....Miss Sinna St. Clair
Officer ....Mr. Edward Merryne
—Apollo.

SOLDIER'S DIVORCE, A, drama, in ten scenes, by Mrs. F. G. Kimberley (September 16, Royal, Wolverhampton). November 11.
Harry Pearson ....Mr. Fred Edouin
Charley Steel ....Mr. Frederick Scarth
Billy Boy ....Mr. Dennis Clyde
Bob Bentley ....Mr. Claude Seaton
Private J. Thorpe ....Mr. Wm. Coake
Philip Steel ....Miss May Harrop
Nurse Alice ....Miss Ethel Masterson
Mary Ann ....Miss Jennie Haydon
Nita Lawson ....Miss Annette Howard
Brenda Steel ....Miss Irene Atchinson
—Elephant and Castle.

SOME FROLICS, revue. Principal artists: Mr. Billy Caryll, Mr. Arthur Carvey, Miss Vena Valma, Mr. Hervey Bruce, Miss Dyson, Miss Eva Farrar. December 30.—Tivoli, Manchester.

SOMETHING DOING, revue, in four acts. Produced under the direction of Lieut. J. W. Fletcher by the 25th (Reserve Battalion) Rifle Brigade in aid of the St. John Ambulance Brigade in France. October 11.—Palace, Truro.

SOMETHING TO HIS ADVANTAGE, playlet, by Dion Titheradge. Produced by Norman McKinnel. May 6.—The Euston.

SON OF THE SEA, A, play, by Clifford Rean (produced under the title of "For Those in Peril on the Sea," July 9, 1917, Grand, Plymouth). January 21.
Paul Tregarron ....Mr. Clifford Rean
Richard Tregarron ....Mr. John Worth
Rev. John O'Farrell ..Mr. Edmund O'Grady
Jacob Polferro ....Mr. Wilford Bailey
Jack Hearn ....Mr. Tom Wheeler
The Coroner ....Mr. George Gormley
Jane Polferro ....Miss Maude Ryder
Edith Tregarron ....Miss Maude Steeples
Aunt Sarah ....Miss Clara Spillard
Poppy Wentworth ......Miss Marie Desmond
—Royal, Woolwich.

SOUL'S AWAKENING, THE, play, in three acts, by J. B. Stewart and Elsie Carlton. October 21.
Prologue.
Nathan ....Mr. J. B. Stewart
Rebecca ....Miss Jennie Deane
The Young Man ......Mr. J. Lister Williams
In the Play.
Maurice Braham ....Mr. Alfred Hearne
Isaac Bernstein ....Mr. J. B. Stewart
Jenkins Pleek ....Mr. Robb Marriott
Bill Slavinski ....Mr. Arthur Whitehead
The Hon. St Albans ....Mr. D'Arcy Salter
Young Philip ....Miss Kathleen Cope
Tommy Dodd ....Mr. Geo. Nicholls
Lady Olive Ormond ..Miss Violet Luddington
Magdala Derwent ....Miss Elsie Carlton
Bill's Missus ....Miss Jennie Deane
Minnie Nichols ......Miss Gwennie Harcourt
Joseph Emanuel ......Mr. J. Lister Williams
—Kennington.

PLAYS OF THE YEAR. 103

SPENDTHRIFT, THE, play, by F. Brooke Warren. September 30.—Royal, Scarborough.

SPOOF, LTD., comedy, with music, by Percival Langley (originally produced as a comedy under the title of "Stolen Fruit," May 28, 1917, Hippodrome, Eastbourne; September 10, 1917, Palace, Hammersmith). August 19. —Empire, Southend.

SPRING, play, in one act, by T. C. Muray. January 7.
Andreesh .... Mr. Fred O'Donovan
Shuvawn .... Miss Margaret Nichols
Seumas .... Mr. Peter Nolan
Judo .... Miss May Craig
Nora .... Miss Irene Kelly
—Abbey, Dublin.

SPY IN THE RANKS, A, military drama, in four acts and eleven scenes, by Mrs. F. G. Kimberley (May 20, Royal, Wolverhampton). July 29.
Colonel Robert Bruce ..Mr. Chas. H. Longden
Capt. John Culling ....Mr. H. Ryeland Leigh
Lieut. Ronald Lee ....Mr. Roy C. Craig
Sam Griggs .... Mr. Lawson Frazier
Pte. Tommy York ....Mr. Frank A. Chapman
Pte. Bill Adams .... Mr. George Sydney
Pte. Nobby Clark .... Mr. Jack Willis
Miri Lee .... Miss May Axon
Barbara Needham .... Miss Mary Hughes
Babetter L'Estrange ..Miss Jeannie Weston
Peggy Merrall .... Miss Marie E. Longden
—Grand, Croydon

ST. GEORGE AND THE DRAGONS, comedy, by Eden Phillpotts. March 30.
Lord Sampford ...... Mr. Christian Morrow
Lady Sampford .... Miss Cathleen Orford
The Hon. Eva Somerset ..Miss Dorothy Taylor
The Hon. Monica Somerset,
      Miss Dorothy Massingham
Sir Moran Tremayne, Bart.,
      Mr. Noel Shammon
Miss Nash-Pomeroy .... Miss Mary Raby
The Rt. Rev. St. George Loftus, D.D.,
      Mr. Joseph A. Dodd
The Rev. Cecil McKinley, M.A.,
      Mr. Ernest Watts-Tye
John Copplestone .... Mr. Frank Moore
Sarah Copplestone ....Miss Margaret Chatwin
Edmund Copplestone ....Mr. Frank D. Clewlow
Unity Copplestone .... Miss Sydney Leon
Nicholas Counter .... Mr. William J. Rea
Bassett .... Mr. Maurice Neville
Polly .... Miss Hilda Vane
Maid .... Miss Nancy Stapies
Footman .... Mr. Sydney Smith
—Repertory, Birmingham.

STONE GINGER, revusical comedy, by J. Aubrey Stanley and A. C. Unwin. Played by Officers of the Command Depôt, Scarborough, and their lady friends. December 12.—Aquarium, Scarborough.

STOPPING THE BREACH, farce, in one scene, by Herbert Thomas. April 8.
The Judge .... Mr. Weedon Grossmith
Mr. Denzil, K.C. ......Mr. Owen Roughwood
Mr. Smithers .... Mr. R. Douglas
Montague Leroy .... Mr. James Whigham
Reggie Pierpont .... Mr. Pat Somerset
Police-Sergeant Blogg ,........Mr. E. Y. Rae
The Usher .... Mr. James Leverett
Mrs. Pierpont .... Mrs. Lena Jameson
Mrs. Niggs .... Miss Drusilla Wills
Lady Emma Jones .... Miss May Palfrey
—London Coliseum.

STORM WRACK, musical play, in one act, by James Lyon, text by T. Barlow. Produced by the H. B. Phillips Opera Company. February 15.
Margot .... Miss Florence Morden
Mathilde .... Miss Gladys Parr

Storm Wrack (Cont.)
René .... Mr. Gwynne Davies
Pierre .... Mr. Lewys James
—Shakespeare, Liverpool.

STORY OF THE ROSARY, THE, revival of Walter Howard's drama (September 17, 1913, Junction, Manchester; December 29, 1913, Princess), by Walter and Frederick Melville. July 8. Last performance (the 102nd).—September 21.—Lyceum.

STROKE OF TEN, THE, dramatic sketch, in one act, by Fred J. Morris. April 4 (matinée).
Jean Cambon .... Mr. Bert Wilson
Captain von Eulenberg ....Mr. Nathaniel Low
Marie Lavellois .... Miss Norah Emerald
—Rehearsal.

STUNTS, revue, books and lyrics by Marriott Edgar, music by Herman Darewski, additional numbers by Callyn Baxter. December 24.—Empire, Bristol.

SUEDUCING OF MACLEAN, THE, comedy sketch, in one act, by R. F. Morrison. December 30.—Royal, Woolwich.

SUMMONS, THE, play, in one act, by Leslie Lynd. March 25.
Thomas Joyce, senr. .... Mr. Walter Kennedy
Thomas Joyce, junr. ...... Mr. Norman Gray
Mrs. Curtin .... Miss Una O'Hagan
Edith Curtin .... Miss Muriel Woods
—Grand Opera House, Belfast

SWITCH NO. 7, sensational episode, in one scene, by George Rollit, originated and devised by Harold Heath. April 1.
Ben Williams .... Mr. Alfred Beale
Captain Fox, V.C. ......Mr. Franklyn Bellamy
The Tramp .... Mr. Harold Heath
Engine Driver .... Mr. George Bogue
Helen Christie .... Miss Dorothy Green
—Victoria Palace.

SWISS V. ROBINSON, sketch, by E. Thornley-Dodge. August 27.—Pier, Eastbourne.

TABS, revue, in two acts and twenty-two scenes, by Harry Grattan, with additional scenes by Ronald Jeans, lyrics by Ronald Jeans, music by Ivor Novello, additional numbers by Pat Thayer, Guy le Feuvre, and Muriel Lillie, dances and ensembles by Gwladys Dillon. Principal artists: Miss Beatrice Lillie, Mr. Alfred Austin, Mr. Hal Bert, Mr. Guy le Feuvre, Mr. Barry Baxter, Miss Ethel Baird, Miss Violet Grey, Miss Tiny Grattan, Miss Margaret Campbell, Mr. Albert Wallace, Mr. Dan O'Neil, Miss Joan Emney, Miss Vera Lennox. May 15. Last performance (the 268th), December 22.—Vaudeville (matinée).

TACTICS, farce, in one act, by Thomas King Moylan (originally produced by the Irish Players at the Irish Club, August 9, 1917). Presented by the Irish Players at the opening of their London season. April 1.—Court.

TACTICAL OFFENSIVE, THE, sketch, by Monckton Hoffe. Produced at the Theatrical Garden Party, June 25.—Royal Botanic Gardens.

TAILS UP, musical entertainment, in two acts, by John Hastings Turner, music by Philip Braham, lyrics by Davy Burnaby and Hugh E. Wright, dances and ensembles by J. W. Jackson. Produced by Harry Grattan. Principal artists: Miss Teddie Gerard, Mr. Clifford Cobbe, Mr. Jack Buchanan, Miss Phyllis Monkman, Mr. Arthur Playfair, Miss Phyllis Titmuss, Mr. Gilbert Childs, Mr. Campbell, Miss Marie Henningway, Miss Babette Tobin, Miss Kathleen Martyn, Miss Gladys Labin,

Tails Up (Cont.).
  Miss Irene Greville, Mr. Arthur Denton, Mr. James Davies, Mr. Rex Anderson. June 1.—Comedy.
TAINTED GOODS, play, by Clifford Rean. March 18.—Royal, Stratford.
TANKS, play, in one act, by Hugh Mytton. February 28
Lady Damity Deerly .... Miss Edith Parker
Mdlle. Tutu .... Mrs. Graeme Robertson
Captain Chancit .... Mr. Gilbert Jacob
P.C. McCrankie .... Mr. H. S. James
  —Vaudeville Pavilion, Devonshire Park, Eastbourne.
TELLING THE TALE, musical farce, in three acts, by Sydney Blow and Douglas Hoare, from the French play "Une Nuit de Noces," by Henri Keroul and Albert Barre, lyrics by Douglas Hoare, music by Philip Braham. August 31. Last performance (the 90th), November 9.
Jules .... Mr. James Crombie
Batnot .... Mr. Douglas Blore
Felicite .... Miss Ruth Siau
Ninette .... Miss Violet Storey
Jeanette .... Miss Betty Beresford
Irene .... Miss Ida Mowbray
Marcel Durosel .... Mr. Denier Warren
Su ette .... Miss Nancy Gibbs
Marguerite .... Miss Winnie Haytor
Jules Duportal .... Mr. Bruce Winston
Mm e. Duportal .... Miss Hannah Jones
Gabrielle .... Mlle. Lucienne Dervyle
Julia .... Miss Birdie Courtney
Yvonne .... Miss Joan Beryl
Sorbier .... Mr. Fred C. Glover
Colette .... Mr. Frank Butt
Henri .... Mr. Gerald Kirby
Claudine .... Mlle. Edmée Dormeuil
Mme. Pigache .... Miss Veda Varrel
Joseph .... Mr. R. A. Swinhoe
Capt. Laverdet .... Mr. Arthur Margetson
Sidonie de Matisse .... Miss Marie Blanche
  —Ambassadors.
TEST KISS, THE, play, in one act, by Keble Howard. June 24.—Palace Pier, Brighton.
THEIR BITTER HARVEST, play, in one act, by Ragna Dehn. October 16.
Major Harry Hetherington
  Mr. Frederick H. U. Bowman.
Doris .... Miss Sylvia Hogarth
Nana .... Miss Ragna Dehn
  —Crane Hall, Liverpool.
THREE BROTHERS, THE, mystery play of the mediæval ages, in four acts, written and produced by Colonel Netterville Barron, lyrics by Colonel Barron, Lieut. F. C. Coulter, and Second Lieut. A. Newberry-Choyce, music by Rifleman Ralph Letts. April 22.
Gomstock, an innkeeper ..Corpl. L. R. Badcoe
Trastomare .... Sergt. A. Downs
Mardelius .... 2nd Lieut. Bridgestock
Cyswithien .... Capt. W. L. Cockcroft
Pamor .... Lieut. Inn Orr-Ewing
Sir Veritas .... Q.M.-Sergt. Cook
Sir Malavise .... Corpl. H. Esgen
Salander .... Corpl. L. R. Badcoe
St. Simplicitas .... Capt. Sheldon
Sir Brien .... Capt. W. L. Cockcroft
The Charcoal Burner ..L-Corpl. H. Thompson
Court Jester .... Corpl. F. Preston
Gardival } The { Lieut. A. C. Cockson
Larcon } Three { 2nd Lieut. Gordon Yates
Julian } Brothers { 2nd Lieut. C. E. Goulding
Tamara .... Miss Cecily Threlfall
Ninith .... Mrs. W. L Cockcroft
Feucassette .... Miss Wynne Pryce
Moreen .... Miss D. Wacher
Lady Damaris .... Miss G. Sallen
Arachne .... Mrs. Arthur J. Brown
  —Opera House, Blackpool.

THREE MONTHS, revusical farce, in three acts, by Clare Estob and Marguerite Storr, music and lyrics by Miss de Llana. Presented by the War Time Players in aid of the R.A.O.B. Widows and Orphans' Fund. March 30.—Margaret Morris, Chelsea.
TITLE, THE, comedy, in three acts, by Arnold Bennett. July 20.
Mr. Culver .... Mr. C. Aubrey Smith
John Culver .... Mr. Leslie Howard
Tranto .... Mr. Martin Lewis
Sampson Straight .... Mr. Nigel Playfair
Mrs. Culver .... Miss Eva Moore
Hildegarde Culver .... Miss Joyce Carey
Miss Starkey .... Miss Gertrude Sterroll
Parlourmaid .... Miss Archie Varre
  —Royalty.
TOBY, comedy, by Herbert Henry Herbert (Major H. H. Woodgate). Produced and played by convalescent officers of the King's Lancashire Military Convalescent Hospital. December 2.—Grand, Blackpool.
TOMMY'S FRENCH WIFE, Anglo-French play, by Charles Darrell (August 5, Her Majesty's, Walsall). August 19.
Cpl. Tom Greystone ....Mr. Tom C. Leybourne
Humphrey Greystone ..Mr. Geo. Osmond Tearle
Dr. Luke Harlow .... Mr. Villiers Stanley
Pte. Freddy Linker ...... Mr. Harry Tilbury
Major Arthur Carr-Lyndon
  Mr. T. Edward Thorne
Miss Abigail Greystone ....Miss Clara Santley
Jessie Malpass .... Miss Cissie Cleveland
Agnes Harlow .... Miss Cissie St. Elmo
Eulalie .... Miss Gipsy Earle
  —Empire, Edmonton.
TOO MUCH MONEY, farce, in three acts, by Israel Zangwill (February 18, Royal, Glasgow. April 9 (matinée). Last performance, (the 62nd), May 25.
Thomas Broadley .... Mr. Marsh Allen
Sir Robert McCorbel, Bart...Mr. M. R. Morand
Grandison Tiptree .... Mr Ernest Hendrie
Sergeant Quizzet .... Mr. Henry Millar
Bewlison .... Mr. Stephen Wentworth
Thisbe Leach .... Miss Lettice Fairfax
Lillian Roseleaf ...... Miss Hilda Bruce Potter
Mrs. Crow .... Miss Mary Brough
Annabel Broadley ...... Miss Lillalf McCarthy
  —Ambassadors.
TRAP, THE, play, in one act, by Alfred Sutro. March 11.
Mr. Longden .... Mr. Herbert Waring
Mr. Gregory Malchas Mr. A. Harding Steerman
The Butler .... Mr. Alan Arthur
The Baroness de Beaumont Miss Miriam Lewes
Mrs. Hennersley Parker....Miss May Congdon
Mrs. Gregory Malchas....Miss Gwen Williams
  —London Coliseum.
TREASURES OF BRITAIN, THE, masque, by Louis N. Parker. Presented at a matinée in aid of the funds of the Charing Cross Hospital. April 19.—Shaftesbury.
TRIMMED IN SCARLET, American play, in four acts, by William Hurlbut. April 25.
Revore Wayne .... Mr. Frank Esmond
David Ebbing................ Mr. Henry Oscar
Benjamin Ebbing .... Mr Edgar Bruce
Charles Knight .... Mr. Clifford Heatherley
Archer Kingston .... Mr. Harold Anstruther
Erroll .... Mr. Gordon Starkey
Janitor .... Mr. R. M. MacDougall
Molly Todd .... Miss Alice Leigh
Mrs. Kipps............. Miss Margot Grenville
Gwen Kennedy .... Miss Eleanor Hommwood
Solly Pierce .... Miss Lola Heatherley
Nursemaid .... Miss Ada Clifford
Housemaid .... Miss May Hase-Wells
Cordelia .... Miss Violet Vanbrugh
  —Royal, Nottingham.

TROJAN WOMAN, THE, Professor Gilbert Murray's translation from Euripides (April 11, 1905, Court). Presented by the Birmingham Repertory Company. April 6.—Repertory, Birmingham.

TRUE VALUES, play, in one act, by Captain Harold Holland. Played by Captain Harold Holland, Miss Shirley King, Miss Irene Barnett, and Miss Violet Rangwale. April 1.—The Surrey.

TWELFTH NIGHT, Shakespeare's comedy revived by Mr. James Bernard Fagan.—October 29.

Orsino	Mr. Terence O'Brien
Sebastian	Mr. E. Pardoe Woodman
Antonio	Mr. Alfred Brydone
A Sea Captain	Mr. Moffat Johnston
Valentine	Mr. Allan Byre
Curio	Mr. Fred Beckett
Sir Toby Belch	Mr. Arthur Whitby
Sir Andrew Aguecheek	Mr. Miles Malleson
Malvolio	Mr. Herbert Waring
Fabian	Mr. Moffat Johnston
Clown	Mr. Edgar Stevens
Olivia	Miss Mary Grey
Viola	Miss Leah Bateman
Maria	Miss Mignon O'Doherty

—Court.

TWISTERS, sketch. Presented by the Strand Productions, Ltd. February 18.—Hippodrome, Poplar.

UNCLE ANYHOW, comedy, in three acts, by Alfred Sutro (produced under the title of "The Two Miss Farndons," May 21, 1917, Gaiety, Manchester). May 1. Last performance (the 52nd), June 15.

Reginald Claughton	Mr. Dennis Eadie
Richard Farndon	Mr. Randle Ayrton
Mr. Floyer	Mr. Dawson Milward
George Floyer	Mr. Geoffrey Douglas
Mr. Petter	Mr. Tewlass Llewellyn
A Porter	Mr. L. de Renzie
Ermyntrude Farndon	Miss Athene Seyler
Christine Farndon	Miss Lila Maravan
Lady Alex. Floyer	Miss Rosa Sullivan
Eliza Jane	Miss Enid Trevor

—Haymarket.

UNCLE BEN'S EXPERIMENT, domestic comedy, in four acts, by John Hobbs. June 17.

Robert Keith	Mr. Harry Cartwright
Jimmy Thompson	Mr. Godfrey Ward
Benjamin Lynch	Mr. Josh. A. Hybert
Christopher Lynch	Mr. Victor Vernon
Mrs. Rogers	Miss Alice May
Mary Jane Smith	Miss Dorothy Lawrence
Elizabeth	Miss Dorothy Hudson

—New, Salisbury.

UPSIDE DOWN, farcical comedy revue, in five scenes, by Mrs. F. G. Kimberley, music by Tom Parsons. Principal artists: Miss Ruby Kimberley, Mr. James D. Hawkes, Mr. Teddy Worth, Mr. H. Solly, Miss Adeline Raby, the Yvonne Troupe. May 6.—King's, Manchester.

UNWANTED CHILD, THE, drama, by Stuart Lomath (produced as "The Wastrel and the Woman," April 23, 1917, Her Majesty's, Walsall; July 16, 1917, Palace, Battersea). April 1.—Palace, Battersea.

US, song-show, songs written and selected by Clay Smith, R. P. Weston, Bert Lee, and others, staged by J. W. Jackson. Principal artists: Miss Lee White, Mr. Clay Smith, Mr. Bert Coote, Miss Tommy Clancy, "Betty," the Eclair Twins, Mr. Bob Cory, Mr. Gerald Valentine, Mr. Billy Wells, Mr. Monte Wolfe. November 28.—Ambassadors

VAGABOND JO, melodrama, in ten scenes, by Charles Hannan (version of his melodrama "The World's Way," May 18, 1903, Pavilion, Mile End; also given as "The Whitechapel King," May 8, 1905, Lyric, Hammersmith). July 8.

Frank Waybourne	Mr. Harry Tresham
Hon. Wilfred Westonberry	Mr. John J. Hooker
Colonel Waybourne	Mr. F. Thorpe Tracey
Samuel Snake	Mr. Will E. Moss
Josiah Dene	Mr. Harry Harrop
Basil Moncrief	Mr. Charles Yorke
Marks	Mr. Arthur Bell
Hopkins	Mr. Charles Auckland
Sergeant	Mr. Fred L. Arthur
Jenkins	Mr. James Laurence
Jones	Mr. Charles Somers
Mary Waybourne	Miss Mysie Monte
Olga Dene	Miss Edith Gregory
Mrs. Hale	Miss Ailie Warde
Ellen	Miss May Payne
Ria Jones	Miss Gertrude Lake
Vagabond Jo	Miss Dora Marriott

—Alexandra, Hull.

VALENTINE, comedy-opera, music by Napoleon Lambelet, book by Arthur Davenport and Charles Wibrow (with acknowledgments to Arthur Sturgess), lyrics by Arthur Davenport. January 24. Last performance (the 87th), April 12.

Valentine	Miss Marjorie Gordon
Gastricus	Mr. Walter Passmore
Citizen Dulacq	Mr. Charles West
Gaston Dulacq	Mr. C. Hayden Coffin
Count Pertino	Mr. Bruce Winston
Broquello	Mr. Henry A. Mather
Captain Odias	Mr. Stephen Bond
Dr. Fubsius	Mr. Leonard Calvert
Baron Boldero	Mr. Arthur Jackson
Pim	Miss Ivy Dewey
Paffe	Mr. Arthur Remey
Pomme	Miss Gwen Carton
Starcus	Mr. Julian Thomas
Diana, Queen of Vimbos	Miss Mabel Twemlow
Pomona, Duchess of Calomello	Miss Hamley-Clifford
Baroness Boldero	Miss Marguerite Wedlake
Princess Gratsia	Miss Prue Temple
Princess Patsia	Miss Gertrude Kaye
Prosia	Miss Gwladys Soman
Carressa	Miss Doris Dean
Princess Petunia	Miss Florence Leigh
Princess Sheila	Miss Hilda Bellamy
Princess Teresa	Miss Beatrice Gomez
Princess Felice	Miss Evelyn Rose

—St. James's.

VALKYRIE, THE, revival of Wagner's opera (presented in English by the Carl Rosa Opera Company, February 3, 1897, at the Garrick), by Sir Thomas Beecham. June 14.—Drury Lane.

VERY GOOD EDDIE, musical play, in two acts, book by Philip Bartholomæ and Guy Bolton, music by Jerome D. Kern (additional numbers by Melville Gideon and Sylvio Hein), dances and ensembles by George Shurley, the play produced by Guy Bragdon (produced in America, November 9, 1915, at the Van Curler, Schenectady; December 23, 1915, Princess's, New York). May 18. Last performance (the 46th), June 22.

Eddie Kettle	Mr. Nelson Keys
Dick Rivers	Mr. Walter Williams
Al Cleveland	Mr. Ralph Lynn
George Francois de Rougemont	M. André Randall
Percy Darling	Mr. Stanley Turnbull
A Purser	Mr. George Grundy
A Coloured Steward	Mr. E. Trimmingham
Elsie Darling	Miss Nellie Briercliffe
Elsie Gray	Miss Madge Saunders

3*

Very Good Eddie (Cont.).
Mme. Matroppo .... Miss Veronica Brady
Georgina Kettle .... Miss Helen Temple
Victoria Lake .... Miss Beryl Harrison
A Booth Girl .... Miss Evie Graham
—Palace.

VERLATEN POST, DE (THE DESERTED POST), play, in three acts, by Dr. Pieter Geyl. Presented by the Dutch Players.—May 12.—Court.

VIOLETTE, comic opera, in two acts, book by Norman Slee, music by John Ansell (revised version of "The King's Bride," June 19, 1911, Kennington). May 15. Last performance (the 57th), June 29.

Maxmilian, King of Celaria
      Mr. Frederick Worlock
Prince Rodolphe .... Mr. Herbert Cave
Baron Pepsicorn .... Mr. George Barrett
Captain Victor St. Pierre .. Mr. Leslie Stiles
Count Van der Kloosh .. Mr. William Cromwell
Leroy .... Mr. J. Kelly
Roche .... Mr. Strafford Moss
Couvin .... Mr. E. Cadle
Jolibert .... Mr. Geo. Dawson
Vanloo .... Mr. Iago Lewys
André .... Mr. Walter Plinge
Georgine .... Miss Prue Temple
Margot .... Miss Freda Le Paye
Princess Fruzelda .... Miss Amy Augarde
Marie .... Miss Beatrice Hunt
Violette .... Miss Violet Essex
—Lyric.

VOICE OF DUTY, THE, play, in one act, by Capt. H. F. Prevost-Battersby (originally produced June 23, 1908, at the Comedy). Revived by Mr. Dion Boucicault. June 24.—London Coliseum.

VOICE ON THE 'PHONE, THE, play, by Clifford Rean (originally produced as "Blackmail"). February 11.
Sir Charles Inglemere ...... Mr. James Stillwell
James Inglemere .... Mr. Geoff. Chate
Julius Dawn .... Mr. Alfred Stretton
Farmer Hulton .... Mr. Charles D. Johnson
Silas P. Judd .... Mr. R. Wilson
Gwendolen Dawn, known as Gwen Ia Vie
      Miss Renée Bevan
Lady Marion Inglemere .... Miss Nita Langford
Miss Hinton .... Miss Nellie Norman
Mrs. Hulton .... Miss Marie D'Yonson
Dorothy .... Miss Florence Lyndon
—Elephant and Castle.

VOLONTE DE L'HOMME, LA, comedy, in three acts, by Tristan Bernard. Presented by the French Players. February 3.
Georges Soubre .... M. Jules Delacre
Mme. Soubre .... Miss Jean Blomfield
Clara .... Mlle. Yvonne Arnaud
Louis .... M. Fernand Léane
Beurdin .... M. Jean Maréchal
Raoul Chavarus .... M. Lucien Mussière
La Bonne .... Mme. Fernande Depernay
Thianville .... M. Yvan Servais
Le Doctor Monireau .... M. Arthur Viroux
Robel .... M. Arthur de Robin
La Petite .... Miss Audrey Hughes
—Garrick.

WANTED—A SPY, play, in two acts, by Philip Mills. May 25.—Polytechnic, Holloway.

WATSON, SHERLOCK'S, HOLMES, skit, by E. B. Norman. March 15.
Dr. Watson .... Mr. Frank Freeman
Sherlock Holmes .... Mr. E. B. Norman
—Gaiety, Manchester.

WAY OF THE WORLD, THE, revival of Congreve's comedy (originally produced 1699, Lincoln's Inn Fields) by the Stage Society. May 12.—King's Hall, Covent Garden.

WEEK-END, a farcical comedy, in three acts, by Walter W. Ellis (August 26, Royal, York). September 12.
Professor Carino .... Mr. Fewlass Llewellyn
Mrs. Beckett .... Miss Clare Greet
Naylor .... Mr. Ernest G. Batley
Ambrose Tibbit .... Mr. Ernest Thesiger
Eric Keats .... Mr. Dennis Neilson-Terry
Lucille de Vivonne .... Miss Yvonne Arnaud
Percy Desborough .... Mr. Sebastian Smith
Sybil .... Miss Evelyn Roselle
Dinah Desborough .... Miss Elsie Craig
Alethea Keats .... Miss Kate Cutler
—Kingsway.

WELL-REMEMBERED VOICE, A, dramatic piece, by J. M. Barrie. Produced at a matinée in aid of Lady Lytton's Hospital. June 23.
M. Don ...... Sir Johnston Forbes-Robertson
M. Rogeri .... Mr. H. V. Esmond
Major Armitage .... Mr. Dawson Milward
Mrs. Don .... Miss Lilian Braithwaite
Laura Bell .... Miss Faith Celli
Another .... Mr. Gerald du Maurier
—Wyndham's.

WHAT A BIRTHDAY! comedy sketch, by A. Myddleton Myles. December 2.
Amelia True .... Miss Amy Bruce
Ben True .... Mr. Fred Moule
Caroline Wilson .... Miss Rita Rees
Nancy Lee .... Miss Betty Anson
Egberta Boyce .... Miss Patty Dene
Popp Stevens .... Mr. Jo Buxton
Jack True .... Mr. W. Carton
—Hippodrome, Putney.

WHAT A SWIZ! sketch, by Stanley Cooke. July 15.
Tom .... Mr. Stanley Cooke
Harry .... Mr. George Miller
Clementine .... Miss Gwendoline Jesson
Ermintrude .... Miss Polly Emery
—Metropolitan.

WHEN THE JOY BELLS ARE RINGING, drama, by Clifford Rean. April 1, Royal, Woolwich.

WHEN LOVE CAME OVER THE HILLS, play, in one act, by W. R. Fearon and Roy Nesbit. January 22.
Kathleen O'Connor .... Miss May Craig
Mrs. Dempsey .... Miss Maureen Delany
Mollie O'Connor .... Miss Irene Kelly
A Tramp .... Mr. Barry Fitzgerald
—Abbey, Dublin.

WHEN OUR LADS COME MARCHING HOME, war drama, in nine scenes, by Sheila Walsh (February 18, Royal, South Shields). June 10.
John Maxwell .... Mr. Arthur Edwards
Sergeant Jack Maxwell .... Mr. Roy Selfridge
Silas Wigglesworth .... Mr. Edgar C. Milton
Private Robert Saunders .. Mr. Ernest Lester
Private William Snooker
      Mr. Courteney Robinson
Private Sam Burrows.... .... Mr. Pat Quinn
Lieutenant Arthur Railton .. Mr. Frank Wilton
Clarence FitzClarence .... Mr. Percy Steven
Dolly Dawson .... Miss Florrie Hall
Elsie Leslie   } Miss Lilian Maitland
Peggy Leslie .... }
—Elephant and Castle.

WHERE THE RAINBOW ENDS, revival of Clifford Mills and John Ramsey's fairy play, music by Roger Quilter (December 21, 1911, Savoy). December 21.—Victoria Palace, (matinée).

WHOSE BABY? farcical comedy, in three acts, by J. H. Darnley. September 2.
Adam Pembleton .... Mr. F. G. Thurstans
Gerald .... Mr. Percy Godfrey
Captain Sandy .... Mr. Cecil Saltmarsh

Whose Baby? (Cont.)
Allan MacTavish ....Mr. George Leslie
James Green ....Mr. Grahame Herington
"9540" ....Mr. H. J. Stafford
Olive ....Miss Norah de Lange
Amy ....Miss Phyllis de Lange
Martha Brown ....Miss Edith Marr
Mrs. Blundell-Staples .....Miss Mary Polson
—Grand, Croydon.

WIDE-AWAKE SLEEPWALKER, THE, somnambulistic scena (with music), in one rap, by G. E. Cornille-Pescud. September 9.
Christopher McFlip ....Mr. Robt. Douglas
Mrs. McFlip ....Miss Margaret Fletcher
Jemima McFlip ....Miss Hilda Barry
Trixie Trevelyan ....Miss Isabel Dorothy
Fred Darrel ....Mr. Kennett Harding
Tweeney Toffin ....Miss Betty Gordon
Tom Toddles ....Mr. Harry Massey
—Alexandra, Stoke Newington.

WIFE'S DILEMMA, A, sketch, by Dion Titheradge. January 7.
Mr. Harker .... Mr. Percival Keitley
Judson .... Mr. Alfred Williams
The Man .... Mr. George Bellamy
Mrs. Harker .... Miss Constance Drever
—Palace, Bath.

WINNING WAY, THE, farcical sketch, by Allan Lane. December 30.
Peter ....Mr. Charles Windermere
Betty ....Miss Pauline Hurgon
Sam ....Mr. Harry Phedora
Servant ....Mr. F. MacKenzie
—Empire, Wood Green.

WOMAN AND WHISKY, play, by Esme Wynee and Noel Coward. January 21.
Major Curtis .... Mr. Cyril Melton
Mr. Loner .... Mr. Kenneth Black
Mrs. Vandeleur .... Miss Aishie Pharall
Norah Chalmers .... Miss Nancy Bevill
—Wimbledon.

WOMAN WINS, THE, playlet, by Robert Desmond. March 18.
Dick Forester .... Mr. Charles Freeman
Angela Morton .... Miss Ivy Carleon
—Hippodrome, Gateshead-on-Tyne.

WOOING O' JANET, THE, comedy sketch, by Patrick Wilson. February 4.
Janet McGregor ....Miss Jean Hamilton.
Helen McGregor ....Miss Stewart Adams.
Willie McFarland ......Mr. George B. Seymour.
Thomas Morrison ....Mr. L. Ross.
Alexander Dalryple ....Mr. Maurice Love.
—Alexandra, N.

YELLOW SPIDER, THE, comedy-dramatic playlet, by Denton Spencer. April 8.
Pearl Browning ....Miss Mabelle F. Barlow
Ruby Sefton ....Miss May Romney
Mr. Fo-Chang .... } Mr. Austin Murdock
Ned Hawkins ....
—Empire, Edmonton.

YOU NEVER KNOW, Y'KNOW, farce, in three acts, adapted from George Feydeau's "La Puce à l'Oreille," by Martin Henry and Hannaford Bennett (June 3, West Pier, Brighton). June 20.
Victor Emanuel Chandebeise
Poche ....} Mr. Rex London
M. Tournel ....Mr. George Bealby
Dr. Finache ....Mr. Cairns James
Camille Chandebeise ......Mr. Douglas Greet
Don Carlos de Histangua
             M. Gaston de Palerme
Etienne ....Mr. Alfred Drayton
Ferraillon ....Mr. Fred Eastman
Rugby ....Mr. Arthur Wellesley
Baptistan ....Mr. James Leverett
A Walter ....Mr. R. C. Scott
Raymonde Chandebeise ....Miss Enid Sass
Lucienne de Histangua ..Miss Daisy Markham
Olympe Ferraillon ....Miss Kitty Barlow
Antoinette ....Miss Betty Gloster
Eugénie ....Miss Honor Byrne
—Criterion.

YVETTE'S DILEMMA, sketch, by Mlle. Juliette Mylo. Presented at an Anglo-French matinée. February 7.—Court.

YELLOW COCKADE, THE, romantic comedy, in three acts, by Bromley Challoner and Wilfred Stephens. November 11.
Capt. Sir Hubert Langton
            Mr. Bromley Challoner
Lord Francis Vaneerlip
            Mr. H. A. Saintsbury
Sir Robert Clynes ....Mr. Alec Crichton
Ensign Humphrey Kemp
            Mr. Charles H. Douglas
Squire Pearce ....Mr. Howard Brenan
Mr. Buffin ....Mr. George Fytche
Footman ....Mr. Temple Mead
Lady Betty Stanhope ....Miss Marjorie Bellairs
Kitty ....Miss Joan Charteris
Caroline Weston.............Miss Jane Seymour
Mrs. Telwit ....Miss Jessie Paget
Jessie ....Miss Josie Hammersley
A Flower Girl ....Miss Elsie Gorse
Pedro ....Miss Rene Summers
—Gaiety, Hastings.

YELLOW STREAK, THE, play, in five acts, by Geoffrey L. Carlile. November 8.
Det. John Shields ..Mr. Geoffrey L. Carlile
Sergt. Simonds ......Mr. Thomas E. Marshall
Terence Lambert ....Mr. William Hayward
Barton ....Mr. George Morris
Esther Mayne ....Miss Clare Huntly
Emily Burden ....Miss Marie de Yonson
Rogers ....Miss Kathleen Harroby
Mrs. Isabel Lambert ...Miss Henrietta Schrier
—Royal, Great Yarmouth.

YULETIDE TALE OF TOMMY TODDLES (THE BOY WHO SAW FATHER CHRISTMAS), children's play, devised and produced by Jeanie Smurthwaite. Presented at a Father Christmas matinée in aid of the Chiswick Red Cross Hospital. December.—Empire, Chiswick.

HAYMARKET.
"Uncle Anyhow." Produced May 1. Ran for 52 performances, ending June 15.
"Marmaduke." Produced June 19. Ran for 47 performances, ending July 27.
"The Freedom of the Seas." Produced August 1.

KINGSWAY.
"Cupid in a Caravan." Produced June 24. Ran for 8 performances, ending June 29.
"A Week End." Produced September 12.

LONDON HIPPODROME.
"Box o' Tricks." Produced March 7.

LONDON PAVILION.
"As You Were." Produced August 3.

LYCEUM.
"The Story of the Rosary." Revived July 8. Ran for 102 performances, ending September 21.
"The Female Hun." Produced October 2.
"Cinderella." Produced December 26.

LYRIC.
"Violette." Produced May 13. Ran for 57 performances, ending June 29.
"The Purple Mask." Produced July 10. (Transferred to Princes, September 16.)
"Roxana." Produced September 18.

MARGARET MORRIS.
"Three Months." Produced March 30. Ran for 11 performances, ending April 6.

NEW.
"The Freaks." Produced February 14. Ran for 51 performances, ending March 30.
"Monica's Blue Boy" and "Belinda." Produced April 8. Monica's Blue Boy finished May 18, with 48 performances; "Belinda," June 8, with 72.
"The Loving Heart." Produced June 12. Ran for 29 performances, ending July 6.
"The Chinese Puzzle." Produced July 11.
"Peter Pan." Revived December 19.

OXFORD.
"In the Night Watch." Produced December 23.

PALACE.
"Very Good Eddie." Produced May 18. Ran for 46 performances, ending June 22.
"Hullo! America." Produced September 25.

PLAYHOUSE.
"The Naughty Wife." Produced April 11.

PRINCES.
"Yes, Uncle." Transferred from Prince of Wales's, March 4.
"Be Careful, Baby." Transferred from Apollo, June 24.
"The Purple Mask." Transferred from Lyric, September 16.
"Jolly Jack Tar." Produced November 29.

PRINCE OF WALES'S.
"Flora." Produced March 12. Ran for 72 performances, ending May 7.
"Fair and Warmer." Produced May 13.

QUEEN'S.
"The Knife." Transferred from Comedy, May 27.
"Lot 79." Produced April 20. Ran for 17 performances, ending May 4.
"General Post." Produced March 14, 1917, at the Haymarket. Ran there until April 28; resumed run at the Queen's, May 6. Ended May 25 with 557 performances.
"The Luck of the Navy." Produced August 5.

ROYALTY.
"The Prime Minister." Produced March 30. Ran for 66 performances, ending May 25.
"The Man from Toronto." Produced May 30. Transferred Duke of York's, July 1.
"The Title." Produced July 20.

SAVOY.
"Nothing But the Truth." Produced February 5.

SCALA.
"The Purple Mask." Transferred from Prince's, November 11.

SHAFTESBURY.
Carl Rosa Opera Season. Began May 6. Finished June 15 with the 50th performance.
"Yes, Uncle." Transferred from Prince's, June 24

ST. JAMES'S.
"Valentine." Produced January 24. Ran for 87 performances, ending April 12.
"Peg o' My Heart." Revived April 24. Ran for 43 performances, ending May 25.
"The Eyes of Youth." Produced September 2.

ST. MARTIN'S.
"The Live Wire." Produced August 30. Ran for 84 performances, ending November 2.
"The Officers' Mess." Produced November 7.

STRAND.
"Cheating Cheaters." Produced February 4. Ran for 67 performances, ending March 30.
"Betty at Bay." Produced April 9. Ran for 53 performances, ending May 18.
"The Hidden Hand." Produced July 4. Ran for 165 performances, ending November 23.
"Scandal." Produced December 7.

VAUDEVILLE.
"Tabs." Produced May 15. Ran for 268 performances, ending December 7.
"Buzz Buzz." Produced December 20.

WYNDHAM'S.
"The Law Divine." Produced August 29.

ROYALTY AT THE THEATRE.

March 1.—Queen Alexandra and Princess Victoria were present at a matinée of "Cheating Cheaters" at the Strand.

March 19.—Queen Alexandra was present at a matinée at the Shaftesbury in aid of the funds of the Charing Cross Hospital.

April 12.—Queen Alexandra, accompanied by the Princess Royal and Princess Maud, attended a matinée at Wyndham's in aid of the War Memorial Actors' Church Union Hostel Fund.

June 10.—Princess Patricia of Connaught was present at the Carl Rosa Opera Company's jubilee matinée, given in aid of the Prisoners of War Fund of the Royal Regiment of Artillery, at the Shaftesbury.

July 2.—Queen Mary, Queen Alexandra, and other members of the Royal Family attended a matinée of "Loyalty" at the St. James's in aid of the funds of the War Service and Women's Legion.

August 12.—Princess Mary and Prince George were present at a matinée of "The Luck of the Navy" at the Queen's.

September 27.—Princess Mary was present at a matinée at Drury Lane, when there was presented "The Pageant of Drury Lane Theatre, 1663-1918," written and presented to Arthur Collins and the Theatrical Charities by Louis N. Parker, in celebration of the twenty-one years of management of the theatre by Arthur Collins.

October 25.—The Queen and Princess Mary were present at a matinée at the "Old Vic.," given in celebration of its centenary.

November 14.—The King and Queen, accompanied by Princess Mary, witnessed "The Bing Boys on Broadway" at the Alhambra.

November 23.—The King and Queen, accompanied by the Prince of Wales, were present at the performance of "The Lilac Domino" at the Empire.

November 25.—The King and Queen were present at the 501st performance of "The Boy" at the Adelphi.

November 25.—The Queen, Queen Alexandra, Princess Victoria, and Princess Christian were present at a special matinée of "The Chinese Puzzle" at the New in aid of the Jubilee Fund of the East London Hospital for Children at Shadwell.

December 3.—The Princess Mary was present at a matinée in aid of Lady Smith-Dorrien's Bag Fund at the St. James's.

December 14.—Princess Patricia of Connaught witnessed the performance of "The Boy" at the Adelphi.

December 17.—The King and Queen, Queen Alexandra, Princess Mary, Prince Albert, and Princess Victoria were present at a matinée at His Majesty's in aid of the King George's Pension Fund for Actors and Actresses.

December 20.—The King and Queen were present at the performance of "The Maid of the Mountains" at Daly's.

December 21.—The Queen of Norway and Prince Olaf, the Princess Royal, Princess Maud, Princess Victoria, and the Princes George and Henry were present at the performance of "Soldier Boy" at the Apollo.

CIRCUITS.

WHERE AND TO WHOM TO WRITE FOR ENGAGEMENTS.

BACON'S PICTURE PALACES.—148, Charing Cross Road, London, W.C.

BOSTOCK TOUR.—Headquarters, Exhibition Hall, Glasgow. Telephone: 498 Douglas. Wires: "Bostock, Glasgow."

BROADHEAD TOUR.—Hulme Hippodrome, Manchester. General District Manager, Mr. H. Winstanley. Telephones: 5928 and 5929 City. Wires: "Broadheads, Manchester."

EDWARDES (T. ALLAN) TOUR.—Grand Theatre, Derby. Telephone: 193

HAMILTON AND HUGHES TOUR.—Co-operative Hall, Crewe.

HAMILTON'S PICTURE PALACES.—213, Buchanan Street, Glasgow.

KENNEDY TOUR.—Empire, Smethwick. Telephone: 127 Smethwick. Telegrams: "Kennedy, Smethwick."

LONDON THEATRES OF VARIETIES, LTD.—Managing Director, Mr. Charles Gulliver, Holborn Empire Buildings, High Holborn, W.C. General Manager, Mr. Harry Masters. Telephones: 9870—9875 Gerrard. Wires: "Randvoll, London," and "Barrasford, London."

MACNAGHTEN VAUDEVILLE CIRCUIT, LTD.—Provinces: King's Chambers, Angel Street, Sheffield. Telephone: 3449. Wires: "Macnaghten, Sheffield." London: Oakley House, Bloomsbury Street, London, W.C. Telephone: 9167 Gerrard. Wires: "Cirvaumac, London."

MIDLAND ELECTRIC THEATRES CO.—Empire Palace, Shirebrook Telephone: 54 Mansfield. Wires: "Ruggins, Shirebrook."

MOSS EMPIRES, LTD.—Cranbourn Mansions, Cranbourn Street, London, W.C. Telephone: 1050 Gerrard. Wires: "Twigsome, London."

PICKARD'S PICTURE PALACES.—115, Trongate, Glasgow.

POOLE'S THEATRES, LTD.—146, Westgate, Gloucester. Telephone: 176 Gloucester. Telegrams: "Myriorama, Gloucester."

THE "C. W." POOLE'S ENTERTAINMENTS.—146, Westgate, Gloucester. Telephone: 176 Gloucester. Telegrams: "Dates, Gloucester."

PRINGLE'S PICTURE PALACES, LTD.—Elm Row, Leith Walk, Edinburgh. Telephone: 288 Central.

ROGERS, STANLEY, TOUR.—Messrs. Arthur Stoker and Co., Waterloo Chambers, Bath Lane, Newcastle.

STOLL TOUR.—Coliseum Buildings, St. Martin's Lane, W.C. Artists' Department. Negotiations: Mr. A. D. Davies. Dates: Mr. Llewellyn Johns. Telephone: 7545 Gerrard. Wires: "Oswastoll, Westrand, London."

SYNDICATE TOUR.—25, Charing Cross Road, London, W.C. Telephone: 2619, 5654, and 5655 Gerrard. Wires: "Minnesia, London."

THOMPSON TOUR.—Cleveden, Linthorpe, Middlesbrough. Telephone, 186, Linthorpe. Telegrams: "Biotint, Middlesbrough."

VARIETY THEATRES CONTROLLING CO., LTD. (De Frece, Barrasford Tours, etc.).—Randvoll House, 15, Bedford Street, Strand, W.C. Booking Manager, Mr. Archie Parnell. Telephone, 9870 to 9875 Gerrard. Wires: "Yellit, London."

VINT TOUR.—142, Long Acre, London, W.C. Telephone: 9549 City. Telegrams: "Vinticon, London." Booking Manager: James J. Welch.

WARD TOUR.—Weymouth House, Salisbury. Telephone: 262 (two lines). Telegrams: "Albany Ward, Salisbury."

WILLMOT TOUR.—33, Norton Street, Liverpool. Telephone: 1758 Royal. Wires: "Vacancies, Liverpool."

AUTHORS OF THE YEAR.

AN ALPHABETICAL LIST OF AUTHORS, COMPOSERS, AND ADAPTORS, WHOSE PLAYS, OPERAS, ETC., HAVE BEEN PRODUCED OR REVIVED DURING THE YEAR 1918. ALSO OF THOSE WHOSE WORKS HAVE BEEN DRAWN UPON BY DRAMATISTS, INCLUDING AUTHORS OF FOREIGN PLAYS FROM WHICH ENGLISH ADAPTATIONS HAVE BEEN MADE.

No references to the familiar operas are included.

ABBOTT, C. H.—"The Just Impediment."
AGATE, EDWARD.—"Le Coq d'Or."
ALLAN, KENNEDY.—"Jack on Leave."
ALLED, ALROD.—"Oh! Boy."
ANDERSON, ARTHUR.—"Just My Luck."
ANSELL, JOHN.—"Violette."
ARMONT, PAUL.—"The Purple Mask."
ARMSTRONG, CAPTAIN CECIL F.—"Home Service."
AUSTIN, MARY.—"Maria Marten; or, The Red Barn."
AYER, NAT D.—"The Bing Boys on Broadway."
AYRE, CHARLES K.—"The Skipper's Submarine."

BAKER, CAPTAIN E. C.—"A Cushy Job."
BAKER, ELIZABETH.—"Miss Robinson."
BALDWIN, CHARLES.—"Great Scott," "Certificates."
BANTOCK, GRANVILLE.—"Arcadian Atalanta," "Cortège."
BARBOR, H. R.—"Cortège."
BARLOW, T.—"Storm Wrack."
BARNES, HERBERT.—"All Over the Shop."
BARRETT, EDWARD F.—"The Grabber."
BARRE, ALBERT.—"Telling the Tale."
BARRIE, SIR J. M.—"Peter Pan."
BARRIE, SIR J. M.—"A Well Remembered Voice," "La Politesse."
BARRON, COLONEL NETTERVILLE, C.M.G., M.V.O., A.M.S.—"The Three Brothers."
BARTHOLOMAE, PHILIP. — "Very Good Eddie."
BARRY, JOSEPH L.—"All Over the Shop."
BATH, HUBERT.—"The Girl in the Bath."
BATLEY, ERNEST G.—"Old Bill's Baby."
BAX, CLIFFORD.—"The Sneezing Charm."
BEALE, ERICA.—"An Egyptian Fantasia."
BECKETT, ALFRED. — "A Face from the Past."
BELLAMY, BRETTONER, O. W.—"Little Miss Vanity."
BENNETT, ARNOLD.—"The Title."
BENNETT, HANNAFORD. — "You Never Know Y'Know."
BENNETT, EX-SERGEANT WILSON. — "Fragments from France."
BERNARD, TRISTAN.—"La Volonté de l'Homme."
BESIER, RUDOLF.—"Robin's Father."
BIESSIPOFF, GREGORY.—"Annajanska, the Wild Grand Duchess."
BIRDHAM, THE VICAR OF.—"His Wife's Secret."
BLOW, SYDNEY.—"Telling the Tale," "The Live Wire," "The Officers' Mess."
BOCCIONI.—"The Green Plums."
BOLTON, GUY.—"Very Good Eddie," "Oh! Joy."

BOTELL, GEORGE W.—"Quits."
BOULTON, MATTHEW.—"A Gold Stripe."
BOWER, MARION.—"The Chinese Puzzle."
BOWMAN, FREDERICK H. U.—"A Cuddlesome Ghost," "Divorce or Dishonour," "Good Old Times," "Private Pinker on Leave."
BOYLE, WILLIAM.—"The Building Fund," "The O'Dempsy."
BRANDON, JOHN G.—"The Pacifist."
BRADSHAW, PERCY.—"Flash Fred."
BRAMAH, ERNEST.—"Blind Man's Buff."
BRAHAM, PHILIP.—"Tails Up," "Telling the Tale," "The Officers' Mess."
BRIEUX, EUGENE.—"Damaged Goods."
BROOKE, SULLIVAN.—"Just My Luck."
BULGER, GODWIN.—"A Second Spring."
BURNABY, DAVY.—"Flora," "Tails Up," "The Officers' Mess," "Jolly Jack Tar."
BURTON, C. E.—"Make Believe."
BUSHELL, CHARLES.—"Smith of the Loamshires."

CAINE, T. HALL.—"The Prime Minister."
CALTHROP, DION CLAYTON.—"Domes of Silence."
CALLISTER, CHRISTIAN.—"A Little Bit of Youth."
CALVERT, HENRY.—"The Girl."
CAMPBELL, COLIN MACLEOD.—"The Princess Gioia."
CANNAN, GILBERT.—"Everybody's Husband."
CANNOT, BRIGADIER-GENERAL J. E., C.M.G., D.S.O.—"The Kiddies in the Ruins."
CARLETON, ROYCE.—"The Secret Service Girl."
CARLILE, GEOFFREY L.—"The Yellow Streak."
CARLTON, ELSIE.—"The Soul's Awakening."
CARR, HOWARD. — "Lavender," "Master Wayfarer."
CARSON, CAPTAIN HARRY.—"An Irishman's Home."
CARTER, ROSALIE.—"Plum and Apple."
CARTON, R. C.—"Nurse Benson."
CASTELL, C. A.—"The Farringdon Case."
CHALLONER, BROMLEY. — "The Yellow Cockade."
CHAPELLE, FREDERICK G — "Hotch Potch," "Box o' Tricks," "Ocean Waves," "Soldier Boy," "Happy-go-Lucky."
CHARSLEY, C. C.—"The Last Vienne."
CLARKSON, BILLY.—"All a Dream," "Fortune's Idol."
COLE, Q.—"The Girl."
CONGREVE, W.—"The Way of the World."
COOKE, STANLEY.—"What a Swiz!"

CORNILLE-PESCUD, G. E. — "The Gay River," "The Rose of Picardy," "The Wide Awake Sleep Walker."
CORNWALL, LEWIS.—"The Marriage of Oberon."
CORRA, BRUNO.—"Passatismo."
COULTER, LIEUT. F. C.—"The Three Brothers."
COURTICE, THOMAS.—"Love and Kisses."
COURTNEIDGE, ROBERT. — "Petticoat Fair."
COWARD, NOEL.—"Woman and Whisky."
COWEN, FREDERIC.—"Monica's Blue Boy."
COWEN, LAWRENCE.—"The Hidden Hand."
CRAVEN, ARTHUR SCOTT.—"Master Wayfarer."
CROOK, JOHN.—"A Celestial Bride."
CUMMINS, G. D.—"Fox and Geese."
CURWEN, HARRY.—"Follow the Girls."
CUVILLIER, CHARLES. — "The Lilac Domino."

DALTON, MAURICE.—"Sable and Gold."
D'ANNUNZIO, GABRIELE. — "The Dead City."
DARRELL, CHARLES.—"Love and the Law," "Tommy's French Wife," "The Airman's Wife."
DAREWSKI, HERMAN.—"Flora," "As You Were," "Jolly Jack Tar," "Buzz Buzz," "Stunts."
DAREWSKI, MAX.—"Jack in the Box," "Jolly Times."
DARNLEY, J. H.—"Whose Baby?"
DAVENPORT, ARTHUR.—"Valentine."
DAVIDSON, JACK.—"Lights Out."
DAY, SUSANNE R.—"Fox and Geese," "Sixes and Sevens."
DEBUSSY, CLAUDE.—"La Boîte à Joujoux."
DE COURVILLE, ALBERT.—"Hotch-Potch," "Box o' Tricks," "Ocean Waves," "Happy-Go-Lucky."
DEHN, RAGNA.—"Their Bitter Harvest."
DE LLANA, AGNESE.—"Three Months."
DENVILLE, ALFRED.—"Reported Missing."
DENNY, ERNEST.—"Marmaduke."
DE MUSSET, ALFRED.—"Le Chandelier."
DE PORTO-RICHE, GEORGES.—"Les Malefilâtres."
DEROYLE, LUCIENNE.—"A Daughter of France."
DESMOND, ROBERT.—"The Woman Wins."
DIX, FRANK.—"The Girl in the Bath."
DORE, JOHN.—"His Kindred Spirit."
DORLAY, GEORGE.—"Make Believe."
DOUGLASS, VINCENT.—"Princess Posy."
DOVE, ALFRED.—"H.M.S. 'Victorious.'"
DRINKWATER, JOHN.—"Abraham Lincoln."
DUFFY, BERNARD.—"The Coiner."
DUMARESQ, BAY.—"Oh! Alexander."
DUNCAN, SARA JEANNETTE.—"His Royal Happiness."
DUNCAN, WM. CAREY.—"Shanghai."
DYMOCK, JOHN.—"The Loving Heart."

EDGAR, MARRIOTT.—"Stunts."
EDMONDS, E. VIVIAN.—"Called Up."
ELLIS, DAVID.—"The Call of the Road."
ELLIS, WALTER W.—"A Week-end."
ELPHINSTONE, CAPT. A. J.—"Good-bye, 1918."
ELSTOB, CLARE.—"Three Months."
ESMOND, H. V.—"The Law Divine."
ESMOND, JOHN.—"High Pressure."
EXLEY, VINCENT.—"Oh, Doctor!" "Flashlights."

FAGGE, ARTHUR.—"H.M.S. 'Victorious.'"
FARRERE, CLAUDE.—"In the Night Watch."
FAYDON, NITA.—"Saving Money."
FEARON, W. R.—"When Love Came Over the Hills."
FEYDEAU, GEORGES.—"You Never Know, Y'Know."
FIELD, SALISBURY.—"Be Careful, Baby."

FINCK, HERMAN.—"Hullo! America."
FITCH, CYRIL.—"A Change of Tactics."
FITZGERALD, S. J. ADAIR.—"The Lilac Domino."
FLEMING, BRANDON.—"Sinners."
FLINT, F. S.—"Philip II."
FOLEY, CAPT. E. GREEN.—"Excuses; or, Why They Were Late."
FORBES, DOUGLAS.—"Box o' Tricks."
FORD, PERCY.—"Betty Wakes Up."
FRANK, JULIAN.—"Oh! Joy."
FRONDAIE, PIERRE.—"The Girl and the Puppet."
FULTON, GRENVILLE.—"The Girl in the Bath."

GALLON, TOM.—"The Call of the Road."
GARROD, W. V.—"What a Wife!"
GERANT, JOHN.—"Phew!!!"
GEYL, DR. PIETER.—"The Deserted Post."
GIBSON, ROLAND R.—"The Girl in the Bath."
GIDEON, MELVILLE.—"Flora," "Very Good Eddie," "Ciro's Frolics."
GILBERT, W. S.—"H.M.S. 'Pinafore.'"
GOLDINI, CARLO.—"The Good-humoured Ladies."
GOMEZ, MANUEL.—"Pan Laughs."
GOODWIN, ERNEST.—"Cupid in a Caravan."
GORDON, SHERIDAN.—"Just my Luck!"
GORING, H.—"Jolly Times."
GORST, MRS. HAROLD.—"Ede's Trouble."
GRAHAM, BERTHA N.—"Sara."
GRAHAM, HARRY.—"Box o' Tricks."
GRATTAN, HARRY.—"Flora," "Tabs."
GRATTAN-CLYNDES, AIMEE.—"Peg of the Pavement."
GREGORY, LADY.—"Hanrahan's Oath."
GREENAWAY, MRS. O. C.—"Dawkins."
GREY, CLIFFORD.—"The Bing Boys on Broadway," "Hullo! America," "Oh! Joy."
GROSSSMITH, GEORGE.—"The Bing Boys on Broadway."
GSELL, PAUL.—"The Kiddies in the Ruins."
GUERNON, CHARLES.—"The Eyes of Youth."

HACKETT, WALTER.—"The Profiteers," "The Freedom of the Seas."
HAINES, HERBERT E.—"Lights Out."
HAMELTON, CICELY.—"Phyl."
HAMILTON, COSMO.—"Scandal."
HAMMOND, LANCE-CPL. H. R. (Kenneth Barton).—"Alice in Sunderland."
HANNAN, CHARLES.—"Vagabond Jo."
HARBAK, OTTO.—"Going Up."
HARDING, MRS. D. C. F.—"Signs of the Times."
HARKER, W. VERE.—"All Dressed Up."
HARRINGTON, JOHN P.—"Jolly Jack Tar."
HARTE, —.—"It's a Walk Over."
HARRIS, CLIFFORD.—"The Passing Show of 1918."
HASLAM, LESLIE.—"Box o' Tricks."
HASTINGS-WALTON, GLADYS.—"Roll of Honour," "A Broken Doll."
HATTON, JOHN.—"Hi-diddle-d'ddle."
HAWKINS, LESLIE.—"Real Sports."
HAYMAN, JOSEPH.—"Jack-in-the-Box."
HAZELTON, GEORGE C.—"Mistress Nell."
HEARD, JAMES.—"Flora," "Jolly Jack Tar."
HEIN, SYLVIO.—"Very Good Eddie."
HELLE, ANDRE.—"La Boîte à Joujoux."
HELMORE, CAPT. W. F.—"Sixes and Sevens."
HENDRIES, FREDERIC.—"The Puritan Girl."
HENN, JAY.—"Devonshire Cream."
HENRY, MARTIN.—"You Never Know, Y'Know."
HERBERT, HENRY H. (Major H. H. Woodgate).—"Toby."
HICHENS, ROBERT.—"Press the Button."
HICKS, SEYMOUR.—"Jolly Jack Tar."
HIRSCH, LOUIS.—"Going Up."
HOARE, DOUGLAS.—"Telling the Tale," "The Live Wire," "The Officers' Mess."

HOBBS, JOHN.—"Uncle Ben's Experiment."
HOFFE, MONCKTON.—"The Tactical Offensive."
HOLLAND, HAROLD.—"True Values."
HOPWOOD, AVERY.—"Fair and Warmer," "Roxana."
HOUSMAN, LAURENCE.—"Bird in Hand."
HOWARD, KEBLE.—"The Test Kiss."
HOWARD, L. G. REDMOND.—"An Irishman's Home."
HOWARD, WALTER.—"The Story of the Rosary."
HOWARD, WILSON.—"Back from Overseas."
HOWITT, JOHN H.—"Jolly Times."
HURLBUT, WILLIAM. — "Trimmed in Scarlet."

IBSEN, HENRIK.—"The Master Builder."
INGLIS, W. BERESFORD.—"Rosette."
ISHAM, FREDERICK.—"Nothing but the Truth."
IVORY, T. W.—"Little Miss Modesty," "Lola."

JACKSON, FRED.—"The Naughty Wife."
JACKSON, J. LEICESTER.—"Fourteen Days' Leave."
JAMES, BENEDICT.—"The Little Brother."
JAZON, E. C.—"The Marriage (K)Not."
JEANS, RONALD.—"Tabs," "Buzz Buzz."
JEFFERSON, ARTHUR.—"Home from the Trenches."
JEFFERSON, G. GORDON.—"Carry On."
JENNINGS, GERTRUDE E.—"After the War."

KARNO, FRED.—"Phew!!!"
KAYE, MARGARET.—"A Change of Tactics."
KEAN, CHARLES.—"Outside the Lines."
KERN, JEROME D.—"Very Good Eddie," "Oh! Joy."
KEROUL, HENRI.—"Telling the Tale."
KIMBERLEY, MRS F. G.—"The Pride of the Regiment," "Upside Down," "A Spy in the Ranks," "How Do You Like It?" "Ruined Lives," "A Soldier's Divorce."

LALLY, GWEN.—"The Great Moment."
LAMBELET, NAPOLEON.—"Valentine."
LANDECK, BEN.—"Jess o' the Caravan."
LANE, ALLAN.—"The Winning Way."
LANE, MARTIN.—"Blame the Cinema."
LANGLEY, PERCIVAL.—"Hi-diddle-diddle," "Spoof, Limited."
LATOUR, CHARLES (MATHESON LANG).—"The Purple Mask."
LE FEUVRE, GUY.—"Tabs."
LEE, BERT. — "Rations," "Any Lady," "Ciro's Frolics," "Us," "Crystals."
LEIGH, W.—"Little Miss Vanity."
LESLIE, HENRIETTA.—"The Loving Heart."
LESTOCQ, GEORGE.—"Just My Luck."
LETHBRIDGE, OLIVE.—"Im."
LETTS, RIFLEMAN RALPH.—"The Three Brothers."
LEWES, EVA.—"Jack On Leave."
LEWIS, MARTIN.—"And Afterwards: A Peace Time Warning."
LEYCESTER, LAURA.—"After the Trial."
LIADOFF, M.—"The Children's Tales."
LION, LEON M.—"The Chinese Puzzle."
LILLIE, MURIEL.—"Tabs."
LINDSAY.—"It's a Walk Over."
LITCHFIELD, EMMA.—"The Queen and the Knave."
LLOYD, GLADYS.—"Money for Nothing."
LOCKE, EDWARD.—"The Bubble."
LOMATH, STUART.—"The Mill Girl and the Miner," "The Unwanted Child."
LOUYS, PIERRE.—"The Girl and the Puppet."
LYND, LESLIE.—"The Summons."
LYON, JAMES.—"Storm Wrack."

"M. P."—"For the Flag."
McARDLE, DOROTHY.—"Atonement."
MACDONALD, BERNARD P.—"A Proper Case."
MACLAREN, JOHN.—"Maria Marten; or, The Red Barn."
MACNAMARA, GERALD.—"Sincerity."
MADDEN, TOM.—"The King of Dublin."
MACARDLE, DOROTHY M. C.—"Asthara."
MACLAREN, CAPT. JOHN.—"Fragments from France."
MAETERLINCK, MAURICE.—"The Burgomaster of Stilemonde."
MAHER, DONOVAN.—"After the Ball."
MALLESON, MILES.—"Maurice's Own Idea."
MANNERS, J. HARTLEY.—"Peg o' My Heart."
MANNING, BURTON.—"Little Miss Vanity."
MANNIX, J. J.—"A German Shell."
MANOUSSI, JEAN.—"The Purple Mask."
MARCIN, MAX.—"Cheating Cheaters," "Eye of Youth."
MARINETTE, F. T.—"A Moonbeam."
MARTIN, GEORGE HENRY.—"Rosette."
MARS, JEAN.—"The Marriage of Oberon."
MASSINE, LEONIDE.—"The Good-humoured Ladies," "The Midnight Sun."
MASSINGHAM, DOROTHY.—"Glass Houses."
MATHE, EDOUARD.—"As You Were."
MAURICE, IVY.—"Back to Blighty."
MAY, LIEUT. E. P.—"Alice in Sunderland."
MAUGHAM, W. SOMERSET.—"Love in a Cottage."
MAYNE, KATHLEEN.—"A Face from the Past."
MAYO, MARGARET.—"Be Careful Baby."
M'CARTHY, J. BERNARD.—"The Men in Possession," "The Romantic Lover."
McCARTHY, JUSTIN HUNTLY.—"Nurse Benson."
McEVOY, CHARLES.—"Her Ladyship."
McGHEE, THOMAS.—"The Ginger Girl."
McKENNA, ROSE S.—"Aliens."
McNULTY, EDWARD.—"The King of Dublin," "Mrs. Mulligan's Millions."
MELVILLE, WALTER.—"The Female Hun."
MERIVALE, BERNARD.—"Fancy Dress."
MILLER, MRS. W. J.—"Dante and Beatrice."
MILLS, CLIFFORD.—"Where the Rainbow Ends."
MILLS, MRS. CLIFFORD.—"The Luck of the Navy."
MILLS, PHILIP.—"Wanted—a Spy."
MILNE, A. A.—"The Boy Comes Home," "Belinda," "Make Believe."
MILLWARD, JOHN S.—"Betty Wakes Up."
MOLIERE.—"L'Amour Médecin."
MONTGOMERY, JAMES.—"Nothing but the Truth," "Going Up."
MORRIS, FRED J.—"The Stroke of Ten."
MORRIS, MICHAEL.—"Dear Sir,—Unless."
MORRISON, KENNETH.—"Lola," "Little Miss Modesty."
MORRISON, R. F.—"Carry On," "The Subduing of Maclean."
MORTIMER, LEONARD.—"The Black Book."
MORSHIEL, GEORGE S.—"Away from the Moss."
MORTON, MICHAEL.—"In the Night Watch."
MOYLAN, THOMAS KING. — "Movies," "Tactics."
MUDIE, WALTER.—"Rose Mary."
MULLORD, DOROTHY.—"Across the Sands of Time," "Married on Leave."
MURRAY, DOUGLAS.—"The Man from Toronto."
MURRAY, PROFESSOR GILBERT.—"The Trojan Women."
MURRAY, T. C.—"Spring."
MYDDLETON-MILES, A.—"Beware Germans," "What a Birthday."
MYLO, MLLE. JULIETTE. — "Loyer D'Olivette," "Yvette's Dilemma," "Pauv'Yette."
MYTTON, HUGH.—"Tanks."

NEPOTY, LUCIEN.—"In the Night Watch."
NESBITT, ROY.—"When Love Came Over the Hills."
NEWBERRY-CHOYCE, LIEUT. A.—"The Three Brothers."
NEWTON, H. CHANCE.—"A Celestial Bride."
NORMAN, E. B.—"Watson, Sherlock's Holmes."
NORMAN, MRS. GEORGE.—"The Call of the Road."
NOVELLO, IVOR.—"Tabs."
NOYES, WING-COMMANDER CHARLES F.—"The Bulldog Breed."
NORDSTROM, FRANCIS.—"All Wrong."

O'BRIEN, SEUMAS.—"Duty."
O'BYRNE, CATHAL.—"The Marryin' of Marget Bella."
O'CONNOR, JACK.—"Mayor for a Day."
O'HANLON, HENRY.—"The All Alone."
O'MAHONY, MICHAEL.—"The Corner Shop."
O'MALLEY, PATRICK.—"Come What May."
ORCZY, BARONESS.—"The Legion of Honour."

PAGE, AUSTIN.—"By Pigeon Post."
PARKER, ALFRED.—"Camouflage."
PARKER, AMOS.—"Princess Posy."
PARKER, LOUIS N.—"The Treasures of Britain," "The Pageant of Freedom," "The Pageant of Drury Lane Theatre, 1663-1918," "L'Aiglon" (The Eaglet).
PARNELL, WALLACE.—"All Dressed Up."
PARSONS, DONOVAN.—"The Girl in the Bath," "Is It Safe?"
PARSONS, TOM.—"Upside Down."
PAYNE, GILBERT.—"It's Topping."
PELHAM, PAUL.—"The Ginger Girl."
PEPPER, HARRY.—"An Old Clown's Idol."
PERCY, LODGE.—"His Good Angel," "For His Lady's Honour," "Her Second Chance," "Mother or Mistress."
PHILLPOTTS, EDEN.—"St. George and the Dragons," "Dante and Beatrice."
PILKINGTON, GEO. W.—"Crystals."
PINERO, SIR ARTHUR.—"The Freaks," "Monica's Blue Boy," "Mind-the-Paint-Girl."
PINK, WAL.—"Hotch-Potch," "Box o' Tricks," "Ocean Waves," "Happy-Go-Lucky."
PORTER, JESSIE.—"Betty at Bay."
POULBOT, FRANCISQUE.—"The Kiddies in the Ruins."
POWELL, DUDLEY.—"Hi-diddle-diddle."
PRICE, ADDISON.—"The Nuns of Ardboe."
PRICE, FRANK.—"The Girl from Canada."
PREVOST-BATTERSBY, CAPTAIN H. F.—"The Voice of Duty."
PROCTOR, C. VERNON.—"The Man Who Made Good," "The Profiteer," "The Plaything of an Hour."

QUILTER, ROGER.—"Where the Rainbow Ends."

RAMSEY, JOHN.—"Where the Rainbow Ends."
RAY, DICK.—"The Fisher Girl."
REILLY, ROBERT.—"Look Pleasant," "Hold Fast."
RELSIE, REGINALD.—"Is It Safe?"
RHODE, A. G.—"The Morals of Vanda."
RICHARDSON, OLIVE.—"The Fairy of the Well."
RIMSKY-KORSAKOFF, N.—"Le Coq d'Or," "The Midnight Sun."
RIP.—"As You Were."
ROBINSON, JEROLD.—"After the Ball."
ROBINSON, LENNOX.—"The Lost Leader."
ROBINSON, SNELL.—"Certificates."
ROBSON, MAISIE.—"Betty Wakes Up."

REAN, CLIFFORD.—"A Son of the Sea," "On Leave for His Wedding," "The Voice on the 'Phone," "When the Joy Bells Are Ringing," "Duty! and the Girl," "The Girl Who Changed Her Mind," "Tainted Goods," "Ignorance."
ROLLIT, GEORGE.—"Switch No. 7," "Money for Nothing."
ROMBEAU, S.—"Soldier Boy."
ROSE, EDWARD E.—"Little Lost Sister."
ROSEBERY, ARTHUR.—"Real Sports."
ROSSETTI, DANTE GABRIEL.—"Rose Mary."
ROSTAND, EDMOND.—"L'Aiglon" (The Eaglet).
ROVETTA, GEROLAMO.—"Romanticismo."
ROWLANDS, GEORGE.—"Boy Wanted."
RUBINSTEIN, H. F.—"The Earlier Works of Sir Roger Athelstane."
RULE, HERBERT.—"Little Miss Vanity."
RUSK, J. WILKIE.—"The Harbury Pearls."

SALTER, JAMES.—"Boy Wanted."
SALTOUN, WALTER.—"The Man She Bought," "The Serpent in the Garden," renamed "A Married Man's Sweetheart."
SANKEY, CECIL.—"High Pressure."
SARGENT, HERBERT C.—"Look Pleasant," "Ocean Waves," "Birds of Paradise."
SCARLATTI, DOMENICO.—"The Good-Humoured Ladies."
SAUNDERS, GERTRUDE M.—"John the Stoic."
SCHRIER, HENRIETTA.—"His Good Angel," "For His Lady's Honour," "Her Second Chance," "Mother or Mistress."
SCOTT, HAROLD.—"Dabchick, M.P."
SEDGEBEER, BERT.—"Devonshire Cream."
SELBIT, P. T.—"Oh, Doctor!" "Fragments," "Flashlights."
SELWYN, EDGAR.—"The Naughty Wife."
SETON, HENRY.—"The Absent-Minded Husband," "The Hon. Gertrude."
SETTIMELLI, EMILIO.—"Passatismo."
SEXTON, JAMES.—"The Corner Shop."
SHAW, GEORGE.—"Boy Wanted."
SHELLEY, HERBERT.—"My Aunt from New York."
SHIRLEY, ARTHUR.—"Khaki and Klogs," "Jolly Jack Tar."
SHORTLAND, KINGSFORD.—"Betty Wakes Up."
SLEE, NORMAN.—"Violette."
SMITH, BRUCE.—"An Old Clown's Idol."
SMITH, CLAY.—"Us."
SMITH, HARRY B.—"The Lilac Domino."
SMITH, JANE.—"Crystals."
SMURTHWAITE, JEANIE.—"Yuletide Tales of Tommy Toddles."
SOLANO, CAPTAIN E. J.—"Salvage."
SOLOMON, JESSICA.—"Below Street Level."
ST. AUBYN, J.—"The Domestic Agency."
SPENCER, DENTON.—"The Yellow Spider," "Settling Day."
STACK, KINGSTON.—"Kitty Breaks Loose."
STAMPER, DAVE.—"Box o' Tricks."
STANFORD, WYBERT.—"Just My Luck."
STANLEY, HORACE.—"Parted at the Church," "Jim Mason, Minesweeper."
STANLEY, J. AUBREY.—"Stone Ginger."
STANLEY, LEEDHAM.—"After Dinner," "Plum and Apple."
STEPHENS, GEORGE A.—"Flashlights."
STEPHENS, H. P.—"The Red Hussar."
STEPHENS, WILFRED.—"The Yellow Cockade."
STEVENS, H. C. GILBARD.—"In the Light of Day."
STEWART, J. B.—"The Soul's Awakening."
STILES, LESLIE.—"Lavender."
STORR, MARGUERITE.—"Three Months."
SULLIVAN, SIR ARTHUR.—"H.M.S. Pinafore."
SUTRO, ALFRED.—"The Trap," "The Two Miss Farndons."

SYKES, PERCIVAL H. T.—"The Cry of the Children."
SYMONS, ARTHUR.—"The Dead City."
SYNGE, JOHN MILLINGTON,—"The Playboy of the Western World."

TAGORE, SIR RABINDRANATH.—"Sacrifice."
TATE, JAS. W.—"The Passing Show of 1918," "Any Lady."
TAYLOR, E. J.—"The Demon's Pawn."
TAYLOR, MRS. EMILY.—"Liza."
TAYLOR, RITA BROMLEY.—"Lift, Sir?"
TCHEKOFF, ANTON.—"The Proposal."
TERRY, J. E. HAROLD.—"Master Wayfarer."
THAYER, PATRICK.—"The Girl in the Bath," "Tabs," "Birds of Paradise."
THOMAS, BRANDON.—"Charley's Aunt."
THOMAS, EVELYN.—"Roses of Picardy."
THOMAS, HERBERT.—"Out of Hell," "Lady Emma's Romance," "Stopping the Breach," "Sinners Both."
THOMAS, VINCENT.—"H.M.S. 'Victorious.'"
THOMPSON, FRED.—"The Bing Boys on Broadway."
THORNLEY-DODGE, E.—"Swiss V. Robinson," "Nibs."
TIERNEY, LOUIS A.—"The Demon's Pawn."
TITHERADGE, DION.—"A Wife's Dilemma," "The K.C.," "Something to His Advantage."
TOMMASINI, VINCENZO. — "The Good-humoured Ladies."
TREMAYNE, W. A.—"The McTaggart," "The Alien."
TURNER, EDWIN.—"Devonshire Cream."
TURNER, JOHN HASTINGS.—"Tails Up," "Hullo! America."
TWINN, SYDNEY.—"Lights Out."

UNWIN, A. C.—"Stone Ginger."

VALENTINE.—"The Passing Show of 1918."
VASEY, WILL.—"The Dog Show."
VEBER, PIERRE.—"The Profiteers."
VERHAEREN, EMILE.—"Philip II."
VERNON, HARRY M.—"The Bing Boys on Broadway."
VOUSDEN, ERNEST.—"Real Sports."

WALKER, SYD.—"Hi-diddle-diddle."
WALLACE, EDGAR.—"Soldier Boy."
WALPOLE, HUGH.—"Robin's Father."
WALTER, EUGENE.—"The Knife."
WALSH, SHEILA.—"When Our Lads Come Marching Home."
WARR, JOHN.—"Maid of the South."
WARREN, F. BROOKE.—"The Spendthrift."
WATSON, MARY.—"Is It Safe?"
WEBB, MILTON.—"The Girl."
WEIGALL, A.—"Pan Laughs."
WEST, JULIUS.—"The Proposal."
WESTON, R. P.—"Rations," "Any Lady," "Ciro's Frolics," "Us," "Crystals."
WESTON-HILL, J.—"Oh Doctor!"
WIBROW, CHARLES.—"Valentine."
WILDE, OSCAR.—"Salomé."
WILLIAMSON, MAUD.—"The Home Wreckers."
WILSON, ARTHUR.—"One of the Birds."
WILSON, A. PATRICK.—"The Wooing o' Janet," "Old Down and Out," "His Dearest Wish," "After Dinner," "Plum and Apple."
WIMPERIS, ARTHUR.—"As You Were," "Buzz! Buzz!!"
WISKIN, GERTRUDE E.—"And Afterwards—A Peace Time Warning."
WITMARK, ISIDOR.—"Shanghai."
WOOD, ARTHUR.—"Petticoat Fair."
WODEHOUSE, P. G.—"Oh! Joy."
WOODERSON, FLORENCE.—"The Fairy of the Well."
WRIGHT, HUGH E.—"Bert and 'Erb," "Tails Up."
WRIGHT, LAWRENCE.—"Camouflage."
WYLIE, LAURI.—"The Passing Show of 1918," "Shanghai."
WYNNE, ESME.—"Woman and Whisky."

YOUNG, RIDA JOHNSON.—"Lot 79," "Soldier Boy."

ZANGWILL, ISRAEL.—"Too Much Money."
ZILLWOOD, LEILA.—"His Australian Wife."
ZILLWOOD, RUTH A.—"The End of the Trail."

ROLL OF HONOUR.—KILLED IN THE WAR.

Addison, Lieutenant George. August 9. Was mortally wounded August 9, and expired a few hours later, in Italy. A nephew of Mrs. F. G. Kimberley. Before enlisting he was showing great promise as an actor in Mrs. Kimberley's plays.

Barrie, K. Scott (Corporal Woolhouse). October. Concert party, France.

Batt, Gunner H. (Harold Batt). November 9. Died of pneumonia in the Military Hospital, Aldershot.

Bartlett, Albert Domett. Aged 28. Killed in action between March 21 and 28. As "The Voyses," he and his wife, Miss Rita Morville, toured with their vocal scena, "A Naval Engagement."

Bennett, Bandsman P. August. From wounds, in Italy. He was a talented clarinet player, and formerly occupied a position in Midland theatre orchestras. He was the son of the late Mr. A. Bennett, for many years trombone player at the Empire, Birmingham.

Bovill, Lieutenant Charles H. Died from wounds. Having eventually been classed as unfit for active service, he was entrusted with the organisation of entertainments at the Front. Although nothing definite is known on the subject, it is believed that he met his death through the bursting of a shell while rehearsing a party of soldiers in a revue written by himself. The deceased, who was highly popular in theatrical and variety circles, and had already made his mark as a writer of witty and polished lyrics and in other forms of humorous writing for the stage, had held a commission in the Coldstream Guards since 1916. He was the son of Major C. E. Bovill, of the Inniskillings, and was born at Coonoor, in India, on September 28, 1878. Among his best-known work are the lyrics for "Come Inside," at the Empire in 1909, and "Peggy," at the Gaiety, in 1911. He was the author (with George Grossmith) of "Everybody's Doing It," at the Empire in 1912; "The Dancing Viennese," at the London Coliseum in 1912; "The Sleeping Beauty" (with George R. Sims), at Drury Lane in 1912; "All the Winners," at the Empire in 1913; and "The Gay Lothario," at the Empire in 1913. He was also concerned, of course, with several popular pieces produced in more recent years at the London Pavilion, the Palace, the Alhambra, and other well-known houses. He was educated at Bedford Grammar School, and was formerly in the Civil Service.

Brannigan, Desmond. August 1. Killed in action in France. Previously to 1915, when he joined the London Scottish, he was leading man in the Esme Percy-Kirsteen Graeme repertory company, and before that he had acted in Miss Hornlman's company and with the Ulster Players.

Calhaen, Lionel, the youngest son of the late Stanislaus Calhaen. Killed in the third Battle of Ypres. He joined up in 1914.

Campkin, Second Lieutenant Reginald E. March 28. Was killed in action. Reg. Campkin was one of those clever young men whom Mr. Oswald Stoll gathered about him in his offices at the Coliseum. He had a great enthusiasm for the theatre, and when Mr. Stoll opened the Chiswick Empire Campkin was installed as assistant-manager. After a considerable period in Western London, he went North as manager of the Queen's, South Shields, subsequently engaging in agency work, and more recently he was lessee of the Empire, Whitehaven. Campkin returned to London to join up, and in February, 1917, he was accepted by the Artists' Rifles. He received his commission in November in the 4th London Regiment.

Carrick, Private Tom E. April 25. Killed in action on April 25. Late acting-manager of the Alhambra, Barnsley, and formerly of the Empire Palace, Barnsley, and Opera House, Scarborough.

Castle, Vernon. In the United States from a flying accident. He had seen service in the Royal Flying Corps in France.

Chasemore, F. E. (Frank Eaglesfield). October 29. Of pneumonia at Alexandria, Egypt.

Chiswell, Sergeant Melville. March 25. Killed in action. He was 32 years of age, and enlisted in the Cheshires in 1916. He went to the front on March 20, and was with the special draft chosen to hold the line. He was killed five days after arriving at the front. Sergeant Chiswell was for several years a leading member of the Raynor Repertory company, and had appeared in Shakespearean revivals under the banner of the late Richard Flanagan at Manchester.

Clifford, Bert. October 28. In France, from pneumonia. He belonged to the 17th Royal Sussex Regiment, having served in France since 1915. He was a member of the late Geo. Edwardes's companies for several years.

Cotterell, Hal (M. Rivkin). April 5. Killed in action.

Donovan, Lance-Corporal Edward, D.C.M., C.O.M. June 18.

Downs, Private Will. July 3. Of pneumonia, while on leave.

Edis, Lieutenant Owen. April. Killed in action, while leading his men. Before joining the Colours he was a member of Miss Florence Glossop Harris's Shakespearean company.

Greensmith, Lance-Corporal G. W. (W. H. Rex). Aged 34. June 2.

Heyel, Private Alfred R. (Al. Kegan). October 22, 1917. (Reported as missing since then; later reported killed.)

Hiatt, Sergeant E. W. Aged 31. April 17. He joined the Army in 1915.

Houghton, Second Lieutenant George. August 26. 12th West Yorks Regiment. Killed in action. He will be remembered as co-partner of the firm of Ambro and Houghton, Kursaal, Whitley Bay, and various touring companies.

Jackson, Will. February. Had appeared in "Bunty Pulls the Strings" and "A Scrape of the Pen."

Johnson, Walter Edward. September 29. At Tooting Hospital. Late of Melville companies and World Tour, Horace Goldin.

Keriston, Wilfred. September 29. 1st Middlesex Regiment. Late of the Graeme-Percy repertory company.

King, Second Lieutenant Norman, the Irish Guards. May 26. From wounds received in action the previous day.

Lax, Second Lieutenant Donald. November. Durham Light Infantry. Killed in action. He was formerly a member of the Dardini Troupe.

Le Couriek, Rupert. August 23. One time a popular member of the Benson company, whom he joined in 1910, when he arrived in England from Australia. He joined up at the outbreak of war. He went to France with the K.E.H., and was sent back in August, 1917, when so many cavalry units were turned over to other units. He went out again with the Northumberland Fusiliers, and was put into the Tanks. On August 23 his tank was hit three times, and he was wounded. The tank then caught fire, but all got out. However, he and his officer were too badly wounded to get away, and the Germans shot them.

Matheson, Lieutenant Herbert. March 24. Was killed in action in France. To the general public he will be remembered for his series of popular songs, written under the nom de guerre of Herbert Mackenzie. His most popular song was undoubtedly "The Trail that Leads to Home," which he wrote as a companion song to "The Long, Long Trail." For over four years he was musical adviser to Messrs. West and Co.

Maxwell, Guy (Lieutenant J. J. Woods). September. In India, whilst on active service. Professionally known originally as Johnnie Woods, and later as Guy Maxwell. Before he joined the Colours Mr. Maxwell was connected with several of Harry Day's revues, including "Excuse Me," "Hullo! Everybody," and "Business as Usual."

Moffat, Sanderson. January 1. He went through the thick of it with his regiment, the South Staffords, until he was finally discharged as unfit in September, 1917, suffering from the effects of enemy gas. Three operations were performed on his throat, where cancer had set in, but without avail, and he passed away at his residence on the first day of 1918. Sanderson Moffat had a long and varied experience on the stage. Beginning in his teens in stock at the Princess, Glasgow, he afterwards joined Ethel Arden, and then went playing leads with the late William Mollison. Following upon several years' touring with his own company came a long run of leading parts at Sadler's Wells, where he proved a great favourite. In later years he created the part of Dan Burrell (the Policeman) in his brother Graham Moffat's famous play "Bunty," and left that to go to America to play the part of Weelum in the New York production of the same play. While in America he also played with the late Lewis Waller. Shortly before the outbreak of the war Sanderson Moffat, together with his brother, Watson Hume Moffat, formed a partnership for the presentation of Scottish plays, among others being the successful "Bauldy."

Mott, Charles. May 22. Died of wounds. He joined the Army in the middle of 1917, and was a lance-corporal in the Artists' Rifles at the time of his death. For several seasons Mr. Mott was a member of operatic companies.

Murray, Lieutenant Arthur. Aged 24. August 8. Killed in action in France. Lieutenant Murray joined the Artists' Rifles on November 16, 1916, gained his commission in March, 1917, and was posted to the 3rd Royal Sussex Regiment, being transferred to the 7th R.S. Regiment in April, 1918. Before joining up Lieutenant Murray played on tour with "A Little Bit of Fluff," "The Land of Promise," and "Diplomacy," also playing at the London Opera House in "Charley's Aunt" the part of Charley.

Newcomb, Sergeant Charles. November 9. 10th London Regiment. Late of Burnaby and Newcomb, comedy duo.

Parker, Charles B. October 20. Was killed in action. He was for some years with Mr. Harrison at the Haymarket, had been under Mr. C. B. Cochran's management, and had assisted his father, Mr. Frank Parker, in a number of his productions.

Payne, Norman. September 13. Killed in action in France.

Pelwar, Robert (Private H. F. Odell). August 21. Killed in action.

Peever, Corporal George. November 20. After a brief illness from dysentery. A popular actor in Ireland before the war, he was understudy for Mr. W. L. Dobell, and played leading parts with him for four years. His performance of Douglas Cattermole will be remembered.

Penny, Al. August 14. At the Military Hospital, Lincoln, from complications arising from wounds received on active service. He was at one time known as the double-voiced coon, and had played with the New York Nippers, Elliot Chocolate Coloured Coons, and David Bliss's "What a Game!" revue, and worked for some time as a single turn. He joined up in 1916, and attained the rank of sergeant in the 3rd South Lancs. He was wounded at Ypres and discharged in January, 1918. Since May he had been working the halls again.

Pollack, Trooper Maurice. October. From wounds received in action. He was an accomplished child actor, best known perhaps as Little Lord Fauntleroy, in which he first appeared at the Grand, Birmingham, under the régime of the late J. W. Turner.

Porter, Private George Leslie. August. From wounds.

Regent, Victor (Victor Holland). Aged 22. March 25. Killed in action. Late Comédie Anglaise Company.

Smith, Lieutenant Sydney G. (Roy G. Sydney). July 26. Accidentally killed on active service.

Taylor, E. S. Sedley. June 9. From consumption brought on by exposure in the firing line. Son of the late Rev. John Gleig Taylor, Minor Canon and Succentor of Hereford Cathedral. For some time he was a member of the Benson's company, and when the war began was with Mr. Granville Barker.

Tomkins, Private Wilfred. Aged 20. October. Devonshire Regiment. Killed in action. He was formerly an acrobat on the vaudeville stage, and also travelled largely in France.

Underhill, Charles (Chowey Thorne). October 23. Killed on the Western Front by shell. Formerly Alexander Marsh company and "When Knights Were Bold" company.

White, Corporal Richard Nelson. October 5. Late of Mr. George Dance's company. He was stationed near an advanced dressing station. He had a duty to perform, and would not be stopped by the shelling, and was hit on the way in the execution of his duty.

OBITUARY.

[THE NAMES OF ACTORS WHO HAVE BEEN KILLED IN THE WAR WILL BE FOUND UNDER THE HEADING "ROLL OF HONOUR."]

Abingdon, W. L. Aged 59. May 17.
Abbott, Rev. W. D., at Dieppe. December.
Alexander, Sir George. Aged 59. March 16.
Anderson, Harry. February.
Andrews, Madge. December 6.
Armytage, Bessie (Bridget Connolly). May 22.
Arthur, George (Arthur George Mack). Aged 44. February 27.
Ashcroft, W. J. Aged 73. January 2.
Austin, Samuel Horatio. Aged 62. January 31.

Baddeley, Cyril Clinton. May 9.
Baines, Florence (Mrs. Albert C. Beattie). Aged 41. December 30.
Barnsley, Tom. July 11.
Barry, Bob. November 14.
Beaumont, Lily. October 7.
Bedford, Harry. March 29.
Bennett, H. G., Dudley. Aged 52. October 16.
Berry, James. December.
Blythe, J. S. November 23.
Boddy, Edward. April 30.
Bolton, Fred. October 31.
Bonnie, Beatrice (Mrs. Will Stylo). October 27.
Beadell, Alfred Thomas. December 2.
Brett, Harry. June.
Brooklyn, Sam. Aged 71. January 19.
Brown, N. Robert (" Buster "). January 30.
Browning, Bonny. September 15.
Bu Val. September 24.
Burge, Dick. Aged 53. March 15.

Caffyn, Laura. November 10.
Carleton, Billie (Florence Leonora Stewart). Aged 22. November 28.
Carlile, Frank. April 26.
Carter, Herbert. November 12.
Carton, Felicia (Alice Happy Butler). Aged 31. October 29.
Channing, Theo. September 29.
Charles, Trevor. August 25.
Chung Ling Soo (Williams Elsworth Robinson). Aged 57. March 23.
Cinquevalli, Paul. Aged 59. July 14.
Collingwood Caird, Hersilia Florence. November 27.
Compton, Edward. Aged 64. July 16.
Conway, Alec. July 14.
Cooke, J. Y. F. January 20.
Cooper, Frank Kemble. Aged 62. December 27.
Cooper, George. November 17.
Coveney, George Howard. Aged 60. May 20.
Coventry, Charles. May 13.
Coventry, Lucy. May 29.
Cowie, A. C. (Stanton Ketchell). October 30.
Cragg, Billy. October 9.
Cresswell, Mary A. (Grace). November 30.
Cross, Victoria. July 28.

Dacre, Henry S. July 13.
Davey, H. B. December.
Delaine, Jack. November 25.
Debussy, Claude.
Dickson, Walter. April 23.

Entwistle, Ethel. November 29.
Evelyn, Mrs. Herbert (Leslie Warner). July 18.
Eversleigh, Clara (Mrs. Edward Trevanion). October 20.

Fairbairn, George. Aged 54. March 3.
Flint, Mrs. Margaret (Quilliam). May 5.
Ffrangcon-Davies, David. Aged 67. April.
Ford, Mrs. Lena Guilbert. March 7.
Fozard, John W. July 25.
French, Marie (Mrs. W. H. Kiddie). January 4.

Gallagher, Beatrice Minnie. November 21.
Gardner, W. M. Aged 38. August 20.
Glyde, Ethel. October 25.
Godwin, Harold, in Canada. January.
Gold, Ben. October 20.
Gordon, Sydney (Sydney William Stuart). December 6.
Gould, Fred. Aged 76. December 30.
Grady, Alfred. February 12.
Graham, Mamie (Ethel Nixon). November

Hamilton, Henry. September 4.
Haslam, René. October 25.
Haydon, Florence. Aged 80. July 21.
Hayes, F. W. September 7.
Hill, Francis. July 16.
Hemsley, Violet Margaret. Aged 16. March 29.
Hemsley, W. T. Aged 68. February 8.
Heron, James. November 2.
Higham, Fred. Aged 63. January 10.
Hilland, Frederick Parkinson. June 14.
Horne, the Rev. Thomas. Aged 68. July.
Howard, Victor. July 26.
Hudson, Eric. Aged 56. October 4.
Hutchinson, James George. July.
Hutchison, William Douglas. August 21.

Imeson, George I. September.
Inch, Minnie. July 23.

Johnson, Chas. W. November 11.

Kibble, Billie. October 24.
Kneller, Zettie. Aged 22. October 29.

Langton, J. D. November 7.
Lecocq, Charles. Aged 86. October 24.
Le Ray, Mme. Elizabeth. June 16.
Lehmann, Mme. Liza. September 19.
"Little Tony." Aged 48. January.
Leigh-Vallas, Evelyn Maud (Cicely Gilbert) October 9.
Longden, Charles H. Aged 63. August 11.
Lukos, Alex. April.
Lynn, Harry. June 8.

MacCabe, James. August 18.
Macfarlane, Jack. December 13.
Maltby, Captain Tom. Aged 70. October 2.
Mannon, Charles H. April 1.
Mayeur, Eugene. January 26.
Mayne, Will. Aged 48. December 1.
Marriott, Hetty (Mrs. Barrett Stewart). August 30.
Middlemas, Henry. March 7.
Milton, Arthur, "Milton Rays" (William James Lunt). Aged 61. November 23.
Mitchell, Charlie. April 2.
Mitchell, Cooper. Aged 37. January 20.
Mudje, George. Aged 59. December 28.
Mulvaney, Constance. Aged 16. June 22.
Murphy, Mrs. Frank (Nellie Clifford). August 28.

Nella, John Edward (Allen). Aged 44. September 5.
Nelson, Thomas Young. June 16.
Nicholls, Norman. October 18.

Ohnet, Georges. Aged 70. May 6.

Paley, John. January 5
Pareezer, Barnett. Aged 59. August 22.
Parker, Florence. Aged 47. October 13.
Parker, Frank. October 24.
Parry, Sir Hubert. Aged 70. October 7.
Phelps, Stella (Estelle Madeleine Osbaldestone). August 28.
Playfair, Arthur. Aged 49. August 28.
Poole, Charles William. Aged 60. March 12.

Quilliam, Madge. May 6

Randle, Percy E. Aged 28. June 19.
Ray, Phil. Aged 46. December 8.
Read, Corporal Jennings November 0.
Reynolds, Charles. Aged 69. March.
Robbins, Herbert. November 25.
Rollason, Marion. November 10.
Romah, Lou. November 20.
Rostand, Edmond. Aged 50. December 2.
Russell, J. O. October 18.

Scarisbrick, C. J Aged 41. January 24.

Scarisbrick, Thomas. May 19.
Shelley, Evelyn. November 20.
Sheridan, Mark. Aged 41. January 15.
Sinclair, Olive. November 19.
Southern, Fred (Cornwell). November 12.
Sprange, Adnam. May.
Stanton, Alfred. Aged 73. October 26.
Stevenson, Esther. November 10.
Stewart, L. M. June.
Storri, Sadrene. April.
Stratford, Frederick G. Aged 53. December 1.
Stratton, Eugene. Aged 57. September 15.
Stuart, Winifred (Mrs. Edwards). October 19.
Subtel, Walter. Aged 37. October 21.
Sudlow, A. V. October 18.
Swanton, Mrs. Mary. Aged 76. December.

Talbot, Alice (Mrs. E. H. Knight). July 3.
Talboys, T. A. Aged 59. February 9.
Thornton, Frank. Aged 74. December 18.
Thornton, Harry. October 19.
Towers, John. Aged 76. January 3.
Tozer, Sir Henry. Aged 67. April 26.
Turner, Alfred Ruddall. Aged 29. December 20
Tyars, Frank. Aged 70. May 11.
Tyrer, Jimmy. Aged 24. November 28.

Vento, Lillie. Aged 52. August 31.
Verdi, Ruby (Mrs. Ben Albert). December 17.
Vince, Colin. December 3.
Vyner, Robert George. July 31.

Wain, Ivy. May 12.
Wake, Richard. March
Wakley, Ronald F. April 9.
Walsh, Minnie (Mrs. Frank Moore). Aged 35. October 23.
Watts, C. F. J. May 5.
Westwood, W. H. April 26.
Whitby, Ethel. November 15.
Wilson, Stanley. November 3.
Woodger, Ben. August 23.
Woods, Graham. March 11.
Warlow, Percy. March 7.
Woolf, Jack. March 20

Yelding, Harry. Aged 50. September 4.
Yuill, Will. February.
Young, T. B. January 12.

THE AMERICAN STAGE.

PRINCIPAL PLAYS PRODUCED IN AMERICA, AND IMPORTANT REVIVALS IN NEW YORK BETWEEN DECEMBER 1, 1917, AND NOVEMBER 30, 1918.

In cases where pieces have been acted previously to presentation in New York the casts given are those of the New York productions.

AFTERMATH, THE, war playlet, presented by Miss Ethel Clifton and company.—Palace, New York, October 28.

ALIEN, THE, melodrama, by W. A. Tremayne. (Produced in England at the Royal Court, Warrington, November 11).—His Majesty's, Montreal, June 3.

ALLEGIANCE, war play, in three acts, by Prince and Princess Troubetzkoy (Amelie Rives).—Maxine Elliott, New York, August 1.

Mr. Hartmann	Carl Sauerman
Karl Hartmann	Carl Anthony
Max Hartmann	Charles Meredith
Elisa Hartmann	Blanche Yurka
Albert Perry	Charles Hampden
Anna Perry	Evelyn Varden
Count von Geier	Harrison Hunter
Billy Elton	Charles Laite
Gottlieb	Charles Kraus
Minna	Margery Lytle
Karlchen	William Read, Jun.

AN AMERICAN ACE, play, in four acts and twelve scenes, by Lincoln J. Carter, produced by Al. H. Woods.—Casino, New York, April 2.

Mrs. Darrow	Camilla Crume
Kate Darrow	Edna Leslie
George Darrow	Joseph McManus
Philip Drake	James L. Crane
Colonel Frank Stace	Robert Fischer
Harry Whitmer	James Dyrenforth
Fritz Mueller	Arthur Klein
Mailman	Henry Dawson
Doctor Mueller	Claude H. Cooper
Rose Matern	Sue MacManamy
Mrs. Noe	Kate Blair
Mr. Noe	Frank Harriman
Claudius Noe	Marcy Breuer
Rev. Dr. Saphore	George E. Murphy
Lieut. Hermancier	Charles Martin
Col. Luffenberg	True S. James
Victor Belois	Richard Barrows
Mariel Dandoy	Marion Coakley
Monsieur Dandoy	Harry Jackson
Sergeant	Claude Peyton
Col. Dodd Beane	David Landau
Lieut. Frank Upham	John Blake
First Soldier	Jimmy McCann
Second Soldier	William C. Loyd
Bomb Thrower	Harry D. Mack
Joe	Harvey Carter
Davis	Joe Bird
Tucker	Charlie Blair
Belgian Woman	Alice May

AN IDEAL HUSBAND, comedy, in four acts, by Oscar Wilde. (Produced in London at the Haymarket, January 3, 1895; presented in New York by the Students of the American Academy of Dramatic Arts and Empire Theatre Dramatic School at the Lyceum, March 10, 1916).—Comedy, New York, September 16.

Lady Chiltern	Beatrice Beckley
Mrs. Marchmont	Elizabeth Deimel
Lady Basildon	Merle Maddern
Vicomte de Nanjac	George Hayes
Lady Jane Barford	Dorothy Clay
The Earl of Caversham	Cyril Harcourt
Mr. Montford	S. V. Phillips
Mabel Chiltern	Gretchen Yates
Lady Markby	Alice Angarde Butler
Mrs. Cheveley	Constance Collier
Count Strelic	Vincent Sartor
Sir Robert Chiltern	Norman Trevor
Lord Goring	Julian L'Estrange
Phipps	Henry Crocker
Mason	Alfred Helton

AN ORIENTAL BREEZE, musical sketch.—Harlem Opera House, New York, August 26.

ANOTHER MAN'S SHOES, comedy, in three acts, by Laura Hinkley and Mabel Ferris, based upon a story by Miss Hinkley, presented by Frederick McKay.—Northampton Mass., October 18, 1914; Thirty-ninth Street, New York, September 12.

Dick	Lionel Atwill
Miss Podmore	Ethel Wilson
Mrs. Wolfe	Lucia Moore
Anne	Carol Lloyd
Hughes	Paul Porter
Dora (Mrs. Craven)	Elsie Mackay
Dr. Worrall	George Backus
Slade (alias Crouse)	Richard Taber
Mr. Wolfe	Aubrey Beattie
Dawson	Erville Alderson
Miles	Cyril Raymond
Mrs. Milson	Gilda Leary

APRIL, comedy, in three acts, by Hubert Osborne.—Punch and Judy, New York, April 6.

The Woman	Pauline Lord
Her Husband	Mitchell Harris
Her Son	Jay Strong
Her Daughter	Margalo Gillmore
Her Father	Burr Caruth
Her Mother	Mrs. Jaques Martin
Her Friend	Julie Herne
Her Neighbour's Boy	Gordon Morris
Her Husband's Wife	Francesca Rotoli
The Strange Gentleman	Charles Hopkins

April (cont.).

A Very Rich Man .... Alphonz Ethir
His Son .... France Bendtsen
His Son's Friend .... Charles Meredith
His Footmen .. Robert Morton, Frederick Macdonald

ARABIAN NIGHTS, THE, drama, adapted by Owen Davis from tales of "The Arabian Nights." Produced by Arthur Hopkins.—Colonial, Boston, December 12, 1917.

ARMY WITH BANNERS, THE, comedy, in five acts, by Charles Rann Kennedy.—Vieux Colombier, New York, April 9.
Mary Bliss .... Edith Wynne Matthison
Julia Manners .... Adrienne Morrison
Job Limp .... Wallace Erskine
Timothy Hodge .... Edmund Gurney
Tommy Trail .... Ernest Anderson
Pomeroy Wragg .... Walter Kingsford
Dafty .... Henry Herbert

ART'S REJUVENATION, musical play, in one act, by Kenneth and Roy Webb. Presented by the Actors and Authors' Theatre.—Fulton, New York, June 10.

ASK DAD, musical play, book and lyrics by Guy Bolton and P. G. Wodehouse, music by Louis Hirsch.—Royal Alexandra, Toronto, November 5.

AWAKENING, THE, love drama, in epilogue and three acts, by Ruth Sawyer, presented by the Tamar and Sabinoff Company, Inc., under the direction of Jacques Coini.—Criterion, New York, October 2.
Prince Alexis .... Wilton Lackaye
Makhail Sabinoff .... Theodore Kosloff
Ivan Feodorovitch Tcherkasky
                               Henry B. Walthall
Rupert Leighton .... Leonard Willey
Roger Penfield .... Oscar G. Briggs
Lucien Thibaut .... Howard Boulden
Charles Saurel .... Edwin Beryl
Louis Le Clerc .... Harry Sothern
Maurice De Brissac .... Bennett Kilpack
Fitzgerald .... Frederick Walter
Zametoff .... Luray Butler
General Petain .... G. H. Moore
Pierre .... Master Charles Eaton
Sergei .... Harry Sothern
Flora Tamar .... Khyva St. Albans
Princess Maria Alexandrovna....Gilda Varess
Mrs. Lewiston .... Laura Burt
Sybil Lewiston .... Shirley Carter
Louise Saurel .... Agnes Ruge
Vigee Delvair .... Betty Prescott
Clarice .... Mary L. Wilson

BACK AGAIN, musical comedy, in two acts, by George V. Hobart and Frank Stammers, lyrics by Louis A. Hirsch.—Chestnut Street Opera House, Philadelphia, April 29.

BACK TO EARTH, play, by William Lee Baron. Produced by Charles Dillingham.—National, Washington, November 25.

BARRIER, THE, playlet, by Tom Barry. Played by Helen Ware.—Palace, New York, April 29.

BE CALM, CAMILLA, comedy, in two acts and four scenes, by Clare Kummer. Produced by Arthur Hopkins.—Booth, New York, October 31.
Junius Patterson .... Walter Hampden
Baxter Poll .... Rex McDougall
Gus Beals .... Arthur Shaw
McNeil Brownlow .... William Sampson
Jo Gibbons .... Harold Salter
Bill Slattery .... John J. Harris
Celia Brooke .... Carlotta Monterey
Alma Robins .... Hedda Hopper
Camilla Hathaway .... Lola Fisher

BEAUTIFUL LEGEND OF POKEY; or, THE AMOROUS INDIAN, play, by Philip Moeller. Presented by the Washington Square Players.—Comedy, New York, January 23

BELINDA, comedy, in three acts, by A. A. Milne (produced in London at the New, April 8).—Empire, New York, May 6.
Belinda Barrington .... Ethel Barrymore
Delia .... Eva Le Gallienne
Harold Baxter .... E. Lyall Swete
Claude Devenish .... Richard Hatteras
John Barrington .... Cyril Keightley
Betty .... Clara T. Bracy

BEST SELLERS, THE, play, by Kenneth and Roy Webb. Presented by the Actors and Authors' Theatre.—Fulton, New York, June 10.

BETTER 'OLE, THE, by Bruce Bairnsfather and Arthur Eliot, music by Herman Darewski, lyrics by James Hurd (Produced in London at the Oxford, August 4, 1917).—Greenwich Village, New York, October 19.

BETROTHED, THE, play, in three acts, and twelve scenes, by Maurice Maeterlinck, translated by Alexander Taixeira de Mattos.—Shubert, New York, November 18.
Tyltyl .... Reggie Sheffield
The Fairy Berylune .... Mrs. Jacques Martin
Milette .... Boots Wooster
Belline .... Winifred Lenihan
Jalline .... Gladys George
Aimette .... May Collins
Roselle .... June Walker
Rosarelle .... Flora Sheffield
Destiny .... Maurice Cass
The Veiled Figure .... Theresa Duncan
The Miser .... Cecil Yapp
Light .... Edith Wynne Matthison
Granny Tyl .... Inda Palmer
Gaffer Tyl .... Wallis Clark
The Great Ancestor .... Augustin Duncan
The Great Peasant .... Henry Carvill
The Great Mendicant .... Elwyn Eaton
The Rich Ancestor .... Allen Thomas
The Sick Ancestor .... Barry Macollum
The Drunken Ancestor ...... Claude Cooper
The Murderer Ancestor .... Georges Du Bois
The Littlest Child .... Ivy Ward
The Last Born .... George Wolcott
Mummy Tyl .... Ethel Brandon
Myltyl .... Betty Hilburne
Daddy Tyl .... Henry Travers
Neighbour Berlingot .. Mrs. Jacques Martin
Joy Berlingot .... Sylvia Field
Other characters were four of Tyltyl's children: eleven grandchildren, and nine great grandchildren.

BETWEEN TRAINS, comedy playlet.—Harlem Opera House, New York, September 23.

BIG CHANCE, THE, play, in three acts, by Willard Mack and Grant Morris.—Shubert, New Haven, September 13; 48th Street, New York, October 28.
Bertie Thorndyke .... Willard Mack
Mrs. Malloy .... Anna Berlein
Margaret Malloy
                Katharine Harris Barrymore
Eddie Crandall .... William E. Meehan
Charles Hickson .... Harry Robert
Mary Delano .... Mary Nash
Pinkey Granville .... Ramsey Wallace
Asa Hickson .... John Mason
Jack Burns .... John Sharkey
Sergeant Todkins .... T. S. James
Fritz .... Nathaniel Sack

BIG SCENE, THE, play, in one act, by Arthur Schnitzler, translated by Charles Henry Meltzer. Presented by the Greenwich Village Players.—Greenwich Village, New York, April 18.

BILLETED, comedy, in three acts, by P. Tennyson, Jesse and H. M. Harwood. (Produced in London at the Royalty, August 21, 1917; in America as Lonely Soldiers, Nixon, Pittsburgh, September 17, 1917.)—Playhouse, New York, December 25, 1917.

Rose	Margaret Hoffman
Emmaline Liptrott	Sally Williams
Rev. Ambrose Liptrott	Roland Rushton
Penelope Moon	Phyllis Birkett
Betty Tarradine	Margaret Anglin
Colonel Preedy	Langdon Bruce
Captain Bymill	Edward Emery
Cook	Myra Burrington
Mr. MacFarlane	Howard Lindsay

BLEST BE, play, by Humphrey W. Pearson. Presented by the Columbus Centre of the Drama League of America.—Knickerbocker, Columbus, April 26.

BLIND YOUTH, play, in three acts, by Willard Mack and Lou Tellegen.—Playhouse, Wilmington, November 22, 1917; Republic, New York, December 3, 1917.

Lolis Delmas	Paul Porcasi
Tubby Mathews	Mark Smith
Bobo	Hazel Turney
Conny Chandoce	Marie Chambers
Maurice Monnier	Lou Tellegen
Henri	Howard Lange
Mrs. Wilton	Jennie Eustace
Harry Wilton	William Courtleigh, Jr.
Nora	Jennie Dumont
Frances Granger	Grace Carlyle

BLUE PEARL, THE, comedy drama, in three acts, by Anne Crawford Flexner.—Newark, June 18; Longacre, New York, August 8.

Rolling Choir Boy	E. H. Bender
Wilfred Scott	William David
Angelica Topping	Dorothy Klewer
Hooper McHugh	G. Oliver Smith
Mrs. H. Augustus Topping	Annie Hughes
Major H. Augustus Topping	J. Palmer Collins
Holland Webb	Orlando Daly
Sybil Kent	Julia Bruns
Laura Webb	Grace Carlyle
Stokes	Hubert Druce
Stephen Drake	George Nash
Alexander Petrofsky	Charles Angelo
Madame Petrofsky	Yolande Duquette
Footman	Lyman-Fink
Penrose Kent	Perce Benton
Ellis	Frederick Kaufman
Monahan	H. B. Tisdale
Mason	Thomas Borden
Mrs. Coombes	Amelia Hendon

BIRDS OF PREY, play, by Joseph Noel. Produced by the Poli Players.—Lyric, Bridgeport, Conn., February 11.

BOOK OF JOB, THE, drama, adapted from the Book of Job in the Bible. Presented by Stuart Walker.—Booth, New York, March 7.

Narrators	{ Judith Lowry / Margaret Mower }
Job	George Gaul
Eliphaz	Henry Buckler
Bildad	Edgar Stehli
Zophar	Eugene Stockdale
Elihu	Walter Hampden
The Voice Out of the Whirlwind	David Bishpam

BOTTLED BABIES, farce, by Mabel S. Keightley. Producer by the Lando Stock Company.—Whalom Park, Fitchburg, August 5.

BRIGHT AND EARLY, play.—Atlantic City, N.J., December 3, 1917.

BRUISED WINGS, drama, by Edward Clark. —Apollo, Atlantic City, May 13.

BY PIGEON POST, melodrama, in three acts, by Austin Page. (Produced in London at the Garrick, March 30).—Broad Street, Philadelphia, November 12; George M. Cohan, New York, November 25.

Blondel	St. Clair Bayfield
Lacken	Harrison Hunter
Captain Paul Chalfont	Jerome Patrick
Madame Chalfont	Ida Waterman
Major Pierre Vaudry	Vincent Serrano
Marie Latour	Phœbe Foster
Colonel Laroque	John Sainpolis
Margot Latour	Peggy O'Neil
General Delapierre	Frank Kemble Cooper
Orderly	John A. Higgins
Orderly	Hugh Schmedes

CAMOUFLAGE, dramatic playlet. Produced by Henry du Vries.—Palace, New York, February 18.

CANARY, THE, musical comedy, book adapted from the French by Harry B. Smith, music by Ivan B. Caryll. Produced by Charles Dillingham.—Nixon, Pittsburgh, September 23.

CAPPY RICKS, play, by Edward E. Rose, adapted from Peter B. Kyne's "Cappy Ricks" stories. Produced by Oliver Morosco.—Apollo, Atlantic City, November 28.

CASEY, THE FIREMAN, sketch, played by Chas. Buckley and company.—Proctor's Fifty-Eighth Street, New York, April 1.

CHINESE PUZZLE, THE, play, in four acts, by Marion Bower and Leon M. Lion. (Produced in England at the Shakespeare, Liverpool, July 1; New, London, July 11.) —Poli's, Washington, June 24.

CLOSE THE BOOK, comedy, by Susan Glaspell. Presented by the Washington Square Players.—Comedy, New York, May 13.

Jhansi	Florence Enright
Peyton Adams Root	T. W. Gibson
Mrs. Root	Elizabeth Patterson
Mrs. Peyton	Helen Westley
George Peyton	J. Luray Butler
Bessie Root	Marjorie Vonnegut
State Senator Byrd	R. E. McDonald
Mrs. Byrd	Jean Robb

COHAN REVUE, 1918, THE, musical revue, in two acts and sixteen scenes, book by George M. Cohan, music and lyrics by George M. Cohan and Irving Berlin.—New Amsterdam, New York, December 31, 1917.

COMMITTEE ON ADMISSIONS, THE, burlesque, by Edwin Milton Royle. Presented at the Lambs' 1918 Gambol.—Hudson, New York, June 14.

COMMON CAUSE, THE, play, by Crane Wilbur. Presented by Ye Liberty Players. —Oakland, September 15.

COPPERHEAD, THE, drama, in four acts, by Augustus Thomas (from a story by Frederick Landis). Produced by John D. Williams.—Parson's, Hartford, January 7; Shubert, New York, February 18.

Joey Shanks	Raymond Hackett
Grandma Perley	Eugenie Woodward
Ma Shanks	Doris Rankin
Captain Hardy	Albert Phillips
Milt Shanks	Lionel Barrymore
Mrs. Bates	Evelyn Archer
Sue Perley	Gladys Burgette
Lem Tollard	Ethelbert Hales
Newt Gillespie	William Norton
Andrews	Harry Hadfield
Sam Carter	Chester Morris
Madeline King	Doris Rankin
Philip Manning	Thomas Carrigan
Mrs. Manning	Grace Reals
Dr. Randall	Hayden Stevenson

CRITIC'S COMEDY, THE, play, in one act, by Samuel Kaplan. Presented by the Washington Square Players.—Comedy, New York, December 3, 1917.

CROPS AND CROPPERS, comedy, in three acts, by Theresa Helburn.—Belmont, New York, September 12.

Annie	Irene Daley
Janie Wimpole	Eleanor Fox
Margot Marbrook	Louise Cook
Peter Weston	Ben Johnson
Allison Marbrook	Eileen Huban
Ray Parcher	Thomas Mitchell
Stetson	J. M. Troughton
Jean	Georges Flateau
Mrs. Bradley	Madeline Valentine
Dr. Truesdale	Vernon Kelso
Stephen Marbrook	Henry Stanford
Mrs. Spencer	Helen Westley
Mrs. Pray	Maud Sinclair
Pete Cobb	Charles Kennedy

CROWDED HOUR, THE, play, in four acts, by Edgar Selwyn and Channing Pollock, produced by the Selwyns. A. H. Woods, Chicago, October 14; Selwyn, New York, November 25.

Matt Wilde	Franklyn Ardell
Charley	Cyril Raymond
Vivian	Mabel Godding
Lawrence	Jane Cowl
Jackson	Jules Epailly
Grace Laidlaw	Christine Norman
Captain Bert Caswell	Henry Stephenson
Dorothy Wayne	Miss Rae Selwyn
General Dalton	George LeSoir
Billy Laidlaw	Orme Caldara
Merrick	John Black
Nevins	Edward Kearney
Davis	Sidney Hall
Wills	Burni Prevost
Grandmère Bauvaise	Michellette Burani
Jean	Henry Call
Pierre	Andy Aubrey
Marie	Mildred Call
Mignon	Antoinette Letienne
Captain René Soulier	Georges Flateau
Marthe	Yahne Fleury
A Veteran	Georges Deschaux
Lieutenant Bailey	Harold Mullane
Lieutenant Epstein	Harry Schwalbe
Lieutenant Williams	Leslie L'Estrange
Lieutenant Walcott	Cyril Raymond
Dr. Beauchamps	Cecil Owen

CURE FOR CURABLES, a comedy, in four acts, by Earl Derr Biggers and Lawrence Whitman, suggested by Curra Harris's short story. Produced by Lee Shubert.—Trenton, October 4, 1917; Thirty-ninth Street, New York, February 25

Mrs. Hamilton Blaine	Ada C. Nevil
Elizabeth Rankin	Adelyn Wesley
Bishop Rutledge	Carson Davenport
Dutton	George Lund
Mrs. Margaret Forster	Edith Shayne
Jeanne	Fanchon Duval
Colonel Fairchild	Charles E. Verner
Philin	Harold White
Phyllis Blaine	Clara Moores
Frederick Jamieson	Edward Wonn
Robert Gleason	George Barr
Herbert Davies	Clarence Bellair
Dr. Parker	Robert Wayne
Corn	Frederick Strong
J. Cunningham Hale	Brigham Royce
Watkins	Davis Marshall
Shep	Jerry Hart
David Manville	Joseph Weber
Dr. James Pendergrass	William Hodge
Judge Luckett	James H. Lewis
Jack Morris	James C. Malaidy
Sheriff	Arthur E. Sprague
Deputy Sheriff	Ford Record

DADDIES, comedy, in four acts, by John Lessing Hobble, produced by David Belasco.—Washington, June 10; Belasco, New York, September 5.

Robert Audrey	Bruce McRae
James Crocket	John W. Cope
Nicholson Walters	Edwards Davis
Henry Allen	George Abott
William Rivers	S. K. Walker
Parker	George Giddens
Ruth Atkins	Jeanne Eagels
Mrs. Audrey	Winifred Fraser
Bobette	Edith King
Madame Levigne	Paulette Noizeux
Lorry	Lorna Volare
Alice ("Little Sammy")	Aida Armand
Francois and Co.	The Quinns
Katie	Mrs. Armand
Nurse	Mrs. Quinn

DARLING OF THE WORLD, THE, play, by Eleanor Gates, presented by the Northampton Players.—Northampton, Mass., September 23.

DAVID'S ADVENTURE, play, by Augustus Thomas, based on the novel "Driftwood Adventure," by Leona Dalrymple. Produced by Cohan and Harris.—Apollo, Atlantic City, June 3.

DEMOCRACY'S KING, Allegorical play, in one act, by Arnold Daly. Produced by Arnold Daly.—Hudson, New York, February 19.

William	Arnold Daly
George	Langdon Gillette
Albert	George Frederichs
Emanuel	Paul Irving
Poincaire	William Frederic
Kerensky	Charles Halton
The American	Harry Mestayer

DEVIL, THE, drama, in three acts. Presented by the Fifth Avenue Theatre Stock Company.—Brooklyn, December 17, 1917.

DOLL'S HOUSE, A, revival of Ibsen's drama (produced in London at the Novelty, June 7, 1889) by Arthur Hopkins.—Plymouth, New York, April 29.

Torvald Helmer	Lionel Atwill
Nora	Mme. Nazimova
Doctor Rank	George Probert
Mrs. Linden	Katharine Emmet
Nils Krogstad	Roland Young
Anna	Amy Veness
Ellen	Charity Finney
A Porter	A. O. Huhn

DOLLY OF THE FOLLIES, farce.—Stamford, Conn, August 12.

DOUBLE EXPOSURE, farce, in three acts, by Avery Hopwood. Produced by Selwyn and company.—Belasco, Washington, June 30; Bijou, New York, August 27.

Tommy Campbell	John Westley
Lecksy Campbell	Francine Larrimore
Sybil Norton	Janet Beecher
Jimmie Norton	John Cumberland
Baba Mahrati	J. Harry Irvine
Maggie	Grace Hayle
William	William Postance
Officer O'Brien	Dan Moyles

DRUMS, THE, allegory, by George V. Hobart (taken from his play Loyalty). Presented at the Lambs' 1918 Gambol.—Hudson, New York, June 14.

ECCENTRIC LORD COMBERDENE, THE, comedy, by R. C. Carton (produced in London at the St. James's, November 19, 1910).—Copley, Boston, March.

EFFICIENCY, dramatic playlet, by R. H. Davis and Perly Sheehan. Played by Lawrence Grant and company.—Palace, Staten Island, February 4.

ELECTRA, tragedy, by Sophocles. Presented by the Symphony Society of New York, in conjunction with Margaret Anglin.—Carnegie Hall, New York, February 6.
Guardian of Orestes .... Fuller Mellish
Orestes .... Fred Eric
Pylades .... Benjamin Kauser
Electra .... Margaret Anglin
Chrysothemis .... Madeline Delmas
Attendants on Chrysothemis—
  Melrose Pitman, Melanie Avery
Queen Clytemnestra ...... Florence Wollersen
Aegisthos .... Mitchell Harris

ENEMIES WITHIN, war play, in four acts, by A. H. Van Buren and Kilgour Gordon. Presented by the Poli Stock Company.—Hartford, Conn., August 19.

EVERYMAN, English Morality play. Revived by Edith Wynne Matthison.—Cort, New York, January 18.
Messenger .... Charles Rann Kennedy
Adonai .... William Raymond
Dethe .... Pedro de Cordoba
Everyman .... Edith Wynne Matthison
Felawshyp .... John S. O'Brien
Cosin .... Percival Vivian
Kynrede .... Ruth Vivian
Goodes .... C. H. Meredith
Good Dedes .... Antoinette Glover
Knowledge .... Adrienne Morrison
Confession .... Charles Rann Kennedy
Beaute .... Elsie Herndon Kearns
Strength .... Elna Larrimore
Fyve Wyttes .... Margaret Gage
Dyscrecion .... Jane Stewart
Red Aungell .... Mercedes de Cordoba
White Aungell .... Constance Bennett
Doctour .... Charles Rann Kennedy

EVERYTHING, spectacle, in three parts and fifteen scenes, lyrics by John L. Golden, music by Raymond Hubbell.—Hippodrome, New York, August 22. Principals:—Wolf Hopper, Belle Story, Charles T. Aldrich, Bluch Landolf, Bert Levy, Will J. Evans, Desiree Lubowska, Gerda Gulda, William A. Weston, Helen Patterson, Arthur Hill, Albert Froom, Four Amaranths, Sisters Breen, George Gifford, Mallia and Bart, Diers and Russell, Two Nelsons, Four Ladellas, Davis Family, Byrnes Brothers, Stella Norelle, Four Guintinis, Octavio Tay, Musical Johnstons, Arthur Geary, Inez Bauer, Peggy H. Barnstead, Cassie Hayden and Marion Saki.

FAMILY PRIDE, play, in one act, by Mrs. Walter M. Broadway (the prize-winning play in the contest conducted by the Drama League of America, Pasadena centre), presented by the Community Players.—Savoy, Pasadena, April 15.

FANCY FREE, musical comedy, book by Dorothy Donnelly, lyrics and music by Augustus Barratt. Produced by Lee and J. J. Shubert.—Ford's, Baltimore, January 28; Astor, New York, April 11.
Elevator Boy .... Alton Weber
Hotel Clerk .... William Tillett
Bell Boy .... Joseph Tinsley
Hotel Manager .... John E. Wheeler
Yvette .... Yvonne Darle
Philip Pike .... Ray Raymond
Betty Pestlewaite .... Marilynn Miller
Albert Van Wyck ...... Clifton Crawford
Flower Girl .... Regina Richards
The Bridegroom .... Hal Peel
The Bride .... Tim Poni
Professor Hyhrower ...... Charles Brown
Pinkie Pestlewaite .... Marjorie Gateson
The Manicurist .. .. Yvonne Gouraud
The Mysterious One ...... Harold Evarts
Benjamin Pestlewaite ...... Harry Conor
Peter Pope .... Robinson Newbold
Gussie Pope .... Violet Englefield

FIDDLES THREE, operetta, in two acts and three scenes, book and lyrics by William Cary Duncan, music by Alexander Johnstone.—Apollo, Atlantic City, August 19; Cort, New York, September 3.
Gilda Varelli .... Louise Groody
Carlo Andreani .... Henry Leoni
Reginald De by, Lord Duffer .... Echlin Gayer
Sam Wrigglesberry ...... Hal Skelley
Rosa .... Betty Dodsworth
Nicolo Colona .... Thomas Conkey
Giuisippe .... Joseph Miller
Suzanne Foppitt .... Josie Intropidi
Bernice Brockway ...... Hazel Kirke
Anina Andreani .... Tavie Belge
Beppo .... Antonio Salerno
Paganini .... Gilbert Clayton
Kubelik .... Antonio Salerno
Giorgio .... Tempe Evans

FINE SYSTEM, THE, comedy, in one act, by George Courteline, played by Olive Wyndham and Jose Ruben.—Palace, New York, May 6.

FISHERMAN'S LUCK, comedy, in three acts, by Arthur Edwin Krows and Norman Lee Swartout. Presented by the Northampton Players.—Academy of Music, Northampton, Mass., March 11.

FLEURETTE'S DREAM AT PERONNE, pantomimic musical fashion revue, in ten scenes, presented by Lady Duff Gordon.—Palace, New York, December 3, 1917.

FLO-FLO, musical comedy, in two acts, book by Fred de Gresac, lyrics by E. Paulton and Fred de Gresac, music by Silvio Hein, produced by John Cort.—Weiting Opera House, Syracuse, November 21, 1917; Cort, New York, December 20, 1917.
Flo-Flo .... Vera Michelena
Isidor Moser .... James B. Carson
Robert Simpson .... Oscar Figman
Billy Cope .... Leon Leonard
Angelina Stokes .... Wanda Lyon
Mrs. R. G. Stokes ...... Louise Beaudet
Count Pedro Di Seguilla ... George Renavent
Carmen Carassa .... Finita De Soria
Pink .... Thomas Handers
Mud .... Arthur Millis
Officer Casey .... W. H. Mack
Maid .... Marie Hollywell
Bella .... Blanche Bellaire
Cora .... Esther Ingham
Rosa .... Anna Sands
Mona .... Kate Stout

FLYING COLOURS, comedy, by John Taintor Foote and John L. Golden.—Atlantic City, N.J., June 23.

FOREVER AFTER, drama, in three acts, by Owen Davis.—Long Branch, N.J., August 12; Central, New York, September 9.
Ted .... Conrad Nagel
Jack .... John Warner
Jennie .... Alice Brady
Mrs. Clayton .... Mrs. Russ Whytal
Mr. Clayton .... Frank Hatch
Nan .... Isabel Lamon
Private Nolan .... Maxwell Driscoll
Tom Lowell .... Frederick Manatt
McNabb, of the Red Cross .. J. Paul Jones
Miss Webb .... Bernice Parker
Doctor Mason .... J. R. Armstrong
Williams .... J. Paul Jones

FOLLOW THE GIRL, musical comedy, by Henry Blossom and Zoel Parenteau. Presented by Raymond Hitchcock and E. Ray Goetz.—Forty-Fourth Street, Roof Theatre, New York. March 2.

FOR OUR BOYS, War playlet, by George Crosman, played by Henrietta Crosman and company.—New Liberty, Staten Island, April 8

FORGOTTEN SOULS, plays, by David Pinski. Presented by the Theatre Workshop.—People's House, New York, January 10.

FORTUNATO, play, translated from the Spanish of S. and J. Alvarez-Quintero. Presented by the Neighbourhood Players.—Neighbourhood Playhouse, New York, February 23.

FOUNTAIN OF YOUTH, THE, comedy, in three acts, by Louis Evan Shipman.—Henry Miller's, New York, April 1.
Gerald Place .... Henry Miller
Longdan Train ...... Frank Kemble Cooper
Jack Forsythe .... Robert Ames
Kenneth Guile .... C. Leslie Austen
Harrison Healey .... Frank Sylvester
Crockett .... Lewis Sealey
Mrs. Forsythe .... Lucile Watson
Mrs. Lupin .... Hilda Spong
Hilda Forsythe ...... Lillian Kemble Cooper
Elizabeth Crichton .... Olive Tell

FREEDOM, play, by C. Lewis Hind and E. Lyall Swete, presented by Julie Opp Faversham and E. Lyall Swete.—Century, New York, October 19.

FRIENDLY DIVORCE, A, comedy, in prologue and three acts, by Tadema Bussiere. Produced by the Cecil Spooner Stock Company.—Grand Opera House, Brooklyn, April 15.

FRIENDLY ENEMIES, comedy, in three acts, by Samuel Shipman and Aaron Hoffman.—Apollo, Atlantic City, February 28; Hudson, New York, July 22.
Walter Stuart .... Felix Krembs
Nora .... Natalie Manning
Marie Pfeiffer .... Mathilde Cottrelly
June Block .... Regina Wallace
Karl Pfeiffer .... Louis Mann
Henry Block .... Sam Bernard
William Pfeiffer .... Richard Barbee

FRIENDS INVITED, play, in one act, by Ray Lee Jackson, presented by the Drama League of Columbus.—Knickerbocker, Columbus, March 8.

GARDEN OF ALLAH, THE, drama, in four acts, by Robert Hichens and Mary Anderson (Century, New York, October 21, 1911), revived by Comstock and Gest.—Manhattan Opera House, New York, February 25.
Domini Enfilden .... Sarah Truax
Suzanne .... Pearl Gray
Count Anteoni .... Howard Gould
Father Roubier .... Albert Andruss
Captain de Trevignac .... Thaddeus Gray
Batouch .... Antonio Salerno
Hadj .... Said Coury
The Sand Diviner .... Saleem Ayobb
Larbi .... Houardi
Ouardi .... Said Ben Hamed
Shiek .... Charles Abbott
Mueddin .... Saleem Ayobb
Garcon .... Alphonso Fabre
Trappist Monk .... Ameen Ayobb
Irene .... Faddma
Tamouda .... Aemasa
Selima .... Frosine
Boris Androvsky .... William Jeffrey

GARDEN OF PARADISE, THE, play, by Edward Sheldon, taken from Hans Andersen's Fairy Tale of the same name. Presented by Russell Janney Players.—Pabst, Milwaukee, June 17.

GARSIDE'S CAREER, comedy, by Harold Brighouse. (Produced in England at the Gaiety, Manchester, February 2, 1914: Coronet, May 11, 1914.) Presented by the students of the Academy of Dramatic Arts, Lyceum, New York, March 1.

GEE-RUSALEM, play. Presented by the Provincetown Players.—133, McDougal Street, New York, November 23.

GENERAL POST, comedy, by J. E. Harold Terry. (Produced in London at the Haymarket, March 1¾, 1917.)—Gaiety, New York, December 24, 1917.
Sir Dennys Broughton .... Thomas A. Wise
Lady Broughton .... Cynthia Brooke
Alec .... Cecil Fletcher
Betty .... Olive Tell
Wilson .... James Kearney
Edward Smith .... William Courtenay
Albert Smith .... Wigney Percyval

GETTING TOGETHER, patriotic play, in three acts and six scenes, by Major Beith (Ian Hay), J. Hartley Manners and Percival Knight, songs by Lieut. Gitz Rice, presented under the auspices of the British-Canadian Recruiting Mission, in co-operation with the American Military and Naval Forces, and for the War Charities of the Allies.—Harmanus Bleecker Hall, Albany, March 11; Lyric, New York, March 18.
Orrin Palmer .... Holbrook Blinn
A Servant .... Edwin Taylor
Mrs. Palmer .... Blanche Bates
Edward Wadsworth .... William Roselle
First Recruit .... Leonard Barry
Second Recruit .... William Rowland
Third Recruit .... James Flint
First Spectator .... E. J. Kennedy
Second Spectator .... John Thorne
Third Spectator .... W. J. O'Neil
Fourth Spectator .... Timothy Conway
Fifth Spectator .... Edwin Taylor
Warrant Officer .... Harrison Brockbank
Lieutenant Gitz Rice .... Lieutenant Gitz Rice
A Retired Bellhop .... Harry Blakemore
A Woman .... Harriet Sterling
British Sergeant .. Sergt. L. Shannon Cormack
British Soldier .... Private Charles Francis
A Poilu .... Gustave Rolland
Sergeant Atkins .... Percival Knight
Santa Claus .... Harris Brockbank
Death .... Private Charles Francis
Sergeant Jennings .... John Thorne
First British Soldier .... Edwin Taylor
First American Soldier .... Arthur Ray
Second American Soldier ...... E. J. Kennedy
War Tank Officer
                Sergt. L. Shannon Cormack
British Surgeon .... Private Charles Cormack
Miss Fletcher .... Dorothy Knight
A Waitress .... Suzanne Feday
A Refugee .... Ruth Benson

GIRL BEHIND THE GUN, THE, musical comedy, in three acts, book and lyrics by Guy Bolton and P. G. Wodehouse, music by Ivan Caryll.—Apollo, Atlantic City, August 26; New Amsterdam, New York, September 16.
Robert Lambrissac .... Donald Brian
Pierre Breval .... Jack Hazzard
Georgette Breval .... Ada Meade
Colonel Servan .... Frank Doane
Lucienne Lambrissac .... Wilda Bennett
Harper Wentworth .... Bert Gardner
Eileen Moore .... Eva Francis
Brichoux .... John E. Young
Zellie .... Virginia O'Brien
Edna .... Florence Delmar
Pollie .... Elaine Palmer
Margie .... Cissie Sewell
Carrie .... June White

GIRL HE LEFT BEHIND THE, play, by Ralph T. Kettering. — Majestic, Milwaukee, July 24.

GIRL IN THE COFFIN, THE, play, in one act, by Theodore Dreiser. Presented by the Washington Square Players.—Comedy, New York, December 3 1917.

AMERICAN PLAYS OF THE YEAR. 129

GIRL O' MINE, musical comedy, in two acts, book and lyrics by Philip Bartholomae, music by Frank Tours. Produced by Elisabeth Marbury and the Shuberts.—Van Curler, Schenectady, N.Y., December 25, 1917; Bijou New York, January 28.

Chef de Gare .... Ernest Perrin
Duc de Bouvais .... James Lounsbery
Toby .... Carl Hyson
Betty .... Dorothy Dickson
Lulu .... Edna Wallace Hopper
Charlie .... Barratt Greenwood
Teddy .... David Quixano
Lily .... Marie Nordstrom
Jack .... Frank Fay
Mildred .... Helen Bee
A Waiter .... Charles Burrows
Greene .... Carlton Macy
Maitre d'Hôtel .... Ernest Perrin

GIRL OF MY HEART, musical comedy, book and lyrics by Arthur J. Lamb, music by Jules Chauvenet.—Duquesne, Pittsburgh, January 14.

GIRL OUTSIDE, THE, play, by Vincent Lawrence. Presented by the Poli Players.—Bridgeport, Conn., January 21.

GLORIANNA, musical comedy, in three acts, book and lyrics by Catherine Chisholm Cushing, music by Rudolf Friml, presented by John Cort.—Apollo, Atlantic City, September 13; Liberty, New York, October 28.

Glorianna Grey .... Eleanor Painter
Dolores Pennington .... Dorothy South
Therese, Ltd. .... Josephine Whittell
Tonio .... Curtis Karpe
Mrs. Sapronia Pennington .... Ursula Ellsworth
Miss Angelica Pennington .... Rose McIntyre
Lt. Dick Pennington .... Joseph Lertora
Jack Pennington .... Ralph Whitehead
Alexander Galloway .... Alexander Clark
Robbins .... James Joseph Dunn
Nenette }
Rintintin } .... Egotti Twins
Jessica .... Emily Lea

Other characters by Gilbert Wells, C. Balfour Lloyd, Misses Marguerite St. Clair, Elsie Lawson, Vera Dunn, Stout, Wynn, O'Connell, Merode, Redding, Burton, Bowhan, White, Sharp, Sitgraves, Smith, Stevens, Hall, Foreman, Scott, Haddone and Warren.

GOING UP, musical comedy, founded on James Montgomery's The Aviator. (Produced in England at the Lyceum, Sheffield, September 28, 1911.) Book and lyrics by Otto Harbach, music by Louis A. Hirsch.—Apollo, Atlantic City, November 15, 1917; Liberty, New York, December 25, 1917.

Miss Zonne .... Ruth Donnelly
John Gordon .... John Park
F. H. Douglas .... Donald Meek
Mrs. Douglas .... Grace Peters
Jules Gaillard .... Joseph Lertora
Grace Douglas .... Edith Day
Madeline Manners .... Marion Sunshine
Hopkinson Brown .... Frank Otto
Robert Street .... Frank Craven
James Brooks .... Arthur Stuart Hull
Sam Robinson .... Edward Begley
Louis .... Francois Vaulry
Sylvia Thorn .... Evelyn Cavanaugh
E. Tompkins Todd .... Richard Dore

GOOD-BYE, BILL, musical play, music by Pte. William B. Kernell, book by Pte. Richard Feckheimer, played by the men of the United States Army Ambulance Service.—Forty-Eighth Street, New York, March 17.

GOOD LUCK, UNCLE SAM, musical comedy, lyrics by Sergeant Edward Anthony, music by Sergeant Louis G. Merrill, produced by the soldiers at Camp Merritt.—Lexington, New York, November 25.

Floyd Dell .... Christopher Hayes
Mrs. Mabel Marshmallow .... Leo Herrup
Second Lieutenant Fred Andrews
            .... Lorenz Gillette
Ulysses S. Grant Johnson ..... N. D. Cohen
Private Sam Esterbrook
                 .... Joseph Le Grange Abbott
Martha Walters .... Corporal F. H. Healy
General Goff .... John P. Stack
The Colonel .... M. T. Collins
The Major .... W. J. Dunn
The Captain .... Joseph R. Flick
The First Lieutenant .... Robert L. Hamilton
The Second Lieutenant .. Robert A. Blackburne
The Orderly .... James J. Sullivan
Entertainment Captain ...... Joseph R. Flick
The Bugler .... Lorenzo W. Brown
Alexander .... George Tripler
Mrs. George Washington Cackle. George Rubin
Mrs. Larson .... J. W. Wujcik

GOOD MEN DO, THE, epilogue, by Hubert Osborne. Presented by the Actors' and Authors' Theatre.—Fulton, New York, May 24.

Nurse .... Grace Griswold
Jenkyns .... H. Asheton Tonge
Jedith .... Victoria Montgomery
Suzanna .... Hilda Spong
Mistress Whately .... Grace Eisher
Anne Hathaway .... Mrs. Thomas A. Wise
Dr. John Hall .... Albert Gran
The Vicar .... Maxwell Ryder

GOOD MORNING, ROSAMOND, comedy, in three acts, by Constance Lindsay Skinner. Produced by the Shuberts and Jessie Bonstelle.—Star, Buffalo, August 13, 1917; Forty-Eighth Street, New York, December 10, 1917.

Rosamond Mearely .... Lily Cahill
Mrs. Lee .... Mrs. E. A. Eberle
Mrs. Witherby .... Annie Hughes
Corinne Witherby .... Marian Morgan
Mabel Crewe .... Lilian Cooper
Wilton Howard .... Dwight Meade
Dr. Frei .... Robert Adams
La-sanavatiewicz .... Herman Gerold
Alfred Marks .... Arthur Allen
Dr. Wells .... Charles H. Riegel
Judge Giffen .... Robert Forsythe
George Andrews .... Sidney Macy
The Vagabond .... Lowell Sherman

GOSH, WE'RE ALL FRIENDS, revue, by Oliver Morosco. Produced for the Stage Women's War Relief.—Morosco, New York, May 19.

GRASS WIDOW, THE, musical comedy, book and lyrics by Channing Pollock and Rennold Wolf, adapted from Bisson and St. Albin's "Le Peril Jaune," music by Louis A. Hirsch.—Apollo, Atlantic City, N.J., October 8, 1917; Liberty, New York, December 3, 1917.

An Ill-Humored Man .... J. C. Klein
Annette .... Helen Lowell
Vincent .... Tom O'Hare
Anatol Pivert .... George Marion
Larry Doyle .... Robert Emmet Keane
Dorothy .... Irene Dixon
Florence .... Edna Waddell
Betty .... Marion Ford
Angie .... May Hopkins
Denise .... Natalie Alt
Colette .... Gretchen Eastman
Fernand Dore .... Victor Morley
Fanchon .... Marion Pollard
Claire .... Anita Francesca
Jacques, Count de Cluny .... Howard Marsh
Lucille .... Marguerite L. Fritts
Monsieur Faveran .... Leon E. Brown

5

GREATER HERO, THE, play, in one act, by William Moore Patch.—Pitt, Pittsburgh, February 18.

GREATER AMERICAN, THE, play, by Ralph T. Kettering.—Shubert, Minneapolis, July 24.

GYPSY TRAIL, THE, comedy, in three acts, by Robert Housum. Produced by Arthur Hopkins.—Plymouth, New York, December 3, 1917.
Frank Raymond .... Robert Cummings
Miss Janet Raymond ...... Katharine Emmet
John Raymond .... Frank Longacre
Stiles .... Charles Hanna
Frances Raymond .... Phœbe Foster
Edward Andrews .... Roland Young
Michael .... Ernest Glendinning
Mrs. Widdimore .... Effie Elsler
Ellen .... Margaret Sayres

HABIT, play, by Frank Dare. Presented by the Washington Square Players.—Comedy, New York, January 23.

HAPPINESS, comedy, in three acts and epilogue, by J. Hartley Manners.—Criterion, New York, December 31, 1917.
Phillip Chandos .... O. P. Heggie
Formoy MacDonagh .... J. M. Kerrigan
John Snowcroft .... Hubert Druce
Walter .... Andrew Stiles
A Boy .... Warner Anderson
Mrs. Chrystal-Pole .... Violet Kemble Cooper
Miss Perkins .... Lynn Fontanne
Mrs. Wreay .... Catherine Proctor
A Girl .... Dorothea Camden
An Assistant .... Edna Jane Hill
An Applicant .... Dorothy Dunn
Jeany .... Laurette Taylor

HARVEST, Irish drama, by Lennox Robinson. Presented by the pupils of the American Academy of Dramatic Arts and the Empire Theatre Dramatic School.—Lyceum, New York, February 1.

HARVEST, THE, play, in prologue and three acts, by Henry Hamilton, presented by the Emerson Players.—Colonial, Lawrence, Mass., December 17, 1917.

HEAD OVER HEELS, musical comedy, in two acts and three scenes, book and lyrics by Edgar Allan Woolf, music by Jerome Kern, produced by Henry W. Savage.—Tremont, Boston, May 25; Cohan, New York, August 29.
Muriel Sterling .... Dorothy Mackaye
Office Boy .... Lambert Terry
Robert Lawson .... Boyd Marshall
Edward Sterling .... Irving Beebe
Anthony Squibbs ...... Robert Emmet Keane
Mitzi Bambinetti .... Mitzi
Signor Bambinetti .... Charles Judels
Miss Edith Penfield .... Grace Daniels
Mrs. Sarah Montague ...... Gertrude Dallas
Baron D'Oultremont .... Ernest Marini
Jarvis .... Edmund Gurney
Molly .... Carrie McManus
Toni .... Joseph Dunn
Oscar .... James Oliver
Buxaume .... George Obey
Henri .... Edward Mathews

HEART OF ANNIE WOOD, THE, sketch, played by Miss Helen Ford and Company.—Harlem Opera House, New York, October 28.

HE DIDN'T WANT TO DO IT, musical comedy, in three acts, book and lyrics by George Broadhurst, music by Silvio Hein. (Produced in London as a farcical play at the Prince of Wales's, March 6, 1915.)—. Stamford, Conn., August 1; Broadhurst, New York, August 20.
Alexander McPherson .... Ernest Torrence
O. Vivian Smith .... Percy Ames
Washington Demming ...... Charles Meakins
Detective .... Ned A. Sparks
Manager of the Hotel ...... Alexander Frank
Waiter .... Robert O'Connor
Lieutenant Rodgers .... Joseph Wilmot
Paula Wainwright ...... Katherine Galloway
Marjorie Thompson .... Helen Shipman
Norma Wallace .... Adele Blood
Mary Manners .... Elsa Thomas
Wilda Wood .... Elsie Gordon
Bertha Barrison .... Natalie Bates
Constance Conover .... Helen Pierre
Roberta Runyon .... Edna Pierre
Frances Farrington .... Mary Cunningham
Neva Norcross .... Carrie DeNoville
Gertrude Glover .... Florence Collier
Dorothy Daniels .... Anna Toddings
Kate Carter .... Mary McDonald
Henrietta Hadley .... Jean Carroll
Janice Godfrey .... Clara Carroll
Katherine Kollis .... Ona Hamilton
Marie Melton .... Dorothy LaRue
Leonore Leonard .... Gladys Clifton
Nanette Norris .... Ida Ross

HEDDA GABLER, Henrik Ibsen's drama (Vaudeville, London, April 20, 1891), revived by Arthur Hopkins.—Plymouth, New York, April 8.
George Tesman .... Lionel Atwill
Hedda Tesman .... Alla Nazimova
Miss Juliana Tesman .. Lizzie Hudson Collier
Mrs Elvested .... Nila Mac
Judge Brack .... Charles Bryant
Eilert Lovborg .... George Probert
Berta .... Charity Finney

HELEN-WITH-THE-HIGH-HAND, adaptation, by Richard Pryce, of Arnold Bennett's novel (produced in London, February 17, 1914, at the Vaudeville).—Stamford, Conn., August 1.

HER BIT, sketch, by Fennimore Merrill. Played by Effie Shannon and company.—Palace, Staten Island, January 21.

HER COUNTRY, drama, in four acts, by Rudolf Besier and Sybil Spottiswoode (produced in London under the title of "Kultur at Home" at the Court, March 11, 1916).—Punch and Judy, New York, February 21.
Major Kolbeck .... Redfield Clarke
Mrs. Kolbeck .... Winona Bridges
Elsa Kolbeck .... Margaret Vaune
Paul, the Kolbeck's servant.... Walter Plinge
Margaret Tinworth .... Rosa Lynd
Kurt Hartling .... Alexander Onslow
Otto Von Oftberg .... George Hallett
Mr. Tinworth .... Charles Fleming
Schmidt .... Edward Broadley
Minna .... Mary Broome
Sophie Von Dorn .... Adele Klaer
Erika Krauss .... Bertha Broad
Mrs. Munroe .... Maude Milton
Ralph Munroe .... William Williams
Lieut. Reinkampf .... Anthony Blair
Lieut. Von Sieb .... Edward Reece
Lieut. Delmann .... Frank Ross
Lieut. Von Prossheim ...... Charles Haines
Mrs. Colonel Von Rapp ...... Marion Kelby
A Waiter .... Adalbert Jones

HER HAPPINESS, play, by Horace Holley. Presented by the Henderson Players.—Bramhall Playhouse, April 20.

AMERICAN PLAYS OF THE YEAR. 131

HER HONOUR THE MAYOR, comedy, in two acts, by Arline Van Ness Hines. Produced by the Actors and Authors' Theatre.—Fulton, New York, May 24.
Miss Midge .... Olive May Windsor .... Arthur Cornell
Mrs. Stimson Barr .... Amelia Summerville
Mrs. Emmy Wilkins .... Ada Gilman
Minnie Scott .... Mary Blair
Julia Kennedy .... Laura Nelson Hall
Mrs. Emmett Potts ...... Florence Pendleton
Miss Lucretia Dobbs .... Julia Reinhardt
Henrietta Holt .... Marion Kerby
Rev. Tanner .... Etienne Girardot
Buddy Martin .... Charles H. Meredith
Jerry McGrath .... J. Irving Southard
Miss Miller .... Auriol Lee
Elsie Harris .... Margalo Gilmore
John Martin .... Brandon Hurst
Frank Stanton .... Edward Fielding
Sofie Wojeska .... Zola Talma

HERITAGE, THE, melodrama, in four acts, by Eugene Walter. Produced by the Shuberts.—Playhouse, New York, January 14.
Antonio .... Cyril Keightley
Giuseppe .... Walter D. Greene
Enrico .... Hermann Lieb
Floretta .... Olive Oliver
Maria .... Madeline Delmar
Emily .... Margaret Vaune
Anna .... Louise Seymour
Georgette .... Eleanor Williams
Inspector X .... Lowell Sherman
Paul Young .... George Burton
Luigi .... Franklin George
Joe Ross .... Howard Sydney
Giovanni .... Antonio Salerno
Police Sergeant Ferris .... John Ward
Police Captain .... Gordon Burby
First Policeman .... Alfred Noone
Second Policeman .... Frederick Grace
Third Policeman .... Frederick Beane

HEMPFIELD, play, produced by the Russell Janney Players.—Pabst, Milwaukee, July 23.

HERO, THE, war episode, in one act, by Alice Brown.—Murat, Indianapolis, May 27.

HIDDEN MENACE, THE, play, by Edward Howard Crosby. Presented by the Somerville Players.—Somerville, Mass., February 11.

HIGH AND DRY, drama, by Lewis B. Ely.—Albany, May 23.

HITCHY-KOO, 1918, musical revue, in two acts and thirteen scenes, written by Glen MacDonogh, music by Raymond Hubbell, presented by Raymond Hitchcock.—Globe, New York, June 6.
Yogi .... Ivan Arbuckle
Yogi's Assistant .... George Spelvin
Plain Clothes Man .... Warren Jackson
Officer .... R. E. Addis
Lem Balliss .... Felix Rush
Stenographer .... Ruth Mitchell
Eve .... Edith Stockham
Helen of Troy .... Esther Wurtz
Circe .... Edith Whitney
Delilah .... Lucille Saunders
Lucrezia Borgia .... Irene Hayes
Pompadour .... Dorothy Koffe
Lola Montez .... Elsie Lawson
Cora Pearl .... Gertrude Rial
Cleo de Merode .... Dorothy Newall
Modern Siren .... Irene Bordoni
A Manager .... Raymond Hitchcock
A Backer .... Leon Errol
Martha Pringle .... Helen Weer
Brass Knuckle Bessie .... George Moore
Agony Al .... Charles Cartmell

Hitchy-Koo, 1918 (cont.).
Tilly .... Emma Haig
Kate .... Ray Dooley
Small Change .... Roy Cummings
Loose Cash .... Frank Bessinger
Carmen .... Sara Kouns
Jacinta .... Nellie Kouns
Verbena .... Laura Harris

HOMEBREAKER, THE, dramatic sketch, by Dodson Mitchell. Presented at the Lambs' 1918 Gambol.—Hudson, New York, June 14.

HOW TO HOLD A HUSBAND, play, in four acts, by Hal Reid. Produced by the Cecil Spooner Stock Company.—Grand Opera House, Brooklyn, December 3, 1917.

HUMPTY-DUMPTY, comedy, in four acts, by Horace Annesley Vachell, presented by Charles Frohman, Inc. (produced in London at the Savoy, June 14, 1917).—Majestic, Buffalo, September 2; Lyceum, New York, September 16.
Albert Mott .... Otis Skinner
John Delamothe .... Fleming Ward
General the Hon. Henry Delamothe
                        Morton Selton
Viscount Loosehanger ...... Robert Harrison
Higginbotham .... Ernest Elton
Jopling .... Robert Entwistle
Puttick .... William Eville
James Wallop .... John Rogers
Sinkins .... Walter Scott
Lady Susan Delamothe ...... Maud Milton
Nancy Delamothe .... Ruth Rose
Mrs. Mott .... Beryl Mercer
Crissie Parkins .... Elizabeth Risdon
Mrs. Rogers .... Clara T. Bracy

IN AND OUT, satirical comedy, in three acts, story and lyrics by Collin Davis and Howard Whitney Swope, music by Joseph C. Howard.—Belasco, Washington, July 22.

IN A NET, play, by Maravene Thompson.—Apollo, Atlantic City, May 16.

INFERNAL MASCULINE, THE, play, in one act, by Alfred Brand. Presented by the Pasadena Community Players.—Savoy, Pasadena, February 18.

I. O. U., melodrama, in three acts, by Hector Turnbull and Willard Mack, presented by William A. Brady.—Belmont, New York, October 5.
" Bobo " Hardy .... Mary Nash
Richard Hardy .... Frederick Truesdell
Ramdah Sima .... Jose Ruben
Kane Cavendish .... Kenneth Hill
Cecil Thornby .... Andrew Higginson
Mrs. Amanda Dodge .... Emily Fitzroy
Lottie .... Martha McGraw
Mrs. Barrows .... Helen Pingree
Ruggs .... George Riddell
Mr. Dorkins .... James Donian
Marie .... Florence Flynn
Ganda .... George Burton
Roy .... Burt West

INDESTRUCTIBLE WIFE, THE, comedy, in three acts, by Frederic and Fannie Hatton—Playhouse, Wilmington, January 1; Hudson, New York, January 30.
Charlotte Ordway .... Minna Gombel
James Ordway .... Lionel Atwill
Benjamin Field .... Frederic Esmelton
Amelia Field .... Mrs. Jacques Martin
Schuyler Horne .... Roland Byram
Paul Brooks .... John Cromwell
Brandy McBride .... Clay Clement
Julia Keith .... Jane Houston
Mary .... Irene Timmons
Ellen .... Esther Howard
Patmore .... Howard Kyle
Clapper .... Edward Leduc

132 THE STAGE YEAR BOOK.

INFORMATION, PLEASE, comedy, in three acts, by Jane Cowl and Jane Murfin.—Selwyn, New York, October 2.
Morrow ....Helen Salinger
Sir John Desmond, M.P. ....Orme Caldara
Lady Betty Desmond ....Jane Cowl
Ivy Druce ....Viola Compton
Simpson ....Henry Graham
Edith Bacon ....Blanche Yurka
Sir George Forrester ....Henry Stephenson
Gerald Forrester ....Robert Rendel
Smithers ....Clifford Brook
Meggs ....Harry Hanlon
Ralph Morse ....Malcolm Duncan
Bell Boy ....Jack McKee
Tom Morgan ....Alan Brooks
Frederick Coningsby ....Cecil Owen
Pierre ....Jules Epailly

INGRATE, THE, melodrama, in three acts, by M. Kellessar. Presented by the Washington Stock Players.—Comet, West New York, N.J., December 31, 1917.

IN THE DARK, play, by Percy Hirschbien. Presented by the Theatre Workshop.—People's House, New York, January 10.

INSIDE OUTSIDE INN, comic sketch. Played by Haviland and Thornton.—Fifth Avenue, New York, April 1.

IRISH LOYALTY, dramatic sketch, in one act, by Lawrence Brooke.—Empire, Lawrence, Mass., December 20, 1917.

IRON HAND, THE, war playlet, by Hall Caine. Played by Derwent Hall Caine and company.—Palace, New York, April 1.

IT PAYS TO FLIRT, comedy, with music, book and lyrics by Frances Nordstrom, music by Joseph McManus. Produced by the Shuberts.—Shubert, New Haven, April 24.

JAPANESE GARDEN, A, Japanese playlet, by Kenneth Webb, with music by Roy Webb. Presented at the Lambs' 1918 Gambol.—Hudson, New York, June 14

JONATHAN MAKES A WISH, play, in three acts, by Stuart Walker.—Murat, Indianapolis, August 12; Princess's, New York, September 10.
Letitia ....Elizabeth Patterson
Susan Sample ....Beatrice Maude
Uncle Nathaniel ....George Gaul
Uncle John ....Ainsworth Arnold
Jonathan ....Gregory Kelly
Mlle. Perrault ....Margaret Mower
Hank ....Edgar Stehli
Albert Peet ....Joseph Graham
Mary ....Elizabeth Black
John III. ....John Talbott

JOSEPHINE, satirical comedy, in a prologue, three acts, and an epilogue, by Herman Bahr, adapted by Dr. Washburn Freund.—Knickerbocker, New York, January 28.
In the Prologue.
Clio, the muse of history ....Grace Harrigan
The author's muse ....Ann Andrews
" Boney " ....George Frederichs
In the Play.
Josephine ....Virginia Harned
Barras ....Hubert Wilke
Louise ....Aimee Dalmores
Napoleon ....Arnold Daly
The Colonel ....Joseph McManus
Moustache ....Harry Mestayer
The Austrian Ambassador ....Paul Irving
La Rose ....Marion Ballou
The Abbe ....Coulton White
Talma ....Arthur Forrest

JULIUS CÆSAR, Shakespeare's play. Presented by the Shakespeare Playhouse.—Court, New York, March 15.

JUST AROUND THE CORNER, comedy, by George V. Hobart and Herbert Winslow.—Apollo, Atlantic City, May 9.

KAISER, BARBARIAN OF GERMANY, THE, play, by Kilpatrick Boone.—Indianapolis, September 8.

KAREN, drama, in four acts, by Hjalmar Bergstrom, translated from the Danish by Edwin Bjorkman. Produced by the Greenwich Village Players.—Greenwich Village Theatre, January 7.
Kristen Borneman ....Frank Conroy
Cecilia ....Grace Henderson
Karen ....Fania Marinoff
Peter ....Edwin Strawbridge
Thora ....Helen Robbins
Dr. Schou ....Joseph Macauley
Strandgaard ....Harold Meltzer
Hanzine ....Margaret Fareleigh
A Living-Out Maid ....Mary Pyne
A Typist ....Louie Earle

KEEP HER SMILING, comedy, in three acts and four scenes, by John Hunter Booth, founded upon a story by Edgar Franklin. Produced by Richard Walton Tully.—Shubert, New Haven, March 18; Astor, New York, August 5.
Mr. Donovan ....Byron Russell
Theodore Brackett ....De Witt C. Jennings
Henry Trindle ....Sidney Drew
Mr. Storer ....Ivan Christy
Stellar Goodwin ....Daisy Rudd
Grapely ....John H. Dilson
Mr. Bland ....John M. Washburne
Marie ....Rosanna Allison
Polly Trindle ....Mrs. Sidney Drew
Jim Merriweather ....Lincoln Plumer
Myra Merriweather ....Maidel Turner
Bentley ....Charles Mylott
Mr. Wainwright ....William T. Hays
Mr. Welburn Otis ....W. A. Whitecar
Middleton's Man ....Stanley Mortimer
William Sampson Truscott ......Page Spencer
Miss Atterbury ....Vira Rial
Hugh R. Stafford ....John F. Weber
Mr. Breckenbridge ....W. H. Post
A. Walter ....L. Tantillo
Mrs. Winston Pierce ....Rose Emerson
Miss Wainwright ....Nell Sandilands
Mrs. Welburn Otis ....Dorothy Quincy
Publicity Agent ....C. L. McVey
Dr. Morrow ....Edmund Dalby
Madlova ....Marie Bantzhaff
Slavarloofsky ....Fred Pena
Maruso ....Enrico Sbordi

KISS BURGLAR, THE, musical comedy, in two acts, book and lyrics by Glen MacDonough, music by Raymond Hubbell.—Academy, Baltimore, April 22; George M. Cohan, New York, May 9.
Aline ....Fay Bainter
E. Chatterton-Pym ....Cyril Chadwick
Mrs. E. Chatterton-Pym ....Grace Field
Miss Harte ....Janet Velie
Bert DuVivier ....Armand Kalisz
Tommy Dodd ....Harry Clarke
Oswald Gayly ....Denman Maley
Colonel Trotovitch ....E. Payton Gibbs
First Aide ....H. Morrison
Second Aide ....George Otto
A Detective ....A. Settle
Miss Tinkle ....Evelyn Cavanaugh
Mr. Toby ....Richard Dore
Proprietor of Inn ....Paul Dulzell
Waiter ....H. Coghlan
Pinkie Doolittle ....Gertrude Harrison
Tissie Baltimore ....June White
Rose ....Virginia Richmond
Natalie ....Betty Dodsworth
Page ....Peggie Ellis

AMERICAN PLAYS OF THE YEAR. 133

LADY OF THE CAMELIAS, THE, revised version of Dumas' play, by Edward Sheldon.—Empire, New York, December 24, 1917.
Armand Duval ....Conway Tearle
Georges Duval ....Holbrook Blinn
Prince D'Aurec ....Charles Wallace
Rene de Vavrille ....Percy Marmont
Gaston Rieux ....Leonard Mudie
Gustave Roger ......Charles F. Coghlan
St. Gaudens ....Maxwell Ryder
Doctor Guerin ....Wallace Erskine
Balliffs,. Frederick Raymond, Charles Webster
Marguerite Gautier ....Ethel Barrymore
Mme. Prudence ....Rose Coghlan
Nichette Duprat ....Mary Worth
Nanine ....Mary Hampton
Olympe Granier ......Edith Campbell Walker
Clemende ....Shirley Aubert
The Old Year ....Herbert Ayling
The New Year ......Cuscaden Blackwood
Baron de Giray ....Allen Ramsey
The Auctioneer ....Douglas Paterson
The Concierge ......John M. Troughton
Mme. La Comtesse D'Alencourt ..Noel Haddon

LAMBS' 1918 GAMBOL, THE.—Hudson, New York, June 14.

LAND OVER YONDER, THE, sketch, by Peter E. Kyne. Played by Charles L. Gill and company.—Palace, New York, July 29.

LET'S GO, revue, in two acts, presented by William Rock and Frances White.—Fulton, New York, March 7.

LAUGHTER OF FOOLS, THE, comedy, by H. F. Maltby. (Originally produced at Carlisle, May 21, 1909; Little, London, March 9, 1911).—Atlantic City, April 1.

LIBERTY GUN, THE, melodrama, by Robert Mears Mackay and Victor Mapes. Produced by the Shuberts.—Shubert, New Haven, May 30.

LIGHTNIN', comedy, in a prologue and three acts, by Winchell Smith and Frank Bacon.—National, Washington, January 28; Gaiety, New York, August 26.
Lightnin' Bill Jones ....Frank Bacon
John Marvin ....Ralph Morgan
Raymond Thomas ....Paul Stanton
Lemuel Townsend ....Thomas MacLarnie
Rodney Harper ....Harry Davenport
Everett Hammond ....E. J. Blunkall
Nevin Blodgett ....Sam Coit
Oscar Nelsen ....George Thompson
Fred Peters ....Sidney Coburn
Walter Lennon ....William F. Granger
Zeb Crothers ....George Spelvin
Liveryman ....Fred Conklin
Hotel Clerk ....James C. Lane
Mildred Buckley ....Beatrice Nichols
Mrs. Jones ....Jessie Pringle
Margaret Davis ....Jane Oaker
Mrs. Harper ....Bessie Bacon
Freda ....Beth Martin
Emily Jarvis ....Sue Wilson
Mrs. Moore ....Phyllis Rankin
Mrs. Jordan ....Minnie Palmer
Mrs. Brainerd ....May Duryea
Mrs. Starr ....Frances Kennan
Mrs. Cogshall ....Ruth Towle
Mrs. Brewer ....Helen Story

LIKENESS OF THE NIGHT, THE, Mrs. W. K. Clifford's play (produced in England at the Court, Liverpool, October 18, 1900; St. James's, London, October 28, 1901). Presented by the pupils of the American Academy of Dramatic Arts.—Lyceum, New York, March 29.

LITTLE BIT OLD-FASHIONED, A, play.—English's, Indianapolis, December 6, 1917

LITTLE BROTHER, THE, play, in three acts, by Milton Goldsmith and Benedict James. (Produced in London at the Ambassadors, February 6).—Royal Alexandra, Toronto, October 7; Belmont, New York, November 25.
Rabbi Elkan ....Walker Whiteside
Father Petrovitch ....Tyrone Power
George Lubin ....Richard Dix
Shinovitch ....Sam Sidman
Rube Samuels ......William St. James
Mr. Vanderlinde ....John Gomar
Marie Breschofska ....Edyth Latimer
Bridget ....Mary Malleson
Judith Elkan ....Mabel Bunyea

LITTLE TEACHER, THE, comedy, in three acts, by Harry James Smith. (Produced as "The Teacher of Goschen Hollow," at the Star, Buffalo, December 22, 1917).—Playhouse, New York, February 4.
Emily West ....Mary Ryan
Mrs. Caldwell ....Lillian Dix
Miss Meech ....Carolyn Lee
Mrs. Hodges ....Marie Haynes
Liz ....Kate Mayhew
Mrs. Tarberry ....Nina Morris
Mrs. Dale ....Viola Leach
Pansy Rollins ....Florence Curran
Aggie Brazee ....Maxine Mazanovich
Marie ....Katherine Brewster
Andy ....Tommy Gillen
Damien Bailey ....James Gillen
Lucius Bowman ....Paul Bryant
Pug ....Curtis Cooksey
Batiste ....Edward G. Robinson
Neal Brockway ....Ethan Allen
Bert Gresham ....Harold Hartzel
Ezekiel Fox ....Waldo Whipple
James McCullon ....Edward L. Snader
Mr. Brown ....William J. Phinney
Mr. Dunham ....Horace James

'LLE, play, in one act, by Eugene O'Neil. Presented by the Greenwich Village Players.—Greenwich Village, New York, April 18.

LOOK WHO'S HERE, musical play, book and lyrics by Harry B. Smith, music by A. Baldwin Sloane.—Trenton, N.J., August 30.

LORD AND LADY ALGY, revival of R. C. Carton's comedy (produced in London at the Comedy, April 21, 1898), by William Faversham.—Broadhurst, New York, December 22, 1917.

LOVE AND BUSINESS, comedy drama, in four acts. Presented by the Strand Players.—Strand, Hoboken, N.J., March 25.

LOVE FORBIDDEN, play, by Jacques Renaud (originally produced in Paris under the title of "L'Amour Defendu"). Presented by Joseph and I. Weber.—Ford's, Baltimore, February 4.

LOVE LIAR, THE, play, by Crane Wilbur.—Macdonough, Oakland, Cal., February 11.

LOVE'S LIGHTNING, comedy, by Ada Patterson and Robert Edeson. Presented by the Masks, Inc.—Lexington Opera House, New York, March 25.
Robert Clark ....Norman Hackett
Herman Langstrom ......Irving Lancaster
Jack Pierce ....J. R. Mason
Dick Lowell ....George M. Clark
Sato ....Thomas Yagin
Mrs. McConnell ......Josephine Williams
Mrs. Chevey ....Josephine Randall
Jerry ....Theodore Westman, Jr.
Constance Chevey ....Grace Carlyle
Marie Dauvray ....June Congreve
Mons. Ferris ....William Seymour
Maurice Ferris ....Alpheus Lincoln
Peter Barry ....Arthur Little

LOVE MILL, THE, musical comedy, in two acts, book and lyrics by Earl Carroll, music by Alfred Francis.—Shubert, New Haven, January 28; Forty-eighth Street, New York, February 8.
Mrs. Carter-Beaumont .... Grace Fisher
Mrs. Thompson .... Jeannette Lowrie
Millie .... Carrie McManus
Lucille .... Emilie Lea
Peggy .... Yolande Presbury
Count Aladin Claman Maria Przeaprodensky
.... Al Roberts
George Dodge .... Harry Tighe
William King .... Victor Morley
Tom Morris .... Clarence Nordstrom
James .... Edward Richards
Henry .... Joseph Bennett
Fifi .... Frances Fielder

LOYALTY, play, by George V. Hobart. Produced by Elliott, Comstock and Gest.—Ford's Opera House, Baltimore, May 20.

MADONNA OF THE FUTURE, THE, satire, in three acts, by Alan Dale.—Broadhurst, New York, January 29. (Title afterwards changed to "The Woman of the Future.")
Iris Fotheringay .... Emily Stevens
Rex Letherick .... Jerome Patrick
Sallie Winborn .... Frances Underwood
Mrs. Van Dusen .... Teresa Conover
Mrs. Wallingford .... Floliott Paget
Reginald .... Douglas Rose

MAGGIE, play, by Ed. Pepple.—His Majesty's, Montreal, January 14. (Title afterwards changed to "Patsy on the Wing.")

MAGIC FIDDLE, THE, comic opera, by Alonzo Price and Antonio Bafunno. Presented by the Opera Players.—Parson's, Hartford, June 24.

MAID OF FRANCE, THE, play, in one act, by Harold Brighouse (produced in London at the Metropolitan Music Hall, July 16, 1917). Presented by the Greenwich Village Players.—Greenwich Village, New York, April 18.

MAID OF THE MOUNTAINS, THE, musical play, in three acts, book by Frederick Lonsdale, lyrics by Harry Graham, music by Harold Fraser-Simson (produced in England at the Prince's, Manchester, December 23, 1916; Daly's, London, February 10, 1917).—Casino, New York, September 11.
Baldasarre, Brigand Chief .. Wm. Courtenay
Tonio .... Bert Clark
Beppo .... Carl Gantvoort
Carlo .... Jackson Hines
Andrea .... M. La Prade
Pietro .... Victor Leroy
General Malona .... William Danforth
Crumpet .... Al. Roberts
Lieutenant Rugini .... John Steel
Mayor of Santo .... William Reid
Zacchi .... Louis Le Vie
Teresa .... Sidonie Espero
Vittoria .... Miriam Doyle
Angela .... Evelyn Egerton
Gianetta .... Gertrude Hamilton
Maria .... Mina Davis
Marietta .... Marguerite May
Beppiria .... Eva Newton
Pepita .... Patricia Frewen

MAID, THE MAN, AND THE MONEY, THE, play. Presented by the B. F. Keith Players.—Hudson, Union Hill, N.J., September 23.

MAN AND HIS SHADOW, THE, Yiddish drama.—Irving Place, New York, August 29.

MAN POWER, play, in one act, by J. C. Nugent and Julie York.—Orpheum, Des Moines, May 31.

MAN THEY LEFT BEHIND, THE, war play, by Barton King. Presented by the Somerville Players.—Somerville, Mass., September 16.

MAN WHO STAYED AT HOME, THE, play, by Lechmere Worrall and J. E. Harold Terry (produced in London at the Royalty, December 10, 1914; in America as "The White Feather," Comedy, New York, February 5, 1915).—Forty-eighth Street, New York, April 3.
John Preston, M.P. .... John L. Shine
Miss Myrtle .... Florence Edney
Fraulein Schroeder .... Louise Muldener
Percival Pennicuick .... Philip Leigh
Dalphore Kidlington .... Nancy Winston
Molly Preston .... Charlotte Ives
Fritz .... John Burkell
Miriam Lee .... Katharine Kaelred
Christopher Brent .... Albert Brown
Mrs. Sanderson .... Amelia Bingham
Carl Sanderson .... A. H. Van Buren
Corporal Atkins .... J. Casler West

MARRIAGE OF CONVENIENCE, A, revival of Sydney Grundy's four-act adaptation of Dumas's comedy (produced in London at the Haymarket, June 5, 1897), by Henry Miller.—Henry Miller's, New York, May 1.
Comtesse de Candale .... Billie Burke
Marton .... Lucile Watson
The General .... Frank Kemble Cooper
Comte de Candale .... Henry Miller
Chevalier de Valclos .... Lowell Sherman
Jasmin .... Frederick Lloyd
An Officer .... Lewis Sealy
A Suisse .... Lynn Hammond

MARRIAGES ARE MADE——, comedy, in one act, by Bess Lipscultz. Presented by the Actors' and Authors' Theatre.—Fulton, New York, June 24.

MARRY IN HASTE, play.—Stamford, Conn., August 5.

MARY; OR, A STRING OF BEADS, play, by Maude Fulton.—Fulton Playhouse, Oakland, September 22.

MARY'S WAY OUT, play, by Ashton Stevens.—Morosco, Los Angeles, January 21.

MASTER, THE, revival of Benjamin F. Glazer's play (adapted from the German of Hermann Bahr), Boston, November 20, 1916; Fulton, New York, December 5, 1916.—Hudson, New York, February 19.

MATINEE HERO, THE, comedy, in three acts, by Leo Ditrichstein and A. E. Thomas, presented by Cohan and Harris.—Parson's, Hartford, September 12; Vanderbilt, New York, October 7.
Miss Hopkins .... Cora Witherspoon
Miss Davis .... Jessie Parnell
Frances .... Josephine Hamner
Frank Fairchild .... Brandon Tynan
Sam McNaughton .... Robert McWade
Giovanni .... William Ricciardi
Richard Leroy .... Leo Ditrichstein
Mrs. Leroy .... Catherine Proctor
Miss Blanche Langlais ...... Vivian Rushmore

MEDEA, by Euripides, revived by Margaret Anglin, in conjunction with the New York Symphony Society.—Carnegie Hall, New York, February 20.

MICHAL, play, by David Pinski. Presented by the Theatre Workshop.—People's House, New York, January 10.

MIDNIGHT, comedy, in three acts, by Samuel Janney and Edward Delaney Dunn. Presented by the Meridian Producing Company. — Playhouse, Wilmington, Del., April 8

AMERICAN PLAYS OF THE YEAR.

MISS BLUE EYES, musical play (based on George V. Hobart's farce, "What's Your Husband Doing?"), music by Silvio Hein.—Apollo, Atlantic City, October 3.

MISS I-DON'T-KNOW, musical play, by Rida Johnson Young and Augustus Barrett.—Stamford, Conn., September 14.

MOONLIT WAY, THE, play, by Sada Cowan. Presented by the pupils of the American Academy of Dramatic Arts and the Empire Theatre Dramatic School.—Lyceum, New York, February 1.

MOONSHINE, dramatic sketch, by Arthur Hopkins. Presented at the Lambs' 1918 Gambol.—Hudson, New York, June 14.

MOTHER'S LIBERTY BOND, melodrama, in four acts, by Parker Fisher.—Park, New York, August 9.
Hubbard Holmes ....Charles Foster
Hannah Trumbull ....Carrie Lowe
Jonathan Bond ....Richard Castilla
Peter Stanhope ....Charles B. Stevens
Alonzo Phelps ....Royal C. Stout
Adele Bond ....Gilda Leary
Alf Trumbull ....Edward Mackay
Suzanne Gilkrist ....Adeline Warwick
Sheriff Stone ....George La Tour
Earl Phelps ....Charles C. Wilson
Gov. Horace Bancroft ......Frank W. Taylor
An Orderly ....Joseph Williams

MOTHERS OF MEN, play, by Percival Wilde. Presented by the Columbus Centre of the Drama League of America.—Knickerbocker, Columbus, April 26.

MR. BARNUM, comedy, in four acts, by Harrison Rhodes and Thomas A. Wise.—Royal Alexandra, Toronto, June 17; Criterion, New York, September 9.
Mr. Barnum ....Thomas A. Wise
Nat Morley ....Richard Gordon
Kid Bailey ....Clyde North
Daddy Price ....Harold De Becker
Con Lonergan ....Jay Wilson
Props ....Leavitt James
Lucien Forterre ....Gaston Glass
Mr. Gerrone ....Albert Sackett
Henry Scratton ....Herbert Rice
Cody ....Francis La Mont
Aristide Letellier ....Albert Sackett
Sheriff ....L. Melton Clodagh
Alonzo Carter ....Luray Butler
Colonel Maurel ....William Seymour
Buckler Genin ....Luray Butler
Bill Collector ....L. M. Clodagh
George Washington Gibson ..Charles Jackson
Cuffy ....George Ford
Ticket Sellers ....John Pratt, J. N. Gaunt
Jeanne Letellier ....Phœbe Foster
Adelina Bonfanti ....Carlotta Monterey
Zueleika ....Ethel Cadman
Emma Morgan ....Adeline Mitchell
Lavinia Warren ....Queenie Mab
Jenny Lind ....Frances Nielson

MUGGINS, Lancashire comedy, by Frank J. Gregory and Hal Forde. Presented by the Actors and Authors' Theatre.—Fulton, New York, June 10.

MY DARK ROSALEEN, play, by Whitford Kane.—Auditorium, Lynn, Mass., December 17, 1917.

MY NEW CURATE, dramatisation of Father Sheehan's Irish novel of the same name. Presented by the St. Peter's Dramatic Society.—St. Peter's College, Jersey City, March 17.

MYSTERY OF LIFE, THE, morality play, by Father J. F. X. O'Conor.—Lexington Opera House, New York, May 6.

NANCY LEE, drama, in prologue and three acts, by Eugene Walter and H. Crownin Wilson. Produced by the estate of Henry B. Harris.—Hudson, New York, April 9.
Miss Nancy Lee ....Charlotte Walker
Mr. Lee ....Clarence Handyside
Miss Grace Lee ....Rosalie Mathieu
Mrs. Lee ....Pauline Duffield
Douglas Wreford ....Ralph Kellard
Andrews ....Charles MacDonald
Molly Day ....Jobyna Howland
Kittie Graham ....Charlotte Carter
Ethel Drayton ....Judith Voss
Johnny Boland ....A. S. Byron
Anthony Weir ....Lewis Stone
Alice ....Marie Pettes
Mrs. O'Neill ....Blanche Moulton
Process Server ....David Adler

NAPOLEON, dramatic sketch, by Edward Everett Rice.—Keith's, Jersey City, January 7.

NEWLY-MARRIED COUPLE, THE, dramatic playlet, by Bjornson. Presented by the pupils of the American Academy of Dramatic Art and Empire Theatre Dramatic School.—Lyceum, New York, March 22.

NIGHT IN JUNE, A, musical fantasy.—Harlem Opera House, New York, August 26.

NIGHT IN SPAIN, A, musical play, by Quinito Valverde. — Cocoanut Grove, Century Theatre, New York, December 6, 1917.

NIGHT IN THE TRENCHES, A, war sketch.—American, New York, August 19.

NOTHING BUT LIES, a "collierism in three acts and a little bit more," by Aaron Hoffman. Produced by Weber and Anderson.—Longacre, New York, October 8.
In the Prologue.
George Washington ....Grant Stewart
Ananias ....Malcolm Bradley
In the Play.
Jefferson Nigh ....Rapley Holmes
Lorna Temple ....Florence Enright
George Washington Cross ....William Collier
Molly Connor ....Jane Blake
Fred Thomas ....Robert Strange
Allen Nigh ....Clyde North
The Hon. Timothy Connor
                      William Riley Hatch
Anna Nigh ....Olive Wyndham
Bryan ....Frank Monroe
Foreman ....Harry Cowley
Bill ....Gordon Burby
Mike ....Malcolm Bradley
Potter ....James Bryson
Rufus Chadwick Pettingill ....Grant Stewart

NOT WITH MY MONEY, melodramatic farce, by Edward Clark.—Academy of Music, Baltimore, September 9.

ODDS AND ENDS, musical revue, in two parts and sixteen scenes, book by Bide Dudley and John Godfrey, lyrics and music by Dudley, Godfrey and James Byrnes. Produced by Norworth and Shannon.—Apollo, Atlantic City, September 24, 1917; Bijou, New York, November 19, 1917.

OFF-CHANCE, THE, comedy, in four acts, by R. C. Carton (produced in England at the Queen's, London, September 19, 1917).—Empire, New York, February 14.
Duke of Burchester ....Cyril Keightley
Lord Cardonnell ....E. Lyall Swete
Sir George Rainsford ....Albert Gran
Cornelius Jeffcott Bayne ....John Cope
Major Bagleigh ....Edward Emery
Mr. Brunson ....Thomas Louden
Deade ....Charles Webster

Off-Chance, T. e (cont.).
Meecher ....J. M. Troughton
Lethridge ....Charles Gibson
Duchess of Burchester ....Eva La Gallienne
Lady Rainsford ....Cecilia Radcliffe
Mme. Maria De Blanca ..Marcelle Roussillion
Mrs. Meecher ....Clara T. Bracy
Watson ....Louise Worthington
Lady Cardonnell ....Ethel Barrymore
OFFER $3,000, sketch. Played by Thomas Swift and Marie Kelly.—Riverside, New York, January 14.
OH! LADY, LADY! musical comedy, in two acts, book and lyrics by Guy Bolton and P. G. Wodehouse, music by Jerome Kern. Presented by Comstock and Elliott.— Albany, New York, January 7; Princess's, New York, January 31.
Parker ....Constance Binney
Mollie Farrington ....Vivienne Segal
Mrs. Farrington ....Margaret Dale
Willoughby French ....Carl Randall
Hale Underwood ....Harry C. Browne
Spike Hudgins ....Edward Abeles
Fanny Welch ....Florence Shirley
May Barber ....Carroll McComas
Cyril Twombly ....Reginald Mason
William Watty ....Harry Fisher
OH, MY DEAR! musical comedy, in two acts, book and lyrics by Guy Bolton and P. G. Wodehouse, music by Louis A. Hirsch. Produced by F. Ray Comstock and William Elliott.—Princess's, New York, November 26.
Hazel ....Evelyn Doru
Dr. Rockett ....Frederick Graham
Broadway Willie Burbank ....Roy Atwell
Grace Spelvin ....Marjorie Bentley
Bagshott ....Joseph Allen
Bruce Allenby ....Joseph Santley
Hilda Rockett ....Ivy Sawyer
Georgie Van Alstyne ....Helen Barnes
Pickles ....Miriam Collins
Babe ....Helen Clarke
Mrs. Rockett ....Georgia Caine
Jenny Wren ....Juliette Day
Joe Plummer ....Francis X. Conlan
Nan Hatton ....Florence McGuire
Miss Lenox ....Clara Carroll
Miss Bryant ....Dorothy LaRue
Miss Schuyler ....Gene Carroll
Miss Stuyvesant ....Frances Chase
Miss Rhinelander ....Victoria Miles
Miss Greeley ....Jennifer Sinclair
Miss Beckman ....Dorothy Bailey
Miss Cortlandt ....Bessie More
Miss Franklin ....Bene Manning
Miss Audubon ....Alfa Lance
Miss Barclay ....Patricia Gordon
Neal Clarke ....Sven Eric
Harry Coppins ....Robert Gebhardt
Willie Love ....Victor Le Roy
Frank Lynn ....Jaque Stone
OH, LOOK! musical comedy, in two acts, book by James Montgomery, lyrics by Joseph McCarthy, music by Harry Carroll.—Vanderbilt, New York, March 7.
Stephen Baird ....Harry Fox
Sidney Rosenthal ....George Sidney
Sam Welch ....Clarence Nordstrom
William Stewart ....A'fred Kappeler
James E. Morgan ......Alexander F. Frank
Hon. John H. Tyler ....Albert Sackett
Jackson Ives ....Frederick Burton
Captain West ....Harry Kelly
Ethel Bennett ....Frances Grant
Neil ....Charles Mussett
James Clark ....Jed Wing
Grace Tyler ....Louise Cox
Genevieve Tyler ....Genevieve Tobin
Mrs. John H. Tyler ....Amelia Gardner
Margy Elliott ....Florence Bruce
Claire Dainton ....Betty Nope Hale
Peggy Warburton ....Mildred Sinclair
Frances Huntley ....Betsy Hamilton
Ida Montaine ....Emily Morrison

ON THE HIGH SEAS, spectacular playlet, by George Melrose.—Palace, New York, February 25.

ON THE WESTERN FRONT, dramatic playlet.—City, New York, May 20.

ONE OF US, comedy, in three acts, by Jack Lait and Jo Swerling, produced by Oliver Morosco.—Morosco, Los Angeles, June 9; Bijou, New York, September 9.
David Strong, Jr ....Arthur Ashley
Elsie Strong ....Helene Montrose
Cyril Roswell ....Murray Stevens
Tony Watson ....Murray Vincent
Harry Miller ....Frank Livingston
Marie Foley ....Ruth Donnelly
"Frisco" Molly ....Isabella Jason
"Jazz Joe" Falk ....Harry Hart
Joan Grey ....Bertha Mann
"Parson" Smith ....Harry C. Bradley
"Coast-to-Coast" Taylor ...Charles Gotthold
Barry ....Frank Raymond
Mullen ....William Balfour
Egan ....Stanley Jessup
Mrs. David Strong ....Mrs. Edmond Gurney
Butler ....Williston Haggard

ONCE UPON A TIME, comedy, in four acts, by Rachel Crothers. Produced by Cohan and Harris.—National, Washington, December 3, 1917; Fulton, New York, April 15.
Bill ....Thomas Williams
Terry ....Mr. Olcott
Annie ....Elsie Lyding
Lizzie ....Jessie Ralph
Patsy ....Bonnie Marie
The Boy ....George Brennan
Mary ....Ethel Wilson
Jack ....Edward Fielding
Lenox ....W. L. Romaine

ONLY GIRL, THE, comedy playlet, book by Henry Blossom, music by Victor Herbert. —125th Street, New York, August 19.

ONLY SON, THE, play, in one act, by Marjorie Sinclair. Presented by the Pasadena Community Players.—Savoy, Pasadena, February 18.

OVER HERE, war play, in four acts, by Oliver D. Bailey.—Fulton, New York, September 11.
Keever ....George Schaefer
Haines ....Elmer Grandin
Daggart ....Harry Sherwood
Kenneth Merrill, Jr. ....Ralph Kellerd
Adolph Von Hellar ....William Ingersoll
Johann Berg ....Fred W. Peters
Kenneth Merrill, Sr. ......Harry Leighton
Beth Grayling ....Lily Cahill
Mrs. Kenneth Merrill, Sr.
                Evelyn Carter Carrington
Karl Von Hellar ....Leo Lindhard
An Officer of the U.S. Navy
                Frank E. McDermott

OVER HERE, dramatic playlet, by Samuel Shipman and Clara Lipman.—Riverside, New York, April 1.

OVER THE TOP, musical revue, in two acts and twelve scenes, words by Philip Bartholomæ and Harold Atteridge, lyrics by Matthew C. Woodward and Charles Manning, music by Sigmund Romberg and Herman Timberg. Produced by the Shuberts.—Forty-fourth Street Roof Theatre, December 1, 1917.

Principals.—T. Roy Barnes, Craig Campbell, Justine Johnstone, Joe Laurie, Aileen Bronson, Harry Sharrock, Emma Sharrock, Charles Mack, Vivian Oakland, Dagmar Oakland, Fred Astaire, Adele Astaire, Ted Lorraine, Ma Belle, Mary Eaton.

AMERICAN PLAYS OF THE YEAR. 137

OVER THERE, war melodrama, by Howard McKent Barnes. Produced under the direction of Oscar Eagle, by arrangement with Charles Hopkins. — Princess, Chicago, May 11.

PACK UP YOUR TROUBLES, "a group of amusing anecdotes of our soldiers in the camps and 'over there,'" by George C. Hazleton. Produced by Wagenhals and Kemper.—New National, Washington, June 17.

Betty Green ....Florence E. Martin
Lieutenant Rollins ....Harold Vosburgh
Mose ....John P. Wade
Private Burke ....H. Roy Beattie
Dr. Reed ....Frazier Coulter
Private Ikey Ikeystein ......Nathaniel Sack
Corporal Rankin ....Louis Fletcher
Miss Irene, Milliner ....Minette Barrett
Mrs. Chauncey Chauncey ......Emily Fitzroy
Miss Worthington ....Clay Carroll
Private Chauncey Chauncey
                              Norval Keedwell
Private Weston Wise ....Timothy J. Daley
Sal ....Martha McGraw
Private Tim O'Shaughnessey ......Joe Weston
Private Tom Shay ......Arthur Guy Empey
Mrs. Andy Shay ....Rose Stahl
Colonel Smith ....Roy La Rue
Private Bill Williams ....W. F. Williams
Fuzz ....Minette Barrett
Schmidt ....Philip Brown

PAIR OF PETTICOATS, A, comedy, in four acts, by Cyril Harcourt. Produced as "Petticoats," New Haven, March 7; Forty-fourth Street Roof, New York, March 18.

General Carew ....George Giddens
Sybil Carew ....Maude Hannaford
Captain Eric Lowndes ....George Mudie
Dr. Ross ....Ray Gordon
Captain Earl of Crowsborough..Cyril Harcourt
Commander Sir Ruqent Yeld ..Norman Trevor
Ferrers ....Byron Russell
Thomas ....Henry Travers
Mrs. Rockingham ....Laura Hope Crews

PAN AND THE YOUNG SHEPHERD, pastoral comedy, in two acts and seven scenes, by Maurice Hewlett (produced in England at the Court, London, February 27, 1906), acting version by Granville Barker, incidental music by W. Franke Harling. Presented by the Greenwich Village Players.—Greenwich Village, March 18.

Geron ....Joseph Macaulay
Neanian ....Sydney Carlisle
Balkis ....Grace Henderson
Teucer ....Everett Glass
Mopsus ....Edwin Strawbridge
Sphorx ....Harold Meltzer
Merla ....Margaret Fareleigh
Aglae ....Fania Marinoff
Erotion ....Ruth Ober
Sitys ....Janet Brownell
Geerna ....Hazel Sands
Phœno ....Anita Day
Dryas ....Helen Robbins
Adora ....Mary Pyne
Pan ....Frank Conroy

PARLOUR, BEDROOM, AND BATH, farce, in three acts, by C. W. Bell and Mark Swan.—Apollo, Atlantic City, July 16, 1917; Republic, New York, December 24, 1917.

Nita Leslie ....Francine Larrimore
Mary ....Mary Vallen
Virginia Embry ....Helen Menken
Leila Crofton ....Carolyn Lilja
Angelica Irving ....Sydney Shields
Reginald Irving ....John Cumberland
Geoffrey Haywood ....Will Deming
Frederick Leslie ....Richard Gordon
Samuel Barkis ....C. W. Butler
Polly Hathaway ....Florence Moore
Wilfred Rogers ....Tommy Meade
Carroll ....Nick Judels

PASSING SHOW OF 1918, musical production, in two acts and fourteen scenes, dialogue and lyrics by Harold Atteridge, music by Sigmund Romberg and Jean Schwartz.—Globe, Atlantic City, July 15; Winter Gardens, New York, July 25.

PATSY ON THE WING, comedy, by Edward Peple. Presented by Harrison Grey Fiske. —Broadway, Long Branch, June 24. (Originally produced under the title of "Maggie" at His Majesty's, Montreal, January 14.)

PEARLS, sketch, played by Robert Edeson and company.—Riverside, New York, January 7.

PEG OF PEACOCK ALLEY, melodrama of the war, by Hugh Stanislaus Stange and Stannard Mears.—Academy, Baltimore, May 20.

Jimmy O'Hara ....George Spelzin
Timothy "Red" Fitzpatrick..Joseph Allerton
Tony Ardelo ....Albert Prisco
Mrs. Parson ....Herbert Portier
Isabelle Wainwright ....Jane Gilroy
Peggy O'Hara ....Antoinette Walker
Mrs. Fitzpatrick ....Mattie Keene
The "Lout" ....George Spencer
Eileen Marcy ....Florence Johns
Mr. Drake ....Richard Allen
Smaltz ....Herman Gerold
Major Edward Turner, U.S.A. ..Orrin Johnson
Gas Man ....Fred Allen
Sergeant, U.S.A. ....George Armstrong
Stretcher-Bearers
                Walter Jones and W. Flannigan

PENROD, comedy, in four acts, by Edward E. Rose, based on Booth Tarkington's stories. —Apollo, Atlantic City, May 20; Globe, New York, September 2.

Tim ....Robert Vaughan
Della ....Flo Irwin
Mary Schofield ....Catherine Emmet
Burns ....Thomas Ford
Robert Williams ....Paul Kelly
Mrs. Laura Rewbush ....Maud Hosford
Jarge ....Leslie M. Hunt
Henry P. Schofield ....Edmund Elton
Margaret Schofield ....Helen Hayes
Mr. Jones ....George Meech
Herbert Hamilton Dada ......John Davidson
Penrod Schofield ....Andrew Lawlor
Sam Williams ....Richard Ross
Rev. Lester Kinosling ....W. F. Canfield
Rodney Magsworth Bitts ......Bevor Alvarez
Maurice Levy ....Henry Quinn
Georgie Bassett ....Ben F. Grauer
Mrs. Bassett ....May Ellis
Mamie Rennesdale ....Lilian Roth
Marjorie Jones ....Helen Chandler
Herman ....Thomas McCann
Verman ....Charles Whitfield
Mr. Coombes ....Jack Ellis

PETER'S MOTHER, play, by Mrs. Henry de la Pasture (originally produced in London at Wyndham's, September 12, 1906). Presented by William A. Brady.—Globe, Atlantic City, October 3

PETTICOATS. (See "A Pair of Petticoats.")

PLACE IN THE SUN, A, play, in four acts, by Cyril Harcourt (produced in England at Devonshire Park, Eastbourne, July 21, 1913; Comedy, London, November 3, 1913). —Comedy, New York, November 28.

Dick Blair ....Norman Trevor
Rosie ....Jane Cooper
A Farmer ....Henry Crocker
Stuart Capel ....John Halliday
Marjorie Capel ....Peggy Hopkins
Mrs. Moutrie ....Merle Maddern
Arthur Blagden ....Cyril Harcourt
Sir John Capel ....George Fitzgerald
Parsons ....Mr. Goodfellow
Agnes ....Florence Fair

5*

138 THE STAGE YEAR BOOK.

POMP, play, in one act, by Sada Cowan. Presented by the pupils of the American Academy of Dramatic Arts and Empire Theatre Dramatic School.—Lyceum, New York, January 11.

PRINCE THERE WAS, A, play, dramatised from the novel "Enchanted Hearts," by Robert Hilliard and Frank H. Westerton.—Apollo, Atlantic City, October 31.

PRINCESS MARRIES THE PAGE, THE, play. Presented by the Provincetown Players.—133, McDougal Street, New York, November 23.

PURPLE POPPY, THE, dramatic sketch, by Paul M. Potter and C. V. de Vonde. Played by Valeska Suratt and company.—Riverside, New York, December 3, 1917.

RAINBOW GIRL, THE, musical play, in three acts and four scenes, adapted from a story by Jerome K. Jerome, book and lyrics by Rennold Wolf, music by Louis A. Hirsch.—Forrest, Philadelphia, December 3, 1917; New Amsterdam, New York, April 1.

Daisy Meade .... Laura Hamilton
Frank Scudder .... William Clifton
Buck Evans .... Billy B. Van
Gus Norton .... Robert G. Pitkin
Robert Vernon Dudley .... Harry Benham
Mollie Murdock .... Beth Lydy
Miss Terris .... Miriam Medie
Miss Gwendolin .... Marguerite St. Clair
Clergyman .... Frederic Solomon
Miss Dudley .... Jane Burby
Miss Dudley .... Margaret Merriman
Girl in Blue .... Florence Ware
Mart'n Bennett .... Sydney Greenstreet
Susannah Bennett .... Claire Grenville
Honoria Bennett .... Kathleen Lindley
Ernest Bennett .... Harry Delf
Jane Bennett .... Lenora Novasio
Matilda Bennett .... Jane Callen
Mary Anne Bennett .... Marion Sitgreaves
Simeon Bennett .... Jesse Willingham
Charles Bennett .... Charles Fulton
Anastasia Bennett .... Julie Eastman
James Bennett .... Charles Hall
John Bennett .... Carlisle Blackton

RAPE OF BELGIUM, THE, melodrama of the war, by Max Marcin and Louis K. Anspacher, presented by A. H. Woods.—Shubert, New Haven, Conn., March 20.

REALIZATION, sketch, by John B. Hymer and Mabel Pierpoint.—Keith's, Jersey City, June 10.

REDEMPTION, drama, in two acts and eleven scenes, by Leo Tolstoy (adaptation of his drama "The Living Corpse"). Presented by Arthur Hopkins.—Plymouth, New York, October 3.

Anna Pavlovna .... Beatrice Moreland
Elizaveta Protosova .... Maude Hanaford
Sasha .... Margaret Fareleigh
Fedor Vasilyevich Protosov ... John Barrymore
Sopia Karenina .... Zeffie Tilbury
Victor Michailovich Karenin .. Manart Kippen
Prince Serghei Obreskov ...... Russ Whytal
Afremo .... John Reynolds
Ivan Makarovich .... Jacob Kingsberry
Nastasia Ivanovna .... Helen Westley
Masha .... Mona Hungerford
Ivan Petrovich Alexandrov .... Hubert Druce
Petushkov .... E. J. Ballantine
Artemyev .... Thomas Mitchell
Voznesenski .... Ernest Hopkinson
Examining Magistrate .... Charles Kennedy
Secretary .... Eugene Lincoln
A Young Lawyer .... William J. McClure
Petrushkin .... Arthur Clare
A Maid .... Ruza Wenclaw
A Nurse .... Gladys Fairbanks
Misha (first act) .... Helen Gaskill
Misha (second act) .... Lois Bartlett

REJUVENATION, musical playlet, by Kenneth and Roy Webb. Presented by the Actors and Authors' Theatre.—Fulton, New York, June 10.

REMNANT, comedy, in three acts, by Michael Morton and D. Niccodemi (produced in London at the Royalty, March 3, 1917).—Apollo, Atlantic City, November 4; Morosco, New York, November 19.

Jules .... Orrin Johnson
Tony .... George Gaul
Alphonse .... Etienne Girardot
Lougon .... Ben R. Graham
Manoa .... Corinne Barker
Emilie .... Dorothy Cheston
"Remnant" .... Florence Nash
Maid .... Marie Bruce

RETURN TO MUTTON, THE, play, by James N. Rosenberg. Presented by the Henderson Players.—Bramhall Playhouse, April 20.

RIDDLE WOMAN, THE, play, in three acts, by Charlotte E. Wells and Dorothy Donnelly.—Harris, New York, October 23.

ROADS OF DESTINY, play, in prologue and three acts, based on O. Henry's story of the same name. Produced by A. H. Woods.—Trent, Trenton, November 15; Republic, New York, November 27.

Prologue.
David Marsh .... Edmond Lowe
"Alec" Harley .... Malcolm Williams
Ann Harley .... Alma Belwin
Lewis Marsh .... John Miltern
A Voice .... Alma Kruger

Road to the Left.
David Marsh .... Edmond Lowe
Alan Harding .... Malcolm Williams
Marion Hardy .... Alma Belwin
"Spider" Lewis .... John Miltern
Rose Le Claire .... Florence Reed
"Pious" McPherson .... John Daly Murphy
Jim Gleason .... Claude Brooke
"Long Tom" Kirk .... Edwin Walter
The Barkeeper .... Charles A. Sellon

Road to the Right.
David Marsh .... Edmond Lowe
Alan Harding .... Malcolm Williams
Annette Harding .... Alma Belwin
Grantland Lewis .... John Miltern
Rosetta Clare .... Florence Reed
Andrew McPherson .... John Daly Murphy
Jennings .... Claude Brooke
Tom Church .... Edwin Walter
The Butler .... Charles A. Sellon

The Road Back Home.
David Marsh .... Edmond Lowe
Ann Marsh .... Alma Belwin
Lewis Marsh .... John Miltern
Rose Carter .... Florence Reed
Robert McPherson .... John Daly Murphy

ROBINSON CRUSOE, English musical comedy, book and lyrics by F. Stuart-Whyte.—Lyceum, Rochester, February 28.

ROCK-A-BYE, BABY, musical version of "Baby Mine" (originally produced in America at Fort Wayne, June 6, 1910; Daly's, New York, August 23, 1910—in London, at the Criterion, February 22, 1911), by Margaret Mayo and Edgar Allan Woolf, lyrics by Herbert Reynolds, music by Jerome Kern.—Shubert, New Haven, April 8; Astor, New York, May 22.

Pasquale .... Arthur Lipson
Archie Drummond .... Carl Hyson
Monte Laidlow .... Allan Hale
George Westbury .... Eddy Myers
Madame Tentelucci .... Edna Munsey
Bellboy .... S. Sydney Chon
Alfred Hardy .... Frank Morgan
Zoie Hardy .... Edna Hibbard
Jimmy Jinks .... Walter Jones

AMERICAN PLAYS OF THE YEAR. 139

Rock-a-Bye, Baby (cont.).
Chauffeur ....Frank Derr
Aggie Jinks ....Louise Dresser
Dorothy Manners ....Dorothy Dickson
Maid ....Claire Nagle
Weenie ....Mae Carmen
Finnegan ....Gus Baci
Weenie's Father ....H. Nelson Dickson
ROPE, THE, PLAY, by Eugene O'Neill. Presented by the Washington Square Players. —Comedy, New York, May 13.
Mary Sweeney ....Kate Morgan
Abraham Bentley.............Whitford Kane
Annie Sweeney ....Josephine A. Meyer
Pat Sweeney ....Robert Strange
Luke Bentley ....Effingham Pinto
ROSES, sketch, played by Schofield, Martin, and company.—Proctor's, Fifth Avenue, New York, December 31, 1917.
ROTTERS, THE, comedy, in three acts, by H. F. Maltby (produced in England at the Winter Gardens, New Brighton, July 10, 1916; Garrick, London, July 29, 1916).—Playhouse, Chicago, October 21.
RUNAWAYS, THE, comedy p'aylet.—125th Street, New York, August 26.
RUSHLIGHT, THE, play, in one act, by Monica Barry O'Shea. Presented by the students of the American Academy of Dramatic Arts.—Lyceum, New York, February 15.
SANDBAR QUEEN, THE, play, by George Cronyn. Presented by the Washington Square Players.—Comedy, New York, January 23.
SAVING GRACE, THE, comedy, in three acts, by C. Haddon Chambers (produced in England at the Gaiety, Manchester, October 1, 1917; Garrick, London, October 10, 1917). —Majestice, Buffalo, September 16.
SCHEMERS, THE, comedy sketch, presented by Hyman, Adler, and company.—Eighty-first Street, New York, February 18.
SEAL OF SILENCE, THE, sketch, played by Walter Law and company.—Folly, New York, January 21.
SECOND LOOK, A, comedy, in three acts, by C. A. de Lima. Presented by the pupils of the American Academy of Dramatic Arts and Empire Theatre Dramatic School. —Lyceum, New York, January 11.
SECRET, LE, revival of Henri Bernstein's drama (Opera House, Detroit, December 8, 1913; Belasco, New York, December 23, 1913).—Théâtre du Vieux Colombier, New York, October 14.
Constant Jannelot..............Jacques Copeau
Denis De Guenn ....Lucien Weber
Charlie Ponta Tulli ....Henri Dhurtar
Gabrielle Jannelot ....Lucienne Bogaert
Henriette Hozleur ....Suzanne Bing
Clotilde de Savageat ....Marcelle France
SEE YOU LATER, musical comedy, book and lyrics by Guy Bolton and P. G. Wodehouse, music by Joseph Szulc (adaptation of "The Girl from Rector's," Weber's, New York, February 1, 1909).—Academy, Baltimore, April 15.
SERVANT IN THE HOUSE, THE, revival of Charles Rann Kennedy's drama (produced in London, at the Bijou, Bayswater, June 19, 1907; Adelphi, October 25, 1909).— Théâtre du Vieux Colombier, New York, April 24.
James Ponsonby Makeshyfte, D.D.
                                Edmund Gurney
The Rev. William Smythe ....Wallace Erskine
Auntie ....Edith Wynne Matthison
Mary ....Adrienne Morrison
Mr. Robert Smith ....Ernest Anderson
Rogers ....Walter Kingsford
Manson ....Henry Herbert

SERVICE, drama, by Henri Lavedan (originally produced at the Théâtre Bernhardt, Paris, 1913). Presented by Harrison Grey Fiske, by agreement with Klaw and Erlanger and George C. Tyler.—Academy, Baltimore, November 5, 1917; Cohan, New York, April 15.
Colonel Eulin ....Lee Baker
Lieutenant Eulin...........Georges Flateau
General Girard ....Roger Lytton
The Minister of War ....Rikel Kent
Madame Eulin ....Mrs. Fiske
Pauline ....Alexa Fior
SEVEN DAYS' LEAVE, melodrama, in four acts, by Walter Howard, arranged for the American stage by Max Marcin (produced in London at the Lyceum, February 14, 1917).—Park, New York, January 17.
Rev. John Sharrow ....Frank E. Jamison
Kitty Sharrow ....Miriam Collins
Mrs. Keys ....Alice Belmore
Percy Skindles ....Edwin Taylor
Colonel George Sharrow ......H. Cooper Cliffe
Captain Cornelius Keys ....Galwey Herbert
Lord Arthur Pendennis ....Percy Ames
Lady Mary Heather ....Elizabeth Risdon
Stephen Darrell ....Frederick Perry
Madame Constance Morrell....Evelyn Varden
Captain Paul Lunmonde ....Edwin Forsberg
Major Terry Fielding ....William J. Kelly
Edgar Parsons ....Warren Hill
Fritz Oberdorf ....J. Fred Holloway
SEVENTEEN, comedy, in four acts, dramatised by Hugh Stanislaus Stange and Stannard Mears from Booth Tarkington's novel.— Shubert, Indianapolis, June 18, 1917; Booth, New York, January 21.
Mr. Baxter ....Lew Medbury
Jane Baxter ....Lillian Ross
Mrs. Baxter ....Judith Lowry
William Sylvanus Baxter ....Gregory Kelly
Johnnie Watson ....Neil Martin
May Parcher ....Beatrice Maude
Lola Pratt ....Ruth Gordon
Genesis ....George Gaul
Joe Bullitt ....Morgan Farley
Mr. Parcher ....Eugene Stockdale
George Cooper ....Paul Kelly
Ethel Boke ....Agnes Horton
Wallie Banks ....Arthur Wells
Mary Brooks ....Henrietta McDannel
SEVEN UP, farce, in three acts, by Alta May Coleman.—Shubert, Murat, Ind., July 1.
SHADOWS, playlet, by Lucie Lacoste, played by Lucie Lacoste and company.—Palace, Staten Island, May 6.
SHE BURNT HER FINGERS, comedy, by Cosmo Hamilton (dramatisation of Mr. Hamilton's story " Scandal ").—Washington, June 17.
SHE MUST MARRY A DOCTOR, play, by Solomon J. Rabinowitsch. Presented by the Theatre Workshop.—People's House, New York, January 10.
SHE TOOK A CHANCE, musical version of " A Full House " (presented by the Manhattan Players, Lyceum, Rochester, May 15, 1916). —Tremont, Boston, Mass, October 25.
SHE WALKED IN HER SLEEP, farce, in three acts, by Mark Swan.—Stamford, Conn., April 1; Playhouse, New York, August 12.
Charles Prescott ....Robert Ober
William Bruce ....Arthur Aylesworth
Dr. Roscoe Keith ....William Jefferson
Ted Lennox ....Walter Lewis
John Arnold ....Walter Walker
Daphne Arnold ....Alberta Burton
Serena Lennox ....Isabel Irving
Maude Bruce ....Helen Lackaye
Mamie Cassidy ....Eva Williams
Katherine Prescott ....Leila Frost
Bellboy ....Albert Bushee

SICK-A-BED, farcical comedy, in three acts, by Ethel Watts Mumford.—Pitt, Pittsburgh, January 22; Gaiety, New York, February 25.
Constance Weems ....Mary Newcombe
Patrick ....Edward O'Connor
Saji ....David Burton
John Weems ....John Flood
Mr. Chalmers ....Frank Connor
Reginald Jay ....Edwin Nicander
Dr. Flexner ....Charles E. Evans
Dr. Widner ....Dallas Welford
Miss Durant ....Mary Boland
Miss Hepworth ....Julia Ralph
Dr. Robert Macklyn ....George Parsons
                                (Specially engaged)
Officer ....Thomas Al'yn
SILENT SMITH, dramatic playlet, presented by Raymond Bond and company.—Eighty-first Street, New York, November 25.
SILENT WITNESS, THE, play, by Butler Davenport.—Bramhall Playhouse, December 15, 1917.
SINBAD, musical extravaganza, in two acts and fourteen scenes, dialogue and lyrics by Harold Atteridge, music by Sigmund Romberg and Al. Johnson, presented by the Shuberts.—Winter Gardens, New York, February 14.
SIRENS, THE, musical sketch, played by Frank Dobson and company.—Riverside, New York, November 4.
SLEEPING PARTNERS, farce-comedy, in three acts, from the French of Sacha Guitry (produced in London at the St. Martin's, December 31, 1917).—Bijou, New York, October 5.
He ....H. B. Warner
She ....Irene Bordoni
The Husband ....Guy Favieres
The Servant ....Arthur Lewis
SLUMWHERE IN NEW YORK, comedy sketch. Presented by Eddie Foy and family.—Palace, New York, August 26.
SOME BRIDE, miniature musical comedy, lyrics by John McGowan and Miss Blair Treynor, music by John Malloy.—Riverside, New York, February 18.
SOME DADDY, comedy, by Harry Allan Jacobs and James L. Campbell.—Apollo, Atlantic City, January 11.
SOME LITTLE GIRL, musical comedy, in three acts. Produced by Anderson and Weber.—Empire, Syracuse, March 14.
SOME NIGHT, musical comedy, in three acts, book lyrics and music by Harry Delf. Presented by Joseph Klaw.—Asbury Park, New York, August 19; Harris, New York, September 16.
John Hardy ....Forrest Winant
Robert ....Charles Welsh-Homer
Mrs. Hardy ....Camilla Crume
Marjorie ....Grace Edmund
Daisy ....Anna Fredericks
Bobby ....Harry Lambert
Joe ....Louis Simon
Dorothy Wayne ....Roma June
Madden ....Thomas H. Wa'sh
Joe Scanlon ....James C. Marlowe
Henry Spiffens ....Charles W. Meyers
SOMEONE IN THE HOUSE, melodramatic comedy, in four acts, by Larry Evans, Walter Percival, and George S. Kaufman. Presented by Klaw and Erlanger and George C. Tyler.—Knickerbocker, New York, September 9.
McVeigh ....Joseph Woodburn
Snowie ....Edwin Redding
The Deacon ....Wm. B. Mack
English ....Dudley Digges

Someone in the House (c.nt.).
Jimmy Burke..................Robert Hudson
Halloran ....Sidney Toler
Peter Spencer ....Robert Barrat
Freddie Vanderpool ....Rex McDougal
Tom Hargreaves ....John Blair
Gerald Fenshaw ....James Dyrenforth
Molly Brant ....Julia Hay
Mrs. Glendenning ....Lynne Fontanne
J. Percyval Glendenning ......Hassard Short
Higgins ....Basil West
Roberta Rollings ....Mona Kingsley
Malone ....John Sparks
Anderson ....James Henderson
Caffery ....George Andrews
O'Brien ....Henry Lawlor
Olson ....Thomas Larsen
SOMETIME, musical comedy, in three acts, book by Rida Johnson Young, music by Rudolf Friml. Presented by Arthur Hammerstein.—Atlantic City, N.J., August 26; Shubert, New York, October 4.
Mayme Dean ....Mae West
Phyllis ....Beatrice Summers
Henry Vaughn ....Harrison Brockbank
Loney ....Ed. Wynn
Enid Vaughn................Francine Larrimore
Dressing Room Girl ....Betty Stivers
Dressing Room Girl ....Virginia Lee
Joe Allegretti ....Charles De Haven
Mike Mazetti ....Fred Nice
Richard Carter ....John Merkyl
Sylvia de Forrest ....Frances Cameron
Argentine Dancer ....Mildred Le Gue
Argentine Singer ....William Dorlan
Apthorp ....Albert Sackett
George Gray ....Harold Williams
Roof Garden Manager ......Francis Murphy
Mr. Jones ....George Gaston
SOMEWHERE IN NEW YORK, sketch. Played by Gibbs and Colwell.—Harlem Opera House, New York, June 3.
SPARERIBS, comedy playlet. Played by Homer B. Miles and company.—Harlem Opera House, New York, April 1.
SPRING IS CALLING, sketch. Played by Leon Kimberley and Helen Page.—Royal, New York, September 16.
SQUAB FARM, comedy, in four acts, by Frederic and Fanny Hatton.—Savoy, Asbury Park, N.J., June 26, 1916; Bijou, New York, March 15.
Bruce Sanford ....Lowell Sherman
Jack Logan ....William L. Gibson
Gus (Gloom) Johnson .....Harry Davenport
Harry Fox ..,.............Charles M. Seay
Jed Burns ....Bert Angeles
"Pinkie" Florsheim ....Fred Kaufman
Eddie James ....Alfred Dayton
Duke Kenyon..............Raymond Bloomer
Randolph Travers ....G. Oliver Smith
Dixie De Vere ....Miss Julia Bruns
Mary Martin ....Miss Vivian Rushmore
Cleo de Montigny ....Miss Ann Austin
"Pop Tracy" ....Miss Susanne Willa
Babette La Mar ....Miss Florence Doyle
Rea St. John ....Miss Dorothy Klewer
Peggy Rogers ....Miss Marie Centlivre
Gladys Sinclair ...Miss Tallulah Bankhead
Martha Ehrlich ....Ester Small
Hortense Hogan ....Miss Helen Barnes
Jane Sanford ....Miss Jeannette Horton
Virginia Leslie ....Miss Alma Tell
SQUARING ACCOUNTS, comedy sketch. Played by John F. Weber and company.—Olympic, New York, April 8.
STARTING SOMETHING. "farmerette" comedy, in three acts, by Elizabeth Tyree Metcalfe. Presented for the benefit of the Red Cross.—Théâtre du Vieux Colombier, New York, June 5.

AMERICAN PLAYS OF THE YEAR. 141

STITCH IN TIME, A, comedy drama, in four acts, by Oliver D. Bailey and Lottie M. Meaney.—Fulton, New York, October 15.
Gilbert Hill ....Earle Mitchell
Lawrence Brockman ....Charles Hampden
Worthington Bryce ....Ralph Kellard
Jenkins ....David Higgins
Richard Moreland ....Robert Cain
Worthington Bryce, Sr. ....J. H. Gilmour
Phœbe-Ann Hubbard ....Irene Fenwick
Lela Trevor ....Grace Carlyle
Mrs. Trevor ....Evelyn Carter Carrington

STOP THAT MAN, comedy, in three acts, by George V. Hobart.—Opera House, Providence, October 31.

SUBMARINE ATTACK, THE, sketch, by Allen Lieber. Played by Helen Gleason and company.—Eighty-first Street, New York, December 10, 1917.

SUCCESS, comedy-drama, in four acts, by Adeline Leitzbach and Theodore A. Liebler, Jun.—Stamford, Conn., November 21, 1917; Harris, New York, January 28.
Dolly Dean ....Carree Clarke
Miss Hamilton ....Mildred Southwick
Willis Potter ....William Hassan
Phil Lawton ....Melton Cladoagh
Jane Arlington ....Helen Holmes
John Treadwell ....Arda La Croix
Mike Lewis ....Jess Dandy
Margaret Hamlin ....Emily Callaway
Gilbert Gordon ....Lionel Glenister
Barry Carleton ....Brandon Tynan
Nick Walker ....George Leffingwell
Henry Briggs ....James Durkin
Rose ....Marion Coakley

SUPPRESSED DESIRES, play, by Susan Glaspell and George Cram Cook. Presented by the Washington Square Players.—Comedy, New York, January 23.

SOUVERAINE, LA, play, by Gustave Vanzype, translated by Barrett H. Clark. Presented by the pupils of the American Academy of Dramatic Art and Empire Theatre Dramatic School.—Lyceum, New York, March 22.

TAMURA, Japanese play. Presented by the Neighbourhood Players.—Neighbourhood Playhouse, New York, February 23.

TEA FOR THREE, comedy, in three acts, by Roi Cooper Megrue. Presented by the Selwyns.—Belasco, Washington, June 3; Maxine Elliott, New York, September 19.
The Friend ....Arthur Byron
The Wife ....Margaret Lawrence
The Husband ....Frederick Perry
The Maid ....Kathryn Keyes
The Valet ....William Postance

TEACHER OF GOSCHEN HOLLOW, THE. (See "The Little Teacher.")

TELL THAT TO THE MARINES, comedy-drama, in three acts, by Adolph Philipp and Edward A. Paulton.—Yorkville, New York, September 24.
Hein Schulz ....Adolf Philipp
Helen Schulz...............Georgia Lee Hall
Charlie Schulz ....Joseph Striker
Jere Thurston ....Philip Lord
Tom Thurston ....Chauncey M. Keim
Maud Hopkins ....Cecil Kern
Bill Hopkins ....Jack Bernard
Abraham Shinegold ....Albert C. Winn
Maria Mueller ....Marie Pert
Carl Frumstadt ....John Hanson
Augusta ....Elsie Smith

THREE FACES EAST, melodrama, in prologue and three acts, by Anthony Paul Kelly.—Apollo, Atlantic City, April 22; Cohan and Harris, New York, August 13.
Kugar ....Joseph Selman
Helene ....Violet Heming
Colonel Von Ritter ......Fred J. Fairbanks
Captain Luchow ....Otto Niemeyer
George Bennett ....Charles Harbury
Lieut. Arthur Bennett ....Frank Westerton
Valdar ....Emmett Corrigan
Thompson ....Herbert Evans
Mrs. George Bennett ....Marion Grey
Dorothy ....Grace Ade
Miss Risdon ....Cora Witherspoon
Hewett ....Harry Lambart
Yeats ....Frank Sheridan
A Fugitive ....David M. Leonard
Lieut. Frank Bennett .....William Jeffirey
Nurse ....Mary Heen Mack

THREE WISE FOOLS, comedy, in three acts, by Austin Strong (produced as "Three Wise Men," Parson's, Hartford, October 15).—Criterion, New York, October 31.
Mr. Theodore Findley ....Claude Gillingwater
Dr. Richard Gaunt ....Harry Davenport
Hon. James Trumbull .....William Ingersoll
Miss Fairchild ....Helen Menken
Mrs. Saunders ....Phyllis Rankin
Gordon Schuyler ....Charles Laite
Benjamin Suratt ....Stephen Colby
John Crawshay ....Charles B. Wells
Poole ....Hayward Ginn
Gray ....Harry H. Forsman
Clancy ....Levitt James
Douglas ....J. Moy Bennett
Policeman ....George Spelvin

THREE WISE MEN. (See "Three Wise Fools.")

THROUGH THE KEYHOLE, playlet.—Eighty-first Street, New York, September 16.

TIGER! TIGER!! play, in four acts, by Edward Knoblock. Produced by David Belasco.—Ford's Opera House, Baltimore, November 4; Belasco, New York, November 12.
Clive Couper, M.P. ....Lionel Atwill
Freddie Staunton ....O. P. Heggie
Stephen Greer..............Wallace Erskine
Sam Tullidge...............Whitford Kane
Bartlett ....Thomas Louden
Sally ....Frances Starr
Evelyn Greer............Dorothy Cumming
Lizzie ....Auriol Lee
Mrs. Wix ....Daisy Belmore

TILLIE, play, by Helen R. Martin and Frank Howe, Jun., based on Helen R. Martin's story, "Tillie, the Mennonite Maid."—Court, Wheeling, W. Va., October 4.

TO ARMS! patriotic playlet. Presented by Lester Lonergan and company.—Olympia, New Bedford, Mass., January 28.

TOMMY'S BIRTHDAY PARTY, musical sketch.—125th Street, New York, August 19.

TOOT! TOOT!! musical play (adapted from "Excuse Me," by Rupert Hughes, Lyceum, Allentown, January 13, 1911; Gaiety, New York, February 13, 1911), book by Edgar Allan Woolf, lyrics by Berton Braley, music by Jerome Kern.—Wilmington, Del., December 25, 1917; George M. Cohan, New York, March 11.
Lieut. Shaw ....Louis A. Templeman
Lieut. Hudson............Anthony Hughes
Porter ....Harry Fern
Mr. James Wellington ......Edward Garvie
Mrs. James Wellington .....Flora Zabelle
Walter Colt, D.D. ....Earl Benham
Mrs. Walter Colt ....Louise Groody
Capt. Jones ....Greek Evans
Sergt. Flint ....Norman Bryan

Toot! Toot!! (cont.).
Lieut. Harry Mallory ......Donald Macdonald
Marjorie Newton ....Louise Allen
Snoozelums ....Himself
Messenger Boy ....Lew Renard
A Ballyhoo ....Alonzo Price
Pardora Buncombe ....Florence Johns
Hyperion Buncombe ....Billy Kent
Train Boy ....Ernie Adams
Conductor ....Ben Hendricks
Gambler ....Alonzo Price
Minister ....Louis A. Templeman
Chief Oskenonton ....Oskenonton
Peter Deerfoot ....Greek Evans
Karontowanen ....Albert Racklin

TRAP THE, dramatic sketch, played by Edwin Arden and company.—Proctor's Fifth Avenue, New York, January 14.

TRENCH FANTASY, A, play, in one act, by Percival Knight (originally produced at the Lambs' Gambol).—Plymouth, New York, January 31.

TRIMMING, comedy playlet. Played by Fitzgibbons and Normand.—Fifty-eighth Street, New York, May 13.

TRIUMPH OF THE PHILISTINES, THE, comedy, by Henry Arthur Jones (produced in London at the St. James's, May 11, 1895). Presented by the students of the American Academy of Dramatic Arts.—Lyceum, New York, February 15.

TWO PAIRS, comedy, by Donald MacLaren.—Shubert, New Haven, March 25.

UNCLE SAM, book by Mrs. Wm. Smith Goldenburg, Ned Hastings, and Horace G. Williamson, music by Wm. Smith Goldenburg. Produced by the Cincinatti Rotary Club.—Emery Auditorium, Cincinatti, December 12, 1917.

UNDER ORDERS, drama, in four acts, by Berte Thomas (produced in London at the Ambassadors' under the title of "Out of Hell," January 5; as "My Boy," Parson's, Hartford, May 6).—Eltinge, New York, August 20.
Arthur Ford ....Shelley Hull
Mrs. Ford ....Effie Shannon
Captain Hartzmann ....Shelley Hull
Frau Hartzmann ....Effie Shannon

UNKNOWN PURPLE, THE, melodrama, in prologue and three acts, by Roland West and Carlyle Moore.—National, Washington, June 24; Lyric, New York, September 14.
Peter Marchmont ....Richard Bennett
James Dawson ....Earle Brown
Phelan ....E. L. Duane
Bobby Dawson ....Arthur Le Vien
Ruth Charleton ....Lorraine Frost
Richard Bradbury ....Edward Van Sloan
George Allison ....Frank McCormick
Bonnie Allison ....Marion Kerby
Mrs. James Dawson ....Helen MacKellar
Johnson ....Herbert Ashton
Burton ....Curtis Benton

VERY GOOD YOUNG MAN, A, comedy, in three acts, by Martin Brown.—Belasco, Washington, August; Plymouth, New York, August 19.
Mrs. Hannigan ....Josephine Meyer
Pearl Hannigan ....Ruth Findlay
Walter Hannigan ....Frank Longacre
Katie Hannigan ....Fannie Bourke
Dutch Grogan ....Harold Salter
Mrs. Mandelharper ....Ada Lewis
Osprey Mandelharper ....Lydia Dickson
Leroy Gumph ....Wallace Eddinger
Elmer Erdwurm ....Alan Dinehart
Alex ....William Williams

Very G.o.l Young Man, A (cont.).
Julius ....Louis Fletcher
Lute ....Timothy Daley
Fred Pantzer ....Wm. H. Elliott
Birdie Pantzer ....Marion Dyer
Al Binne ....Eddy Meyers
Platina Gonne ....Virginia Curtis
Mr. Honey ....Glenn Kunkel
Minnie Pintitten ....Grace Knell
George Wemyss-Daingerfield..St. Clair Bayfield
Pebolita Berrigan ....Eleanor Boardman
The Roaches' Second Cousin..Clarke Williams

VILLAGE TINKER, THE, comedy. Presented by Fred J. Ardath.—Alhambra, New York, March 18.

VOICE OF McCONNELL, THE, play, by George M. Cohan.—Ford's Opera House, Baltimore, October 28.

WATCH YOUR NEIGHBOUR, play, in three acts, by Leon Gordon and Le Roy Clemens. Produced by Oliver Morosco.—Booth, New York, September 2.
Corporal Greene ....Le Roy Clemens
Commissioner ....Alexander Loftus
Major Tomms ....Frederick Esmelton
Capt. Fielding ....General Pring
Capt. Bennett ....Leon Gordon
Sergt. Birdseye ....Stanley Harrison
Edith ....By Herself
Dorothy Farnham ....Mary Servoss
Mr. Dudley ....Emil Hoch
Mrs. Patch ....Ruby Hallier
Comrade Deversalles ....Harold Vosburgh
Karl ....Dore Rogers
Comrade Olganoff ....Bertram Marburgh
Comrade Nagle ....Dodson L. Mitchell
Comrade Pastorelli ....Edward Colebrook
Comrade Beaubein ....John De Briac
Comrade Bergstoff ....Charles Fisher

WALK-OFFS, THE, comedy, in three acts, by Frederick and Fanny Hatton. Presented by Oliver Morosco.—Morosco, New York, September 16.
Mary Carter ....Frances Underwood
Sonia Orloff ....Fania Marinoff
Ah Foo ....Elmer Ballard
Carolyn Rutherford ....Roberta Arnold
Rose ....Mae McGinn
Peter Grandin ....Charles A. Stevenson
Schuyler Rutherford ....William Roselle
Judge Charles Brent ....Percival T. Moore
Mrs. Alicia Elliott ....Janet Travers
Fay Marsh ....Alison Bradshaw
Kathleen Rutherford ....Carroll McComas
Murray Van Allan ....Fred L. Tilden
Robert Shirley Winston ......Edmond Lowe
George Washington White ...E. Shackelford

WHAT NEXT? musical play, written, staged and produced by soldiers and sailors. Presented under the auspices of the Long Island Chapter for War Camp Activities.—Academy of Music, Brooklyn, November 4.

WHEN A WOMAN LOVES, play, by Mrs. Christian Hemmick. Produced by the Cecil Spooner Stock Company.—Grand Opera House, Brooklyn, December 17, 1917.

WHEN HE COMES BACK, playlet. Presented by Mrs. Gene Hughes and company.—Royal, New York, November 18.

WHEN ROGUES FALL OUT, comedydrama, in four acts, by C. W. Bell.—Lexington, New York, February 25.
Reda Colville ....June Congreve
Bobby Prichard ....George H. Clark
A Waiter ....J. R. Mason
"Bill" Truman ....J. Harry Jenkins
Helen Stanton ....Grace Carlyle
"Flukey" Haines ....Alpheus Lincoln
George Scott ....Joseph Hyland
"Doggy" Grice ....John D. O'Hara
Richard Farwell ....Irving Lancaster
Mrs. Ellison ....Leslie Leigh
Frederick Ellison ....Norman Hackett

AMERICAN PLAYS OF THE YEAR. 143

WHERE POPPIES BLOOM, melodrama, in three acts, by Roi Cooper Megrue, founded on the French of Henri Kistemaeckers.—Globe, Atlantic City, August 12; Republic, New York, August 26.
Guido ....By Himself
Breval ....Jean Gautier
Charlie ....Will Deming
Lagarde ....Laurence Eddinger
Pierre ....Alfred Hesse
Henry ....Percival Knight
Velieres ....Marcel Rousseau
Brochier ....Paul Doucet
Theuret ....Roy Walling
Bertolle ....Lewis S. Stone
Shorty ....Frank Nelson
Marianee ....Marjorie Rambeau
Rene ....Pedro de Cordoba

WHERE THE CROSS IS MADE, play. Presented by the Provincetown Players.—133, Macdougal Street, New York, November 23.

WHERE THINGS HAPPEN, war playlet, by Richard Madden. Played by Emily Ann Wesman and company.—Palace, New York, May 27.

WHY MARRY? comedy, in three acts, by Jesse Lynch Williams. Produced by Selwyn and company.—Cohan's Grand Opera House, Chicago, November 5, 1917; Astor, New York, December 25, 1917.
Jean ....Lotus Robb
Rex ....Harold West
Lucy ....Beatrice Beckley
Theodore ....Ernest Lawford
Everett ....Nat C. Goodwin
Helen ....Estelle Winwood
Ernest ....Shelley Hull

WHY NOT ME?—A WOMAN, play, by Stephen Gardner Champlin.—Dixon's Third Avenue, New York, September 16.

WHY WORRY? melodramatic farce, with songs, by Montague Glass and Jules Eckert Goodman.—Belasco, Washington, July 29; Harris, New York, August 23.
Dora ....Fannie Brice
Stella ....May Boley
Mrs. Harris ....Vera Gordon
Shapiro ....Ezra C. Walck
Felix Noblestone ....George Sidney
Louis ....Carl Dietz
Steffens ....Edwin Maxwell
Wolter ....Harry Dumont
David Meyer ....Charles Trowbridge
Devlin ....Jack Sharkey
Thorpe ....John Wallace
Dan ....Ralph Belmont
A Lady ....Francesca Rotoli
A Gentleman ....True S. James
Rashkind ....Joe Smith
Margolius ....Irving Kaufman
Dubin ....Harry Goodwin
November ....Charles Dale
Flo ....Frances Richards
Frost ....Kalman Matus
Bedell ....James Cherry

WIDOW'S WEEDS, THE, comedy-drama of rural life, in four acts, by Alfred H. Brown. Presented by the Masks, Inc.—Lexington, New York, March 11.
Bruce Weston ....Theodore Westman, Jr.
Peachy Jones ....Grace Carlyle
Spencer Martin ....J. J. Hyland
Mrs. Shattuck ....Lisle Leigh
Jennie Wrenn ....June Congreve
Jack Clover ....Alpheus Lincoln
Mrs. Helen Mabie ....Mildred Southwick
Bob Mable ....Geo. M. Clark
Florence Wrenn...............Letha Walters
Tip Banning ....Norman Hackett
Mrs. Martin................Margaret Macklyn
Ina Shattuck ....J. Jenkins
Jeff Sparks ....Irving Lancaster
Silas Blin ....John J. O'Hara
Matt Buell ....J. H. Price
Nancy Buell ....Persis Atwood Smith

WILD DUCK, THE, play, by Ibsen (produced in London at the Royalty, May 5, 1894). —Plymouth, New York, March 12.
Werle ....Dodson Mitchell
Gregers Werle ....Harry Mestayer
Old Ekdal ....Edward Connelly
Hjalmar Ekdal ....Lionel Atwill
Gina Ekdal ....Amy Veness
Hedvig ....Mme. Nazimova
Mrs. Sorby ....Nora Lamison
Relling ....Lyster Chambers
Molvik ....St. Clair Bayfield
Graberg ....Adelbert Knott
Pettersen ....A. O. Huhn
Jensen ....Frederick Gibbs
A Flabby Gentleman ....Walter C. Wilson
A Thin-Haired Gentleman ....J. H. Wright
A Short-Sighted Gentleman ......George Paige

WINNING OF MA, THE, comedy, dramatised from the "Fackinger" stories of Isaac and Michael Landman by Bessie R. Hoover. Produced by Cohan and Harris.—Apollo, Atlantic City, July 8.

WOMAN OF THE FUTURE, THE. (See "The Madonna of the Future.")

WOMAN ON THE INDEX, THE, drama, in a prologue and three acts, by Lillian Trimple Bradley and George Broadhurst, based on a story by Frank M. O'Brien.—Harmanus Bleecker Hall, Albany, N.Y., February 21; Forty-eighth Street, New York, August 29.
Sylvie Angot ....Julia Dean
Mme. Zenlon ....Eugenie Blair
Police Captain Zenlon ....Lee Baker
Dr. Anderson ....Walter Ringham
Jacques Despard ....Curtis Karpe
Louis Ganz ....James Grace
David Maber ....Lester Lonergan
Henri Delcasse ....George Probert
Robert Alden ....Lee Baker
General Sir William Thorndyke
                                Walter Bingham
M. Deschamps ....George Le Soir
Zetts ....Bennett Southard
Johnson ....Harry Hadfield
Oki ....T. Tamamoto
Helen Maber ....Julia Dean
Lady Millicent Thorndyke..Alison Skipworth
Madame Deschamps ....Camilla Dalberg
Mme. Barrios ....Constance De Vois

WORDS AND MUSIC, musical revue, words said to be by Shakespeare and music by Beethoven.—Fulton, New York, December 24, 1917.
A Yogi ....Wellington Cross
A Distinguished Playwright ....Frank Mayne
A Famous Composer ....Ben Hendricks
The Yogi's Assistant ....Harry Seymour
A Commuter ....Gladys Logan
A Stenographer ....Anna May Seymour
A Gambler ....Jay Wilson
A Theatrical Manager ....Richard Carle
Eve ....Mildred Colby
Helen of Troy ....Ellen Cassidy
Circe ....Edythe Whitney
Delilah ....Evelyn Monte
Lucretia Borgia ....Lillian Davis
Madamella Pompadour ....Dorothy Koffee
Lola Montez ....Evelyn Kerner
Cora Pearl ....Flo Hart
Gaby Delys ....Marion Davies
A Plain Clothes Man ....Harry Tanner
Gazzoleen ....Ray Dooley
Al Radish ....William Dooley
Inbad ....Gordon Dooley

WORK FOR UNCLE SAM, war sketch, by Clara Lipman and Samuel Shipman.—Alhambra, New York, November 25.

YES OR NO, drama, in a prologue, three acts, and an epilogue, by Arthur Goodrich, produced by Anderson and Weber.—Murat, Indianapolis, October 11, 1917; Forty-eighth Street, New York, December 21, 1917.

Nell	Eva Francis
General Kent	Kalman Matus
Margaret Vane	Willette Kershaw
Donald Vane	Frank Wilcox
Phil	Walter Regan
Paul Derrick	Byron Beasley
Dr. Malloy	Halbert Brown
Minnie	Emilie Polini
Jack	Robert Kelly
Emma	Marjorie Wood
Tom	John Adair, Jr.
Ruth	Louis Bartlett
Dan	William Read
Ellen	Margaret Lytle
Leach	Malcolm Duncan
Hooker	John Butler
Kittie	Bliss Milford
Daniel Berry	Frank Aberwald
Ruth Berry	Alice Smyth
Nicholas Rankin	Irving Dillon

YIP, YIP, YAPHANK, words and music by Irving Berlin. Produced by the soldiers at Camp Upton.—Century, New York, August 19.

YOUNG GIRL'S ROMANCE, A, play. Produced by the Cecil Spooner Company.—Grand, Brooklyn, December 3, 1917.

YOUTH, comedy, in three acts, by Miles Malleson (only produced by the Stage Society, Court, London, March 26, 1916). Presented by the Washington Square Players.—Comedy, New York, February 20.

Nina Geoffreys	Marjorie Vonnegut
Douglas Hetherly	Saxon Kling
Joe	John King
Frank Denton	Robert Strange
Ferris	Edward Balzerit
Cecil Wainwright	Arthur Hohl
May	Jay Strong
Antony Gunn	Edward F. Flammer
Tom	James Terbell
The Rev. John Hetherly	Samuel Jaffe
Estelle	Helen Westley

YUM CHAPAB, pantomime, by J. Garcia Pimental and Beatrice de Holthoir. Presented by the Washington Square Players.—Comedy, New York, December 3, 1917.

ZIEGFELD FOLLIES of 1918, revue, in two acts and twenty-six scenes, lines and lyrics by Rennold Wolf and Gene Buck, music by Louis Hirsch, Dave Stamper, Irving Berlin and Victor Jacobi.—New Amsterdam, New York, June 18.

FIRES IN AMERICAN THEATRES.

December 8, 1917.—Strand, Spokane, Wash., severely damaged.
January 14.—Victoria, Dayton, damaged.
January 15.—Chicago Theatre, Chicago, destroyed.
May 20.—Clifford, Urbana, Ohio, destroyed.
July.—Family, Rochester, damaged.
August 8.—Pastime, Columbia, S.C., destroyed.

NEW THEATRES OPENED IN AMERICA.

January 7.—Pantages, Tacoma. Drama.
January 28.—Norworth, New York. Drama.
March 11.—Al. H. Woods, Chicago. Drama.
March 19.—Liberty, Staten Island. Drama.
April 1.—Henry Miller's Theatre, New York. Drama.
May 13.—Diamond, New Orleans. Vaudeville and Pictures.
July.—Pantages, Spokane. Variety.
August 26.—Sam S. Shubert Memorial, Philadelphia. Drama.
September 9.—Central, New York. Drama.
September 16.—Metropolitan, Brooklyn. Vaudeville.
October 2.—Selwyn, New York. Drama.

AUTHORS (PLAYS IN AMERICA) OF THE YEAR

AN ALPHABETICAL LIST OF AUTHORS, COMPOSERS, AND ADAPTORS, WHOSE PLAYS, OPERAS, ETC., HAVE BEEN PRODUCED OR REVIVED BETWEEN DECEMBER 1, 1917, AND NOVEMBER 30, 1918, ALSO OF THOSE WHOSE WORKS HAVE BEEN DRAWN UPON BY DRAMATISTS, INCLUDING AUTHORS OF FOREIGN PLAYS FROM WHICH AMERICAN ADAPTATIONS HAVE BEEN MADE.

ANDERSON, MARY.—" The Garden of Allah."
ANSPACHER, LOUIS K.—" The Rape of Belgium."
ANTHONY, SERGEANT EDWARD.—" Good Luck, Uncle Sam! "
ATTERIDGE, HAROLD.—" Over the Top," " Sinbad," " The Passing Show of 1918."

BACON, FRANK.—" Lightnin'."
BAFUNNO, ANTONIO.—" The Magic Fiddle."
BAILEY, OLIVER D.—" A Stitch in Time," " Over Here."
BAIRNSFATHER, BRUCE.—" The Better 'Ole."
BAHR, HERMAN. — " Josephine," " The Master."
BARKER, GRANVILLE.—" Pan and the Young Shepherd."
BARON, WILLIAM LEE.—" Back to Earth."
BARTHOLOMAE, PHILIP.—" Over the Top," " Girl o' Mine."
BARNES, HOWARD McKENT.—" Over There."
BARRETT, AUGUSTUS. — " Fancy Free," " Miss I-Don't-Know."
BARRY, TOM.—" The Barrier."
BEITH, MAJOR (Ian Hay).—" Getting Together."
BELL, C. W.—" Parlour, Bedroom, and Bath," " When Rogues Fall Out."
BENNETT, ARNOLD.—" Helen-with-the-High-Hand."
BERGSTROM, HJALMAR.—" Karen."
BERLIN, IRVING.—" The Cohen Revue, 1918," " Ziegfeld Follies of 1918," " Yip, Yip, Yaphank."
BERNSTEIN, HENRI.—" Le Secret."
BESIER, RUDOLF.—" Her Country."
BISSON.—" The Grass Widow."
BJORKMAN, EDWIN.—" Karen."
BJORNSON.—" The Newly Married Couple."
BOLTON, GUY.—" Oh, Lady, Lady," " See You Later," " The Girl Behind the Gun," " Ask Dad," " Oh, My Dear."
BOONE, KILPATRICK.—" The Kaiser, Barbarian of Germany."
BOOTH, JOHN HUNTER.—" Keep Her Smiling."
BOWER, MARION.—" The Chinese Puzzle."
BRADLEY, LILLIAN T.—" The Woman on the Index."
BRAILEY, BERTON.—" Toot! Toot!! "
BRAND, ALFRED.—" The Infernal Masculine."
BRIGHOUSE, HAROLD.—" Garside's Career," " The Maid of France."
BROADHURST, GEORGE.—" The Woman on the Index," " He Didn't Want to Do It."
BROADWAY, MRS. WALTER.—" Family Pride."
BROOKE, LAWRENCE.—" Irish Loyalty."
BROWN, ALICE.—" The Hero."

BROWN, ALFRED H.—" The Widow's Weeds."
BROWN, MARTIN.—" The Very Good Young Man."
BUCK, GENE.—" Ziegfeld Follies of 1918."
BUSSIERE, TADEMA.—" A Friendly Divorce."
BYRNES, JAMES.—" Odds and Ends."

CAINE, HALL.—" The Iron Hand."
CAMPBELL, JAMES L.—" Some Daddy."
CARROLL, EARL.—" The Love Mill."
CARROLL, HARRY.—" Oh, Look! "
CARTER, LINCOLN J.—" An American Ace."
CARTON, R. C.—" The Eccentric Lord Comberdene," " The Off Chance," " Lord and Lady Algy."
CARYLL, IVAN.—" The Girl Behind the Gun," " The Canary."
CHAMBERS, C. HADDON.—" The Saving Grace."
CHAMPLIN, STEPHEN GARDNER.—" Why Not Me—a Woman? "
CHAUVENET, JULES.—" Girl of My Heart."
CLARK, EDWARD.—" Bruised Wings," " Not with My Money."
CLEMENS, LE ROY.—" Watch Your Neighbour."
CLIFFORD, MRS. W. K.—" The Likeness of the Night."
COHAN, GEORGE M.—" The Cohan Revue, 1918," " The Voice of McConnell."
COLEMAN, ALTA MAY.—" Seven Up."
COOPER, ROI MEGRUE.—" Tea for Three."
COURTELINE, GEORGE.—" The Fine System."
COWAN, SADA.—" Pomp," " The Moonlit Way."
COWL, JANE.—" Information, Please."
CRONYN, GEORGE.—" The Sandbar Queen."
CROSBY, EDWARD HOWARD. — " The Menace."
CROSMAN, GEORGE.—" For Our Boys."
CROTHERS, RACHEL.—" Once Upon a Time."
CUSHING, CATHERINE CHISHOLM. — " Glorianna."

DALE, ALAN.—" The Madonna of the Future."
DALRYMPLE, LEONA.—" David's Adventure."
DALY, ARNOLD.—" Democracy's King."
DARE, FRANK.—" Habit."
DAREWSKI, HERMAN.—" The Better 'Ole."
DAVENPORT, BUTLER.—" The Silent Witness."
DAVIS, COLLIN.—" In and Out."
DAVIS, OWEN.—" The Arabian Nights," " Forever After."
DAVIS, R. H.—" Efficiency."
DE GRESAC, FRED.—" Flo-Flo."
DE HOLTHOIR, BEATRICE.—" Yum Chapab."
DE LA PASTURE, MRS. HENRY.—" Peter's Mother."

DELF, HARRY.—"Some Night."
DE LIMA, C. A.—"A Second Look."
DE MATTOS, ALEXANDER TEIXEIRA — "The Betrothed."
DERR BIGGERS, EARL.—"A Cure for Curables."
DE VONDE, C. D.—"The Purple Poppy."
DITRICHSTEIN, LEO.—"The Matinée Hero."
DONNELLY, DOROTHY.—"Fancy Free," "The Riddle Woman."
DREISER, THEODORE.—"The Girl in the Coffin"
DUDLEY, BIDE.—"Odds and Ends."
DUMAS, ALEXANDRE.—"A Marriage of Convenience," "The Lady of the Camellias."
DUNCAN, WILLIAM CARY. — "Fiddlers Three."
DUNN, EDWARD DELANEY.—"Midnight."

EDESON, ROBERT.—"Love's Lightning."
ELIOT, ARTHUR.—"The Better 'Ole."
ELY, LEWIS B.—"High and Dry."
EVANS, LARRY.—"Someone in the House."

FECKHEIMER, PTE. RICHARD.—"Good-bye, Bill."
FERRIS, MABEL.—"Another Man's Shoes."
FISHER, PARKER.—"Mother's Liberty Bond."
FLEXNER, ANNE CRAWFORD.—"The Blue Pearl."
FOOTE, JOHN TAINTOR.—"Flying Colours."
FORDE, HAL.—"Muggins."
FRANCIS, ALFRED.—"The Love Mill."
FRANKLIN, EDGAR.—"Keep Her Smiling."
FREUND, E. WASHBURN.—"Josephine."
FRASER-SIMSON, HAROLD.—"The Maid of the Mountains."
FRIML, RUDOLPH.—"Sometime," "Gloriana."
FULTON, MAUDE.—"Mary; or, A String of Beads."

GATES, ELEANOR.—"The Darling of the World."
GLASPELL, SUSAN.—"Suppressed Desires," "Close the Book."
GLASS, MONTAGUE.—"Why Worry?"
GLAZER, BENJAMIN F.—"The Master."
GODFREY, JOHN.—"Odds and Ends."
GOLDEN, JOHN L.—"Flying Colours," "Everything."
GOLDENBURG, MRS. WM. SMITH.—"Uncle Sam."
GOLDENBURG, WM. SMITH.—"Uncle Sam."
GOLDSMITH, MILTON. — "The Little Brother."
GOODMAN, JULES ECKERT. — "Why Worry?"
GOODRICH, ARTHUR.—"Yes or No."
GORDON, KILGOUR.—"Enemies Within."
GORDON, LEON.—"Watch Your Neighbour."
GRAHAM, HARRY.—"The Maid of the Mountains."
GREGORY, FRANK J.—"Muggins."
GRUNDY, SYDNEY.—"A Marriage of Convenience."
GUITRY, SACHA.—"Sleeping Partners."

HAMILTON, COSMO.—"She Burnt Her Fingers."
HAMILTON, HENRY.—"The Harvest."
HARBACH, OTTO.—"Going Up."
HARCOURT, CYRIL.—"A Place in the Sun."
HARLING, W. FRANKE.—"Pan and the Young Shepherd."
HARRIS, CURRA.—"A Cure for Curables."
HARTLEY, RANDOLPH.—"The Daughter of the Forest."
HARWOOD, H. M.—"Billeted."
HASTINGS, NED.—"Uncle Sam."
HATTON, FANNY. — "The Indestructible Wife," "Squab Farm," "The Walk-offs."

HATTON, FREDERIC.—"The Indestructible Wife," "Squab Farm," "The Walk-offs."
HAZELTON, GEORGE C.—"Pack Up Your Troubles."
HEIN, SILVIO.—"Flo-Flo," "He Didn't Want to Do It," "Miss Blue Eyes."
HELBURN, THERESA. — "Crops and Croppers."
HEMMICK, MRS. CHRISTIAN.—"When a Woman Loves."
HENRY, O.—"Roads to Destiny."
HERBERT, VICTOR.—"The Only Girl."
HEWLETT, MAURICE.—"Pan and the Young Shepherd."
HICHENS, ROBERT.—"The Garden of Allah."
HILLIARD, ROBERT.—"A Prince There Was."
HIND, C. LEWIS.—"Freedom."
HINES, ARLINE VAN NESS.—"Her Honour, The Mayor."
HINKLEY, LAURA.—"Another Man's Shoes."
HIRSCH, LOUIS A.—"The Grass Widow," "The Rainbow Girl," "Going Up," "Back Again," "Ziegfeld Follies of 1918," "Ask Dad," "Oh, My Dear."
HIRSCHBIEN, PERCY.—"In the Dark."
HOBART, GEORGE V.—"Back Again," "Just Around the Corner," "Loyalty," "The Drums," "Miss Blue Eyes," "Stop that Man."
HOBBLE, JOHN LESSING.—"Daddies."
HOFFMAN, AARON.—"Friendly Enemies," "Nothing but Lies."
HOLLEY, HORACE.—"Her Happiness."
HOOVER, BESSIE R.—"The Winning of Ma."
HOPKINS, ARTHUR.—"Moonshine."
HOPWOOD, AVERY.—"Double Exposure."
HOUSUM, ROBERT.—"The Gypsy Trail."
HOWE, FRANK, JUN.—"Tillie."
HOWARD, JOSEPH E.—"In and Out."
HOWARD, WALTER.—"Seven Days' Leave."
HUBBELL, RAYMOND.—"The Kiss Burglar," "Hitchy-Koo, 1918," "Everything."
HUGHES, RUPERT.—"Toot! Toot!!"
HURD, JAMES.—"The Better 'Ole."
HYMER, JOHN B.—"Realisation."

IBSEN, HENRIK.—"The Wild Duck," "Hedda Gabler," "A Doll's House."

JACKSON, RAY LEE.—"Friends Invited."
JACOBS, HARRY ALLAN.—"Some Daddy."
JACOBI, VICTOR.—"Ziegfeld Follies of 1918."
JAMES, BENEDICT.—"The Little Brother."
JANNEY, SAMUEL.—"Midnight."
JEROME, JEROME K.—"The Rainbow Girl."
JESSE, F. TENNYSON.—"Billeted."
JOHNSTONE, ALEXANDER. — "Fiddlers Three."
JOLSON, AL.—"Sinbad."
JONES, HENRY ARTHUR.—"The Triumph of the Philistines."

KANE, WHITFORD.—"My Dark Rosaleen."
KAPLAN, SAMUEL.—"The Critic's Comedy."
KAUFMAN, GEORGE S.—"Someone in the House."
KEIGHTLEY, MABEL S.—"Bottled Babies."
KELLEY, ANTHONY PAUL.—"Three Faces East."
KELLESSAR, M.—"The Ingrate."
KENNEDY, CHARLES RANN.—"The Army with Banners," "The Servant in the House."
KERN, JEROME.—"Toot! Toot!!" "Oh, Lady, Lady," "Rock-a-bye, Baby," "Head Over Heels."
KERNELL, PTE. WILLIAM B.—"Good-bye, Bill."
KETTERING, RALPH THOMAS.—"The Girl He Left Behind," "The Greater American."
KING, BARTON.—"The Man They Left Behind."

KISTEMAEKERS, HENRI.—"Where Poppies Bloom."
KNIGHT, PERCIVAL.—"A Trench Fantasy."
KNOBLOCK, EDWARD.—"Tiger! Tiger!!"
KROWS, ARTHUR EDWIN.—"Fisherman's Luck."
KUGELMAN, F. B.—"The Hermit and His Messiah."
KUMMER, CLARE.—"Be Calm, Camilla."
KYNE, PETER B.—"The Land Over Yonder," "Cappy Ricks."

LACOSTE, LUCIE.—"Shadows."
LAMB, ARTHUR J.—"Girl of My Heart."
LAIT, JACK.—"One of Us."
LANDIS, FREDERICK.—"The Copperhead."
LAVEDAN, HENRI.—"Service."
LAWRENCE, VINCENT.—"The Girl Outside."
LEITZBACH, ADELINE.—"Success."
LIEBER, ALLEN.—"The Submarine Attack"
LIEBLER, THEODORE A., JUN.—"Success."
LIPMAN, CLARA.—"Work for Uncle Sam."
LION, LEON M.—"The Chinese Puzzle."
LIPMAN, CLARA.—"Over Here."
LIPSCHUTZ, BESS.—"Marriages are Made—"
LONSDALE, FREDERICK.—"The Maid of the Mountains."

MACK, WILLARD.—"Blind Youth," "I.O.U.," "The Big Chance."
MACKAY, ROBERT MEARS.—"The Liberty Gun."
MACLAREN, DONALD.—"Two Pairs."
MADDEN, RICHARD. — "Where Things Happen."
MAETERLINCK, MAURICE. — "The Betrothed."
MALLOY, JOHN.—"Some Bride."
MALLESON, MILES.—"Youth."
MALTBY, H. F.—"The Laughter of Fools," "The Rotters."
MANNING, CHARLES.—"Over the Top."
MANNERS, J. HARTLEY.—"Happiness," "Getting Together."
MAPES, VICTOR.—"The Liberty Gun."
MARTAN, MAX.—"Seven Days' Leave," "The Rape of Belgium."
MARTIN, HELEN R.—"Tillie."
MAYO, MARGARET.—"Rock-a-bye, Baby."
McCARTHY, JOSEPH.—"Oh, Look!"
McDONOUGH, GLEN.—"The Kiss Burglar," "Hitchy-Koo, 1918."
McGOWAN, JOHN.—"Some Bride."
McMANUS, JOSEPH.—"It Pays to Flirt."
MEANEY, LOTTIE D.—"A Stitch in Time."
MEARS, STANNARD.—"Seventeen," "Peg of Peacock Alley."
MEGRUE, ROI COOPER.—"Where Poppies Bloom."
MELROSE, GEORGE.—"On the High Seas."
MELTZER, CHARLES HENRY.—"The Big Scene."
MERRILL, FENNIMORE.—"Her Bit."
MERRILL, SERGT. LOUIS G.—"Good Luck, Sam!"
METCALFE, ELIZABETH TYREE.—"Starting Something."
MILNE, A. A.—"Belinda."
MITCHELL, DODSON. — "The Lambs' Gambol."
MOELLER, PHILIP.—"The Beautiful Legend of Pokey; or, The Amorous Indian."
MONTGOMERY, JAMES. — "Oh, Look!" "Going Up."
MOORE, CARLYLE.—"The Unknown Purple."
MORRIS, GRANT.—"The Big Chance."
MOROSCO, OLIVER.—"Gosh! We're All Friends."
MORTON, MICHAEL.—"Remnant."
MUMFORD, ETHEL WATTS.—"Sick-a-Bed."
MURFIN, JANE.—"Information, Please."

NEVIN, ARTHUR.—"The Daughter of the Forest."
NICCODEMI, D.—"Remnant."

NOEL, JOSEPH.—"Birds of Prey."
NORDSTROM, FRANCES.—"It Pays to Flirt."
NUGENT, J. C.—"Man-Power."

O'CONNOR, FATHER J. F. X.—"The Mystery of Life."
O'NEILL, EUGENE.—"The Rope," "Ile."
OSBORNE, HUBERT.—"April," "The Good Men Do."
O'SHEA, MONICA BARRY.—"The Rushlight."

PAGE, AUSTIN.—"By Pigeon Post."
PARENTEAU, ZOEL.—"Follow the Girl."
PATCH, WILLIAM MOORE.—"The Greater Hero."
PATTERSON, ADA.—"Love's Lightning."
PAULTON, E.—"Flo-Flo."
PAULTON, EDWARD A.—"Tell That to the Marines."
PEARSON, HUMPHREY W.—"Best Be."
PEPPLE, ED.—"Maggie."
PERCIVAL, WALTER.—"Someone in the House."
PHILIPP, ADOLPH.—"Tell That to the Marines."
PIERPOINT, MABEL.—"Realisation."
PIMENTAL, J. GARCIA.—"Yum Chapab."
PINSKI, DAVID. — "Forgotten Souls," "Michal."
POLLOCK, CHANNING.—"The Grass Widow," "Roads to Destiny," "The Crowded Hour."
POTTER, PAUL M.—"The Purple Poppy."
PRICE, ALONZO.—"The Magic Fiddle."
PRYCE, RICHARD. — "Helen-with-the-High-Hand."

RABINOWITSCH, SOLOMON J.—"She Must Marry a Doctor."
RADIN MAX.—"Come Across."
REID, HAL.—"How to Hold a Husband."
RENAUD, JACQUES.—"Love Forbidden."
REYNOLDS, HERBERT.—"Rock-a-bye, Baby."
RHODES, HARRISON.—"Mr. Barnum."
RICE, EDWARD EVERETT.—"Napoleon."
RICE, LIEUT. GITZ.—"Getting Together."
ROBINSON, LENNOX.—"Harvest."
ROMBERG, SIGMUND.—"Over the Top," "Sinbad," "The Passing Show of 1918."
ROSE, EDWARD E.—"Penrod," "Cappy Ricks."
ROSENBERG, JAMES N.—"The Return to Mutton."
ROYLE, EDWIN MILTON.—"The Committee on Admissions."

SAWYER, RUTH.—"The Awakening."
SCHNITZLER, DR. ARTHUR.—"The Big Scene."
SCHWARTZ, JEAN.—"The Passing Show of 1918."
SELWYN, EDGAR.—"The Crowded Hour."
SHEEHAN, PERLY.—"Efficiency."
SHELDON, EDWARD.—"The Lady of the Camellias," "The Garden of Paradise."
SHIPMAN, LOUIS EVAN.—"The Fountain of Youth."
SHIPMAN, SAMUEL.—"Friendly Enemies," "Over Here," "Work for Uncle Sam."
SINCLAIR, MARJORIE.—"The Only Son."
SKINNER, CONSTANCE LINDSAY.—"Good Morning, Rosamund."
SLOANE, BALDWIN A.—"Look Who's Here."
SMITH, HARRY B.—"The Canary," "Look Who's Here."
SMITH, HARRY JAMES.—"The Little Teacher."
SMITH, WINCHELL.—"Lightnin'."
SPOTTISWOODE, SYBIL.—"Her Country."
ST. ALBIN.—"The Grass Widow."
STAMMERS, FRANK.—"Back Again."
STAMPER, DAVE.—"Ziegfeld Follies of 1918."
STANGE, HUGH STANISLAUS.—"Seventeen," "Peg of Peacock Alley."

STEVENS, ASHTON.—"Mary's Way Out."
STRONG, AUSTIN.—"Three Wise Fools."
STUART-WHYTE, F.—"Robinson Crusoe."
SWAN, MARK.—"Parlour, Bedroom, and Bath," "She Walked in Her Sleep."
SWARTOUT, NORMAN LEE.—"Fisherman's Luck."
SWERLING, JO.—"One of Us."
SWETE, E. LYALL.—"Freedom."
SWOPE, HOWARD WHITNEY.—"In and Out."
SZULC, JOSEPH.—"See You Later."

TARKINGTON, BOOTH.—"Seventeen," "Penrod."
TELLEGREN, LOU.—"Blind Youth."
TERRY, J. E. HAROLD.—"General Post," "The Man Who Stayed at Home."
THOMAS, A. E.—"The Matinée Hero."
THOMAS, AUGUSTUS.—"The Copperhead," "David's Adventure."
THOMAS, BERTE.—"My Boy."
THOMPSON, MARAVENE.—"In a Net."
TIMBERG, HERMAN.—"Over the Top."
TOLSTOY, LEO.—"The Living Corpse."
TOURS, FRANK.—"Girl o' Mine."
TREMAYNE, W. A.—"The Alien."
TREYNOR, BLAIR.—"Some Bride."
TROUBETZKOY, PRINCESS (AMELIE RIVES).—"Allegiance."
TROUBETZKOY, PRINCE.—"Allegiance."
TURNBULL, HECTOR.—"I.O.U."

VACHELL, HORACE ANNESLEY.—"Humpty Dumpty."
VALVERDE, QUINITO.—"A Night in Spain."
VAN BUREN, A. H.—"Enemies Within."
VANZYPE, GUSTAVE.—"La Suveraine."

WALKER, STUART.—"Jonathan Makes a Wish."

WALTER, EUGENE.—"The Heritage," "Nancy Lee."
WEBB, KENNETH.—"The Best Sellers," "Art's Rejuvenation," "A Japanese Garden."
WEBB, ROY.—"The Best Sellers," "Art's Rejuvenation," "A Japanese Garden."
WELLS, CHARLOTTE E.—"The Riddle Woman."
WEST, ROLAND.—"The Unknown Purple."
WESTERTON, FRANK H.—"A Prince There Was."
WHITMAN, LAWRENCE.—"A Cure for Curables."
WILBUR, CRANE.—"The Love Liar," "The Common Cause."
WILDE, OSCAR.—"An Ideal Husband."
WILDE, PERCIVAL.—"Mothers of Men."
WILLIAMS, JESSE LYNCH.—"Why Marry?"
WILLIAMSON, HORACE G.—"Uncle Sam."
WILSON, H. CROWNIN.—"Nancy Lee."
WINSLOW, HERBERT.—"Just Around the Corner."
WISE, THOMAS.—"Mr. Barnum."
WODEHOUSE, P. G.—"Oh, Lady, Lady," "See You Later," "The Girl Behind the Gun," "Ask Dad," "Oh, My Dear."
WOLF, RENNOLD.—"The Grass Widow," "The Rainbow Girl," "Ziegfeld Follies of 1918."
WOODWARD, MATTHEW C.—"Over the Top."
WOOLF, EDGAR ALLAN.—"Head Over Heels."
WOOLF, EDGAR ALLAN.—"Toot! Toot!!" "Rock-a-bye, Baby."
WORRALL, LECHMERE.—"The Man Who Stayed at Home."

YOUNG, RIDA JOHNSON.—"Sometime," "Miss I-Don't-Know."
YORK, JULIE.—"Man-Power."

AMERICAN OBITUARY.

DECEMBER 1, 1917, TO END OF NOVEMBER, 1918.

Affleck, Mrs. Edward T., singer. Toledo, Ohio, January.
Allen, Jennie, actress. New York, November 3.
Alvin, Mercedes, vaudeville artist. Hattiesburg, Miss., June.
Arden, Edwin, actor. Aged 54. New York, October 16.
Arline, Annie, actress. New York, July 27.
Armstrong, James J., booking agent. Aged 62. Jersey City, February 3.
Arnold, Richard, musician. Aged 73. New York, June 21.
Arthur Lee, playwright. Aged 40. Los Angeles, December, 1917.
Asbury, W. S., former musician. Aged 44. Ottumwa, Ia., July 11.
Aveling, Edward Willett, vaudeville artist. Aged 30. New York, October 13.

Bagley, Robert A., former theatrical producer. Aged 66. New York, January 28.
Bailey, Molly (Mrs. A. H. Hardesty), circus proprietress. Aged 82. Houston, Tex., October 2.
Barclay, Delancy, actor. New York, December 9, 1917.
Barnabee, H. C., actor. Aged 84. Jamaica Plain, December 16, 1917.
Barron, Charles, former actor. Aged 76. Boston, February 13.
Bassett, Russell, actor. Aged 72. New York, May 8.
Beeson, Thomas J., comedian. Aged 56. Coney Island, February 18.
Bennett, Charles W., manager. Aged 45. Jersey City, N.J., January 3.
Benton, Jay, dramatic critic. Aged 49. Boston, June.
Bishop, Mrs. Josephine (Jennie Parker), former actress. Aged 81. Philadelphia, May 28.
Bittner, William B., actor and manager. Aged 52. New York, July 4.
Bixby, Frank, theatrical manager, producer, and director. Aged 68. New York, February 8.
Blake, Arthur J., financial manager. Philadelphia, October.
Blakeney, William, former orchestra leader. New York, February 8.
Blett, Cleda Udora, actress. Aged 22. New York. December 25, 1917.
Boardman, True, actor. Aged 39. Los Angeles, October.
Bonheur, Lucien, manager. Aged 54. New York, August.
Borrow, Robert E., manager. Aged 33. Philadelphia, October 3.
Bowser, Cecil, actor. Fort Wayne, May 28.
Boyle, John Francis, actor and singer. Aged 45. New York, March 8.
Braman, Charles E., actor. Aged 44. Terre Haute, Ind., February 16.
Brooks, Una, actress. Cleveland, O., November 26.
Brown, Colonel T. Alston, former manager and agent. Aged 80. Philadelphia, April 2.

Bruce, Lilian (Mrs. Lilian Stilson Phillips), former actress. Brooklyn, August 22.
Bryson, William G., actor. Aged 41. Boston, September.
Burke, J. Frank, actor and stage director. Aged 50. Los Angeles, January 23.
Bush, John L., vaudeville artist. July 24.
Burns, Bernadetta, actress. Kansas City, Mo., August 6.
Buskirk, Frederick, vaudeville artist. New York, March 10.
Byron, Benny, vaudeville artist. Chicago, September.

Cahill, May, vaudeville artist. Aged 24. Chicago, August 11.
Callahan, Joseph, actor. Los Angeles, December 20, 1917.
Camp, M. Ralph, manager. Boston, September.
Campbell, Charles J., playwright. Aged 60. New York, February 27.
Campbell, J. W., former advance agent. Bedford, Va., October.
Cameron, Peggy, actress. Boston, September 26.
Carey, Joseph P., actor. Aged 47. New York, May 31.
Carl Lyle, John, actor. Aged 60. New Rochelle. July 25.
Carmichael, Ermina, vaudeville artist. Aged 23. Minneapolis.
Carroll, Charles A., actor. Aged 47. New York, December 3, 1917.
Carroll, Edna, musician. Aged 36. New York, December 8, 1917.
Carter, Carl vaudeville artist. Chicago, February 1.
Carter, Robert Peyton, actor. Monrovia, Cal., June.
Castle, George, manager. Aged 67. Miami, Fla., December, 1917.
Cave, George, vaudeville artist. Boston, Mass., March 17.
Chapin, Benjamin Chester, actor and lecturer. Aged 44. Liberty, N.Y., June 2.
Charters, Charles, actor. New York, January 18.
Chase, Sergt. Dave, actor. Camp Lee, Petersburg, Va., September 26.
Chester, Mrs. Sam K., former actress. Aged 78. Staten Island, April 2.
Clapham, Harry J., theatrical manager. Aged 77. Flemmingsville, N.Y., February 19.
Clarke, Birchet, former Press agent. Aged 85. Flatbush, L.I., July 4.
Clarke, Henry G., former actor. Aged 77. New York, April 12.
Clayton, Sergt. Jerry, actor. August 16 (killed in action).
Clifton, Cathleen B., actress. Aged 37. New York, March 29.
Cleef, Augustus Van, writer upon art and the drama. Ward's Island, February 14.
Collins, Marie Barrett (Mrs. George W. Collins) actress. St. Louis, January 22.
Collyer, Dan, actor. Aged 65. Chicago, March 30.
Connelly, Thomas J., actor. Aged 26. Killed in action in France.

THE STAGE YEAR BOOK.

Conroy, former circus clown. Aged 59. Brooklyn, January 3.
Converse, Charles Crozart, composer. Aged 86. Englewood, N.J., October 18.
Cook, Lillian, actress. Age 19. New York, March.
Cook, Pearl L., actress. Portland, Oregon, December 16, 1917.
Cooley, Hollis E., manager. Aged 59. New York, August 2.
Cooley, Lillian (Mrs. Hollis Cooley), actress and vocalist. Great Kills, Staten Island. February 6.
Course, John, musician. Aged 23. Trenton, N.J.
Courtleigh, Wm., jun., actor. Aged 26. Philadelphia, March 13.
Cowper, William C., actor. Aged 65. June 13.
Crauford, Russell, actor. Aged 71. New York. November 25.
Cross, Will H., actor. Chicago, May.
Crotty, Joe, vaudeville artist. Columbus, O., July 12.

D'Acre, Louise, vaudeville actress. Aged 48. New York, September.
Dahn, William, vaudeville artist. Aged 49. Springfield, Ill., July 9.
Darling, Ruth (Mrs. Chester Franklin), actress San Francisco, September.
Davenport, Edgar Loomis, actor. Aged 56. Dorchester, Mass., July 25.
Davies, Matilda, operatic and concert singer. New York, February 11.
Davis, Mrs. Mary, former actress. Aged 72. Hornell, N.Y., June 24.
Dawn, Billy, vaudeville artist. Springfield, Ill., July 19.
De Lesser, Alfred M., former actor. Aged 55. Brooklyn, N.Y., September 9.
Dempsey, James A., song writer. Philadelphia, October 12.
Dickerman, Goodwal, actor, vocalist, and dramatic instructor. Omaha, March 22.
Dingwall, A. W., manager. Aged 61. New York, July 27.
Dixon, Joe, actor. Aged 42. New York, December 27, 1917.
Dobson, Thomas, musician. Aged 29. New York, November 25.
Donald, Arthur S. August 25.
Donohue, George, clown. Hammond, Ind., July 6.
Doolin, George, vaudeville artist. Aged 26. Rochester, N.Y., October 11.
Dougherty, Hughey, former minstrel. Kirkbrides, Philadelphia, August.
Douglas, Virginia, actress. Minneapolis, Minn., March 20.
Dow, Max, vaudeville artist. New York, June 1.
Downer, John (Cpl. John Downer Yount), actor. Aged 38. Camp Wadsworth, February 14.
Drew, Sidney Rankin, motion picture director. Aged 27. May 18. Killed in action.
Duffy, Michael, vaudeville artist. Aged 43. Pittsburgh, December 22, 1917.
Dunn, Arthur, agent. Milwaukee, July.

Earle, Bessie (Mrs. Val Vino), singer. Aged 55. Pottsville, Pa., September 18.
Eberts, Fred C., manager. Aged 44. Chicago, January 25.
Eckert, Eddie, circus clown. Aged 25. Kansas City, December 25, 1917.
Edel, Harold E., manager. Aged 29. New York, November 3.
Edgard, Louis, actor. Aged 38. New York, December, 1917.
Eddy, Jerome H., theatrical press agent. Aged 83. Brooklyn, N.Y., June 7.
Elliott, Winnie, vaudeville artist. New York, February 25.

Ellwood, William (Billy), business manager. Pittsburgh, Pa., June 2.
Enoch, Harry, minstrel. Aged 86. Philadelphia, November 30.
Erwood, Robert J., actor and manager, Greenridge, Staten Island, December 15, 1917.

Fairchild, Roy, actor. Aged 42. Columbus, O., April 29.
Feinler, Louis A., musician. Aged 65. Wheeling W. Va., April 14.
Felix, Frank, musician. Tillson, Ulster County, New York, January.
Ferguson, Terry, actor. Aged 57. Buffalo, N.Y., December 7, 1917.
Findlay, John, actor. New York, April 9.
Fisher, George H., manager. Fort Wayne, January 23.
Fisher, Mrs. Jennie, former actress. Aged 81. Staten Island. May 3.
Fohs, Professor Alfred D., bandmaster. Aged 58. New York, May.
Foil, Harry Gil (Frank B. Graff), actor. Bayshore, L.I., August 10.
Ford, John, former vaudeville artist. New York, March 5.
Foy, Mrs. Eddie, actress. Aged 48. New Rochelle, N.Y. June 14.
France, Sydney, vaudeville artist. Seton, May.
Frankel, Gus, actor. Aged 56. New York, May 14.
Fraser, Eugene, actor. Aged 48. Brooklyn, N.Y., February 17.
Friebus, Theodore, actor. Aged 45. New York, December 25, 1917.

Galvani, Joseph, actor. Cincinnati, October 11.
Gardner, May, vaudeville artist. Aged 23. North Hackensack, N.J., June 21.
"Gerald" (of Moore and Gerald), vaudeville artist. Spokane, May.
Gill, Edith, actress. Brooklyn, October.
Gilbert, James, theatrical producer. Aged 66. Somerville, Mass., March 10.
Gillespie, Edward Charles, actor. Aged 44. New York, July 23.
Gill, Capt. Robert S., actor. Paris, September 23.
Gilmore, Dwight O., manager. Aged 80. Springfield, Mass., June 10.
Golden, Anna Carson (Mrs. Mayer Lautz), actress. Cincinnati, October.
Goodman, Lieut. Kenneth Sawyer, playwright. Chicago, November.
Gorton, Lew H., actor. Neenah, Wis., January 11.
Graff, Genia de Aria, singer. Camp Humphreys, Virginia, October.
Gray, Gloria, actress. Aged 18. Walla Walla, Wash., April 4.
Grey, Leonard, actor. Aged 56. New York, August 3.
Griffin, Emma, actress. Aged 44. Chicago, August 23.

Hale, Walter, actor, artist, and war correspondent. Aged 49. New York, December, 1917.
Hall, Laddie, vaudeville artist. New York, September.
Hamilton, Leah, actress. October 16.
Hamilton, Virginia Marshall, actress. Aged 27. New York, August.
Hampton, Albert Russell, actor. Ware, Mass., June 24.
Hardesty, Mrs. A. H. (Molly Baily), former actress. Houston, Tex., October.
Harding, Charles, actor. Aged 58. New York, November 4.
Harold, Donald, actor. Baltimore, January 24.
Harold, Mrs. May Thompson, former actress. Aged 79. Baltimore, February 6.
Harris, Charles E., actor and stage manager. Aged 35. Lake Saranac, April 27.

AMERICAN OBITUARY. 151

Harrison, Neva, actress. Aged 45. New York, August 28.
Hart, William J., song writer. New York, August 9.
Haydock, John, actor. Aged 74. New York, January 19.
Hedges, Mrs. Fred, actress. New York, November 3.
Held, Anna, actress. Aged 45. New York, August 19.
Helston, Gussie, vaudeville artist. Brooklyn, July 8.
Henry, Charles W., manager. North Ferrisburg, November 14.
Herbert, Harry Maurice, actor. Aged 50. New York, February 7.
Henry, Charles W., author and artist. North Ferrisburg, Vt., November 14.
Hinckley, William, actor. Aged 25. New York, May 4.
Hines, William E., vaudeville artist. Aged 60. New York, December 13, 1917.
Hodges, D. B., former advance agent. Aged 88. Bedford, Va., October 17.
Holcomb, Burt H., showman. New Rochelle, N.Y., January 13.
Holman, Alfred D., actor. Aged 65. London, Can., September 14.
Holmes, Capitola, actress. Aged 17. New York, May 2.
Holmes, W. Hodge, manager. Albany, N.Y., June 26.
Horn, Clara, actress. Kensington, Pa., October.
Howell, Earl, actor. Aged 42. Boston, July 18.
Huber, Harry, actor. El Dorado, Kan., June 4.
Hunter, Thomas Marion, actor. Worcester, Mass., March 4.

Irwin, Erina, actress. Aged 22. New York, June 21.
Isaacson, Mark N., violinist. Aged 62. Brooklyn, N.Y., June 20.

Jackson, Billy, producer and former actor. Little Rock, Ark., March 10.
Jacobs, Maurice, manager. Brooklyn, N.Y., March 6.

Karmont, Charles, actor. Aged 40. Troy, N.Y.
Kaufman, Joseph, former actor and director of motion pictures. Aged 35. New York, February 1.
Krause, Otto H., manager. Aged 59. Bedford, Va., February 28.

Lamb, Frank E., actor and stage director. New York, February 5.
Lamar, Al. (John A. Ryder), manager and actor. New York, June 12.
Lawrence, W. B., manager. Aged 48. Winnipeg, Manitoba, June.
Lee, Frankie (Mrs. Franlin Lee Prentice), actress. Aged 37. New York, December 12, 1917.
Leester, Richard (Bob Watts), actor. Port Nichols, November 4.
Leo, Jose, actor. El Dorado, Kan., June 4.
Leonard, Harry W., former actor and singer. Aged 55. New York, January 21.
Lewis, Albert J. (James Edwards), actor. Los Angeles, May 23.
Licalzi, Mitchell, manager. Aged 42. Chicago, August 6.
Lipzin, Mme. Kenny, actress. Aged 63. New York, October 12.
Lockwood, Harold, actor. New York, October 27.
Long, Freemont, former showman. Aged 65. Columbus, O., March 13.
Lorraine, Fred F., advance agent. Aged 30. Hagerstown, Pa., October.

Lotto, Arthur A., actor, manager, and newspaper man. Aged 54. Tacoma, Wash., January 19.
Ludick, M. S., former theatrical manager. Chicago, November.
Lyon, Damon, actor. Aged 55. White Plains, N.Y., July 5.
Macdona, Harry, actor. Philadelphia, March 30.
McCarthy, Edward Lionel, vaudeville artist. Aged 27. Buffalo.
Mack, Edward J. (M'Dermott), vaudeville artist. Aged 38. Pine Bluff, Ark., December 7, 1917.
Madden, Arthur, vaudeville artist. Aged 28. Memphis, Tenn., November 16.
Maddern, Richard H., musician. Aged 78. New York, December 24, 1917.
Magie, Mrs. Katherine Fisher, former actress. Aged 85. Brooklyn, July.
Mann, W. F., theatrical producer. Fennville, Mich., December 15, 1917.
Mansfield, Richard Gibbs, actor. Aged 20. San Antonio, Tex., April 3.
Marble, Ellen Bloom, actress. Aged 69. Staten Island, January 14.
Mark, Mitchell H., motion picture exhibitor. Buffalo, N.Y., March 20.
Marriott, Charles, actor. Aged 58. Los Angeles, December 8, 1917.
Marshall, Charles A., manager, Duluth, Minn. October.
Mason, Lowell, manager. Aged 69. Bayport, L.I., May 17.
Mastbaum, Stanley V., picture theatre manager. Aged 38. Philadelphia, March 7.
Matthews, Robert, actor. Aged 45. New York, October 20.
Maurice, Mary, actress. Port Carbon, Pa., May 3.
Mayer, Marcus, manager. Aged 77. Amityville, L.I., May 8.
McCabe, George F., actor. New York, December 7, 1917.
McCarthy, Lawrence J., manager. Aged 57. Boston, April.
McCourt, John J., vaudeville artist. Aged 50. New York, June 6.
McCree, Junie, actor. Aged 52. New York, January 13.
McDonald, Alex. A., business manager and advertising agent. Aged 56. Ocean City, Md., July 20.
M'Henry, Charles F., actor. Aged 28. June 8.
M'Kee, William, actor. Aged 56. New York, January 3.
McNess, Willmot, vaudeville actor. Aged 38. New York, January.
McGarry, Billy, vaudeville artist. Aged 31. Philadelphia, May 23.
McGinn, Francis, actor. Aged 42. New York, February 16.
McVntcheon, Walter, manager and advance agent. Bath Beach, Brooklyn, October 3.
Melarkey, William J., manager. Aged 32. New York, March.
Meldon, Percy, stage director. Trenton, June.
Merwin, Ray, vaudeville agent. Chicago. February 19.
Milliken, Sandal (Carlos French Stoddard), actress. New Haven, April.
Miron, Joseph, singer. Webster, Mass., March 27.
Mitchell, Lorey, vaudeville artist. Little Rock, Ark., May 15.
Mitchell, Maggie (Mrs. Charles Abbott), actress. Aged 86. New York. March 22.
Moffatt, Clinton W., theatrical producer and agent. New York, June 6.
Morrell, Billy, vaudeville artist and manager. Hamburg, Pa., May 4.
Moretti, Eleanor (Mrs. Charles T. Huntington), former actress. New York, July.
Moseley, Pte. Harry J., actor. Aged 30. Camp Meade, October 12.

Mull, Eva, actress. New York, October 13.
Mullally, Jack (Dinny Mack), vaudeville artist. New York City, March 22.

Naugle, Harry D., manager. Aged 29. Omaha, November 23.
Nelson, John, circus performer. Gary, Ind., July 12.
Newman, Mrs. Laura B., actress. Aged 52. New York, November.
Nichols, Marion A., actress. Aged 29. Taunton, Mass., March 24.
Nicholls, Will M., manager. Aged 63. Indianapolis, January 12.
Nitram, Bessie (Mrs. Joe J. Smith), vaudeville artist. Aged 47. St. Louis, Mo., January 26.

Odell, Thomas, minstrel. New York, November 13.
O'Neil, Barry (Thomas J. McCarthy), actor and manager. New York, March 23.
O'Neill, Frank (James Barter Freel), actor, Brooklyn. December 8, 1917.
O'Neill, Paula, vaudeville artist. Los Angeles, February 6.
Owens, William, former circus performer. Aged 73. Red Bank, N.J., May 15.
O'Rourke, Stephen, actor. Aged 38. New York, October 10.

Paine, Matilda Scott, former operatic singer. Aged 70. New York, January.
Parent, Harry F., manager. Detroit, April 8.
Pastor, G. W., vaudeville artist. Arbroath, November 17.
Pickering, Mayien J., former actor. Aged 59. Philadelphia, January 15.
Pilkington, Paul, actor. Fresno, Cal., January 26.
Poloff, Elsie, vaudeville artist. New York, March 5.
Porte, Professor Edouard Hippolyte, musician. East Liverpool, O., November 30.
Prior, Thomas W., theatrical agent. Venice, Cal.
Pruette, William, opera singer. Aged 55. Liberty, N.Y., July 15.
Pubillones, Antonio, circus proprietor. Mexico City, May 23.

Quicksell, Fern, actress. Philadelphia, October 10.

Radcliffe, Minnie (Mrs. M. R. Williams). New York, October 1.
Reilly, James A., actor. Philadelphia, January 15.
Rice, Major Charles E., former manager. Aged 81. Allston, Mass., May.
Rice, Myron B., manager. Aged 57. New York, December 22, 1917.
Ringling, Henry, circus owner. Baraboo, Wis., October 11.
Richardson, Leander, playwright, critic, and novelist. Aged 62. New York, February 2.
Ritchie, Frank, actor. Los Angeles, January.
Rhodes, Eileen, child actress. Aged 12. Pittsburgh, April.
Rhodes, James E., manager. Aged 52. Albany, N.Y., June 8.
Roberts, Lillian, actress. San Francisco, June.
Roeder, Mrs. Geraldine (Geraldine Morgan), musician. New York, May 20.
Romer, Mae, actress. New York, May 4.
Roschke, Carl, stage manager. St. Paul, Minn., March 29.
Ross, Charles J., actor. Asbury Park, June.
Rose, Annie E., musician. New York, October 6.

Ross, Charles J., actor. Aged 59. Asbury Park, N.J., June 15.
Russell, Hattie, actress. Aged 69. Long Branch, August.
Russell, Sarah Elizabeth Weston, musician. Aged 81. Belmont, Mass, April 5.
Ryan, Mary Isabelle, trapeze performer. Aged 63. New York, October.

Samuel, Mrs. Kate (Kitty Mitchell), actress. Aged 50. Brooklyn, January 10.
Sarjeantson, Kat, actress. New York, February 16.
Schoeifel, John B., actor. Boston, August 30.
Schoenfield, Maurice J., former actor. Aged 26. Pittsburg, April 17.
Searles, Mrs. Harriet Jane, former circus performer. Denver, Colo., June 12.
Sears, Alice, actress. Aged 22. New York, June 19.
Semple, William K., theatrical representative. Aged 46. Washington, April 9.
Shaw, Mrs. Alice, whistler. Aged 62. Elmira, N.Y., April 22.
Sheridan, Margaret, actress. Philadelphia, October 25.
Shirley, Jessie, actress. Aged 40. Spokane, May 28.
Silvo, Louis, vaudeville artist. Aged 52. January 1.
Smith, Harry G. (Robert Crane), actor. Marshfield, Wis., October.
Smith, Harry James, playwright. New Westminster, British Columbia, March 16.
Spirescu, Oscar, musical conductor. New York, September 7.
Stanley, Charles H., former actor. Aged 61. Washington, January.
Stanley, Frank M., actor and singer. New York, March 13.
Staples, Mrs. Freda, former actress. Aged 38. New York, June 6.
Stein, Nathan, manager. Washington, June 19.
Steppe, Mrs. Bertie Wyatt, actress. Aged 27. Toronto, October 5.
Stern, Louis, advance agent. New York, November 22.
Stevens, Robert E., manager. Aged 80. New York, July 21.
Stevens, Sadie, vaudeville artist. New York, February 21.
St. Vrain, Joseph R., actor. New York.
Sweet, George H., dancer. Brooklyn, March 21.

Taylor, Charles W., actor. New York, October.
Thayer, Sarah, former actress. Aged 98. December 4, 1917.
Thericault, Billie, actor. Buffalo, February 4.
Thomas, D. C., manager. Gadsden, Ala., November 22.
Thompson, Molly (Mrs. Edward Garvie), actress. Aged 51. Mount Vernon, N.Y., January 21.
Thompson, W. C., Press representative. October.
Thorpe, James R. (James Ranza), vaudeville artist. New York September 30.
Tomlinson, J. Wilder, actor. Texas, September.
Towne, Fennimore Cooper, actor-author. Aged 25. New York, January 4.
Turner, Otis, actor, stage director, and motion picture director. Aged 55. Hollywood, Cal., March 28.

Vanda, Alice (Mrs. Willard Lee), vaudeville artist. Aged 27. Chicago, February 19.
Van der Werken, Albert, theatrical scene builder. Aged 51. Boston, February 10.
Varrey, Colin actor. Elgin, Ill., May 16.
Von Doenhoff, Mme. Helen, operatic singer. New York, August 29.
Vreeland, C. W., musician. Aged 65. Friendship, N.Y. April 27.

AMERICAN OBITUARY. 153

Waixel, Mrs. Julia, musician. Stamford, Conn., August 2.
Wallace, J. W. (Isaac W. Topping), actor. Aged 61. Morristown, Tenn., January 14
Warren, John B., showman. Aged 52. Chicago June 30.
Washburn, John H., former theatrical manager. Aged 70. New York, December 11, 1917.
Weis, Clarence, manager. New York, October.
Weiss, Albert, manager. Aged 76. New York, May 1.
Welch, Joe, actor. Westport, Conn., July 15.
Welch, George T., actor. Freeport, L.I., May 8.
Welch, Joseph, actor. Aged 45. Westport, Conn., July 22.
Welty, George, manager. New York, October 10.
West, W. C., actor. New York, September 13.
Wheeler, Zelma, actress. Aged 36. Pittsburgh, November 17
Whipple, Clifford, actor. Chicago, October.
Williams, Clee, manager. Alameda, Cal., March 18.
Williams, Evans, singer. Aged 55. Akron, O., May 24.

Williams, John J., actor. New York, October.
Wills, Nat M., actor. Aged 44. New York, December, 1917.
Wilson, Jessie, actress. Toledo, October.
Wilson, Sam, vaudeville artist. New York, February 17.
Wiltse, Simon H., actor. Aged 70. Englewood, N.J., January 12.
Winchester, Alfred N., vaudeville artist. St. Joseph, Mo., May 10.
Woodhull, Wayne, actor. Waco, Tex., April 24.

Yager, Walter D., manager. Aged 46. New York, March 8.
Yerance, William, actor. Aged 64. Boston, December 19, 1917.
Young, David R., actor. Aged 68. New London, Conn., March 13.
Young, Ernest, actor. Camp Upton, Yaphank, January 30.

Zentay, Mary, musician. Aged 21. New York, October 3.

LEGAL CASES OF THE YEAR.

MARCH.

14 **WEST v. PHILLIPS—CLAIM FOR SALARY.**
Before the Common Serjeant (Mr. H. F. Dickens, K.C.), in the Lord Mayor's Court, a claim was made by Mr. Charles West, stage manager, 42, Randolph Gardens, Kilburn Park Road, against the H. B. Phillips Opera Company, Limited (and another), 489a, Oxford Street, for arrears of salary, and salary in lieu of notice, due to him under an agreement dated August 22, 1917, which was entered into between the plaintiff and Mr. H. B. Phillips on behalf of the defendant company. Under the agreement the plaintiff was engaged to stage manage for the H. B. Phillips Opera Company for the season commencing September 17, 1917, at a salary of £6 a week, subject to the termination of the agreement by the company at any time by giving the plaintiff a fortnight's previous notice in writing. Plaintiff alleged that he duly performed his duties under the agreement, but that when he came to the weeks commencing October 15, October 22, and October 29, the defendants, instead of paying him the full salary of £6 a week, only paid him £4 each week, and that, therefore, in respect of those three weeks there were arrears of salary amounting to £6. Then he said he was dismissed on November 3 before the expiration of the season, and without such notice having been given as required by the agreement. He was claiming the loss of two weeks' salary from November 3, £12 in all by way of damages. The defendants set up in the proceedings that the plaintiff was verbally given a fortnight's notice to determine the agreement on October 13, and on October 15 a verbal agreement was entered into employing the plaintiff week by week at £4 a week, and that the plaintiff himself determined that employment by giving a week's notice on October 27, 1917.

The Common Serjeant, after hearing the evidence, gave judgment for the defendants with costs.

---

18 **BROTHERS LUCK v. GUS ELTON.**
At the Southwark County Court an action was brought by the Six Brothers Luck against Gus Elton for £15.—Counsel explained that defendant was under contract with the Six Brothers Luck, but had accepted an engagement to play in pantomime for Mr. Salberg, of Birmingham. Mr. Luck arranged that defendant should terminate his engagement on the understanding that he paid Mr. Luck £15 out of the pantomime engagement. When Mr. Luck applied to Mr. Salberg for this consideration, he received intimation that Mr. Elton refused to pay the money. Mr. Elton counter-claimed for £15 for being billed, but Mr. Luck stated that this was the result of a mistake.—His Honour gave judgment for the plaintiffs for £15, and on the counter-claim with costs.

APRIL.

25 **AFRICAN THEATRES TRUST v. JESSE JACOBSON—A SOUTH AFRICAN TOUR.**
At the Westminster County Court an action for damages for breach of contract was brought by the African Theatres Trust, Limited, against Mr. Jesse Jacobson, who had failed to proceed to South Africa in connection with the act entitled "Two Rascals and Jacobson." Another action was brought by the International Variety and Theatrical Agency, Ltd., for loss of commission in connection with the same breach of contract. After hearing counsel on behalf of the plaintiffs, who stated that Mr. Jacobson had contracted to proceed to South Africa and had agreed date of sailing, but had failed to proceed to fulfil his engagement, and was apparently performing in this country. Judgment was given against Mr. Jesse Jacobson in both cases for the sum of £50 and £60 respectively, with costs.

MAY.

1 **BOGANNY'S (LIMITED) v. MARNER—WRONGFUL DETENTION OF PROPERTIES.**
In this case, heard before Mr. Justice Shearman and a common jury, in the King's Bench, Boganny's (Limited), of Central House, Oxford Street, W., sued Chris. Marner, of the Palladium, W., for damages for the detention of goods, conversion, and trespass.

Mr. Patrick Hastings appeared for the plaintiffs, and Mr. Charles Doughty for the defendant.

The plaintiffs were the proprietors and producers of a sketch. They alleged that the defendant retained possession of the properties and effects used by them for producing the sketch, which prevented them from performing an engagement during the week beginning October 15, 1917, at the Palladium, Southport. They claimed £70 salary forfeited under the Southport contract and £70 liquidated damages payable under the contract. The case arose out of a dispute between the parties at the Palladium, London, where the Boganny company were performing. It was alleged that because of that dispute the defendant declined to permit the property to be removed from the theatre on the Saturday night or Sunday morning.

His Lordship directed the jury that the dispute did not entitle the defendant to take the law into his own hands, and it was a question of the damage suffered by the plaintiffs owing to the detention of the property.

The jury returned a verdict for £140. They expressed a desire that the troupe should be paid their full salaries for the period in question, and Mr. Patrick Hastings said that that would be done.

GILBERT v. DYSON—CLAIM FOR COMMISSION.

10 At the Westminster County Court, before Judge Lush, an action to recover £69 commission on engagements was brought by Cyril Gilbert, Limited, Charing Cross Road, W., against Miss Laura Dyson (Mrs. Lennard), residing at Acre Lane, Brixton. The defendant appeared in person.

Mr. H. W. Lever said the plaintiffs were variety agents and the defendant was the proprietor of the revue "All Plums." Half the amount claimed was in respect of engagements obtained for her at the Middlesex (London), the Newcastle Pavilion, and the Oldham Music Hall. The sum of £31 10s. was in respect of commission on the salaries of four artists employed by her in the revue, and whose engagements were obtained by the plaintiffs. She was to deduct the commission from their salaries and forward the amount to the plaintiffs, but failed to do so.

Mr. Gilbert said in March, 1917, when the revue was at the Middlesex, where she had a sharing agreement, the takings for the week were £185.

The defendant said her husband acted as her manager and collected the moneys and made all arrangements with Mr. Gilbert.

Mr. Lennard stated that he was the salaried manager, and before going on tour he made an arrangement that he should collect the commission from four artists and set off the amount against £40 balance of a loan of £90 made by his wife to Mr. Gilbert. The £90 was advanced to buy a motor-car, which Gilbert expected to sell at a profit, to be divided between him and Miss Dyson. He (defendant) only collected the commissions for four weeks, and afterwards they were taken by the managers at the various theatres. One artist claimed for got £40 the first week, and it was reduced to £30 and then to £15.

Mr. Gilbert (recalled) denied that the £90 was lent to him, and said he sold a car for the defendant for that amount to a gentleman at the Strand Theatre. The gentleman paid £50 on account, which was sent to the defendant, but there was £40 due, and no arrangement was made to set off the commissions collected against his balance. He wrote several times to the defendant for the commission due, and in one letter she wrote, "Cannot you get the £40 from the gentleman who has bought the car?"

Ultimately Judge Lush gave judgment for the plaintiffs for £53 8s., with costs.

KAHN v. BEATIE AND BABS—A QUESTION OF COPYRIGHT.

10 In the Chancery Division, before Mr. Justice Neville, a copyright case was heard, in which plaintiff, Mr. Arthur Kahn, optician, who was formerly an actor and a theatre manager in America, claimed an injunction restraining the performance of the sketches entitled "A Pavement Rehearsal," "A Little Sagg-ragette," and "Kitchen Frolics" by his nieces, Miss Beatrice and Miss Hilda Samuels, better known as Beatie and Babs. A third defendant was the mother of the young ladies, Mrs. Emily Samuels, a sister of plaintiff, who claimed that she, and not plaintiff, was the author of the last-named sketch, and, further, that as it was not original, it was not a subject of copyright. Mr. Jenkins, K.C., and Mr. S. P. Kerr were for plaintiff; and Mr. Patrick Hastings for defendants.

Mr. Jenkins stated that some years ago plaintiff and Mr. Charles Kahn rendered pecuniary assistance to the family of the defendants but it did not appear to have enabled them to carry on business with success. Miss Beatrice, who was then aged ten, and Miss Hilda, aged eight, developed some talent in singing and dancing, and he wrote a sketch for them in 1906, entitled "A Pavement Rehearsal," which they performed successfully. In 1911 he wrote another sketch, entitled "A Little Sagg-ragette." As the girls grew up another sketch was desirable, so plaintiff wrote "Kitchen Frolics."

In the course of his cross-examination of plaintiff Mr. Hastings stated that Beatie and Babs were receiving £200 a week.

Mr. Hastings submitted, for the defence, that there was nothing in the sketch "Kitchen Frolics" which could be called composition, or could in itself be described as a show.

After various evidence had been taken, Mr. Hastings announced that he had advised his clients that, in his opinion, the proper course for them to adopt was to consent to the plaintiff retaining the copyright in the plays, and to pay him 10s. for each performance from the date of a letter he had written them last September revoking his consent for their performance of the pieces.

His Lordship said that it had been a most unfortunate quarrel, and regretted that it had arisen.

ENTERTAINMENT CATERER FINED.

13 At the Hayward's Heath Petty Sessions Gordon White, an amusement caterer, of Birmingham, was summoned for failing to comply with Regulation 4 of the Entertainment Duty Regulations, 1916.—Mr. Clark, who appeared for the Customs and Excise, said the offence charged against the defendant was issuing tickets for an entertainment at Hassocks on December 1 without their having the price of admission printed on them, and without stating whether the price paid included the Entertainment Tax or otherwise. Although purely technical, the offence was a serious one. Defendant did not appear to the original summons, and a warrant had to be issued for his arrest, and he now asked for costs owing to defendant's non-appearance on the last occasion.—Defendant, who now pleaded guilty, said the whole thing was done in ignorance. The tickets were such as were used at a number of different entertainments, and the colours denoted the prices. He was not aware of the summons, which was the reason for his non-appearance on the first occasion.—He was fined 5s., and ordered to pay the costs, £1 4s. 7d.

PIER BAND CONCERTS AND THE ENTERTAINMENT TAX.

31 A case to determine the liability of piers to the payment of the entertainments tax for their band concerts was heard at the Brighton Police Court, when the West Pier Company were summoned for failing to pay the tax in respect of the West Pier Concert Hall on March 17.

The case, it was explained, was a test one, to determine whether the entertainments duty was payable in respect of the charge made for chairs at band performances.

Inspector Horace Bingham deposed to attending an afternoon performance on March 17, when there was an audience of about 1,100 people, and when a charge of twopence was made upon each person who occupied a seat. Witness paid twopence for the ticket produced, which had no entertainment duty tax upon it. Before the concert was finished from 1,200 to 1,300 persons were present, and he heard a number of pieces played by the Municipal Orchestra.

The defence was that it was the ordinary case of the payment of twopence by a person who took a chair, and there was not a shadow of evidence to show that it was a payment for the entertainment.

After legal argument, the chairman announced that the Bench had decided to impose a fine of £10. [See report of appeal, July 1.]

JUNE.

PEMBERTON BILLING TRIAL—ALLEGED CRIMINAL LIBEL ON MISS MAUD ALLAN—VERDICT OF ACQUITTAL.

4 On June 4 the charges at the Central Criminal Court, before Mr. Justice Darling and a jury, against Noel Pemberton Billing, M.P., of libelling Maud Allan and J. T. Grein, failed, the jury returning a verdict of Not Guilty after a hearing extending over the better part of six days. Mr. Billing was charged on three indictments: (1) Publishing a false and defamatory libel on Miss Maud Allan, the dancer; (2) publishing a similar libel on Mr. J. T. Grein; and (3) publishing an obscene libel.

Mr. Hume Williams, K.C., Mr. Travers Humphreys, and Mr. Valetta appeared for the prosecution; and Mr. Billing conducted his own defence.

The libel complained of appeared in a propagandist newspaper called the *Vigilante*, conducted by the defendant, and (apart from the heading, in respect of which the charge of obscene libel was preferred) was as follows:—

To be a member of Miss Maud Allan's private performance in Oscar Wilde's Salomé one must apply to Miss Valetta, 9, Duke Street, W.C. If Scotland Yard were to seize the lists of those members I have no doubt they would be able to secure the names of some thousands of the 47,000, and the necessary means should be taken to bring some of them to justice.

Of the first five days of the trial three were taken up by Mr. Billing's defence in reference to the first charge, to which he pleaded not guilty and urged a plea of justification.

Miss Maud Allan, in the witness-box, gave evidence concerning her career. Her own dance, "The Vision of Salomé," had nothing to do with the play of "Salomé," in which a different dance was given. Except for her rôle in the play, she had nothing to do with the performance. She was not a member of the Independent Theatre Society.

The defendant called a number of witnesses, including medical men and dramatic critics, and also Mr. Grein.

On the conclusion of the evidence on June 3 the Judge directed the attention of the jury to his ruling with reference to the matters that had been raised. He should leave to the jury whether the passages mentioned were libels on Miss Allan, and of course the question as well whether they were justified. As to the book which had been mentioned, his Lordship said it was not necessary for Mr. Billing to prove that there were the 47,000 in question, or that anyone was or was not included in it. He would confine the case to the question whether the quoted passage was a libel upon Miss Maud Allan, and whether it was for the public benefit that that statement should be made. As to all the mention about the 47,000 and German agents, he would rule that that was absolutely irrelevant to these proceedings, and no question would be left to the jury about it.

In his summing up on June 4 the Judge said that the libel on Miss Allan charged her with being a lewd, unchaste, and immoral woman, and the performance in which she appeared was said to be obscene and indecent. The defendant had said he never intended to accuse Miss Allan of immoral practices, and that, if he had been so understood, he now withdrew any such suggestion. "That," said the Judge, "cannot be too well known, and the case stands in that position as regards Miss Allan, namely, that the defendant does not allege, and if he ever had alleged, and could have been understood to be alleging, that she had been guilty of any such practices, he withdraws it, and no one is entitled henceforth to say that any such charge as that is made against her, or that she rests under any such imputation." That cleared away a great deal, but it still left to be dealt with the question of what was the meaning of the cult referred to in the libel. He understood that what was relied upon was that she took part in playing in an indecent and obscene play, which did not represent simply a natural, although exaggerated, passion of a young girl for a man, but an unnatural passion. Dealing with the question as to what was the effect, nature, and intention of the play, his Lordship said it was common knowledge that one could go to a theatre and see a piece played decently and go to another and see the same piece played very vulgarly. There were some actors who, without any words being said, did very indecent things. Then the play might itself be an indecent play, and yet it might be played with a restraint and refinement which might conceal the indecency.

The jury were absent for an hour and twenty-five minutes, and on their return the foreman returned a verdict of "Not guilty."

Mr. Hume Williams said he would not proceed with the other indictments.

The jury, on the direction of the judge, then returned a verdict of "Not guilty" on the charge of publishing a defamatory libel against Jack Thomas Grein and of publishing an obscene libel.

At this point the Judge said:—I desire to say a word on this case. This case arose entirely from the production of a play by Mr. Oscar Wilde, the play of "Salomé," which it is perfectly clear the Censor would not permit to be played in public. People who cannot get the leave of the Censor to produce plays in the ordinary way are able, apparently, as the law stands, to produce them in this sort of fashion privately by subscription or by some way in which apparently they cannot be stopped. This play should never have been produced, either in public or in private, and the Censor could not be expected to allow such a thing to be produced before audiences which he could control.

There has been a great deal said in the course of this case regarding the kind of dances and the costumes worn. In fact, worse than nothing are some of the things they wear, and to my mind the law wants altering in these two respects. It ought to be made impossible for plays of this kind to be produced before any audience, either privately or by subscription, or by any other means, and those who have the power, or believe that they have the power, to prevent improper dances from being danced or such costumes worn on the stage ought to exercise their powers most stringently to put a stop to that kind of thing.

LENA v. VICTORIA PALACE, LTD.—BREACH OF CONTRACT.

19 In the King's Bench Division, before Mr. Justice McCardie and a common jury, Lily Lena (Mrs. Lily Turpin) claimed damages from the defendant company for alleged repudiation and determination of an agreement entered into with them to perform at the Victoria Palace on various dates. The defence was that the plaintiff herself repudiated the contract by refusing to perform, and they counterclaimed for damages.

Mr. J. B. Matthews, K.C., and Mr. E. F. Lever (instructed by Messrs. Bevan and Co.) for the plaintiff; Mr. McCall, K.C., and Mr. Scanlan, M.P. (instructed by Messrs. Beyfus and Beyfus) for the defendants.

Plaintiff stated that on May 19, 1916, she entered into the agreement now in dispute to appear at the Victoria Palace in the weeks commencing March 12, 1917; October 1, 1917; June 10, 1918; December 9, 1918; June 9, 1919; March 20, 1920; and September 7, 1920, at £25 a week. When she attended the rehearsal on March 12, 1917, she found that, although a "star," she was inconspicuously "billed," that her "turn" was the first after the interval—a very unsatisfactory position—and that her performance was cut down from fifteen to twenty minutes to eight to ten minutes. She remonstrated over the telephone with Mr. Hayman, the booking manager, and in consequence of his replies she broke down and could not appear that night. She sent a doctor's certificate stating that she was suffering from nervous prostration, but, notwithstanding, Mr. Hayman engaged substitutes, and the agreement was determined.

Evidence was given by Mr. Fred Russell, chairman of the V.A.F., as to the nature of the agreement, and by Mr. Turpin, husband of the plaintiff.

Mr. Matthews analysed the agreement, pointing out that the word "engagement" was used in different senses, the reference in some clauses being to the week's appearances, in others to the whole series of appearances, and in others to both. Each week, he contended, must be taken as a separate engagement.

Mr. Hall, defendants' manager, giving evidence for the defence, said he never received the doctor's certificate.

Mr. John Hayman, the booking manager, said he considered plaintiff's position on the bill and the programme quite suitable. She told him she preferred to cancel all her engagements if an alteration could not be made, and as it could not, he said he agreed to that proposition.

The case was continued on June 20.

His Lordship said that he would direct the jury to consider the question of damages under two distinct heads—(1) Loss of salary, and (2) loss of the benefit of publicity.

The jury found (1) that there had been no cancellation of the contract by consent on March 12, 1917; (2) that the plaintiff had supplied a medical certificate of inability to appear, as required by the contract; (3) that the defendants had not determined the contract within a reasonable time; and (4) that the evidence of a customary meaning of the word "engagement" was insufficient. They assessed damages for loss of salary at £100 and for loss of publicity at £100.

Judgment was entered for the plaintiff for £100, with costs, under the first head of damages. The second head, his Lordship said, involved a novel point in the law of the measure of damages. It was decided accordingly that the case should come up for argument by counsel.

On June 24 the case was again before the Court.

Mr. J. B. Matthews, K.C., submitted that the plaintiff was entitled to recover under both heads, because the defendants must have known that if they deprived her of the opportunity of appearing at a West End hall her general professional career would be prejudiced.

Mr. Scanlan, for the defendants, contended that the contract was to pay salary alone, and contained no implied terms to give publicity. The defendants were not bound to allow the plaintiff to appear. In all contracts like that under discussion there was mutuality. Both the parties gave consideration, the plaintiff consideration to perform a "turn," the defendants' consideration to pay the plaintiff £25 a week. The salary was the measure of damages.

His Lordship said the point was an important one, touching several professions and a vast body of contracts, and he would put his judgment in writing and endeavour to deliver it on June 28.

In his considered judgment his Lordship said that the plaintiff's claim for damages for loss of publicity was based on the fact that the Victoria Palace was regarded as a West End place of entertainment with a large and critical audience, whose approbation would open to a performer the gateway of London success. If the plaintiff's contention was correct, a new and serious head of damages might be asserted in many future cases, for the considerations involved touched not only the class of agreement in question, but many branches of contractual obligation. In actions for breach of contract such elements as malice, ignominy, and aggravation, which were generally admissible in tort, could be regarded in certain exceptional cases only (Addis v. Gramophone Co., Limited) (1909).

The learned Judge referred to Bostock v. Nicholson, Fitzgerald v. Leonard, and Cointat v. Myham, and went on to say that all these cases concerned damages to existing reputation, and did not determine the somewhat different question that might arise where the plaintiff asserted that he had been deprived of an accretion of future reputation by the defendants' default. The mere fact that such a loss would be difficult to assess would afford no reason for refusing damages (Chaplin v. Hicks); and he could see no reason in law against the recovery of damages for loss of publicity if the contract and circumstances of the case were appropriate, and on that ground the decisions in Bunning v. Lyric Theatre, Limited, and Marcus v. Myers and Davis were clearly sound in principle. It was clear that where, e.g., a young and gifted performer agreed to work for a famous impresario at a nominal salary for a period of years on the express terms that the latter should advertise the former and endeavour to secure his popularity and success substantial damages might be obtained if the impresario wrongly repudiated. Counsel for the defendants pointed out that in both those cases the contracts contained express provision for advertisement. The crucial question, therefore, was, Did the contract in the present case present any juristic similarity to the contracts in Bunning v. Lyric Theatre and Marcus v. Myers and Davis?

Before that question could be answered it was essential to decide whether the present contract imposed on the defendants any obligation at all to allow the plaintiff to appear at their music-hall on the dates fixed by the agreement. If no such obligation existed, then damages for loss of publicity could not be recovered. The leading authority was Turner v. Sawdon and Co., in which the Court of Appeal held that an agreement to "engage and employ" the plaintiff did not import any obligation on the defendants to provide him with actual work. As was said by A. L. Smith, M.R.:—"It is within the province of the master to say that he will go on paying wages, but that he is under no obligation to provide work."

The learned Judge also cited Lagerwall v. Wilkinson and Co., Limited, and Konski v. Peet. All these authorities, he said, were seriously adverse to the plaintiff unless a distinction existed between the employment of a public performer and the employment of an ordinary commercial agent. That the two classes of employment might well differ in essential features was indicated by Sir John Romilly in Fechter v. Montgomery. Nevertheless, the fact that a man who was an actor or public singer or the like could not affect the settled principles of construction applicable to every contract. It was an important circumstance, but it was only a circumstance.

THE TERMS OF THE CONTRACT.

The learned Judge then discussed the terms of the contract, which, he said, was somewhat remarkable, as out of thirty-nine clauses one only was in favour of the artist, namely, the clause providing for the payment of salary.

The contract was a perfectly good business arrangement without any such implied obligation, for the artist had the right to full salary though she might never perform, while the employer had a right to call for such performances as he wished. The terms of the contract tended to negative rather than support the implication asserted by the plaintiff, for there was nothing in the bargain which denoted that the parties treated the alleged obligation on the basis of the agreement. Clause 33 ran: "The management shall have the sole right to determine the position of the artist's name, the size and nature of the type . . . on the bills and programme and in the advertisements." This wide and dominating discretion of the employer pointed clearly to the fact that it was for the defendants to determine the artistic standing of the plaintiff for the performance at their hall, and to decide upon the collateral points involved. On an examination of the contract he was satisfied that the contention of counsel for the defendants was correct—that there was nothing that could be said to place on the defendants an express obligation to allow the plaintiff to appear and perform. There being no express obligation of the kind, was there any implied obligation?

With regard to the contract before the Court, it must be observed that if any such obligation had been intended it would have been easy to express it in the contract. His conclusion was that there was no implied obligation on the defendants to allow the plaintiff to appear at their hall during the contract periods. From that conclusion it followed that the plaintiff's claim to the second head of damages could not be supported in law. To allow it would involve a dangerous extension of the right to damages.

His Lordship said that he came to this conclusion with regret. He trusted a new form of contract might be devised which would give a wider measure of protection to the legitimate interests of the music-hall artist. He was satisfied that the Victoria Palace, Limited, made the contract upon no other basis than a business engagement of an artist at a salary they agreed to pay. No element of publicity of the plaintiff entered into their part of the bargain. They were a business company, and the Victoria Palace was, after all, a dividend-paying concern rather than an academy for the advancement of ambitious artists. He should therefore enter judgment for the plaintiff for £100 only, for loss of salary, and costs.

His Lordship accordingly gave judgment for the plaintiff for £100. Costs were allowed on the High Court scale, but the plaintiff was ordered to pay the costs of the argument.

On the application of Mr. McCall, a stay of execution was granted on the usual terms. [See report of appeal, December 6.]

JULY.

ENTERTAINMENTS TAX—PIER SEATS—BRIGHTON CONVICTION UPHELD.

At the Brighton Quarter Sessions the management of the Brighton West Pier Company appealed against a conviction of Mr. Albert William Scholey, the secretary, on May 31, when a fine of £10 was imposed by the justices for an alleged infringement of the statute relating to the entertainments tax. The appeal was heard before Mr. W. P. G. Boxall, Recorder, and the counsel engaged were Mr. Huntley Jenkins, for the Excise Commissioners, and Mr. G. Edwardes Jones, with whom was Mr. A. Hutchinson, for the West Pier Company.

Mr. Scholey, called by the counsel for the appellants, said there were ten double doors to the concert hall, and people went in and out as they pleased. Payment was for admission to the pier, and it entitled anyone to hear the band performances without further payment. Anyone paying twopence for a chair outside the concert hall was perfectly free to take the chair inside the hall whilst the band was playing, and it was frequently done. Considerable numbers of people stood without paying, and he had never received a complaint as to inconvenience caused through people standing in the hall. When the concert hall was originally opened a charge of 2d. was made at the door, but this was found to be unpopular, and so it was abandoned. Cross-examined: A large proportion of the company's income was derived from the concert hall, which was provided with about 1,000 seats in summer and rather fewer in winter. Twopence was charged in respect of every seat occupied, and nothing had as yet been paid in the way of tax, although he agreed that the public were entertained by the band performances. He agreed that if twopence were charged for admission to the concert hall a tax would have to be paid.

In reply to the Recorder, he said that there was no charge for the chairs except during the hours the band was playing. The concert hall was not closed when the band was not playing. Very few people visited the hall between the band performances.

Evidence was heard confirming the evidence of Mr. Scholey.

Mr. Edwardes Jones submitted that the section did not apply to this case, seeing that no charge was made for admission to the place of entertainment. It was a perfectly free place, to which persons were admitted without any payment whatever. The mere fact that a charge was made for a chair after admission had been obtained without charge would not make it a charge for admission to a place of entertainment. A movable chair could not be held to be a place within the meaning of the Act. Any person who went on the pier had an absolute right to hear the concert, and it did not make it a payment for the entertainment if the person chose to take a chair in order that he might hear it in more comfort. The payment was payment for the chair whether inside or outside the hall.

Mr. Huntley Jenkins, on behalf of the respondents, contended that it did not matter whether people got their entertainment outside or inside the concert hall, which was built for the purpose of giving concerts. The original system of collecting money at the door was not found to be a convenient way of carrying on, and so they got their money for the concert by means of these chairs, which practically filled the room. The whole object of the concerts was to increase the revenue.

In the course of his judgment the Recorder said the point raised was not without difficulty, nor was it at all a simple case, but on the evidence before him he had come to the conclusion that the conviction by the Justices must stand, and his reasons for that decision would probably be clear to anyone who had considered the provisions of the Act. In substance it seemed to him that the charge for the chairs came within Section 1 and the definition in Section 6. He had less difficulty in coming to that decision because it was pretty obvious that any decision he gave would be reviewed by a higher authority, and he was quite prepared to state a case in order that this test case might be considered elsewhere. The appeal would be dismissed, the penalty imposed by the Justices to stand. The question of costs was ordered to stand over until after the hearing of the appeal. [See report of original case, May 31.]

GORDON v. GILBERT.

10 At the Bolton County Court, before the Registrar, Mr. C. E. Hulton, the case of Gordon v. Gilbert was up for hearing. The plaintiff, Mr. Kenneth Gordon, claimed from the defendants, Messrs. Cyril Gilbert, Limited, the sum of £6 4s. 3d. for services rendered in respect of a curtain-raiser, "The Woman in the Case," as performed in a Bolton theatre. The action was undefended, and judgment was entered accordingly for the amount claimed and costs, payable within seven days.

BLAIBERG v. MONTEFIORE.

15 At Westminster County Court Judge Lush heard an action to recover £84 7s. 6d. on a cheque, the plaintiff being Benjamin Blaiberg, proprietor of the Grand, Croydon, and the defendant Eade Montefiore, theatrical manager, Haymarket, S.W. The defence was that the cheque and the agreement under which it was given were obtained through fraud by the plaintiff's agent.

Mr. A. Powell, K.C., and Mr. Tindal Davies were for the plaintiff, and Mr. Wallington for the defendant.

Mr. Powell said that defendant was touring with his piece, "The Widow's Might," and when at Bedford telephoned to Mr. Royce, plaintiff's manager, asking what he would take for his expenses for a week. Royce replied £160, and defendant signed a contract agreeing to pay that sum for the week commencing March 18. During the week defendant was at the Grand, but not on the Saturday, but he had given his manager, Mr. Mandeville, a signed cheque with the figure space left blank. Then it was found that after deducting the takings there was the sum of £84 7s. 6d. due to plaintiff, so that amount was filled in the cheque. It was paid into the bank, but was returned marked "Not to pay." No complaint had been made, but now the defendant said that the theatre's weekly expenses were not £160, as represented to him. The defendant counter-claimed £251 for fraud, and alleged that he was told the takings at the theatre would reach £400, that the orchestra was insufficient, as well as the billposting.

Cyril Royce, plaintiff's manager, said the p'ay was extensively advertised. The total receipts for the week were £88 4s. 6d., and there was a rebate of £5 on account of the band being small. Cross-examined, witness denied that he told defendant he anticipated the takings for the week would be £400. Defendant never asked what their expenses were, but simply what they would take for expenses.

Wm. Peet, the theatre auditor, put in balance-sheets showing that the theatre's average expenses each week were £134. In addition, £40 was put down each week on account of capital.

The defendant said he had twenty-eight years as theatrical manager. When touring with "The Widow's Might" the theatre takings at Bedford were £276, at Norwich £330, and at Hull £443. On March 6 he saw Mr. Royce, and saying he would like to play at Croydon asked what his idea of takings were. Royce said it might be £400. Later he asked what they would take to play the piece, and ultimately £160 was the figure agreed upon and the agreement signed. Just before signing, Royce said they expected £50 for the Monday's house. Royce could not find his billing man, so he (defendant) sent him one for the Saturday in the week he (defendant) was away, but on Monday following, when he got a report from Mr. Mandeville, his manager, he telegraphed for the cheque to be stopped.

Judge Lush said the evidence did not support in the slightest the charge of fraud made for the defence, nor did Mr. Montefiore's evidence suggest it. Therefore the counter claim could not stand. There would be judgment for the plaintiff for the amount claimed, and the counter-claim would be dismissed.

THOMPSON (MERSON) v. LONDON THEATRES OF VARIETIES, LTD. WHAT IS A MATINEE?

16 The suit brought by Wm. Henry Thompson professionally known as Billy Merson, against the London Theatres of Varieties, Ltd., was heard before Mr. Justice Peterson in the Chancery Division on July 16 and 18. Mr. Compston, K.C., and Mr. Patrick Hastings appeared for the plaintiff; and Mr. Tomlin, K.C., and Mr. Stamp for the defendants.

Mr. Compston said that the case raised a point of the construction of a contract between the parties with regard to daytime performances. The plaintiff was a well-known comedian, and the defendants owned many houses of entertainment. The contract was dated November 29, 1915, and was entered into by Mr. Charles Gulliver, manager of the Palladium, acting in behalf of the defendant company. It engaged the services of Mr. Merson for five years, beginning in 1916 and extending to 1921, on certain specified dates in each year, and the places of entertainment at which he was to appear as comedian and burlesque artist were to be such theatres or music-halls of the defendants within the Metropolitan Police area as the management desired. The agreement was that he should perform twice daily, each turn lasting thirty minutes. If the contract had stopped there no difficulty would have arisen, but it went on to provide "except that the artist shall appear and perform at any matinée the management may reasonably desire, in addition to the said two performances per day." It was upon that the difficulty had arisen. At the time the contract was entered into the Palladium, which was the house over which the dispute had arisen, gave three matinées per week. It was expressly agreed that Mr. Merson's salary was to include two matinées at the Palladium when he was appearing at that hall in 1916, 1917, and 1918, and one matinée in 1919, 1920, and 1921. Any additional matinées were to be paid for at the rate of one-twelfth of his weekly salary. It had since happened that the Palladium decided to have a daytime performance every day, except Sunday, in addition to the two evening performances, and they had required the plaintiff to appear at the three performances. He did so, apparently without protest, and he would tell his lordship that he did not want to object so long as his health was not over-taxed; but the conditions under which he had been required to give his performances lately had put such a strain upon him that he could not continue it, and was obliged to come and ask the Court if he was compelled to give these extra performances. The rule was twice daily, with the exception of matinées, and, in the case of the Palladium, the exception had been turned into the rule, which Mr. Merson said was not right. Counsel said he was going to rely strongly upon the provision in the contract with respect to the Coliseum, in which a sharp distinction was drawn between a matinée and a daily performance in the afternoon. The agreement provided that the afternoon performance in that case should not be treated as a matinée, but put it on the same footing as an evening performance. The defendant company had the option of extending Mr. Merson's contract for a further five years, and under the present conditions of three performances daily this would be a great hardship. Counsel said that the public, who knew nothing of the rules and regulations under which the artists performed, probably imagined that they had a very easy and pleasant time, but Mr. Merson was under an obligation to introduce something original or an old song at a moment's notice; he had to sing three songs at each performance, and to give encores if the management so desired. It was very hard work, requiring a great deal of strain. Mr. Merson had been suffering lately from throat trouble, which had compelled him to take the step he had taken. The question his lordship had to decide was, to put it in the form of a conundrum—When is a matinée not a matinée? The answer was that in the music-hall profession the word had a very clear and definite meaning. A matinée was a performance that met the convenience of certain sections of the community who were at liberty on certain afternoons and not at liberty on others. Wednesdays and Saturdays were well known in that respect.

His Lordship: Would a performance on Tuesday afternoon be a matinée?

Mr. Compston said he could not explain Tuesdays himself. With regard to Monday, this was a valuable day for soldiers on weekend leave. He urged that a matinée was something wholly different from a regular daytime performance. The Palladium was the only house that gave a performance every afternoon and two performances nightly. In plaintiff's previous contract the words appeared, "afternoon performances," not being regular matinées.

Mr. Merson, giving evidence, said he had seventeen years' experience of the music-hall stage. When he signed the contract the Palladium was giving two performances nightly and matinées on Monday, Wednesday, and Saturday. He had no indication of the proposed change until shortly after the agreement was signed. He did not object to the three performances so long as his health was not taxed too much. He was paid extra for all afternoon performances over two a week. He had to devote a good deal of time during the day to his kinema contracts, and had he known that the Palladium was going to run a daytime performance every day he would not have signed the agreement with the defendants.

Asked if the word "matinée" had a well-understood meaning in the profession, witness replied: "I do not think any artist would say that the Palladium performance is a matinée. It is a recognised daily performance, and is not treated as a matinée. A matinée is an exceptional performance put on in the case of successful plays or at holiday times.

Mr. George Robey, in giving evidence in support of the plaintiff's case, said that if there were five afternoon performances a week they were matinées, but if there were six they ceased to be matinées. An habitual afternoon performance was not considered in the music-hall world to be a matinée.

Mr. H. M. Vernon said that if the afternoon performances exceeded three they ceased to be matinées.

Mr. Charles Gulliver, called for the defence, said that a matinée meant any afternoon performance. The plaintiff had never complained to him about the three performances daily.

Mr. Tomlin said that the contract was perfectly plain. The Oxford Dictionary defined a matinée as "a musical or theatrical afternoon performance." There was a recent case before the Privy Council, where it was held that the Court was entitled to look at the conduct of the parties to a document for the purpose of interpreting that document. Here the plaintiff had accepted the conditions at the Palladium for two years.

Mr. Justice Peterson, in giving judgment, said that three witnesses had given evidence for the plaintiff, but, on looking at their evidence, he found that none of them agreed about the meaning of the word matinée: It was, therefore, impossible to say that there was any general meaning given to the word in music-hall circles, and he was thrown back on the contract. He found that the plaintiff had contracted to perform at any matinées that the defendants might desire. It appeared, therefore, that on the true construction of the contract a matinée meant any performance given in the afternoon, and the action must be dismissed with costs.

AUGUST.

COWEN v. ROLLS.

28 In the Vacation Court, before Mr. Justice Roche, Mr. Laurence Cowen applied for an interim injunction to restrain Mr. Ernest Charles Rolls from further producing or performing in public in its present form the play entitled "The Hidden Hand," which was then running at the Strand Theatre. Mr. Cowen, who conducted his own case, said his complaint was that since he wrote the play certain prominent public persons had either voluntarily joined up or been conscripted into the service of altering, rewriting, or generally improving out of all knowledge what was once his work. By an agreement, dated March 23 last, Mr. Rolls acquired the producing and performing rights of "The Hidden Hand," together with certain other of the applicant's dramatic works. Interpolations and alterations of a prejudicial character had been made in the play without his sanction or approval, with the result that his literary reputation had suffered and ridicule had been cast upon him in the Press.

Mr. Harold Smith, for the defendant, read an affidavit to the effect that certain passages in the original play, which were received with laughter by the public and were much criticised in the Press, were struck out and other alterations were made without any protest from the plaintiff, and in some cases at his instance. Minor alterations were in the discretion of the producer. The present proceedings had come as a surprise to Mr. Rolls, who would, however, be delighted to meet Mr. Cowen and go into the matter with him with a view to an agreement being come to.

His Lordship said that Mr. Cowen had made his public protest. It was impossible to try the issues on affidavit, and there would be no order on the motion except that the costs be costs in the action.

LIGHTING REGULATIONS AND STAGE SCENERY—BOGNOR PROSECUTION—CHARGE DISMISSED.

31 Considerable interest was taken in a case—the first of the kind—heard at the Chichester County Bench. William Nathaniel Tate, proprietor and manager of the Kursaal Theatre, Bognor, and Ernest

Reginald Lambert, the stage carpenter, were summoned for unlawfully consuming electric current at the Bognor Theatre on August 3 and 11.

Mr. A. Dixon, who prosecuted for the police, said that proceedings were taken under the Lighting, Heating, and Power Order, 1918, which came into force in April, 1918. The Order was made under the D.O.R.A. by the Board of Trade, and had to be construed by the Court. It was not for the people who made this Order to say what it meant; it was for the magistrates to do so. The Order clearly specified that no gas or electric current should be used on the stage at theatres and other places of entertainment between the hours of 10.30 p.m. and 1 p.m. on the following day, except such as might be needed for the necessary cleaning and washing thereof, or for the exhibition of kinema films, etc., to the trade, to which the general public would not be admitted. On August 3, at 11.15 p.m., Special Constable Browning found that lights were on the stage, and on investigating he found six electric bulbs were being used for the removal of scenery to a lorry in York Road. The facts were not disputed. The company appearing at the Kursaal had finished their performance, and the scenery was being taken away. That was distinctly contrary to the Order, as no gas or electric current was to be consumed for other purposes than those he had named. When Mr. Tate was fetched the bulbs were immediately reduced to two, clearly showing that the work could have been carried out with less light. This work, he submitted, could have been done with candles or lamps, thereby not breaking the Order made by the Board of Trade. He admitted that on the decision of the Bench the whole of the theatres in England would be affected, but he had nothing to do with that. The Order was made to be carried out, and was quite clear to every manager and theatre-owner in the kingdom.

Special Constable Browning gave formal evidence as to the consuming of the electric current, and stated that the lights were full on when he visited the theatre.

Mr. E. B. Wannop, for the defence, said that if the suggestion of the police was accepted by the Bench, and they held that no lights should be used for removing scenery, then theatres could not go on, for the reason that the contracts of theatre companies contained a clause that the scenery should be moved the evening after their contracts terminated. Lights were used in London for the "striking" of scenery, and when Mr. J. B. Williams, the secretary representing the Amusements Industry Committee, raised a similar question respecting a theatre, the Board of Trade then said that under the Order the use of lights for the removal of scenery was permissible, and was included in the terms of the Order. Were the Bench going to put such an interpretation on the Order as would mean the closing of theatres? It was impossible to use candles, because they would invalidate the insurance policy and were held to be contrary to the terms of the license granted by the Bench.

Mr. Tate, in his evidence, said that there were no means of lighting the stage except by artificial light, and at whatever time scenery was moved it would be necessary to use artificial light. They could not use candles or lamps, for the Bench would not grant them permission, and it would not be permitted by the insurance company.

Mr. H. W. Rowland, secretary to the Theatrical Managers' Association, and manager of various theatres, said that it was customary for light to be used for the removal of scenery. He spoke of the interviews he had had with the Board of Trade and Mr. Hills on the point raised in the present case.

Correspondence from the Board of Trade on the subject submitted by the witness was objected to by Mr. Dixon.

The witness went on to explain methods in vogue in the London and suburban theatres. He referred to a settlement of the question in regard to the Royal, Plymouth. If the contention of the police was correct in the present case, then all theatres would have to close down.

The Chairman: Surely not. Do you know if this is the first prosecution?

Witness: Yes, it is. The Chief Constable of Plymouth wrote to the Board of Trade, and their answer I sent to THE STAGE and other professional papers, and it was accepted as settling the point.

In cross-examination the witness said that it would be impossible for the theatres to carry on if the Court held that this Order was to stand and be carried out. It would apply to every theatre in London, as well as the provinces.

Having deliberated in private, the Chairman said: This case is no doubt a very important one for managers and proprietors of theatres. Although the removal of the scenery was for the purpose of taking it out of the theatre, it was also preliminary to cleaning. We, therefore, after very careful consideration, dismiss the case. We think light can be used for that purpose.

The following are the letters—referred to by Mr. Rowland in his evidence—which were objected to by the prosecution as inadmissible:—

Public Utilities and Harbour Department,
Board of Trade,
7, Whitehall Gardens, London, S.W.,
August 26, 1918.

Sir,—With reference to your interview to-day on the subject of Section 10 of the Lighting, Heating, and Power Order, 1918, I am directed by the Board of Trade to state that, as already intimated to Mr. J. B. Williams from Mr. Wardle's private secretary, on April 11 last, the Board of Trade are of opinion that the removal from the place of entertainment of scenery and effects belonging to travelling companies may be regarded as " cleaning " for the purposes of that section; and I am to enclose for your information a copy of a communication to that effect which was sent on April 17 last to the manager of the Royal, Plymouth.—I am, Sir, your obedient servant, .

(Signed) HERBERT C. HONEY.

H. W. Rowland, Esq.,
  Secretary,
    Theatrical Managers' Association,
    52, Shaftesbury Avenue, W.1.
April 17, 1918.

[COPY.]

Sir,—With reference to your letter of April 5 on the subject of Section 10 of the Lighting, Heating, and Power Order, 1918, I am directed by the Board of Trade to state that they are of opinion that the removal from a place of entertainment of scenery, properties, etc., belonging to performers or theatrical companies, may be regarded as " cleaning " for the purposes of the section.—I am, your obedient servant,

(Signed) GARNHAM ROPER.

J. M. Glover, Esq.,
  Royal, Plymouth.

SEPTEMBER.

PEARL v. TURNER—CLAIM FOR SALARY.

2 At Clerkenwell County Court Arthur Pearl, comedian, of Guildford Road, Stockwell, sued Percy M. Turner, theatrical manager, for salary in lieu of notice.

Mr. Boney said that his client was a variety artist, and was engaged to appear in a concert party at a salary of £7 per week for the first four weeks and £8 per week afterwards. The engagement was subject to a fortnight's notice on either side. The party went on tour in Wales, and at the end of the second week plaintiff was handed a note saying that his engagement was terminated.

Plaintiff said that in the second week of the tour the party went to Porth, in Wales. At the conclusion of the Saturday night performance he was paid and a note was handed him. The note, evidently intended to date from the previous Monday, stated, "Please note that your engagement will terminate on Saturday next." He got an engagement at the same salary in the second week after his dismissal.

Defendant, in evidence, said he was professionally known as Dex Shirland, illusionist. During the performance at Porth plaintiff had to do a single number—a single song—and at the end of the song people got up and walked out. Those who remained gave plaintiff "the bird."

His Honour (to defendant): There is no condition in the engagement that he should please the audience.

Defendant: But if he comes with a West-End reputation and recommendation, surely that is good enough?

His Honour: He may please a West-End audience very well, but in Porth they may not like it.

Defendant: A comedian of reputation should be able to adapt his business to suit any audience.

His Honour: He warrants reasonable proficiency as a music-hall artist, but I don't think he warrants that he will please every audience.

Defendant: The majority of music-hall artists, if they go North, adapt themselves to suit the audiences of the North, and so on with regard to other places. I was not prepared to go on losing with a man like Mr. Pearl.

His Honour: You were bound to give a fortnight's notice unless he had committed some breach of warranty—some expressed condition—that his employment is conditional upon giving satisfaction to all audiences.

Defendant: Plaintiff caught a cold and lost his voice. It may be due to that.

His Honour: I think you must pay a week's salary. There will be judgment for plaintiff for £7 and costs.

Plaintiff, who said he had come from Whitstable to attend court, was allowed expenses.

OCTOBER.

WHAT IS A "NO. 1" COMPANY?— GRIFFITHS v. SEEBOLD.

7 At the Worthing County Court, on Monday before his Honour Judge Mackarness, Mr. Gilbert Griffiths, theatrical agent, of 18, Charing Cross Road, London, sued Mr. Adolf Seebold, proprietor of the Worthing Theatre Royal, to recover £28 9s. 6d., alleged to be due under an agreement, and defendant counterclaimed for £33 15s.

Mr. Harold Simmons was for the plaintiff, and Mr. A. B. Dixon was for the defendant.

Mr. Simmons said the defendant, finding himself without a company for a certain week in June, telephoned to plaintiff to see if his No. 1 Company playing "The Chorus Lady" was at liberty. An agreement was made for defendant to provide the scenery, plaintiff bringing ten people in the company with twelve parts. The contract stated that plaintiff should receive 60 per cent. of the gross takings, with a guarantee of £70. Plaintiff had only received £41 10s. 6d.

Plaintiff, in his evidence, said that when defendant asked for his company to come to Worthing he asked 65 per cent. with a guarantee of £70. At the last moment Kenneth Gordon, a leading man in the company, was taken ill, and another man had to be substituted at a double salary.

Mr. Dixon: According to the heading on your notepaper Cyril Gilbert is running this company. Why, then, is Gilbert Griffiths taking the action?

Plaintiff replied that his business was Cyril Gilbert, Ltd.; there were two members of the limited liability company.

In cross-examination Mr. Dixon elicited that Mr. Kenneth Gordon left the company at Bolton on account of his health.

Mr. Dixon: I put it to you that Mr. Gordon left because he was not paid his salary?— I know nothing about that.

Did you pay all your artists last week?— Yes, I always pay them, even in the poorest business.

Mr. Dixon: Well, I can produce two artists who left you because they were not paid.

Mr. Carl Adolf Seebold, the defendant, said that from a conversation over the telephone with Mr. Gilbert he understood that "The Chorus Lady" was a West-End production with a West-End company of twelve, and that the salary list was £70. He therefore thought he was getting hold of something good. He asked Mr. Gilbert to mention some names in the cast, and he heard the name of Kenneth Gordon. Knowing that that actor had left a favourable impression from a previous visit to the town, he thought it was a good guarantee. He sent two contracts to Mr. Gilbert, signed one himself, and later received the other back from Mr. Gilbert, signed, but with the clause relating to scenery deleted. But there was no letter drawing witness's attention to the deletion. On arrival of the company he heard that the show was not up to expectations. He (witness) took good care to be away from the theatre at the conclusion of the performance, as he considered it was taking money under false pretences. It was a disgrace to the profession and to the theatre, and the takings were very much below the usual average. Witness told the plaintiff's manager that he had understood the company was a "No. 1" company, and that it was a West-End production. He explained to plaintiff's manager that he would only receive 55 per cent. of the takings, as there was no scenery. Witness received a letter from Mr. Kenneth Gordon at the beginning of the week explaining his absence from the cast, but he heard nothing about a doctor's certificate until the end of the week.

Cross-examined: The company's week at Worthing was a bad week; it was at the worst time of the year (November), and the takings were just over £46. He did not see the show right through; he had not the courage, but he heard it was terrible.

Mr. John Henry Lynch, acting manager for Mr. Seebold, said eight performers appeared on the first night. He saw a portion of the show that night, and thought it was a very bad one; there were interruptions from the audience. The man who took Kenneth Gordon's part did not know it, and needed much prompting. Members of the audience went out complaining, and some of them asked for their money back.

Frederick Henry Gates, stage carpenter at the theatre, said "The Chorus Lady" was the worst show he had ever seen there; there were but eight performers and the manager.

The Judge said he understood a No. 1 company to be a company of first-rate actors, which, as was shown by the evidence, this was not; therefore it was not a "No. 1" company, and he gave judgment for Mr. Seebold.

J. LYONS AND CO. v. REX—RESTAURANTS AND ENTERTAINMENTS TAX.

13 In the Divisional Court this appeal came on for re-argument before five judges after an undecided hearing by three judges last sittings, raising the question whether music, either instrumental or vocal or both, given in restaurants during meal hours, constitutes an entertainment for which payment is made, so as to be liable to entertainment tax under the provisions of Section 1 of the Finance (New Duties) Act, 1916. Appellants, Messrs. J. Lyons and Co., caterers, had been fined £10 under each of two separate convictions in respect of the Trocadero, and appealed on a case stated by the convicting magistrate, Mr. Graham Campbell, Bow Street stipendiary. One summons related to a Sunday evening dinner and the other to an afternoon tea.

Submitting that the Act did not apply to the music in question, Mr. Upjohn, K.C., said the whole question was whether the patron paid for admission to an entertainment. His contention was that he did not. At some of the firm's large establishments there was no music, but the charge for meals was the same. The graduated scale of tax imposed by the Act made it impossible to apply its provisions to circumstances such as these, because two people might pay different sums for a meal—one, say, 7s. 6d., and the other 25s.—yet the music was the same. The Act laid it down that the expression "admission" meant admission "as a spectator or one of an audience." The object of patrons of the restaurant was to enjoy a meal, not to be spectators or members of an audience.

Sir Gordon Hewart, K.C., said it was no part of the policy of the Commissioners to prosecute in every case where there was an orchestra, because they held the view that the music was purely incidental or auxiliary to a restaurant. It was only where the music offered and paid for was a real, substantial performance that proceedings were taken.

Mr. Justice Salter and Mr. Justice Shearman held that the appeal failed, as payment was made for admission to a meal and a concert.

Mr. Justice Bailhache thought the appeal succeeded, on the ground that the words "pay for admission" in the Act were used in the ordinary, and not in a special, sense, and that patrons did not "pay for admission" in the ordinary sense.

Mr. Justice Lawrence took the same view. In his opinion the Act was not intended to hit this class of entertainment.

Mr. Justice Darling likewise thought the appeal succeeded. If the Legislature intended to hit this kind of entertainment they had not used the proper language to enable them to do so. In taxation statutes the words must plainly impose a tax, and the Court could only decide for the revenue by straining the words of this Act. What convinced him that the Legislature did not intend to hit this class of entertainment was that by the Act a penalty of £5 was imposed on every person who failed to pay the tax. If they had intended that in the case of restaurants they would have said so in plain terms, because they knew such places existed.

WOODS v. FARADAY WOODS v. FARADAY. HORSFIELD AND WOODWARD, AND THE FARADAY SYNDICATE— WITHIN THE LAW CONTRACTS.

17 On October 17, 18, and 19 these cases were before Mr. Justice Bailhache in the King's Bench. In the first case, plaintiff, Mr. Albert Herman Woods, sued Mr. Philip Michael Faraday and the executors of Sir Herbert Beerbohm Tree for an account of the proceeds of the London production and a declaration as to whether or not the production in the provinces in the beginning of 1914 was a breach of the contract. If so, then damages were claimed. His lordship, in giving judgment, dismissed plaintiff's action in the first case, with costs. In the second action, in which the plaintiffs were Mr. Woods and Mr. Selwyn, who had the American copyright in the play, his lordship held that Mr. Selwyn had not shown in evidence that he was entitled to the English copyright, and therefore his action failed. Mr. Faraday, by giving a licence to Messrs. Horsfield and Woodward for the provincial production without the consent of Mr. Woods, had committed a breach of the contract. As no damage had been suffered, but profits made from the play, nominal damages of 20s. would be awarded to Mr. Woods. The action against Messrs. Horsfield and Woodward for alleged infringement of the copyright failed.

NOVEMBER.

HUGHES v. SALTER—BREACH OF CONTRACT.

15 Before Judge Shand, at the Widnes County Court, an action was brought by William Hughes, proprietor of the Co-operative Hall there, to recover damages from Joseph Salter, music-hall artist, for damages in respect of a breach of a contract into which defendant entered to appear at the Co-operative Hall for the week beginning September 2. The plaintiff appeared by solicitor, the defendant being unrepresented. The plaintiff adduced in evidence that the defendant attributed his non-appearance to his being called up by the military authorities, but upon inquiries being made this was found to be incorrect, a shorter journey and more lucrative engagement being preferred by defendant. The defendant in court said "the military gag was a good stunt at the time." Addressing the defendant, the judge said if he (the defendant) would take his advice he would never do anything so foolish again. The plaintiff was acting generously towards him when he accepted judgment for £5 and costs.

PHILPS v. NORTH-WESTERN RAILWAY CO.—DAMAGE AT A CLOAK-ROOM.

18 At the Bloomsbury County Court, before Judge Bray, Arthur Carlton Philps, professionally known as Carlton, sued the North-Western Railway Co. to recover £5, the value of an Oriental fiddle, which had been placed in the company's cloakroom at London Road Station, Manchester.

Mr. J. Harris said plaintiff purchased the fiddle from a member of the Chinese Labour Battalion from Manchuria. The plaintiff really bought the fiddle as a curio, but it was possible that he could introduce it into a performance by his troupe. When the fiddle was handed out it was broken into three pieces.

The plaintiff said that the fiddle was placed in the cloakroom just before he went to Dublin. When the fiddle was handed up there was a label stuck on it, "Broken when left by owner."

Mr. Muller, solicitor for the company, said they wrote to the plaintiff and told him that the damage was done by a Japanese basket being placed on the top of the fiddle by the plaintiff's servant, and the company could not admit liability.

Plaintiff said that when the fiddle was handed back he at once drew the clerk's attention to it. He did not go away from the cloakroom and return ten minutes later and then make the complaint. It was obvious that the fiddle was broken when it was handed out.

Mr. Pratley, a member of the plaintiff's company, said that the fiddle was deposited by Mr. Leggatt, who was in the service of the plaintiff, and was in good order. Witness took a Japanese basket to the cloakroom, but he did not touch the fiddle.

The judge gave judgment for the plaintiff for the amount claimed, with costs.

VAUDEVILLE PRODUCTIONS, LTD., v. DANCE—PRODUCER'S CLAIM.

28 In the King's Bench, before Mr. Justice McCardie, Gus Scholke, of the plaintiff company, claimed from George Dance the sum of £200 for producing two touring versions of the Alhambra revue, "The Bing Boys," alleged to be due under an agreement made on February 13, 1917. The defendant denied liability, and counterclaimed for damages in respect of the plaintiffs' alleged failure to put on the road another "Bing Boys" company in December, 1917.

Mr. Patrick Hastings (instructed by Messrs. J. B. and G. S. Beirnstein) for the plaintiff; Sir Edward Marshall Hall, K.C., and Mr. van den Berg (instructed by Messrs. J. D. Langton and Passmore) for the defendant.

Mr. Hastings stated that the original rights in the revue "The Bing Boys" having passed from Oswald Stoll to the defendant, the plaintiff and the defendant entered into an agreement whereby the former was to produce the revue at the Alhambra in April, 1916, in consideration of a fee of £250, paid in advance, and a weekly royalty of £5 "for the run at the Alhambra or elsewhere," and, further, he was to receive £100 and a weekly royalty of £5 for any touring versions. The first touring version (No. 2 Company) was out from October, 1916, till April, 1917, and the second (No. 1 Company) was out from January, 1917, till May, 1917. The plaintiff was paid £400 in respect of each of these tours. In August, 1917, three companies went on tour (No. 1, No. 2, and No. 3), but he was paid only for No. 3 (a two-houses-a-night show), the defendant contending that No. 1 and No. 2 were not "productions," but merely continuations of the earlier tours. The claim was in respect of those versions. Plaintiff claimed in the alternative that under the agreement he was entitled to the sum of £200 for services rendered, because if he was not bound to produce the two versions he was asked to do so, and actually did so. The defendant said it was an express or implied term that he should do this work or rehearsal. With regard to the counter-claim, the plaintiff said the defendant did not give him sufficient notice to enable him to produce the version in December, 1917.

Plaintiff, in the witness-box, explained as to the meaning of "production," he, in conjunction with the costumier, thought out the general scheme of the dresses and the scenery and the dances, but did not interfere with the singing. In conjunction with the author, he also made necessary alterations in the book. The touring versions of "The Bing Boys" were in all essentials reproductions of the Alhambra revue, but on a smaller scale, requiring changes to be made to fit in with smaller stage accommodation.

Mr. Wylie, of the plaintiff company, said with regard to the counter-claim that it was November 15, 1917, the day after the writ in this action was issued, that he was first told by Mr. Wray, acting for Mr. Dance, that Mr. Scholke would be wanted to run the tour of December, 1917. As Mr. Scholke was then preparing his annual Christmas pantomime for Manchester, he told Mr. Wray that Mr. Scholke could not possibly undertake the work, although he knew that under the contract the work could not be given to anybody else.

Cross-examined, the witness said Mr. Scholke was engaged by his company, and they "let him out."

Before the defence was opened counsel consulted with a view to a settlement, and eventually a settlement was come to on agreed terms, and an order for taxation of costs made, by consent.

His lordship remarked that it was desirable when a settlement took place between those who had to work together in the future, and were leading and well-known members of the theatrical profession, that it should not be of a litigious character, but one that would lead to a continuance of friendly feelings. He was very glad that this action had ended in an atmosphere of general friendliness.

DECEMBER.

POSTERS PROSECUTION.

5 Messrs. Moss' Empires, Limited, were summoned at Swansea Police Court for exhibiting, or causing to be exhibited, on a wall or hoarding in Ivy Place, Swansea, a number of posters which in the aggregate exceeded a superficial area of 2,400 sq. inches, contrary to the Paper Restriction (Posters and Circulars) Orders, 1918.

Mr. George Henry Richardson, manager, Swansea Empire, was summoned for aiding and abetting.

It was stated that there were three posters, on one of which was the weekly contents bill, and on the other two were lithos. Around the hills "blanking" had been used.

The defence submitted that the lithos were stock posters and that the "blanking" also was in stock, and that posters, etc., which were printed prior to the date of the Order were exempted from the Order.

The Bench said they considered there had been no breach of the regulations. The case was dismissed.

LENA v. VICTORIA PALACE, LTD.—THE LENA CASE—UNSUCCESSFUL APPEAL BY DEFENDANTS.

6 In the Court of Appeal, before Lords Justices Bankes, Warrington, and Scrutton, the appeal was heard in the case of Turpin v. Victoria Palace, Ltd.

The plaintiff, Mrs. Lily Turpin, professionally known as Lily Lena, of Loughborough Park, recovered £100 damages against the Victoria Palace, Ltd., for breach of contract. An agreement was entered into in May, 1916, for the plaintiff to appear at the Victoria Palace on a series of dates commencing on March 12, 1917, and she was to receive a salary of £25 a week. Her turn took from fifteen to twenty minutes, consisting of songs, and allowing a margin for encores. She went on March 12, 1917, for a rehearsal, and found that she was placed on the bill in a position lower than she considered her merits justified. She raised an objection, and after a consultation with the manager she broke down and returned home feeling ill. She sent a medical certificate to say that she could not appear, the defendants in the meantime having engaged another turn. It was contended by the defendants that the plaintiff had cancelled the contract. When she presented herself for the second week she was not allowed to fulfil her engagement. The jury awarded her £100 loss of salary, but a further award of £100 for loss of publicity Mr. Justice McCardie set aside. Judgment was entered for the loss of salary.

The defendants' appeal was on the grounds that there had been misdirection by the judge, that the verdict was against the weight of evidence, and that the damages were excessive.

Mr. McCall, K.C., who appeared for the appellants, said that there was no cross-appeal by the plaintiff against the judge's decision on the loss of publicity. The first question that arose was what took place on March 12, when the plaintiff saw the defendants' manager, and a heated conversation took place as to her position. According to the manager, when the plaintiff raised an objection to the place in which she was put in the bill she said that she would not appear at all, and would throw up the engagement. She, however, denied that, but soon after another artist was procured to take her position in the bill. She went home, and said that she was unable to see her doctor immediately she got home, but she did see him later in the evening, and he gave her a certificate that owing to her hysterical condition she was unable to appear. That certificate was given to her husband, and posted to the defendants the next morning. The defendants said that they never received the certificate.

His first point was that the plaintiff did not comply with the condition under the contract. This was necessary in order that the management could secure someone to take her place in the programme. A day or two later the plaintiff was quite able to take her place on the stage, but she didn't appear, and upon that the defendants contended that they were entitled to put an end to the contract.

Dealing with the question whether the plaintiff was entitled to £100 damages, Mr. McCall said that in 1917 there was a great demand for star artists, owing to the war and other causes, and the plaintiff was a star artist, according to her own statement, but she took no steps whatever to find other employment, except that she gave instructions through her husband. The agent was not called, and no evidence was given that she had done anything to effectively minimise the damages. In reply to a judge, Mr. McCall said that the defendants acted entirely on the assumption that the plaintiff had cancelled her contract, and would not perform at all.

Mr. J. B. Matthews, K.C. (for the plaintiff): I challenge that entirely.

Mr. McCall said that the evidence in support of the defendants was strongly in favour of the cancellation. If she was ill at twelve o'clock she was bound to send as soon as possible notice to the defendants to enable them to get someone to take her place.

Lord Justice Scrutton: As soon as possible must depend on circumstances.

Mr. McCall said that if the lady was crying at twelve o'clock it was not likely that she would be so at half-past seven.

Lord Justice Bankes: They can if they try. (Laughter.)

Mr. McCall: It requires a great stretch of imagination, and the contract does not give that stretch.

Mr. Matthews, K.C. (for respondent), was not called upon.

(See report, June 19.)

JUDGMENT.

Lord Justice Bankes, in giving judgment, said that the application was for a new trial in an action in which the plaintiff contended that the defendants had committed a breach of an agreement they had entered into with her, under which they had given her an engagement for a certain number of weeks commencing March, 1917, and running until September, 1920. Mr. Justice McCardie had put certain questions to the jury, who had answered in favour of the plaintiff. The plaintiff went to a rehearsal on March 12 for her week's engagement commencing on that day. She found her position on the bill was such as she considered degrading to her, and she was also given a dressing-room which she thought was one not suited to her position, and she was apparently extremely disturbed, and complained at the Victoria Palace and also on the telephone to Mr. Hayman, the manager. After the conversation she could not appear that night because she was so upset through what had happened. No doubt she said a great deal more, because she was undoubtedly very much disturbed, but she disputed that she said anything which could be reasonably construed into a repudiation of the agreement engaging her during that week or any subsequent occasions. She went home, and was in such a hysterical state that she tried to get a certificate from her doctor, which was inconsistent if she considered the agreement at an end, because a certificate would only be wanted if she intended to comply with the agreement. Somebody else was engaged for the week, and the question which was before the jury and upon which they were directed by the judge was whether the plaintiff repudiated the agreement or sent any cancellation of it. That question was answered in favour of the plaintiff. As to setting aside the evidence, it was not for him to express an opinion as to the conclusion he would have come to on the evidence, and upon which reasonable men might come to either one way or the other. In the circumstances it was quite impossible to interfere with that part of the case.

To the next point taken—that, even assuming the plaintiff did not repudiate the agreement, she was under an obligation to send a doctor's certificate immediately she discovered she was ill and could not perform, in order to give the management an opportunity of procuring somebody else in her place, her answer was that she did it immediately, and immediately meant within a reasonable time as the expression used in the agreement. The husband said the certificate was given to him, that he put it in a letter, and addressed it to Mr. Hayman, at the Palace Theatre, but the receipt of the certificate was denied or disputed. It seemed that no great fight was made on that point, and the jury were certainly entitled to accept the view that the certificate had been posted and had been received. Was it sent immediately? In any case some time must elapse before it could be received, whichever way it was sent. The defendants knew that the plaintiff could not appear that night, for help was obtained. Again, on that point the jury had abundant evidence before them upon which they could choose to take the view that the certificate was sent in time.

The only point remaining was that the damages were excessive. That was a question purely for the jury. It was remarked that the lady made no effort apparently to bring anyone to corroborate her story that she was not able to get an engagement in respect of the future weeks she had been originally engaged by the defendants. The jury had considered that, and it was put forward that it was difficult for a star to obtain such a position as she had held. The jury might have taken into consideration the circumstances that there was a great deal of questioning whether she was a star, or whether she had not fallen from the high estate of £60 a week to something below £25 a week, and that it might be difficult for the lady in that position to obtain an engagement which would not possibly affect her market value, if he might use that expression. There was something more to be considered, namely, whether there was a pool in stars. He did not think they could find the award excessive, and it was within the jury's province to give the amount they had awarded. The appeal, therefore, failed.

Lord Justices Warrington and Scrutton agreed, and the appeal was dismissed, with costs.

CHARLOT v. THOMPSON—QUESTION OF TITLE.

Mr. Justice Astbury, sitting in the Chancery Division, dealt with an ex parte application made on behalf of Mr. André Charlot for an injunction restraining Mr. P. Mawsey Thompson from presenting a revue at the Empire, Southend-on-Sea, under the title "Coupons," on the following Monday, on the ground that a revue bearing the same name, "Coupons," had been advertised for production at the Vaudeville on December 18. Mr. Williams, for Mr. Charlot, contended that the production at Southend-on-Sea would forestall his own, and thereby do him injury, and that Mr. Thompson would secure all the advantages of his extensive advertising of "Coupons" at the Vaudeville.

His Lordship observed that there was no suggestion that Mr. Thompson was passing off his production as that of the applicant. He could not see how a revue at Southend-on-Sea could affect a revue of the same name at the Vaudeville.

Mr. Williams submitted that at any rate it was a dishonest trick.

His Lordship: There is no evidence that Mr. Thompson has seen your advertisements.

Mr. Williams: He has presumably seen the theatrical papers, and has done a most improper act by taking my title.

His Lordship: The impropriety depends on whether he knows.

Mr. Williams: I do not want to stop his play. I only want to stop him using the name "Coupons." He has only to give it some other name.

His Lordship: My own view is that this won't do you the slightest bit of harm.

Mr. Williams observed that the opportunity of first production was an important asset. The production at Southend-on-Sea would damp down public interest in the production of the Vaudeville.

His Lordship declined to grant an injunction.

CURRY v. HACKNEY AND SHEPHERD'S BUSH EMPIRE—THE RIGHT TO DEMAND TICKETS IN THEATRES AND MUSIC HALLS.

The question of the right of music halls or theatres to demand the production of a ticket was discussed by Judge Cluer in the Shoreditch County Court. The plaintiff in the action was Philip Curry, of 127, Dalston Lane, N.E., an artificial teeth manufacturer, and he sued the Hackney and Shepherd's Bush Empire Palace, Limited, and Bernard Fleming, the assistant manager of the Hackney Empire, Mare Street, Hackney, to recover £50 damages. His claim set out that he bought a grand circle ticket, and later was accused of having fraudulently obtained admission on an old ticket, was ejected, and seriously assaulted by the defendant Fleming.—Mr. Zeffertt appeared as counsel for the plaintiff, and Mr. Lever, barrister, for the defence.—In opening the case, counsel said that the plaintiff purchased a grand circle ticket. Later on, at the interval, he asked for a pass-out ticket to the buffet. He was directed past the promenade at the back of the orchestra stalls. He stayed in the buffet until it closed at 9.30. He then went on his way back to the grand circle, when the defendant Fleming came up, and in a most offensive manner demanded to know what he was doing there, and also to see his ticket. He produced his pass-out, when he was immediately accused of having fraudulently obtained admission on an old ticket and of being a swindler. He was hustled out into the street, and defendant struck him a violent blow in the eye. The plaintiff gave evidence bearing out this statement, and swore that he paid 1s. 3d. per admission on this night, and that the pass-out which he handed to the assistant manager was given him by the attendant.

Two witnesses were called, who swore that they saw the plaintiff assaulted.

The defendant Fleming then gave evidence, and denied that the plaintiff came from the buffet, but said he was certain he came in from the corridor. He politely asked for his ticket, when the plaintiff became highly indignant, spoke in a loud, excited tone, upsetting the audience, so that he was asked to walk outside the door. Then the manager and attendants were called, the plaintiff finally producing the pass-out ticket. This was an old one, and witness decided to have him put out. He was then persuasively edged to the door by himself and the police. No blow of any kind was struck, and no suggestion made that he was a swindler.

Mr. Zeffertt: Why did you demand the ticket?

Witness: He was not entitled to be in the theatre unless he produced his ticket on demand.

Judge Cluer: Where is that on your tickets, and when is it ever told to the visitors to your halls? Do you think I have never been to a theatre? You are not a corporation to pass bye-laws as you think fit. You know that the statement is deliberately false. You have no more right to demand a ticket from a visitor than a conductor of an omnibus has from a passenger.

Witness: I have always been under the impression that there was a right.

Mr. Zeffertt: How long have you been in the profession?

Witness: All my life.

Judge Cluer: He has always thought that if a visitor is in the stalls his ticket can be demanded of him.

Witness: I mean on his admission.

Judge Cluer: You did not say so.

In answer to counsel, witness said he wished the plaintiff to be put out, although he produced a ticket, as he had created a disturbance. The hearing was adjourned for want of time.

Judge Cluer gave judgment on December 16. He said that in his view the plaintiff came by the pass-out ticket honestly, and was lawfully in the music hall. It was a case for general damages. The probability was that he was given the pass-out check by mistake, otherwise it would have been a mean and contemptible fraud. It might have been the manner that he was asked for the ticket that unreasonably annoyed him, and that he unwisely did not show the ticket when asked. It had been put to him as an argument in law that an unreasonable refusal to produce the ticket, coupled with a subsequent showing of an out-of-date ticket, justified ejectment, but he did not agree. Had he created a disturbance, "yes," but he had not acted in any way that justified ejectment. It seemed clear that as he was turned out Fleming banged him against the door. He could not couple Fleming in the action with the assault, but he would give the plaintiff general damages of £10 10s., with such costs as the verdict gave.

Mr. Lever: Then what about Fleming's costs, as we succeed in the action for assault?

Judge Cluer: Oh, no; there was the banging against the door.

Judgment was then entered in the terms stated.

LEONARD v. HORSFIELD AND WOODWARD — ACTOR'S NOTICE CASE FAILS.

16 At the Westminster County Court, his Honour Judge Lush heard an action to recover £24 in respect of a fortnight's notice, the plaintiffs being H. Leonard, actor, and Leah Douglas, actress, of New Street, W.C., and the defendants Horsfield and Woodward, Limited, Charing Cross Road, W. Mr. Leonard also claimed £5 in respect of services over a sketch.

Mr. Cox Sinclair, counsel for the plaintiffs, said that on January 16 last they entered into a contract with the defendants to go on tour and play in "The Three Musketeers." Mr. Leonard was to receive £8 a week and the lady £4. In the contract it was stipulated that where there was a week or part of a week out there would be no pay, but there was also the usual clause that the engagement was subject to two weeks' notice on either side.

Mr. Leonard, in his evidence, said that the last week he appeared was that ending April 6. During that week they were several times informed, and finally on the Thursday, that nothing had been settled as to whether Dundee was to be visited in the following week, and that the company was to return to London. Then on getting to town on April 8 he called at the company's offices, but did not receive, as he contended he ought by the custom of the profession, a fortnight's salary in lieu of notice.

Two witnesses gave evidence as to custom.

Mr. O'Malley, counsel for the defendants, said that the notice had been given on March 23, when the company was at Kilmarnock. Further, the plaintiff Leonard had given notice himself on March 15, when he wrote the manager that unless an engagement he had accepted for Dublin was put back by his agents they would not be able to play at Kilmarnock. From March 15 to 20 nothing was heard, and then Leonard sent a telegram: "Understand tour continuing. Decided not to play at Dublin." The plaintiffs were informed that a week might be fixed up at Sunderland, but they must take the risk. On March 23, at Kilmarnock, all the company were informed by a notice put up that the tour would not be continued. Efforts were being made to fix another week, but, after the formal notice, all knew that it was a speculative matter.

Plaintiffs were never told that Sunderland was fixed definitely.

Judge Lush said that under ordinary circumstances there ought to be a fortnight's notice that a tour was about to end, and, in fact, he found that it was given on March 23. Further, it was within the knowledge of all the parties that the tour was ending, and that it was doubtful whether they would go on. There would be judgment for the defendants in respect of the claim for a fortnight's salary in lieu of notice. As to the claim for £5 in respect of the production of a sketch, he found in favour of the plaintiff, who would have judgment for that amount.

ST. SWITHIN'S SYNDICATE v. MAYO — A PANTOMIME SONG.

20 Before Mr. Justice P. O. Lawrence, in the Chancery Division, an application was made for an injunction restraining the defendant, Mr. Sam Mayo, from parting with the copyright of the Song "Many Happy Returns of the Day," except to the plaintiffs, who claimed to be the owners by reason of a verbal agreement.

Mr. C. E. E. Jenkins, K.C., and Mr. Henn Collins (instructed by Messrs. Beirnstein) for plaintiffs; Mr. Martin O'Connor (instructed by Messrs. Edmond O'Connor and Co. for the defendant.

Mr. Jenkins read the affidavit of Mr. Herman Darewski, the managing director of the plaintiff syndicate, in which he said that on Monday, December 9, Mr. Mayo offered him the song. He sang it over to him, and it was arranged that the syndicate should pay Mr. Mayo £6 down and a royalty of 10 per cent. on the selling price of the song. Mr. Darewski offered the defendant a cheque at the time, but he was hurrying off to fulfil an engagement at Nottingham, and asked that the cheque and contract should be posted to him. Mr. Darewski said the cheque and contract were duly posted on the following day, but two days after the interview he received a telegram from the defendant to the following effect — "Not having received confirmation of the song, our arrangements are cancelled. — MAYO."

In the meantime, said counsel, Mr. Darewski, following out the terms of the verbal agreement, had had the song copied by one of his assistants, and it was in process of engraving.

Mr. O'Connor read an affidavit by Mr. Mayo in which he stated that he was the author, composer, and owner of this new song. He was of opinion that it would be eagerly sought after by artists all over the world. He had already received an offer of £200 for it from Miss Alice Lloyd, and an offer of a similar amount from Miss Hetty King. He was anxious that the song should be placed with a well-known publisher, and, knowing that Mr Darewski was characterised by his quick and clever business tactics, he approached him. His object was to get the song published in time for the Christmas pantomimes. The time was, of course, very important, and when he did not receive the contract from the plaintiffs he sent his telegram.

Mr. Jenkins, at this stage, said that during the reading of the affidavits the parties had met, and terms had been arranged between them, so, with the consent of his lordship, the matter would be adjourned generally.

His lordship agreed.

INDEX TO LEGAL CASES.

Plaintiff.	Defendant.	Date.	Nature of Contract.
African Theatres' Trust	Jacobson	April 25	Breach of Contract
Blaiberg	Montefiore	July 15	Claim on a Cheque
Boganny's, Ltd.	Marner	May 1	Wrongful detention of Properties
Charlot	Thompson	Dec. 7	Question of Title
Cowen	Rolls	Aug. 28	Application for Injunction
Curry	Hackney Empire	Dec. 10	The Right to demand Tickets
Gilbert	Dyson	May 10	Claim for Commission
Gordon	Gilbert	July 10	Claim for payment for services rendered.
Griffiths	Seebold	Oct. 7	What is a No. 1 Company?
Kahn	Beatie and Babs	May 10	Question of Copyright
Hughes	Salter	Nov. 15	Breach of Contract
Lena	Victoria Palace, Ltd.	June 19 & Dec. 6	Breach of Contract
Leonard	Horsfield and Woodward	Dec. 16	Question of Notice
Luck	Elton	March 18	Breach of Contract
Merson	London Theatre of Varieties	July 16	What is a Matinee?
Pearl	Turner	Sept. 2	Claim for Salary
Philps	North Western Railway Co.	Nov. 18	Claim for Damages
St. Swithin's Syndicate	Mayo	Dec 20	Dispute over Song
Vaudeville Productions, Ltd.	Dance	Nov. 28	Producer's claim
West	Phillips	March 14	Claim for Salary
Woods	Faraday	Oct. 17	Alleged Infringement of Copyright

PROSECUTIONS.

Billing	June 4	Alleged Criminal Libel
Brighton Pier Co.	May 31 & July 1	Entertainments' Tax
Lyons	Oct. 13	Music in Restaurants
Tate	August 31	Lighting Regulations
White	May 13	Entertainments' Duty
Moss Empires	Dec. 5	Posters

Printed by ST. CLEMENTS PRESS, LTD., Portugal Street, Kingsway, W.C. 2.

Lightning Source UK Ltd.
Milton Keynes UK
UKHW010802290720
367358UK00001B/222